JUSTICE FOR CRIMES AGAINST HUMANITY

The aim of this book is to assess recent developments in international law in bringing to justice those accused of war crimes and crimes against humanity. The book was originally conceived while the editors were engaged, in different capacities, in proceedings relating to the detention of Senator Pinochet in London. Recent developments including that case, the trial of former President Milošević, and the creation of the International Criminal Court, have transformed international criminal law and also sparked vigorous public debate. Under what circumstances can those accused of grave crimes under international law now be brought to justice in national or international courts? When can immunity from jurisdiction still be claimed? In addressing these questions and attempting to clarify the applicable law, this book also acknowledges the wider moral and political questions raised, which in turn will influence the further development of the law.

Justice for Crimes Against Humanity

Edited by

MARK LATTIMER

and

PHILIPPE SANDS QC

•HART•
PUBLISHING

HART PUBLISHING
OXFORD AND PORTLAND, OREGON
2003

Published in North America (US and Canada) by
Hart Publishing
c/o International Specialized Book Services
5804 NE Hassalo Street
Portland, Oregon
97213-3644
USA

Hart Publishing is a specialist legal publisher based in Oxford, England.
To order further copies of this book or to request a list of other publications please write to:

Hart Publishing, Salters Boatyard, Folly Bridge,
Abingdon Rd, Oxford, OX1 4LB
Telephone: +44 (0)1865 245533 Fax: +44 (0) 1865 794882
email: mail@hartpub.co.uk
WEBSITE: http//:www.hartpub.co.uk

British Library Cataloguing in Publication Data
Data Available

ISBN 1-84113-413-9 (hardback)

Typeset by John Saunders Design & Production
Printed and bound in Great Britain by
Biddles Ltd, *www.biddles.co.uk*

For Katya and Clara

Preface

The aim of this book is to provide an assessment of recent developments in international law (including its domestic application) in bringing an end to impunity for persons accused of the most serious international crimes, namely genocide, war crimes and crimes against humanity. The book was conceived while we were both engaged, in different capacities, in the arguments on the *Pinochet* case before the Judicial Committee of the House of Lords. The great public interest in that case—and other developments in international criminal law since the late 1990s—demonstrated the close connections between the law and wider political and moral questions. In the field of international criminal justice there appeared, therefore, a clear need to distinguish legal from essentially political issues—promoting the application of the law in as objective a manner as possible—while at the same time enabling each to legitimately inform the development of the other. This book thus seeks to provide a broad perspective on the legal issues raised, from scholars, practitioners and a judge.

We are very grateful to a number of people whose efforts and encouragement helped make this book possible, including Maggie Paterson, Derek Cross, Tala Dowlatshahi, Noémi Byrd, Helen Ghosh and Ruth Mackenzie. The editors and Benjamin Ferencz would like to thank the Development and Peace Foundation and the Columbia Journal of Transnational Law for permission to use substantial revised extracts from, respectively, SEF Policy Paper 8, 'From Nuremberg to Rome: Towards an International Criminal Court' (Bonn, Development and Peace Foundation, 1998) and 'A Prosecutor's Personal Account' in *Columbia Journal of Transnational Law* 37, Spring 1999. We also owe a debt of gratitude to our respective colleagues more generally, including those at the Faculty of Law at University College London and the Law Department at the School of Oriental and African Studies, the PICT Centre for International Courts and Tribunals, Matrix Chambers, Amnesty International, Human Rights Watch, Minority Rights Group International, the Redress Trust, and the Medical Foundation for the Care of Victims of Torture. A particular research debt is owed to Reed Brody and Michael Ratner, who in compiling *The Pinochet Papers* (Kluwer Law International, The Hague, 2000) have greatly facilitated the task of *Pinochet* scholarship.

At Hart Publishing we would like to thank Richard Hart, April Boffin and our copy editor Rosemary Mullins. We would also like to record our gratitude to John Louth at Oxford University Press for the numerous suggestions, including from other sources, which have improved the book considerably.

The strength of an edited collection such as this is that it reflects a wide range of different voices gathered together in a single volume. This is also a potential weakness, since diversity of style and substance necessarily imposes a challenge for coherence. In bringing together these different voices and perspectives we have tried to strike an appropriate balance between uniformity of style and the individual tone of the contributors.

A word of explanation is necessary about the style used in referring to the crimes which form the subject matter of this book. They broadly include genocide, torture, crimes against humanity, war crimes and other serious violations of international law attracting criminal liability. There is no precise catch-all phrase which covers all these categories of offence (which in some cases overlap) and a number are favoured by different contributors, including 'international crimes' or 'crimes under international law', 'human rights crimes', 'human rights atrocities' or (as in the book's title) simply 'crimes against humanity'. The individual contributor's preferred term has been retained where a summary expression is clearly being used; where the context requires reference to a particular category of offence or source of law, the correct specialist term is used, applied consistently through the book. An outline of the different sources of law—and their interrelationship—may be found in the introduction.

Mark Lattimer
Philippe Sands
London, December 2002

Contents

List of Contributors

William J Aceves is Professor of Law and Director of the International Legal Studies Program at California Western School of Law. He works with human rights organisations on projects involving international law and its domestic application. He has represented several of these organisations as Counsel of Record in cases before US courts, including the Ninth Circuit Court of Appeals and the United States Supreme Court. He has also appeared before the United Nations Special Rapporteur on Migrants, the Inter-American Commission on Human Rights, and the US Commission on Civil Rights.

M Cherif Bassiouni is Professor of Law and President of the International Human Rights Law Institute, DePaul University College of Law (Chicago). He chaired the UN Commission of Experts on the former Yugoslavia and was Chairman of the Drafting Committee of the UN Diplomatic Conference on the Establishment of the International Criminal Court. He is President of the International Association of Penal Law in Paris, France and of the International Institute of Higher Studies in Criminal Sciences in Siracusa, Italy.

Geoffrey Bindman is the senior partner in Bindman & Partners Solicitors, and a visiting professor of law at University College London. He represented Amnesty International and other human rights groups and individual victims in the *Pinochet* case. He is author (with Lord Lester of Herne Hill) of *Race and Law* (Harmondsworth, Longmans/Penguin, 1972).

Graham T Blewitt, a career prosecutor, has been the Deputy Prosecutor at the International Criminal Tribunal for the former Yugoslavia since February 1994. Prior to that, from 1988 until 1993, he was the Deputy Director and then the Director of the Special Investigations Unit (Nazi War Crimes) in Sydney, Australia. He was formerly Senior Legal Adviser to the National Crime Authority in Sydney.

Alex Boraine was the Deputy Chairman and coordinator of the South African Truth and Reconciliation Commission. He is President of the International Center for Transitional Justice based in New York and Adjunct Professor at the School of Law, New York University. He is the author of *A Country Unmasked*, an inside history of the Truth and Reconciliation Commission in South Africa.

Reed Brody is Special Counsel of Human Rights Watch (HRW). He coordinates the International Committee for the Trial of Hissène Habré and directed HRW's intervention in the *Pinochet* case in Britain's House of Lords. Previously, he led UN teams investigating massacres in the Democratic Republic of Congo and observing human rights in El Salvador. In 1995–1996, he coordinated an international legal team convened by President Aristide to prosecute human rights crimes in Haiti.

Andrew Clapham is Professor of Public International Law at the Graduate Institute of International Studies in Geneva and, until recently, was the Representative of Amnesty International at the UN in New York. His publications include *Human Rights in the Private Sphere* (Oxford University Press, Oxford, 1993).

Eric David is Professor of Public International Law at the Université Libre de Bruxelles and President of the Center of International Law of the Law Faculty. He is the author, *inter alia*, of *Principes de droit des conflits armés* (Bruylant, Brussels, 3rd edition (2002)).

Benjamin B Ferencz is a former Nuremberg prosecutor. He was Chief Prosecutor in the *Einsatzgruppen* trial before the US Military Tribunal at Nuremberg. A graduate of Harvard Law School, he served in the Army under General Patton in every campaign in Europe and was among the liberators of Buchenwald, Mauthausen and other Nazi concentration camps. He is the author of numerous books including *New Legal Foundations for Global Survival* (1994). He was an Adjunct Professor of International Law at Pace University in the US and founder of the Pace Peace Center.

Christopher Keith Hall is the Legal Adviser at Amnesty International.

Paul L Hoffman is a civil rights lawyer from Los Angeles, California. He is the former Legal Director of the American Civil Liberties Union Foundation of Southern California, in which capacity he litigated numerous international human rights cases in US courts. He is the Chair of the International Executive Committee of Amnesty International and is widely published in the field of human rights litigation.

Sadakat Kadri is a barrister at Doughty Street chambers in London. He is currently writing a history of the British and American criminal trial.

Mark Lattimer is the Executive Director of Minority Rights Group International, which works with partners in some 60 countries worldwide to protect the rights of minorities and indigenous peoples. Formerly he was the Communications Director for Amnesty International UK, where he was the director responsible for managing work on the *Pinochet* case.

Richard May is a Judge of the International Criminal Tribunal for the former Yugoslavia. He is the Presiding Judge, Trial Chamber III and Presiding Judge for the trial of Slobodan Milošević.

Timothy L H McCormack is Australian Red Cross Professor of International Humanitarian Law and the Foundation Director of the Asia-Pacific Centre for Military Law at the University of Melbourne. He was recently appointed amicus curiae on international law matters to the judges of Trial Chamber III of the International Criminal Tribunal for the Former Yugoslavia for the trial of Slobodan Milošević

Fiona McKay is Director of the International Justice Program at the Lawyers Committee for Human Rights, based in New York. She was formerly Deputy Director of the Kurdish Human Rights Project, and Legal Officer at Redress, an NGO that works to secure reparation for the survivors of torture.

Clare Montgomery QC is a barrister at Matrix Chambers in London. She represented Senator Pinochet in the *Pinochet* case. She is the co-author of *The Law of Extradition and Mutual Assistance* (Cameron May, London, 2001).

Diane F Orentlicher is Professor of Law and Director of the War Crimes Research Office at Washington College of Law, American University. She has published extensively on issues relating to the nature and scope of states' obligations under international law in the aftermath of mass atrocity and on the work of international criminal tribunals.

Sir Nigel Rodley is Professor of Law at the University of Essex. He is a member of the UN Human Rights Committee and was, until recently, the UN Special Rapporteur on torture. His numerous publications include *The Treatment of Prisoners under International Law* (Clarendon Press, Oxford, 2nd edn. 1999).

Philippe Sands QC is Professor of Laws and Director of the PICT Centre for International Courts and Tribunals at University College London, and a barrister at Matrix Chambers. He served as counsel for Human Rights Watch and then Belgium in the *Pinochet* proceedings in England.

Brigitte Stern is Professor of International Law at the University of Paris I, Panthéon-Sorbonne, and Director of the CEDIN-Paris I, Centre of Research in International Law. She also works as an arbitrator and as expert counsel for international organisations and governments, including the Bosnian Government in the Genocide Case against the Federal Republic of Yugoslavia before the International Court of Justice. She is a Member of the United Nations Administrative Tribunal (UNAT) and is also the President of the French Commission for the Elimination of Landmines.

Introduction

MARK LATTIMER AND PHILIPPE SANDS

On Monday 27 September 1999, the clerk at London's Bow Street Magistrates Court began to read out the charges against the accused. It took over 15 minutes to reach the end of the list. The 35 charges of torture and conspiracy to torture included inflicting torture:

— on Marcos Quezada Yañez, aged 17, by inflicting electric shocks causing his eventual death;
— on Avelino Villarroel Muñoz by beating him, inflicting electric shocks on him, restricting his breathing and allowing him to hear the infliction of severe pain and suffering upon others;
— on Jessica Antonia Liberona Niñoles by depriving her of sleep, making threats about her nine-year old daughter and conducting repeated interrogations while she was naked;
— on Marcos Antonio Mardoñes Villarroel by beating him, inflicting electric shocks and burning him; and
— on Andrea Paulsen Figuera by depriving her of sleep, food and water for several days and threatening that her five-year old daughter would be tortured.

They were, said counsel, 'some of the most serious allegations of crime ever to come before English criminal courts'.

Over the next five days, the details of this extraordinary hearing were followed avidly around the world. This was less on account of the gravity of the charges than the identity of the accused: Augusto Pinochet Ugarte, member of the Chilean Senate, former President of the Republic of Chile and former Commander in Chief of Chile's armed forces. But more than anything it was because Chile's former head of state was in detention and subject to proceedings in the United Kingdom on an extradition request from Spain and three other European states. Justice had gone global and the world was watching.

What made possible these events which would have been unthinkable just one year before? Most immediately, UK Home Secretary Jack Straw had allowed extradition proceedings to go ahead following an unprecedented set of legal proceedings in the Judicial Committee of the House of Lords which eventually led to a judgment[1] which found that, even as a former head of state, Senator Pinochet had no immunity from the jurisdiction of the English courts in respect of a prosecution for the crime of torture over which states party to the 1984 UN Convention against Torture[2] had given universal jurisdiction to all courts, no matter where the crime was committed.

More broadly, the proceedings against Senator Pinochet must be seen against the background of normative and institutional developments in international law: the emergence of human rights instruments providing for universal jurisdiction, the establishment of international criminal tribunals for the former Yugoslavia and Rwanda and, in the summer of 1998 in Rome, the adoption of the Statute of the International Criminal Court, providing for a permanent institution to address crimes against humanity, war crimes, and genocide.

Against this background, Senator Pinochet's detention in the United Kingdom was triggered by the actions of Balthazar Garzón, the Spanish investigating magistrate. Judge Garzón had been investigating the deaths of Spanish citizens in Chile during the period of Senator Pinochet's governance, and seized his chance to issue an international arrest warrant when Senator Pinochet visited London in October 1998. Behind that warrant lay several years of research and coordinated legal preparations by Spanish and Chilean jurists—as well as jurists in other jurisdictions, including Belgium, France and Switzerland—working on the cases of those tortured, murdered and forcibly disappeared under Latin American dictatorships. These jurists were emboldened by the developing notion of a 'universal' jurisdiction for crimes against humanity as advocated by human rights groups and torture victims worldwide, and increasingly supported by states. In a significant decision that paved the way for the case to proceed, Spain's jurisdiction over the case was upheld by the *Audiencia National* in November 1998.[3]

But much of the debate in the proceedings against Senator Pinochet turned on points of UK statutory interpretation. Working within a strong dualist tradition, the English courts required the identification of sufficient jurisdictional authority in national legislation to prosecute substantive and established norms of international law. It is clear that the Judicial Committee of the House of Lords would not have affirmed English jurisdiction over Senator Pinochet were it not for the United Kingdom's ratification, by Margaret Thatcher's Government in 1988, of the UN Convention against Torture. This followed the adoption of the Criminal Justice Act 1988, which made torture committed abroad a criminal offence in the UK.

[1] *R v Bow Street Metropolitan Stipendiary Magistrate Ex p. Pinochet Ugarte (No 3)* (HL(E)) [2000] 1 AC 147, hereafter *Pinochet No 3*; the earlier judgments were *R v Bow Street Metropolitan Stipendiary Magistrate Ex p. Pinochet Ugarte* (HL(E)) [2000] 1 AC 61, hereafter *Pinochet No 1* and *R v Bow Street Metropolitan Stipendiary Magistrate Ex p. Pinochet Ugarte* (HL (E)) [2000] 1 AC 119, hereafter *Pinochet No 2*.

[2] UN Doc A/39/51 (1984). See Appendix I.

[3] Order of the Criminal Chamber of the *Audiencia Nacional*, 5 Nov 1998. See www.derechos.org/nizkor/chile/juicio/audi.html for a copy of the order; an unofficial English translation is included in Reed Brody and Michael Ratner (eds), *The Pinochet Papers* (Kluwer Law International, The Hague, 2000).

Behind the immediate causes of Senator Pinochet's arrest and detention therefore stands the wider subject addressed by this book: the recent rapid development of an emerging system of international criminal justice, which may be traced back to the Nuremberg trials of Nazi leaders in 1945–1946. The *Pinochet* case, and the indictment and trial of Slobodan Milošević which closely followed it, may be seen as landmarks within a broader set of developments, whose central principle is that leaders and other individuals should be held personally responsible for their role in committing gross abuses of human rights and violations of the laws of war. In many ways these developments signal a shift in the basic foundations of the established international legal order, away from an order which promotes the primacy of the interests of the state towards one which promotes the interests of individuals.

HUMAN RIGHTS, THE LAWS OF WAR AND INTERNATIONAL CRIMES

The years following the end of the Second World War and the adoption of the United Nations Charter in 1945 saw a number of historic developments in international cooperation and standard-setting, many of which were aimed at preventing a re-occurrence of the massive human suffering that the world had just endured. Legally, those developments followed two main strands: the emergence of international human rights law following the 1948 Universal Declaration of Human Rights; and the further development of international humanitarian law with the Geneva Conventions of 1949 and subsequent standards.

Although the 1948 Universal Declaration of Human Rights was not in itself legally binding, it spawned a series of human rights treaties, including the International Covenant on Civil and Political Rights (ICCPR) and the International Covenant on Economic, Social and Cultural Rights (ICESCR) of 1966.[4] Under these treaties, states accepted obligations to respect and protect the human rights of their citizens and other inhabitants. Some states further accepted the scrutiny of UN monitoring committees regarding individual complaints of violation (for example, the UN Human Rights Committee considers complaints from individuals or groups in those states which have ratified the Optional Protocol to the ICCPR).[5] The obligations under this new body of human rights law therefore fall squarely on states, as do any legal enforcement mechanisms established by treaty. In times of war or national emergency, states can derogate from these obligations, but not in respect of certain absolute rights (termed non-derogable) including the right to life and the rights not to be tortured or enslaved.

The specific need to protect civilians and other non-combatants in times of war was the aim of the 1949 Geneva Conventions, the cornerstone of what has come to be known as international humanitarian law. Building on customary law as well as earlier treaties signed at Geneva and The Hague, the four Geneva

[4] ICCPR, 999 UNTS 171; ICESCR, 993 UNTS 3.
[5] 999 UNTS 302.

Conventions established specific protections for the injured, ship-wrecked, prisoners-of-war and all civilians in wartime.[6] This protection was based on the fundamental obligation to distinguish at all times between military objects, which were legitimate targets of war, and civilians and civilian installations, which states were strictly forbidden to target and obliged to take positive measures to protect. Certain serious violations of the Geneva Conventions were expressly designated as 'grave breaches' thereby attracting a further duty on states to suppress them as war crimes and prosecute the individuals responsible. The protections established by the Geneva Conventions were in the main applicable in situations of international armed conflict and occupation, but Article 3 common to the four Conventions outlawed the killing or inhumane treatment of civilians and other non-combatants in situations of internal as well as international armed conflict (a prohibition without, however, any specific means of enforcement). This rudimentary protection in cases of civil conflict was enlarged on in the second of two additional protocols to the Geneva Conventions agreed in 1977,[7] although it remains to be ratified by some 40 states, including many with ongoing civil wars.

In certain respects international criminal law can be seen as a melding of principles of human rights law and international humanitarian law, with some specific sources of its own, including from national law. By applying a serious criminal sanction on the individual, it fixes in its sights the civilian or military leaders who are prepared to ignore their states' international legal obligations and the officials or forces who are given domestic licence to abuse human rights with impunity. Its *locus classicus* is the Charter of the International Military Tribunal at Nuremberg,[8] adopted as binding international law by resolution of the UN General Assembly in 1946.[9] The Nuremberg Charter established definitively the personal criminal responsibility of both military and political leaders for violations of the laws of war and for gross abuses designated crimes against humanity. The grave breaches provisions of the Geneva Conventions further defined those acts which attracted personal criminal liability. The development of international human rights law also played a key role in that human rights treaties place an obligation on states to suppress violations and provide a remedy to victims. In many cases this will mean the obligation to prosecute those responsible for such acts.

[6] Geneva Convention for the Amelioration of the Condition of the Wounded and Sick in Armed Forces in the Field, 75 UNTS 31; Geneva Convention for the Amelioration of the Condition of Wounded, Sick and Shipwrecked Members of Armed Forces at Sea, 75 UNTS 85; Geneva Convention relative to the Treatment of Prisoners of War, 75 UNTS 135; Geneva Convention relative to the Protection of Civilian Persons in Time of War, 75 UNTS 287.

[7] Protocol Additional to the Geneva Conventions of 12 Aug 1949, and Relating to the Protection of Victims of Non-International Armed Conflicts (Protocol II), 1125 UNTS 609. Protocol I relates to the protection of victims of international armed conflicts, 1125 UNTS 3.

[8] The Charter is contained in the 'Agreement for the Prosecution and Punishment of the Major War Criminals of the European Axis (London Agreement)', 8 August 1945, 82 UNTS 280.

[9] 'Affirmation of the Principles of International Law recognised by the Charter of the Nuremberg Tribunal', UN GA Res 95 (I), 11 Dec 1946.

The existence of a universal jurisdiction in customary law over crimes against humanity was confirmed in the 1962 trial in Israel of Adolf Eichmann, the Nazi Gestapo chief responsible for administering the 'final solution'. The Jerusalem District Court ruled that such 'abhorrent crimes'

> ... are not crimes under Israeli law alone. These crimes, which struck at the whole of mankind and shocked the conscience of nations, are grave offences against the law of nations itself.[10]

In 1973 the UN General Assembly adopted a set of principles which declared that all states were to co-operate with each other in the detection, arrest, extradition and punishment of persons guilty of war crimes and crimes against humanity.[11] Both the Geneva Conventions and some human rights conventions, such as the UN Convention against Torture 1984, confirmed by treaty a universal jurisdiction to enable states to suppress the specified crimes, giving rise to an obligation *aut dedere aut judicare*—either to prosecute the alleged offenders or extradite them to a country willing to do so. Finally, a series of treaties have been agreed aiming at particular crimes of a trans-national character whose suppression requires international cooperation—such as hijacking, hostage-taking and other acts of international terrorism—developing some of the principles reflected in the long-established universal jurisdiction over piracy on the high seas.

All of these sources of law were drawn on in the early 1990s when the UN Security Council established international criminal tribunals for the former Yugoslavia[12] and for Rwanda[13]—the first since the tribunals at Nuremberg and Tokyo after the Second World War. The International Law Commission, a UN body of international lawyers, was also asked by the UN General Assembly to revive its work codifying international crimes and produce a draft statute for a permanent tribunal.[14] The Statute of the International Criminal Court was finally agreed at a UN conference of plenipotentiaries in Rome in 1998, and now provides the most comprehensive, definitive and authoritative list of war crimes and crimes against humanity attracting individual criminal liability.[15]

THE CASE OF SENATOR PINOCHET

Just three months after the Rome conference, Senator Pinochet was arrested in London by the Metropolitan Police, acting on a request from Interpol. The

10 *Attorney-General of the Government of Israel v Eichmann*, (1961) 36 ILR 5.

11 'Principles of International Co-Operation in the Detection, Arrest, Extradition and Punishment of Persons Guilty of War Crimes and Crimes Against Humanity', GA Res 3074 (XXVIII), UN Doc A/9030/Add1 (1973).

12 UN Security Council Res 827, 25 May 1993.

13 UN Security Council Res 955, 8 Nov 1994.

14 'Draft Statute for an International Criminal Court', Report of the ILC on the work of its forty-sixth session, 2 May–22 July 1994, GA, 49th session, supplement No 10 (A/49/10), 29–161.

15 UN Doc. A/CONF.183/9 (1998). See appendix II. Hereafter 'ICC Statute'.

arrest galvanised interest worldwide in international criminal justice, in a way that a diplomatic conference could not have done. Formally, the case involved six states: Chile, the UK and the four countries—Spain, Belgium, France and Switzerland—seeking Senator Pinochet's extradition for crimes against their nationals or against mainly Chilean nationals under the principle of universal jurisdiction. But other states were also closely involved, not least the USA which was immediately conscious of the revelations that a trial would bring about its own role in Senator Pinochet's rise to power. A timeline summarising the main events in the case is set out below.

Timeline: the *Pinochet* case

1996

1 July Initial criminal complaints against Augusto Pinochet on charges of genocide and terrorism are submitted to the *Audiencia Nacional*, the Spanish national court.

1997

February Spanish judicial investigations are initiated in respect of alleged crimes against Spanish citizens in Chile under Pinochet's military government and crimes committed as part of Operation Condor.

1998

22 September Pinochet travels to the United Kingdom for an operation on his spine.

25 September Amnesty International issues a news release publicising Pinochet's presence in the UK and questioning whether the authorities will act according to their obligations under the UN Convention against Torture.

14 October Spanish judges Manuel Garcia-Castellon and Baltasar Garzón Real file an official petition with the UK authorities to question Augusto Pinochet.

16 October Augusto Pinochet is served at a London clinic with a provisional arrest warrant, issued by a metropolitan stipendiary magistrate, and is placed in police custody.

18 October Judge Garzón issues a second international warrant of arrest against Augusto Pinochet in order to prepare the request for extradition. Criminal proceedings are subsequently announced in Italy, Luxembourg, Norway, Sweden and the USA.

22 October Augusto Pinochet's lawyers submit an appeal against his detention to the UK High Court of Justice.

28 October The UK High Court rules that Augusto Pinochet is entitled to immunity as a former head of state from both criminal and civil proceedings in the English courts. Leave is granted to appeal to the House of Lords.

5 November The *Audiencia Nacional* upholds Spain's jurisdiction in the case. The Spanish government subsequently files a formal request with the UK authorities for Augusto Pinochet to be extradited to Spain to face trial for genocide, terrorism, kidnapping, torture, enforced disappearances, and for conspiracy to commit these crimes.

11–12 November The Swiss and French governments also file extradition requests with the UK authorities.

17 November The UN Committee against Torture recommends to the UK government that the case of Augusto Pinochet 'be referred to the office of the public prosecutor, with a view to examining the feasibility of and if appropriate initiating criminal proceedings in England, in the event that the decision is made not to extradite him'.

25 November The Judicial Committee of the House of Lords, the highest UK court, reverses the High Court judgment. By a majority of three to two, the Law Lords rule that Pinochet's status as a former head of state does not give him immunity from prosecution. This ruling leaves the way open for Pinochet to be extradited to Spain on charges of mass murder, terrorism and torture. The final decision on whether to allow the extradition to proceed rests with the UK Home Secretary, Jack Straw.

9 December On the eve of the 50th anniversary of the Universal Declaration of Human Rights, the Home Secretary issues the authority to proceed with Pinochet's extradition.

10 December Pinochet's lawyers challenge the House of Lords' decision, citing a conflict of interest on behalf of one of the judges.

11 December Augusto Pinochet attends a bail hearing at Belmarsh Magistrates' Court in London. He remains under police guard in the UK, at an estate in Wentworth, while the legal proceedings continue.

15 December The Belgian government also files an extradition request with the UK authorities.

17 December Another panel of Law Lords sets aside the earlier House of Lords' ruling, on the basis that one of the judges, Lord Hoffman, had links with Amnesty International, which had intervened in the proceedings. A new panel of seven Law Lords is scheduled to reconsider the case in January 1999.

1999

January-February A new hearing extends over 12 days before the House of Lords. The Chilean government is granted leave to participate, as are Amnesty International, the Medical Foundation for the Care of Victims of Torture, the Redress Trust, Mary Ann and Juana Francisca Beausire, British torture victim Sheila Cassidy and the Association of Relatives of the Disappeared in Chile.

*24 Marc*h By a majority of six to one, the Law Lords rule that Augusto Pinochet does not have immunity from prosecution for acts of torture committed when he was head of state and that he could be extradited, but only for the crimes of torture and conspiracy to torture alleged to have been committed after 8 December 1988—the date on which the UN Convention against Torture became binding on Chile, Spain and the UK.

30 March The UN Human Rights Committee states that the Chilean Amnesty Law of 1978 violates the right to have an effective remedy and is incompatible with the obligation of the state to investigate human rights violations.

15 April The UK Home Secretary gives authority for the extradition application to proceed for a second time. Extradition hearings are scheduled for September.

27 May The High Court rejects a challenge to Jack Straw's second authority to proceed.

July–August It is reported that separate discussions on a lawful means of halting Pinochet's extradition have been held between Chile, Spain and the UK at Foreign Minister level and between President Eduardo Frei of Chile and Prime Minister Tony Blair. A regular channel of communication between officials is established. The Chilean 5th Court of Appeals cites Pinochet's parliamentary immunity in rejecting a judicial request to include him in an investigation related to the killing of 72 people in the 1973 'Caravan of Death' operation.

September In the year following his arrest in London, 40 lawsuits are filed against Augusto Pinochet before Chilean Courts.

4 September A request from Chile to submit the Pinochet case to international arbitration is rejected by the Spanish government.

24 September For the second time, Spain's *Audiencia Nacional* affirms Spain's jurisdiction over Pinochet following a challenge from the state prosecutor.

27 September A hearing begins at Bow Street Magistrates' Court to determine whether Pinochet should be committed for extradition on 35 cases of torture or conspiracy to torture committed after 8 December 1988, and on further cases of torture resulting from 1,198 enforced disappearances submitted by Spanish judge Baltasar Garzón.

8 October The Bow Street Magistrate, Ronald Bartle, commits Pinochet on all charges to await the decision of the Home Secretary on extradition. The Chilean government subsequently requests the UK authorities to undertake medical tests on Augusto Pinochet in order to consider releasing him on humanitarian grounds. Pinochet's lawyers appeal against the Magistrate's decision through application for a writ of *habeas corpus*.

5 November The UK Home Office asks that Augusto Pinochet undergo independent medical tests following a request from the Chilean government that he be released on health grounds.

19 November Spain's *Audiencia Nacional* rejects, for the third time, attempts by the Spanish Public Prosecution Office and by the Public Prosecutor's Department to stop the proceedings against Augusto Pinochet in Spain. The *Audiencia* reaffirms the jurisdiction of the Spanish courts and authorises Judge Garzón's investigations.

December Two High Court judges schedule the hearing for Augusto Pinochet's appeal against the ruling of Magistrate Bartle for March 2000.

2000

5 January A medical team led by Sir John Grimley Evans examines Pinochet at Northwick Park Hospital and submits a report to Jack Straw.

11 January The UK Home Secretary Jack Straw announces that he 'is minded' to halt extradition proceedings on medical grounds. He invites representations but states that the contents of the medical report are confidential.

25 January Belgium and a group of human rights organisations led by Amnesty International make an application for judicial review of the Home Secretary's decision not to disclose the medical report on Pinochet.

31 January Application dismissed by Mr Justice Kay in the High Court. The application for judicial review is subsequently renewed by Belgium and the human rights organisations.

15 February High Court allows the application and requires disclosure of the medical report on Pinochet to the four states requesting extradition. The conclusion of the medical report states that Pinochet is not 'mentally capable of meaningful participation in a trial' due to brain damage from cerebro-vascular disease.

18 February Spanish medical experts commissioned by Judge Garzón submit that the evidence in the medical report does not establish that Pinochet's physical and mental condition is not sufficiently normal to face trial and that the tests performed on him are not the most suitable to determine unfitness to stand trial. Other states requesting extradition also make representations.

2 March UK Home Secretary Jack Straw halts the extradition proceedings on the grounds that Pinochet is unfit to stand trial. Solicitor General Ross Cranston announces that there will be no criminal prosecution of Pinochet in England. Pinochet flies back to Chile.

Sources: *Amnesty International Report 2000*; Brody and Ratner, *The Pinochet Papers*; authors' own sources.
Note: Further legal proceedings against Pinochet after his return to Chile are summarised in ch 14.

For the development of international criminal law, the principal outcome of the case was to clarify the scope and application of the 1984 Convention against Torture and related rules of international law and recognise the principle that a claim to jurisdictional immunity was incompatible with the requirements of the 1984 Convention. In *Eichmann* it had been established that there existed a *permissive* universal jurisdiction over crimes against humanity, but never before had a domestic court refused a claim of immunity in respect of criminal proceedings against a former foreign head of state.[16] In *Pinochet*, decisions of Spain's *Audiencia Nacional* and the UK House of Lords confirmed that the exercise of criminal jurisdiction was *mandatory* for certain crimes under international law (where specified by treaty applicable to the facts in question) in the sense that the state of custody was *obliged* either to prosecute or extradite, and in that the exercise of jurisdiction did not require consent or a waiver of immunity from the state of nationality. According to these courts any continuing immunity held by former heads of state and other public officials in respect of acts undertaken while in office did not extend to treaty crimes such as torture for which the exercise of jurisdiction was stipulated by the treaty.

Commentators and human rights campaigners recognised the *Pinochet* judgments as amongst the most important human rights cases since Nuremberg, and spoke of a 'Pinochet effect', whereby prosecuting authorities and courts around the world would find support for moves against others suspected of torture, crimes against humanity or war crimes that came to their country. Cases have since followed in several states, including Belgium, France, Germany, the Netherlands, Senegal, Spain, Switzerland and the UK, concerning cases of crimes in, inter alia, the Democratic Republic of Congo, Mauritania, the former Yugoslavia, Suriname, Chad, Argentina, Rwanda and Sudan.[17]

A combination of excitement and concern about the implications of the case was heightened by at least two factors that reached far beyond the text of the legal judgements. The first was concrete evidence of a relatively new principle of motivation in international relations. From a realist perspective, states traditionally acted to promote or defend their interests, narrowly defined as the pursuit of economic or strategic advantage. International action motivated primarily by humanitarian considerations was comparatively rare, usually multilateral in nature, and typically only followed intense public and diplomatic pressure. But in undertaking prosecutions of foreign nationals under universal jurisdiction, states (or at least independent prosecutors in certain states) were acting unilaterally in furtherance of human rights. To the extent that they were still pursuing state interest, it was action premised on the articulation of a

[16] But see ch3 for a discussion of related cases. In the *Noriega* case, which provides perhaps the closest recent parallel, the court noted that Noriega had never been recognised as head of state by the US (*United States v Noriega* (1990) 746 F Supp 1506).

[17] See Menno T Kamminga, 'Lessons Learned from the Exercise of Universal Jurisdiction in Respect of Gross Human Rights Offenses', *Human Rights Quarterly* 23 (2001); and Redress, *Universal Jurisdiction in Europe* (Redress, London, 1999). See also the contributions in this volume by Christopher Hall and Reed Brody.

universal interest: the common interest of all states in suppressing crimes that offended against humanity.

That this was possible was partly due to the fact that governments, and in particular the executive branch, were no longer entirely able to control developments. Extradition proceedings were initiated and pursued against Senator Pinochet despite the serious reservations of political leaders in Chile, Spain and the UK. A second factor, then, is the proliferation of actors in the field of international law and a relative shift of power away from the executive branch of government. Historically the executive has jealously guarded its prerogative in international relations from interference by the judiciary. Treaty-making, national security and the conduct of foreign relations generally are all areas not amenable to judicial review. But the expansion of international treaty law, and the multiplication of cases in which domestic courts are called upon to apply international law, have begun to enhance the role and influence of national judicial authorities in its further development and implementation.[18]

The expansion of international actors within the state is mirrored by a similar phenomenon in civil society. When the *Pinochet* case reached the House of Lords, Amnesty International, the Redress Trust, the Medical Foundation for the Care of Victims of Torture, the Association of Relatives of Disappeared Persons in Chile, the family of William Beausire, Sheila Ann Cassidy and Human Rights Watch joined the case as intervenors with the aim of ensuring that comprehensive arguments in comparative and international law were presented (although the arguments were principally put by counsel for the Spanish prosecutor, Senator Pinochet, Chile—which intervened in *Pinochet No 3*—and an *amicus curiae* appointed by the Judicial Committee).

ONE LAW FOR ONE WORLD?

As he committed Senator Pinochet for extradition in 1999, the Bow Street magistrate Ronald Bartle made some telling observations about the legal developments that had brought the former Chilean President within the grasp of international justice:

> These Conventions [on extradition and human rights] represent the growing trend of the international community to combine together to outlaw crimes which are abhorrent to civilised society... This development may be said to presage the day when, for the purposes of extradition, there will be one law for one world.[19]

Clearly, the developments in international law identified above aim at the creation of global or universal minimum standards for the protection of human life

[18] See most recently *R ex parte Abbassi and another v Secretary of State for Foreign and Commonwealth Affairs and the Secretary of State for the Home Department*, Court of Appeal (Lord Phillips MR, Lord Justice Waller and lord Justice Carnwath), judgment of 6 Nov 2002.

[19] *Kingdom of Spain v Augusto Pinochet Ugarte*, judgment in the Bow Street Magistrates' Court, 8 Oct 1999; reproduced in *The Pinochet Papers*, (Kluwer Law International, The Hague, 2000) 398.

and liberties, binding on all states and international actors. But equally clearly, the world is a long way from accepting the rule of one law, even as regards the suppression of torture and crimes against humanity.

Although international human rights law and international humanitarian law in theory create overlapping systems of protection, the gaps in that protection are sufficiently large to allow much blood to flow in between. Even in war, states are under an obligation to protect non-derogable human rights, but in practice in a situation of armed conflict, the general law of human rights will be subject to the more specialised laws of war. And under international humanitarian law it is always salutary to remember that the killing of civilians in the course of an attack on a military object is not of itself unlawful: a violation only occurs if the anticipated impact on civilians is disproportionate or the attack is indiscriminate. (Even the sort of indiscriminate killing that likely would attend the use of nuclear weapons has left the International Court of Justice divided as to its legality.)[20]

The existence of effective international criminal sanctions is particularly patchy. One important omission is the fact that common Article 3 of the Geneva Conventions, covering violations in internal armed conflict and by armed opposition groups as well as by states, does not provide a basis for international criminal prosecutions. Yet even as the Geneva Conventions established in 1949 a system of international criminal justice covering grave breaches of the Conventions in international conflict—war crimes—the nature of warfare was changing. The great majority of wars in the world today are internal armed conflicts, thus escaping the 'grave breaches' provisions. In some cases, such as Somalia, civil wars result in the disintegration of the state itself. This pattern of warfare is the principal reason why 90 per cent of the casualties of war at the start of the twenty-first century were civilian and only 10 per cent military, reversing the proportions of a century earlier.[21] Add to this the fact that international hostility is now more often pursued through covert means such as support for dissident armed groups and other encouragement of low-intensity civil conflict, rather than through open international conflict, and it becomes depressingly evident that the penal sanctions established by the Geneva Conventions fail to cover most atrocities of war perpetrated today.

Those treaties which create international jurisdictions for a specific crime or closely-related group of crimes vary greatly in scope and application, leading to more gaps. It was not for nothing that the central crime alleged in the *Pinochet* case was torture, after the English court had ruled that it had no jurisdiction over the crime of murder committed abroad (by a non-British national) and that the allegations did not match the definition of the international crime of

[20] See Laurence Boisson de Chazournes and Philippe Sands, *International Law, the International Court of Justice and Nuclear Weapons* (Cambridge University Press, Cambridge, 1999).

[21] Christa Ahlstrom, *Casualties of Conflict* (Dept of Peace and Conflict Research, Uppsala University, Sweden, 1991); Amnesty International UK, *In the Firing Line: War and Children's Rights* (AIUK, London, 1999).

hostage-taking. The UN Convention against Torture was concluded relatively recently in 1984 and, unusually, establishes an extraterritorial jurisdiction over even single instances of the crime of torture.[22] Even here, the final decision of the House of Lords in the *Pinochet* case was ambiguous, with the judges divided over whether a single instance of torture was sufficient to trump the immunity Senator Pinochet claimed as a former head of state, or whether this required torture perpetrated on a sufficiently widespread or systematic basis as to constitute a crime against humanity.

That crimes against humanity are contrary to customary international law has been accepted, as noted above, since at least 1946. This is the reason why the International Criminal Tribunals for the former Yugoslavia and Rwanda could be established without offending against the fundamental principle of *nulle crimen sine lege*, the prohibition on retrospective justice. But in the absence of such specific enforcement mechanisms, prosecutions for crimes against humanity were, at least until very recently, few and far between. Judicial practice has lagged a considerable way behind the theory of a customary universal jurisdiction for crimes against humanity, with few states realistically claiming the domestic legal competence to prosecute or extradite suspects. Political will lags behind even that.

The Rome Statute of the International Criminal Court provides unambiguously for criminal liability for war crimes in international and internal armed conflicts alike. Yet even when the Court comes into operation, its jurisdiction will not be general. It can only act if the offence occurred on the territory of a state that has ratified the Court's statute, or where the suspect is a national of such a state, and it has no retrospective application. In practice, therefore, the Court's jurisdiction will be limited to consenting states and to situations referred by the UN Security Council under its peace enforcement powers under Chapter 7 of the UN Charter.[23]

This highlights a gap which raises particular concerns: the enforcement gap. At the turn of the twenty-first century, the perpetrator of a simple assault may be more likely to be brought to justice than a person responsible for mass torture. Those responsible for killing a single human being may have a greater chance of being convicted than those who commit or contribute to genocide.

THE POLITICS OF INTERNATIONAL JUSTICE

Yet it cannot be denied that international criminal justice is developing at some speed. The last five years have seen the conviction for genocide of a former African prime minister (Jean Kambanda of Rwanda), the indictment of a serving European head of state and his subsequent arrest and trial (Slobodan Milošević), and assertions of extended jurisdiction by a number of European

[22] Arts 4–7 (torture is defined in Art 1). See appendix I.
[23] ICC Statute, Arts 12–13.

states in several cases, including those of Senator Pinochet, President Gaddafi and former Minister of Defence Sharon. In addition to the International Criminal Tribunals for the former Yugoslavia and Rwanda, established in 1993 and 1994, internationalised tribunals with a criminal jurisdiction were either created or are at an advanced stage of planning for East Timor, Cambodia and Sierra Leone. The International Criminal Court will become operational in 2003, now that it has received more than the 60 ratifications required to bring its Statute into force.

These changes establish their own momentum, but their speed also makes it difficult to predict future developments. It is also important to recognise that different voices are also being raised, most notably that of the International Court of Justice in the *Democratic Republic of Congo v Belgium* case, affirming the absolute immunity of a serving foreign minister from the jurisdiction of foreign national courts, and implying differences with the Pinochet decision.[23a] Inevitably these developments will have significant implications for international relations generally, in particular for sovereignty and the status of states as the privileged subjects of international law. And that means that international politics, rather than judicial innovation, is likely to remain the key driver.

International justice is necessarily dependent on political will, which makes it in turn susceptible to allegations that decisions permitting of a discretion may be taken on political rather than legal grounds. This may be illustrated by looking at the mixed record of states in cooperating with the International Criminal Tribunal for the former Yugoslavia (ICTY). Established in 1993 by the UN Security Council under its chapter 7 powers, the Tribunal received guarantees of cooperation in 1995 from the states or territorial entities party to the Dayton Peace Accord. Yet in the two or three years that followed, Balkan politicians made no effort to hand over indicted suspects and troops of the NATO-led Stabilization Force (S-FOR) showed little appetite for arresting them by force.

But a change in US policy and a pro-active approach by troops in the British sector of Bosnia-Herzegovina led to a series of high profile arrests in the course of 1997–1998. The death of Franjo Tuđman, Croatia's nationalist President, also marked a change in Croatia's relations with the international community and real moves towards cooperation with the Tribunal. By mid-1998, over a third of those publicly indicted by the ICTY Prosecutor had been delivered to The Hague. However, in Croatia there was a widespread perception that the Tribunal was anti-Croat, and in the Federal Republic of Yugoslavia and the Republika Serpska an equal conviction that it was anti-Serb.

With the Kosovan war in 1999 the allegations of political bias intensified. During the NATO bombing campaign, UK foreign secretary Robin Cook publicly handed over to the Tribunal intelligence intercepts, aerial photographs and other evidence of alleged Serbian war crimes. When the Tribunal subsequently

[23a] *ICJ* General List No 121, judgment of 14 Feb 2002. See generally Philippe Sands 'After Pinochet: the role of national courts', in Philippe Sands (ed), *From Nuremberg to The Hague* (CUP, Cambridge, 2003); see also chs 3 and 12.

issued a public indictment of Slobodan Milošević and three other Yugoslav and Serbian leaders, it had to face the accusation that its action was just a part of NATO's war effort. Under some pressure the ICTY Prosecutor initiated a preliminary investigation of NATO's record during the war in respect of a number of incidents when civilians were killed in bombing raids, including most notably an attack on a Belgrade television station. The Prosecutor found, however, that there was not sufficient evidence to justify issuing any indictments, despite the fact that human rights organisations had pointed to possible violations of the Geneva Conventions by NATO, and Amnesty International went as far as to name one action—the bombing of the Serbian state television station on 29 April 1999 with the loss of 15 civilian lives—as a war crime.

By 2001, cooperation with the Tribunal had become a key political issue in both Croatia and the Federal Republic of Yugoslavia. A proposal in Croatia to hand over two indictees to the Tribunal led to the resignation of four ministers from the Croatian cabinet and a confidence vote in Parliament, which the government survived. In Yugoslavia, following the fall of Milošević, the new President Vojislav Koštunica had begun moves to bring him to justice domestically on fraud and corruption charges. But the decision by the US and other governments to make a major package of aid dependent on the transfer of Milošević to the Tribunal increased pressure within Yugoslavia for his transfer. Despite the expressed opposition of President Koštunica and a federal court ruling halting an extradition order, the Serbian government of Prime Minister Zoran Djindjić handed Milošević over for transfer to The Hague on 28 June 2001—on the eve of an international donor conference to approve $1 billion in aid for Yugoslavia. The continuation of diplomatic pressure linked to aid ensured that further surrenders of high profile military and political indictees followed, including the surrender in April 2002 of Dragoljub Ojdanić, the General who commanded Yugoslav armed forces in Kosovo in 1998–9.

Timeline: the *Milošević* case

1993

25 May The International Criminal Tribunal for the former Yugoslavia (ICTY) is established by the UN Security Council. Resolution 827 expresses 'grave alarm at continuing reports of widespread and flagrant violations of international humanitarian law occurring within the territory of the former Yugoslavia, and especially in the Republic of Bosnia and Herzegovina, including reports of mass killings, massive, organized and systematic detention and rape of women, and the continuance of the practice of "ethnic cleansing"'.

1995

14 December The Federal Republic of Yugoslavia, the Republic of Croatia, and the Republic of Bosnia and Herzegovina sign the General Framework Agreement for Peace in Bosnia and Herzegovina, negotiated at Dayton, Ohio, USA. In Article IX the Agreement confirms the obligation of the parties 'to cooperate in the investigation and prosecution of war crimes and other violations of international humanitarian law'.

1997

7 May ICTY secures its first conviction, against Duško Tadić, for war crimes and crimes against humanity committed in Bosnia and Herzegovina. He is later sentenced to 20 years' imprisonment.

1999

27 May ICTY formally issues an indictment against Slobodan Milošević, President of the Federal Republic of Yugoslavia (FRY), and four others, accusing them of crimes against humanity, including deportation, murder and persecution, and murder as a violation of the laws or customs of war, committed in Kosovo. The co-accused are Milan Milutinović, President of Serbia, Nikola Sainović, Deputy Prime Minister of FRY, General Dragoljub Ojdanić, Chief of the General Staff of the VJ (Yugoslav army), and Vlajko Stojiljković, Minister of Internal Affairs of Serbia. Judge Hunt orders international arrest warrants sent to all UN member states, Switzerland, and the Minister of Justice of FRY, and orders each member state to freeze the assets of the accused.

2000

5 October Milošević falls from power in a popular uprising after the Democratic Opposition of Serbia claims victory in the 24 September presidential elections.

2001

28 February A criminal investigation is confirmed into Milošević's affairs, regarding allegations of fraud and theft of state property.

30 March Serbian authorities attempt to arrest Milošević, the day before the expiry of a US deadline to arrest him, linked to financial aid. The attempt fails.

31 March A second attempt to arrest Milošević, with a special forces team, also fails.

1 April After a prolonged stand off, Milošević hands himself over to police in the early hours of the morning. He is transferred to Belgrade Central Prison where he becomes prisoner 101980, charged with defrauding the state treasury.

23 June The Yugoslav government passes a decree paving the way for indicted suspects to be transferred to ICTY.

28 June The Yugoslav Constitutional Court suspends enactment of the decree, pending the outcome of an appeal against it by Milošević.

The Serbian Cabinet of Prime Minister Zoran Djindjić votes to surrender Milošević to The Hague. Milošević is taken from Belgrade Central Prison and flown by helicopter to a US-run airbase in Tuzla, Bosnia and Herzegovina. From there he is put on a NATO plane bound for The Hague.

29 June Milošević is transferred to the custody of ICTY. An amended indictment is confirmed charging Milošević and his co-accused with crimes committed in Kosovo between January and June 1999.

2 July Milošević declines to appoint defence lawyers, saying he will represent himself.

3 July Milošević appears in court for the first time. He refuses to plead, stating that he does not recognise the authority of the court. A 'not-guilty' plea is entered for all counts on the indictment relating to Kosovo.

2 August General Radislav Krstić is convicted by ICTY of genocide and sentenced to 46 years in prison in connection with the murder of over 7,000 men and boys at Srebrenica in July 1995.

31 August A Dutch court rejects a challenge by Milošević to the jurisdiction of ICTY, which Milošević had argued was illegal.

September–November The ICTY Registrar appoints Steven Kay QC, Branislav Tapuskovic and Michail Wladimiroff to act as *amici curiae* in the three cases. The trial chamber had considered their appointment 'desirable and in the interests of securing a fair trial', noting that their role was 'not to represent the accused but to assist in the proper determination of the case'.

8 October Judge Almiro Rodrigues confirms an indictment charging Milošević with grave breaches of the 1949 Geneva Conventions, violations of the laws or customs of war and crimes against humanity committed in Croatia in 1991-2.

29 October A second amended indictment is confirmed by ICTY in the case relating to Kosovo, charging Milošević, Milutinović, Ojdanić, Sainović and Stojiljković with one count of violations of the laws or customs of war and four counts of crimes against humanity, committed in 1999. A 'not-guilty' plea is entered for Milošević for all counts on the indictment relating to Croatia.

22 November Judge Richard May confirms an indictment charging Milošević with 27 counts of crimes against humanity, grave breaches of the Geneva Conventions and violations of the laws or customs of war, and two counts of genocide and complicity in genocide, committed between 1992 and 1995 in Bosnia and Herzegovina.

11 December A 'not-guilty' plea is entered for Milošević for all counts on the indictment relating to Bosnia and Herzegovina.

2002

1 February The appeals chamber orders that the three indictments concerning Kosovo, Croatia and Bosnia and Herzegovina be joined together in one single trial.

12 February The Milošević trial begins in trial chamber III, before Judge Richard May from the UK (presiding), Judge Patrick Robinson of Jamaica and Judge O-Gon Kwon of South Korea. The trial begins with evidence only on the charges relating to Kosovo.

14 February Milošević begins his opening statement in his own defence, claiming that 'the whole world knows that this is a political trial'.

March Vlajko Stojiljković commits suicide.

25 April General Ojdanić surrenders voluntarily to ICTY.

2 May Ibrahim Rugova, President of Kosovo, tells the Tribunal that 'Belgrade clearly decided to destroy Kosovo through violence and war'. Nikola Sainović surrenders to ICTY.

11 September Prosecution case regarding Kosovo concludes.

26 September Prosecution begins the presentation of its case regarding Croatia and Bosnia and Herzegovina.

1 October Stipe Mesić, President of Croatia, appears as a prosecution witness. 'He was always working for the war option', Mesić testifies, saying that Milošević had planned to create a Greater Serbia 'on the ruins of the former Yugoslavia', and the Yugoslav army had obeyed Milošević alone.

22 November Timothy McCormack designated to act as *amicus curiae*, replacing Professor Wladimiroff.

6 December Milan Babić, a former Croatian Serb leader and mayor of Knin, testifies that Milošević played a key role in the Croat Serb uprising in 1991 after Croatia proclaimed its independence.

2003

9 January A former member of the paramilitary Special Operations Unit or 'Red Berets' during the Bosnian war testifies that it had operated under the direct command of Milošević's government.

13 January The trial is adjourned for the sixth time on account of Milošević's ill health (influenza).

20 January Milan Milutinović surrenders voluntarily to ICTY.

Autumn Milošević's defence scheduled to begin.

Sources: ICTY, BBC, authors' own sources.

Political policies and events thus impact heavily on the work of the International Criminal Tribunal outside the strict confines of the courtroom, where by contrast the Tribunal has succeeded in building up a strong reputation for judicial integrity and impartiality. This is not to say, however, that proceedings in the courtroom may not themselves have a political impact. Broadcast live throughout Serbia, the Milošević trial quickly became one of the most widely watched in history. Milošević began his defence by denouncing the legitimacy of the court, arguing that it was a propaganda exercise sponsored by NATO, but he continued to participate actively as the trial went on. Having refused to appoint counsel, Milošević used the opportunity of conducting his own defence to score political points while his legal interests were safeguarded by three *amici curiae* appointed by the court. The resulting impression made by the opening phase of the proceedings led at least one human rights activist to argue that the Tribunal should pay more attention to public relations, mindful of the impact the proceedings would have on public opinion and reconciliation in the former Yugoslavia.[24] Tribunal staff cannot of course ignore the public impression created by the Tribunal's work, which continues to be dependent on international co-operation for funding, as well as for the gathering of evidence, the arrest and delivery of indictees, and for appropriate pressure on those states which are initially unwilling to co-operate.

Outside the courtroom at least, international criminal justice cannot be immune from strategic influences. It is plain that global and regional politics renders the commitment of some states to international justice more decisive than that of others. This leads to some uncomfortable conclusions: for example, one could speculate that if the Tribunal *had* issued indictments against NATO personnel over incidents in the Kosovan war, it might have seriously undermined Western support for the Tribunal and possibly compromised the whole project of international criminal justice, including the International Criminal Court.

Much has been written on the increasingly vociferous hostility of the United States to the ICC,[25] which most often dwells on the threat of politically-

[24] Vojin Dimitrijević, 'Justice must be done and be seen to be done: the Milošević trial', *East European Constitutional Review*, 11/1-2, Winter/Spring 2002, 59–62.

[25] See for example Sarah B Sewall and Carl Kaysen, (eds), *The United States and the International*

motivated prosecutions against US personnel. The legal arguments deployed by the US against the ICC include the claim that US nationals abroad should not be in jeopardy of prosecution under a jurisdiction created by a treaty which the US has not ratified. State parties to the ICC Statute counter that there exist extensive safeguards to check any abuse of power by the ICC prosecutor,[26] that US nationals abroad already fall under the territorial criminal jurisdiction of foreign states, and that numerous other treaties exist which establish international criminal jurisdictions covering the nationals of non-ratifying states. Nevertheless, there is no doubt that the sustained opposition of the US represents a potentially significant impediment to the ICC securing widespread international cooperation.[27]

That said, it is equally clear that the international legal order is sufficiently mature to mean that the support of any particular state—even a permanent member of the Security Council—is unlikely to constitute a *sine qua non* for the success of the International Criminal Court. Despite the opposition of China and the United States, the Rome Statute of the ICC has attracted widespread support and exceeded the required 60 ratifications at a speed that few would have predicted following the adoption of the Statute in 1998.

WHAT IS INTERNATIONAL CRIMINAL JUSTICE FOR?

Professor Antonio Cassese, the first President of the ICTY, has argued that international criminal justice is an imperfect but necessary alternative to the existing mechanisms available for enforcing norms against war crimes and crimes against humanity, namely peace-keeping operations, and counter-measures or 'peaceful reprisals', such as sanctions. He has sought to justify the development and application of international criminal justice by reference to five key attributes: justice for victims, reconciliation, the establishment of truth, imposition of the rule of law, and deterrence.[28]

Developing Professor Cassese's classification, it is possible to identify eight justifications for international criminal justice. These are considered briefly below, together with some of the common countervailing arguments.

Criminal Court; National Security and International Law (Rowman and Littlefield, Lenham MD, 2000); and for a recent overview, David P Forsythe, 'The United States and International Criminal Justice', (2002) *Human Rights Quarterly 24* .

[26] See ch 7.

[27] US opposition to the ICC led in July 2002 to the USA threatening to block renewal of the UN's peacekeeping mandate in Bosnia and Herzegovina unless its personnel were exempted from prosecution before the ICC. In a compromise deal, the UN Security Council adopted a resolution which requests the ICC not to proceed for a 12-month period with investigation or prosecution of any case involving personnel from a non-state party to the ICC Statute engaged in UN operations: UN Security Council Resolution 1422, 12 July 2002. Furthermore, the US has pressured over 20 governments to sign agreements not to surrender to the ICC US nationals who are alleged to have committed crimes on the territory of a state party to the ICC Statute.

[28] Lecture at London School of Economics and Political Science, 13 Nov 2000 (unpublished).

1. Providing justice for victims

The cry for 'justice', as voiced insistently by the relatives of those forcibly disappeared in the *Pinochet* case, provides the first and foremost argument for the application of international criminal law, given that the relevant state is itself frequently unwilling or unable to act. International standards provide that reparation to victims may take the form of restitution, compensation, rehabilitation, and satisfaction and guarantees of non-repetition,[29] and the ICC Statute makes provision for such reparation.[30] Although crimes against humanity, by definition, offend against the whole of humankind, the case for justice for their immediate victims has an overwhelming moral force that is generally recognised even by those opposed to international criminal justice on political or strategic grounds.

2. Establishing truth for reconciliation

This justification is, together with the objective of removing criminals from power (see number 5 below), probably the most contentious. The transitional period following violent repression or conflict is generally a difficult and dangerous one, and it is sometimes argued that normal legal and moral imperatives can be suspended in the face of the overwhelming necessity to avoid the further outbreak of violence or even war. Atrocities, so this argument runs, are frequently committed by both sides in a conflict, and insistently raking up the past is an obstacle to people forgetting and moving on. To this, the victims' representatives counter that a crime against humanity is not something that anyone is every likely to forget, and that the public establishment and acknowledgement of the truth, as provided in a court of law, is a necessary condition for genuine reconciliation.

It is now widely recognised that one of the most important legacies of the Nuremberg Tribunal was its role in amassing and publishing incontestable evidence of Nazi crimes against humanity, making it rationally impossible for partisan historians to re-write history subsequently. So-called 'truth' commissions may perform a useful function in uncovering some facts publicly, but their investigations are generally strictly circumscribed, and they do not establish responsibility for the crimes they describe.[31]

3. Providing an alternative to vengeance

Civil conflicts typically exhibit a cyclical pattern of violence with killings perpetrated in retaliation for other killings—or at least justified in this way. In delivering legal retribution focused strictly on those responsible, criminal justice provides an

[29] See 'Basic Principles and Guidelines on the Right to a Remedy and Reparation for Victims of Violations of International Human Rights and Humanitarian Law', UN Doc E/CN.4/2000/62, annex.

[30] ICC Statute, Art 75.

[31] See the discussion in ch 14; see also the contribution by Alex Boraine in ch 13.

alternative to vengeance. This may help break the cycle of violence, with international legal mechanisms once again applying where domestic courts are not considered capable of guaranteeing a fair trial for suspects from either side in a conflict.

4. Distinguishing individual from group responsibility

The responsibility for an atrocity is often ascribed to a collectivity, whether it be a particular ethnic, religious or social group, a nation or a state. This invites retribution on all the members of that group, once again helping perpetuate cycles of inter-group violence. Yet despite some commentators' references to 'ancient tribal hatreds', the different ethnic groups in areas of conflict have often lived together peacefully for centuries; violence is often linked to leaders' exploitation of ethnic difference for their own political gain. Targeting solely those individuals responsible for atrocities, criminal justice is preferable to measures which target a whole group, of whom the vast majority are generally innocent.

Sanctions and other inter-state measures are aimed at governments and leaders but their effect is invariably felt by a wider population. The punitive Versailles settlement imposed on Germany after the First World War, which led to a deep-seated resentment easily exploited by the Nazi party, can be contrasted with the Allied response to Germany after the Second World War, combining war crimes trials with the Marshall Plan for reconstruction.

5. Removing criminals from power

Those most likely to commit war crimes or crimes against humanity are often those who have done so already. This makes their removal from positions of power an imperative for the suppression of such crimes. The public indictment of Bosnian Serb leaders Radovan Karadzić and Ratko Mladić ensured their exclusion from the Dayton peace talks and their subsequent political marginalisation in Bosnian Serb politics.

However, this argument is challenged by sceptics of international criminal justice, who contend that the threat of criminal trials will dissuade human rights abusers from ever relinquishing power. More practically, they suggest that insistence on the application of international criminal law severely impacts on the freedom to negotiate at peace talks, constraining, for example, the scope of amnesties that can be offered. (Interestingly, however, this was not the case at Dayton, where all the parties, including President Milošević, signed up to cooperate with the ICTY.)

6. Deterring future crimes

It has not been established that international trials will make dictators 'think again' and deter the commission of future crimes against humanity. The slaughter of over 7,000 men and boys at Srebrenica in 1995, the worst single crime in Europe since the Second World War, occurred two years *after* the ICTY was set up (although before it had shown its teeth and proved itself to be more than just a sop to international conscience). At a more junior, operational level, impunity clearly contributes to the spread and institutionalisation of abuses by military and police personnel, while their clear prohibition and the consistent imposition of disciplinary measures can effectively suppress them (for example, the concern of US troops for the respect of international humanitarian law in the Gulf War of 1991 can usefully be contrasted with their earlier conduct in Vietnam). But establishing whether the deterrent effect can be seen at the level of a country's leadership may have to wait until international criminal justice is sufficiently widely enforced to constitute a real threat.

Two conclusions can, however, be made. The first is that political and military rulers, or former rulers, are increasingly showing a wariness of the consequences of the development of a system of international justice. There are numerous examples of individuals avoiding international travel, or fleeing or avoiding countries where they have reason to fear possible arrest, or seeking specific guarantees of immunity.[32] Secondly, the grant of amnesties—the negation, in other words, of criminal justice—is at best ineffective and at worst counterproductive in preventing further atrocities. Following a brutal eight-year conflict, rebel forces in Sierra Leone were awarded amnesties and seats in a government of national unity in a peace agreement signed at Lomé in 1999. Encouraged by its success, the main Revolutionary United Front quickly resumed the campaign of killings, rape and mutilations for which it had become notorious, and within a year was again threatening the capital Freetown.

7. Supporting the rule of law

The credibility of the United Nations and the whole edifice of international standard-setting is damaged when flagrant abuses of human rights or humanitarian law are repeatedly committed despite diplomatic condemnation. This is particularly the case when a lack of political will impedes the implementation of the UN's own agreed mechanisms, for example in the international response to the Rwandan genocide in 1994. By targeting those responsible for the worst abuses of all, international criminal justice provides essential support for the international rule of law, not least because it places a similar sanction on the rulers of a state as domestic criminal law places on a state's citizens.

Critics argue that this is to mistake the nature of international law, the foundation of which is the sovereignty of independent states. To the extent that moves at international justice challenge state sovereignty, they threaten the comity of nations and by extension undermine the international legal order itself.

[32] See the contribution by Reed Brody in ch 13 for some examples.

8. Filling the enforcement gap created by the advance of human rights and humanitarian norms

Few jurists today, however, would defend an absolute notion of state sovereignty in the face of continued advances in international treaty law. Every treaty, by definition, is a voluntary acceptance of limits on a state's absolute freedom to act, and the UN Charter imposes the greatest limitations of all. The mere existence of over 100 multi-lateral treaties with normative human rights or humanitarian content—to say nothing of the undiminished frequency of atrocities round the world—raises the question of implementation and enforcement. In addition to the general sense in which this question was raised above, a specific enforcement gap has been created by the fact that instruments of humanitarian law in some cases themselves limit states' ability to act.

The oldest method of enforcing international law, and still the one with the widest scope, is self-help. Without a centralised global authority or judicial order, states are still heavily reliant on their own action to enforce their rights and defend their interests. But in extreme situations, the action they can take is now strictly constrained by the absolute interdiction on certain practices and targets of war. Although disputed by some states, it is now generally accepted that international law protects non-combatants from any form of armed reprisal (that is, a proportionate response to compel another state to stop acting illegally). Similarly, the use of certain weapons, such as biological weapons, is banned by treaty even in circumstances when they are employed by the other side. In low-intensity conflicts, armed groups frequently coerce the civilian population into sustaining or shielding their activities, making any form of effective military response highly problematic. What can a state do when confronted by such illegal actions, other than denounce them to the international community? Without the sanction provided by international criminal law, the law-abiding state is left vulnerable with no proportionate means of response to a wide range of illegal violence perpetrated by another state or by armed groups.

It is apparent that the arguments explaining the justifications for international justice fall into three overlapping categories, corresponding to the main functions of modern systems of criminal justice: reparation (arguments 1–4), retribution (3–6) and prevention (5–8). One function which is familiar to penal theory is absent, namely rehabilitation.

INTERNATIONAL LAW AFTER PINOCHET AND MILOŠEVIĆ

Where do we stand following the *Pinochet* case, the indictment and trial of Milošević, and the founding of the International Criminal Court? The contributors to this book seek to provide detailed answers to that question, both for the international legal order and for the situation in particular states.

In the opening chapter, Benjamin Ferencz gives a personal account of the development of international criminal law from Nuremberg to the International Criminal Court. His own experience highlights two aspects of the legacy of Nuremberg that have received comparatively less attention: the successor trials conducted at Nuremberg before US judges after the International Military Tribunal had closed, which first confirmed that crimes against humanity could be committed in peacetime; and the huge programme of work to secure compensation for survivors of the Holocaust. He argues that one part of the legacy that has sadly not been realised by future generations, despite being of central importance at Nuremberg, is the recognition of the waging of aggressive war as the supreme war crime.

Far from starting at Nuremberg, as is often assumed, the history of international jurisdictions over grave crimes goes back many centuries, as Christopher Hall explains in chapter 2. He describes the concept of 'universal' jurisdiction, and underscores the practical, legal and other rationales for its emergence. In his opinion 'none of the objections to the principle of universal jurisdiction have merit'; although some of the problems with its exercise are noted by him and other contributors to this book.

In chapter 3 Brigitte Stern assesses the state of the rules of international law concerning the entitlement of serving and former heads of state to claim jurisdictional immunities from criminal proceedings, both at the international and national levels. She considers the different meanings ascribed to the term 'immunity' and its relationship to the 'act of state' doctrine, which in some jurisdictions (mainly common law) has limited municipal courts from examining the validity of the acts of foreign governments, including from a human rights or criminal law perspective. She concludes that following the judgment of the House of Lords in *Pinochet* it will be difficult to characterise 'international crimes' as official acts, and that this will make claims of immunity more difficult to uphold. Nevertheless she expresses a hint of caution, noting that it may yet be preferable not to open the door 'too widely' at the national level, at least at this time, and that the answerability of heads of state may best be addressed at the international level (for example, before the International Criminal Court) in order to limit the possibilities of political bias.

Timothy McCormack reviews the reasons for the willingness—or unwillingness—of states to subject their own nationals to municipal justice for international crimes. His contribution indicates the background against which the 'internationalisation' of criminal justice has occurred, leading first to municipal proceedings in the courts of third countries and, more recently, proceedings before international tribunals. He identifies three sets of circumstances which influence the likelihood of domestic proceedings in the 'home' state: whether there has been a change of political regime; whether there exists the possibility—or threat—of international proceedings; and whether the violations relate to violations by a state's own armed forces outside the territory of the state. His historical review concludes that the 'critical distinction in terms of the likelihood of domestic trials of own nationals is undoubtedly the "us" and "them" distinction': it is more likely that the 'other' will be subjected to domestic proceedings, and this factor he considers provides a 'compelling argument for the establishment of an international criminal law regime', including the internationalisation of domestic institutions (as is occurring in East Timor, Kosovo and Sierra Leone).

Part Two of this book addresses 'Justice in International and Mixed Law Courts'. Graham Blewitt describes the work of the International Criminal Tribunals for the former Yugoslavia and for Rwanda. Amongst the various topics he addresses, he focuses on the relationship between national and international criminal proceedings and the early jurisprudence of the ICTY. Amongst the challenges facing the ICTY he signals the particular importance of ensuring the arrest of all high level fugitives,[33] the need to ensure that trials are conducted without undue delay, and the possible future relationship between the ICTY and the ICC. By way of conclusion he focuses on the possible deterrent effect of fully functioning international criminal courts, and the contribution of such bodies to the termination of impunity.

At the heart of an effective international criminal justice system is the need to ensure appropriate rules governing the collection and admissibility of evidence, in the context of significant cultural and legal differences, and to ensure the rights of the accused who face charges of the utmost gravity. Richard May, presiding judge at the trial of Slobodan Milošević at the International Criminal Tribunal for the former Yugoslavia, recognises the challenges this poses for the emerging system of international criminal justice. His chapter is of particular interest given the criticisms sometimes voiced of the workings of international tribunals by those from common law countries who are unfamiliar with rules of evidence and procedures drawn from civil law systems.

Judge May considers issues and problems associated with the age of the evidence, the scope of the trials, and the rules governing the admissibility of the evidence. He focuses in particular on the circumstances in which rules of evidence might be relaxed (for example by permitting the admission of affidavits), and the importance of ensuring equality between the parties in any proceedings. He also addresses two particular problems: the need to provide adequate protection of witnesses, and the difficulties associated with the gathering of evidence from different countries and organisations. His contribution indicates a range of issues which will need to be addressed both at the national and international levels, as the 'system' of international criminal justice matures.

M Cherif Bassiouni describes the circumstances leading to the adoption of the Statute of the International Criminal Court, in Rome in the summer of 1998. He provides a detailed commentary on the particular characteristics of the Court, including its jurisdiction, procedural rules, and related issues, clarifying in the process some of the misconceptions that have arisen about how the

[33] We note here the transformative effect on public perceptions of the ICTY which followed the arrest and transfer of Slobodan Milošević to the ICTY.

Court will operate. He concludes that although the ICC is a product of compromise, it is nevertheless an historic step in the direction of providing international criminal justice.

Diane Orentlicher looks to the future of international criminal law and in particular at the growing number of criminal tribunals around the world which combine international and national elements. In this practice and in the communication between national, international and mixed law courts trying atrocious crimes she sees the construction of a transnational jurisprudence, 'developing a common code of humanity'. As potential fora proliferate, however, there needs to be a way of deciding which has priority. She suggests that jurisdictional clashes should be resolved by considering the respective interests of relevant communities. Although they draw on the principle of universality, most of the new mechanisms retain a territorial or nationality link with the crimes in question. The legitimacy of prosecutions in fora outside the territorial state will be enhanced, she concludes, if priority has been given to the jurisdictional claims of states that have substantial nationality links with the defendant and/or victim: an approach that can be described as 'universality plus'.

The third part of the book considers the pursuit of international criminal justice in national courts. William Aceves and Paul Hoffman assess the pursuit of crimes against humanity in the United States, and conclude by identifying the need for a comprehensive liability regime to prosecute crime against humanity. They note the United States' general support for the codification and prosecution of crimes against humanity, following historical opposition, as well as the more recent opposition of that country to the ICC Statute, in its adopted form. Their contribution then goes on to describe the regime governing criminal liability for crimes against humanity (including hostage taking, genocide, torture and war crimes), which has been little utilised. By contrast, the regime for civil liability for crimes against humanity—emanating from the Alien Tort Claims Act of 1789—is 'robust' and has led to a growing case-law (the controversial implications of which are more usually noted outside the United States than within, we would observe).

By comparison, the situation in the United Kingdom is discussed in a separate contribution by Clare Montgomery who explores the implications of the House of Lords' judgment in *Pinochet No 3* for the enforcement of other international crimes within the national jurisdiction. She considers the main rationale of the judgment is that the liability of other public officials alleged to have committed a crime outside the United Kingdom will turn on whether the offence in question was incorporated into English law by statute and it occurred after the entry into force of such legislation. With regards to immunity, she concludes that the various judgments in *Pinochet* indicate that a serving head of state would continue to enjoy immunity *ratione personae* before national courts for acts of torture. She also considers that a 'predicament' which remains to be addressed is the disparity between the jurisdiction of national and international courts, an issue that will be heightened now that the ICC Statute has come into force. She explores this question more broadly by reference to the case of Tharcisse Muvunyi, whose arrest and extradition from the United Kingdom was requested by the ICTR in February 2000. By way of conclusion, and urging greater consistency and clarity, she notes the many questions that remain unanswered, including the circumstances in which universal jurisdiction over international crimes will exist in the absence of national legislation creating a jurisdictional basis.

Turning from criminal proceedings to civil actions, Fiona McKay considers the prospects for US-style (Alien Tort Claims Act) civil proceedings in the United Kingdom and elsewhere in Europe. She notes the conflict between, on the one hand, the emergence of public international law norms committing states to combat impunity and, on the other, rules of private international law which restrict the exercise of extraterritorial jurisdiction in civil matters. She reviews a series of recent cases on the right of reparation under international law through civil actions in the national courts of third states and identifies the difficulties which plaintiffs are likely to face in bringing cross border cases (rules of evidence, limitation periods, tracing and freezing assets, and costs). In relation to human rights issues she identifies three of particular importance: establishing a cause of action, establishing jurisdiction, and immunity. She concludes that although there are some signs of movement towards the emergence of 'civil universal jurisdiction', the law is likely to develop differently in common law and civil law jurisdictions, and law reform is needed.

Andrew Clapham takes the reader from these more general and cross-cutting issues to a single case at the crossroads of national and international law, namely the case brought by the Democratic Republic of Congo against Belgium at the International Court of Justice, challenging the issue of an international arrest warrant pursuant to the principle of universal jurisdiction. He considers that the case, whose outcome was seen by many human rights activists as a reverse, prompts us to consider the limits of state action with regard to the quest to ensure justice for international crimes through national action. He analyses the fundamental concepts raised by the case (issues which lie at the heart of the emerging international criminal justice 'system'): sovereignty, diplomatic immunity, universal jurisdiction. He concludes that presently international law does not prohibit the exercise of universal jurisdiction over certain international crimes and that it does not expressly prohibit that application of national criminal law to a person located outside the territorial jurisdiction of the investigating state. He questions whether the ICJ's 'prioritisation of smooth inter-state relations over the emerging regime of international criminal law' will be followed by other courts.

The rapid pace of recent developments in securing justice for crimes under international law has involved legal practitioners working on issues of the utmost gravity but having to navigate in relatively uncharted waters. Chapter 13 brings together a set of personal perspectives from a prosecutor, national and international advocates, UN officials and human rights activists who, like other contributors to this book, have been closely involved in the developments concerned. They provide a range of insights into the workings of truth commissions, international tribunals and national prosecutions, and the combination of practical and theoretical questions that confront them.

In the concluding chapter, Mark Lattimer revisits some of the major international legal developments covered in this book by seeing them in the context of an enforcement crisis in the international system of human rights protection. He begins by exploring the emergence of the concept of enforced disappearance as an international crime, a development which was pivotal in the *Pinochet* case and has been of major significance to the application of justice in transitional societies. He then turns to the 'collision' between those norms of international law requiring prosecution for international crimes such as torture and those norms establishing principles of sovereign immunity. His conclusion here is that the judgment in *Pinochet No 3* marked a turning 'away from absolute deference before sovereign authority towards the international enforcement of justice'. This relates to his broader conclusion, that recent international criminal law developments have lent new credence to the practicability of enforcing human rights which is already being felt in other jurisdictions around the globe.

* * *

From these contributions emerge a number of common themes. The characterisation of certain acts as international crimes is broadly recognised. With such characterisation there has also emerged a growing application of an extended criminal jurisdiction, and this in turn has given rise to a transformation in some of the basic assumptions underpinning the traditional international legal order, shifting the balance from a system designed presumptively to protect the interests of the sovereign to a system which places greater emphasis on the rights of the individual. With this shift national and international criminal jurisdictions are forced to confront issues for which the international community has not yet legislated responses: the circumstances in which a court (national or international) should recognise an amnesty granted by a state; the conditions governing the assessment of claims to immunity from jurisdiction; and the proper balance in the relationship between competing national jurisdictions, and between national and international jurisdictions. Beyond these broad systemic issues, the contributors identify a range of other procedural and institutional issues which will give rise, in coming years, to difficult questions. If it is now possible to talk of a 'system' of international criminal justice, as part of the broader international legal order, such a 'system' remains in its early stages of development.

PART I

Atrocity, Impunity, Justice

1

From Nuremberg to Rome: A Personal Account

BENJAMIN FERENCZ

Prosecuting crimes against peace and humanity was not invented at Nuremberg in 1945. Since ancient days, the legality of war itself and how wars were waged had been debated by renowned scholars from Plato to Grotius. Over 200 years ago, Immanuel Kant's *Zum Ewigen Frieden* called for the protection of peace and human rights through the rule of international law.

A major effort to curb war-related crimes by international law arose after World War I. In 1919, a commission—appointed by the victors—concluded: 'All persons belonging to enemy countries, however high their position. . . who have been guilty of offences against the laws and customs of war or the laws of humanity are liable to criminal prosecution.' To avoid allegations that the enemy was being subjected to *ex post facto* law, the German Kaiser was not charged with the crime of aggression since no sovereign had ever before been brought to trial for making war. Instead, the Treaty of Versailles provided that Wilhelm II would be tried by an Allied court for 'a supreme offence against international morality and the sanctity of treaties'. Lesser leaders, accused of various atrocities, were also to be handed over for trial.

Germany promptly denounced the treaty as a *Diktat*. The Kaiser found refuge in the Netherlands which refused to extradite him, noting that there existed no international criminal tribunal competent to try a head of state. The frustrated Allied Commissioners recommended that German aggression be formally condemned and that 'for the future penal sanctions should be provided for such grave outrages against the elementary principles of international law'. Some German officers accused of atrocities were eventually brought to trial by the German Supreme Court which handed down a few light sentences. The inability to bring to court those primarily responsible for war and its atrocities emphasised the need to create a more effective system of international criminal justice.

In 1927, the League of Nations declared that 'a war of aggression can never serve as the means of settling international disputes and is, in consequence, an international crime'. In 1928, the Kellogg–Briand Pact renounced war as an instrument of national policy and a Pan–American Conference declared a war of aggression to be 'a crime against mankind'. But nothing was done to create a court to punish violators. Japan invaded Manchuria in 1931 and Mussolini brazenly seized Ethiopia. In 1935, following the assassination in Marseilles of King Alexander of Yugoslavia, the outraged League appointed a committee to draft a convention for the repression of such terrorist acts. The committee appended a complete text—about five pages long—for an international criminal court. No nation was willing to accept it. Humankind would pay dearly for the indecision of the decision-makers.

Hitler began the German march of conquest over Europe. Behind the *Blitzkrieg* of the German tanks came the *Einsatzgruppen* to murder without pity or remorse every Jewish man, woman or child, every gypsy or perceived adversary they could catch. Prisoners of war were executed or starved to death, millions of civilians were forced into slave labour, while those unable to work were simply annihilated in gas chambers and concentration camps. Japanese troops committed similar crimes in areas they occupied. Repeated Allied warnings that those responsible for atrocities would be held to account went unheeded. The British proposed that, when the war was won, prominent Nazis be taken out and simply executed. It could have come as a relief but not as a surprise when defeated German and Japanese leaders found themselves in the dock to answer for their deeds in a court of law.

PRELUDE TO NUREMBERG

When the United States entered World War II, I applied for an assignment in army intelligence but was disqualified because of my foreign birth. The Air Force turned me down because I was only five feet one-half inch tall. As soon as I received my law degree I became a private in the supply room of an anti-aircraft battalion being trained for the invasion of France. In due course, we landed on the beaches of Normandy, and joined General Patton's Third Army pursuing Germans back across the Rhine and on to the final 'Battle of the Bulge'. After almost three years of military service, I was honourably discharged as a Sergeant and was awarded five battle stars which, as far as I could make out, was a reward for not having been wounded or killed.

The most formative events of my army career had to do with war crimes. Professor Sheldon Glueck, for whom I had worked as a research assistant at Harvard, had written a book on the prosecution of war criminals. When Washington turned to him for guidance, he suggested that the army try to locate me, noting that I had just written an article on the rehabilitation of army offenders which identified me as a corporal with the 115th AAA Gun Battalion. Much to my surprise, in December 1944, I was transferred to a new Judge Advocate section of Third Army Headquarters in Luxembourg that had been ordered to set up a war crimes branch.

The first persons targeted for trial were Germans who had committed atrocities against American troops, such as killing prisoners or downed allied flyers. Captured Nazi concentration camp commanders would also be called to account before an American military court. Investigations were carried out by a few enlisted men. After digging up bodies of American flyers murdered by enraged German mobs, I prepared reports identifying the suspects and listing the laws of war that had been violated. Witnesses were ordered to write out a complete description of the criminal event—under penalty of being shot. Confessions from accused were obtained by similar persuasions—even though they were usually rewritten under more sympathetic circumstances before being validated by an officer who would offer it in evidence. It was a grisly assignment. But the worst was yet to come.

I entered several concentration camps, such as Buchenwald and Mauthausen strewn with putrid bodies of the dead and dying. My primary goal was to capture all official camp records, including registries of inmates killed in the camps and the roster of German officers and guards, and have the crimes certified by survivors' affidavits describing their ordeals and naming their torturers. Amid the overwhelming stench of burning skeletons, I was exposed to the filth of dysentery, typhus and other diseases that racked the emaciated bodies of the liberated inmates. I uncovered many mass graves as I followed trails of starving prisoners who had been whipped through the woods by fleeing guards—only to have their brains blown out when they could no longer go on. To keep from going mad, my senses became numbed as my mind built an artificial barrier and refused to be derailed by what my eyes saw. But the trauma was indelible and will remain with me forever.

As a form of symbolic justice, the army decided to try the captured criminals in a former Nazi concentration camp near Munich. I hammered up the sign saying 'U.S. ARMY WAR CRIMES TRIALS, DACHAU'. The proceedings were in the nature of traditional military commissions following rules similar to those of regular army courts martial, where judges, prosecutors and defence counsel were US army officers—many with no legal training. No great new principles of law were established and the trials were abruptly discontinued when Pentagon policy toward Germany was reversed. The less said about the US Army war crimes trials the better. I left Germany as soon as I could after the war and hoped never to return there again.

The highly publicised trial of German Field Marshal Hermann Goering and other Nazi leaders accused of war crimes was already underway before the International Military Tribunal (IMT) at Nuremberg. Shortly after I arrived in New York I received a telegram from the War Department inviting me to come to Washington. I was urged to return to Germany as a civilian with the simulated rank of full Colonel to continue doing essentially what I had done as an army sergeant. I was also interviewed by Colonel Telford Taylor, a key member of the US prosecution team at the IMT. The US had decided to conduct a number of additional trials at Nuremberg after the IMT trial was completed. These 'subsequent proceedings' were to portray the broad panorama of Nazi criminality. Taylor was the man in charge and he was looking for help. He was a Harvard lawyer with a distinguished career in government and I agreed to join him. I was married in New York intending to leave for Nuremberg with my bride—like myself also a refugee from Transylvania—for a pleasant European sojourn at army expense. It turned out to be quite an unusual honeymoon.

THE TRIALS AT NUREMBERG

On 8 August 1945, three months after the end of World War II, culminating six-weeks of intensive negotiations in London, the United States, Great Britain, the Soviet Union and France signed the Charter creating the International Military Tribunal for the Prosecution and Punishment of the Major War Criminals of the European Axis. Only three crimes for which there would be individual responsibility were to be within the jurisdiction of the court: crimes against peace (planning and waging aggressive war); war crimes (prohibited by custom and the Hague Conventions); and crimes against humanity (such as genocide and similar persecutions against civilian populations).

Only leaders and organisers or instigators who conspired to commit the crimes would be held responsible by the IMT. Superior orders would be no defence but could be considered in mitigation of punishment. The official position of the defendants would not free them from responsibility. The provisions of the 30 Articles were carefully designed to assure a fair trial for the accused.

The principal architect of the IMT Charter was Robert H Jackson, on leave from the US Supreme Court. Justice Jackson's opening statement as the Chief Prosecutor for the United States was an inspiring call for universally binding international law:

> The privilege of opening the first trial in history for crimes against the peace of the world imposes a grave responsibility... That four great nations, flushed with victory and stung with injury, stay the hand of vengeance and voluntarily submit their captive enemies to the judgment of the law is one of the most significant tributes that Power has ever paid to Reason.... We must never forget that the record on which we judge these defendants is the record on which history will judge us tomorrow.[1]

Twenty-four major Nazi war criminals were placed on trial. Defendants were represented by competent counsel of their own choice—paid for by the Allies. The judges from the victor states regretted that there were no real neutrals to sit in judgment but vengeance was never their goal. The trial, in four languages, was open to the public so that all could see that it was conducted to 'commend itself to posterity as fulfilling humanity's aspirations to do justice'. Of the 24 original defendants, one hanged himself before trial and one was pronounced

[1] 21 Nov 1945; see *Trial of the Major War Criminals before the International Military Tribunal* (the 'Blue Series'), 14 Nov 1945–1 Oct 1946 (US GPO, 1947–1949); T Taylor, *The Anatomy of the Nuremberg Trials* (Knopf, New York, 1992).

medically unable to attend. Twelve were sentenced to hang, including Goering, Martin Bormann, Ernst Kaltenbrunner, Hans Frank, Joachim Ribbentrop and Alfred Jodl. Seven others received prison sentences of between 10 years and life. Three defendants were acquitted.

The judgment rendered by renowned Allied jurists was clear, comprehensive and persuasive. The judges pointed to the many treaties and international declarations that made aggressive war an illegal act ('the supreme international crime') for which even a head of state would be accountable. It traced the origins of crimes against humanity. The judges held that the Charter was not *ex post facto* law designed to punish Germans only. 'The law is not static' said the Tribunal, 'but by continued adaptation follows the needs of a changing world.' True, by confirming that aggressive war and crimes against humanity were violations of established legal norms, the IMT was taking a step forward, but its judgment was based on evolving customary law and it was a step long overdue. Both the Charter and Judgment of the IMT were unanimously affirmed by the first General Assembly of the United Nations. Its principles were thereby confirmed as valid expressions of binding international law.

Crimes of the enormity revealed by the IMT required collaboration from many segments of German society but the four occupying powers were unable to agree upon additional joint trials. Instead, they enacted Control Council Law No 10—very similar to the IMT Charter—authorising unilateral trials in their respective zones of occupation. The United States decided to continue with a dozen subsequent proceedings in the same courthouse at Nuremberg. The Chief of Counsel was General Telford Taylor. The accused included medical doctors responsible for illegal human experiments, jurists who distorted law to achieve Nazi goals, high-ranking military officers responsible for atrocities, Foreign Ministry officials who helped plan aggression and industrialists who seized foreign properties and worked concentration camp inmates to death.[2]

There were 177 defendants in all put on trial, of whom 35 were acquitted. These 12 trials, with only American judges on the bench, further clarified international law and made plain (contrary to the view of the IMT) that crimes against humanity could be punished even if committed in peacetime. The law had taken another step forward to protect humankind.

My first assignment from Taylor was to head a team of about 50 researchers to scour the German archives in Berlin—including nearly ten million Nazi Party files—in search of incriminating evidence adequate to convict leading Nazi suspects under arrest in Nuremberg. My wife joined me and became a member of the staff. Time and budget was tight and only a tiny sampling of criminals, those against whom overwhelming evidence of crime was available, could be

[2] See *Trial of War Criminals before the Nuremberg Military Tribunals Under Control Council Law No 10* (the 'Green Series'), Oct 1946–April 1949 (US GPO, 1949–1953); T Taylor, *Final Report to the Secretary of the Army on the Nuremberg War Crimes Trials Under Control Council Law No 10* (Washington DC, 1949); B Ferencz, 'Nuremberg Trial Procedure and the Rights of the Accused', July–Aug 1948, *Journal of Criminal Law and Criminology*, 144.

brought to trial. The rest would have to be left to other allied courts or possible prosecution by the Germans themselves. A surprise discovery in the ruins of Berlin brought another unanticipated change to my life.

THE *EINSATZGRUPPEN* TRIAL

As German troops invaded Poland and the Soviet Union, they were followed by special military units, known as *SS Einsatzgruppen* (EG), whose task it was to annihilate anyone who might present a current or future threat to Germany. Totalling some 3,000 men, these extermination squads were in fact to murder Jews, gypsies and perceived opponents of the Hitler regime. EG daily reports were consolidated, marked 'Top Secret' and then distributed in about 100 mimeographed copies to higher echelons of the Nazi and military hierarchy. The reports often contained the date, time, place and name of the unit commanders responsible for the killings. One of our researchers searching the remains of the Foreign Ministry in Berlin stumbled upon a nearly complete set of the EG reports. They showed beyond doubt that, over a two-year period, the EG had systematically slaughtered over a million helpless men, women and children.

I flew to Nuremberg, showed the discovery to General Taylor and urged that a new trial be prepared against the genocidal killers. Taylor recognised the importance of the evidence but expressed regret that all lawyers were already assigned and it was too late to organise new prosecutions. In exasperation, I offered to handle the prosecution myself—in addition to my other duties. Taylor smiled but agreed. I was promoted to Chief Prosecutor in the Nuremberg trial against the *Einsatzgruppen*. I scrounged three associate counsels from other cases and 30 days before trial made available to the 44 German defence lawyers every bit of evidence to be used at the trial. Relying on the official German documents, and without calling a single witness, the prosecution rested its case in three days. All 22 defendants, including six SS generals, were convicted of murdering over a million innocent people. The trial dragged on for about nine months while phoney alibis of the defendants were systematically rebutted. The 13 death sentences were hailed as a great victory and the press called it 'the biggest murder trial in history'. I was then 27 years old. It was my first case.

It was clear to me that no punishment against 22 fanatic killers, no matter how severe, could ever compensate for the murder of over a million people slain because they did not share the race or creed of their executioners. If the trial was to have enduring significance it should articulate principles of international law that might prevent the repetition of such enormous crimes against humanity. That was the primary goal as I addressed the tribunal:

> It is with sorrow and with hope that we here disclose the deliberate slaughter of more than a million innocent and defenceless men, women and children. Vengeance is not our goal, nor do we seek merely a just retribution. We ask this Court to affirm by

international penal action man's right to live in peace and dignity regardless of his race or creed. The case we present is a plea of humanity to law.

After outlining the proof to be presented, I concluded:

> The defendants in the dock were the cruel executioners, whose terror wrote the blackest page in human history. Death was their tool and life was their toy. If these men be immune, then law has lost its meaning and man must live in fear.

Little did I dream then, that my last sentence would resonate in the halls of the UN half a century later. In September 1997, in his annual report to the General Assembly and the Security Council, Professor Antonio Cassese, President of the International Tribunal for the Former Yugoslavia, concluded his presentation by quoting verbatim the warning I had articulated in September 1947.[3]

COMPENSATING VICTIMS OF CRIMES AGAINST HUMANITY

My life again took another unexpected turn when, in the summer of 1948, I was invited to come to Paris by the American Joint Distribution Committee, the largest Jewish relief organisation assisting survivors of Nazi persecution. A new military government law allowed heirless and unclaimed property taken from Nazi victims to be retrieved by a charitable organisation that would benefit survivors.[4] Of course, there was no precedent for such an undertaking and there was no money available to carry out the assignment. Although we wanted to return home, my wife and I decided that the chance to help the persecuted was a challenge not to be refused.

I designated myself the Director-General of the Jewish Restitution Successor Organization (JRSO), managed to borrow money from occupation funds, recruited staff and promptly proceeded to file claims for over 163,000 properties in thc US Zone of Germany. German possessors adamantly refused to surrender their homes or businesses, arguing that they had paid a fair price or were bona fide purchasers who had improved the properties. Difficult legal issues had to be litigated through German agencies and courts and finally be resolved by an Allied Court of Restitution Appeals that was also set up in the Nuremberg courthouse.

In 1951, I joined a team negotiating a 'reparations' agreement between West Germany, Israel and the world's largest Jewish organisations that were consolidated in a 'Conference on Jewish Material Claims Against Germany' (Claims Conference). After difficult negotiations in The Hague, Germany promised to compensate Nazi victims—Jews and non-Jews alike—for a complicated variety of losses. I set up an office in Bonn to work with legislators to be sure that

[3] A/52/375, S/1997/729, 19 Sept 1997 46

[4] US Military Government Law No 59, 10 Nov 1947

Germany lived up to its promise. When the restitution and indemnification laws were enacted, every claim had to be verified by a complex administrative apparatus that put a strict burden of proof on every claimant. Jews were unwilling to turn to former Nazi lawyers for assistance. It was necessary to organise a non-profit United Restitution Organisation (URO) to assist needy claimants. It was probably the biggest legal aid society in the world with a combined staff exceeding 1,200 persons in 19 countries, including 250 screened German lawyers supervised by former Nazi victims.

Considering that there were no precedents for such programmes and that Germany was totally impoverished, it is gratifying that so many Nazi victims have received some measure of recompense. To the survivors, of course, no payment will ever be adequate, but the more than 100 billion DM (about 60 billion US dollars) already paid by the German government has made a significant difference in the lives of hundreds of thousands of persons, and the end is not yet in sight. (Nazi victims resident in communist countries, with which Germany had no diplomatic relations, received nothing.) In 1948, when I first started work on restitution of heirless property and in the following years when I pleaded for compensation and rehabilitation for survivors of persecution, I felt like a voice in the legal wilderness. I could not foresee that in 1998, in Rome, the overwhelming majority of states would affirm, in the statute of a new International Criminal Court, that victims of crimes against humanity were entitled to restitution, compensation and rehabilitation as a legal right.[5]

ESTABLISHING INTERNATIONAL NORMS

In addition to the trials at Nuremberg, trials also took place in the other zones of occupied Germany as well as in countries that had been overrun by the German armies. These were basically consistent with the Nuremberg precedents and added to the growing body of international criminal law.

On the other side of the globe, General Douglas MacArthur, Supreme Commander for the Allied Powers in the Far East, guided by the IMT Charter, appointed tribunals to try Japanese leaders accused of aggression, war crimes and crimes against humanity. Many Japanese viewed these trials as hypocritical and more vengeance than justice—arguing that the US nuclear bombing of Hiroshima was a crime against humanity. A dissenting opinion by Tokyo Judge Pal of India (who would have acquitted all 28 defendants) maintained that all nations must share some responsibility for war and its inevitable consequences.

Further elaboration of norms to govern civilised society was taken up by the United Nations. The UN Charter expressed the determination of 'We the peoples' to 'save succeeding generations from the scourge of war'. Its preamble stressed the need for justice and respect for international law. Shocked by the

[5] ICC Statute, Art 75

enormity of Nazi crimes revealed at Nuremberg, the Assembly, after affirming the validity of the Nuremberg Charter and Judgment, called for a convention to punish the crime of genocide. A draft Convention was quickly prepared in 1947 and the Secretariat, with the help of experts (Vespasian Pella, Donnedieu de Vabres and Raphael Lemkin) appended two versions of proposed statutes for an international criminal court. Appendix I contained 43 Articles and Appendix II had only 36. But nations were still not ready. How genocide was to be punished was left in Article 6 of the Convention to the jurisdiction of the state where the genocide took place or to such international penal tribunal as states might later accept.

UN committees were appointed to draft a Code of Crimes against the Peace and Security of Mankind as well as a new statute for an international criminal court to enforce the Code. After long debates, a statute for the court was submitted in 1951 (55 Articles) and revised in 1953 (54 Articles). But cold-war rivalries, coupled with mistrust and reluctance to yield sovereign rights to any new international institution, blocked effective action. It was argued that until there was agreement on a Code of Crimes there was no need for a criminal court to enforce it. Until there was agreement on the definition of aggression—'the supreme international crime'—there could be no Code. The Code, the definition of aggression and the court were thus linked and conveniently put into the deep freeze by the cold war. The UN was stymied and the world went back to killing as usual.

In 1974—with a thaw in US-Soviet relations—it was possible, with General Assembly approval, to reach a consensus definition of the crime of aggression. It confirmed (as prescribed by the UN Charter) that only the Security Council had authority to determine when aggression by a state had occurred. The definition contained illustrations of aggressive acts but it allowed considerable flexibility in deciding whether such acts, or others, were criminal. Once the definitional hurdle had been overcome, the General Assembly asked the International Law Commission to resume work on drafting the Code of Crimes and the statute for an international criminal court. In the meanwhile, many areas of the world became killing fields where millions of innocent and helpless people were victimised by aggression and outrageous crimes against humanity which the international community failed to prevent or punish—to their everlasting shame.

The situation changed dramatically when reliable television reports streaming out of former Yugoslavia around 1992 vividly portrayed starved and beaten prisoners and described mass rapes of thousands of Muslim women by Serbian forces determined to 'cleanse' the area for their own national hegemony. The Security Council established a Commission, later headed by legal expert Professor M Cherif Bassiouni, to investigate. He confirmed and documented massive atrocities reminiscent of World War II. The time had finally come—for the first time since Nuremberg—to reach for the rule of an international tribunal to punish shocking international crimes that could no longer be ignored.

THE SECURITY COUNCIL ACTS: THE NEW *AD HOC* TRIBUNALS

In response to cries of public outrage—particularly by women everywhere—the somnolent political will of powerful nations was aroused. On 22 February 1993, the Security Council in Resolution 808 called upon the Secretary-General of the UN to submit statutes for an International Criminal Tribunal *within sixty days*. It was done! The statute prepared by the UN Office of Legal Affairs contained 34 articles that spelled out the legal basis and competence of the court, its organisation and procedures, the assistance it was to receive from states and similar essentials.[6] The jurisdiction of the proposed tribunal was limited to serious violations of international humanitarian law (genocide, crimes against humanity, grave breaches of the Geneva Conventions of 1949 and customary war crimes) committed in the territory of the former Yugoslavia since 1991.

In due course the new criminal court, with its seat in The Hague, was born. It was not an easy birth. There were problems of funding, recruiting prosecutors, judges and defence counsel, training administrators, investigators and translators, overcoming difficult logistical, legal and procedural hurdles and obtaining cooperation from states before any indictments could be drawn, suspects arrested and trials begun. But it was done. The 11 judges from various regions of the world (including the first President Antonio Cassese from Italy, later succeeded by Gabrielle Kirk McDonald of Texas) agreed upon detailed rules for fair trial. Defence lawyers and prosecutors (led initially by Richard Goldstone of South Africa's Supreme Court and later by Louise Arbour of Canada and Carla Del Ponte from Switzerland) earned respect for their competence and dedication. Tribunal decisions, including the appeals, were thoroughly researched and persuasive.

At the outset, the number of cases was very limited but by 1998 there were two convictions (the first convict, Dusko Tadić, was sentenced to 20 years) and four trials were in progress simultaneously. Two new courtrooms were built with donations from Britain, the Netherlands and the US. Some accused were surrendering voluntarily. Witness protection programmes, especially for women, were in place. The staff grew to over 400 and the UN approved annual budget approached $70 million with 22 states donating over $9 million. A few years after the Tribunal was established, Antonio Cassese was able to report to the UN that the International Criminal Tribunal for the former Yugoslavia (ICTY) was 'a vibrant, fully functioning judicial body'.

Every newborn child must crawl before it can walk. The new Tribunal was not free of problems. Co-operation by states like the Federal Republic of Yugoslavia (as well as Croatia and Bosnia), whose nationals were indicted and whose Constitution prohibited their extradition, was less than exemplary. The Tribunal had absolutely no enforcement mechanism of its own and the failure of

[6] S/25704, 3 May 1993

states to arrest indicted suspects, like former Bosnian Serb political leader Radovan Karadzić and army commander General Ratko Mladić, charged with massive war crimes and crimes against humanity, diminished respect for both the Security Council and its ad hoc criminal tribunal. David Scheffer, special US Ambassador for War Crimes, warned: 'their day before the Yugoslav Tribunal will come'.

The initial hesitation to use UN forces to arrest wanted suspects was gradually overcome as the political situation was further stabilised and risks reduced, and more and more indictees have been detained by international forces. In 1999 the Prosecutor's Office issued its most high-profile indictment: that of the then-serving Yugoslav President, Slobodan Milošević, for crimes against humanity. By April 2003, there were 76 outstanding public indictments, in respect of which 50 people were in detention, eight provisionally released and 24 accused still at large. By that same date, the Tribunal had handed down sentences to 32 accused and found five not guilty.

In 1994, a brutal ethnic war erupted in Rwanda. A Security Council investigative commission confirmed that perhaps half-a-million Tutsi—men, women and children—and their supporters were savagely massacred by being hacked to pieces by machetes or bludgeoned to death by the dominant Hutu tribe. Hundreds of thousands fled in terror to neighbouring countries where brutalities fired by vengeance continued in refugee camps until the Tutsi returned to power. The Security Council again responded to public outrage by quickly creating another criminal court to bring mass murderers to justice and help restore peace. The International Criminal Tribunal for Rwanda (ICTR) was established at the end of 1994 under Resolution 955 and followed the pattern of the ICTY. An international war of aggression was not an issue and only human rights crimes were made punishable. Only a few specified crimes, committed within the defined territory during the year 1994, could be prosecuted. The statute made explicit that genocide, war crimes and crimes against humanity would not be tolerated even if the conflict was national and not international.

To save money and personnel, the ICTY and ICTR shared the same Chief Prosecutor and the appellate chambers in The Hague. Because Rwanda was devastated by the civil war, the ICTR was located in Arusha, in Tanzania. In Rwanda, the administrative problems for the justice system were enormous. Over 100,000 Hutus were jammed into local jails and charged by the new Tutsi government with genocide, mass rape or similar atrocities. There were few lawyers or judges left in the country. Tutsi who had seen their families slaughtered demanded that Hutu murderers be put to death. But the Security Council statutes for both *ad hoc* tribunals—following European human rights conventions—outlawed the death penalty. Lesser criminals might face death imposed by summary national courts in Rwanda while the 'big fish' under arrest in The Hague for planning the genocide might escape with only imprisonment.

Despite such enormous political and logistical obstacles, progress has slowly been made. High-ranking officials are under indictment and in detention in

Arusha. Witnesses who dare not reveal their identity lest lives be endangered are being heard under special procedures that also protect the rights of the accused. In September 1998, the ICTR announced the first-ever judgment convicting a defendant—former Rwandan Prime Minister Jean Kambanda—for the crime of genocide. The landmark decision was hailed by the UN Secretary General as 'A defining example of the ability of the United Nations to establish an effective legal order and the rule of law'.[7]

A PERMANENT INTERNATIONAL CRIMINAL COURT

The two special tribunals created by the Security Council met an important need by responding quickly to strong public demand that mass rapists and perpetrators of genocide be brought to justice. Instant worldwide communications brought an end to the age of impunity in which national leaders could commit atrocious crimes and still be sure to escape punishment. Consideration was being given to creating another ad hoc tribunal to deal with the crimes against humanity committed during the terror reign of Pol Pot in Cambodia. But a string of temporary tribunals created after the event and with only limited jurisdiction to deal with a few particular crimes in certain areas during a limited time frame is a very primitive and unsatisfactory way to assure that universal justice will prevail. International law must be known in advance and apply equally to everyone. What is needed as a deterrent to international crimes is an impartial, competent and permanent international criminal tribunal.

The initiative for putting an International Criminal Court (ICC) back on the UN agenda came in 1989 when Prime Minister ANR Robinson of Trinidad and Tobago called for help in curbing international drug-traffickers. The International Law Commission (ILC), 34 legal experts from diverse regions, prodded by the General Assembly, completed its 60-article *Draft Statute for an International Criminal Court* in 1994. UN committees began to review the ILC proposals. The ILC *Draft Code of Offenses against the Peace and Security of Mankind* was submitted in 1996. With these stated hurdles overcome, and political tensions between the super-powers abated, the time seemed ripe to move ahead in closing a glaring gap in the international legal order.

Beginning in 1996, a UN preparatory committee, under the skilful leadership of Adriaan Bos of the Netherlands, held half-a-dozen lengthy sessions at the UN trying to cobble together an accord. UN Secretary-General Kofi Annan (echoing sentiments of his predecessor Boutros Ghali) called the ICC 'the symbol of our highest hopes for this unity of peace and justice'. US President Clinton declared to the General Assembly at the end of 1997: 'Before the century ends, we should establish a permanent international court to prosecute the most serious violations of humanitarian law.' Everyone seemed agreed that

[7] UN *Press Release SG/SM/6687, L/2896,* (2 Sept 1998)

an ICC would be needed and activated only when, and if, national courts were unable or unwilling to put perpetrators on trial. The ICC had to be established by a treaty open to all states, independent and competent to deal only with the most serious international crimes. It also had to be 'fair, efficient and effective'.

Translating these shared sentiments into a coherent text acceptable to lawyers representing 185 nations with different legal and social systems—and possibly with different degrees of commitment to the goals—was a test of their ingenuity and dedication. Intensive efforts by several working groups sought consensus on each article of the proposed statute: how to establish the court; the crimes to be tried by the ICC and precisely how those crimes were to be defined; the principles of criminal law to be applied; the composition and administration of the court; the powers of the Prosecutor to investigate and inaugurate prosecutions; applicable rules of evidence; penalties; procedures for appeal and review; enforcement; and how the entire package was finally to be put into effect. When the PrepCom concluded its work in April 1998, much progress had been made but many differences, indicated by squared brackets around alternative texts, remained unresolved.

The final negotiating conference took place in Rome that summer. After intensive wrangling, compromises and a dramatic climax, the Rome Statute for an International Criminal Court received a wild ovation when it was adopted on 17 July 1998 by a vote of 120 in favour, seven against and 21 abstentions. Despite threats from US Senate and Pentagon representatives that sanctions would be imposed against any state that supported the Court, the entire European community and many other American allies voted for it. Chairman Philippe Kirsch of Canada, called in at the last moment to replace the respected but ailing Dutch Chairman Adriaan Bos, quivered with emotion as he hailed the historical moment as one of great importance for the future of humankind. UN Secretary-General Annan flew to Rome and called the Statute 'a gift of hope to future generations, and a giant step forward in the march towards universal human rights and the rule of law'.[8] In a letter I received from ANR Robinson, now President of Trinidad and Tobago, he wrote that he considered the establishment of the ICC to be the major achievement of his life.[9]

The United States, China and a reluctant Israel were among the seven states that voted against the Statute—each for different reasons. (Since the vote was not recorded, the identity of the other four negative voters is uncertain, but has been reported to include Iraq and Libya.) The US was not willing to subject its military to the risk of trial by a foreign court. China, mired in old traditions, was unwilling to yield sovereign rights. Israel said it would have been honoured to sign but reneged when words were inserted making population transfers a possible war crime.[10] US efforts to block the final vote suffered a resounding defeat. It was painful to me to hear the sustained rhythmic applause of defiant

[8] *Press Release, L/ROM/23* (18 July 1998)
[9] Letter to the author dated 3 Sept 1998.
[10] Statement by Eli Nathan, Head of the Israel Delegation, (17 July 1998)

delegates who glared at the large US delegation as if to show their resentment against what many perceived as a superpower bully that wanted to be above the law.

Article 1 of the ICC Statute declared: 'An International Criminal Court ('the Court') is hereby established.' Unfortunately, the declaration that the Court was *established* on 17 July 1998 was a bit of an exaggeration. Under Article 126, the Statute could only go into force after it was ratified by at least 60 nations. Financing and other important transitional and administrative matters had to be left for later consideration. The Court would have jurisdiction over genocide, war crimes and crimes against humanity, and the crime of aggression. But there were severe limitations on that jurisdiction: the Court could act only in those cases where national states were unwilling or unable to grant the accused a fair trial; the Prosecutor could not act without prior approval by judicial supervisors; and in certain cases, the defendant could not be indicted unless the state of his nationality consented to the trial. In addition, the Court could only deal with the crime of aggression if, at a distant and uncertain future date, it would be possible to reach near-unanimous agreement on its definition. Some powerful states were eager to omit aggression from the Court's jurisdiction altogether and it was included upon the insistence of a host of smaller nations.

In 1945, Justice Jackson, after analysing emerging law, reported to President Truman: 'It is high time that we act on the juridical principle that aggressive war-making is illegal and criminal'.[11] The 'crime against peace' was enshrined as the primary target of the Charter of the International Military Tribunal at Nuremberg. Telford Taylor agreed that the most important crime was war-making itself.[12] I had appealed to US President Clinton and many officials of many nations and written a host of articles arguing that aggressive war must be curtailed by law. Failure to include aggression within the ICCs jurisdiction would have been a repudiation of Nuremberg's main achievement. Its omission might imply that aggressive war was not considered a punishable crime, the glorified 'war-ethic' would be enhanced and the advocates of a world without war would be disabled.

Until the final session in Rome, it was uncertain whether aggression would be subject to the Court's jurisdiction at all. States that had power were unwilling to give it up and those without power seemed helpless. Since I had fought harder and longer than anyone I know to have aggression subject to punishment in an international court, I welcomed its inclusion on any basis. The fact that it was listed as one of the four core crimes was a demonstration of unrelenting human determination to move toward a more peaceful world. Its inclusion opened the possibility that upon further reflection, nations will overcome their fears and understand that building on the cornerstone of the Nuremberg Charter—and

[11] Report to the President, 6 June 1945, *International Conference on Military Trials* (London, 1945) 52; reproduced in B Ferencz, *Defining International Aggression* (Oceana, Dobbs Ferry NY, 1975) at 370.

[12] *Ibid*, at 64.

not discarding it—remains the best way to protect human rights and the peace of people everywhere.

On 11 April 2002, more than half a century after Nuremberg, the number of ratifications needed to bring the ICC Statute into effect on 1 July 2002 was exceeded in a ceremonial presentation at the United Nations. In appreciation for having placed the item of an international criminal court back on the UN's agenda, President Robinson of Trinidad and Tobago was invited to address the assemblage. In his moving remarks, he paid tribute to my dedication to our shared goal for so many years. He noted that I was sitting in the balcony. I cannot deny that I was very touched when the hall burst into loud applause. A dream of my youth was becoming a reality. A milestone had been reached in advancing the rule of law for the protection of all humanity.

2

Universal Jurisdiction: New Uses for an Old Tool

CHRISTOPHER KEITH HALL

It is not widely known that universal jurisdiction has been an accepted part of international law since the Middle Ages. It is also not widely known that approximately three-fifths of all countries have incorporated the principle of universal jurisdiction in their national legislation. However, apart from a flurry of interest in the aftermath of the Second World War, its potential to deter and punish crimes under international law such as war crimes, crimes against humanity, genocide, torture, extrajudicial executions and 'disappearances' only began to be realised in a sustained way in the final decade of the last century. The following account describes the various types of geographic jurisdiction of courts, briefly reviews the history of the principle, discusses the reasons for universal jurisdiction, answers objections to the principle, describes state practice with respect to particular crimes and explains how obstacles to universal jurisdiction can be overcome. The chapter concludes with an assessment of the future of universal jurisdiction.[1]

FIVE TYPES OF GEOGRAPHIC JURISDICTION

National criminal justice systems can exercise five different types of geographic jurisdiction. The most common form of such jurisdiction is *territorial jurisdiction*, that is, jurisdiction of a court over the territory of the state (forum state) in which it sits. This has been interpreted to extend to include jurisdiction over ships carrying the national flag and aircraft registered in the state, although this is not strictly speaking territorial jurisdiction. It also includes jurisdiction over conduct commenced outside the forum state with effects inside that state (objective territorial jurisdiction) and conduct which occurred in the forum state with effects abroad (subjective territorial jurisdiction).

[1] This chapter is largely based on research by Amnesty International published in 2001 on state practice concerning universal jurisdiction in approximately 125 countries, *Universal jurisdiction: The duty of states to enact and implement legislation*, IOR 40/002-018/2001, September 2001 (obtainable from <http://www.amnesty.org> A comprehensive listing of all sources used in this chapter can be found in that study.

The second most common form of geographic jurisdiction is *active personality* jurisdiction or jurisdiction over crimes committed abroad by nationals of the forum state. Although it has been claimed that active personality jurisdiction includes jurisdiction over alien residents at the time of the crime and aliens who become residents or citizens after the crime, such jurisdiction is not, strictly speaking, active personality jurisdiction and, particularly in the context of crimes under international law, better seen as universal jurisdiction. A third, less widely accepted form of geographic jurisdiction is *passive personality* jurisdiction or jurisdiction over crimes committed abroad against a state's own nationals. A fourth form is *protective jurisdiction* over crimes committed against the forum state's particular interests, such as harming its national security or counterfeiting its currency. Each of these forms of jurisdiction has some link to the state whose criminal justice system is seeking to investigate and prosecute conduct committed abroad.

The fifth form of jurisdiction, *universal jurisdiction*, is the ability of states to investigate and prosecute conduct abroad which is not linked to the forum state by the nationality of the suspect or of the victim or by harm to the forum state's own interests. Customary international law permits any state to exercise universal jurisdiction over three types of crimes: crimes under international law (that is, crimes defined by customary international law, such as war crimes, crimes against humanity, genocide, torture, extrajudicial executions and 'disappearances'), ordinary crimes under national law of international concern (most commonly, crimes identified in treaties, such as hijacking of aircraft, attacks on aircraft or diplomats, theft of nuclear material, drug trafficking) and ordinary crimes common to most legal systems, such as murder, abduction, assault or rape. Whether crimes under international law which are not common to most legal systems, such as criminal anti-trust laws or criminal prohibitions for violating restrictions on trade with certain countries, are subject to universal jurisdiction is controversial and outside the scope of this chapter.

As explained below, the label 'universal jurisdiction' is not that helpful when discussing jurisdiction over conduct which is a crime under international law, but defined as a crime under national law, since the national court is really acting as an agent of the international community, rather than enforcing its own law. This is not simply a terminological quibble; since the state is enforcing international, rather than national, law, none of the restrictions which might be appropriate for crimes under national law, such as dual criminality, statutes of limitations or official immunities, are appropriate.[2] The exercise of such jurisdiction is sometimes described as the decentralised prosecution of crimes under international law, but for the purposes of this chapter, the more common term is used.[3]

[2] See ch 3 for an explanation of why such official immunities for crimes under international law are inconsistent with international law.

[3] For the origin of this term, see Rüdiger Wolfrum, 'The Decentralised Prosecution of International Offences through National Courts', (1994) *Israel Y.B. Int'l L.* 24, 183–89.

NATIONAL LAW RESTRICTIONS ON THE SCOPE OF UNIVERSAL JURISDICTION

National law restricts the scope of universal jurisdiction in a number of ways, although none of the limitations are required by international law and some would be contrary to a state's obligations under international law. The most common restriction under national law is to require that the suspect be in the forum state before the criminal justice system can exercise jurisdiction, in some cases apparently precluding the police, prosecutor or investigating judge from even investigating a crime with a view to prosecution if the suspect were expected to enter the state or to seeking the suspect's extradition for trial (universal jurisdiction conditioned on presence of suspect at time of investigation). Of course, the suspect should be present in the forum state for any trial and not be tried *in absentia*, but the inability to investigate or seek extradition when a suspect is not present is a major limitation on the effectiveness of the current international system of justice. It is also unwarranted by international law. Indeed, the Geneva Conventions of 1949 expressly authorise each of the 189 states parties to seek extradition of persons suspected of grave breaches of those Conventions based on universal jurisdiction. A number of states have enacted legislation that does not preclude the opening of an investigation with a view to requesting extradition or to be able to act quickly if a suspect enters the territory.[4]

Another common restriction is a requirement that the suspect be a resident of the forum state, either at the time of the crime or thereafter. This approach was followed in Australia's War Crimes Amendment Act 1988, the United Kingdom's War Crimes Act 1991 and Article 12 (1) of the 1996 Russian Criminal Code.[5] Customary international law does not require that an extradition request have been made or refused before a state may exercise universal jurisdiction, although some states have imposed such a restriction. A number of states, such as Brazil and Germany, have double-criminality legislative provisions with regard to certain crimes that require the conduct be a crime in both the forum state and the state where the crime occurred (territorial state).[6] Some states limit the scope of their legislation to crimes committed in certain states or regions. There are two types of temporal limits on universal jurisdiction. Special legislative provisions may limit the jurisdiction to crimes committed in a certain

[4] Such states include Belgium and Spain. Thus, assertions in several of the separate opinions in the *Democratic Republic of the Congo v Belgium* case that state practice does not support the exercise of universal jurisdiction to open an investigation or to issue an arrest warrant when the suspect is abroad are not correct.

[5] War Crimes Act, 1945 (as amended by the War Crimes Amendment Act, 1988) (Australia), s 11; War Crimes Act 1991 (United Kingdom), s 1; Russian Criminal Code, adopted 13 June 1996 and entered into force 1 Jan 1997, Art 12 (1) (English translation in *Criminal Code of the Russian Federation* (Kluwer Law International and Simmonds & Hill Publishing Ltd., 3rd edn.The Hague/New York/Boston, 1999) (trans William E Butler)).

[6] Brazilian Criminal Code, Art 7 (Part II) (a), s 2 (b); German Penal Code, Art 7 (2).

period, such as the Second World War, as in Australia's War Crimes Amendment Act 1988. Other legislation, such as that of New Zealand, may limit the crimes to those committed at a date long after the conduct was recognised as a crime under international law.[7]

A SHORT HISTORY OF THE PRINCIPLE OF UNIVERSAL JURISDICTION

The concept of universal jurisdiction has a long history and has been traced at least to the sixth century Code of Justinian. It has been recognised as a general principle of law applicable to crimes under international law, and even ordinary crimes under national law, in the work of many international scholars since the Middle Ages, including Grotius. However, this chapter focuses largely on state practice. A brief review of the origins of the practice of universal jurisdiction is useful, not only since it demonstrates that the law is well established, but also since many of the same rationales for the principle apply to contemporary practice.

During the Middle Ages, northern Italian city states exercised jurisdiction over brigands who were suspected of committing crimes outside the borders of the city state, based on the argument that there was no effective state control in the area where they committed their crimes and that if the city state did not exercise jurisdiction, the brigands would have complete impunity. These precedents appear to have shaped the thinking of those who drafted the Nuremberg Charter and Allied Control Council Law No 10 Universal jurisdiction over war crimes appears to date to at least the fourteenth century, when the *jus militaire* (law of arms governing professional soldiers) became recognised as part of the *jus gentium* (international law). Trials of persons suspected of violations of the law of arms could be conducted by any country for violation of a universal code, both because of the gravity of the crime and because of the lack of an adequate judicial system where the crimes took place. States began to exercise universal jurisdiction over piracy on the high seas as early as the sixteenth century. Among the justifications advanced for such jurisdiction were that the pirate was an outlaw who was an enemy of all mankind (*hostis humani*) whom any state could punish in the interest of all, that the crime was one of extreme gravity, that the crime took place on the high seas outside the jurisdiction of any state and that in the absence of universal jurisdiction the crime would go unpunished and that since the pirate attacked international commerce, the attack was on the international community and the international legal order. Similarly, states began to exercise extraterritorial jurisdiction in the middle of the nineteenth century over slave traders and later over slave owners. Like piracy, the slave trade took place largely on the high seas outside the jurisdiction

[7] International Crimes and International Criminal Court Act 2000 (New Zealand), Art 8 (universal jurisdiction over war crimes on or after 1 Oct 2000); Art. 9 (universal jurisdiction over genocide after 21 March 1979).

of any state and the crimes were seen as particularly atrocious, deserving of international condemnation.[8]

This state practice was supplemented in the last century by international law associations before the Second World War, which called upon states to provide for universal jurisdiction over a number of crimes under international law, other crimes of international concern and even ordinary crimes under national law.[9] Indeed, nearly two centuries ago, beginning with Austria in 1803, states started to provide their courts with universal jurisdiction over ordinary crimes under national law.[10] By the eve of the Second World War, at least 26 states (approximately half of all states at the time) had either enacted legislation providing for universal jurisdiction over ordinary crimes or had considered proposals which subsequently became law.

Although the jurisdiction of the Nuremberg Tribunal over crimes that had no particular geographic location has usually been justified on principles other than universal jurisdiction, the Tribunal implicitly recognised the existence of universal jurisdiction over crimes against peace, war crimes and crimes against humanity by stating that, in addition to the ground that the parties to the London Agreement could legislate for Germany as occupying powers, in setting up the Tribunal they had 'done together what any one of them might have done singly; for it is not to be doubted that any nation has the right thus to set up special courts to administer law'.[11] Some of the thousands of trials by Allied military courts and commissions at the end of the War of other persons who

[8] The above brief account draws upon a wide number of sources, including, in particular, M Cherif Bassiouni, *Crimes against Humanity in International Law* (Kluwer Law International, 2nd edn. The Hague/London/Boston, 1999) 227-242; Willard Cowles, 'Universality of Jurisdiction over War Crimes', (1945) *Cal. L Rev* 33 , 177; Henri Donnedieu de Vabres, *Les Principes Modernes du Droit Pénal International* (Libraire du Recueil Sirey, Paris, 1928); GIAD Draper, 'The Modern Pattern of War Criminality', (1976) *Israel Y.B. Hum. Rts* 6, 9; Marc Henzelin, *Le Principe de l'Universalité en Droit Pénal International: Droit et Obligation pour les Etats de Poursuivre et Juge Selon le Principe de l'Universalité* (Helbing & Lichtenhahn et Bruxelles, Bruylant, Bâle/Genève/Munich, 2000); Thomas H Sponsler, 'The Universality Principle of Jurisdiction and the Threatened Trials of American Airmen', (1968–1969) *Loy. L Rev* 15 , 43.

[9] Resolutions were adopted at a number of meetings of such associations, including: the Institute of International Law at Munich in 1883; International Law Association (Japanese Branch) (1926); the Conference for the Unification of Penal Law, Warsaw, 5 November 1927; the Institute of International Law at Cambridge, 31 July 1931; the International Congress of Comparative Law, The Hague, 2–6 Aug 1932; and the Third International Conference of Penal Law, Palermo, 1933. In addition, after a major research project reviewed contemporary state practice, it proposed a draft treaty providing for universal jurisdiction over ordinary crimes under national law, subject to a number of conditions: 'Research in International Law (Harvard Research), Draft Convention with Respect to Crime' (Supp. 1935), 29 *Am J Int'l L*. 439, 573, Arts 9 and 10.

[10] In addition to Austria, states that had enacted such legislation before 1939 included: Hungary (1878), Argentina (1885), Italy (1889), Bulgaria (1896), Norway (1902), Russia (1903), Turkey (1926), Albania (1927), Yugoslavia (1929) and Poland (1932). Six other states had considered proposals by that date to provide courts with such jurisdiction that were subsequently adopted in essentially the same or expanded form, including: Switzerland (1913), Sweden (1923), Cuba (1926), Czechoslovakia (1926), Germany (1927) and Rumania (1928).

[11] Judgment of the International Military Tribunal for the Trial of German Major War Criminals (With the dissenting opinion of the Soviet Member), Nuremberg, 30 Sept and 1 Oct, 1946, 38 (HMSO Cmd. London, 6964, 1946).

had served the Axis Powers for war crimes and crimes against humanity were based on universal jurisdiction or expressly recognised the doctrine as applicable to these crimes.[12]

However, apart from the trial of Adolf Eichmann by Israel in 1961,[13] there appear to have been no other trials for war crimes or crimes against humanity based on universal jurisdiction until the establishment of the International Criminal Tribunals for the former Yugoslavia (Yugoslavia Tribunal) in 1993 and for Rwanda (Rwanda Tribunal) in 1994 acted as a catalyst for national prosecutors and investigating judges to investigate and prosecute persons suspected of war crimes, crimes against humanity and genocide in these two regions. Since 1993, there have been investigations and prosecutions based on universal jurisdiction for such crimes in former Yugoslavia and Rwanda and neighbouring countries by prosecutors and investigating judges in Austria, Belgium, Denmark, France, Germany, the Netherlands and Switzerland.

Two important developments in 1998, both of them covered extensively in this book, have led to a renewed interest in the use of universal jurisdiction as part of a broader struggle to end impunity for crimes under international law. On 17 July 1998, a diplomatic conference in Rome adopted the Rome Statute of the International Criminal Court, more than a century after it was first proposed in 1872 by Gustave Moynier, one of the founders of the International Committee of the Red Cross. Although the ICC Statute did not provide the Court with universal jurisdiction or expressly require states parties to exercise such jurisdiction, in the Preamble, states parties affirm that 'the most serious crimes of concern to the international community as a whole must not go unpunished and that their effective prosecution must be ensured by taking measures at the national level and by enhancing international co-operation', determine 'to put an end to impunity for the perpetrators of these crimes' and recall that 'it is the duty of every State to exercise its criminal jurisdiction over those responsible for international crimes'.[14] The arrest of the former President of Chile, Augusto Pinochet Ugarte, on 16 October 1998 in London in response to a extradition request seeking his trial in Spain based on universal jurisdiction for genocide, torture, murder and hostage-taking in Chile, Spain and other countries, marked a significant shift in the use of universal jurisdiction. For the

[12] See, for example, *In re List (Hostages* case*)*, judgment, Case No 47, US Mil Trib Nuremberg, 19 Feb 1948, 8 *Law Reports of Trials of War Criminals* 35, 54 (HMSO London, 1949); *Trial of Wilhelm von Leeb and Thirteen Others* (*German High Command* case), judgment, US Mil Trib Nuremberg, 28 Oct 1948, 12 *Law Reports of Trials of War Criminals,* above, 61; *In re Eisentrager,* judgment, case No 84, US Mil Comm'n, Shanghai 1947, 14 *Law Reports of Trials of Major War Criminals,* above, 8, 15; *The Hadamar Trial*, judgment, Case No 4, US Mil Comm'n, Weisbaden, 8–15 Oct 1945, 9 *Law Reports of Trials of War Criminals,* above, 46, 53; *The Almelo Trial,* judgment, Case No 3, Brit Mil Ct, Almelo, 24–26 Nov 1945, 1 *Law Reports of Trials of War Criminals,* above, 35, 42; *The Zyklon B Case,* judgment, Case No 9, Brit Mil Ct., Hamburg, 1946, 1 *Law Reports of Trials of War Criminals,* above, 93, 103.

[13] 'Attorney General of Israel v. Eichmann', 36 *Int'l L Rep.* 18 (Israel Dist Ct Jerusalem 1961), *aff'd,* 36 *Int'l L Rep.* 277 (Sup Ct Israel 1962).

[14] ICC Statute, Preamble, paras 4–6.

first time since the *Eichmann* case nearly four decades before, an investigation was based on universal jurisdiction for crimes in a country that was not already within the jurisdiction of an existing international court.

The final decision by the House of the Lords in *Pinochet* was limited to permitting the extradition of a former head of state to another country to face trial on charges of torture and conspiracy to torture, based largely on interpretation of the United Kingdom's obligations under its legislation implementing the Convention against Torture, and each of the six judges in the majority wrote different opinions.[15] Moreover, the Home Secretary, after a series of judicial challenges, subsequently permitted the suspect to leave on the disputed ground that he was mentally unfit to stand trial. However, the decision remains of enormous significance to the practice of universal jurisdiction and to efforts to end impunity in territorial states.

Although the *Pinochet* judgment has not led to an explosion of investigations and prosecutions based on universal jurisdiction, as many had hoped and others had feared, it has lent a new legitimacy to an old tool. Prosecutors and investigating judges are now more willing to consider launching an investigation into war crimes, crimes against humanity, genocide and torture than they were before and political officials, who often have to power to prevent investigations or prosecutions, are less likely to stop them. For example, there have been investigations opened in other cases since 16 October 1998 in Austria, Belgium, France, Germany, the Netherlands, Paraguay, Senegal (although that effort was ultimately unsuccessful) and Switzerland.[16] National authorities have been somewhat more willing in certain cases to co-operate with states seeking to exercise universal jurisdiction, either by extraditing suspects or providing mutual legal assistance, such as searching for evidence, locating witnesses or tracing, freezing and transferring assets. For example, in January 2001, a judge in Mexico authorised the extradition of an Argentine suspect to Spain for a trial based on universal jurisdiction over torture and other crimes, although that decision was subsequently limited by a decision that the charges of torture were barred by statutes of limitation (a decision that has been appealed to the Supreme Court). National legislatures are moving to amend existing legislation providing for universal jurisdiction or to include it for the first time, usually in the context of the enactment of implementing legislation for the ICC Statute. For example, Canada and New Zealand have enacted such implementing legislation with universal jurisdiction over crimes in the ICC Statute and other countries, including Argentina, Australia, Germany, Ghana, Norway, Senegal, South Africa, Sweden and Switzerland, are expected to follow suit.[17]

[15] *Pinochet No 3*.

[16] See also the contribution in ch 13 by Reed Brody.

[17] Only the United Kingdom, in its legislation for England and Wales, has decided not to extend its existing universal jurisdiction over grave breaches of the Geneva Conventions and Protocol I and torture to the full range of crimes in the ICC Statute.

PRACTICAL REASONS FOR UNIVERSAL JURISDICTION

There are at least four practical reasons for universal jurisdiction. First, territorial states fail to investigate and prosecute crimes under international law. Despite the millions of acts of genocide, crimes against humanity, war crimes, cases of torture, extrajudicial executions and 'disappearances' since the end of the Second World War, only a handful of individuals have ever been brought to justice by national courts in the territories or jurisdictions where they occurred. Many of those responsible for these crimes have been able to travel outside their countries—either voluntarily on state business or pleasure trips or involuntarily after going into exile—with complete impunity. Indeed, in most cases when suspects are at liberty abroad one can presume—absent a convincing showing to the contrary—that the reason is that the territorial state has not only failed to fulfil its responsibilities under international law, but that it also is unlikely to do so.

Secondly, the jurisdiction of international criminal courts is limited. The jurisdiction of the Yugoslavia and Rwanda Tribunals is limited to certain time periods, to certain crimes under international law and to two limited geographic areas. The jurisdiction of the latter is further limited to persons of one nationality when the conduct occurred outside Rwanda. The jurisdiction of the International Criminal Court will be limited to certain crimes committed after the entry into force of the ICC Statute and, apart from referrals by the Security Council of situations that breach or threaten to breach international peace and security, to crimes committed in the territory of a state party or state recognising the Court's jurisdiction over the crime, and by a national of such a state. In addition, the Court will have limited resources and will be able to try only a fraction of all the cases that fall within its jurisdiction.

Thirdly, the exercise of universal jurisdiction often acts as a catalyst for prosecutors and investigating judges in territorial states to investigate and prosecute crimes. One of the most important and generally unforeseen benefits of universal jurisdiction is that it has prompted or reinforced such action in territorial states. The most well known example is the case of former President Pinochet. His prolonged absence from Chile while he was on conditional bail in the United Kingdom awaiting a decision on the extradition requests by Belgium, France, Spain and Switzerland sparked a debate in Chile on his immunity as Senator for Life that fuelled the efforts of a courageous investigating judge to seek to have his immunity lifted and may well have strengthened the resolve of the Supreme Court to lift that immunity when he returned. The arrest and indictment of Hissène Habré in Senegal encouraged victims and their families to file complaints in Chad against persons alleged to have tortured them. The trial of Eichmann in Israel gave renewed impetus to investigations and prosecutions in Germany of former Nazis for war crimes and crimes against humanity.

Fourthly, the exercise of universal jurisdiction will act as a deterrent, at least to some extent. The effectiveness as a deterrent will depend, as with ordinary crimes, on such factors as the certainty of arrest, prosecution and conviction, the severity of punishment and the amount of reparations the convicted person must pay. The empirical evidence at this early stage is inconclusive. However, the very possibility of arrest abroad has led to persons alleged to have committed crimes under international law to changing travel plans, a sure sign that the seriousness of the risk of prosecution is understood.

LEGAL, PHILOSOPHICAL AND MORAL RATIONALES FOR UNIVERSAL JURISDICTION

Why is universal jurisdiction necessary? There are four main contemporary legal, philosophical and moral rationales that have been advanced for universal jurisdiction over crimes under international law and ordinary crimes under national law of international concern. Although any one of them would be sufficient, the first two are particularly compelling grounds for the exercise of universal jurisdiction.

First, war crimes, crimes against humanity, genocide and torture are a threat to the international legal fabric. Crimes under international law undermine the international framework of international law and it is appropriate that states, as creatures of international law whose rights and duties are defined by international law, act as agents of the international community in bringing to justice anyone who has committed such crimes.[18] This role is consistent with the current international legal framework, which largely depends on implementation and enforcement of international law by national authorities and courts on behalf of the international community. As the Supreme Court of Israel explained in the *Eichmann* case,

> '[t]he State of Israel therefore was entitled pursuant to the principle of universal jurisdiction and in the capacity of a guardian of international law and an agent for its enforcement, to try the appellant'.[19]

Secondly, these crimes attack fundamental legal values shared by the international community. As a United States court stated in affirming a decision to extradite a person suspected of war crimes and crimes against humanity during the Second World War to Israel for a trial based on universal jurisdiction, 'This

[18] Amnesty International has stated that the concept of national sovereignty is no longer seen as permitting states unrestricted licence, but as describing their rights and concomitant obligations within an international framework of law. Amnesty International, *The international criminal court: Making the right choices—Part III: Ensuring effective state co-operation,* AI Index: IOR 40/13/97, Nov 1997, Section II.A.2.c. Other exponents of this general view include Robert Jennings & Arthur Watts (eds), *Oppenheim's International Law* 1 (9th edn. Longman, London and New York1992) (paperback edition 1996), 12, and Marc Weller, 'On the hazards of foreign travel for dictators and other international criminals', (1999) *Int'l Aff.* 75, 599.

[19] 'Attorney General of Israel v. Eichmann', *Int'l L Rep* 36 (Israel Sup Ct 1962), 277, 304.

[20] *Demjanjuk v Petrovsky,* 776 F2d 571, 582 (6th Cir 1985), *cert. denied,* 475 US 1016 (1986).

universality principle is based on the assumption that some crimes are so universally condemned that the perpetrators are the enemies of all people. Therefore, any nation which has custody of the perpetrators may punish them according to its law applicable to such offences.'[20]

Thirdly, the universal character of these crimes has sometimes been suggested as a sufficient basis for universal jurisdiction. Fourthly, in some cases, the crimes are a threat to international peace and security. However, this particular rationale has less force in the case of a single act of torture, over which there is universal jurisdiction.

A fifth rationale, that articulated in the *Lotus* case in 1927, that states are permitted to exercise any form of extraterritorial jurisdiction not expressly forbidden by international law, has fallen out of favour, but it has not been rejected entirely and is one ground which is continued to be cited in support of universal jurisdiction over ordinary crimes under national law when the conduct does not also amount to a crime under international law or a crime of international concern.[21] In any event, the widespread use of legislation providing such jurisdiction and the almost universal failure of other states to object to it may well be a stronger argument.

ANSWERS TO CRITICISMS OF UNIVERSAL JURISDICTION

None of the objections to the principle of universal jurisdiction have merit. These fall into three main categories: political and other considerations, legal objections, and the legal and practical difficulties of obtaining evidence abroad.

One of the most common objections to the exercise of universal jurisdiction has been that it is inconsistent with national sovereignty of the territorial state. Whatever the merit of such an argument with respect to the exercise of extraterritorial jurisdiction over ordinary crimes under the national law of the forum state, it has no relevance to the exercise of universal jurisdiction over crimes under international law and crimes of international concern when the forum state is acting on behalf of all states in the international community. This contention was made by Chile in the *Pinochet* case and squarely rejected by the House of Lords.

It is often argued that it is preferable to try a person in the territory where the crime occurred. As a general rule, this is the best course. However, in every case so far when national courts have exercised universal jurisdiction, it is because the territorial state was unable or unwilling to do so in a trial which is neither a sham nor unfair, and the burden of proof that the territorial state is the best forum must be on the territorial state, not the forum state. For example, Chile argued in the *Pinochet* case that it was a better forum to try the former

21 *The Lotus (France v Turkey)*, PCIJ, Ser A, No 9 (1927).

22 See above, n 1.

President. However, not only did it fail to request his extradition at any point during the litigation in the United Kingdom, it had made any trial in Chile for crimes committed between 1973 and 1978 almost impossible at the time of the hearings by granting him an amnesty and by giving him immunity as a Senator for Life for any crimes which occurred between 1973 and 1990. Many would agree that a trial in Chile in the political climate after the former President returned would have far greater impact on the re-establishment of the rule of law in that country and in developing national bulwarks against the repetition of such crimes in the future than a trial abroad. However, such a trial would have been politically impossible in Chile in October 1998. It was only the impact of the prolonged absence of the former President on Chilean society, the persistence of a Chilean investigating judge and the courageous decisions of the appellate courts to lift the former President's immunity which finally opened the possibility of a trial in the territorial state.

A related contention made in the *Pinochet* case by the former President's supporters was that the exercise of universal jurisdiction would destabilise the democratic transition in the territorial state. However, national elections took place peacefully in December 1999 and courts had permitted certain criminal investigations and prosecutions of crimes under international law to proceed even before the former President returned home. International and Chilean observers generally agree that the impact of the arrest of the former President in the year since his return has strengthened, rather than weakened, democratic institutions and restored the independence of the judiciary.

It has also been claimed that the exercise of universal jurisdiction would lead to international tensions. This argument is frequently made by opponents of justice and the inevitable tensions resulting from criminal investigations and prosecutions of such crimes are often exaggerated. The international tensions in the *Pinochet* case between Chile, on the one hand, and Belgium, France, Spain, the United Kingdom and Switzerland, on the other, never led to a break in diplomatic relations, but were resolved in a judicial process. Similarly, the Democratic Republic of the Congo invoked the jurisdiction of the International Court of Justice to challenge an international arrest warrant issued by a Belgian investigating judge for its acting foreign minister and Israel has supported the efforts of its Prime Minister Ariel Sharon to block a criminal investigation of his role in the 1982 killings of civilians at the Shabra and Chatila refugee camps in Lebanon. It has been claimed that it could lead to retaliatory mock trials against nationals of the forum state. However, there is no evidence that any of the cases in which states have exercised universal jurisdiction have led to such retaliation.

A number of observers have suggested that states will use universal jurisdiction to achieve political ends. However, there is no convincing evidence that prosecutors or investigating judges, who have to make the difficult decisions on the allocation of scarce investigative resources, have sought since Nuremberg and Tokyo to advance political goals of the government of the day or even their own political goals through the exercise of universal jurisdiction. Indeed, the investigating judges who have exercised universal jurisdiction most actively in Belgium and Spain have investigated suspects from a wide variety of political backgrounds in different regions of the world. The factual basis for the charges in the indictments issued so far based on universal jurisdiction has been thoroughly and carefully documented with extensive eyewitness testimony and documentary evidence in each case. There are a number of safeguards against any possible abuse. For example, in Spain, investigating judges are chosen by lot for cases, as was Judge Baltazar Garzón in the investigation that led to the request for Pinochet's extradition from the United Kingdom, and investigating judges must wait for a complaint by a prosecutor, victim or other person.

Moreover, there has been a widespread reluctance by prosecutors and investigating judges to initiate investigations or prosecutions based on universal jurisdiction. In marked contrast to this remarkable degree of prosecutorial responsibility in the investigation and prosecution of crimes based on universal jurisdiction, is the widespread and routine abuse of territorial jurisdiction in many countries around the world documented on a depressingly regular basis in Amnesty International's annual reports and other publications.

Some members of the public have claimed that the exercise of universal jurisdiction so far has been largely by courts in the North over suspects from the South or by courts of former colonial powers over suspects from former colonies. However, as indicated below in this chapter, a large number of states in the South and former colonies have legislation permitting the exercise of universal jurisdiction, but simply have not yet exercised it over suspects from other countries. This situation has already begun to change with the arrest of the former President of Chad in Senegal on 3 February 2000 for crimes against humanity and torture, although the charges of torture were dismissed on appeal. Further changes can be expected in the near future as persons in northern countries who have been responsible for grave crimes in the South travel to states in the South where courts may exercise universal jurisdiction. In any event, when national courts exercise universal jurisdiction over crimes under international law they are acting as agents of the international community. They are not simply enforcing their own national law and values.

A different type of argument is that universal jurisdiction would lead to chaos among competing states. However, there has been no such competition in the limited number of cases in the past few centuries in which universal jurisdiction has been recognised, any more than there has been among states seeking to exercise extraterritorial jurisdiction over transnational crimes such as drug-trafficking. For example, in the *Pinochet* case, Chile did not seek to extradite its former President, the United Kingdom did not seek to prosecute him in preference to extradition to Spain and the other states seeking his extradition, Belgium, France and Switzerland, did not seek priority over the Spanish extradition request as long as Spain continued to pursue its extradition request. Indeed, the main problem in universal jurisdiction cases is not competition between requesting states to investigate and prosecute suspects, but the lack of political will by prosecutors, investigating judges and political officials with power to decide on extradition requests.

In the unlikely event that more than one state claimed priority to investigate and prosecute a suspect for the same crimes under international law based on the same conduct, the state whose prosecutor or investigating judge first opened a criminal investigation would normally have the better claim to act on behalf of the international community, provided, however, that its exercise of sovereignty evidenced an ability and willingness to investigate and prosecute in accordance with international standards for fair trial which would not result in the death penalty or other cruel, inhuman or degrading treatment or punishment and a commitment not to conduct sham proceedings. In any event, the concepts of conflict of laws, comity and *forum non conveniens*, which were developed to determine which was the appropriate law to apply or the best forum for civil litigation, have little or no bearing in the determination of which state should act on behalf of the international community in a criminal case. Evidence that such concepts have no place in the context of universal jurisdiction is their omission from the numerous treaties requiring states to extradite or prosecute suspects.

NATIONAL LEGISLATION AND JURISPRUDENCE

The results of an extensive study by Amnesty International concerning universal jurisdiction, the first effort to undertake a global survey of state practice since the Harvard Research in 1935, indicate that approximately 125 states around the world from all the major legal systems have constitutional or legislative provisions permitting their courts to exercise universal jurisdiction over conduct amounting to war crimes, crimes against humanity, genocide or torture.[22]

Such constitutional or legislative provisions fall into one of five models. Many states have a number of provisions, each following a different model. The first model is legislation expressly providing for universal jurisdiction over one or more crimes. For example, many states, particularly in Commonwealth countries, have enacted Geneva Conventions Acts providing their courts with universal jurisdiction over grave breaches of the Geneva Conventions, some of which have been updated to include grave breaches of Protocol I.[23] Some recent legislation expressly provides for universal jurisdiction over all the crimes in the ICC Statute, including war crimes in both international and non-international armed conflict, crimes against humanity and genocide.[24]

[23] See, for example, Ireland's Geneva Conventions (Amendment) Act 1998, extending the scope of universal jurisdiction of the Geneva Conventions Act 1962 to include grave breaches of Protocol I.

[24] See, for example, *Loi relative à la répression des violations graves du droit international humanitaire,* 10 Feb 1999 (Belgium); Crimes against Humanity and War Crimes Act of 2000 (Canada), Art 6 (1); and International Crimes and Criminal Court Act 2000 (New Zealand), Arts 8–10.

[25] *Code Pénal Zairois, 1982, Livre premier,* SI, Art 3 (Democratic Republic of the Congo);

The second model simply provides for universal jurisdiction over ordinary crimes under national law that would constitute war crimes, crimes against humanity, genocide or torture in certain circumstances. A number of states, including the Democratic Republic of the Congo and Norway, have such legislative provisions in their penal codes.[25] This model suffers from the serious drawbacks in most cases that the legislation will not cover all aspects of the crime under international law, will often not incorporate the same principles of criminal responsibility, or will permit defences prohibited by international law (such as superior orders). In addition, such legislation may be subject to limitations applicable to ordinary crimes under national law that are inappropriate when the conduct is a crime under international law, such as the requirement that the conduct have been a crime under the law of the territorial state (dual criminality), statutes of limitation, recognition of official immunities, requirements that an extradition request have been made and refused and recognition of national amnesties.

Legislation following a third model authorises courts to exercise universal jurisdiction over crimes in treaties. Sometimes, the legislation simply refers to treaties listing or defining the crime. In other cases, it provides that the treaty must require the state to exercise such jurisdiction or to extradite. In the latter case, courts probably may not rely on such legislation to try cases of genocide, since the Convention on the Prevention and Punishment of the Crime of Genocide of 1948 does not expressly require—although it does not prohibit—states to exercise universal jurisdiction over genocide. A few states have adopted legislation following a fourth model that authorises courts to exercise universal jurisdiction over crimes under customary international law or general principles of law. Finally, another group of states provide in their constitutions or legislation that conventional or customary international law is part of national law having precedence over contrary national legislation.

As explained in more detail in the following section, the third, fourth and fifth models are not always effective. Even in states following a monist tradition (where international law is considered part of national law without need of any implementing legislation), many courts are reluctant to try persons for crimes under international law directly and follow a dualist approach by requiring that the crime under international law and its punishment be defined in national law.[26] Other courts find that if the conduct abroad is an ordinary crime under

Norwegian Penal General Civil Penal Code of 1902, Art 12 (4).

26 Perhaps the most well known example is the recent decision by the *Cour d'appel* (Court of Appeal) in Dakar holding that Senegalese courts did not have jurisdiction to try Hissène Habré, the former President of Chad, for torture. It held that a provision of the Senegalese Constitution stating that treaties ratified by Senegal were part of national law with precedence over national law did not permit courts to try persons suspected of torture abroad pursuant to Art 7 of the Convention against Torture when there was no provision in national legislation giving courts such jurisdiction. This decision was upheld by the *Cour de cassation* (Court of Cassation). See the contribution in ch 13 by Reed Brody. The text of these decisions and other court documents is obtainable from <http://www.hrw.org>.

27 It is likely that investigations or prosecutions based on universal jurisdiction could take place

national law, such as murder, then the requirement of legality (*nullum crimen sine lege, nulla poena sine lege*) is satisfied by such models.

Approximately 125 countries appear to permit their courts to exercise universal jurisdiction under one or more of these models over certain conduct amounting to one or more of the following crimes under international law: war crimes, crimes against humanity, genocide or torture.[27] However, in a few of these countries ambiguities in the legislation or translations that are available mean that, without any authoritative commentary or jurisprudence, it is possible that courts would not be willing to exercise jurisdiction. For example, Equatorial Guinea recognises universal jurisdiction in its penal code, but it is not clear to what crimes this principle applies. This handful of countries where the meaning of provisions is uncertain may well be offset by other countries which have universal jurisdiction where it has not been possible to locate up-to-date legislation. In addition, there are a number of countries that do not have universal jurisdiction that are expected to include it in their implementing legislation for the ICC Statute for all crimes within the jurisdiction of the International Criminal Court, including Angola, Senegal and South Africa. States that are parties to the Convention against Torture are under the obligation in Articles 5 and 7 to enact legislation providing for universal jurisdiction in those cases when a suspect is found in their territories and the suspect is not extradited. The Committee against Torture, a body of experts established under the Convention to monitor its implementation, reminds states parties, such as Tunisia, on occasion of this obligation and, slowly but surely, these states are fulfilling their obligations by enacting such legislation.

in approximately 125 of the following 129 countries; in a handful of them, such as Equatorial Guinea, which simply recognise the principle, there is some doubt whether prosecutors or investigating judges could open investigations: Algeria, Antigua and Barbuda, Argentina, Armenia, Australia, Austria, Azerbaijan, Bahamas, Barbados, Belarus, Belgium, Belize, Bolivia, Bosnia and Herzegovina, Botswana, Brazil, Bulgaria, Burundi, Cameroon, Canada, Chile, China, Colombia, Costa Rica, Côte D'Ivoire, Croatia, Cuba, Cyprus, Czech Republic, Democratic Republic of the Congo, Denmark, Dominica, Ecuador, Egypt, El Salvador, Ethiopia, the Federal Republic of Yugoslavia, Fiji, Finland, France, Gambia, Georgia, Germany, Ghana, Greece, Grenada, Guatemala, Guinea Bissau, Guyana, Honduras, Hungary, Iceland, India, Iran, Ireland, Israel, Italy, Jamaica, Japan, Jordan, Kazakhstan, Kenya, Kiribati, Kyrgyzstan, Lao People's Democratic Republic, Latvia, Lebanon, Lesotho, Liberia, Liechtenstein, Lithuania, Luxembourg, Macedonia (The former Yugoslav Republic of), Malawi, Malaysia, Malta, Mauritius, Mexico, Moldova, Monaco, Mongolia, the Netherlands, New Zealand, Nicaragua, Nigeria, Norway, Panama, Papua New Guinea, Paraguay, Peru, Philippines, Poland, Portugal, Romania, Russian Federation, Saint Kitts and Nevis, Saint Lucia, Saint Vincent and the Grenadines, Samoa, San Marino, Seychelles, Sierra Leone, Singapore, Slovakia, Slovenia, Solomon Islands, Spain, Sri Lanka, Swaziland, Sweden, Switzerland, Syrian Arab Republic, Tajikistan, Tanzania (United Republic of), Trinidad and Tobago, Turkey, Turkmenistan, Tuvalu, Uganda, Ukraine, United Kingdom, United States, Uruguay, Uzbekistan, Vanuatu, Venezuela, Vietnam, Yemen and Zimbabwe. In addition, East Timor provides for universal jurisdiction over all four crimes.

[28] See ch 6.

[29] Amnesties, pardons and similar measures of impunity have been rejected at the international

OVERCOMING OBSTACLES TO UNIVERSAL JURISDICTION

Although approximately three-fifths of all states have national legislation permitting their courts to exercise universal jurisdiction over certain conduct amounting to crimes under international law, few of these states have legislation covering all of these crimes and the universal jurisdiction provisions in the legislation of most states fall short in certain respects, thus posing the danger that persons responsible for the worst crimes in the world could travel to or even reside in those states with complete impunity.

One of the most common problems in many states has been the failure to define crimes under international law as crimes in the national criminal code and to specify the punishments applicable under national law. These problems are particularly an issue in states which have followed the models of legislation providing national courts with jurisdiction generally over offences defined in treaties or over offences which treaties require states to investigate and punish. They are also a problem in those states with legislation giving courts jurisdiction over crimes under customary international law or defined under general principles of law. However, these problems also apply to legislation expressly providing courts with jurisdiction over specific crimes defined in treaties or customary law. Many national courts are willing to give direct effect in civil litigation to international law. However, since the trials in military courts after the Second World War, national courts appear now to be less willing to do so in criminal cases, even in jurisdictions adhering to a monist view of international law. Courts are concerned that, without precise definitions in the national criminal code of the crimes and punishments, prosecutions would be inconsistent with the fundamental principle of legality (*nullum crimen, nulla poena sine lege*). However, the Yugoslavia and Rwanda Tribunals have been able to prosecute effectively on the basis of customary international law and generally in a manner which has been consistent with due process of law, although with respect to sentencing they take into account the general practice regarding prison sentences in the national courts of the former Yugoslavia and Rwanda. To a great extent, these problems have been avoided in states which have enacted Geneva Conventions Acts, including those which have amended them to include grave breaches of Protocol I and violations of Protocol II.

Reliance on national constitutions or legislation that provide that international law, either conventional or customary, is part of national law, either automatically or after acceptance by the state, and generally overriding national legislation, sometimes is sufficient to permit courts to exercise universal jurisdiction over crimes under international law. It is not always clear, however, whether such provisions incorporate only the substantive criminal law provisions of treaties or also the procedural ones, such as those concerning universal jurisdiction, and often the answer will not be known until tested in a criminal investigation or prosecution. In some of these states there are authoritative interpretations by executive officials, courts, scholars or international treaty monitoring bodies indicating that they are insufficient to permit a court to exercise universal jurisdiction.

A number of states fail to define the crimes consistently with international law. A similarly common weakness in national legislation has been the failure to extend universal jurisdiction to all crimes under international law. Most states do not include crucial principles of criminal responsibility, such as command responsibility for military commanders and superior responsibility for civilians. Some states have inappropriate or prohibited defences, such as superior orders. Other states have statutes of limitations that apply to all crimes, including crimes under international law.

One practical problem in some countries is that they have slow or inadequate procedures for arresting persons suspected of crimes under international law which could permit suspects to flee before effective action could be taken. The lack of awareness of, and training for, lawyers for victims, prosecutors and judges concerning legal opportunities has been a serious obstacle to initiating and conducting criminal prosecutions based on universal jurisdiction in some jurisdictions. It is often difficult to locate up-to-date legal commentaries discussing universal jurisdiction or to obtain comprehensive collections of extradition or mutual legal assistance treaties in law libraries in many countries. The lack of public awareness concerning the purposes of universal jurisdiction has been identified as a factor in the limited interest of prosecutors to undertake universal jurisdiction investigations and prosecutions.

The most serious obstacles to the effective exercise of universal jurisdiction probably are the lack of political will by all three branches of national governments: legislative, judicial and executive. Even where international treaties such as the Geneva Conventions and the Convention against Torture expressly require states to enact legislation providing for universal jurisdiction, many states have yet to fulfil their obligations to do so. The factors responsible, which vary from country to country, include the slowness of parliamentary processes, inertia and low priority in comparison to other matters.

Even when legislation exists permitting courts to exercise universal jurisdiction over crimes under international law, prosecutors and investigating judges (and political officials, when their approval is needed to initiate an investigation or prosecution) have often lacked the political will to investigate or prosecute crimes under international law committed abroad. In some countries a political official makes the ultimate decision whether a criminal prosecution based on universal jurisdiction should proceed and they are often reluctant to permit an investigation or prosecution based on universal jurisdiction.

Sometimes the obstacle is not the lack of political will, but political interference. The current international framework permits political officials to interfere with judicial decision-making. This problem arises in two ways. First, national legislation giving courts universal jurisdiction or providing for extradition to a state that might try a suspect based on universal jurisdiction often requires approval of one or more political officials. Secondly, sometimes political officials are accused of preventing the exercise of universal jurisdiction by other means, such as by tipping off suspects about investigations or even assisting them to leave the country. A related problem is the continued use of military, rather than civilian, courts to try cases involving crimes under international law.

A common challenge in investigations and prosecutions is how to obtain evidence of crimes committed abroad. Although this can be a serious problem in some cases, it has been surmounted in criminal proceedings based on universal jurisdiction and by the Yugoslavia and Rwanda Tribunals, without infringing the rights of suspects and accused.[28]

Experience has demonstrated that the investigation and prosecution of crimes under international law requires specialised legal knowledge of international law, just as tax evasion, securities fraud and crimes of sexual violence require specialised legal knowledge both among investigators and prosecutors. They also require special practical skills and experience in investigating and prosecuting crimes committed abroad, including evidence gathering, interviewing victims of crimes of sexual violence, witness protection, negotiation with other law enforcement agencies, language ability or translation and interpretation facilities.

Special units can be set up within police forces and prosecution offices (or units combining both), drawing upon the experience of the special units established in Australia, Canada, Ethiopia and the United Kingdom to investigate war crimes, crimes against humanity or other crimes under international law. These units generally conducted thorough and effective investigations; their limited success in completing prosecutions should be seen as the result of other factors, such as weak legislation, restrictive jurisprudence and the evidentiary problems—particularly with respect to eye-witness testimony—half a century after the crimes occurred.

Many of the underlying problems with respect to gathering evidence abroad are rooted in the inadequate system of mutual legal assistance treaties and agreements. First, there are only a few multilateral treaties and usually they have limited scope. Secondly, there is a complex patchwork of bilateral treaties or arrangements among more than 189 states, which leads to widely varying mutual legal assistance regimes. Thirdly, these mutual legal assistance treaties provide a broad range of grounds of refusal which are inappropriate when crimes under international law are involved, including double criminality requirements, the political offence exception, *ne bis in idem* and statutes of limitation. These grounds are improper when the crimes are crimes under international law which the requesting state is seeking to prosecute on behalf of the international community. Fourthly, determinations whether grounds for refusal exist are left to political officials—rather than courts—in the requested state to make. In the absence of an international monitoring mechanism for mutual legal assistance, a requested state should be able to refuse to provide such assistance to a state

level by the UN Secretary-General, the UN Security Council, the UN General Assembly, the UN

which it considers would not be able to afford the suspect a fair trial or might impose the death penalty. However, such decisions are best decided by a court, on the basis of law, rather than by a politician, on the basis of discretion.

In many cases, neither the court, the prosecutor nor the accused will be able to conduct an on-site investigation. However, as described below in the following paragraphs, there are often alternative means of obtaining evidence which may be almost as effective. In those cases where the territorial state is willing to permit such investigations, it may require that the investigation be carried out solely by its own authorities—who may be implicated in the crimes—or carried out under their supervision. In addition to making such investigations less efficient than if they had been carried out directly by the investigators and prosecutors preparing the case, they may discourage witnesses from speaking to investigators. A similar problem has plagued the work of the Yugoslavia and Rwanda Tribunals and could limit the effectiveness of the International Criminal Court. It will be essential for states to revise the existing international system of mutual legal assistance to permit investigators from the state exercising universal jurisdiction to conduct on-site investigations.

One way for states exercising universal jurisdiction to address the practical problems in conducting investigations is for the international community to share the burden through a UN or other multilateral framework. For example, Amnesty International has recommended that the UN establish an independent international body of impartial professional investigators to conduct investigations of human rights violations or abuses or to assist national authorities in conducting such investigations. In addition to this mechanism, states exercising universal and other forms of extraterritorial jurisdiction could establish such an independent and impartial body themselves to conduct investigations or to assist national investigators by providing the necessary expertise and resources.

Either of the proposed approaches would have at least two advantages. First, each would enable small states with limited resources or expertise to fulfil their international responsibilities. Secondly, investigators in a UN body or a multilateral body might well be more acceptable to some national authorities than investigators from certain other states.

In addition to recognising that they must co-operate with international criminal courts in the investigation and prosecution of crimes under international law, states have recognised that they have a duty to co-operate with each other in investigating and prosecuting crimes under international law, particularly genocide, crimes against humanity and war crimes. They have also expressly obliged themselves in treaties to co-operate with each other in the investigation and prosecution of crimes under international law, including war crimes and torture. These obligations are part of a broader, but still emerging and fragmentary system of bilateral and multilateral commitments to co-operate with other states in the investigation and prosecution of ordinary crimes and crimes under national law of international concern.

Despite these extensive obligations of states to co-operate with each other, the courts and other authorities in the foreign state may sometimes be unwilling to co-operate for a variety of non-legal reasons, such as a restrictive view of sovereignty, unfamiliarity with international law or state-to-state co-operation, lack of independence or even implication in the crimes. Such problems may arise not only in the territorial state, but also in other states where evidence is located, such as states which contributed personnel to a United Nations peacekeeping operation or another multinational operation in the territorial state.

There are a variety of solutions to these problems which have been used by national courts and by the Yugoslavia and Rwanda Tribunals. For example, given the usual scale of the crimes and the number of the victims, alternative sources of evidence are often available for many of the crimes. For example, although the Spanish investigating judge in the *Pinochet* case was not able to obtain co-operation in the related Argentine and Chilean cases from the executive authorities in the territorial states, he was able to obtain voluminous evidence from official truth commissions in both states, as well as the testimony of hundreds of victims, information from police and prosecutors in other states conducting investigations of the crimes and information from certain non-governmental organisations. To the extent that executive authorities in the foreign state refuse to co-operate, it may be possible, as in the *Pinochet* case, for the investigators to obtain co-operation from judicial authorities in that state. In addition, persistence by the authorities of the forum state and diplomatic pressure to co-operate by other states may encourage co-operation. Such persistence by the Yugoslavia and Rwanda Tribunals has led to increased co-operation by both territorial states and states where evidence is located. External pressure also led to co-operation by Chile in an investigation in its territory by Federal Bureau of Investigation investigators of the murder in Washington, DC of Orlando Letelier and Ronni Moffit.

Similarly, the London Metropolitan Police, which do not have a specialised unit to investigate crimes under international law committed since the Second World War, have relied heavily on experienced non-governmental organisations such as Redress and the Medical Foundation for the Care of Victims of Torture. One or both have helped them to obtain the names and addresses of witnesses willing to testify and to contact witnesses abroad, provided impartial background information on matters ranging from the political context to cultural or language issues, acted as liaison between the authorities and community groups in the territorial state, assisted in obtaining qualified translators and interpreters, identified appropriate experts and obtained expert legal opinions on questions of evidence and international and foreign law. They have also provided moral support and other assistance and other support to victims, witnesses and groups who have provided information. Redress has explained the unfamiliar legal procedures in the United Kingdom to victims and witnesses and kept them informed of developments in cases. National victims groups in Chile and in Chad have performed similar functions in the *Pinochet* and *Habré* cases.

It may be difficult for a national prosecutor in some circumstances to locate witnesses in another state. However, as in all the prosecutions based on universal jurisdiction so far, the prosecutor will be able to rely on victims' groups, either in the territorial state, other states or in the state where the court is located, to assist in locating witnesses. It has been claimed that it is too costly to transport witnesses from the territorial state to the state exercising universal jurisdiction, but with the increasing amount of transnational criminal and civil litigation in all types of cases, this is increasingly a cost which must be incurred in the ordinary course of many cases. Indeed, forum states have been willing to transport witnesses to testify in criminal cases based on universal jurisdiction. For example, Belgium and Switzerland have transported witnesses from Rwanda so that they could testify at trials of persons accused of committing crimes in that country.

As an alternative to transporting witnesses to the forum state, such costs, as well as fears for security, can be minimised by the use of video-conferencing facilities in the territorial state or in a neighbouring state. As in ordinary organised crime cases, witnesses predisposed to co-operate may need protection. In such cases, governments as a matter of course will provide security, relocate witnesses and their families and, if necessary, provide them with new identities. They should do no less in the case of far more serious crimes. Similarly, if witnesses are not willing to co-operate by travelling to the forum state, they can be encouraged to do so by providing testimony through video-conferencing, or, if necessary, compelled to provide testimony through such facilities, subject to appropriate due process guarantees. It may be difficult to locate experienced and qualified translators and interpreters. Nevertheless, to some extent, expatriates from the territorial state may be able to assist in locating such persons or in doing some of the translation and interpretation themselves, subject to careful revision or monitoring.

Another way that some of these difficulties can be surmounted, if some of the authorities in the territorial state, such as investigating judges in Chile in the *Pinochet* case, are willing to help, or there is access to the territorial state where the government has collapsed but a peace-keeping force is present, is for the forum state to send the prosecutor or investigating judge to the state. In some cases, the territorial state may even permit part of the trial to take place in its territory, as in the *Sawoniuk* case where the judge and jury in a United Kingdom court sat for several days in Belarus at the sites of massacres during the Second World War.

If an uncooperative witness who is in the forum state asserts an immunity of his or her own state, that national immunity should not be recognised by the forum state in a trial involving crimes under international law (see the discussion in the following chapter by Brigitte Stern). In addition, the territorial state can be urged to waive an immunity such as diplomatic immunity in the rare case when the witness is an ambassador accredited to the forum state or a head of state. Most countries recognise some privileges with regard to certain communications and documents, such as the confidentiality of lawyer-client communications concerning past actions and memoranda on legal strategy. However, to the extent that the witness asserts a privilege under his or her national law, the scope of that privilege, when crimes under international law are involved, should be measured in accordance with international standards. If perjury or other offences against the administration of justice by a witness are discovered while the witness is in the forum state, it will normally be possible for the judicial system to take effective action. If the offence is discovered after the departure of the witness, however, the ability of the forum state to take effective measures will be limited and largely depend on the existence of bilateral or multilateral extradition agreements.

There are a number of problems associated with documentary and physical evidence. These include authentication of documents, transport of physical evidence out of the state, excavation of graves, claims of national security and imbalances in power to obtain evidence between the prosecution and defence. Each of these problems can be surmounted in individual cases. However, it would be useful for states to adopt a multilateral treaty open to all states which would facilitate state co-operation with respect to mutual legal assistance in the investigation and prosecution of crimes under international law.

There are many grounds in extradition agreements and legislation for requested states to refuse extradition. As with mutual legal assistance, most of these grounds of refusal, including the prohibition of the extradition of nationals, double criminality requirements, advanced age, the political offence exception, *ne bis in idem*, statutes of limitation and general discretion, are not appropriate grounds when the crimes are crimes under international law which the requesting state is seeking to prosecute on behalf of the international community. Other grounds for refusing extradition are factors which, as a general rule, should be considered by the courts (as opposed to the executive authorities) in the requesting—rather than the requested—state, such as fitness to stand trial. When these decisions, as in the *Pinochet* case, are left to political officials in the requested state to decide in secret on the basis of discretion, instead of the courts of the requesting state, in a fair and open process on the basis of legal criteria, the public perception of the fairness and integrity of the proceedings is undermined. In the absence of an international monitoring mechanism for extradition, a requested state should be able to refuse to extradite a person to a state which it considers would not be able to afford the suspect a fair trial or might impose the death penalty or other cruel, inhuman or degrading punishments. Once again, such decisions are best decided by a court, on the basis of law, rather than by a politician, on the basis of discretion.

A number of states have given those responsible for war crimes, crimes against humanity, genocide, torture, extrajudicial executions and enforced disappearances impunity through amnesties, pardons and similar measures. However, national amnesties, pardons and similar national measures of impunity for the worst imaginable crimes not only have no place in an international system of justice, but also are prohibited under international law.[29] They are also inconsistent with the duty to bring to justice those responsible for such violations recognised in the Preamble to the ICC Statute. They deny the rights of victims to justice. Therefore, such steps cannot prevent the courts of another state or an international criminal court from investigating and prosecuting persons suspected of such crimes. Indeed, for such reasons, Amnesty International has consistently opposed, without exception, amnesties, pardons and similar measures of impunity that prevent the emergence of the truth, a final judicial determination of guilt or innocence and satisfactory reparations to victims and their families.

CONCLUSION: PROSPECTS FOR UNIVERSAL JURISDICTION

The adoption of the ICC Statute and the arrest of the former President of Chile in 1998 mark a sea change in international law. No longer are war crimes, crimes against humanity, genocide and torture seen as political events to be resolved by diplomats and politicians, but as crimes to be investigated and prosecuted, just like murder, kidnapping, assault and rape. We are still too close to these events to understand their full import, but it is safe to say that efforts to end impunity around the world have been significantly strengthened. All three branches of national governments are more likely to look more favourably on using international jurisdiction to this end. Legislatures are moving to amend existing universal jurisdiction legislation or enact legislation where none exists as they draft implementing legislation for the ICC Statute. Prosecutors and investigating judges have been breathing life into legislation that has remained unused—in some cases for more than a century—to investigate and prosecute crimes under international law. Even more importantly, political officials have been somewhat more reluctant to prevent investigations and prosecutions based on universal jurisdiction, whether in their own courts or abroad in states seeking extradition. When they still do obstruct justice, in some cases they risk facing a public uproar.

However, whether the lasting legacy of these developments will be a new commitment to justice in the states where such crimes occur to steps not only to investigate and prosecute such crimes, but also to prevent them, remains to be seen. Moreover, apart from the judgment in June 2001 by a Belgian court in the case of four Rwandans accused of war crimes in Rwanda in 1994, the period since the highwater mark of the second judgment of the House of Lords in the

Commission on Human Rights, the International Criminal Tribunal for the former Yugoslavia, the Committee against Torture and the Human Rights Committee. They have also been determined to be contrary to international law by the Inter-American Commission on Human Rights and the Inter-American Court of Human Rights.

Pinochet case has been marked by a series of judicial and executive setbacks in universal jurisdiction cases at the international and national level.

On 14 February 2002 the International Court of Justice declared in the *Democratic Republic of the Congo v Belgium* case, without citing any evidence of state practice and *opinio juris*, that customary international law prevented an investigating judge in Belgium from issuing an arrest warrant for an acting foreign minister of another country for war crimes and crimes against humanity committed abroad because the acting foreign minister had immunity for such crimes while in office. Although the Court did not directly rule on the question whether the Belgian court could exercise universal jurisdiction by issuing an arrest warrant for a foreign suspect when the suspect was not present in the country, a number of the separate opinions suggested that this step was not permitted under international law, despite state practice suggesting that only a handful of the approximately 125 states with universal jurisdiction legislation expressly prevent the opening of a criminal investigation or the request for extradition of a suspect when the suspect is outside the forum state (see the chapter on this case by Andrew Clapham).

At the national level, after intervention by the United States Department of State, a former Peruvian army officer was permitted to leave the United States on 10 March 2000 after he had been detained by the Federal Bureau of Investigation for questioning in a Texas airport concerning allegations of torture. The decision by a Senegalese court on 3 February 2000 to indict the former President of Chad for crimes in that country was overturned on appeal on 4 July 2000. In March 2002, a Mexican judge, while authorising the extradition of a former Argentine naval officer to face trial in Spain on charges of committing genocide and 'terrorism' in Argentina, limited an earlier decision by the Minister of Foreign Affairs permitting extradition on charges of torture (who in turn had rejected a previous court decision to the contrary) by refusing to permit extradition on these charges on the ground that they were barred by statutes of limitation. On 16 April 2002, a Belgian court decided, despite evidence to the contrary, that the Parliament had intended that national courts could not even open a criminal investigation based on universal jurisdiction if the suspect was outside the country. Lawyers for the Prime Minister of Israel and others had argued on 15 May 2002 in another Belgian court that, based on the 16 April decision, it should determine that an investigating judge had no jurisdiction to conduct an investigation of the 1982 killings at the Sabra and Chatila refugee camps on the outskirts of Beirut, Lebanon. The decision was upheld by the Brussels Court of Appeal on 26 June 2002 but at the time of writing was being appealed. In April 2002, the United Kingdom Home Office refused to implement requests by French and Spanish judges to question a former United States Secretary of State concerning crimes committed in Chile and a United Kingdom magistrate refused to arrest that former official in connection with allegations he was responsible for grave breaches of the Geneva Conventions of 1949 in the bombing of Cambodia in the 1970s, partly on the ground that the Attorney General would not authorise a criminal investigation. These unfortunate developments indicate that the future of universal jurisdiction remains in danger.

3

Immunities for Heads of State: Where Do We Stand?

BRIGITTE STERN

Some very important steps have been taken during the last few years in the field of international criminal justice, as previous chapters in this book have already noted: the landmark developments include the adoption on 17 July 1998 of the Statute of a permanent International Criminal Court (ICC), which can prosecute cases against heads of states, in spite of any protection or immunities they enjoy; the decisions in November 1998[1] and March 1999[2] in the United Kingdom of the House of Lords, according to which Augusto Pinochet could claim no immunity for acts of torture he was accused of, a decision which appears like a milestone in the history of international law; and the indictment the same month of Slobodan Milošević by the International Criminal Tribunal for the Former Yugoslavia (ICTY) for his actions in Kosovo, this being the first time a serving head of state had been indicted before an international criminal tribunal. A step backwards seems however to have been made with the recent decision of the International Court of Justice (ICJ) in the case concerning the *Arrest Warrant of 11 April 2000 (Democratic Republic of Congo v Belgium)*.[3]

All these decisions must be analysed, in order to see where we stand today as far as immunities are concerned, and to evaluate these evolutions, focusing on their positive aspects, but also on some of the critical questions they raise.[4]

[1] *Pinochet No 1*.

[2] *Pinochet No 3*.

[3] *Arrest Warrant of 11 April 2000 (DRC v Belgium)*, 14 Feb 2002, General List 121. A similar step backwards, although in a civil claim and not a criminal case, was made by the European Court of Human Rights (ECHR) in the case *Al-Adsani*, Application N° 35763/97, judgment of 21 Nov 2001. See below.

[4] Among the extensive literature on the topic of heads of state immunities, see some recent contributions, Hervé Ascensio, 'L'immunité des chefs d'Etat et des gouvernants', in CEDIN, *L'immunité pénale des gouvernants* (Pedone, Paris, forthcoming); Michel Cosnard, 'Les immunités du chef d'Etat' in SFDI, *Le chef d'Etat et le droit international* (Pedone, Paris, 2002), 189; Marc Henzelin, 'Corruption, pillage des ressources et détournements de fonds étatiques: la fin des immunités pénales pour les chefs d'Etats ? Situation en droit suisse', (June 2002) *Rev. suisse de dr. int. et de dr. eur.* ; Mary Margaret Penrose, 'It's Good to Be the King!: Prosecuting Heads of State and Former Heads of State Under International Law', (2000–1) *Columbia J Int'l L.* 193; Jill M Sears, 'Confronting the 'Culture of Impunity': Immunity of Heads of State from Nuremberg to *ex parte Pinochet*', (1999) *German Y. Int'l L.*, 42, 125; Joe Verhoven, 'Les immunités de juridiction et

RELEVANT CONCEPTS

The immunities of present or former heads of state are just one category of immunities among others,[5] sometimes having the same character and scope as more general immunities, sometimes being totally specific to the head of state. Some of the tenets used in order to grant immunity to heads of state have their origin in customary international law, some have been codified in conventional international law and some merely reflect national approaches.

The Different Meanings of Immunity

As a matter of fact, immunity is a word used in several ways which should be distinguished for the sake of clarity.

Immunity can first refer to a kind of *substantive immunity*, meaning that the person benefiting from this kind of immunity would not have to abide by the existing laws. In this first meaning, immunity would amount to complete *irresponsibility*. This kind of immunity has been denounced in very strong terms by Jackson in his *Report to President Truman on the Basis for Trial of War Criminals*:[6]

> Nor should such a defence be recognised as the obsolete doctrine that a head of state is immune from legal liability. There is more than a suspicion that this idea is a relic of the doctrine of divine rights of kings... We do not accept the paradox that legal responsibility should be the least where power is the greatest. We stand on the principle of responsible government declared some three centuries ago to King James by Lord Justice Coke, who proclaimed that even a King is still "under God and the law".

Of course, if such substantive immunity does not exist, then the consequences have to be drawn on the procedural level, and no general procedural immunity should be granted to heads of states. As stated by the ILC '(t)he absence of any procedural immunity with respect to prosecution and punishment in appropriate judicial proceedings is an essential corollary of the absence of any substantive immunity or defence'.[7]

But *procedural immunity* can exist without necessarily implying impunity: this is so, if this procedural immunity is only immunity from some procedures and not immunity from all possible procedures, or alternatively even when it is

d'exécution du chef d'Etat et de l'ancien chef d'Etat en droit international', *Rapport provisoire, Institut de droit international* (Institute of International Law, 2001), doc. mim.; and a reminder of an older but important contribution, Sir Arthur Watts, 'The Legal Position in International Law of Heads of States, Heads of Governments and Foreign Ministers', *RCADI*, 247 (1994/III), 9.

[5] See for example, Christian Dominicé, 'Quelques observations sur l'immunité pénale de l'ancien chef d'Etat', (1999) *RGDIP*, 2, 298.

[6] (1946) *Temp. L Q* 19, 148.

[7] Report on the work of its 48th session, 6 May–26 July 1996, UN Doc. A/51/10, 41.

immunity from all procedures, if this immunity exists only for a certain period of time.

Usually, when one speaks of procedural immunities—immunity from jurisdiction[8] and from execution[9]—reference is generally made to immunities for the acts attributable to one state or its representatives before the courts of a foreign state. But the concept of immunity is also used before national courts, even if the legal justification behind it is different, as will be seen later.[10]

It is also an open question whether immunities have the same scope in criminal matters and civil matters arising from the criminal act, this difficult question having led to a split in the European Court of Human Rights in the *Al-Adsani* case.[11]

Quite often, it is even used in a broader sense, meaning also that no procedure can be launched before an international tribunal, but strictly speaking the concept of immunity does not apply before the international courts.[12] It is interesting that this idea has been expressed by the Tokyo Tribunal, in the case of *Oshima*, Ambassador of Japan in Germany:

> Oshima's special defence is that in connection with his activities in Germany he is protected by diplomatic immunity and is exempt from prosecution. Diplomatic privilege does not import immunity from legal liability, but only exemption from trials by the Courts of the state to which an Ambassador is accredited. In any event this immunity has no relation to crimes against international law charged before a tribunal having jurisdiction.[13]

Lastly, it happens sometimes that the expression 'immunity' is used in order to convey the idea that a head of state is protected from the jurisdiction of another state, even if that protection results from a theory other than immunity (like for example the Act of State doctrine, or the doctrine of *forum non conveniens*[14]).

In order to clarify things we shall speak of the absence of impunity before international tribunals, and only speak of immunities before national courts; and we shall try to distinguish immunities from the other defences put forward by heads of states having the same protective effect as immunity.

[8] Immunity from jurisdiction implies that a state cannot be arraigned before the courts of another state without its consent.

[9] Even if a judgement is duly entered into by the courts of one state against an act or an agent of another state, it is still impossible to execute that judgement against the property of that state: this is known as immunity from execution, or immunity from attachment.

[10] On this question in general, see Michel Cosnard, *La soumission des Etats aux tribunaux internes* (Pedone, Paris, 1996).

[11] See below.

[12] Christian Dominicé, for example, writes: 'The notion of immunity from jurisdiction is irrelevant before an international tribunal', our translation, above n5, 307.

[13] Röling and Rüter (eds), *The Tokyo Judgment. The International Military Tribunal for the Far East, 29 April 1946–12 November 1949*, I (UP Amsterdam BBV, Amsterdam, 1977), 456.

[14] That is, the doctrine under which a court can decline to hear, or can transfer, a case on the grounds that there is a more appropriate court (eg. in the home state) in which it could be heard; see the chapter in this book by Fiona McKay.

The Diverse Immunities of a Head of State

It is usually considered that the ancestor of all immunities of the head of state is *sovereign immunity*, which seems to have existed before the state came into existence, and was granted to the person of the sovereign—the King, the Emperor, the Chief. This immunity, based on the necessary respect for the person of the sovereign, protects the latter from any interference by the courts of his own state or of another state, for all his acts, whether public or private, and whether concerning civil, administrative or criminal matters.

In addition, a rule developed in international law in order to confer state immunity to the entity that emerged in the XIV century, meaning that a state enjoys immunity of jurisdiction and of execution in civil and administrative matters—criminal responsibility of states having so far no existence in international or national law—before the authorities of all other foreign states. This idea is based on the principle of the sovereign equality of all states. Thus, state immunity appears more restricted than sovereign immunity, as it does not concern criminal matters, and concerns only acts done by an agent or organ of the state in an official capacity, not acts done in a private capacity. Naturally, in theory, in case his acts were not already covered by sovereign immunity, the head of state's acts would be liable to enjoy such immunities.

But international law has also developed so-called *diplomatic immunities* for the special agents of the state that represent the state in other countries and which are therefore particularly liable to the risk of being brought before the court of a foreign state. These immunities have first been developed in customary international law and are now codified in the Vienna Convention on Diplomatic Relations, 1961. They are granted in order to afford protection to the state more than to the person of the diplomat: as stated in the Preamble of the Convention, 'the purpose of such privileges and immunities is not to benefit individuals but to ensure the efficient performance of the functions of diplomatic missions as representing states'. It is generally admitted that the diplomatic immunities apply also, *mutatis mutandis,* to heads of state, whether one considers that customary international law applicable to heads of state has embodied more or less the same rules as expressed in the Vienna Convention, or that the Convention applies either directly or by virtue of a reference from a national law (as is the case in England), to heads of state. These diplomatic immunities, strictly speaking according to some writers, should apply only when the head of state is abroad within the territory of another state. As stated by Hazel Fox:[15]

> Immunity from civil and administrative jurisdiction is generally restricted to acts performed in the exercise of official functions,[16] but when the Head is in the territory of

[15] The Resolution of the Institute of International Law on the Immunities of Heads of State and Government, (2002), *ICLQ* 51 119, at 122.

[16] However, it is generally accepted that property personally belonging to a head of state located in the territory of another state shall not be subject to any measure of execution, except to give effect to a final judgment. See Art 4 (1) of the Institute of International Law Resolution of 2001.

> another State in the exercise of official functions no such civil or administrative proceedings may be taken.

However, again, it seems to me that in fact sovereign immunities granted to the head of state while in office supersede the diplomatic immunities.

Finally, to be complete, one must also mention the great variety of *national immunities* given on the basis of the theory of separation of powers to Members of Parliaments and government or to heads of state before the courts of their own state: parliamentary immunities, among which was the senatorial immunity granted to Augusto Pinochet, immunities granted to the Presidents of most countries and so on.[17]

The Act of State Doctrine

To these diverse immunities—rooted, with the exception of purely national immunities, in international law—must be added, among the national theories, the Act of State doctrine—a doctrine developed as such in the Anglo-Saxon world, but which has equivalent approaches in the civil law countries: it is not, it must be insisted, a rule of international law but a judicial self-restraint doctrine.[18] However, it is worth mentioning, although it is not *stricto sensu* immunity, because it has often been invoked to justify a court's refusal to try former heads of state, and therefore plays exactly the same protective role as immunity. It should also be said that even if the Act of State doctrine does not concern criminal responsibility, it can be relevant in the pursuit of justice for crimes against humanity, as the granting of reparation in a civil case can participate in justice being done.

The idea behind the Act of State doctrine is that municipal law will refrain from examining the validity of the acts of foreign governments performed in their capacities as sovereigns within their territory. It is considered as being best described in the statement of the US Supreme Court in the often quoted citation of *Underhill v Fernandez*:[19]

> Every sovereign state is bound to respect the independence of every sovereign state, and the courts of one country will not sit in judgement on the acts of the government of another done in his own territory.'

The Act of State doctrine has been expressed in the *Restatement (Third) of the Foreign Relations Law of the United States*:[20]

[17] Recently a report to Tony Blair showed the responsibility of many officials in the spreading of the 'mad cow' disease in England. But, as stated in *Le Monde*, 28 Oct 2000, 1, 'The tens of politicians and civil servants cited are protected by "Crown immunity"', '"Vache folle": le mea culpa britannique'.

[18] As a matter of fact it can be set aside by the Executive, asking either that it not be used or that it be used in cases where it does not apply.

[19] 1897, 169 US 456. The English landmark precedent is *Buttes Gas v Hammer*, (1981) 3 AER 616 and (1982) AC 888.

[20] St Paul, American Law Institute, I (1987) 366–67.

> . . . courts in the United States will generally refrain from examining the validity of a taking by a foreign state of property within its own territory, or from sitting in judgement on other acts of governmental character done by a foreign state within its own territory and applicable there.

In a nutshell, the Act of State doctrine is applicable to acts attributable to another sovereign state, not exclusively to the head of state. Some limitations are inherently linked to the formulation of the doctrine itself: the act must be a sovereign act; the act must be performed within the territory of the state invoking it.

The fact that the act must be a sovereign act—and not an act performed by the state as a merchant—in order to benefit from the Act of State doctrine has been clearly expressed by the United States Supreme Court in *Alfred Dunhill v Republic de Cuba*,[21] where it refused to recognise a repudiation by the state of Cuba of commercial obligations as an act of state.

The fact that the act has to be performed in a foreign territory means that the US courts for example will not consider themselves prohibited from examining the taking by a foreign state of property situated in the US. A good example of such a restrictive interpretation was given in the case *Republic of Iraq v First National City Bank*,[22] where the revolutionary government tried to recover former King Faysal's assets held in a New York bank, after passing a decree depriving him of those assets; in this case, it has been stated that '(w)hen property confiscated is within the United States at the time of attempted confiscation, our courts will give effect to acts of state only if they are consistent with the policy and law of the United States'. In other words, self-restraint does not apply.

Many examples could illustrate the use of this doctrine by former heads of state in order to try to protect themselves. In the case *The Republic of Philippines v Marcos*,[23] the Republic of Philippines tried to recover or freeze assets it regarded as improperly acquired by former President Marcos and his wife Imelda, but the court ruled that 'adjudication is barred by the act of state doctrine'.[24]

It is precisely in order to avoid such an outcome that Iran, which wanted to get back assets of the former Shah it considered improperly acquired, included a specific provision in paragraph 14 of the Algiers Accords of 1981, stating that 'the claims of Iran should not be considered legally barred by the act of state doctrine'. The problem was then raised before the Iran-US Claims Tribunal in Case A/11 between the Islamic Republic of Iran and the United States concerning the former Shah's assets, each country presenting a different interpretation of the consequences that could be drawn from Article 14. In the view of Iran,

[21] 425 US 682 (1976), 15 *ILM* 735, *ILR* 66, 212.

[22] 241 F Supp 567 (SDNY 1965) affirmed, 353 F. 2d 47 (2d Cir 1965), certiorari denied, 382 US 1027, 86 S Ct.648, 15 L Ed 2d 540 (1966).

[23] United States Court of Appeals, 9th Cir, 818 F 2d 1473 (9th Cir 1987).

[24] *Ibid*, at 1490.

the United States had undertaken in this provision not to bar the claims of Iran before the American courts for the return of the Shah's assets situated in the United States, either by the presentation of preliminary objections based on sovereign immunity or other defences, or by arguments based on the Act of State doctrine. In the view of the United States, however, the commitment to ensure that the Shah's assets would be returned to Iran through procedures before the American courts was not really one, as they invoked the separation of powers and the freedom of the courts to decide. And in fact the four suits brought by Iran were dismissed on *forum non conveniens*. In the Partial Award adopted on 7 April 2000,[25] the Iran-US Claims Tribunal, sitting in Full Tribunal, decided that the refusal of the courts of the United States to return the Shah's assets did not violate the Algiers Declaration:

> With respect to paragraph 14 of the General Declaration:
> Iran has not been denied access to United States courts to pursue its Pahlavi-assets claims and the United States did not guarantee Iran access to United States courts for the consideration of Iran's Pahlavi-assets claims on the merits.
> The United States is obliged to make known to all appropriate United States courts in which Pahlavi-assets litigation is pending that it is the United States Government's position that Iranian decrees and judgements relating to Pahlavi-assets should be enforced by United States courts in accordance with United States law. The phrase 'United States law' covers both procedural and substantive federal and state law in force in the United States. The United States did not guarantee that United States courts would enforce all Iranian decrees and judgements relating to the nationalisation and expropriation of Pahlavi-assets.[26]

In other words, the Iran-US Claims Tribunal, disregarding the rule of the *effet utile*, considered that nothing more was conceded to Iran by the provision of paragraph 14 than the application of the normal rules flowing from the Act of State doctrine.

Besides the two traditional limitations to the Act of State doctrine, there is a trend towards the development of new limitations to the use of the Act of State doctrine to protect states, mainly for acts performed on the territory of the state, but which are in flagrant violation of important rules of international law. Interestingly, it seems that in the United States this trend has started with the protection of property, then of human rights, while in the United Kingdom the evolution has started with human rights and developed in the field of the protection of property.

First, in the field of the protection of private property, it is well known that in the United States, an act of Congress, the Second Hickenlooper Amendment, has added a third limitation, to the extent that it will not apply for an act of confiscation of property in violation of international law. The same position seems to have been adopted very recently in the United Kingdom, in the case *Kuwait Airways*

[25] *The Islamic Republic of Iran v The United States of America*, Award N° 597-A11-FT.
[26] *Ibid*, para 313 D.

Corporation (KAC) v Iraqi Airways Company (IAC) and others,[27] where it was decided for the first time that the acts of a foreign state within its territory may be refused recognition because they constitute flagrant breaches of public international law.[28] Therefore, Resolution 369 of 9 September 1990—by which Iraq transferred all property of KAC, worldwide, including ten aircraft that had been seized in Kuwait and brought to Iraq, to IAC—was not recognised as valid, as it was linked with the illegal aggression towards Kuwait by Iraq on 2 August 1990.

Secondly, in the field of the protection of human rights, the position in the United States is less affirmative and has not been adopted by an act of Congress:[29] however, the *Restatement* considers that '(a) claim on behalf of a victim of torture or genocide—*would*. . . probably not be defeated by the act of state doctrine, since the accepted international law of human rights is well established and contemplates scrutiny of such acts'.[30] Some time ago in the UK, courts restricted the application of such a doctrine, when they were asked to take into consideration a Nazi decree depriving German Jews residing abroad of their citizenship and taking their properties: they considered the decree as being incapable of being a law, thus considering that it could not be an act of state entering in the functions of a state: the House of Lords held that 'so grave an infringement of human rights'[31] should lead to the refusal of recognition of the decree as law.

[27] This position was adopted first by the Court of Appeal (Nov 2000, 3 WLR 1117, 1127H–1128E) and then by the House of Lords (16 May 2002, [2002] UKHL 19, http://www.parliament.the-stationary-office.co.uk/pa/ld200102/ldjudgmt). However, it is possible that the English courts will not accept as easily as the US courts that private individuals have been deprived of their property by an act contrary to international law, as the remarks made in the judgment of *Oppenheimer v Cattermole*, 1976 AC 249 suggest. See n32. In the *KAC v IAC* case, the violation was recognised by the Security Council, which requested all states to refrain from recognising any effects to the aggression of Iraq on Kuwait. Lord Nicholls of Birkenhead of the House of Lords expressed this idea: 'RCC resolution 369 [transferring the KAC planes to IAC] was simply not a governmental expropriation of property within its territory. Having forcibly invaded Kuwait, seized its assets, and taken KAC's aircraft from Kuwait to its own territory, Iraq adopted this decree as part of its attempt to extinguish every vestige of Kuwait's existence as a separate state. An expropriatory decree made in these circumstances and for this purpose is simply not acceptable today', 16 May 2002, para 28. Lord Steyn wrote along the same line: 'An English court may not give direct or indirect recognition to Resolution 369 for any purpose whatsoever. An English court may not recognise any Iraqi decree or act which would directly or indirectly enable Iraq or Iraqi enterprises to retain the spoils of illegal invasion', para 117.

[28] As stated by Lord Steyn, '(i)t is true that the Court of Appeal broke new ground. It was the first decision to hold that the acts of a foreign state within its territory may be refused recognition because they are contrary to public international law… In my view the Court of Appeal was right to extend the public policy exception beyond human rights violations to flagrant breaches of public international law', see preceding note, para 114.

[29] At least not as a general rule. But in specific circumstances the rule has also been set aside. A new exception has been added in the Foreign Sovereign Immunities Act, introduced by s 221 of the Anti-Terrorism and Effective Death Penalty Act of 1996, which applies in respect of a claim for damages for personal injury or death caused by an act of torture, extra-judicial killing, aircraft sabotage of hostage taking, against a state designated by the US as a sponsor of terrorism, were the claimant or victim was a national of the US at the moment of the facts.

[30] Our emphasis. As suggested by Lord Steyn, in this citation from *The Restatement* in his opinion of 25 Nov 1998 in the *Pinochet* case, the word 'probably' should today be replaced by the word 'generally'.

[31] *Oppenheimer v Cattermole*, 1976 AC 249.

All in all, in order for the Act of State doctrine to protect an act from review in a foreign court, it must be a sovereign act and be performed on the territory of the state adopting the act, and not be in flagrant contradiction with the basic principles of international law, for example on the protection of property [32] or on the protection of fundamental human rights.

The Act of State doctrine seems to have been developed in order to give to the agents of the state acting in their official capacities the same protection that was formerly given to a sovereign, and did not seem to be of any use to the head of state benefiting from sovereign immunities. However, being of general application to all acts attributable to a state—to Parliament, the Executive power and so on—the Act of State doctrine is naturally applicable to the acts of the head of state as representing the state, and has indeed frequently be referred to by heads of state.

How Does All This Fit Together?

As stated earlier, it happens sometimes that the word 'immunity' is wrongfully utilised to signify that a person benefits from impunity or is not prosecuted, for reasons other than the technical legal bar of immunity.

What is quite clear is that, in order for the question of immunity to be raised before a court, the competence of the court has to be ascertained first. For example, in the *Pinochet* case, it was only after the Spanish judge was considered to have jurisdiction to prosecute and ask for extradition[33] and after the Law Lords ascertained in the UK that there existed an extradition crime, that they went on to consider the question of immunity.[34]

By the same token, although the ICJ in the *DRC v Belgium* case was not asked to rule on the existence of universal jurisdiction of the Belgian courts, the Court declared quite clearly that:

> ... in its Application instituting these proceedings, the Congo originally challenged the legality of the arrest warrant of 11 April 2000 on two separate grounds: on the one hand, Belgium's claim to exercise a universal jurisdiction and, on the other, the alleged violation of the immunities of the Minister of Foreign Affairs of the Congo then in office. However, in its submissions in its Memorial, and in its final submissions at the close of the oral proceedings, the Congo invokes only the latter ground.
>
> As a matter of logic, the second ground should be addressed only once there has been a determination in respect of the first, since *it is only where a State has jurisdiction*

[32] In the case cited in the preceding note, it is indeed suggested that English courts should only enforce 'clearly established rules of international law', adding: 'Of course on some points it may be by no means clear what the rule of international law is. Whether, for example, legislation of a particular type is contrary to international law because it is "confiscatory" is a question upon which there may well be wide differences of opinions between communist and capitalist countries', 1976, AC 249, at 278.

[33] The *Audiencia Nacional* had rejected on 29 Oct 1998 the challenge by state prosecutors to the jurisdiction of the Spanish judiciary to try Pinochet.

[34] This is very clear in the second decision of the Law Lords on these issues (*Pinochet No 3*).

> *under international law in relation to a particular matter that there can be any question of immunities* in regard to the exercise of that jurisdiction.[35]

In other words immunity is a preliminary exception that is normally raised after the jurisdictional question is solved.

If immunity is a bar to the admissibility of the case at the procedural level, the existence of an Act of State is a bar to adjudicating on the merits of a case. In order to understand how state immunity and the Act of State doctrine overlap, while being distinct, reference can be made to the explanations given on this issue by Lord Berwick:

> Act of State is a confusing term. . . So it is better to refer to non-justiciability. The principles of sovereign immunity and non-justiciability overlap in practice. But in legal theory they are separate. State immunity, including head of state immunity, is a principle of public international law. It creates a procedural bar to the jurisdiction of the court. Logically therefore it comes first. Non-justiciability is a principle of private international law. It goes to the substance of the issues to be decided. It requires the court to withdraw from adjudication on the grounds that the issues are such as the court is not competent to decide. State immunity, being a procedural bar to the jurisdiction of the court, can be waived by the state. Non-justiciability, being a substantive bar to adjudication, cannot.[36]

Whatever analysis is made, it is clear that they are not at the same level.

The Act of State doctrine has been defined by Lord Nicholls in his opinion of 25 November 1998 as 'a common law principle of uncertain application which prevents the English courts from examining the legality of certain acts performed in the exercise of sovereign authority within a foreign country, or occasionally outside it'. Lord Nicholls explains that this Act of State doctrine yields to a contrary intention shown by Parliament; and, in his view, this contrary intention exists as far as torture is concerned, since the Criminal Justice Act of 1988 has embodied in English law the Torture Convention which makes clear that officials acting in an official capacity are to be prosecuted. They are even the only ones likely to be prosecuted under its terms.

In my view, in practical terms, the immunities benefiting heads of state by application of the Act of State doctrine duplicate the different immunities conferred to their acts, at least for the immunities *ratione materiae*. The protection granted to a head of state by sovereign immunities is broader than the protection granted by reference to the Act of State doctrine. One can however imagine that if the sovereign immunities are waived, then the Act of State doctrine can take over.

[35] Judgment of 14 Feb 2002, paras 45 and 46. Our emphasis.

[36] I would make a slightly different analysis, saying that immunity being a protection of the state can be waived by that state, while non-justiciability resulting from the Act of State doctrine being a decision of the prosecuting state can be waived by it and not by the prosecuted state.

A good example of how the two theories interplay can be found in the above mentioned case of *Kuwait Airways Corporation (KAC) v Iraqi Airways Company (IAC) and others*. In a first judgment, the House of Lords, concerned with challenges to the jurisdiction of the English Court toward Iraq, decided first that Iraq was entitled to state immunity in relation to the removal of the aircraft from Kuwait to Iraq which was an exercise of governmental power by Iraq. But once the aircraft were handed over to the Iraqi public company by the legal act considered as an act of state, it decided secondly that the use by that company—IAC—of the airplanes was not covered by the immunity:

> IAC could not claim state immunity regarding the acts of which KAC was complaining, in so far as they were done after RCC resolution 369 came into force. IAC's retention and use of the aircraft as its own did not constitute acts done in the exercise of sovereign immunity'.[37]

In other words, Iraq was immune, but not IAC, against which KAC continued proceedings.

But then, in the discussion of IAC's liability toward KAC, the question of the validity of the acts undertaken by Iraq came to the forefront, as the situation of IAC was not the same if it was lawfully entitled to the property of the aircraft or not. At this stage, that is the discussion of the merits, the doctrine of Act of State was discussed and received a novel interpretation as mentioned. From the comparison between the two decisions of the House of Lords it appears that a gross violation of international law does not in itself suppress state immunity, while it can be used to decide that the Act of State doctrine does not apply. Immunity thus seems a stronger protection than Act of State.

International Rules Granting Immunities to an Acting Head of State

It is generally considered that the status of an acting head of state is defined by customary international law.

There is no specific international general convention on that topic, even if some international conventions refer expressly to the situation of an acting head of state.[38] The *Institut de droit international* attempted to codify the rules applicable to heads of state before foreign courts in 1891:[39] a distinction was then

[37] 1995, 1 WLR 1147, para 3.

[38] The Convention on the Punishment of Crimes against Internationally Protected Persons of 1973 includes the head of state in the definition of the protected persons, but does not deal with immunities. The Draft Articles of the ILC on Jurisdictional Immunities of States and their Property adopted in 1991 (*Yearbook ILC*, 1991, vol II, Part 2, 13), Art 3 declares: 'The present articles are ...without prejudice to privileges and immunities accorded under international law to Heads of State *ratione personae*'. See also the Convention on Special Missions of 1969 that mentions the privileged status of the head of state.

[39] 'Projet de règlement international sur la compétence des tribunaux dans les procès contre les Etats, les souverains ou chefs d'Etats étrangers', Hamburg session, (1889–1892, revised in 1892) *Ann. Inst dr int* 11 , 436–38

drawn between the head of state acting as representing his state and the head of state acting as a private person. But this project never became positive law.

It is generally admitted that the immunities granted to diplomats by the Vienna Convention on Diplomatic Relations of 1961 apply, with the necessary modifications, to heads of state. If we turn then to the Convention on Diplomatic Relations, we find several articles dealing with immunity.

Article 29 provides that '(t)he person of a diplomatic agent shall be inviolable. He shall not be liable to any form of arrest or detention. . . '; in other words, the diplomatic agent, to which the head of state is assimilated, enjoys absolute immunity from execution.

Article 31 draws the extent and limits of his immunity from jurisdiction: 'A diplomatic agent shall enjoy immunity from criminal jurisdiction of the receiving state. He shall also enjoy immunity from its civil and administrative jurisdiction', except in some cases, involving real property he does not hold for the purpose of his mission, succession questions and commercial activities.

The question is open here as to whether the head of state enjoys the same immunities as diplomats or stronger immunities. If it is considered that he enjoys the same immunities, the question remains open whether this is so only when he is abroad, or also when he is in his home country. If it is considered that he has different immunities, they will certainly be broader. Here we see how sovereign immunity and diplomatic immunity are articulated together, and that some necessary modifications are to be applied to the head of state.

Mainly, for the head of state, it seems that unlike the diplomat he is absolutely immune from criminal prosecution as well as from civil proceedings while he is abroad. No exceptions exist for certain matters, as it does for the diplomats.[40]

This means that heads of state benefit, according to customary international law, from absolute immunity from prosecution in another state while in office. They have an absolute immunity *ratione personae* while in office: their person is protected for all acts, whether public or private, before criminal courts.

On the contrary, it seems that their immunity from civil or administrative matters is far from absolute. This is, at least, how the Institute of International Law has restated its understanding of customary international law in Article 3 of the Resolution adopted in Vancouver in 2001:

> In civil and administrative matters, Head of State does not enjoy any immunity from jurisdiction before the courts of a foreign State, unless that suit relates to acts performed in the exercise of his or her official functions. Even in such a case, the Head of State shall enjoy no immunity in respect of a counterclaim. Nonetheless, nothing shall be done by way of court proceedings with regard to the Head of State while he or she is in the territory of that State, in the exercise of official functions.[40a]

[40] Either a restriction concerning the subject matter, or a restriction depending on his presence abroad.

[40a] See n 15

International Rules Granting Immunities to a Former Head of State

It is less clear what rules govern the former head of state's immunities. In general, international law is quite silent on the situation of a former head of state.

The question of the extent to which a diplomatic agent—and by analogy a head of state—enjoys immunity, after he has left office, is provided in Article 39 of the Convention, which might be of some help in answering this question:

1 Every person entitled to privileges and immunities shall enjoy them from the moment he enters the territory of the receiving state. . .
2 When the functions of a person enjoying privileges and immunities have come to an end, such privileges and immunities shall normally cease at the moment when he leaves the country. . . However, with respect to acts performed by such a person in the exercise of his functions as a member of the mission, immunity shall continue to subsist.

This last provision can give some information on the status of a former head of state. A distinction is usually drawn between the immunity *ratione personae* which is only enjoyed by the acting head of state, as mentioned earlier, and a more restricted immunity *ratione materiae* benefiting the former head of state. An acting head of state has an immunity based on his person's status, a former head of state on the category of acts performed.

Traditionally, the immunity *ratione materiae* was interpreted as based on a distinction between private acts and official acts, that is acts committed as part of the discharge of the head of state's functions.

Today however, the question is raised whether the acts for which a former head of state does not benefit from any immunity are not only private acts which are *functionally outside* the exercise of official duties, but also crimes under international law, which even if performed as part of the exercise of power, have to be considered as *teleologically outside* the functions of a head of state. The answer to this question was clearly affirmative in the decision of the House of Lords in the *Pinochet* case, but is less clear after the judgment of the ICJ in the *DRC v Belgium* case.

LIMITS TO IMPUNITY FOR PUBLIC OFFICIALS AND HEADS OF STATE BEFORE INTERNATIONAL COURTS

Strictly speaking, one does not deal here with immunity, but rather with impunity. It is quite clear that the theory of immunity has developed in order to protect a state and its agents from being tried in states' courts, primarily in the courts of another state. The immunity from arrest as well as the immunity from jurisdiction or execution is based on the sovereign equality of states. But naturally, the sovereign equality of states does not prevent a state's representative from being prosecuted before an international court, if this court is given jurisdiction over former or acting heads of state.

Early International Criminal Law

Before an international tribunal, no procedural bar exists and it has also been asserted, so that things are unambiguous, that no excuse can exist on the merits, because of the official position of a defendant. In other words, immunity is not an issue before the international tribunals and irresponsibility has been clearly swept out. This has been asserted in the Versailles Treaty, in Article 227, indicting the Emperor Wilhelm de Hohenzollern, and then, more effectively, in the two Statutes of the Nuremberg and Tokyo Tribunals.

Article 7 of the Charter of the Nuremberg Tribunal states:

> The official position of defendants, whether heads of states or responsible officials in government departments, shall not be considered as freeing them from responsibility or mitigating punishment.

Article 6 of the Statute of the Tokyo Tribunal reads:

> Neither the position, at any time, of an accused, nor the fact that an accused acted pursuant to order of his government or a superior shall, of itself, be sufficient to free such accused from responsibility for any crime with which he is charged. . .

These principles of international criminal law were restated in the seven Principles of Nuremberg by the International Law Commission in 1950. Principle III provides:

> The fact that the author of an act which constitutes a crime under international law has acted in his capacity as head of state or of government does not release him from his responsibility under international law.

The Recent Developments

When adopting the Draft Code of Crimes against the Peace and the Security of Mankind, the ILC adopted the same position, and explained why it was so necessary:

> . . . crimes against the peace and the security of mankind often require the involvement of persons in positions of governmental authority who are capable of formulating plans and policies involving acts of exceptional gravity and magnitude. These crimes require the power to use or to authorise the use of the essential means of destruction and to mobilise the personnel required for carrying out these crimes. A governmental official who plans, instigates, authorises or orders such crimes not only provides the means and the personnel required for carrying out the crime, but also abuses the authority and power entrusted to him. He may, therefore, be considered to be even more culpable than the subordinate who actually commits the criminal act. It would be paradoxical to allow the individuals who are, in some respect, the most responsible for the crime. . . to invoke the sovereignty of the state.[41]

[41] Above n 38, 39.

Articles 7(2) of the Statute of the International Criminal Tribunal for Former Yugoslavia (ICTY) and 6(2) of the International Criminal Tribunal for Rwanda (ICTR) also repeat that heads of state do not benefit from any impunity. Both state that '(t)he official position of any accused person whether as a head of state or Government or as a responsible Government Official shall not relieve such person of criminal responsibility.'

Article 27 of the Statute of the International Criminal Court entitled 'Irrelevance of official position' is also quite explicit, and treats a head of state like any other person, as far as its substantive obligations are concerned and as far as the procedures against him are concerned (see appendices).

A word has to be said here of another article of the Statute which could at first sight seem to be in contradiction with this provision. Article 98 reads:

> The Court may not proceed with a request for surrender or assistance which would require the requested state to act inconsistently with its obligations under international law with respect to the state or diplomatic immunities of a person or property of a third state, unless the Court can first obtain the cooperation of that third state for the waiver of immunity.

It seems that this article's only purpose is to guarantee for example that a head of state of a country that is not a party to the Statute and thus has not accepted the jurisdiction of the Court, will not be arrested and surrendered while travelling to another state party to the Statute.

These rules asserting that heads of state must assume their responsibility and have no impunity before international tribunals apply naturally to former heads of state as well as to heads of state in office, as is shown by the indictment of Milošević by the ICTY in May 1999, for crimes committed in Kosovo, when he was still in office.

LIMITS TO IMMUNITY FOR PUBLIC OFFICIALS AND HEADS OF STATE BEFORE THE NATIONAL COURTS OF THEIR OWN STATE

Limits According to National Laws

It is evident that the best solution, when politically and legally feasible, is for the criminal head of state to be prosecuted before the courts of his own country. As stated by Human Rights Watch, '(c)rimes are far easier to prove in the country in which they were committed. . . and justice delivered locally. . . may be the most meaningful to the victims'.[42]

The extent to which a public official or a head of state will benefit from immunity from justice will depend on the content of the different national laws. These laws are based on the theory of separation of powers, and the necessity to afford a certain protection to the main political actors from judicial harassment.

[42] *The Pinochet Precedent* (HRW, New York, 2000), 18.

In France, as is the case in many other countries, several immunities exist for categories of political leaders, and are even granted by the Constitution. In order that the immunities do not end up in irresponsibility, some special courts have been instituted: in other words, the immunities are accompanied by some privileges of jurisdiction.

Members of Parliament—whether of the National Assembly or of the Senate—benefit from an immunity in criminal matters, unless the Assembly to which they belong lifts that parliamentary immunity in order for them to be prosecuted before the ordinary courts. This protection of their function as representatives of the people of France is granted by Article 26 of the French Constitution of 4 October 1958:

> No member of Parliament may be prosecuted, sought out, arrested, held in custody or tried on account of opinions expressed or votes cast by him in the exercise of his functions. No member of Parliament may be prosecuted or arrested on account of any crime or misdemeanour, without the authorisation of the bureau of the Assembly of which he is a member. This authorisation is not required in case of *flagrante delicto*, or existence of a final sentence.
>
> The detention, measures of privation or restriction of liberty, or the prosecution of a member of Parliament may be suspended during the parliamentary session if the Assembly of which he is a member so demands.

The *members of the Government*—and among them the Prime Minister—also have immunities as far as criminal matters are concerned. In fact, their immunities are not expressly stated as for the members of Parliament, but result implicitly from the fact that they have to be prosecuted before a special court named *Cour de Justice de la République*, which means that they must be considered as benefiting from immunities of jurisdiction and cannot be prosecuted before the ordinary courts. Article 68-1 of the Constitution provides:

> Members of the Government are criminally responsible for actions performed in the carrying out of their duties and qualified as crimes or misdemeanours at the time they were committed. They are tried by the Court of Justice of the Republic (*Cour de Justice de la République*).[43]

And of course, the head of state—*the President of the Republic*—also has extensive immunities, stated in Article 68 of the Constitution:

> The President of the Republic is responsible for actions performed in the carrying out of his duties only in case of high treason. He can be indicted only by identical motions passed by the two assemblies by open ballot and by an absolute majority of their members; he is tried by the High Court of Justice (*Haute Cour de Justice*).[44]

[43] According to Art 68-2 this special court is composed of 12 members of Parliament elected by the National Assembly and the Senate and three judges from the *Cour de cassation*, one of them presiding the Court.

[44] Unlike the *Cour de Justice de la République*, no judge is a member of this *Haute Cour de Justice*, which appears more like a political organ than a court, as it is composed only of elected

The existence of these privileges of jurisdiction appeared problematic when France wanted to ratify the Statute of the International Criminal Court. Since this Statute provides for the possible prosecution of a head of state or other state officials before the ICC, which was not envisioned by the Constitution, a modification of the Constitution had to be adopted, after the Constitutional Council had declared the Statute to be contrary to the French Constitution. This was done by the introduction of a new article in the Constitution, Article 53-2, after which the ICC Statute was ratified.

Other developments have recently occurred, as far as the immunities of the head of state are concerned. A debate arose on the issue of what happens regarding acts not committed in the discharge of official functions, for example private acts or, even more importantly, acts committed before coming into office. Strictly speaking, the Constitution deals only with acts performed as part of the head of state's function, as Article 68 refers to 'actions performed in the carrying out of his duties'. The issue was raised because of accusations of financial misappropriations that could have been committed when President Chirac was Mayor of Paris, of which he might be accused. The legal question was whether the case could be prosecuted before the ordinary courts while he was in office. The Minister of Justice, Mrs Guigou, declared bluntly that 'as any citizen, the President of the Republic can be brought to court if he commits misdemeanours',[45] but other voices were heard to the contrary.

The controversy was first resolved by the aforementioned decision[46] rendered by the Constitutional Council (CC), when it was asked to decide whether or not Article 27 of the ICC Statute was contrary to the French Constitution: in an *obiter dictum*, the CC decided that Article 68 of the French Constitution implies that the President of the Republic enjoys absolute immunity from criminal prosecution while in office for acts accomplished in the exercise of his functions except in the case of *haute trahison*:

> By Article 68 of the Constitution, the President of the Republic may not be held liable for acts performed in the exercise of his duties except in the case of high treason; moreover, he may be indicted only in the High Court of Justice by the procedure determined by that article.

As a matter of fact, two interpretations could have been given to the decision of the Constitutional Council. It could be understood that he can indeed be brought to the *Haute Cour de Justice* for acts committed outside his official functions—whether private acts committed while in office or acts committed before he was in office[47]—or, alternatively, that while in office he is absolutely

members of Parliament (Art 67 of the Constitution). In the United States, the personal responsibility of the President for acts committed outside his functions is set in motion by the procedure of impeachment.

[45] Declaration of 17 May 1998, cited in *Le Monde*, 20 Mar 2000, 8.

[46] Decision no. 98-408, 22 Jan 1999.

[47] This was the interpretation given by Arnaud de Montebourg, a socialist Member of Parliament, who had started to collect signatures to have Jacques Chirac tried by the *Haute Cour de*

immune, except in the case of high treason, the only hypothesis under which he can be tried by the *Haute Cour de Justice*. As the question was heavily debated in France, the CC decided to give its authoritative interpretation of its own decision in a 'Communiqué'. Such a move is without precedent.[48] According to the CC, it is the second interpretation that has to prevail.

The *Cour de cassation,* then faced with a prosecution that could implicate Jacques Chirac, adopted the same position as the CC, in a decision rendered on 10 October 2001.[49] The question was whether he could be asked to give testimony before the French courts. The *Cour de cassation* first ruled that it had to decide that question by itself, and was not bound by the decision of the CC, which was only final and binding as far as the question of the constitutionality of Article 27 of the ICC Statute was concerned, but then it ended up with the same solution as the CC, stating that:

> *... L'article 68 doit être interprété en ce sens qu'étant élu directement par le peuple, pour assurer, notamment, le fonctionnement régulier des pouvoirs publics ainsi que la continuité de l'Etat, le Président de la République ne peut, pendant la durée de son mandat, être entendu comme témoin assisté, ni être mis en examen, cité ou renvoyé pour une infraction quelconque devant une juridiction de droit commun.*

Finally, it should be mentioned that just as there exists an Act of State doctrine of judicial self-restraint towards the acts of a foreign state, doctrines of self-restraint towards certain domestic acts of a governmental nature have also developed in the different national systems: in France, for example it is called the doctrine of acts of government (*actes de gouvernement*), in the United States, the doctrine of 'political acts'.[50] These theories can also be of some relevance for heads of state in their own country.

Limits According to International Law where an International Crime is Concerned

More and more voices are heard stating that international human rights law imposes limitations on the legal possibility of a state adopting an amnesty law or other measures implying a waiver of investigation or prosecution for certain crimes. In other words, national laws should no longer deal with immunities as they see fit, at least where crimes of international law are concerned.

For example, the Inter-American Commission on Human Rights adopted two important decisions on 2 October 1992 referring respectively to the amnesty laws of Argentina and Uruguay. Although these laws were adopted with a view to favouring national reconciliation and helping the transition from dictatorship to democracy, the Commission considered that they were in violation of

justice. He is also the author of a book in which he accuses Jacques Chirac of criminal acts, *La Machine à trahir* (Denoël, Paris, 2000).

[48] See Frédéric Thiriez, 'Le communiqué de presse, source de droit ?', *Le Monde*, 21 Oct 2000.

[49] http://www.courdecassation.fr/agenda/arrets/arret/01-84922arr.htm, 3.

[50] They concern mainly the relations between the Executive and the Legislature, foreign relations and the conduct of war and in addition, for the United States, federal-state relations.

international law, and more specifically of the American Convention of Human Rights and the American Declaration on the Rights and Duties of Man. It adopted the same analysis as far as the Chilean Amnesty law is concerned: according to the Inter-American Commission, 'Amnesty Law 2191 and its legal effects form part of a general policy of human rights violation by the military regime that governed Chile from September 1973 to March 1990'.[51]

The lawyers of victims in Chile have tried to use this analysis, linked with the superiority of international law over national law stated in the Chilean Constitution, in order to have the Chilean courts set aside the Amnesty Law protecting Pinochet.

An important precedent was set recently by the ICTY in the case of *Prosecutor v Anto Furundzija*,[52] where it was stated that if an amnesty law were passed for absolving torturers, this law should be disregarded—by international tribunals, foreign courts and national courts—because of the *erga omnes* value of the prohibition of torture:

> Prosecutions could be initiated by potential victims if they had *locus standi* before a competent international or national judicial body with a view to asking it to hold the national measure to be internationally unlawful; or the victim could bring a civil suit for damage in a foreign court, which would therefore be asked *inter alia* to disregard the legal value of the national authorising act. What is even more important is that perpetrators of torture acting upon or benefiting from those national measures may nevertheless be held criminally responsible for torture, whether in a foreign state, or in their own state under a subsequent regime.[53]

LIMITS TO IMMUNITY FOR PUBLIC OFFICIALS AND HEADS OF STATE BEFORE THE NATIONAL COURTS OF FOREIGN STATES

Limits to State Immunity in Civil Matters, According to National Laws and International Law

As mentioned previously, the principle of sovereign equality implies that the acts attributable to one state cannot be judged in the courts of another state. Therefore, immunities of jurisdiction and execution were granted to foreign states, these immunities naturally benefiting heads of state.

For a long time, state immunity was *absolute*. This immunity applied to all the acts of the state—laws, decrees—as well as to the organs and agents representing the state, the head of state being one of them. Naturally, state immunity was supposed to protect the state in its specific functions performed for the common good. As the principal beneficiary, the state could lift this immunity. In

[51] Cases 11.505 and 11.532 v Chile, Report of the Comision Interamericana de Derechos Humanos (CIDH), no. 36/96 and no. 25/98 of 7 April 1998, para 76.

[52] Decision of 10 Dec 1998, case no. TI-95-17/1-T, 38 *ILM*, (1999), 317.

[53] Para 155.

addition, the state being considered unable to bear criminal responsibility, state immunity concerned only civil and administrative matters.

Today, it is the rule of *relative* immunity of states that prevails. The question is dealt with by principles of international law and sometimes by international conventions like the European Convention on State Immunities and its Additional Protocol of 1972, and is regulated in detail by the different national laws or precedents on state immunities. Generally speaking, it can be said that the state enjoys immunities only for its sovereign acts and not for its commercial activities.

As far as civil actions for torts are concerned, the well known Alien Tort Claims Act and Torture Victim Protection Act give the US courts jurisdiction over civil actions brought by aliens, for tortuous conduct by a person acting under the actual or apparent authority or under colour of law of a foreign state in violation of the law of nations, and have been mainly used in cases of abuses of human rights.[54] The English legislature has also adopted laws to the same effect: for example, the Criminal Justice Act 1988[55] has excluded immunity for acts of torture and the Taking of Hostages Act for acts of taking of hostages.[56]

Some instances involve not only public officials but also former heads of state. A good example is the case *In re Estate of Ferdinand Marcos*,[57] holding that Marcos could not hide behind his immunities, when sued in an action for damages by victims of acts of torture or wrongful deaths, as those acts could not be regarded as official acts committed within the scope of his authority. Another recent example is the case in which immunity was denied to Ayatollah Khamenei, Supreme Leader of the Islamic Republic of Iran and to Rafsanjani, former President, in a case brought against them by US victims of terrorism,[58] by application of the so-called 'Flatow Amendment' amending the Foreign Sovereign Immunities Act of the United States, providing for the denial of immunity to foreign states and their officials that facilitate and encourage terrorism.

International law has also started to limit immunities, as for example in Article 11 of the 1972 European Convention on State Immunity (the Basel Convention):

> A Contracting State cannot claim immunity from the jurisdiction of a court of another Contracting State in proceedings which relate to redress for injury to the person or damage to tangible property, if the facts which occasioned the injury occurred in the territory of the State of forum, and if the author of the injury or damage was present in that territory at the time when those facts occurred.

[54] See for example the landmark case, *Filartiga v Pana Irala*, 630 F 2d 876 (2nd Cir 1980) and 577 F Supp 860 (EDNY, 1984); see also *Kadic v Karadzić*, 70 F. 3d 232 (2nd Cir 1995). See the chapter in this volume by William Aceves and Paul Hoffman.

[55] Art 134.

[56] Art 1 para 1.

[57] *In re: Estate of Ferdinand Marcos Human Rights Litigation*, 25 F 3d 1467 (9th Cir 1994); see also *Trial of former President General Luis Garcia Meza and his collaborators on multiple charges relating to gross human rights violations*, Bolivian Supreme Court of Justice, 21 April 1993.

[58] *Flatow v Islamic Republic of Iran and al*, 99 F Supp 1 (DC Columbia, 1998).

Limits to Immunities According to European Human Rights Law

This question of the limits to immunities in cases of torture has been strongly debated before the European Court of Human Rights (ECHR) in 2001 in the case *Al-Adsani v The United Kingdom* (torture and state immunity). The question raised in that case was whether a government can claim immunity for torture in civil proceedings against it.[59]

Mr Al-Adsani, who had dual British and Kuwaiti nationality, was tortured in Kuwait, and brought proceedings in the English courts. The High Court in a decision entered on 15 May 1995 held that the State Immunity Act of 1998 meant that he could not pursue a claim against the Government of Kuwait, stating:

> It was prepared provisionally to accept that the Government were vicariously responsible for conduct that would qualify as torture under international law. However, international law could be used only to assist in interpreting lacunae or ambiguities in a statute, and when the terms of a statute were clear, the statute had to prevail over international law.[60] The clear language of the 1978 Act bestowed immunity upon sovereign States for acts committed outside the jurisdiction and, by making express provision for exceptions, it excluded as a matter of construction implied exceptions. As a result, there was no room for an implied exception for acts of torture.[61]

The Court of Appeal having confirmed that decision, the Applicant, among others, complained of a violation of this right of access to a court under Article 6.1 of the European Convention on Human Rights.

The ECHR accepted the idea that the prohibition of torture has now become a rule of *jus cogens*, and quoted extensively the decision of the ICTY in the *Prosecutor v Furundzija* case:[62]

> It should be noted that the prohibition of torture laid down in human rights treaties enshrines an absolute right, which can never be derogated from, not even in time of emergency… This is linked to the fact … that the prohibition of torture is a peremptory norm or *jus cogens* … Because of the importance of the values it protects, this principle has evolved into a peremptory norm or *jus cogens*, that is, a norm that enjoys a higher rank in the international hierarchy than treaty law and even 'ordinary' customary rules.[63]

The ECHR then suggests that there is a distinction to be drawn, as was done by Lord Millet in the *Pinochet* case, between immunity *ratione materiae* from

[59] See the chapter in this book by Fiona McKay for a detailed discussion of the case.

[60] It can be stressed that this statement is an illustration of the reluctance of national courts to apply international law, when national law is in contradiction with it.

[61] As restated in the decision of the ECHR, para 17.

[62] Above n 52.

[63] Paras 144 and 151. Similar statements were made in *Prosecutor v Delasic and Others*, 16 Nov 1998, Case no. IT-96-21-T, para 454, and in *Prosecutor v Kunarac*, 22 Feb 2001, Case no. IT-96-23-T and IT-96-23/1, para 466.

criminal jurisdiction and immunity *ratione personae* of sovereign states from civil jurisdiction for acts of torture.

And relying on that distinction, the ECHR considers that 'the grant of sovereign immunity to a State in civil proceedings pursues a legitimate aim of complying with international law, to promote comity and good relations between States through the respect of another State's sovereignty',[64] even if these civil proceedings are in pursuance of reparation for acts of torture and even if other considerations enter into play for the lifting of immunity of a former head of state in criminal proceedings for the same acts.

In a concurring opinion, Judge Pellonpää joined by Judge Bratza suggested that this decision was also taken for practical reasons:

> The somewhat paradoxical result, had the minority's view prevailed, could have been that precisely those States which so far have been most liberal in accepting refugees and asylum seekers, would have imposed upon them the additional burden of guaranteeing access to court for the determination of perhaps hundreds of refugees' civil claims for compensation for alleged torture.

There was been a dissenting opinion by Judge Rozakis and Caflish joined by Judges Wildhaber, Costa, Cabral Barreto and Vajic, in which all these judges criticised the distinction made by the majority, as far as the granting of immunities is concerned, between a criminal action against a head of state or other state agent and a civil action against the state stemming out of the same criminal act: according to them,

> (t)he distinction made by the majority between civil and criminal proceedings, concerning the effect of the rule of the prohibition of torture, is not consonant with the very essence of the operation of the *jus cogens* rules. It is not the nature of the proceedings which determines the effects that a *jus cogens* rule has upon another rule of international law, but the character of the rule as a peremptory norm and its interaction with a hierarchically lower rule.[65]

The serious split in the ECHR—the decision was adopted by a majority of 9 against 8 votes—illustrates the on-going debate on the question of restricting immunities protecting states and their heads or agents.

In fact, the head of state accumulates both state immunity and sovereign immunity, the two having become in my view quite indistinguishable: it seems to me that sovereign immunity in its quasi-absolute formulation is the rule when the head of state is in office, while when he is no longer in office there operates a combination between state immunity in civil and administrative matters with its contemporary limitations, and sovereign immunity in criminal matters for the acts he performed in the exercise of his functions, with its contemporary uncertainties.

64 *Al-Adsani* judgment, para 54.
65 Para 4.

Limits to Sovereign Immunities in Criminal Matters when an International Crime is Concerned[66]

The development of universal jurisdiction extends the cases where a foreign court will assert jurisdiction over a foreigner and thus a foreign head of state: this explains why the problems of immunities of former heads of state have come to the forefront in criminal matters. Universal jurisdiction is based on the idea that every state in the world has an interest in bringing to justice the authors of certain acts qualified as crimes under international law, wherever the crime was committed, by whomsoever it was committed and against whomsoever it was perpetrated. It is a matter of discussion among lawyers whether universal jurisdiction has to be based on a specific treaty like the 1984 UN Convention against Torture, or whether it can also be granted by a customary rule of international law, like the *jus cogens* rule prohibiting torture, crimes against humanity or genocide.[67]

There are several precedents that can be invoked, based on a specific interpretation of international law, according to which immunities of public officials or heads of state are to be disregarded when international crimes are at stake. As far as criminal suits are concerned, the most relevant case, before the *Pinochet* case, is the well known case of *Attorney-General of the Government of Israel v Eichmann*.[68]But the most relevant precedent to the effect that international law limits the immunities of a former head of state when an international crime has been committed is, of course, the *Pinochet* case.[69]

[66] According to the Resolution of 2001 of the Institute of International Law, it is stated in Art 13 that a former head of state enjoys only immunity for acts performed as part of his official functions, adding: 'Nevertheless, he or she may be prosecuted and tried when the acts alleged constitute a crime under international law, or when they are performed exclusively to satisfy a personal interest, or when they constitute a misappropriation of the State's assets and resources.'

[67] See Brigitte Stern, 'La compétence universelle en France: le cas des crimes commis en ex-Yougoslavie et au Rwanda', (1998) 40, *German YIL* 280. International conventions create in general a compulsory universal jurisdiction, while customary law provides for a faculty to use universal jurisdiction. This explains the fact that although the Genocide Convention only provides for compulsory territorial jurisdiction, it can be asserted that a state can, on the basis of customary international law, bring someone accused of genocide before its own courts on the basis of universal jurisdiction.

[68] 36 ILR (1961) 5, para 30; see also *Trial of nine military commanders who had ruled Argentina between 1976 and 1982*, Arg Fed Court of Appeals, 9 Dec 1985 and Arg Supreme Court of Justice, 30 Dec 1986.

[69] For further discussion on the case, see the chapters in this book by Clare Montgomery and Mark Lattimer. Discussions of the case in French include: Jean-Yves de Cara, 'L'affaire Pinochet devant la Chambre des Lords', (1999), *AFDI*, 72; Michel Cosnard, 'Quelques observations sur les décisions de la Chambre des Lords du 25 Novembre 1998 et du 24 mars 1999 dans l'affaire Pinochet', (1999), *RGDIP*, 309; Isabelle Fichet et David Boyle, 'Le jugement de la Chambre des Lords dans l'affaire Pinochet: Un commentaire, http://www.ridi.org/adi/1998; Anne Muxart, 'Immunités de l'ex-chef d'Etat et compétence universelle: quelques réflexions à propos de l'affaire Pinochet', http://www.ridi.org/adi/1998; Brigitte Stern, 'Pinochet face à la justice', *Etudes*, Jan 2001, 7; 'International Decisions, (1999), *AJIL* 93, 696; Article in *Le Monde,* 'Les moyens d'oser', 29 Oct 1998,19; Article in *Le Monde,* 'Tremblez, anciens dictateurs', 26 Mar 1999, 17; Santiago Villalpando, 'L'affaire Pinochet: beaucoup de bruit pour rien? L'apport au droit international de la décision de la Chambre des Lords du 24 mars 1999', (2000) *RGDIP*, 394.

THE QUESTION OF IMMUNITY IN THE *PINOCHET* CASE

Pinochet tried to invoke three different immunities: senatorial immunity, sovereign immunity and diplomatic immunity.

Before examining whether a former head of state can benefit from one or the other of those immunities, it must be ascertained that the person claiming them really is a former head of state.

The Status as Head of State, a Prerequisite for Immunities to Apply

During the first hearings before the House of Lords, one counsel against Pinochet argued that he never was a legal head of state, whether as the President of the Military Junta, the Supreme Chief of the Nation or the President of the Republic of Chile.

Most of the Lords denied this could be even discussed: Lord Lloyd of Berwick declared that '(i)t is clear beyond doubt that he was', Lord Nicholls of Birkenhead stated that

> the evidence shows he was the ruler of Chile from 11 September 1973, when a military junta of which he was the leader overthrew the previous government of President Allende, until 11 March 1990 when he retired from the office of president. I am prepared to assume he was head of state throughout the period.[70]

Only Lord Slynn of Hadley really discussed the issue: considering that Pinochet 'was not, in any event, appointed in a way recognised by the Constitution', he added that '(i)t seems clear, however, that the respondent acted as head of state', and was recognised *de facto* by other states to have the powers of a head of state, as they accepted for example that he could sign the letters of accreditation of ambassadors; therefore, he considered that he should be treated as a former head of state. The same type of reasoning was used in the case brought in the United States against Karadzic, considered as a head of state as he 'acted under the colour of law'.[71]

On the other hand, sovereign immunity was sometimes refused precisely because a head of state was not recognised by the state in which he was prosecuted: this is the reasoning used in the United States to refuse to grant sovereign immunity to Noriega, who, although the ruler of Panama, was never recognised by the United States.[72]

Another question of qualification can be briefly mentioned here. It must be recalled that under the Torture Convention, torture must be committed by a 'public official or a person acting in an official capacity'.

70 Lord Steyn and Lord Browne-Wilkinson make the same type of assumption.
71 Cited n 54.
72 *United States v Noriega* (1990) 746 F Supp 1506.

In the first decision of the House of Lords in *Pinochet*, Lord Slynn of Hadley declared that Pinochet as head of state was neither a public official, nor a person acting in an official capacity, in the sense of the Convention. The reason given for such a surprising interpretation was that the head of state was not mentioned as such and should therefore be considered as excluded from the reach of the Convention. This of course would produce strange results, because it implies that minor officials having participated in the actions of the Chilean government could be prosecuted, whereas the person orchestrating it all could not.

The Reliance on the State Immunity Act

In order to deal with the question of immunity, the Law Lords referred to UK law, more precisely to the State Immunity Act of 1978, which itself refers to international law.

Part I of the State Immunity Act deals with state immunity: this means that a foreign state 'is immune from the jurisdiction of the courts of the United Kingdom' (Article 1) except in some of the cases provided for in the Act, mainly the cases when the state acts not *jure imperii* but *jure gestionis*, in other words when it acts not as a sovereign, but as a merchant. Article 14 specifies that 'references to a state include references to (a) the sovereign or other head of that state in his public capacity; (b) the government of that state; (c) any department of that government, but not to any entity (hereafter referred to as a "separate entity") which is distinct from the executive organs of the government and capable of suing and being sued'. Article 16(4) states that this first part of the Act dealing with state immunity 'does not apply to criminal matters'.

Part III of the Act deals with another type of immunity, diplomatic immunity, and refers to the Diplomatic Privileges Act 1964, which incorporates into the UK legal system the Vienna Convention on Diplomatic Relations.

Two points deserve to be mentioned. First, it must be noted that diplomatic protection as granted by the international convention shall apply to a sovereign or other head of state 'subject ... to any necessary modifications' (Article 20(1)). Secondly, this diplomatic immunity has to be added to the state immunity and does not enter in conflict with it, as is stated twice, in two different articles, one in Part I and one in Part III: Article 16(1) in Part I states that '(t)his Part of the Act does not affect any immunity or privilege conferred by the Diplomatic Privileges Act 1964. . . '; Article 20(5) in Part III provides that '(t)his section applies to the sovereign or other head of any state on which immunities and privileges are conferred by Part I of this Act and is without prejudice to the application of that Part to any such sovereign or head of state in his public capacity'. In other words, it means that the different immunities must be added to each other instead of being considered as exclusive or contradictory.

A Consensus on the Existence of Absolute Immunity for Acting Heads of State

All the Lords asserted that a current head of state is protected by an absolute and complete immunity both in civil and criminal matters, deriving from the historic immunity accorded to the king or emperor,[73] and expressed by analogy in the Vienna Convention on Diplomatic Relations.

In order to know which immunities an acting head of state enjoys in criminal matters, one must look at the situation of a diplomat sent to his post in a foreign state. Referring to Article 39,[74] the analogy is easy to make and was expressed by Lord Slynn of Hadley in his opinion of 25 November 1998:

> The necessary modification to "the moment he enters the territory of the receiving state. . . " and to "the moment when he leaves the country" is to the time when he "becomes head of state" to the time "when he ceases to be head of state". It therefore covers acts done by him whilst in his own state and in post. Conversely there is nothing to indicate that this immunity is limited to acts done within the state of which the person concerned is head.

The head of state in office, in other words, enjoys immunities as such, *ratione personae*: he has absolute immunity from civil, administrative and criminal jurisdiction, that is to say immunity for public as well as private acts.

The fact that a head of state has absolute immunity was stated by all the Lords: Lord Steyn for example, in his opinion of 25 November 1998 declared that '(i)t is common ground that a head of state in office has an absolute immunity against civil and criminal proceedings in the English Courts'.

The Situation of a Former Head of State

The picture changes for a former head of state, who sees his immunities restricted, as he only enjoys immunity *ratione materiae*: his immunity is restricted to 'acts performed in the exercise of his functions'. The whole question is to interpret what kind of acts are covered by this expression.

Some acts are undoubtedly private acts, some acts are beyond discussion public acts, but in-between, there is a grey zone where acts can be found to be clearly linked to the exercise of power without being performed in furtherance of the head of state's functions. 'Acts performed in the exercise of his functions' can mean that only private acts are excluded from the ongoing immunity and that *all official acts performed while he was in function* are covered by immunity from criminal jurisdiction; but it can also mean that only *acts possibly entering into the functions of a head of state* will continue to enjoy immunity after he has left power.

As stated in the decision of 25 November 1998 by Lord Slynn of Hadley, '(t)he sole question is whether (Pinochet) is entitled to immunity as a former head of

[73] Lord Hope went even as far as to consider this absolute immunity as a *jus cogens* rule.

[74] See p 84 of this chapter.

state from arrest and extradition proceedings in the United Kingdom in respect of acts alleged to have been committed whilst he was head of state.' This issue is even more important when a specific category of illegal acts, crimes under international law, are involved: as stated by Lord Slynn of Hadley, 'the question is what effect, if any, the recognition of acts as international crimes has in itself on. . . immunity'.

Three answers can be given to that question, two of them being extreme positions: the first is that the existence of an international crime has no effect whatsoever on immunities, the author of such a crime committed in his capacity as head of state enjoying impunity before national courts; the second is that all crimes recognised as international crimes are outside the protection of the immunity for a former head of state; the third is that some official acts benefit from immunities and others not. What interpretation did the judges in the UK choose? How to define the functions of a head of state? Is a reference to the way international law defines the functions of a head of state possible? As we know, there was no unanimity on these questions.

At the High Court level,[75] the judges decided that Pinochet did enjoy absolute immunity for the acts performed in the exercise of his functions, whatever their nature. One of the judges, Justice Collins, rejected the argument that crimes under international law could never be part of the sovereign functions of a head of state, in recalling that quite often heads of state have committed such acts: 'Unfortunately, history shows that it has indeed on occasions been state policy to exterminate or to oppress particular groups. One does not have to look very far back in history to see examples of that sort of thing having happened'.

In the first decision of 25 November 1998, by a three to two majority, the Law Lords adopted an historic ruling, revoking the granting of sovereign immunity to Pinochet. And in the second decision of 24 March 1999, by a six to one majority, the Law Lords upheld the same position and decided that Pinochet could not benefit from immunity so as to prevent its extradition to Spain.

Three Law Lords in Favour of Immunity

A narrow textual reading was adopted by Lord Slynn of Hadley, Lord Lloyd of Berwick and Lord Goff of Chieveley who considered that all acts committed as part of the official activities of the head of state were immune from prosecution in national courts.

If one considers the official acts that enjoy immunity, it must be conceded that it is not because an act is illegal that it is *ipso facto* disqualified from being an official act: if this were true, the institution of immunity would make no sense, as it is precisely to protect the head of state from prosecution that it was instituted. As stated by Lord Slynn of Hadley,

[75] 28 Oct 1998, Lord Bingham of Cornhill, *Smith Bernal Official Court Reporters*.

> the fact that. . . a head of state commits an illegal act does not mean that he is no longer to be regarded as carrying out one of his functions. If it did, the immunity in respect of criminal acts would be deprived of much of its content. I do not think it right to draw a distinction for this purpose between acts whose criminality and moral obliquity is more or less great.

Lord Slynn of Hadley however leaves the door open for an evolution of this classical position: he admits in fact the possibility that the immunity enjoyed by a former head of state might be affected in the future, but only on the condition that it is clearly provided for by an international convention incorporated by legislation into the English legal system, which he doesn't think is the case yet with the Torture Convention.

The opinion of Lord Berwick follows a reasoning in several steps that brings him to the conclusion that immunity is maintained even when an international crime is committed. Under customary international law, it is accepted that a former head of state benefits only from immunity for his public acts. Naturally, the distinction between personal or private acts on the one hand and public or official acts done in execution or under the colour of sovereign authority on the other hand is not always easy: for example, in the *Noriega* case, the Fifth Circuit Court of Appeals concluded that Noriega's alleged drug trafficking could not conceivably constitute public acts on behalf of Panama.[76]

It is by a strict application of the dichotomy private acts/public acts that Lord Berwick refused to consider the crimes of which General Pinochet was accused as lifting the immunity:

> He was acting in a sovereign capacity. It has not been suggested that he was personally guilty of any of the crimes of torture or hostage taking in the sense that he carried them out with his own hands. What is alleged against him is that he organised the commission of such crimes, including the elimination of his political opponents, as head of the Chilean government, and that he did so in co-operation with other governments under Plan Condor, and in particular with the government of Argentina. I do not see how in these circumstances he can be treated as having acted in a private capacity.

It is worth noticing however that Lord Berwick could not help recognising that '(o)f course it is strange to think of murder or torture as 'official' acts or as part of the head of state's 'public functions''. Strange indeed.

Finally, Lord Berwick considers that even if there were no valid claims to sovereign immunity, the Court should decline jurisdiction on a question of extradition which involves sensitive questions of foreign relations.

The second time the House of Lords considered the matter, the only judge to be in favour of immunity, Lord Goff of Chieveley, considered to the same result that 'the fact that the head of state performs an act, other than a private act, which is criminal does not deprive it of its governmental character'.[77]

[76] Case cited n 72.

[77] He considered that it was too dangerous to introduce a distinction among official acts, for it could be used in a political manner: he gave the example of a Minister of her Majesty that could be sued for acts of torture in Northern Ireland in another state that supported the IRA.

Nine Law Lords Against Immunity

Most of the Lords could not accept that acts of torture could be qualified as official acts and considered that they must be disqualified *per se*.

For example, in the first decision, Lord Nicholls introduces an interpretation of the functions of a head of state according to international law, stating that 'it hardly needs saying that torture of his own subjects or of aliens, would not be regarded by international law as a function of a head of state'. And he adds: 'International law has made it plain that certain types of conduct, including torture and hostage taking, are not acceptable conduct on the part of anyone. This applies as much to heads of state, and even more so, as it does to anyone else. The contrary would make a mockery of international law.'

In the same vein, Lord Steyn declared:

> ... by the time of the 1973 coup d'état, and certainly ever since, international law condemned genocide, torture, hostage-taking and crimes against humanity... as international crimes deserving of punishment. Given this state of international law, it seems to me difficult to maintain that the commission of such high crimes may amount to acts performed in the exercise of the functions of a head of state.

These acts are necessarily 'conduct falling beyond the scope of his functions as head of state'.

And Lord Steyn added: 'It follows inexorably from the reasoning of the High Court that when Hitler ordered the "final solution" his act must be regarded as an official act deriving from the exercise of his functions as head of state.'

The decision in *Pinochet No 3* of 24 March 1999 is rather disappointing as far as a general statement on the limits to immunities of former heads of state is concerned: only Lord Millett endorsed the idea that immunity is always overridden by the existence of international crimes. All the other Lords relied exclusively on the Torture Convention and interpreted it as meaning that, in this specific case, no immunity should be granted: they considered that immunity would be incompatible with the Convention, as its express provisions refer to the official character of torture as a constituent element of the international crime giving rise to universal jurisdiction.[78]

This of course, restricts considerably the scope of the decision taken. For example, Lord Browne-Wilkinson declared: 'I believe there to be strong ground for saying that the implementation of torture as defined by the Torture Convention cannot be a state function'. Also, in the words of Lord Saville:

> So far as the parties to the Convention are concerned, I cannot see how, so far as torture is concerned, this immunity can exist consistently with the terms of the Convention. Each state party has agreed that the other states parties can exercise jurisdiction over alleged official torturers found within their territories... and thus to my

[78] In other words, an act of torture committed by an armed group fighting against the government would not qualify as torture under the Convention.

> mind can hardly simultaneously claim an immunity from extradition or prosecution that is necessarily based on the official nature of the alleged act.

Although he did not refer expressly to the Convention, Lord Hutton seems to have taken a similar general approach:

> The alleged acts of torture by Senator Pinochet were carried out under colour of his position as head of state, but they cannot be regarded as functions of a head of state under international law when international law expressly prohibits torture as a measure which a state cannot employ in any circumstances whatsoever and has made it an international crime.

But, by the same token, this means that such a conclusion cannot be generalised for all crimes under customary international law.

The Lifting of the Senatorial Immunity in Chile

In Chile, it is well known that Pinochet took a series of measures in order to protect himself and those in power with him from prosecution after they left power. First, an Amnesty Law[79] was passed in 1978 deciding that 'all persons... who in their capacity as perpetrators, accomplices or accessories before or after the fact committed criminal acts during the operative period of the State of Siege, extending from 11 September 1973 until 10 March 1978' benefited from a broad amnesty and could therefore not be prosecuted. Then, as if this self-amnesty was not sufficient, Pinochet included, in 1980, another protection in the new constitution providing for himself and eight others to become 'senator for life' and therefore immune from prosecution because of parliamentary immunity. However, if the Amnesty Law and the parliamentary immunity could protect him in Chile, these texts had no extraterritorial effect and could well be disregarded by the courts of other countries.

It is well known that the court of Santiago first, on 23 May 2000, and the Chilean Supreme Court afterwards, on 8 August 2000, lifted the parliamentary immunity. Parliamentary immunity is not granted in order to ensure impunity for the members of Parliament, but only in order to avoid unfounded prosecutions. Therefore three conditions are to be met for a parliamentary immunity to be lifted according to the Chilean Code: that the judge has jurisdiction, that the crimes are defined by the law and that there is a prima facie responsibility of the accused. Moreover, the suggestion has been made before the Chilean court that the Amnesty Law should be set aside because it violates international law, this point having been discussed earlier.[80]

[79] Decree Law 2191, adopted on 19 April 1978.

[80] For the cases of disappearances, it has been considered that they are continuous offences, and therefore their prosecution is not barred by the Amnesty Law. For this analysis, see UN Declaration on the Protection from Enforced Disappearances, adopted by the UN General Assembly in Resolution 47/133, 18 Dec 1992. See also ch 14.

The Lesson of the *Pinochet* Case

Whatever the restrictions in the reasoning used by the Lords, it seemed that what emerged is that *'international crimes in the highest sense' cannot per se be considered as official acts*, just as commercial acts have been distinguished from sovereign acts according to their finality. Gross human rights violations cannot be qualified as sovereign acts. This is a consequence of the inderogable character of the international rule prohibiting torture and crimes against humanity.

Finally the position adopted by the House of Lords, in spite of its many ambiguities, seemed to indicate 'that the emerging notion of an international public order based on the primacy of certain values and common interests is making its way into the legal culture and common practice of municipal courts'.[81] A huge step has been made towards combating impunity. In the *Pinochet* case, it has been accepted that a former head of state cannot hide behind his immunities, whatever their name, in order to escape his responsibility, if he has committed a crime under international law.

As stated by Christine Chinkin,

> (t)he challenge to the immunity *ratione materiae* claimed by a former head of state for official acts of torture represented a choice between two visions of international law: a horizontal system based upon the sovereign equality of states and a vertical system that upholds norms of *jus cogens* such as those guaranteeing fundamental human rights.[82]

The decisions of the House of Lords undoubtedly mark progress. But some questions remain. If the solution is based on the *jus cogens* nature of the prohibition of a crime that overrides any other rule, it is hard to explain why it should not apply also to heads of state in office, unless their absolute immunity is also considered as a *jus cogens* rule.[83] Of course, the regression of impunity must be welcomed, but maybe not at any price. Personally, I think that the next step, called for by some NGOs, allowing prosecution of acting heads of state in any national court should not be admitted. The example of a Belgrade court condemning, on the 21 September 2000, fourteen Western leaders, among them Bill Clinton, Tony Blair and Jacques Chirac, to 20 years imprisonment for the

[81] Andréa Bianchi, 'Immunity v Human Rights: The Pinochet Case', (1999-2), *EJIL*, 238.

[82] 'International Decisions', (1999), *AJIL* 3 703, at 711; see also for a similar conclusion, Andréa Bianchi, above n 81, at 240: 'The divide between the Law Lords sitting in the First Appellate Committee is evidence of the sense of uncertainty over which values and principles should be accorded priority in contemporary international law. The two opposite poles of the spectrum are evident. On the one hand, stands the principle of sovereignty with its many corollaries including immunity, on the other, the notion that fundamental human rights should be respected and that particular heinous violations, be they committed by states or individuals, should be punished. While the first principle is the most obvious expression and ultimate guarantee of a horizontally-organised community of equal and independent states, the second view represents the emergence of values and interests common to the international community as a whole which deeply cuts across traditional precepts of state sovereignty and non interference in the internal affairs of other states.'

[83] This position was adopted by Lord Hope, see n 73. However it is difficult to admit that the rules on immunities are *jus cogens* rules, as they can be set aside, which a *jus cogens* rule cannot.

actions of NATO in Yugoslavia shows some of the possible counterproductive effects of opening the door too broadly.

However, the risk currently might not be to open the door too broadly, but to close the door, as could well result from the decision of the ICJ in the *DRC v Belgium* case.

THE QUESTION OF IMMUNITY IN THE *DRC v BELGIUM* CASE

In the recent *DRC v Belgium* case,[84] the International Court of Justice has found that not only acting heads of state but also incumbent ministers for foreign affairs benefit under international law from a complete immunity from criminal jurisdiction in foreign courts.[85]

The positions of the two parties were quite opposite. For the Congo, there exists an inviolability and immunity from criminal process that is 'absolute or complete': in its terms 'the immunity accorded to Ministers for Foreign Affairs when in office cover all their acts, including any committed before they took office, and ... it is irrelevant whether the acts done whilst in office may be characterised or not as official acts'.[86] Belgium on the contrary adopted a position closer to the one of NGOs acting against impunity, and stated that 'while Ministers for Foreign Affairs in office generally enjoy an immunity from jurisdiction before the courts of a foreign State, such immunity applies only to acts carried out in the course of their official functions, and cannot protect such persons in respect of private acts or when acting otherwise than in the performance of their official functions'.[87]

The ICJ considered implicitly that the immunities of the minister for foreign affairs in office were the same as the ones benefiting an acting head of state,[88] as it declared 'that the functions of a Minister for Foreign Affairs are such that, throughout the duration of his or her office, he or she when abroad enjoys full immunity from criminal jurisdiction and inviolability'. And to make things

[84] For a full discussion of this case, see ch 12. See also Brigitte Stern, 'Les dits et les non dits de la Cour internationale de Justice dans l'affaire RDC contre Belgique', *International Law FORUM du droit international*, (2002) 102; see also, Antonio Cassese, 'When May Senior State Officials Be Tried for International Crimes? Some Comments on the *Congo v Belgium* Case', *EJIL*, (2002) 853; Marina Spinedi, 'State Responsibility v Individual Responsibility for International Crimes: *Tertium Non Datur*? *ELIL*, (2002) 895. Steffen Wirth, 'Immunity for Core Crimes? The ICJ's Judgment in the *Congo v Belgium* Case', *EJIL* (2002) 877. Sir Robert Jennings, 'Jurisdiction and Immunity in the ICJ Decision in the *Yerodia* Case', *International Law FORUM du droit international*, (2002) 99; Christophe Schreur and Stephan Wittich, 'Immunity and Accountability: the ICJ's Judgment in the *Yerodia* Case', *International Law FORUM du droit international*, (2002) 117.

[85] *Arrest Warrant of 11 April 2000 (DRC v Belgium)*, 14 Feb 2002, General List 121.

[86] Para 47 of the judgment.

[87] Para 49 of the judgment.

[88] It must be noticed that in its original form, the Draft Resolution of the Institute of International Law adopted the same assimilation, but that in its final form the Resolution on 'The Immunities from Jurisdiction and Execution of Heads of States and Heads of Government in International Law' adopted by the Institute on 26 Aug 2001 limited the beneficiary of the Resolution

crystal clear, the Court added : 'In this respect, no distinction can be drawn between acts performed by a Minister for Foreign Affairs in an "official" capacity, and those claimed to have been performed before the person concerned assumed office as Minister for Foreign Affairs and acts committed during the period of office'.[89]

Moreover, on the situation of a former minister for foreign affairs, the ICJ has adopted a 'regressive' position compared to the position adopted in the *Pinochet* case. The decision is naturally also important for heads of state, as it is quite clear that if an international crime does not imply a suppression of the immunities of a former minister for foreign affairs, it will even less have this effect for a former head of state, usually considered as the most protected public person in the state.

Having affirmed the existence of absolute immunity, the ICJ goes on to distinguish the granting of immunities and impunity:

> The Court emphasises, however, that the *immunity* from jurisdiction enjoyed by incumbent Ministers for Foreign Affairs does not mean that they enjoy *impunity* in respect of any crimes they might have committed, irrespective of their gravity... the immunities enjoyed under international law by an incumbent or former Minister for Foreign Affairs do not represent a bar to criminal prosecution in certain circumstances.[90]

The Court endeavours then to list the four 'exceptions' to immunity. Let us first mention the exception that the ICJ mentions last, as this is not strictly speaking an exception to immunity, as formerly explained: according to the ICJ, '(f)ourthly, an incumbent or former Minister for Foreign Affairs may be subject to criminal proceedings before certain international criminal courts'.[91] Then, if one looks at the two first exceptions, they do not appear to be very far reaching. The Court states that '(f)irst, such persons enjoy no criminal immunities under international law in their own countries';[92] this is absolutely true, but as seen earlier, quite often they benefit from extensive immunities in their own countries under national laws. Then the ICJ goes on with the second exception: 'Secondly, they will cease to enjoy immunity from foreign jurisdiction if the State which they represent or have represented decides to waive that immunity'.[93] This is indeed true too, but will probably only happen after a change of power and thus it is likely that this situation will only concern former ministers.

But it is in the statement concerning the third exception that the Court is the more disappointing:

> Thirdly, after a person ceases to hold the office of Minister for Foreign Affairs, he or she will no longer enjoy all the immunities accorded by international law in other

to the central political figure.

[89] Paras 54 and 55 of the judgment.

[90] Paras 60 and 61 of the judgment (the Court's emphasis).

[91] Para 61 of the judgment.

[92] *Ibid.*

> States. Provided that it has jurisdiction under international law, a court of one State may try a former Minister for Foreign Affairs of another State in respect of acts committed prior or subsequent to his or her period of office, as well as in respect of acts committed during that period of office in a private capacity.[94]

Not a word on acts that cannot be considered ever as part of the functions of a head of state, as acts considered as crimes under international law. This is why I share the regrets of the *ad hoc* Judge of Belgium, Mrs Van den Wyngaert, when she states:

> The Court's conclusion is reached without regard to the general tendency toward the restriction of immunity of the State officials (including even Heads of State), not only in the field of private and commercial law where the *in par parem* principle has become more and more restricted and deprived of its mystique, but also in the field of criminal law, when there are allegations of serious international crimes.[95]

CONCLUSION

Naturally a balance has to be found, and in the name of combating impunity, chaos should not be introduced. This does not mean that impunity should be favoured. Heads of state in office must definitely be answerable for their acts, but in order to avoid political bias as far as possible, this should be done before the International Criminal Court.

[93] *Ibid.*
[94] *Ibid.*
[95] Dissenting opinion, para 23.

4

Their *Atrocities and* Our *Misdemeanours: The Reticence of States to Try Their 'Own Nationals' for International Crimes*

TIMOTHY L H McCORMACK*

One of the most compelling arguments for the early establishment of an effective international criminal regime is the frustrating experience of all but exclusive reliance upon domestic enforcement of international criminal law. A number of studies of national war crimes trials have exposed inconsistencies and selectivities riddling the approaches of various nations to prosecute international crimes pursuant to their own domestic law.[1] Gary Jonathan Bass persuasively exposes the limits of 'legalism'—a term he uses to describe the belief that it is right for war criminals to be put on trial. Bass identifies a significant tension between idealism and selfishness in the conduct of war crimes trials. His assessment is that states will rarely put their own soldiers at risk to bring alleged war criminals to justice and will always take war crimes committed against their own population more seriously than those committed against 'innocent foreigners'.[2] States are also often reluctant to try their own soldiers for alleged atrocities committed against a foreign population. Despite the rhetoric of a commitment to the principle of trying war crimes, the practice of states

* The author gratefully acknowledges the excellent research assistance of Chelsea Candy and Jadranka Petrović in the preparation of this chapter. I am also indebted to Helen Durham, Robert Mathews, Jadranka Petrović and Lisa Tickell for their helpful comments on earlier drafts.

[1] See, for example, Rüdiger Wolfrum, 'The Decentralised Prosecution of International Offences Through National Courts', in Yoram Dinstein and Mala Tabory (eds), *War Crimes in International Law* (1996), 233–49; Various contributions to Section II, 'National Prosecutions for International Crimes', in M Cherif Bassiouni (ed), *International Criminal Law: Vol III—Enforcement,* 2nd edn., (1999), 217–390; Gillian Triggs, 'National Prosecutions of War Crimes and the Rule of Law', in Helen Durham and Timothy LH McCormack (eds), *The Changing Face of Conflict and the Efficacy of International Humanitarian Law* (1999), 175–92; Ruth Wedgwood, 'National Courts and the Prosecution of War Crimes', in Gabrielle Kirk McDonald and Olivia Swaak-Goldman (eds), *Substantive and Procedural Aspects of International Criminal Law: The Experience of International and National Courts: Vol I: Commentary* (2000), 389–413.

[2] Gary Jonathan Bass, *Stay the Hand of Vengeance: The Politics of War Crimes Tribunals* (2000), 8.

confirms glaring inconsistencies between those acts which are tried and those which are not—inconsistencies most readily explicable on the basis of an 'us' and 'them' mentality.

Existing studies of national approaches to the prosecution of international crimes tend to focus on the utilisation of universal jurisdiction to try non-nationals for alleged atrocities committed outside the territory of the prosecuting state. It is for others in this volume to assess the utilisation of universal jurisdiction as a basis for domestic trials of international crimes.[3] The intention in this chapter is to provide an overview of various domestic trials of 'own nationals'. The intention is not to attempt a broad survey of military courts martial and related disciplinary proceedings but to focus on judicial responses to serious violations of international criminal law. The chapter attempts to provide some analysis of the reasons why the selected trials have been undertaken and argues that there is a discernible shift towards increased domestic trials of own nationals as a direct result of, or perhaps more accurately, as an integral aspect of, the recent and remarkable developments in the enforcement of international criminal law.

CIRCUMSTANCES CONDUCIVE TO DOMESTIC TRIALS OF OWN NATIONALS

One could be forgiven for assuming that, with atrocities committed around the world at an alarmingly frequent rate, the amount of domestic jurisprudence would be too voluminous to contemplate. The contrary is the unfortunate reality and the disparity between perpetration and prosecution is staggering. However, it is not the case that there is an absence of material. If anything, I have been surprised to unearth much more material than I knew existed. The jurisprudential experience, dating back at least as far as post-World War I, is certainly substantial enough to support the identification of three distinct sets of circumstances which may result in what Gerry Simpson so neatly describes as the 'unusually propitious constellation of political factors' required for war crimes trials to occur.[4]

The most obvious situation, and certainly the reason behind the overwhelming majority of domestic trials of own nationals, is transition within states to a new political regime. Trials against officials or participants in a former regime can be undertaken to distance the nation from the sins of the past, and/or to legitimate the new political regime, and/or to educate the contemporary generation. Irrespective of the precise motivation for instituting trials, literally thousands of individuals have been tried pursuant to their own domestic penal

[3] See ch 2.

[4] See Gerry Simpson, 'War Crimes: A Critical Introduction', in Timothy LH McCormack and Gerry J Simpson (eds), *The Law of War Crimes: National and International Approaches* (1997), 28.

legislation for their participation in international crimes most commonly perpetrated in their own national territory. This is certainly the case for Germany and Austria especially, and for other states generally, post-World War II. It is also the case for more contemporary atrocities in post-military ruled societies—in Greece after the 'Rule of the Colonels'; in Argentina following the end of the '*Guerra Sucia*' or 'Dirty War'; and in Ethiopia following the demise of the Mengistu Regime.

Domestic trials such as these will no doubt continue to occur around the world irrespective of current and foreseeable multilateral developments in the enforcement of international criminal law. I am not suggesting that it is axiomatic that trials follow political transition from dictatorship to democracy. General amnesties are often instituted to increase the likelihood of smoother transition. However, such trials do tend to occur in the aftermath of a catalytic transition and only if the new political regime has had no close ties with the activities of the ousted regime. The many examples of domestic trials of own nationals in transitional states hardly constitutes an argument against the need for an effective international criminal court—too many former and current political leaders continue to enjoy impunity for their crimes.

In both the other sets of circumstances conducive to domestic trials of own nationals, there is a closer correlation between multilateral developments and increased prospects for domestic trials than is the case for states in political transition. The second distinct set of circumstances relates to concurrent domestic and international jurisdiction—or at least the threat of it. In the aftermath of World War I, the German Government could not accept the domestic political ramifications of international tribunals prosecuting German nationals for alleged atrocities in the conduct of the war. The threat of an international tribunal was sufficient motivation for the German Government to conduct its own trials at Leipzig avoiding the ignominy of perceived diminution of national sovereignty. In Istanbul the Turks also tried their own nationals and hoped for Allied leniency in the terms of the Peace Treaty as their *quid pro quo*.

Much more recently, the Rwandan Government faces an unprecedented challenge with 120,000 suspected *genocidaires* languishing in abject prison conditions awaiting trial while the International Criminal Tribunal for Rwanda (ICTR) in Arusha holds only 51 indictees in detention pending trial.[5] The Rwandan Government, unlike Germany in 1922, is not fighting to retain jurisdictional sovereignty. In relations with Kigali, the multilateral community seems to have missed opportunities to establish significant precedents in national capacity building and mutually beneficial co-operation. The situation in the Balkans stands in stark contrast. There the existence of the International Criminal Tribunal for the Former Yugoslavia (ICTY) has not only resulted in the detention of Slobodan Milošević in The Hague but has also influenced an increase in domestic trials within various Balkan states. These trials

[5] See website of the ICTR for list of indictees currently held in detention in Arusha: www.ictr.org/english/factsheets/detainee.htm

commenced as vengeful initiatives against 'other' ethnic minorities but slowly the tide has turned so that now trials have also been instituted against those from the dominant ethnic majority. These recent developments surely support the arguments for an effective international criminal law regime—not to displace national court processes but to supplement them and, in some cases, to galvanise them into action.

The third set of circumstances conducive to domestic trials of own nationals relates to unacceptable violations of the laws of war committed by a state's own armed forces on deployment outside the territory of the state. As already mentioned, there appears to be a very high threshold of tolerance for lack of discipline by 'our own troops'. The number of trials for serious violations of international criminal law in such circumstances is tragically inadequate. The proceedings against Lieutenant Calley for the atrocities committed at My Lai during the Vietnam conflict are the best known of all such cases and those particular proceedings expose serious challenges to the more effective enforcement of international criminal law. Some examples of more recent disciplinary actions for the perpetration of international crimes by a state's own armed forces provide greater reasons for optimism. Here again it seems that multilateral developments in the enforcement of international criminal law have raised expectations globally that atrocities will not go unpunished. Consequently, there appears to be greater pressure on governments to take significant breaches of discipline by their own forces much more seriously than might have been the case in the past.

DOMESTIC TRIALS BY STATES IN POLITICAL TRANSITION

Post-World War II

The domestic trials of individuals for World War II atrocities which have received the most public attention have tended to be those of foreign nationals—the US trial of General Yamashita, the Israeli trials of Adolf Eichmann and of John Demjanjuk, the French trial of Klaus Barbie, the Italian trial of Erich Priebke, the Canadian trial of Imre Finta, the Australian trial of Ivan Polyukhovich. The intention here is to go beyond the high public profile cases and to briefly consider some of the experiences of those states which have tried some of their own nationals.

Germany

Those who assume a scarcity of jurisprudence involving the trial of a state's own nationals pursuant to domestic criminal law would benefit from scrutiny of the German national experience. More than 91,000 German defendants have been tried for their alleged participation in international crimes during World

War II in the Federal Republic of Germany alone[6]—a huge number of trials which does not include those German nationals tried by courts in the Democratic Republic of Germany prior to German reunification.[7] This willingness to take responsibility for the prosecution of German defendants pursuant to German domestic criminal law stands in stark contrast to the attitude of the German Government following World War I.[8] It has been suggested that Germany struggled with its own national responsibility for the prosecution of Nazi criminality for the first decade after the end of World War II. John Herz, for example, argues that the combination of Allied war crimes trials (at Nuremberg and through the subsidiary trial processes) and the imposition of sanctions (usually fines and temporary detentions) pursuant to various denazification procedures were considered by many to have absolved the nation from further collective responsibility.[9] The failure to investigate and prosecute proactively in the period in which many crimes would most readily have been exposed inevitably resulted in impunity for an unspecified number of German nationals.[10]

However, from the late 1950s, a national attitudinal shift resulted in an ongoing commitment to try German nationals. Trials have continued right up to the end of the twentieth century and, although authorities in Bonn were occasionally frustrated by protracted extradition proceedings and increasingly complex trial processes so long after the alleged events,[11] the commitment to prosecute German nationals has not abated. Now, of course, nearly 60 years since World War II, the prospect of Nazi-era trials is greatly diminished. Not only are alleged perpetrators harder to find alive and in sound mental and physical health but the complexities of adducing evidence to satisfy a criminal standard of proof is increasingly difficult.

Austria

Unlike Germany, post-World War II Austria responded expeditiously to the wartime involvement of Austrian nationals with Nazism. This contrast is hardly surprising because Austria was dealing with crimes of collaboration with a

[6] See Axel Marschik, 'The Politics of Prosecution: National Approaches to War Crimes', in McCormack and Simpson, *The Law of War Crimes,* 74–77. The most authoritative study of many of the trials is Adelheid L Rüter-Ehlermann, C F Rüter, and ors. (eds), *Justiz und NS-Verbrechen: Sammlung Deutscher Strafurteile wegen Nationalsozialististicher Tötungsverbrechen 1945–1966* (1966–1981).

[7] Irina Lediakh, for example, claims that the German Democratic Republic tried a total of 12,828 East German nationals for their participation in Nazi war crimes and crimes against humanity. See I A Lediakh, 'The Application of the Nuremberg Principles by Other Military Tribunals and National Courts', in Georg Ginsburgs and V N Kudriavtsev (eds), *The Nuremberg Trial and International Law* (1990), 282.

[8] See discussion of the Leipzig Trials below.

[9] John H Herz, 'Denazification and Related Policies', in John H Herz (ed), *From Dictatorship to Democracy: Coping With the Legacies of Authoritarianism and Totalitarianism* (1982) 19–20.

[10] *Ibid*; See also I A Lediakh, above n 7 at 279.

[11] Marschik, above n 6, at 75–76.

foreign, occupying power. In Germany's case, the society was confronted with its own national guilt. The Austrian denazification programme extended to a range of sanctions for differing levels of allegiance to the party including trials for alleged participation in war crimes and crimes against humanity. By 1955 more than 13,000 Austrians had been convicted of involvement in such crimes and 41 of those convicted defendants had been subjected to the death penalty.[12] The mid-1950s marked a significant shift in prevailing sentiment towards the prosecution of Austrian nationals. Other Western governments had already become more preoccupied with the Cold War and anti-communism than with anti-facism and, in Vienna, the Government was keen to communicate a positive, futuristic vision rather than a preoccupation with the failures of the past.[13] By 1957 Vienna had passed a general amnesty decriminalising membership of the Nazi party and, although it was still possible for war crimes and crimes against humanity to be prosecuted on the basis of the domestic criminal law operating in Austria at the time of the alleged acts, the momentum for trials had clearly diminished.[14] In some specific cases, trials were rendered impossible by the mid-1950s because senior Austrian Nazis had either committed suicide or fled their homeland.[15]

France

In the aftermath of World War II French society engaged in a comprehensive and often vengeful response to the national suffering endured during Nazi occupation of France. In extra-judicial acts, thousands were assassinated and tens of thousands interned for their allegiance throughout the war to pro-Vichy or pro-German organizations.[16] Special Tribunals were also established with a legislative mandate to try both foreigners and French nationals. In a discriminatory and revealing approach to social purging, foreign nationals were tried for their participation in war crimes while French nationals were charged with the 'major' crimes of treason and/or collaboration or with the less serious charge of *indignité nationale*.[17]

These trials terminated in the early 1970s once the statutory limitation period had been reached. However, the French Parliament had adopted a law in 1964 declaring the imprescriptibility of crimes against humanity and thus ensuring the non-applicability of a statutory limitation period to the prosecution of this

[12] Marschik, above n 6, at 78.

[13] *Ibid*, particularly at footnote 66.

[14] Frederick C Engelmann, 'How Austria Has Coped With Two Dictatorial Legacies', in Herz, *From Dictatorship to Democracy,* 144; Marschik, above n 6, at 78.

[15] Engelmann, *ibid*, at 44.

[16] See Roy C Macridis, 'France: From Vichy to the Fourth Republic', in Herz, *From Dictatorship to Democracy,* 171; Leila Sadat Wexler, 'The Interpretation of the Nuremberg Principles by the French Court of Cassation: From Touvier to Barbie and Back Again', (1994) 32 *Columbia Journal of Transnational Law*, 316–22.

[17] Macridis, *ibid.*, 171–172. See also Eugène Aroneanu, *Le Crime Contre L'Humanité* (1961), 225.

category of crimes as defined in the Nuremberg Charter.[18] This new legislation was invoked in relation to three French nationals charged with participation in crimes against humanity in the 1990s. Christian Bousquet, the former Secretary-General of the Vichy Police, had been arrested in 1945 for his collaboration with the Germans but was then released from detention in 1947 and not subsequently tried.[19] He was charged with crimes against humanity in 1990 but was killed in 1993 before the commencement of his trial.[20]

Paul Touvier, the former head of information services in the Lyon *Milice*[21] and, as such, a close collaborator with Klaus Barbie, was the first French national to be tried for crimes against humanity pursuant to the 1964 law. Touvier had been tried and sentenced to death twice *in absentia* for 'treason and intelligence with the enemy'[22]— in 1945 and in 1947[23]—but had managed to evade justice in person by hiding until after the passage of the statutory limitation period had elapsed. President Pompidou officially pardoned Touvier in 1971 but then fresh charges were laid against him. After a protracted judicial process to clarify the state of French law in relation to the prosecution of crimes against humanity, the *Cour de Cassation* confirmed the imprescriptibility of crimes against humanity which could be tried before the ordinary criminal courts of France.[24] Touvier was finally convicted of complicity in crimes against humanity in 1994.

In 1998 Maurice Papon became the second French national to be convicted of complicity in crimes against humanity. Papon had served as a high ranking civil servant in the Vichy Government and was charged in relation to his involvement in the deportation of almost 1,600 Jews from the Bordeaux Region.[25] Papon's trial process was also protracted although the courts benefited from the clarifications in the law declared in the context of the trial of Paul Touvier some years earlier. The *Cour de Cassation* sentenced Papon to 10 years' imprisonment. He unsuccessfully appealed his conviction in 1999 and was then captured in Switzerland and returned to France to serve out his sentence.[26]

[18] See Leila Sadat Wexler, 'The French Experience', in M Cherif Bassiouni (ed), *International Criminal Law: Vol III—Enforcement* 2nd edn, (1999), 275. For a French critique of the 1964 law see Jacques-Bernard Herzog, 'Étude des lois concernant la prescription des crimes contre l'humanité' *Revue de Science Criminelle de Droit Pénal Comparé* (1965), 337.

[19] Axel Marschik, above n 6, at 83.

[20] *Ibid.*

[21] Wexler describes the *Milice* as the special military force for combating the Resistance and other enemies of the Vichy Government. See Leila Sadat Wexler, above n 18, at 276.

[22] Wexler, above n 16, at 323.

[23] Marschik, above n 6, at 84.

[24] The intricacies of the proceedings against Paul Touvier are explained in detail in Wexler, above n 16, at 322–31.

[25] Wexler, above n 18, at 288.

[26] For a detailed collection of essays on various aspects of the criminal proceedings against Papon, see Richard J Golsan (ed), *The Papon Affair: Memory and Justice on Trial* (2000).

Other States Post World War II

Several other states have also tried their own nationals for alleged war crimes and crimes against humanity committed during World War II. Hungary, like Austria was allied to Germany during World War II and, following the War, also had to face the unsavoury reality of collaboration with the Nazis. In Budapest several high-ranking political figures including the former Premier Bela Imredy, the former Prime Minister Ferenc Szalasi and Szalasi's Cabinet members were all tried, convicted and subsequently sentenced to death for their participation in Nazi crimes directed against the Jewish population of Hungary.[27] Other East European states have also tried their own nationals. Croatia, for example, established by the Axis Powers in 1941, has more recently confronted its fascist past in the trials of two senior figures in former regimes. In 1986 the Republic of Yugoslavia successfully extradited Andreja Artuković, formerly the Croatian Minister of the Interior during the early 1940s, from the US. Artuković was tried in Zagreb for the murder of more than 230,000 persons, found guilty and sentenced to death.[28] Croatia has continued to pursue its World War II war criminals even after independence. In 1998, for example, Argentina extradited Dinko Šakić to Zagreb. Šakić was tried for crimes committed during his command of the Jasenovac Concentration Camp where up to 85,000 inmates allegedly lost their lives. Šakić was convicted and sentenced to 20 years' imprisonment.[29]

Other European states occupied by Germany during World War II have tried some of their own nationals for their participation in Nazi crimes during the War. While Estonia was under Soviet occupation in 1986, for example, Moscow successfully extradited Karl Linnas from the US. Linnas was to have faced trial in relation to charges of his involvement in the death of more than 2,000 persons in the Tartu Concentration Camp in Estonia. Linnas died in a military hospital in Moscow before the commencement of his trial.[30] Following the break-up of the former Soviet Union and the resumption of independence for the Baltic states, Latvia has initiated attempts to try former Latvians for war crimes allegedly committed on its territory during World War II. In December 2000, for example, Latvia formally requested the extradition of Konrads Kalejs from Australia to be tried for his alleged involvement in the Salspils Camp in Latvia in the 1940s.[31] The Netherlands tried several German nationals for crimes committed in Dutch territory during the War but also tried Pieter Menten, a Dutch national. Menten was convicted for his participation in a number of atrocities committed in Poland where he became involved in pro-Nazi activities while pur-

[27] See Howard S Levie, *Terrorism in War—The Law of War Crimes*, a volume in *Terrorism: Documents of International and Local Control,* 3, Ser 2 (1993), 135.

[28] Axel Marschik, above n 6, at 92.

[29] Jann K Kleffner, 'Correspondents' Reports: Croatia', *Yearbook of International Humanitarian Law* 2 (1999), 353–54.

[30] Axel Marschik, above n 6, at 91.

[31] Timothy L H McCormack, 'Correspondents' Reports: Australia' *Yearbook of International Humanitarian Law* 3 (2000), 414–15.

suing business interests.[32] Menten was originally sentenced to 15 years imprisonment—a term subsequently reduced to10 years.[33]

Another less well known but intriguing experience of domestic prosecution of 'own nationals' involved the Israeli trials of the *Judenrat* (or Jewish councils appointed by the Nazis to organise the relocation of Jewish communities and to collect Jewish valuables and property for the Nazis) and the *Kapos* (Jewish policemen in the concentration camps). The trials of such individuals has been a painful and divisive experience in Israeli society.[34] Although none of the defendants were Israeli nationals at the time of the alleged offences (given that the State of Israel was not established until 1948) the fact that Israel has been prepared to try Jewish people as well as former Nazis for war crimes is certainly significant.

One glaring omission from those states which have tried their own nationals for World War II related crimes is Japan. Despite the high public profile trials of Japanese defendants by the Tokyo Tribunal and the thousands of Japanese defendants tried and sentenced pursuant to the subsidiary trial process, the Japanese people have never demanded national trials of Japanese defendants. On the contrary, following the end of the War, Tokyo relentlessly sought custody of those convicted Japanese war criminals serving out their sentences in various locations throughout the Pacific and, having successfully gained custody of many of them, released them from further incarceration and fully restored their rights.[35] To this day, the issue of Japan's national reticence to accept the reality of atrocities committed by Japanese forces in World War II is controversial.

Greece's 'Rule of the Colonels'

In July 1974 the newly appointed government of Constantine Karamanlis took office and signalled the end of a seven year military dictatorship in Athens. Throughout the period of military rule—often referred to as the 'Rule of the Colonels'—allegations were rife of widespread and systematic practices of torture and mistreatment against opponents of the military regime.[36] Following the transition to civilian rule, the new government was under intense political pressure to deal with crimes committed by the military regime. Karamanlis implemented several initiatives to deal with some of the excesses of the previous regime.[37] Several of the most senior military leaders were tried for insurrection against the democratically elected government and for their own involvement in

[32] Summary of decision: *Prosecutor v P N M,* District Court of Amsterdam, Extraordinary Penal Chamber (Bijzondere Strafkamer), 14 Dec 1977, NJ (1978) No. 26, in *Netherlands Yearbook of International Law* (1978), 337–48.

[33] Axel Marschik, above n 6, at 89.

[34] For an excellent account of some of the key issues raised in several of these trials see Jonathan Wenig, 'Enforcing the Lessons of History: Israel Judges the Holocaust', in McCormack and Simpson, *The Law of War Crimes*, at 118–21.

[35] Arthur E Tiedemann, 'Japan Sheds Dictatorship', in Herz, above n 9, at 199.

[36] See Taki Theodoracopulos, *The Greek Upheaval: Kings, Demagogues and Bayonets* (1978).

[37] *Ibid*, 246–54. See also Harry J Psomiades, 'Greece: From the Colonels' Rule to Democracy', in Herz, above n 9, at 262–65.

the original *coup d'etat* which delivered political power to the military. This particular trial was inevitably politicised and produced carefully scripted sentences—including death penalties all commuted to life sentences for each of the three major military leaders. Other, less politically motivated, trials were also conducted against various military figures—not for their involvement in the implementation of the coup but for their participation in torture and other inhumane practices perpetrated throughout the period of military rule.

Trials were held in Athens, Salonica, Halkis, Patras and Crete. It is estimated that more than 120 individuals have been tried although it has been difficult to determine precise figures because some defendants have been tried on two or three separate occasions in respect of different alleged offences and because no central records appear to have been kept in respect of the trials.[38] The trials established a systemic pattern of torture, beatings, threats, deprivations and humiliations imposed on detainees considered to be opponents of the military regime. Taki Theodoracopulos argues that the evidence adduced at the trials disproved the development of a policy of torture at the highest political levels of the military leadership and that, instead, the practices became routine at lower levels of the military hierarchy.[39] Many defendants were convicted and sentenced to terms of imprisonment ranging from 28 years to 18 months.[40]

Argentina's 'Dirty War'

Argentina's ill-fated decision to invade the Falkland/Malvinas Islands resulted in a serious loss of credibility for the ruling military *junta*. In 1983, the democratically elected Government of President Raúl Alfonsín took office and restored civilian rule to Argentina. In circumstances redolent of Greece's 'Rule of the Colonels', Argentina's period of military rule had been characterised by systematic human rights violations including forced disappearances, arbitrary detention, imprisonment and torture. [41] The reign of the military *junta* is commonly referred to as Argentina's '*guerra sucia'*, or the 'dirty war', waged relentlessly and ruthlessly against left-wing civilians opposed to military rule.[42]

President Alfonsín had the unenviable task of balancing the public demand for retribution with respecting the latent political power of the military. Although the *junta* was a discredited political entity, the military were still very much in control of the means of military force and could not be pushed beyond their limits of tolerance. Alfonsín's first announcements were of the trial of the

[38] Taki Theodoracopulos, above n 36 at 251; Harry Psomiades cites the Amnesty International Report: *Torture in Greece: The First Torturers' Trial 1975* (1977), 75 which claims that between 100 and 400 torture trials were conducted in Greece. See Psomiades, preceding note, at 265.

[39] Theodoracopulos, at 251.

[40] *Ibid*.

[41] See Steven R Ratner, and Jason S Abrams, *Accountability for Human Rights Atrocities in International Law: Beyond the Nuremberg Legacy,* 2nd edn. (2001), 169–171.

[42] For a brief account of the conduct of the 'dirty war' see Alejandro M. Garro and Henry Dahl, 'Legal Accountability for Human Rights Violations in Argentina: One Step Forward and Two Steps Backward', (1987) 8 *Human Rights Law Journal*, 287–300.

nine principal military leaders by military tribunal and the establishment of the National Commission on the Disappearance of Persons to investigate the fate of the so-called '*desaparecidos*'. Both initiatives were criticised by human rights activists and by the military as being either too lenient or too intrusive—unnecessarily accommodating or politically motivated.[43]

The National Commission released its report in 1984 and forwarded over 1,000 cases to civilian judicial authorities for investigation.[44] Although President Alfonsín's legislation paving the way for trials provided for original jurisdiction in military courts, the legislation also allowed for appeal to the civilian federal courts and reserved a contingent jurisdiction to civilian courts in the event of procrastination in the military court process.[45] The military court process did not proceed and so trials were conducted by a civilian appellate court acting on the basis of its contingent jurisdictional competence. Despite legal challenges to the civilian court processes, the Supreme Court upheld the assumption of jurisdictional competence and trials proceeded.[46] However, after the trial against the military leaders had concluded, sweeping amnesties were granted by Alfonsín's successor, President Menem, before many of the trials against middle-ranking military officers had commenced. Consequently, many of those responsible for implementing the policies of the 'dirty war' were not brought to justice in Argentina.

Many people still criticise the whole Argentine national experience of attempting to respond to the human rights abuses of the 'dirty war' since so many offenders still enjoy impunity for their acts. Ratner and Abrams are more positive and point to the uniqueness of Argentina's approach in the Latin American region.[47] The fact that some trials happened at all and that, in the process of those trials, victims of the atrocities gave evidence and policies and practices were exposed in a transparent judicial process were significant for the nation of Argentina itself as well as for the Latin American region as a whole.

Ethiopia's Mengistu Regime

In 1991 the Ethiopian Peoples' Revolutionary Democratic Front (EPRDF) captured Addis Ababa and ended the 17 year military reign of the *Dergue* regime led by Mengistu Haile Mariam.[48] The EPRDF installed a transitional government and appointed Meles Zanawi Acting President. After taking control of the

[43] *Ibid*, 301–13. See also Emilio Fermin Mignone, Cynthia L Estlund and Samuel Issacharoff, 'Dictatorship on Trial: Prosecution of Human Rights Violations in Argentina', (1984)10*Yale Journal of International Law* 10 (1984), 124–30.

[44] Steven Ratner and Jason Abrams, above n 41 at 169.

[45] *Ibid*.

[46] See Alejandro M Garro, 'Nine Years of Transition to Democracy in Argentina: Partial Failure or Qualified Success?', 13 *Columbia Journal of Transnational Law* 31, 13–16.

[47] Steven Ratner and Jason Abrams, above n 41 at 171.

[48] See Yacob Haile-Mariam, 'The Quest for Justice and Reconciliation: The International Criminal Tribunal for Rwanda and the Ethiopian High Court', (1999) 22 *Hastings International and Comparative Law Review*, 675–79.

capital, the EPRDF arrested and detained approximately 2,000 people alleged to have participated in gross human rights violations perpetrated throughout the years of the Mengistu regime. By 1997 more than 5,000 individuals had been charged with offences although less than half of those were actually held in custody.[49]

When the *Dergue* first seized power in Ethiopia in 1974, they deposed and gaoled the then Emperor Haile Sellassie, suspended the constitution and dissolved the Parliament. In the following year the *Dergue* leaders summarily executed 60 former government officials including two prime ministers, senior military officers and leading civilians and then purported to justify the executions as a 'political measure' against the enemies of the regime.[50] Although deplorable, these executions were only a precursor to the unleashing of a systematic campaign of terror and unrestrained violence against the 'opponents of the regime'.[51] By 1977, for example, estimates suggest that as many as 30–50,000 individuals were summarily executed[52]—often for no more than a suspicion of sympathy for anti-*Dergue* sentiment. In addition to summary executions, the period of Mengistu's rule was characterised by torture, forced disappearances and widespread imprisonment.[53]

Although more than ten years have passed since more than 2,000 alleged offenders were first incarcerated, the overwhelming majority of them are still waiting for trial proceedings to commence. The principal trial to date has involved 71 defendants, 25 of whom, including Mengistu Haile Mariam himself, have been tried *in absentia*. That particular trial first commenced in December 1994 and, despite death sentences handed down in November and December 1999 against two defendants *in absentia*, the trial has still not concluded.[54] During 2000 some other lesser trials commenced and, in some cases, concluded. However, the vast majority of the detainees still have little prospect of their trials commencing in the short term.[55]

One consequence of the debilitating rule of the *Dergue* and the subsequent national preoccupation with the border war with Eritrea has been a malfunctioning legal system and few resources to rectify it. Various human rights groups have expressed concern about the need for Ethiopia to balance the demands for justice following the rule of the Mengistu regime with the human rights of those detained for a decade without trial.[56] Some international assistance has been provided to Ethiopia to assist the Office of the Special Prosecutor in the conduct

[49] *Ibid*, 679.

[50] *Ibid*, 676–77.

[51] One of the most comprehensive accounts of the atrocities perpetrated throughout the years of *Dergue* rule is Alexander de Waal, *Evil Days: Thirty Years of War and Famine in Ethiopia* (1991).

[52] Yacob Haile-Mariam, above n 48 at 678.

[53] See Steven Ratner and Jason Abrams, above n 41 at 173–74.

[54] *Ibid*.

[55] See Amnesty International, *Annual Report 2000: Ethiopia,* available at: http://www.web.amnesty.org/web/ar2001.nsf/webafrcountries/ETHIOPIA

[56] *Ibid*. See also. Julie V Mayfield, 'The Prosecution of War Crimes and Respect for Human Rights: Ethiopia's Balancing Act', (1995), 9 *Emory International Law Review*, 553.

of trials[57] but serious problems remain. In this particular situation, the evident political will to undertake trials of some of those responsible for atrocities perpetrated against fellow Ethiopians has not translated into the means to make the trials a reality.

Other States in Political Transition

The circumstances leading to domestic trials in the states already referred to have been affirmed in the experiences of two Latin American states in transition from military to civilian rule: Guatemala and Haiti. In December 1996, the signing of Peace Accords signalled the end of more than 30 years of military rule in Guatemala. Part of the political compromise to reach agreement on the Accords involved the passage of legislation known as the 'National Reconciliation Law' extending a general amnesty for those committing crimes during the period of military rule but with explicit exclusions from the amnesty for those responsible for torture, forced disappearances or genocide.[58]

The UN-sponsored *Comisión de Esclarecimiento Histórico* (CEH—or Historical Clarification Commission) was mandated to investigate and report upon the acts of violence and human rights violations that occurred during the civil war. The CEH was expressly directed not to exercise a trial function and not to attribute individual criminal responsibility but it was authorised to pass general judgements based on international human rights law.[59] The Final Report of the CEH, entitled *Memory of Silence*, detailed gross and systematic human rights abuses perpetrated by the Guatemalan Security Forces throughout the period of their rule. In particular, the CEH found that genocide had been perpetrated against indigenous Guatemalan communities. The identification of non-amnestied offences has cleared the way for prosecution of crimes and some trials have already taken place.[60] Amnesty International has criticised the small number of trials to date and the concomitant lack of justice for the thousands of victims of the atrocities and for their families.[61] The organisation has reported on, and expressed its support for, the prosecution of civil actions by individual

[57] For one example of assistance see Todd Howland, 'Learning to Make Proactive Human Rights Interventions Effective: The Carter Centre and Ethiopia's Office of the Special Prosecutor', (2000), 18 *Wisconsin International Law Journal*, 407.

[58] See Jan Perlin, 'The Guatemalan Historical Clarification Commission Finds Genocide', (2000), 6 *International Law Students Association Journal of International and Comparative Law*, 390.

[59] For a discussion of the limitations of the CEH mandate see Andrew N Keller, 'To Name or Not to Name?: The Commission for Historical Clarification in Guatemala, Its Mandate, and the Decision not to Identify Individual Perpetrators', (2001) 13 *Florida Journal of International Law*, 289.

[60] See David Stoelting, 'Enforcement of International Criminal Law', (2000) 34 *The International Lawyer*, 670.

[61] See Amnesty International, *Guatemala—Breaking the Wall of Impunity: Prosecution for Crimes Against Humanity,* (AI, London: 2000). Text of report available at: http://www.amnesty.org/ai.nsf/print/AMR34202000

and collective survivors against former officials of the military regime allegedly responsible for the atrocities perpetrated against them[62]

In 1994 the UN Security Council authorised military force to overthrow the ruling *junta* in Haiti and to reinstate the democratically elected Government of Jean-Bertrand Aristide.[63] The intervention ended almost four years of rule by the military regime of Raoul Cedras—a period which had been characterised by state-sanctioned massacres, disappearances, assassinations, systematic rape, torture, arbitrary arrests and detentions in brutal conditions.[64] Upon his reinstatement, Aristide established the *Commision nationale de verite et justice (CNVJ)* to investigate the human rights violations perpetrated during military rule. The report of the Commission was tabled in 1996 and entitled *Si M Pa Rele* ('If I Don't Cry Out'). To date there has only been one major trial for crimes committed by the military rulers. In November 2000, 16 co-accused former soldiers were convicted for their part in an attack on civilians in the Aristide-friendly shanty town of Raboteau on the outskirts of Gonaives. Twelve of the convicted were sentenced to life imprisonment and the other four to between four and nine years imprisonment. A further six defendants in the trial were acquitted. Thirty-seven others, including Raoul Cedras and other senior leaders of the military regime involved in masterminding the Raboteau massacre but all living outside of Haiti, were tried *in absentia* and sentenced to life imprisonment.[65]

Whereas in Guatemala the main obstacle to further trials in respect of human rights abuses throughout more than 30 years of military rule appears to be the lingering political influence of the military, in Haiti the major obstacle is a dysfunctional judicial and legal system. As training and capacity building measures are implemented in Haiti, it is likely that additional trials will occur. These fundamentally different reasons for relatively few domestic trials in both Guatemala and in Haiti are indicative of prospects for domestic trials in transitional states generally. That is, the extent of trials conducted against members of a former regime will always be commensurate with the extent of that former regime's ongoing political relevance and influence.

[62] *Ibid*, 2.

[63] See UN Security Council Resolution 940, 49 UN SCOR (3413th mtg.), UN Doc. S/RES/940 (1994).

[64] Michael P Scharf, 'Swapping Amnesty for Peace: Was There a Duty to Prosecute International Crimes in Haiti?', (1996), 31 *Texas International Law Journal*, 1, citing various reports from human rights NGOs on the atrocities committed by the military regime in Haiti.

[65] See Amnesty International, *Haiti: Steps Forward, Steps Back: Human Rights 10 Years After the Coup* (2001). Text of Report available at: http://www.amnesty.org/ai.nsf/print/AMR36102001

[66] See 'Report on the Responsibility of the Authors of the War and on Enforcement of Penalties to the Preliminary Peace Conference, March 1919', reproduced in (1920), 14 *American Journal of International Law*, 95. For accounts of the background to the proposal for international criminal trials see James F. Willis, *Prologue to Nuremberg: The Politics and Diplomacy of Punishing War Criminals of the First World War* (1982); James W. Garner, 'Punishment of Offenders Against the Laws and Customs of War', *American Journal of International Law,* 14 (1920), 70; David Matas, 'Prosecuting Crimes Against Humanity: The Lessons of World War I', (1989–90), 13 *Fordham International Law Journal,* 86.

DOMESTIC TRIALS INFLUENCED BY INTERNATIONAL CRIMINAL TRIBUNALS

Post-World War II

Prior to the cessation of hostilities in World War I, the Allied Commission on the Responsibility of the Authors of the War and on Enforcement of Penalties recommended the establishment of an ad hoc tribunal to try defendants from among the soon to be defeated Northern Powers.[66] The tribunal was to be constituted by judges from among the Allied governments and was to derive its jurisdictional competence from the inclusion of provisions in the envisaged peace treaties after the War.[67] With this procedure in mind, the Commission drafted pro forma provisions on the competence of a tribunal which were subsequently inserted into the texts of each of the peace treaties.[68] Despite this detailed work by the Commission and the widespread political support for international trials throughout the conduct of the War, the proposed tribunal was never established and the envisaged international trials failed to materialise. Instead, the Allied governments agreed to allow both Germany and the Turks to try some of their own nationals. Although many people within Allied societies were contemptuous of the decision not to proceed with international trials, it is intriguing that the threat of the establishment of an international tribunal acted as a catalyst for the domestic trials of at least some German and Turkish nationals.[69]

The Leipzig Trials

In order to implement Article 228 of the Treaty of Versailles, the Allies compiled lists of 896 alleged German war criminals, handed those names to the German Government and then demanded custody of the individuals for subsequent Allied trial.[70] Nationalistic opposition to the diminution of German sovereignty inherent in any surrender of German nationals to an Allied Tribunal was extensive and, ultimately, effective. The political opponents of the Weimar Republic manipulated the issue in an attempt to focus responsibility for agreeing to the

[67] Willis, *Prologue to Nuremberg*, 122–23.

[68] See Annex IV of the Commission Report entitled 'Provisions for Insertion in Treaties with Enemy Governments', above n 66, at 153–54. See also Arts 227–30, Treaty of Peace with Germany, signed at Versailles, 28 March 1919, T.S. No. 4 (1919) (Cmd 153); Arts 173–76, Treaty of Peace with Austria, signed at Saint-Germain-en-Layé, 10 Sept 1919, T S No. 11 (1919) (Cmd 400); Arts 118–20, Treaty of Peace with Bulgaria, signed at Neuilly-sur-Seine, 27 Nov 1919, TS No 5 (1920) (Cmd 522); Art 157–60, Treaty of Peace with Hungary, signed at Trianon, 4 June 1920, TS No 10 (1920) (Cmd 896); Arts 226–30, Treaty of Peace with Turkey, negotiated at Sèvres but never signed.

[69] See Timothy L H McCormack, 'From Sun Tzu to the Sixth Committee: The Evolution of an International Criminal Law Regime', in McCormack and Simpson, *The Law of War Crimes*, at 45–48.

[70] *Ibid*, 49.

terms of the Versailles Treaty squarely on the shoulders of the political leadership.[71] The Allied governments accepted a compromise proposal from Germany that specified defendants be tried before the German Supreme Court (*Reichsgericht*). The reluctant Allied agreement was a pragmatic one—based on the recognition that insistence on international trials was so sensitive for the Germans that it could bring down their Government to be replaced by a regime much less palatable to the Allies.[72] In accepting the compromise, Allied governments insisted on reserving the right to enforce Article 228 if they were not satisfied with the bona fides of the German national process.

Although the original list of 896 names was culled to 45, some of those individuals had either already died, could not be found or otherwise could not be taken into German or Allied custody. German authorities were only able to initiate proceedings against 12 defendants and the majority of those were acquitted—most commonly for lack of evidence.[73] Of the convicted defendants, most were given seemingly lenient sentences. The two co-defendants convicted of their involvement in the strafing of survivors in life-rafts after the sinking of the hospital ship *Llandovery Castle* were sentenced to four years' imprisonment. One of them was dismissed from the German Navy and the other deprived of the right to wear an officer's uniform.[74] However, both defendants escaped from incarceration and never served out their full prison sentences. James Willis notes that the *Reichsgericht* met in a special closed session in 1928 to hear fresh evidence in the case and consequently declared the two men innocent annulling its earlier convictions.[75]

Allied reaction to the trials was overwhelmingly critical—comments such as 'a scandalous failure of justice'[76] and a 'judicial farce'[77] indicative of the depth of the emotive reaction to Leipzig. The French Government, for example, responded by reverting to Articles 228 and 229 of the Versailles Treaty and claiming a unilateral right to conduct its own trials against German

[71] See Willis, *Prologue to Nuremberg*, at 116–20.

[72] Willis quotes Lloyd George who claimed that 'the last thing the Allies wanted was to destroy the present Government and have it succeeded by a Spartacist or militarist government, which would inevitably be the case', *ibid*, 124.

[73] Lieutenant-Captain Karl Neumann was acquitted in more controversial circumstances. He was responsible for the U-boat sinking of the British hospital ship the *Dover Castle*. Although he admitted his responsibility for knowingly sinking a hospital vessel, he successfully argued a defence of obedience to superior orders. The German Admiralty had ordered the sinking of hospital ships within specified zones on the basis that the Allied forces were abusing the traditional immunity of such vessels by illegally using them for the transport of troops. As the *Dover Castle* was within one of the specified zones when it was destroyed, the Court accepted Neumann's plea of obedience to superior orders which he believed were legal. See Claud Mullins, *The Leipzig Trials: An Account of the War Criminals' Trials and a Study of German Mentality* (1921), 99–107; James Willis, above n 66, at 133–34. See also Yoram Dinstein, *The Defence of 'Obedience to Superior Orders' in International Law* (1965), 12–13.

[74] See Claud Mullins, *The Leipzig Trials*, 133.

[75] Willis, above n 66, at 146.

[76] Willis, above n 66, at 139 quoting *The Times* newspaper.

[77] To use the words of Yoram Dinstein, above n 73, at 11.

defendants.[78] Only the British Government seemed satisfied with the conduct of the trials and attempted to move on from retribution after Leipzig.[79] Despite the overwhelmingly negative reaction to the trials, some have pointed to key precedents emerging from them. For example, Claud Mullins, a British observer throughout the trials, claimed that:

> Certainly the number of convictions in the Leipzig War Crimes Trials was a very small fraction of the number of men originally accused. But great principles are often established by minor events. The Leipzig Trials undoubtedly established the principle that individual atrocities committed during a war may be punished when the war is over.[80]

Mullins is surely correct. For all the selectivities inherent in the choice of defendants and the relative leniency of sentences, German courts tried and, in some cases convicted, German nationals for the perpetration of international crimes. They did so because it was considered more acceptable that the particular defendants be tried in German courts than before an international tribunal composed of victorious Allied judges. But the fact remains that the trials took place and set an important precedent for future trials—both before international tribunals and before national courts in defendants' own states.

The Istanbul Trials

The post-World War I Istanbul (then Constantinople) trials of Turkish nationals for their alleged involvement in the massacre of Armenians have, undeservedly, received much less attention than the Leipzig Trials. The lack of analysis of the trials themselves is bewildering given the relatively significant literature on Ottoman atrocities against the Armenian People. This disparity of attention between Leipzig and Istanbul is mirrored in the post-World War II context between Nuremberg and Tokyo (and more recently between the International Criminal Tribunal for the Former Yugoslavia and that for Rwanda) and provides substance to those who have alleged a Eurocentric bias in the literature analysing trials of international crimes.[81]

[78] See Meringhac, 'Sanctions des Infractions au Droit des Gens Commissés au Cours de la Guerre Européene', (1917), 24 *Revue Génerale de Droit International Public* 10. James Willis, above n 66, at 142 indicates that France tried more than 1,200 German defendants post World War I. Willis also points out that Belgium also tried approximately 80 German defendants.

[79] Willis, above n 66, at 139–47 describes the various Allied reactions to Leipzig including the British reaction.

[80] Claud Mullins, above n 73, at 224.

[81] See, for example, Payam Ahkavan, 'The International Criminal Tribunal for Rwanda: The Politics and Pragmatics of Punishment', (1996) 90 *American Journal of International Law*, 501. In discussing the establishment of the ICTR, Akhavan claims that: 'On the basis of international responses to other situations, it has been suggested that the plight of African victims would not generate the same outcry as the suffering of Europeans. In other words, the Rwanda Tribunal was established because of the precedential effect of the Yugoslav Tribunal.'

The Istanbul Trials differed from the Leipzig Trials in a number of important respects. First, at Istanbul dozens of defendants were tried. Although the number of those tried fell well short of the total number suspected of involvement in the massacres and identified in the Report of the Mazhar Inquiry Commission,[82] the proportion of suspects brought to trial was significantly higher than at Leipzig. Secondly, many of those convicted in Istanbul were awarded severe penalties, including the death penalty, in a number of cases. Both of these differences are explicable on the basis of the differing motivations for the trials. In Leipzig, the German Government wanted to avoid the trial of German nationals before an international tribunal whereas in Istanbul it was thought that the institution of proceedings would 'impress and mollify' the victorious Allies and diminish the severity of the terms of the Peace Treaty yet to be imposed.[83] But the Ottomans were also a nation in transition following their defeat in World War I. In addition to the desire to placate the victorious Allies, many within the Sultan's Government saw the trials as an opportunity to inculpate the Ittihadist Party leadership for atrocities perpetrated against the Armenians and, in so doing, exculpate the rest of the Turkish People.[84] This example of political expediency provided a motivation for the trials independently of the threat of an international tribunal imposed by the Allied Powers.

The majority of trials were conducted on the basis of the physical locality of the massacres (or in the case of the Büyükdere Trial Series, allegations of plunder and pillage) and involved multiple defendants for each locality—Yozgat, Trabzon, Harput, Bayburt, Erzincan, Mosul and Büyükdere.[85] Two other trial series involved senior leaders—the Ittihadist wartime ministers and senior military leaders in one trial and the responsible Ittihadist secretaries in the other.[86] The Special Military Tribunal found sufficient evidence of pre-meditated mass murder to convict many of the defendants appearing before it. Fifteen individuals were sentenced to death with a number of other defendants awarded substantial prison sentences.

Despite the awarding of these sentences, however, criticisms of the whole trial experience abound. Vahakn Dadrian is particularly caustic in his assessment of the trials being 'dismally abortive as far as justice was concerned'.[87] Dadrian's assessment is that:

[82] See Vahakn N Dadrian, 'The Turkish Military Tribunal's Prosecution of the Authors of the Armenian Genocide: Four Major Court-Martial Series', (1997), *Holocaust and Genocide Studies* VII (1997) 32.

[83] See Annette Höss, 'The Trial of Perpetrators by the Turkish Military Tribunals: The Case of Yozgat', in Richard G Hovannisian (ed), *The Armenian Genocide: History, Politics, Ethics* (1992), 209; See also Dadrian, preceding note, 31.

[84] Dadrian, *ibid*.

[85] Vahakn N Dadrian, 'The Documentation of the World War I Armenian Massacres in the Proceedings of the Turkish Military Tribunal', (1991), 23 *International Journal of Middle East Studies*, 561. Vahakn N Dadrian, above n 82, discusses the Yozgat and the Trabzon Trial Series in some detail (at 33–42). Annette Höss, above n 83, discusses the Yozgat Trial Series in some detail (at 212–21).

[86] Again, Dadrian, above n 82, discusses both trial series in some detail, at 42–50.

[87] *Ibid*, 50.

> The most salient feature of the present case is the remarkable chasm between the determination of guilt and the indulgence through which so many of the guilty escaped retribution. . . A *nation* was murdered in its ancestral territories and the Tribunal could convict and condemn to death only fifteen men, of whom only three—indeed only the most insignificant of the pack—were actually executed; the rest escaped, or were allowed to escape, and become 'fugitives from justice'. As British Acting High Commissioner at Istanbul, Rear Admiral Webb, reported to London, 'it is interesting to see. . . the manner in which the sentences have been apportioned among the absent and present so as to effect a minimum of real bloodshed'.[88]

Having earlier attempted to differentiate the Istanbul trial experience from that in Leipzig, this criticism from Dadrian exposes some of the similarities in the two Post-World War I national trial processes. The Sultan's Government in Istanbul was replaced by the regime of Mustapha Kemal on a nationalist platform and the trials were terminated before proceedings were instituted in relation to alleged atrocities committed in Adana, Aleppo, Bitlis, Diarbekir, Erzerum, Marash and Van.[89] Under Kemal, none of those defendants already sentenced to imprisonment actually served out their full sentences.[90]

However, for all the limitations and the selectivities inherent in the Ottoman trial experience, the significance of the trials cannot be underestimated. In an attitude redolent with the sentiments expressed by Claud Mullins reflecting on the Leipzig Trial experience, Dadrian acknowledges both the national and international contributions the Istanbul Trials have made. Here, for the first time in Turkish history, Ottoman Turkish leaders were held accountable before a Special Military Tribunal for atrocities committed against a non-muslim minority traditionally considered inferior and systematically the subject of discrimination. The Tribunal's proceedings record the evidence establishing the case and that record will be preserved in perpetuity in Turkish legal history. The international implications, both legal and political, are self evident. The Istanbul trial experience is an important historical precedent for the use of domestic courts and domestic law to try nationals of the state for their participation in international crimes.[91]

Domestic Trials Concurrent with Ad Hoc International Criminal Tribunals

Commonalities between Leipzig and Istanbul on one hand and the national trial experiences of Rwanda and the Balkan states on the other may not be readily apparent. After World War I, Germany and Turkey were only threatened with

[88] *Ibid.*
[89] Annette Höss, above n 83, at 210.
[90] Vahakn N Dadrian, above n 82, at 50.
[91] See Vahakn N Dadrian, 'Genocide as a Problem of National and International Law: The World War I Armenian Case and Its Contemporary Legal Ramifications', (1989), 14 *Yale Journal of International Law*, 221.

the establishment of international tribunals. Contemporary Rwanda and the states of the Former Yugoslavia face quite distinct issues of concurrent jurisdiction with existing ad hoc international criminal tribunals. Despite that obvious distinction, it is suggested here that there are important convergent observations to make. It is interesting, for example, to observe similarities between Germany post-World War I and Croatia, Serbia and, to some extent, even the Republika Srpska in the years following the establishment of the ICTY. In each case the international community has been able to push for the conduct of domestic trials of 'own nationals' with the 'leverage' of either the threat, or the reality, of international trials.

Rwanda and the ICTR

The Rwandan situation, with over 120,000 suspects incarcerated and awaiting trial years after the alleged atrocities, is unique. Only the German national experience in the aftermath of World War II comes close to Rwanda's situation in the enormity of the number of defendants. Germany, however, unlike Rwanda, had an effectively functioning judicial system with the resources to embark on the process of trying more than 90,000 defendants. The Government in Kigali has reason for frustration when it sees the ICTR operating across the border in Arusha. The Rwandan Government is operating on only a tiny fraction of the International Tribunal's multi-million dollar annual budget while Kigali houses more than 2,000 times the number of detainees currently held in Arusha.

The Rwandan Government called for the establishment of an international criminal tribunal to 'internationalise' the response to the Tutsi genocide and to avoid perceptions of national vengeance in the trial process.[92] Ironically, Rwanda, as a non-permanent member of the UN Security Council at the time, ultimately voted against Resolution 955. The Government in Kigali opposed, inter alia, the establishment of the Tribunal in neighbouring Tanzania and the Security Council's refusal to allow the Tribunal to award the death penalty.[93] Despite this opposition to the Security Council's model for the Tribunal, Kigali has consistently stated that it will co-operate fully with the Tribunal in its fulfilment of the mandate encapsulated in Resolution 955. The ICTR is engaged in the process of trying the leaders of the genocide in Rwanda but it was always anticipated that the majority of defendants would be tried by Rwandan national courts.[94] Olivier Dubois has reflected on the Security Council's explicit

[92] Olivier Dubois, 'Rwanda's National Courts and the International Tribunal', (1997), 321 *International Review of the Red Cross* 718; See also Payam Ahkavan, above n 81, at 504–05.

[93] For a fuller discussion of the stated reasons for Rwanda's negative vote on Resolution 955 see Olivier Dubois, preceding note, at 718–20.

[94] See generally, Madeline Morris, 'The Trials of Concurrent Jurisdiction: The Case of Rwanda', (1997), 7 *Duke Journal of Comparative and International Law*, 349; William Schabas, 'Justice, Democracy and Impunity in Post-Genocide Rwanda: Searching for Solutions to Impossible Problems', (1996), 7 *Criminal Law Forum*.

recognition that international co-operation would be required to strengthen the courts and the judicial system of Rwanda in anticipation of the large number of suspects to be tried domestically[95] and laments the lost opportunities on the part of the international community as a whole, and the Tribunal itself, to make more of a contribution in this respect.[96]

Domestic trials for the *genocidaires* only commenced in Rwandan courts late in 1996.[97] Since then, some 2,500 suspects have been tried, several hundred sentenced to death and 800 sentenced to life imprisonment.[98] Most of those held in detention have not been charged with specific offences and the detainees include children and the elderly.[99] Prisons are so overcrowded and conditions so bad that literally thousands have died in detention. In a bold attempt to overcome the obstacles to more expeditious handling of the trials of detainees, the Rwandan Government announced its intention to reinvigorate the *gacaca*—a traditional, community-based non-judicial system of justice. Although concerns were raised—particularly about the capacity of the system to protect the rights of the accused—the UN Commission on Human Rights appointed Special Representative on the Situation of Human Rights in Rwanda has given his tentative approval to the utilisation of the system and approved the trial of the pre-*gacaca* phase of proceedings.[100] The Rwandan Government expects *gacaca* trials to commence by the end of 2001 and this prospect increases hope for a significant reduction in the huge number of detainees in the not too distant future.

Balkan States and the ICTY

The relationship between the ICTY and the domestic jurisdictions of each of the Balkan states is significantly more complex than is the case for the ICTR and Rwanda. In the Balkans, national trials have occurred but the tendency has been to focus on trials of ethnic minorities in each of the Balkan states as a way of shifting blame for atrocities away from the ethnic majority. However, there are encouraging signs that the existence and the operation of the ICTY has given the international community new opportunities to pressure authorities in different Balkan states to increase co-operation with the Tribunal itself as well

[95] See preambulatory para 9 of Resolution 955, 50 UN SCOR (3453rd mtg), UN Doc S/RES/955 (8 Nov 1994).

[96] Olivier Dubois, above n 92, at 720.

[97] For an analysis of the Rwandan legislation to be the basis of domestic trials, see Catherine Cissé, 'The End of a Culture of Impunity in Rwanda?: Prosecution of Genocide and War Crimes Before Rwandan Courts and the International Criminal Tribunal for Rwanda', *Yearbook of International Humanitarian Law* 1 (1998), 175–86.

[98] See Ratner and Abrams, above n 41, at 176.

[99] The Rwandan Government later agreed to release all prisoners under 14 years of age and by the end of Dec 2000, the Government had released 400 such prisoners. See Report of the UN Commission on Human Rights' Special Representative on the Situation of Human Rights in Rwanda, Mr Michel Moussalli: 56 UN ECOR, UN Doc E/CN.4/2001/45/Add.1 (21 March 2001), at 2.

[100] *Ibid*.

as to redress legal inadequacies in domestic judicial processes and the issue of partiality in the ethnic identity of those on trial.

Bosnia-Herzegovina

The Government of Bosnia-Herzegovina supported the initiative to establish the ICTY from the first discussions of the concept and has co-operated fully with the work of the Tribunal ever since. In addition to the provision of assistance to the work of the ICTY, the authorities in Sarajevo have instituted a number of their own war crimes trial proceedings. Although most of these national trials have been against ethnic Serbs, the suggestion that the Bosnian approach to the prosecution of war crimes is prejudiced against the Serbs seems unfounded. Bosnian trials have also been held against ethnic Croats and Muslims and, in some trials, including of ethnic Serbs, some defendants have been acquitted for lack of evidence. The Bosnian authorities do not proceed with national trials without the approval of the ICTY's Office of the Prosecutor—an administrative procedure which ensures that Sarajevo does not obstruct the work of the Tribunal but which also adds some external objectivity to the selection of particular defendants and the decision to institute proceedings.

In May 1997 the Bihac Cantonal Court convicted Mustafa Odobašić and Zuhidja Rizvić for war crimes perpetrated by them as members of the Bosnian Serb militia against members of the Bosnian Government forces in the region of Velika Kladuša in northern Bosnia. The commander of the defendants' Bosnian Serb unit was named as a third defendant and charged with individual criminal responsibility for the acts of his subordinates. The Bihac Cantonal Court acquitted the commander on the basis that there was insufficient evidence that he either ordered the commission of the specific acts or knew that his subordinates were acting as they did in excess of their orders. On appeal to the Supreme Court, the judgment of the Cantonal Court in relation to all three defendants was upheld.[101]

Also in 1997 the Tuzla Cantonal Court tried Drago Ilić for war crimes during his involvement as a Bosnian Serb military policeman in the Batković concentration camp in the Eastern Bijeljina Region of Bosnia. Up to 1,700 mainly Muslims and Croats were held in the camp—many of them subject to physical abuse and mistreatment. Ilić was convicted of severely beating prisoners and of withholding essential medical supplies and was sentenced to seven years imprisonment. His conviction and sentence were upheld on appeal to the Supreme Court.[102]

Trial proceedings against five members of the Bosnian Croat militia (the so-called 'Mostar Five Group') commenced in the Herzegovina-Neretva Cantonal Court in Mostar in relation to the co-defendants' involvement in the mistreat-

[101] Jann K Kleffner, 'Correspondents' Reports: Bosnia-Herzegovina', *Yearbook of International Humanitarian Law* 2 (1999), 340–41.

[102] *Ibid*, 341–43.

ment and summary executions of Muslim civilians and members of the Bosnian Government Forces held as prisoners of war by the Bosnian Croat Army. Three of the five co-defendants, Zoran Soldo, Erhard Poznić and Željko Džidić, surrendered voluntarily to Bosnian Government authorities. The other two accused, Mato Aničić and Ivan Škutor, are being tried *in absentia*.[103] A second trial against six Bosnian Muslims has also commenced in Mostar. The co-accused, Zikrija Ljevo, Vernes Zahirović, Bećir Omanović, Meho Kaminić, Habib Čopelj and Husnija Oručević, have been charged with war crimes relating to their involvement in the torture of imprisoned Croat soldiers.

At least two defendants have been acquitted after appealing against their trial convictions to the Supreme Court of Bosnia-Herzegovina. Miodrag Andrič was originally convicted by the Sarajevo Magistrate's Court and sentenced to 20 years imprisonment for killing civilians in the Bosnian village of Bjelogorcre SO Rogatica. On appeal, the Supreme Court ordered a retrial on the basis of procedural irregularity and questionable interpretation of fact. The Sarajevo Magistrate's Court reversed its original decision on retrial and acquitted Andrič of the charges against him.[104] Ibrahim Đedović had been charged with war crimes allegedly perpetrated during his role as head of the Velika Kladuša police station against internees of the nearby Drmljevo concentration camp. The Magistrate's Court dismissed the charges for lack of sufficient evidence to convict the accused and the Prosecution then appealed the decision. The Supreme Court dismissed the appeal and upheld the decision of the Magistrate's Court.[105] Both cases demonstrate the sensitivities involved in balancing the need for justice with a commitment to legal principles in the administration of criminal procedure. The cases also provide a basis for confidence in the independence of the Bosnian judicial system—a confidence that cannot be shared in relation to the administration of criminal justice within the Republika Srpska.

Quite apart from the refusal of authorities in Pale to co-operate with the ICTY in the arrest and transfer of custody of either Radovan Karadžić or Ratko Mladić, other incidents have raised serious concerns about the Republika Srpska's refusal to countenance the prosecution of Serbs for war crimes against other ethnic communities. Three Bosnian Serbs, Savo Ivanić, Duško Pašalić and Milan Hrvačević, had been convicted of war crimes and sentenced to terms of imprisonment by the courts of Bosnia-Herzegovina. After serving some of their terms in Bosnian prisons, the three were transferred to the Republika Srpska under the terms of an agreement between Sarajevo and Pale which explicitly required the serving out of the full term of imprisonment. Three days before Nikola Poplašen was dismissed as President of the Republika Srpska, he granted amnesty to the three prisoners and they were released back

[103] Jann K Kleffner, 'Correspondents' Reports: Bosnia-Herzegovina', *Yearbook of International Humanitarian Law* 3 (2000), 435–36.
[104] *Ibid*, at 432–33.
[105] *Ibid*, at 433–35.

into the community.[106] But even in Pale the situation is not entirely forlorn. The Parliament of the Republika Srpska passed a first reading of a new Bill on co-operation with the ICTY in July 2001. The Bill must pass a second reading before it becomes law but, given the intransigence of authorities in Pale in their relations with the Tribunal to date, the mere tabling of the Bill is reason for some optimism that perhaps, finally, positive developments are occurring.

Croatia

Despite promises to the contrary, the former President of Croatia, Franjo Tuđman, not only failed to co-operate with the International Criminal Tribunal for the Former Yugoslavia but often took positive steps to obstruct the Tribunal's work. It is well known, for example, that Croatia withheld documentary evidence from the Tribunal in its proceedings against the Bosnian Croat General Tihomir Blaškić in relation to his command responsibilities in the Lasva Valley region of Bosnia-Herzegovina. President Tuđman defied the *subpoenae duces tecum* order against the Government of Croatia instituted initially by Trial Chamber II and reaffirmed by the Appeals Chamber of the Tribunal.[107] President Tuđman also refused to allow ICTY investigators access to sites within Croatia and failed to take Croatians indicted by the Tribunal into custody for transfer to The Hague. Croatian authorities have instituted trial proceedings against Croatian nationals alleged to have perpetrated war crimes but, until recently, the overwhelming majority of those trials have been against ethnic Serbs and not against ethnic Croats. In the few instances of trials of ethnic Croats during the regime of President Tuđman, the charges proved and the sentences imposed were suspiciously more lenient than in the trials of ethnic Serbs.

Some of the trials of ethnic Serbs have also been heavily criticised as unfair. In 1996, for example, the Split County Court found Mirko Graorac, the Bosnian Serb commander of the external guard of the Manjača Camp in Bosnia-Herzegovina, guilty of war crimes perpetrated by himself and by guards under his command at Manjača. Graorac was sentenced to 20 years' imprisonment. Amnesty International challenged the impartiality of the proceedings on the basis that Graorac was precluded from calling his own witnesses or otherwise conducting his own defence. Although the Supreme Court of Croatia heard an appeal from Graorac and ordered a retrial, the Supreme Court did so only to

[106] Jann K Kleffner, above n 101, at 344.

[107] Trial Chamber II—Decision on the Objection of the Republic of Croatia to the Issuance of *Subpeonae Duces Tecum, Prosecutor v Timohir Blaškić,* case no. IT-95-14-PT, 18 July 1997; Appeals Chamber—Judgment on the Request of The Republic of Croatia for Review of the Decision of Trial Chamber II of 18 July 1997, *Prosecutor v Timohir Blaškić,* case no. IT-95-14-PT, 29 Oct 1997. For a brief analysis of the Appeals Chamber's review of the decision of Trial Chamber II see Peter Malanczuk, 'A Note on the Judgement of the Appeals Chamber of the International Criminal Tribunal for the Former Yugoslavia on the Issuance of *Subpeonae Duces Tecum* in the *Blaškić* Case', *Yearbook of International Humanitarian Law* 1 (1998), 229.

clarify one issue of fact and confirmed all other aspects of the Split County Court's decision at first instance.[108]

In contrast, in the first Croatian trial of ethnic Croats for war crimes, six defendants were charged in relation to the deaths of up to one hundred ethnic Serbs in the area of Pakrac, south-east of Zagreb. One of the defendants, Miro Bajramović, was convicted on charges of house breaking and extortion at gun point and sentenced to imprisonment for twenty months. A second defendant, Branko Sarić-Kosa, was convicted of illegally detaining and assaulting a Serb villager and sentenced to 12 months imprisonment. The other, more serious charges of murder, attempted murder and kidnapping against all six defendants were dismissed by the court for lack of evidence.[109] There is no suggestion here that the six defendants were not given the opportunity to defend themselves. In another trial before the District Court of Zagreb, three ethnic Croats were charged in relation to the killing of nine members of a Bosniak family in the village of Mokronoge, Tomislavgrad in the breakaway region of Bosnia-Herzegovina known as the Croatian People's Republic of Herzeg-Bosnia. The three defendants, Ivan Baković, Albert Topić and Petar Majić, were all charged with murder and not with war crimes. Baković did not appear in court and was tried *in absentia*. The court acquitted Topić and Majić but convicted Baković of nine counts of murder and sentenced him to 15 years imprisonment. Baković's whereabouts in Bosnia-Herzegovina is well known but no warrant for his arrest has been issued by Croatian authorities. The decision to only convict one defendant *in absentia* and to acquit the two defendants actually in the custody of Croatian authorities has raised serious questions about the impartiality of the process.[110]

The appointment of President Stipe Mesić and the election of the new Government of Prime Minister Ivica Račan following the death of President Tuđman in December 1999 and the new elections in January 2000, have heralded a new era for Croatia in the prosecution of international crimes. Within weeks of the election, Croatia had made key documentary material available to the ICTY in The Hague, transferred the Bosnian Croat Mladen Naletilić (also known as 'Tuta') to The Hague and permitted ICTY investigators full access to the site of the alleged massacre of Serb civilians in the town of Gospić.[111] The District Court of Osijek has also handed down a decision to acquit five Croatian Serbs of war crimes. The five defendants had been convicted by the

[108] See Amnesty International, *Croatia: Mirko Graorać, Shortchanging Justice: War Crimes Trials in Former Yugoslavia* (Dec 1998). Text of the Report is available at:http://web.amnesty.org/ai.nsf/Index/EUR640101998?OpenDocument&of=COUNTRIES\CROATIA

[109] Jann K Kleffner, 'Correspondents' Reports: Croatia', *Yearbook of International Humanitarian Law* 2 (1999), 352.

[110] See Suzannah Linton, 'Correspondents' Reports: Croatia', *Yearbook of International Humanitarian Law* 3 (2000), 463–65.

[111] See Human Rights Watch, *World Report 2001: Croatia: Human Rights Developments* available at: http://www.hrw.org/wr2k1/europe/croatia.html

same Court in 1999 for their alleged involvement in attacks on Croatian towns in 1991. All five had been sentenced to terms of imprisonment ranging in length from eight to fifteen years. The Supreme Court of Croatia overturned the original trial decision on the basis that the District Court had committed 'significant breaches of criminal procedure' and required a retrial of the five defendants. The District Court annulled its earlier decision and ruled that there was no evidence to link the defendants to the shelling of Croatian towns in 1991.[112]

While some of the unfair trial proceedings against Croatian Serbs have been overturned, the authorities in Zagreb have also stepped up their investigations of alleged war crimes by ethnic Croats. In September 2000 Ante Slišković, former military intelligence chief in Kiseljak, and his deputy, Tomislav Vlajić, were arrested by police in the city of Zadar. Both have been charged with war crimes in respect of the attack on the Bosnian village of Ahmići in 1993 in which more than 100 Muslim civilians were killed. President Mesić has also persisted with the unpopular prosecution of former Croatian General, Mirko Norac, and four other defendants for their alleged involvement in the attack on the Serb village of Gospić in 1991. Norac is the highest ranking Croatian Army officer to be tried in his own country. More than 100,000 demonstrators protested in Split against his trial because he is considered a national hero for his part in the war against the Serbs.[113] President Mesić dismissed seven Croatian generals who criticised him for insulting the memory of the country's war for independence by announcing his willingness to prosecute Croats for alleged crimes against Serbs.[114]

Serbia

At the time the UN Security Council was contemplating the establishment of the International Criminal Tribunal for the Former Yugoslavia, the Federal Government of Serbia and Montenegro opposed the initiative on the basis that the Tribunal was discriminatory and partisan.[115] This was, of course, the Government of Slobodan Milošević. Who would dare to have dreamed that within seven years of the establishment of the Tribunal Milošević would be brought before the very institution whose creation and operation he opposed? While the developments in Serbia leading to the transfer of Milošević to The Hague were remarkable, it is premature to argue that Serbian attitudes to the impartial administration of criminal justice have fundamentally changed. There

[112] See Jann K Kleffner, 'Correspondents' Reports: Croatia', *Yearbook of International Humanitarian Law* 3 (1999), 465.

[113] Amnesty International, 'Croatia: War Crimes Prosecutions Should not be Obstructed', (Press Release, 13 Feb 2001). Text available at: http://web.amnesty.org/ai.nsf/Index/EUR640012001

[114] See Jonathan Steele, 'Croatia's President Gives Seven Generals Their Marching Orders', *The Guardian* (30 Sept 2000), 19.

[115] See, for example, the letter dated 17 May 1993 from the Deputy Prime Minister and Minister for Foreign Affairs of the Federal Republic of Yugoslavia to the UN Secretary-General, UN Doc S/25801 (21 May 1993).

is evidence that many in Belgrade hoped that the transfer of Milošević would relieve some of the international pressure for the additional transfers of former Interior Minister Vlajko Stojilković, retired Head of the Army Dragoljub Ojdanić, current Serbian President Milan Multinović and Nikola Sainović, a senior official in Milošević's Socialist Party. The Serbian Minister for Justice, Vladan Batić, indicated his preference for these four, and other Serbian indictees of the ICTY, to be tried in Belgrade rather than in The Hague.[116] Domestic trials in Belgrade to supplement the work of the ICTY are desirable in principle. However, concerns have been expressed about the independence and impartiality of the Serbian judicial system and its administration of criminal justice.[117]

Some trials have already been held in Serbia against ethnic Serbs. In November 1994, for example, the Šabac District Court commenced trial proceedings against Dušan Vučković, a member of a volunteer Yugoslav Army Unit , for alleged war crimes against Bosnian Muslim civilians near Zvornik.[118] In November 1999, the Belgrade Regional Court commenced a criminal investigation of charges of war crimes and espionage against five Serbian members of the Yugoslav Army Reserve for their alleged activities in Kosovo.[119] While some domestic trials of Serbs have taken place, those trials seem few in number compared to questionable trial processes, particularly against ethnic Albanians, resulting in multiple convictions. Amnesty International, for example, has recently welcomed the decision of Serbia's Supreme Court to release the so-called 'Đakovica Group'—a group of 143 ethnic Albanians arrested in 1999 by Serb forces and convicted in a mass trial of charges of 'association for the purposes of hostile activity in connection with terrorism'. All 143 co-accused were sentenced to terms of imprisonment ranging from seven to 13 years and Amnesty International claims that international standards were breached at every stage of the proceedings against the members of the group.[120] Amnesty International has called for a review of the cases of an additional 400 ethnic Albanians currently held in Serbian prisons—the majority of whom are similarly held on the basis of allegedly unfair trial processes.[121]

It is too simplistic to assume that the transfer of custody of Slobodan Milošević to The Hague, or other significant, albeit less dramatic, developments elsewhere in the Balkans indicates an irreversible momentum towards a

[116] 'Djindjić Hopes for Belgrade Trials', CNN.com/World, 2 July 2001 at: http://europe.cnn.com/2001/WORLD/europe/07/02/serbia.salzburg/ Following the passage of legislation on cooperation with ICTY in 2002, however, Ojdanić and Sainović agreed to surrender to the Tribunal and Stojilković committed suicide.

[117] See, for example, the Helsinki Committee for Human Rights in Serbia, *Report of the Judicial System in Serbia in July 2001* at: http://www.helsinki.org.yu/hcs/HCSreport2001JulJudical.htm

[118] 'Trial Begins of Serb Accused of Killing and Raping Muslims', *BBC Summary of World Broadcasts*, 24 November 1994.

[119] 'Yugoslav Army Reservists Charged with Kosovo War Crimes, Espionage', *BBC Worldwide Monitoring (Europe—Political)*, 17 Nov 1999.

[120] Amnesty International, 'Yugoslavia: Amnesty International Demands Fair Trials', (24 April 2001) at: http://web.amnesty.org/ai.nsf/Index/EUR700112001

[121] *Ibid.*

commitment to the end of impunity for international crimes. The ICTY cannot possibly prosecute even a significant proportion of all the crimes which fall within its jurisdictional competence because of the sheer magnitude of that task. Domestic trials are essential to supplement the work of the Tribunal and yet, those domestic trials are only credible if the judicial processes in each of the Balkan states are independent and impartial. Although there are still varying degrees of improvement required across all of the national jurisdictions in the Balkans, developments to date confirm the fact that the existence and the operation of the ICTY in The Hague provides a degree of leverage to the international community in respect of domestic trial processes within the Balkan states which might not otherwise exist in the absence of the Tribunal.

DOMESTIC TRIALS FOR SERIOUS BREACHES OF MILITARY DISCIPLINE

In the absence of a transition from military to civilian rule, the domestic trial of members of a state's own military forces for war crimes is the most politically sensitive of any domestic prosecution for international crimes. We have observed some circumstances in which the threat of, or actual establishment of, an international criminal tribunal can provide leverage to encourage states to initiate their own prosecutions. But what of the many circumstances where there is no relevant international criminal tribunal? What are the circumstances in which states are ready to prosecute members of their own military?

The infamous US trial proceedings for the My Lai massacre in Vietnam are particularly illustrative. Where military forces are engaged in war against a foreign enemy, vilified and dehumanised in the domestic war propaganda effort, it can be very difficult for the nation as a whole to accept atrocities against 'enemy' civilians for what they really are. In contrast, when troops are deployed as peacekeepers—sent in to protect a civilian population which has not been dehumanised at home, it ought to be easier for the sending state to expect trials of their own troops for serious breaches of discipline. Different national examples arising out of serious breaches of military discipline during the UNOSOM II deployment to Somalia are offered here to illustrate emerging expectations about accountability for peacekeepers. The examples used here are only illustrative—there are, of course, other examples which could be drawn upon if space permitted.

The My Lai Massacre in Vietnam

The trial of Lieutenant William Calley for his involvement in the massacre of 504 unarmed civilians[122] in the South Vietnamese hamlet of My Lai is the

[122] For a list of names and other details of the victims see Trent Angers, *The Forgotten Hero of My Lai: The Hugh Thompson Story* (1999), 223–26. Angers indicates that the list was provided by staff at the Vietnamese Embassy in Washington DC. The Peers Inquiry (the official US inquiry into the affair conducted by retired Lt Gen. William Peers) concluded that between 175 and 200 civilians had been killed and the US Army Criminal Investigation Division estimated the death toll to be 347.

leading *cause célèbre* for the domestic trial of a member of a state's own military forces. This particular case attracted intense media scrutiny because although the US prosecuted a number of other servicemen for various offences in the conduct of the war[123] 'all the crimes alleged to have been committed in Vietnam pale into insignificance when compared with the extent of the killings perpetrated at My Lai'.[124]

The facts of the massacre at My Lai are extensively documented elsewhere.[125] It is sufficient here to indicate that Calley was court-martialled for his involvement in the issuing of orders to his troops in relation to the villagers herded into groups by US forces—'to waste them', 'to kill them', and 'I want them dead'—as well as for his own actions in summarily executing some of the Vietnamese villagers.[126] Although there was extensive evidence of an attempt by military commanders initially to cover up the incident,[127] too many individuals were involved to successfully suppress the story indefinitely. Eventually information reached the media and extensive coverage of the story exposed much of what had transpired.

Calley was convicted by court-martial of three counts of pre-meditated murder and one count of assault with intent to commit murder. He was sentenced to hard labour for the term of his natural life, dismissed from military service and stripped of all pay and allowances. Calley's sentence was reviewed by the convening authority, the Commander of the Third Army, who affirmed the dismissal and forfeitures but reduced the period of incarceration to 20 years hard labour. Calley's appeal to the US Army Court of Military Review was dismissed and the reviewed sentence affirmed. Despite this judicial process, Calley actually only served three and a half years under house arrest after his 20 year sentence was commuted to 10 years by the Secretary of the Army and was subsequently paroled after serving just one third of his already reduced sentence.[128]

see Matthew Lippman, 'War Crimes: The My Lai Massacre and the Vietnam War', (1993), 1 *San Diego Justice Journal*, 309.

[123] See, for example, *US v Griffen* (1968) 39 CMR 586; *US v Potter* (1968) 39 CMR 791; *US v Keenan* (1969) 39 CMR 108; *US v Schultz* (1969) 39 CMR 133; *US v. Bumgarner* (1970) 43 CMR 559; *US v Goldman* (1970) 43 CMR 711; *US v Willey and Cameron* (1971) 44 CMR 390; *US v Crider* (1972) 45 CMR 815; *US v Duffy* (1973) 47 CMR 658.

[124] Leslie C Green, *Superior Orders in National and International Law* (1976), 134.

[125] See the judgment of the US Army Court of Military Review, *US v Calley* (1973) 46 CMR 1131, at 1164–1174 and the personal account of his conduct of the official inquiry into the incident: Lieutenant General William R Peers (ret), *The My Lai Inquiry* (1979), particularly 165–98. See also Seymour M Hersh, *My Lai 4: A Report on the Massacre and its Aftermath* (1970); Joseph Goldstein, Burke Marshall, and Jack Schwartz, (eds), *The My Lai Massacre and Its Cover-Up: Beyond the Reach of Law?* (1976); Captain Norman G Cooper, 'My Lai and Military Justice: To What Effect?', (1975), 59 *Military Law Review*, 92–104; Major Jeffrey F Addicott, and Major William A Hudson Jr, 'The Twenty-Fifth Anniversary of My Lai: A Time to Inculcate the Lessons', (1993), 139 *Military Law Review*, 154–62; Matthew Lippman, above n 122, 302–14.

[126] See judgment of the US Army Court of Military Review, preceding note, at 1168–1173.

[127] Lieutenant General William R. Peers, above n 125, at 199–209; Seymour M. Hersh, above n 125, at 91–102; Goldstein, Marshall and Schwartz, above n 125, at 1–17; Matthew Lippman, above n 122, at 310–14.

[128] For a summary of Calley's case history, see Matthew Lippman, above n 122, at 318–19.

In 1974 Calley instituted civil proceedings and filed a writ of *habeas corpus*. Judge Elliot of the District Court found in favour of Calley on the basis that he had been denied a fair trial because of the prejudicial nature of the media publicity surrounding the case to which the jury members had been exposed.[129] On appeal to the Fifth Circuit Court of Appeals before a 13 judge court, Judge Eliot's decision was reversed and the verdict of the Court of Military Review reinstated.[130] By the time of the Court of Appeals judgment, however, Calley had already been paroled and was not required to serve an additional sentence.

At least the institutionalised military justice system worked in Calley's case. As painful as it was for the US Army to face the reality of the My Lai atrocities perpetrated by men from the Service, the court-martial and appeal process adduced and tested the available evidence, Calley was convicted and sentenced accordingly, the story of the massacre has been faithfully recorded in the official reports series of the judgments of the US Army Court of Military Review and the lessons from the incident can be used repeatedly in the training of soldiers in the US and elsewhere. However, the military court proceedings are only part of the Calley story. The most perturbing aspect of the affair was the reaction of US society to the news of Calley's conviction.

The day after the announcement of Calley's conviction, the US President, Richard Nixon, ordered Calley released from military prison to be returned to his apartment and kept under house arrest. Two days later Nixon indicated that he would personally review Calley's case. Nixon's actions prompted a letter of protest from Calley's prosecutor against Presidential interference in the case.[131] Matthew Lippman states that Members of Congress publicly condemned the conviction, Draft Board members resigned in protest and members of the court-martial were verbally abused. A song entitled *The Battle Hymn of Lt Calley* sold over 200,000 copies in three days after the conviction was announced. The Governor of Georgia, Jimmy Carter (later President Carter), organised an 'American Fighting Men's Day' and exhorted the citizens of Georgia to turn their motor vehicle headlights on in order to 'honour the flag as 'Rusty' [Calley's nickname] had done'.[132]

While Calley's conviction was greeted with dismay, one soldier who had intervened in My Lai to save some of the villagers from slaughter was vilified in the US. Chief Warrant Officer Hugh Thompson was flying a US Army helicopter over the hamlet of My Lai and saw some of the carnage below. He landed his craft between advancing US troops and a group of cowering Vietnamese villagers and ordered his gunner to train his weapon on US soldiers. Thompson indicated to Calley that the troops would be shot if they attempted to kill the civilians. He then coaxed the civilians onto his helicopter—seriously overloading it—and flew

[129] *Calley v Callaway* (1974) 382 F. Supp. 650 (MD Ga).
[130] *Calley v Callaway* (1975) 519 F. 2d 184 (5th Cir).
[131] Matthew Lippmann, above n 122, at 318 citing Richard Hammer, *The Court-Martial of Lt Calley* (1971), 379–81.
[132] *Ibid*, at 362.

them to safety.[133] Thompson received abusive mail and phone calls after his testimony against Calley and had been questioned by the Congressional Armed Services Committee in such a way as to suggest that members of the Committee thought he should be court-martialled for his actions at My Lai.[134] The US Army finally recognised the heroism of Thompson and his gunner with the award of the Soldier's Medal to both men on the thirtieth anniversary of the massacre at My Lai on 16 March 1998.[135]

Prosecution of Peacekeepers Post-Somalia

In the course of the deployment of the UN Security Council approved Unified Task Force for Somalia (UNITAF), and then the United Nations Operation in Somalia II (UNOSOM II),[136] the Canadian, Belgian and Italian contingents were all embroiled in allegations of serious crimes committed against Somali civilians. The fact that peacekeeping troops from three Western nations deployed to ensure the safe delivery of humanitarian assistance to the desperately needy Somali people were involved in the commission of serious crimes, some of which were captured on film and broadcast on television around the globe, shocked the world and raised grave concerns about responsibility for military discipline in the context of peace operations.

Canadian Contingent

On the evening of 4 March 1993, Canadian soldiers shot at two Somali intruders who were attempting to flee the Canadian contingent's compound in Betet Huen. One of the intruders was killed and the other seriously wounded. Less than two weeks later a third Somali youth, sixteen year old Shidane Arone, was caught sneaking in to the compound and was tortured and beaten to death. Evidence suggests that initially the Canadian Military attempted to cover up the incidents[137] but, eventually, information came to light and the Canadian Minister of National Defence ordered a military board of inquiry to investigate the Somalia Operation. Nine soldiers of the Canadian Airborne Regiment Battle Group were charged with offences in relation to the two separate incidents and court-martials were conducted. The convicted soldiers were sentenced to various terms of imprisonment and discharged from the Canadian Forces.[138] The level of national

[133] See Trent Angers, above n 122, at 101–34; Addicott and Hudson Jr, above n 125, at 158–59.

[134] Trent Angers, above n 122, 167–85.

[135] For the text of the citation accompanying the award of the medal see Trent Angers, above n 122, at 230.

[136] UNITAF was mandated pursuant to Resolution 794, 47 UN SCOR (3145 mtg.), UN Doc S/RES/794 (3 Dec 1992); UNOSOM II was established under the terms of Resolution 814, 48 UN SCOR (3188 mtg), UN Doc S/RES/814 (26 March 1993).

[137] See Robert M Young and Maria Molina, 'IHL and Peace Operations: Sharing Canada's Lessons Learned From Somalia', *Yearbook of International Humanitarian Law,* 1 (1998), 362.

[138] For a summary of the court-martial proceedings and outcomes see vol 1 of the *Report of the Somalia Commission of Inquiry,* 'The Somalia Mission: Post Deployment—The Courts Martial' accessible at: http://www.dnd.ca/somalia/vol1/v1c14e.htm

shame associated with the behaviour of Canadian troops in Somalia was such that the Canadian National Defence Forces took the unprecedented step of disbanding the Canadian Airborne Regiment—a unit of the Canadian Forces with a proud deployment history.[139] The Canadian Government decided that the procedures of the Military Board of Inquiry were insufficiently transparent[140] and so established a civilian Royal Commission to investigate the performance of the Canadian Forces in the Somalia Operation. The Commission of Inquiry rendered its five volume report in 1997 with a long list of recommendations.[141]

Belgian Contingent

Some years after the Belgian contingent returned from Somalia a Belgian newspaper carried photographs of Belgian peacekeepers holding a Somali youth over an open fire and of peacekeepers forcing other Somalis to drink heavily salted water.[142] The Belgian Military investigated the conduct of its troops deployed to Somalia and subsequently instituted criminal proceedings against a number of defendants. In the first of several trials arising from Belgian participation in UNOSOM II a number of Belgian paratroopers were tried for human rights abuses including torture, killings and mock executions of children.[143] Most of the paratroopers were acquitted of the charges although some were convicted and one of those sentenced to a prison term of five years.[144]

In a later trial two Belgian peacekeepers were charged with serious violations of international humanitarian law for their involvement in the incident of holding the Somali youth over an open fire during their participation in UNOSOM II. The two soldiers, Kurt Coelus and Claude Baert, were acquitted of the specific charges laid against them because the Military Court, sitting as an appellate court, decided that in the absence of an armed conflict in Somalia, the Geneva Conventions of 1949 and the two Additional Protocols of 1977 did not apply.[145] The decision of the Military Court was heavily criticised and raised serious concerns about the lack of accountability for peacekeepers on the basis of legal technicalities.[146] There is a glaring incongruence between, on one

[139] For brief history of the Canadian Airborne Regiment see Vol I of *Dishonoured Legacy: Report of the Somalia Commission of Inquiry* available at: http://www.dnd.ca/somalia/vol1/v1c9e.htm

[140] See Report of the Special Rapporteur on the Situation of Human Rights in Somalia to the UN Commission on Human Rights, 53 UN ESCOR, UN Doc E/CN.4/1998/96 (16 Jan 1998), 21.

[141] The complete text of *Dishonoured Legacy: Report of the Somalia Commission of Inquiry* is available at: http://www.dnd.ca/somalia/somaliae.htm

[142] See Report of the Special Rapporteur on Somalia, above n 140, at 20.

[143] *Ibid.*

[144] *Ibid.*

[145] See Marc Cogen, 'Correspondents' Reports: Belgium', *Yearbook of International Humanitarian Law,* 1 (1998), 415. Cogen provides the following citation for the case: Judgment of the Belgian Military Court regarding violations of IHL committed in Somalia and Rwanda, Nr 54 AR 1997, 20 Nov 1997. Published in *Journal des tribunaux,* 24 Avril 1998, 286–89.

[146] See Olivier Dubois, 'Implementation of International Humanitarian Law: Biannual Update of National Legislation and Jurisprudence—January to June 1998', 325 (1998), *International Review of the Red Cross* 732.

hand, the instigation of criminal proceedings in Belgium against Ariel Sharon, a foreign head of state, for his lack of intervention as the then Israeli Defence Minister in the massacre of Palestinians in the Sabra and Shatila refugee camps in Beirut while, on the other hand, acquitting Belgian peacekeepers for serious violations of human rights on narrow technical legal grounds. At first sight this incongruence smacks of blatant partiality in the Belgian legal system. However, the evidence does suggest that the problem of lack of accountability for the Belgian peacekeepers in Somalia had more to do with prosecutorial selection of charges than with any national attempt to avoid convictions.

In a third Belgian case involving the actions of a peacekeeper in Somalia, the Military Court convicted Sgt Dirk Nassel of several offences involving serious mistreatment of Somali youths. Sgt Nassel forcibly fed a Somali child with pork and salted water until the child vomited; tied a Somali child to a military vehicle and ordered the vehicle to move off; and procured and offered a Somali girl as a 'present' at the birthday party of a paratrooper under Sgt Nassel's command. The Somali girl was subsequently subjected to sexual abuse.[147] It is significant that the charges against Sgt Nassel were not in relation to violations of international humanitarian law but to human rights violations. This choice of charges ensured that the Military Court did not repeat its judgment resulting in the acquittal of Kurt Coelus and Claude Baert. According to the International Committee of the Red Cross, the Belgian Military Court made no reference to the question of the applicability or otherwise of international humanitarian law to the acts of Sgt Nassel.[148]

Italian Contingent

In June 1997, the Italian weekly magazine *Panorama* carried photographs of Italian peacekeepers in Somalia allegedly torturing young Somali detainees with electrodes attached to their naked bodies and by stubbing out cigarettes on the bodies of Somali prisoners who had been hooded and tied up.[149] The alleged incidents had occurred four years before the publication of the photographs and yet no disciplinary measures had apparently been implemented.

The release of the photographs shocked the nation and the Italian Government responded by establishing a Commission of Inquiry on the Italian Mission to Somalia to investigate the allegations against the Italian contingent and to report on the management of the Italian involvement in the Somalia Operation.[150] The Inquiry Commission tabled two reports—the first in August 1997 on 'Events Which Occurred in Somalia'[151] and the second in June 1999 on

[147] See Amnesty International's 1999 Annual Report for Belgium, available at: http://www.amnesty.org/ailib/aireport/ar99/eur14.htm

[148] See Olivier Dubois, above n 146, at 732.

[149] See Report of the Special Rapporteur on Somalia, above n 140, at 23–24.

[150] Natalia Lupi, Report by the Enquiry Commission on the behaviour of Italian Peace-Keeping Troops in Somalia', *Yearbook of International Humanitarian Law,* 1 (1998), 377.

[151] *Ibid,* 377–79.

the 'Investigation of Behaviour of the Italian Military Contingent in Somalia in the Context of the UN Mission "Restore Hope"'.[152] The Inquiry was not tasked to determine individual responsibility for the particular practices exposed by the *Panorama* photographs. That responsibility fell to the Commission of the Army General Staff for Discipline which has been conducting trials to determine criminal responsibility.[153] The Inquiry Commission did, however, confirm at least three incidents of torture and rape. Although the Commission indicated its view that these acts were 'absolutely individual' in nature, the members of the Commission did make recommendations to strengthen the system of military discipline and justice in the Italian Armed Forces which the Somalia deployment had exposed.[154]

CONCLUSION

The circumstances leading to domestic trials of own nationals are not always as neatly compartmentalised as the foregoing analysis might suggest. The German national trials post-World War II, for example, were preceded by Nuremberg as well as by literally dozens of 'subsidiary trials' conducted either pursuant to Control Council Law No.10 or to national legislation of one or other of the victorious Allied states. It could be argued, consequently, that the German national experience was very much influenced by the preceding international jurisprudence—the quintessential case study for the second category of trials analysed in this chapter rather than for the first. Another example of the blurring of the categories of circumstances conducive to domestic trials of own nationals are the Istanbul trials post-World War I. We have already seen that the trials were used by the ruling regime to distance itself from the wartime reign of the Ittihadists—akin to the circumstances of those states in political transition analysed at the beginning of the chapter—more than that the trials were influenced by the threat of the creation of an international tribunal by the victorious Allied nations.

A dogmatic insistence on strict compartmentalisation is hardly necessary. The critical distinction in terms of the likelihood of domestic trials of own nationals is undoubtedly the 'us' and 'them' distinction. States will always find it easier to try their own nationals in situations where the particular defendants are readily identifiable as belonging to an 'other' or a 'them'. Sometimes that 'other' will be the former members of a military or political regime responsible for perpetrating atrocities against the civilian population—the population responsible for democratically electing the new political elite which now represents the 'us'. The Greek, Argentinean, Ethiopian, Guatemalan, Haitian and

[152] See Fabio Raspadori, 'Correspondents' Reports: Italy', 2 *Yearbook of International Humanitarian Law* (1999), 385.

[153] *Ibid.*

[154] See Natalia Lupi, above n 150 at 378–79 and Fabio Raspadori, above n 152, at 385.

post-World War II German trials all affirm this phenomenon to varying degrees. Those variations, often expressed in the number of prosecutions, are regularly determined by the extent, if any, of the former regime's ongoing relevance and political influence. Sometimes the 'other' is an ethnic minority as was the case in the early national trials in Croatia, Serbia and the Republika Srpska. In the Former Yugoslavia, one state's ethnic 'other' is another state's ethnic 'us' and that is precisely the reason for much of the violence just as it explains why some national trials were possible. In the Israeli trials of members of the *Judenrat* or of Jewish *kapos*, as well as the Austrian (and other European states') trials post-World War II, the 'other' were traitors who sided with an occupying, enemy Power and were complicit in the perpetration of atrocities against their own fellow citizens.

Trials of those fellow nationals who are representative of the predominant 'us' will always be more difficult to prosecute. The popular reaction to the trial of William Calley and the concomitant vilification of Hugh Thompson pose a sobering challenge. According to prevailing public sentiment, Calley was, after all, only killing 'gooks' and Thompson ordered his gunner to train his weapon on American soldiers in order to protect the very creatures who wanted Americans dead—the wrong guy is on trial here! It is fallacious to single out the US and to suggest that this sort of sentiment is exclusively a US problem. The French nation found the trial of Klaus Barbie relatively easy—he was an 'other'—a German Nazi. But the trials of Maurice Papon and Paul Touvier were divisive and threatening because, to some extent at least, Vichy France itself was on trial. The trials proceeded despite the heartache—the Vichy regime had sided with the enemy occupier and most of the 'us' had resisted the occupation. However, some have queried: why was Papon not tried for the murder of Algerians by Paris Police? Between 1942 and 1944 Papon was a 'junior official in an occupied country. But in 1961 he was the most senior police official in the capital city' at the height of the French campaign in Algeria when Paris Police killed a large number of Algerian demonstrators who had defied a French Government curfew.[155] The answer surely has much to do with French perceptions of the 'us'. Former General Paul Aussaresses has recently published his autobiographical account of French involvement in the Algerian War and has, unashamedly, told of systematic torture and extra-judicial killings of Algerian prisoners—policies, he claims, which were implemented with the highest military and political level of approval.[156] He has been charged as an apologist for war crimes and his claims have evoked intense and divisive reactions in France. At least Calley was tried and convicted by the military courts-martial process. France is yet to come to terms with alleged atrocities by French military personnel in Algeria. These US and French examples are symptomatic of what other

[155] Richard Vinen, 'Papon in Perspective: Implications of Maurice Papon's Trial for Crimes Against Humanity', (1998), 48 *History Today* 10.

[156] See 'Le TGI de Paris examinera les plaites deposes pour "apologie de crimes de guerre" après la parution de son livre sur la torture en Algérie', *le nouvel Observateur*, 5 Aug 2001.

nations are also guilty of—an aversion to accept the ugliness of what their own troops have done against the enemy they have come to dehumanise.

This aversion, common to each of our own states if we are honest with ourselves, is a compelling argument for the establishment of an international criminal law regime. The efforts to internationalise the prosecution of crimes which might otherwise go unpunished—in East Timor, in Kosovo, in Sierra Leone and even in Cambodia—have facilitated a focus on the need for international pressure to help overcome some of the naturally occurring reticence to hold a state's own nationals to account. Not that merely proposing the establishment of a new ad hoc international criminal tribunal (or even a hybrid international/domestic tribunal) will automatically guarantee the prosecution of crimes. The Cambodian national experience is an excellent illustration of the fact that internationalisation does not automatically alter domestic political will.[157]

There is a tendency amongst those fixated with international criminal institution-building to overlook the role of domestic trials of a state's own nationals. International trials, as well as domestic trials of foreign nationals utilising universal jurisdiction, are essential to ensure that impunity for international atrocity does not enjoy its protracted dominance. Domestic trials of own nationals will always be essential complements to international developments—in substantial part because of the overwhelming numbers of those who should be tried and are simply too numerous for international institutions to cope with. But there are other, more substantial, arguments for domestic trials of own nationals. The Balkan experience is helpful here. Until recently, different histories of the conflict have been affirmed in the trial of the 'other' ethnic communities—the ones who are 'really responsible' for the worst atrocities of the conflict. Domestic trials of a state's own nationals—or in the Balkan experience, of a state's own ethnic majority—help redress the view that the 'us' can never do as much wrong as the 'them'. As states contemplate domestic penal legislation prior to participation in the ICC Statute, the international community may yet see an increased willingness on the part of states to try their own nationals in preference to transfer of custody, and jurisdictional competence, to The Hague.[158] That could prove to be one of the most significant outcomes of the entire ICC initiative and a prospect that certainly warrants greater attention than it currently receives.

[157] See the chapter in this volume by Diane Orentlicher.

[158] On the possibility of the complementarity formula in the ICC Statute having this catalytic effect for increased domestic trials of own nationals in the future, see Katherine L Doherty and Timothy L H McCormack, 'Complementarity as a Catalyst for Domestic Penal Legislation', (1999), 5 *University of California Davis Journal of International Law and Policy* 147.

PART II

Justice in International and Mixed Law Courts

5

The International Criminal Tribunals for the Former Yugoslavia and Rwanda

GRAHAM T BLEWITT

Following the work of the Nuremberg and Tokyo Tribunals, very little was accomplished in terms of creating a permanent international criminal court to prosecute persons who were guilty of serious violations of international humanitarian law.[1] There were, however, several countries involved, some rather belatedly, in pursuing domestic war crimes prosecutions. Germany certainly had undertaken thousands of investigations and prosecutions following the work of the Nuremberg Tribunal, and during the 1980s and 1990s, other countries like the United States of America, Australia, Canada, England and Scotland also conducted war crimes investigations involving Nazi collaborators (who migrated to those respective countries following World War II).[2] These domestic prosecutions had mixed success in terms of convictions, but nevertheless they sent a clear and unambiguous message to war criminals: it does not matter whether they flee to the other side of the world to seek refuge, and even if it is 50 years since the commission of the crimes, if the evidence still exists, it is still possible to bring them to justice.

Apart from these domestic initiatives in pursuing war criminals, the first most important development, following the legacy of the Nuremberg and Tokyo Tribunals, was the creation of the United Nations International Criminal Tribunal for the former Yugoslavia (ICTY) in 1993 and the International Criminal Tribunal for Rwanda (ICTR) in 1994. The creation of the ICTY in May 1993 took most of the world by surprise, particularly in light of the painfully slow progress then being experienced in setting up a permanent international criminal court. Not many anticipated that the UN Security Council would create a judicial sub-organ under Chapter VII of the UN Charter, as a means of maintaining international peace and security. This remarkable, drastic and unprecedented step was taken only after it was realised by the international community that another Holocaust, with widespread ethnic cleansing in the

[1] See ch 1.
[2] See ch 4.

form of genocide and crimes against humanity, was actually occurring in Europe, within living memory of Nazi attempts to wipe all trace of the European Jews from the face of the earth.

One very important feature of the Security Council's actions in creating the ICTY and ICTR under Chapter VII of the UN Charter, is that all Member States of the UN are legally obliged to co-operate with the Tribunals and to comply with their orders and warrants. Thus, if an ICTY warrant of arrest is directed to a State, that State has the obligation to apprehend and surrender the fugitive to The Hague, and failure to do so could result in a report being submitted to the Security Council by the ICTY, which could in turn lead to the imposition of sanctions against the non-conforming State.

The Chapter VII mandate gives the ICTY a clearly defined function in contributing to the restoration and maintenance of peace and security in the Balkans. In other words, the ICTY is essentially an instrument of peace: the criminal prosecution of persons responsible for serious violations of international humanitarian law is regarded as being central to the peace process in the former Yugoslavia. The same is true of the ICTR in Rwanda.

ESTABLISHMENT OF THE INTERNATIONAL CRIMINAL TRIBUNAL FOR THE FORMER YUGOSLAVIA

The ICTY, which is a sub-organ of the Security Council, has undergone some structural change over the years. When it was first established in 1993, it consisted of three separate and independent organs, namely a Chambers of 11 judges, the Registrar's Office, and the Office of the Prosecutor. The judges, who are elected by the General Assembly of the United Nations, formed two Trial Chambers, each with three judges, and an Appeals Chamber of five judges. Each Trial Chamber presides over trials of indicted accused and there are no juries to determine the guilt or innocence of the accused. This task falls to the three trial judges. The judges elect a President, who holds term for a period of two years, and the President can be re-elected for one term. The Prosecutor, who is appointed by the UN Security Council, on the Secretary-General's nomination, undertakes investigations and prosecutions. The Registry is headed by the Registrar, who is appointed by the UN Secretary-General, after consultation with the President of the Tribunal. The Registrar is responsible for the administration of the Tribunal and for providing support to the other two organs of the Tribunal. The first structural change occurred in May 1998, when the Security Council amended the Tribunal's Statute to provide an additional Trial Chamber of three judges to meet the demands being created by a backlog of trials. On 30 November 2000 the Security Council made a further structural change to the ICTY, by creating a pool of nine *ad litum*, or part time, judges, again with a view of moving the increasing backlog of trials.

The ICTY was somewhat slow in gaining momentum at the beginning, following its creation in May 1993. The 11 judges were appointed in November 1993, the Deputy Prosecutor was appointed in February 1994, the first investigators started to arrive in June 1994, and the first Prosecutor was only appointed in August 1994. Notwithstanding this slow start, the first indictment was issued and confirmed in November 1994. Since that time, the ICTY has grown steadily, and it is now a fully functioning judicial institution, conducting trials and hearing resulting appeals in a manner which meets international standards and approval.

JURISDICTION OF THE ICTY

The ICTY was established by United Nations Security Council Resolution 827, in May 1993. It has the power and the mandate to both investigate and prosecute individuals responsible for the commission of serious violations of international humanitarian law, namely grave breaches of the 1949 Geneva Conventions,[3] violations of the laws or customs of war,[4] genocide,[5] and crimes

[3] Art 2 of the Tribunal's Statute provides:
The International Tribunal shall have the power to prosecute persons committing or ordering to be committed grave breaches of the Geneva Conventions of 12 August 1949, namely the following acts against persons or property under the provisions of the relevant Geneva Convention:
a wilful killing;
b torture or inhuman treatment, including biological experiments;
c wilfully causing great suffering or serious injury to body or health;
d extensive destruction and appropriation of property, not justified by military necessity and carried out unlawfully and wantonly;
e compelling a prisoner of war or a civilian to serve in the forces of a hostile power;
f wilfully depriving a prisoner of war or a civilian of the rights of fair and regular trial;
g unlawful deportation or transfer or unlawful confinement of a civilian;
h taking civilians as hostages.

[4] Art 3 of the Statute provides:
The International Tribunal shall have the power to prosecute persons violating the laws or customs of war. Such violations shall include, but not be limited to:
a employment of poisonous weapons or other weapons calculated to cause unnecessary suffering;
b wanton destruction of cities, towns or villages, or devastation not justified by military necessity;
c attack, or bombardment, by whatever means, of undefended towns, villages, dwellings, or buildings;
d seizure of, destruction or wilful damage done to institutions dedicated to religion, charity and education, the arts and sciences, historic monuments and works of art and science;
e plunder of public or private property.

[5] Art 4 of the Statute provides:
1 The International Tribunal shall have the power to prosecute persons committing genocide as defined in paragraph 2 of this article or of committing any of the other acts enumerated in paragraph 3 of this article.
2 Genocide means any of the following acts committed with intent to destroy, in whole or in part, a national, ethnical, racial or religious group, as such:
a killing members of the group;
b causing serious bodily or mental harm to members of the group;
c deliberately inflicting on the group conditions of life calculated to bring about its physical destruction in whole or in part;
d imposing measures intended to prevent births within the group;
e forcibly transferring children of the group to another group.

against humanity,[6] committed on the territory of the former Yugoslavia since 1991. That temporal jurisdiction continues to this day, and hence if there were any further outbreak of war in the future, the ICTY would have the authority to investigate and prosecute any war crimes committed in such a conflict. In this way, following the cessation of hostilities throughout the former Yugoslavia in 1995, the ICTY was nevertheless able to investigate the crimes being committed in Kosovo in 1998 and 1999, which in turn led the an indictment being issued, in May 1999, against President Slobodan Milošević, the first time that a sitting head of state had been indicted by an international criminal tribunal.

Further, there have been allegations received by the Prosecutor in late 1999 and during 2000, that after the withdrawal of Serb military and police forces from Kosovo in June 1999, and following the deployment of the NATO-led peace-keeping force, KFOR, into Kosovo, some militant Kosovo Albanians were undertaking a campaign of violence against the remaining Serb civilian population, with the intention of driving them from Kosovo, thus committing what is now known as ethnic cleansing.

The ICTY's Statute, however, limits the Tribunal's jurisdiction to offences committed *during an armed conflict,* for all offences except genocide. Generally speaking, all violations of the laws or customs of war and grave breaches of the 1949 Geneva Conventions are offences which can only be committed during an armed conflict. Under general international law, however, it is possible for crimes against humanity to be committed at any time. Under Article 5 of the ICTY Statute, the Tribunal is limited to only prosecuting crimes against humanity which occur during an armed conflict. To overcome this situation, the ICTY Prosecutor has requested the Security Council to amend Article 5, to remove this limitation, so the ICTY may prosecute crimes against humanity occurring after the cessation of hostilities in Kosovo in June 1999.

An interesting development occurred in 1999 during the NATO air campaign in Yugoslavia. Since the ICTY has jurisdiction over serious violations of

3 The following acts shall be punishable:

a genocide;
b conspiracy to commit genocide;
c direct and public incitement to commit genocide;
d attempt to commit genocide
e complicity in genocide.

[6] Art 5 of the Statute provides:

The International Tribunal shall have the power to prosecute persons responsible for the following crimes when committed in armed conflict, whether international or internal in character, and directed against any civilian population:

a murder;
b extermination;
c enslavement;
d deportation;
e imprisonment;
f torture;
g rape;
h persecutions on political, racial and religious grounds;
i other inhumane acts.

international humanitarian law committed on the territory of the former Yugoslavia since 1991, it has jurisdiction over any such violations committed by any party involved in an armed conflict in the former Yugoslavia, and of course this includes members of NATO forces during the 1999 bombing campaign throughout Yugoslavia, as NATO was involved in an international armed conflict when it launched the air campaign. It is important to note, however, that the ICTY has jurisdiction over crimes committed by individuals, not over NATO itself or its member states. Also, it does not have jurisdiction over crimes against peace, such as waging aggressive war, and the question of the legality of the use of force by the NATO members is beyond the Tribunal's competence.

Following receipt of allegations concerning the NATO air campaign, the ICTY Prosecutor reviewed all available material and evidence to determine whether there was any justification to conduct an investigation related to incidents occurring during the bombing campaign. In a report released on 8 June 2000, the Prosecutor decided against commencing such an investigation because it did not appear that it would result in indictments against any high level person or for that matter against low level persons who had committed particularly heinous acts. The Prosecutor indicated she would not commence an investigation on the basis of information available. It is interesting to note that the USA has consistently indicated its opposition to the new International Criminal Court, in part, because of fear that the ICC Prosecutor would act as a loose cannon. One might hope that the responsible and balanced approach of the ICTY Prosecutor to allegations arising from NATO bombing will allay any such fears.

Like the Nuremberg tribunal the ICTY is concentrating on the leaders, that is, those who were responsible for the planning and implementation of genocide, ethnic cleansing and other atrocities. The Prosecutor's office commenced its investigations on a broad basis, with a view to being able to establish what happened on the ground throughout the entire territory—to prove a systematic attack against the civilian population and to prove that it was not just an outbreak of general violence, which had no direction or purpose. The Prosecutor's office has to establish what was happening throughout the country, so as to be able to prove the cases against the leaders.

In relation to such leaders, Article 7 of the ICTY Statute addresses the question of the basis of individual criminal responsibility. Civilian or military leaders may be held responsible for planning, instigating, ordering, committing or aiding and abetting in the commission of offences under Article 7(1). They may also be held responsible for failure to act to control their subordinates, or to punish them when they are guilty of war crimes, under the doctrine of command responsibility, which is incorporated into the Statute through Article 7(3). It is also essential to note that the ICTY and ICTR are prosecuting the individuals who were responsible for the atrocities; nations or ethnic groups are not being investigated or prosecuted. In that way that all notions of collective guilt can be put aside, and this is very important for achieving a lasting peace based on justice.

RELATIONSHIP BETWEEN INTERNATIONAL LAW AND NATIONAL LAW

The ICTY enjoys jurisdictional primacy vis-à-vis national criminal justice systems. Not only can the Tribunal take over cases from domestic courts at any stage of the procedure,[7] but the Statute even makes exceptions to the *non bis in idem* principle, allowing the ICTY to take over cases *after* the suspect has been tried if, for example, the domestic proceedings were not impartial or independent.[8] This jurisdictional pre-eminence has been reversed in the Statute of the International Criminal Court (ICC), where the admissibility test for the Court is based on a principle of complementarity, whereby the Prosecutor must show either unwillingness or inability on the part of a State that has jurisdiction over a case to genuinely investigate and prosecute it. This places an unusual burden on the Prosecution, but it should at the same time provide comfort to any State that might fear the reach of the ICC, as long as it operates in good faith with regard to its international obligations to investigate and prosecute the international crimes which fall within the ICC's subject-matter jurisdiction.

The primacy of the ICTY is balanced by the equally important principle that the Tribunal and national courts have concurrent jurisdiction.[9] As a matter of fact, the ICTY has encouraged States to investigate and prosecute crimes committed in the former Yugoslavia from the very beginning of its existence. This is essential, if impunity is not to be extended to the majority of perpetrators, insofar as an international Tribunal can necessarily only prosecute those most responsible for serious violations. The Office of the Prosecutor of the ICTY has co-operated closely with domestic criminal justice systems involved in the prosecution of war criminals from the former Yugoslavia. In the case of territorial States directly affected by large scale atrocities, it is particularly important to observe the ability and willingness of the domestic criminal justice system engaged in such prosecution to do so independently, impartially and with appropriate diligence.

As mentioned above, the ICTYs jurisdiction to prosecute war crimes perpetrators is concurrent with that of national courts, although the Tribunal is able to exercise primacy in any case it chooses. It is also imperative that national courts play a role in bringing perpetrators to justice, because it will never be possible for the ICTY to deal with all cases. The ICTY plays an important role in domestic war crimes prosecutions in Bosnia and Herzegovina, by giving the Prosecutor of the ICTY a guiding hand in such prosecutions.

This came about as a consequence of an incident in Sarajevo in January 1996, almost immediately after the signing of the Dayton Peace Accords at the end of 1995. The incident involved the apprehension by the Bosniaks of General Djukić, a member of the Bosnian Serb army, on war crimes charges. The ICTY

[7] Art 9(2) of the ICTY Statute.
[8] Art 10(2) of the ICTY Statute.
[9] Art 9(1) of the ICTY Statute.

exercised its primacy in this case and General Djukić was surrendered to the Tribunal, but the circumstances surrounding the arrest put the Dayton Peace Accords at serious risk. As a consequence of this incident, which was seen as a real impediment to freedom of movement throughout Bosnia and Herzegovina, one of the corner stones of the Dayton Agreement, a conference was held in Rome in February 1996, at which the parties of the former Yugoslavia agreed to a scheme, subsequently called the Rules of the Road programme. The scheme envisaged that no person would be arrested in Bosnia and Herzegovina for war crime charges, unless the Prosecutor of ICTY first agreed, in writing, that there were sufficient grounds, by international legal standards, to justify a domestic prosecution. The scheme also envisaged that any of the parties to the conflict in Bosnia and Herzegovina could submit investigation files and other papers to the ICTY, and that once examined, the Prosecutor of the ICTY would return the file to the party submitting the file, with a written opinion that there was either sufficient or insufficient evidence to support a local prosecution. This scheme has been operating since 1996 and the ICTY has examined hundreds of cases and notified the submitting party of the result of the examination. Thereafter many local prosecutions have been launched, with the parties having some confidence in the proceedings by reason of the ICTY Prosecutor's involvement in the process. Apart from examining the file, the ICTY takes no other part in the domestic proceedings, either by monitoring those proceedings or in any way acting as a court of appeal. It is expected that the Rules of the Road scheme will continue for the foreseeable future.

Ideas have surfaced from time to time, suggesting that a truth and reconciliation process is required for Bosnia and Herzegovina, for the Federal Republic of Yugoslavia, or for the entire territory of the former Yugoslavia. The ICTY has recognised the interests underlying such proposals, and has not excluded that in time, it may be advisable to institute such a process. It is clear, however, that we have not reached this point in time yet. The simplified dichotomy between *reconciliation and justice* serves academic discourse more than it accurately describes reality. The ICTY was established, in part, as a measure for the maintenance of international peace and security, through its ability to contribute to reconciliation in the territorial States torn by violence and disunity.

Reconciliation through criminal justice is characterised by a certain slowness and tediousness on the one hand, but on the other the strict procedures followed for the determination of the truth, combined with the sacrosanct principles of judicial independence and impartiality, permeate the factual findings produced by the criminal justice process with a particular authority. It is important that the elaborate factual discussions and findings in ICTY judgements be properly received in the republics of the former Yugoslavia, so that their reconciliatory potential is appropriately made use of in those war-torn societies, especially for the benefit of their emerging generations of citizens.

It should be noted that there is also an important distinction to be drawn between normal extradition procedures and the surrender and transfer of persons to the custody of the Tribunal. The process is not one of extradition, which is traditionally dependant on the existence of an extradition treaty between the states concerned, which amounts to an agreed and specialised set of rules to regulate and protect the handing over of fugitives between sovereign states. Rather, where the ICTY is concerned, it is the case that all member states of the UN are obliged to take all necessary steps, which may involve making special provisions in their domestic laws or constitutions, to comply with any binding obligation to execute the Tribunal's orders, to arrest and surrender indicted accused. [10]

It is sometimes said that the Tribunal's existence is a threat to the peace process. This was said during the Dayton peace negotiations at the end of 1995, and again during the NATO air campaign in Kosovo in the early part of 1999. This issue has also been raised following many arrests under sealed indictments, when it was said that the very existence of sealed indictments was threatening the peace process in Bosnia. Criminal justice, however, is not a pleasant process in any system, and criminals often seek to resist criminal law sanctions. Clearly the ICTY is affecting the situation on the ground in the former Yugoslavia, but if there is ever to be a long term and lasting peace in the Balkans, it is clear that the war criminals must be brought to justice, particularly those who were most responsible for the atrocities. The international community cannot afford to allow shortsighted arguments interfere with what is proving to be an important development in international affairs, namely, the creation an effective system of international criminal law enforcement.

EARLY JURISPRUDENCE OF THE ICTY

Rule 61 Proceedings

One unique feature concerning the early work of the ICTY relates to proceedings that occurred when accused persons were not surrendered to the Tribunal, following the issue of warrants of arrest. These were proceedings under Rule 61 of the Tribunal's Rules of Procedure and Evidence. When the judges of the Tribunal were framing the Tribunal's Rules in the early days of the ICTY, there was no certainty that the States of the former Yugoslavia would co-operate by handing over indicted accused, and consequently the judges devised a process which was aimed at alleviating this problem—but which fell short of having a trial *in absentia*, which is not permitted under the Tribunal's Statute.

The rule 61 procedure envisaged holding a public hearing or proceeding, at which the Prosecutor would call the evidence which was being relied upon in support of the indictment. This proceeding took place in the absence of the

[10] Rule 58 of the ICTY's Rules of Procedure and Evidence provides: 'The obligations laid down in Article 29 of the Statute shall prevail over any legal impediment to the surrender or transfer of the accused or of a witness to the Tribunal which may exist under the national law or extradition treaties of the State concerned.'

accused in a public hearing. By calling the evidence in public, the world could determine whether the indictment was justified and whether the evidence was sufficient for the accused to be placed on trial. If the Trial Chamber was satisfied that the evidence was sufficient to support the indictment, it issued an international arrest warrant at the conclusion of the hearing, thus making an international pariah of the accused. The President could also report to the United Nations Security Council the fact that a particular State had failed to surrender the accused to the Tribunal, leaving it to the Security Council to take appropriate action. There were in fact several rule 61 hearings but when arrests started to occur in numbers in 1997, the need for rule 61 hearings disappeared, and there has been no such hearing since that time.

Rules of Procedure and Evidence

The Rules of Procedure and Evidence of the ICTY were drafted by the judges pursuant to the Statute of the Tribunal. The ICTY Rules have been amended more than twenty times since 1994, which has ensured that the Rules have adapted to changing practical needs. At the same time, this has created an ever-changing procedural infrastructure, to which the parties have had to adapt. The practice of judicial amendments of Tribunal Rules has been criticised by some states during the ICC process, but such criticism ignores the fact that international law has to remain flexible and change with the times. One must hope that the very detailed draft Rules of Procedure and Evidence prepared by the Preparatory Commission for the ICC will serve interests of justice at least as well as the Tribunal Rules have.

Information to Assist the Prosecutor in Investigations

Early in the ICTYs existence, during 1994 and 1995, it was apparent that the discovery obligations imposed on the Prosecutor under the Tribunal's Rules of Procedure and Evidence, that is to disclose certain information and evidence to an accused person, to help in the preparation and conduct of the defence case, created problems for the Prosecutor in developing investigations. Many nations had information which could be provided to the Prosecutor, but because of the confidential nature of the information, or more often because either the source of the information or the manner in which it was collected had to be kept confidential, those nations were unwilling to provide the information if it meant that it may have to be disclosed to the accused. To overcome this problem, the Tribunal's Rules (rule 70(B)) were amended to protect the Prosecutor, and providers of confidential information, so that the Prosecutor's obligations to disclose information to the defence did not apply to information or material provided under that Rule, if the provider did not consent to the information being used in evidence.

In 1997, the Appeals Chamber issued a judgment in the *Blaškić* case in which it indicated the Tribunal had the authority to issue binding orders and requests to States and that States were not entitled to withhold requested documents or other evidentiary material by simply asserting a need to protect their national security.

High Profile Indictments and Convictions

It is important to consider the thoroughness with which all ICTY indictments are prepared and confirmed, not only those against persons who held senior positions. There is internal scrutiny at several levels within the Office of the Prosecutor, pursuant to standard operating procedures, including indictment reviews during which the investigation team faces a panel of lawyers and analysts who may challenge any aspect of its draft indictment. When the Prosecutor and Deputy Prosecutor are satisfied that a prima facie case exists, the indictment will be transmitted for review to a judge.[11] The judge may only confirm the indictment if he or she, upon considering the text of the indictment and any supporting material, determines that a prima facie case has been established by the Prosecutor.[12] Upon confirmation of the indictment, the judge may issue warrants for the arrest, detention, surrender or transfer of persons.[13] States are obliged under Article 29 of the Statute to comply without undue delay with arrest warrants transmitted to them and to surrender the accused person to the Tribunal.

For some time, in the early stages of the life of the ICTY, when public indictments were being issued, there was a reluctance on the part of the international security forces and civilian presences in the former Yugoslavia to undertake arrests or detentions of persons indicted by the Tribunal. This reluctance put the credibility of the Tribunal to the test during 1996 and the first half of 1997. The Prosecutor of the Tribunal made systematic efforts to explain to States the importance of respecting the international legal obligations generated under the Statute of the Tribunal. Commencing in July 1997, gradually the international military presence in Bosnia and Herzegovina has fulfilled its mandate to apprehend indicted persons if encountered in course of duty. However, a number of accused persons continue to enjoy impunity, including some of the leaders who were behind the atrocities which occurred in the former Yugoslavia, because they remain fugitives in situations where they could and should be apprehended and surrendered to the ICTY.

Sealed Indictments

At the time of writing the practice in the case of the ICTY, however, is no longer to issue public indictments, nor to seek international arrest warrants through

[11] Art 18(4).
[12] Art 19(1).
[13] Art 19(2).

rule 61 hearings. It was becoming obvious in most instances, in particular in the case of the Bosnian Serbs and the Federal Republic of Yugoslavia, that the issuing of public indictments was futile, as Tribunal's warrants of arrest were being ignored. In some instances this situation continues to this day.

It became clear that other solutions were necessary. This led to the practice, which involves the non-public disclosure of the existence of indictments and warrants of arrest. When an indictment is confirmed by a judge of the Tribunal, the Prosecutor seeks an order that the indictment be kept confidential. This provides the Prosecutor with the opportunity to seek other means to secure the arrest of the indicted accused. In most instances, in the case of Bosnia and Herzegovina, this involves serving a copy of the warrant on SFOR, which under its own mandate has the power and authority to detain indicted war criminals and to transfer them to the Tribunal. This has proved to be a most successful weapon and has the added benefit of encouraging some indicted accused to surrender themselves voluntarily to the Tribunal. Given the success of the practice of issuing what has been termed 'sealed indictments', it is the Prosecutor's intention to maintain this initiative in appropriate circumstances.

EVALUATION OF THE TRIBUNALS' RECORD TO DATE

Some of the jurisprudence that has emerged from the tribunals is very significant insofar as it has clarified the exact scope of the protection regimes of international humanitarian law. Take for example, the three landmark decisions on sexual violence which were handed down in 1998, in the *Akayesu* (ICTR),[14] *Delalić et al* (ICTY)[15] and *Furundžija* (ICTY)[16] cases. Collectively, these judgments concluded that rape and other forms of sexual violence constitute acts of genocide, crimes against humanity, violations of the laws or customs of war, or grave breaches of the 1949 Geneva Conventions. The accused were convicted of sexual violence in all three cases. The judgments also interpreted the scope of sex crimes under the Statutes of the ICTY and ICTR and substantively advanced the jurisprudence of sexual violence under international law.[17]

The ICTY has achieved remarkable results, although it is far from perfect. It took some time to get started; yet despite its imperfections and at times insurmountable difficulties, it has demonstrated that it is possible to create, at the international level, a fully-functioning criminal justice system, and it has proved that international tribunals are capable of conducting and completing investigations, having indictments confirmed, effecting arrests of indicted accused, holding fair trials and dispensing a satisfactory standard of justice which is open to public scrutiny.

[14] *Prosecutor v Akayesu*, judgjment and Opinion, case No ICTR-96-4-T, 2 Sept 1998.
[15] *Prosecutor v Zejnil Delalić et al*, judgment, case No IT-96-21-T, 16 Nov 1998.
[16] *Prosecutor v Anto Furundžija*, judgment, case No IT-95-17/I-T, 10 Dec 1998.
[17] See Patricia Viseur-Sellers, 'The Culture Value of Sexual Violence', *ASIL Proceedings* (1999), 1.

KEY CHALLENGES FOR THE FUTURE

Arrest of All High Level Fugitives

One of the main challenges facing the ICTY is the arrest of all remaining fugitives. The fact that fugitives like Radovan Karadzić and Ratko Mladić remain at large constitutes a major obstacle to maintaining a lasting peace in the former Yugoslavia. There have been opportunities to apprehend these individuals, but those opportunities have been lost. There is still no satisfactory explanation as to why these fugitives have been allowed to remain at large and to influence the political landscape long after they were indicted.

The Right to a Trial Without Undue Delay

One of the main problems currently confronting the ICTY is the number of detainees in custody awaiting trial. The Statute of the Tribunal guarantees all accused persons the right to a fair trial without delay. There are several factors contributing to the delays, and a very important one is the fact that not all States of the former Yugoslavia are co-operating with the Tribunal. For instance, many accused are indicted as co-accused in one indictment, but because the accused are not surrendered at the same time, it means that it is not possible to conduct a single trial of all accused. In one indictment containing six accused, the accused were surrendered at different times, which meant that the Tribunal was forced to have three separate trials relating to the one indictment, and two of these trials were very lengthy.[18]

In most national jurisdictions, when there are many accused in custody awaiting trial, there are normally two ways to relieve the problem, namely, either releasing the accused on bail, or appointing more judges to move the back log of cases. With the ICTY, most accused are not good candidates for provisional release on bail, particularly if the State from which the accused comes is not co-operating with the Tribunal or if SFOR was required to apprehend the accused in the first place.

To overcome the problem being created by accused spending lengthy periods in pre-trial custody, the ICTY is adopting procedures to shorten trials, and in addition the Security Council has appointed more judges to enable the Tribunal to conduct more trials.

Possible Transfer of Remaining Trial Cases to ICC

Another challenge for the future, which the Security Council may have to address at some stage, concerns the longer-term implications of a likely co-existence between the ICTY and the ICC. The question, which will beg attention, is

[18] The three trials involved Blaškić, Aleksovski and Kordić.

whether the ICC, as a permanent jurisdiction, should be authorised to absorb some of the functions of the ICTY and ICTR under their Statutes. Take for example the responsibility of the Tribunals to supervise the serving of sentences of persons they have convicted, some of whom have already been given prison terms of 40 years and longer.[19] This seems to be a function which the Security Council could transfer to another agency, for example the ICC. Given the prolific appeals record in both Tribunals to date, it is quite likely that there will be appellate proceedings beyond the conclusion of the last Tribunal trial. Should these and maybe other appellate and trial proceedings be taken over by the ICC at some stage?

It is essential to retain the fundamental Chapter VII nature of the jurisdiction and powers of the ad hoc Tribunals. The ICC will not possess the same jurisdictional efficacy and powers as the ad hoc Tribunals when it operates in its normal mode.[20] It has been pointed out, however, that the Security Council is unlikely to make use of its ability to refer situations to the ICC under Chapter VII of the UN Charter, unless it can ensure that the powers of the Prosecutor and Chambers and the State co-operation regime are as effective as in the ad hoc Tribunals it has established.[21]

The Council retains its Charter-based power to establish new ad hoc jurisdictions even after the ICC has been established, and may find it necessary to consider doing so if the efficacy of its international judicial intervention would be significantly diluted by referring a situation to the ICC. Likewise, it seems unthinkable that the Security Council would transfer functions of the existing ad hoc Tribunals to the ICC without ensuring that the Chapter VII nature of those functions be fully retained.

THE INTERNATIONAL CRIMINAL TRIBUNAL FOR RWANDA

Having established the principle that a threat to international peace and security could be addressed by the creation of a sub-organ in the form of a criminal tribunal, the Security Council responded to the explosion of violence in the Great Lakes Region of Africa in 1994, in particular the genocide in Rwanda, by creating the International Criminal Tribunal for Rwanda (ICTR). In its resolution 955, adopted on 8 November 1994, the Security Council established a sister Tribunal to the ICTY, with jurisdiction to prosecute persons responsible for genocide and other serious violations of international humanitarian law

[19] See Art 27 *in fine*.

[20] See Louise Arbour and Morten Bergsmo, 'Conspicuous Absence of Jurisdictional Overreach', in HAM von Hebel, JG Lammers and J Schukking (eds), *Reflections on the International Criminal Court: Essays in Honour of Adriaan Bos* (TMC Asser Press, The Hague, 1999), 139–40.

[21] See Morten Bergsmo, 'Occasional remarks on certain State concerns about the jurisdictional reach of the International Criminal Court, and their possible implications for the relationship between the Court and the Security Council' (2000), 69 *Nordic Journal of International Law*, at 110.

committed in the territory of Rwanda and Rwanda citizens responsible for genocide and other such violations committed in the territory of neighbouring states between 1 January 1994 and 31 December 1994.

Whereas the ICTY had been given jurisdiction over crimes that can be committed either during an international armed conflict or in a civil war, the subject matter jurisdiction of the ICTR was designed to cover the situation of internal armed conflict only. Thus, the statute of the ICTR covers genocide, crimes against humanity, and violations of Article 3 common to the Geneva Conventions and of Additional Protocol II (applicable to non-international armed conflict). The two Tribunals therefore deal with very similar areas of international criminal law, and it was considered important that they develop the law in a consistent fashion. For that reason, and partly for reasons of economy, the two Tribunals share a common Appeals Chamber, and by Statute the Prosecutor of the ICTY also serves as Prosecutor for the ICTR. These institutional links are designed to ensure that a consistent approach is taken from the investigation stage of a case, through the legal arguments presented at trial, right up to the final authoritative pronouncement of the law by the judges of the Appeals Chamber.

The seat of the ICTR was established in Arusha, Tanzania, but the Office of the Prosecutor was set-up in the capital of Rwanda itself, Kigali, recognising not only the practical demands of on-site investigations and access to witnesses, but also the need to let the people of Rwanda see at first hand the involvement and relevance of the International Tribunal in the process of reconciliation.

The ICTR enjoyed a greater initial success than the ICTY in terms of the arrest of persons indicted. Perhaps reflecting the fact that many of the senior figures of the former Rwandan regime had been forced to flee the country and seek refuge in other African States, where they were unable to control territory and protect themselves militarily, early arrests of leading accused occurred with regularity. An important factor in this success was the excellent co-operation extended to the Tribunal by the governments and authorities in the countries concerned. The substantial number of accused in custody, and the corresponding need to bring their cases to trial resulted in the expansion of the capacity of the ICTR. In its resolution 1165 (1998) the Security Council increased the number of judges from six to nine, so that three Trial Chambers were available to process the trial workload. By March 2002, 58 detainees had been arrested under the authority of the Tribunal, of whom eight had been convicted, one acquitted, 17 were on trial and a further 32 were awaiting trial. Many of these were former ministers and military commanders. In a further recognition of the need to expand the capacity of the Tribunal, the Security Council, in its resolution 1329 (2000) of 30 November, agreed to increase the number of ICTR judges by two and thereafter to have two ICTR judges serve in the shared Appeals Chamber to deal with its increasing workload.

As trials commenced and were completed, the ICTR created groundbreaking jurisprudence. The historic conviction of Jean-Paul Akayesu, sentenced to life imprisonment in September 1998, was the first judgement of an international court on the 1948 Convention on the Prevention and Punishment of the Crime of Genocide. That case also made important statements about sexual offences. For the first time rape (as now broadly defined in international law by the Chamber) was viewed as constituting an element of genocide, in that sexual violence, systematically directed against Tutsi women, was seen to involve the necessary specific intent to destroy an ethnic group required for the crime of genocide.

Not all accused insisted on going to trial to contest the charges against them. The former Prime Minister of Rwanda, Jean Kambanda, entered a plea of guilty to the indictment and admitted his involvement in the planning and the execution of the genocide in his country. He too was sentenced to life imprisonment, the Chamber describing genocide as 'the crime of crimes'. That sentence was subsequently upheld on appeal.

Other prosecutions before the ICTR have dealt with accused in the categories of Prefects and Bourgmestres, army and police commanders, *interahamwe* (local militia) leaders, prominent politicians and businessmen, journalists and media figures, and even individuals in the fields of medicine and religion. In addition to genocide and sexual crimes, charges have included conspiracy to commit genocide, crimes against humanity, murder, extermination, torture, and other inhumane acts. By the end of the year 2001, a large 'media' trial was exploring the question of incitement of the population by the transmission of radio 'hate broadcasts', and other major trials were underway, including two 'government' trials involving various ministers, and the 'military' trial of senior army commanders.

Although the temporal jurisdiction of the ICTR is limited to the calendar year 1994, and although the situation in Rwanda itself is less tense than in the aftermath of the genocide, the military and political situation in the great Lakes Region and in the Congo is still fraught with difficulty, and the contribution of the International Tribunal to the restoration and maintenance of international peace and security remains critically important. Much still remains to be done in the field of criminal justice, both at the international and local level to bring a lasting end to the cycles of impunity that have ravaged this part of the world for too long.

CONCLUSION

When the ICTY first commenced operations in 1993–1994, the prospect of creating a permanent international criminal court was merely a dream. As the ICTY and ICTR gained momentum, however, the realisation was achieved that it was possible to have criminal justice at the international level, and that in many conflicts in the world which had a component of never ending cycles of violence, the achievement of justice was an important component in achieving a lasting peace. Thus, support for a permanent international criminal court grew at a tremendous pace and the world eventually saw, on 17 July 1998, the Statute for a permanent International Criminal Court being adopted in Rome. In his chapter in this volume, M Cherif Bassiouni describes in detail the creation of the court and outlines its jurisdiction.

In all countries throughout the world, the existence of laws to regulate human behaviour, and to punish wrong doers in the criminal courts, has never wiped out crime or criminal behaviour. The criminal justice system in most countries is a busy jurisdiction and over-crowding in prisons is a common problem. It is nevertheless an accepted fact, that if there were no laws to regulate human behaviour or to punish criminal acts, there would be anarchy in the streets and it would not be safe for anyone to go about their daily lives. The same is true at the international level.

The existence of internationally recognised and accepted criminal sanctions and the creation of an international criminal court will not, unfortunately, prevent the commission of all crime. However, with the creation of a fully functioning international criminal court, there will be a permanent deterrent, at the international level, to prevent or punish the commission of genocide, crimes against humanity and other breaches of international humanitarian law. No longer will political, military or police leaders of countries be able to commit such crimes with impunity. There will be a realistic likelihood that they will be held accountable for their actions in an international criminal court. The developments in the *Pinochet* case, following the House of Lords decisions and the subsequent charging of Pinochet in Chile, are another indicator of the trend towards terminating impunity for alleged major malefactors in the world community.

This important and long awaited permanent deterrence will certainly prevent some (and hopefully most) future atrocities and will moderate the behaviour of those world leaders who would otherwise not hesitate to utilise unlawful means such as the mass murder and torture of their enemies, minorities, or opponents, as a means to achieve their political goals. One important consequence of the creation of the permanent international criminal court is that humanity is coming closer to achieving international peace and security. This is a wonderful legacy to leave to future generations.

6

The Collection and Admissibility of Evidence and the Rights of the Accused

RICHARD MAY*

Courts trying war crimes follow procedures similar to those followed in ordinary criminal trials. However, collecting the evidence, putting it before the court and establishing the truth involves greater challenges. For a start, there may be few survivors to act as witnesses. Next, documents may have been destroyed by the criminals. Finally, the passage of time does not make things easier. This led one of the leading Nuremberg prosecutors to refer to 'the necessity for liberal rules of evidence concerning events transpiring in the Third Reich where the lips of many potential witnesses were sealed by violence and many records have disappeared either by intention or by the fortunes of war'.[1]

On the other hand, sentences for such crimes may be lengthy and the stigma attached to conviction profound. The rights of the accused, therefore, must be protected and the fairness of the trial secured. It is for the court to balance the interests of the prosecution (acting for the international community) and the interests of the accused.

AGE OF THE EVIDENCE

The age of the relevant evidence is a particular problem facing war crimes trials; especially those arising out of the Second World War. For instance in *Sawoniuk*[2] the accused was tried and convicted, in England, under the War Crimes Act 1991, for the murder of two Jewish civilians in Domachevo, Belorussia in 1942. On appeal the defendant argued that his trial was an abuse of the process of the

* The author wishes to thank Marieke Wierda, former Assistant Legal Officer, ICTY, for her considerable assistance in this chapter.

[1] Brigadier-General Telford Taylor, *Trials of War Criminals Before the Nuremberg Military Tribunals Under Control Council Law No 10* (1946-1949), Vol 15, at p 894.

[2] *Sawoniuk* [2000] 2 Cr App R, 230.

court and that the judge erred in not staying the proceedings due to:

1 the passage of over 56 years from the date of the alleged crime to the date of trial;
2 the fact that the sole witness of the crime had made no statement on the subject for over 50 years and that his evidence was unsupported; and
3 the inability of the defence, after the lapse of time, to locate witnesses who may have been present during the incident.

The Court of Appeal held that the judge could have only granted a stay if he had been persuaded that continuance of the proceedings would cause serious prejudice to the defendant by denying him a fair trial; and the judge was correct in not so finding, because:

1 he regarded it as entirely speculative whether the unavailability of other witnesses represented a detriment to the appellant or a bonus; and
2 he was confident that the evidence of the single eyewitness could be properly and rigorously tested within the confines of the trial process.

The Court, therefore, upheld the decision of the trial judge 'despite the unprecedented passage of time since 1942'.

The witness to the execution was a boy of 13 at the time; on appeal the defendant argued that his conviction on the basis of an unsupported identification made by a single witness well over 50 years ago, at a considerable distance and in an uncertain light, was unsafe. The Court of Appeal, however, pointed out that the witness was standing within feet of the appellant when the murder was committed and that 'it was not a case of an identification made 56 years after the event, but one of contemporaneous recognition to which the witness deposed after that lapse of time. It is not easy to imagine any event which, if witnessed, would impress itself more indelibly on the mind of a 13 year old boy'.[3] The Court noted that the jury must have found the witness to be honest and reliable and saw no reason to question its conclusions. His appeal was, therefore, dismissed.

However, time does not need to span 50 years for doubt to be cast on the credibility of identification. In the case of *Kupreškić* before the International Criminal Tribunal for the former Yugoslavia (ICTY), one witness, a former UNPROFOR soldier, identified one of the accused in court as a Bosnian Croat whom he had met during the conflict in Central Bosnia in 1993, who had identified himself as 'Dragan' and who had indicated that he had killed 32 Muslims by drawing his hand across his throat. The witness stated that 'When someone tells you they have killed 32 people you don't forget their face in a hurry.' The Trial Chamber, however, was not sure that the witness identified the correct man in court five years after the event, there having been no prior identification; and the accused was acquitted.[4]

[3] *Ibid*, 246.

[4] *Kupreškić*, judgment, 14 Jan 2000, paras 356, 368. The ICTY decisions cited in this chapter are available on the ICTY website: http://www.un.org/icty

Other factors may have an impact on eyewitness evidence in war crimes trials. Due to the excessively violent nature of the crimes many witnesses have suffered a degree of trauma and some will have Post Traumatic Stress Disorder. A Trial Chamber of the ICTY however said 'even when a person is suffering from PTSD, this does not mean that he or she is necessarily inaccurate in the evidence given. There is no reason why a person with PTSD cannot be a perfectly reliable witness'.[5]

SCOPE OF THE TRIALS

Another feature of war crimes trials is that they usually cover a much broader span of events than ordinary criminal trials. Thus, the Nuremberg trial involved events which covered a decade and an entire continent. Modern war crimes trials are more limited in their scale but that scale may still be extensive. For instance, the complexity and international nature of the trials may require the court to hear evidence of the background and context in which the crimes were committed. As the Court of Appeal in *Sawoniuk* said:

> Criminal charges cannot be fairly judged in a factual vacuum. In order to make a rational assessment of evidence directly relating to a charge it may often be necessary for a jury to receive evidence describing, perhaps in some detail, the context and circumstances in which the offences are said to have been committed. ... The approach seems to us of particular significance in an exceptional case such as the present, in which a London jury was asked to assess the significance of evidence relating to events in a country quite unlike our own, taking place a very long time ago in the extraordinary conditions prevailing in 1941–1942.[6]

The result has been long and complex trials. The trials before the ad hoc tribunals commonly last more than a year and most of the time is taken up with hearing the evidence of witnesses. This is illustrated by some of the trials before the ICTY: in *Tadić* 126 witnesses gave evidence; in *Kupreškić* 157 and in *Blaškić* 161.

ADMISSIBILITY OF EVIDENCE

How then do the Tribunals seek to address these problems? One answer is through the rules governing the admissibility of evidence. National courts, of course, have their own rules of evidence. In general, in countries following the civil law tradition and the inquisitorial criminal process, liberal rules for the admission of evidence apply. For instance, the German Code provides that in its search for the truth the Court is obliged to take into account all facts and

[5] *Furundžija*, judgment, 10 Dec 1998, para 109.
[6] *Sawoniuk* [2000] 2 Cr App R 234–35, *per* Lord Bingham C J.

evidence relevant for the Judgement.[7] On the other hand, in those countries following the common law tradition and an adversarial criminal process, restrictive rules apply to admissibility.

Against this background, international courts and tribunals have been left to establish their own rules of evidence. From the post-World War II military tribunals to the modern ad hoc United Nations tribunals, international tribunals have generally taken a liberal approach to the admission of evidence. The Charter of the International Military Tribunal at Nuremberg said that the Tribunal was not to be bound by technical rules of evidence, but should apply expeditious and non-technical procedure and admit any evidence which it considered to have probative value.[8] The modern tribunals have followed this lead. The Appeals Chamber of the ICTY, commenting on the sometimes elaborate rules of evidence in some national jurisdictions, declared that 'there is no reason to import such rules into the practice of the Tribunal, which is not bound by national rules of evidence. The purpose of the rules (of the Tribunal) is to promote a fair and expeditious trial and Trial Chambers must have the flexibility to achieve this goal'.[9] Those rules provide that 'in cases not otherwise provided for in the Rules, the Trial Chamber shall apply rules of evidence which will best favour a fair determination of the matter before it and are consonant with the spirit of the Statute and the general principles of law'.[10] A Trial Chamber may thus admit any relevant evidence which it considers to have probative value,[11] however, it may exclude evidence if its probative value is substantially outweighed by the need to ensure a fair trial.[12] (The Statute of the International Criminal Court indicates that the ICC will also take a similar liberal approach to issues of admissibility of evidence).[13]

The tendency, therefore, in international tribunals is to admit evidence, leaving its weight to be assessed by the court at the end of the case. Restrictive common law rules have not been followed. One reason for these rules is the need to protect jurors from exposure to prejudicial material of little probative value which they may not be able to put out of their minds. This consideration does not apply in international tribunals where trials are conducted by professional judges.[14] The safeguard against a wrong appraisal of the evidence lies in the fact

[7] Code of Criminal Procedure (*Strafprozessordnung*), S 244.2; *see* also the Dutch Code of Criminal Procedure (*Wetboek van Strafvordering*), Arts 338, 339.

[8] Art 19 of the Charter of the International Military Tribunal. An identical provision is found in Art 15 of the Charter of the International Military Tribunal for the Far East at Tokyo which provides for specific types of evidence being admissible. 'Probative value' means evidence tending to prove or disprove a fact in issue: *Black's Law Dictionary* (7th edn).

[9] *Aleksovski*, Appeal on Admissibility of Evidence, 16 Feb 1999, para 19.

[10] Rule 89(B) of the Rules of Procedure and Evidence of the ICTY. The Rules of Procedure and Evidence of the International Criminal Tribunal for Rwanda ("ICTR") contain the same provision in Rule 89(B).

[11] ICTY Rule 89(C), ICTR Rule 89(C).

[12] ICTY Rule 89(D).

[13] ICC Statute, Art 69.3, 4.

[14] *Delalić et al*, Decision on Admissibility of Evidence, 19 Jan 1998, para 20.

that the judgements are fully reasoned, thus reflecting which evidence the judges have relied on for their findings.[15]

Whereas the historical tribunals were able to rely largely on documentary evidence, the modern tribunals have to rely (primarily) on the evidence of live witnesses: indeed the rules of the ICTY originally provided that in principle witnesses be heard in this way.[16] This course has the advantage that the evidence is given in court under declaration and is subject to cross-examination, thus enabling the judges to see and hear the witness and observe his or her demeanour.

However, direct evidence may well not be available and the courts must have recourse to indirect evidence. The most common example of such evidence is hearsay, ie when 'A' tells a court what 'B' told him. Hearsay evidence is usually inadmissible in common law systems; however it has generally been admitted by international tribunals. Early rulings by Trial Chambers of the ICTY[17] enabled the Appeals Chamber to say that it was well settled in the practice of the Tribunal that hearsay evidence was admissible.[18]

Some common law courts have followed suit and relaxed technical rules of evidence in the light of the special circumstances of war crimes trials. For instance, the Supreme Court of Canada has recognised that a flexible approach to the hearsay rule is appropriate provided that the evidence is necessary and reliable.[19] The court said:

> It is essential, in a case where the events took place 45 years ago, that all material evidence be put before the jury. With the passage of time it becomes increasingly difficult to get at the truth of events; witnesses die or cannot be located, memories fade and evidence can be so easily forever lost. It is then essential that in such a case all available accounts are placed before the court.[20]

In Israel, special rules of evidence have been provided for allowing courts to depart from rules of evidence ordinarily applicable to criminal trials, such as the hearsay rule, in cases of war crimes or crimes against humanity.[21]

THE EXTENT OF RELAXATION

The rules of evidence apply equally to both parties. Accordingly, any relaxation in those rules should in principle be applied equally to both. However, the prosecution has the burden of proving the case whereas the accused is entitled to the protection of certain rights in order to ensure that the trial is fair, eg the right to

[15] Nuremberg Charter, Art 26; ICTY Statute, Art. 23(2). Civil law systems follow the same approach: *see* the Dutch Code of Criminal Procedure, Art 359.

[16] Rule 90(A) (now deleted).

[17] *Tadić*, Decision on Hearsay, 5 Aug 1996; *Blaškić*, Decision on the Admission of Hearsay, 21 Jan 1998.

[18] *Aleksovski*, Appeals Chamber Decision on Admissibility of Evidence, 16 Feb 1999, para 15.

[19] *R v Finta* [1994] 1 SCR 701.

[20] *R v Finta*, 707.

[21] Kenneth Mann, 'Hearsay Evidence in War Crimes Trials', in Yoram Dinstein and Mala Tabory (eds), *War Crimes in International Law* (Martinus Nijhoff, London/The Hague/Boston,1996), 351.

examine the witnesses against him.[22] Accordingly, there is a potential for conflict between these principles. The question arises: how far should the rules be relaxed, in particular to accept evidence not subject to cross-examination?

As already noted, the trials are long and complex and much time is taken up in hearing the evidence of numerous witnesses. Therefore, other methods of putting evidence before the Tribunal must be found: for instance, the transcripts of evidence given by witnesses in other, related, cases before the Tribunal. Although such evidence is open to the objection that strictly it constitutes hearsay, and counsel for the accused in the instant case is not able to cross-examine the witness, this disadvantage is mitigated by the fact that the witness will have been cross-examined by counsel in the related case on legal and factual aspects relevant to both cases.[23]

Another method, which at least has the sanction of being subject to oath or other solemn declaration, is by means of an affidavit or sworn statement. Thus, an affidavit is usually made before a judge or other legal official and the maker swears to the truth of its contents. The Nuremberg and Tokyo Trials relied heavily on affidavits produced by both parties: their admission resulted in significant time-saving and enabled more trials to be held.[24] The ICTY followed this lead and the Rules provided for the admission of affidavits, subject to objection by the other party, in which case it was for the Trial Chamber to decide whether to require cross-examination of the maker or not. Therefore, the right to cross-examine was not lost altogether but was subject to the ruling of the Trial Chamber. (This rule has now been deleted, see below.)

On the other hand, unsworn witness statements have not generally been admitted. In *Kordić and Čerkez*[25] the Appeal Chamber held that such a statement was not admissible. The statement had been taken by a prosecution investigator in 1995 from a witness who had since died. The Trial Chamber had admitted the statement but noted that it would not be possible to convict the accused on the basis of this statement alone if that evidence was uncorroborated. This decision was overturned by the Appeals Chamber, who said that the relevant rule 'must be interpreted so that safeguards are provided to ensure that the Trial Chamber can be satisfied that the evidence is reliable'. The Appeals Chamber remarked that the statement was not given under oath or before a judge. The deceased witness could not be cross-examined. The statement, taken by an investigator, who worked through an interpreter, was not just 'first-hand' hearsay but more removed. It was made some years after the conflict. (This Appeals Chamber ruling adopts a stricter approach than the one taken by Trial Chambers previously, determining that lack of reliability should be a bar to admissibility rather than a matter of weight—thus giving less discretion to the Trial Chambers in admitting evidence).

22 ICTY Statute, Art 21(4)(e).

23 *Aleksovski*, Appeals Chamber Decision on Admissibility of Evidence, 16 Feb 1999.

24 15 NMT at 746.

25 *Kordić and Čerkez*, Appeals Chamber Decision Regarding Statement of a Deceased Witness, 21 July 2000.

The same statement had been admitted in another case but this was at the request of the accused,[26] and so, as the Appeals Chamber observed, the accused's right to cross-examine the witnesses was not involved. This ruling indicates a certain leeway for the defence in that it can present uncross-examined evidence, as opposed to the prosecution.

The ICTY has recently deleted the rule relating to affidavits and adopted a more liberal rule for the admission of statements and transcripts (Rule 92*bis*). This rule allows a Trial Chamber to admit a written statement which goes to proof of a matter other than the acts and conduct of the accused and which has been attested to by the person making it. However, a Trial Chamber must decide whether to require the witness to attend for cross-examination. The same rule allows for the admission of statements made by persons who have subsequently died, cannot be traced or by reason of bodily or mental condition are unable to testify: before such a statement is admitted there must be satisfactory indicia of its reliability. Thus there is now a greater opportunity for both parties to put written evidence before the Tribunal.

Should there, in principle, be a more liberal treatment of defence evidence in order to ensure maximum protection against unjust convictions?

Support for such an approach is found in national case law such as the Canadian case of *R v Finta*.[27] Finta was alleged to have been the commander of troops at Szeged in Hungary where over 8,000 Jews were detained in a brickyard, forcibly stripped of their valuables and deported to the extermination camps as part of the Nazi 'final solution' in 1944. He was charged under the Canadian Criminal Code with war crimes and crimes against humanity. The Crown case against him depended largely on the testimony of 19 witnesses who had been interned at Szeged, six of whom were eyewitnesses. During the trial the judge admitted an exculpatory statement made before a Hungarian court by a witness whose evidence, pointed to another man as the person responsible. The witness had since died (in 1963). The trial judge admitted the evidence even though it was hearsay, holding that it was both necessary and reliable evidence.[28] The defendant was acquitted and the Crown appealed to the Court of Appeal, which upheld the trial judge's decision but stated that this exception to the hearsay rule could only be invoked by the defence. The Crown appealed to the Supreme Court, which upheld the decision of the Court of Appeal and said that 'a court has a residual discretion to relax in favour of the accused a strict rule of evidence where it is necessary to prevent a miscarriage of justice'.[29] The Supreme Court went on to say:

[26] *Blaškić*, Decision on the Defence Motion to Admit into Evidence the Prior Statement of Deceased Witness Midhat Haskić, 29 April 1998.

[27] *R v Finta* [1994] 1 SCR 701, (Supreme Court of Canada).

[28] These requirements were laid down in an earlier Canadian Supreme Court case, that of *R v Khan* [1900] 2 SCR 531.

[29] Quoting Judge Martin in *R v Williams* (1985), 18 CCC (3d) 356 at 378.

> The importance of putting all relevant and reliable evidence that is available before the trier of fact in order to provide the clearest possible picture of what happened at the time of the offences is indisputable. It would have been unfair to have deprived the respondent of the benefit of having all relevant, probative and reliable evidence before the jury. This is particularly true of evidence that could be considered helpful to his position.[30]

A similar relaxation of the rules of evidence in favour of the defence led to the acquittal of *Demjanjuk* who was tried for war crimes and crimes against humanity in Israel in 1987. The Prosecution alleged that Demjanjuk, an extradited US citizen, was Ivan Grozny, or Ivan the Terrible, who had been a member of the Nazi SS who operated the gas chambers in the Treblinka and Sobibor extermination camps: he had perpetrated acts of particular cruelty on the Jewish inmates of those camps and had actively participated in their extermination. The Prosecution relied on three types of evidence:

(a) records showing that Demjanjuk had served as a member of the SS unit which trained guards to serve at the camps;
(b) identification evidence by eye-witnesses who had identified him from photographs as Ivan the Terrible; and
(c) hearsay accounts of identification by eyewitnesses who had died before the time of the trial.[31]

The accused argued that he was not Ivan the Terrible; his defence being one of mistaken identity.[32] At trial the court convicted him on the basis that 'the possibility of the identifiers having substituted the defendant for Ivan Grozny because of an amazing similarity between them, is farfetched and beyond the limits of reasonable doubt'.[33]

When the case was heard on appeal the Supreme Court dismissed defence objections to the reliability of the eye-witness testimony and upheld the trial court's findings in this regard. However, new evidence was introduced at the appellate stage. This evidence consisted of statements and records of testimonies of former members of the SS unit. These statements raised the possibility that another man, named Marchenko, may have been Ivan the Terrible. There was no evidence before the Supreme Court as to where exactly these statements had come from or who had obtained and recorded them and the makers were not available to give evidence or for cross-examination.[34] The Supreme Court found that although there were problems with the origins and reliability of the statements, it could find no way of rejecting completely the possibility contained in them, ie that Marchenko was Ivan the Terrible. The court therefore concluded that 'in the absence of a rational conclusion whatsoever with regard

[30] *R v Finta* [1994] 1 SCR 701, 855; *Cory*, J at 855.
[31] Kenneth Mann, 'Hearsay Evidence in War Crimes Trials', in Dinstein and Tabory, *War Crimes in International Law*, 356.
[32] *Ibid*, p 355.
[33] *Ibid*, p 359; The Opinion, at 215–52.
[34] *Ibid*, pp 359–60.

to the statements, there remains a deadlock, ie a reasonable doubt, and if there is a reasonable doubt, the appellant is entitled to benefit from it… Therefore justice demands that he be acquitted'.[35]

In a commentary on *Demjanjuk*, Kenneth Mann argues that while it is appropriate to limit the types of evidence admissible in international war crimes trials, there should be a 'clear rule of asymmetry permitting the defendant to rely on certain kinds of evidence that the prosecution would not be allowed to rely upon, as actually occurred in the trial of *Demjanjuk*'.[36]

However, this is not the approach taken by the ICTY, which has based its jurisprudence on the principle of 'equality of arms', originating from the European Court of Human Rights. This principle has been interpreted to mean procedural equality between the parties, implying that each party must be afforded a reasonable opportunity to present his evidence under conditions that do not place him at a substantial disadvantage vis-à-vis his opponent.[37] This interpretation of the principle of 'equality of arms' was endorsed by the ICTY Appeals Chamber in *Aleksovski*:[38]

> This application of the concept of a fair trial in favour of both parties is understandable because the Prosecution acts on behalf of and in the interests of the community, including the interests of the victims of the offence charged (in cases before the Tribunal the prosecutor acts on behalf of the international community). This principle of equality does not affect the fundamental protections given by the general law or the Statute to the accused and the trial proceeds against the background of those fundamental protections. Seen in this way, it is difficult to see how a trial could ever be considered to be fair where the accused is favoured at the expense of the Prosecution beyond a strict compliance with those fundamental protections.

It should also be noted in this connection that the prosecution has claimed that in some trials before the ICTY the defence are more likely than the prosecution to have the assistance of the relevant government: this, of course, is completely contrary to what occurs in national jurisdictions. However, in many other cases the defence has fewer resources than the prosecution; it is thus for Trial Chambers to be vigilant to ensure that the balance between the parties is not disturbed.

WITNESS PROTECTION

The experience of the modern tribunals has shown a broad need for the protection of witnesses. Many of these witnesses may have survived atrocities of the

35 *Ibid*, 363.

36 *Ibid*, 377.

37 *Ekbatani v Sweden* (1988) 10 EHRR 510 at para 30; *Barbera v Spain* (1988) 11 EHRR 360 at para 18; *Brandsetter v Austria* (1991) 15 EHRR 213 at para 67; *Dombo Beheer BV v The Netherlands* (1993) 18 EHRR 213 at para 33.

38 *Aleksovski*, Appeals Chamber Decision on Admissibility of Evidence, 16 Feb. 1999, para 25.

39 *Tadić*, Decision on Protective Measures, 10 Aug 1995, paras 31–44.

worst kind, their home countries may be unstable and some may fear reprisals, which render them unwilling to come and give testimony. The question of whether 'protective measures' (as they are called) are warranted for a particular witness has to be assessed in the circumstances of the particular case. The Trial Chamber must balance the need for a public trial against the witness's need for protection. Protective measures are available for prosecution and defence witnesses alike. Some of the measures available are:

(a) Confidentiality: in the first case before the ICTY the Trial Chamber held that the protection of victims and witnesses is an acceptable reason to limit the right of an accused to a public trial.[39] Witnesses may, therefore, testify in closed session under a pseudonym, so that their identity remains hidden from the press and the public. Image and voice distortion on the video recording are available to further obscure witness identity.
(b) Anonymity: in *Tadić* a majority of the Trial Chamber held that in exceptional circumstances it could grant full anonymity to a witness. The majority said that anonymous testimony could be relevant and probative and that the right of the accused to examine, or have examined, the witness against him is not necessarily violated if the defence is allowed to question the witness in accordance with certain procedural safeguards.[40] This measure has been granted in no case since.
(c) Safe Conduct: Some witnesses may be reluctant to come to The Hague to testify out of fear that they themselves will be prosecuted. For these reasons a Trial Chamber has the power to grant limited immunity from prosecution in the form of safe conduct.[41]

One difficulty with ICTY witness protection is that the Trial Chamber does not know the situation on the ground and lacks its own enforcement agency. However, it can employ a variety of means to prevent intimidation or harassment of witnesses, including delayed, limited and monitored disclosure of their statements and identity, under threat of contempt of court.[42]

COLLECTION OF EVIDENCE FROM DIFFERENT COUNTRIES AND ORGANISATIONS

Many war crimes trials involve witnesses from states other than those directly involved in the conflict, for instance, witnesses from peacekeeping forces. States, therefore, may have access to relevant evidence. National or international courts may request, or order, such evidence to be produced.[43] Normally, national

[40] *Tadić*, *ibid.*, paras. 74–75.
[41] ICTY Rule 54.
[42] *Kupreškić*, Decision on Motion to Delay Disclosure of Witness Statements, 20 May 1998.
[43] *See* Göran Sluiter, 'Obtaining Evidence for the International Criminal Tribunal for the Former Yugoslavia: An Overview and Assessment of Domestic Legislation', (1998), XLV *Netherlands International Law Review*, 87–113.

courts would make such a request under a mutual legal assistance treaty; and many countries have taken a similar approach towards the ICTY. However, the ICTY itself defines its power more broadly, as is demonstrated in the litigation concerning subpoenas in the *Blaškić* case. A subpoena was issued in that case to the Republic of Croatia, against which Croatia appealed. The Appeals Chamber held that the Tribunal cannot issue subpoenas to states. This is because the Tribunal does not have the power to take enforcement measures against states and, since the sanction for non-compliance with a subpoena is typically penal, and since states are not subject to criminal sanctions, it follows that a subpoena cannot be issued to states. However, the Appeals Chamber held that the Tribunal can issue orders to states, noting that although its primary jurisdiction is over individuals, it has ancillary (or incidental) powers vis-à-vis states. Any such order should (1) identify specific documents; (2) set out succinctly the relevance of the documents to the trial; (3) not be unduly onerous; (4) allow the requested state reasonable time to comply. In case of non-compliance, the Appeals Chamber ruled that the appropriate remedy was for the President of the Tribunal to transmit the relevant judicial finding to the United Nations Security Council which could decide whether or not to impose sanctions.[44]

Croatia also argued in *Blaškić* that states have a blanket right to withhold documents because to disclose them would prejudice a state's national security interests. The Appeals Chamber considered this argument but said that such interests could not always prevail and could not prevent the Tribunal from obtaining crucial material. However, special procedures have now been developed to accommodate national security concerns.[45] It should also be noted that the ICC Statute provides for elaborate procedures to meet the national security concerns of states. Under Article 93.4 of the Statute, states may deny a request for assistance in whole or in part only if the request concerns the production of any documents or disclosure of evidence which relates to its national security.

International or non-governmental organisations such as the UNHCR or the ICRC may also have access to materials of significance to war crimes cases. Thus the question arose in an ICTY case whether a former employee of the ICRC could be compelled to testify. The Trial Chamber (by a majority) decided that the ICRC had a right, under customary international law, to non-disclosure of the information at its disposal, since states party to the Geneva Conventions and its Protocols must be taken to have accepted the fundamental principles on which the ICRC operates, ie impartiality, neutrality and confidentiality. The majority said that although the Tribunal and the ICRC share common goals, their functions and tasks are different: the ICRCs activities are 'preventive', ie to prevent breaches of international humanitarian law, while the International Tribunal prosecutes such breaches after they have occurred.[46] (Judge Hunt, in a

[44] *Blaškić*, Judgement on the Request of the Republic of Croatia for Review, 29 Oct 1997.

[45] Rule 54*bis*. The Rule allows for the designation by the Trial Chamber of a single judge to scrutinise the materials in closed, *ex parte* proceedings.

[46] *Simić*, Decision, 1 Oct 1999.

separate opinion, said that a balancing exercise had to be carried out and the interests of the ICRC had to be weighed against the importance of the evidence, but held that in the instant case the balance favoured the ICRC.)

However, if evidence is obtained through means which go beyond the powers of the Tribunal, it is to be excluded, in accordance with international human rights law. The rules require Trial Chambers to exclude evidence if it was obtained by methods which cast substantial doubt on its reliability or if its admission is antithetical to, and would seriously damage, the integrity of the proceedings.[47] Examples of such methods would include evidence obtained by torture or duress or by other involuntary means or evidence seized by irregular or illegal means. In *Kordić and Čerkez* the defence sought to exclude materials obtained by the prosecution during the execution of a warrant to search offices in a municipal building in Bosnia. The defence submitted that the evidence should have been excluded since the prosecution did not have the power to search for and seize evidence in a sovereign state without the consent of the state or its participation and the prosecution should have resorted to customary rules of judicial assistance in its attempts to obtain this evidence. Accordingly, the defence submitted that its admission would be antithetical to the integrity of the proceedings. The prosecution submitted that the accused had no standing to challenge the admissibility of the evidence since only a state could challenge any violation of its sovereignty. Secondly, the prosecution had the power, under the Statute and Rules, to conduct on-site investigations and there was no need to resort to the rules of judicial assistance.

The Trial Chamber held that (1) the accused was entitled to challenge the admissibility of the evidence; but (2) the submission failed since the prosecution was within its powers in searching for and seizing the material. The Trial Chamber pointed out that all states have an obligation to lend co-operation and assistance to the Tribunal under Article 29 of the Statute, stemming from the Charter of the United Nations (in particular Article 25 and Chapter VII) and, therefore, there was no need to resort to customary international rules of judicial assistance.[48]

CONCLUSION

It is too early in the lives of the ad hoc Tribunals to come to any definite conclusion about the way in which they have tackled the particular problems facing the collection and presentation of evidence. As in any criminal process, new problems crop up all the time. The determined effort that is being made to surmount these problems combines the civil and common law traditions, in an effort to present a balanced and coherent system suitable for this type of trial.

[47] ICTY Rule 95. ICC Statute, Art 69(7).

[48] *Kordić and Čerkez*, Decision, 25 June 1999.

7

The Permanent International Criminal Court

M CHERIF BASSIOUNI*

THE NEED FOR AN INTERNATIONAL CRIMINAL COURT

World War I was to be 'the war to end all wars'. However, a relatively short time later, the world again found itself embroiled in another conflict of even greater proportions. After the atrocities of World War II were revealed, the world community promised: 'never again.' Since then, however, some 250 international, regional, and internal armed conflicts have occurred.[1] These conflicts, along with human rights violations perpetrated by repressive regimes, have produced an estimated number of casualties that ranges from 70 to 170 million deaths.[2] Cumulatively, the harmful consequences are almost beyond comprehension, but these stark realities must be faced and addressed. Tragically, there have been few mechanisms for accountability, and thus no deterrence. Since the trial of the Nazi leadership at Nuremberg, governments have for the most part receded to the convenient practices of *realpolitik*, whereby accountability and justice are bargained for political compromises.[3] One of the outcomes of this approach has been that *jus cogens* crimes,[4] such as aggression, genocide, crimes against humanity, war crimes, slave related practices, and torture, have increased in almost all parts of the world. Moreover, governments in a position to prevent or mitigate these tragic events, or to pursue restorative and retributive justice, have

* Portions of this article are derived from M Cherif Bassiouni, 'Negotiating the Treaty of Rome on the Establishment of an International Criminal Court', (1999) *32 Cornell Int'l L. J. 443*; M. Cherif Bassiouni, 'Explanatory Note on the ICC', (2000) *71 International Review of Penal Law 1*.

[1] M Cherif Bassiouni, 'Searching for Peace and Achieving Justice', *Law & Contemp Probs* 59 (1996), 9, 10; see also Daniel Chirot, *Modern Tyrants: The Power and Prevalence of Evil in our Age* (1994). Pierre Hassner, *Violence and Peace: From the Atomic Bomb to Ethnic Cleansing* (1995); Rudolph J Rummel, *Death by Government* (1994). See also Eric Hobsbawm, *The Age of Extremes: A History of the World, 1914–1991* (1995); SIPRI Yearbooks 1975–1996. See also the newsletters, progress reports and conflict maps produced by PIOOM (Interdisciplinary Research Program on Causes of Human Rights Violations, Leiden, The Netherlands).

[2] See above n 1.

[3] M Cherif Bassiouni, 'Impunity for International Crimes', (2000), 71 *U. Colo L Rev* 409.

[4] See M Cherif Bassiouni, 'Sources of International Criminal Law', in M Cherif Bassiouni (ed), 2nd edn., (1999), 71 *International Criminal Law* 1 (1999), 38–46, 62–81 (3 vols).

regrettably remained, for the most part passive, indifferent, and at times even supportive of these practices.[5]

Consequently, instead of being held accountable for these international crimes, most of the perpetrators have benefited from impunity either *de facto* or *de jure*.[6] International civil society has, however, expressed a growing opposition to the practices of granting impunity, particularly for the leaders who ordered the commission of atrocities and those senior commanders who executed these unlawful orders. As a result, some charges are already occurring.[7]

Since World War I, the demands for justice have brought about the establishment of five international investigative commissions[8] and four ad hoc international tribunals.[9] These institutions benefited from the support of governments

[5] The Rwandan genocide is a striking example of passivity on the part of the world community in violation of its pledge 'never again'. While a criminal tribunal was ultimately enacted in the wake of the genocide which occurred in 1994, the world community watched as the slaughter unfolded over the course of a year. See generally Gerard Prunier, *The Rwanda Crisis: History of a Genocide* (1997); Philip Gourevitch, *We Wish to Inform You That Tomorrow We Will Be Killed with Our Families* (1998); 'Frontline: The Triumph of Evil', *PBS television broadcast*, 1 Jan 1999 (recounting the passivity of the international community during the Rwandan genocide).

[6] *De facto* impunity may occur either when the failure to investigate or prosecute is intentional, though not sanctioned by law, or when a legal system is unable to meet its obligations to investigate and prosecute. In some instances, a given state may be willing but unable to carry out investigation and prosecution. This may occur in the aftermath of conflict, when states are faced with many competing priorities. In these situations, governments often fail to prioritise effective criminal justice and limit resources for prosecutions or fail to ensure that positions are staffed with competent professionals who pursue their functions with diligence and ethics. Thus, states without functioning judicial systems impede the goals of international civil society to provide accountability and justice. *De jure* impunity occurs when any of a number of appropriate accountability mechanisms are preempted by the granting of amnesties or like measures. These may include blanket amnesties covering a given period of time or applying to a given group of persons or may be specifically given to an individual. The following accountability mechanisms have been employed in the resolution of conflicts: international prosecutions, international investigatory commissions, national investigatory and truth commissions, national prosecutions, lustration mechanisms, civil remedies, mechanisms for victim compensation. See Bassiouni, 'Searching for Peace', above n 1, at 18–22. It should also be noted that *de jure* impunity also can result when a state selects an inappropriate accountability mechanism, given the nature of the violation. This is especially true when the selection of a particular mechanism excludes all other forms. Thus, for example, a state may be fostering a policy of impunity if it opts for a truth commission as an accountability mechanism for genocide with an absolute bar on prosecution. Cumbersome legal procedures or inadequate periods of limitations that operate to frustrate prosecution or civil claims for damages are further examples.

[7] For example, the indictment of former and current leaders such as Augusto Pinochet of Chile, Slobodan Milošević of Serbia, Radovan Karadzić of the former Republika Srpska in Bosnia, Hissène Habré of Chad, and Foday Sankoh and other members of the Revolutionary United Front in Sierra Leone, all cases which are described elsewhere in this book. See M Scharf and W Schabas, *Slobodan Milošević on Trial: A Companion* (2002).

[8] The five international investigative commissions are: (1) The 1919 Commission on the Responsibilities of Authors of War and on the Enforcement of Penalties; (2) The 1943 United Nations War Crimes Commission; (3) The 1946 Far Eastern Commission; (4) The 1992 Commission of Experts Established Pursuant to Security Council Resolution 780 (1992) to Investigate War Crimes and other Violations of International Humanitarian Law in the Former Yugoslavia; and (5) The 1994 Independent Commission of Experts Established Pursuant to Security Council Resolution 935 (1994) to Investigate Grave Violations of International Humanitarian Law in the Territory of Rwanda. See generally M. Cherif Bassiouni, 'From Versailles to Rwanda in Seventy-Five Years: The Need to Establish a Permanent International Criminal Court', (1997), 10 *Harv Hum Rts J* 11–49.

[9] The four ad hoc international tribunals are: (1) The 1945 International Military Tribunal to

motivated by humanistic values and also by those governments who recognised the importance of international criminal accountability mechanisms as a means to maintain world order and restore peace. These developments reflect the emergence of accountability and justice as internationally recognised values or policies that are necessary for the maintenance of world order and for the restoration and maintenance of peace. However, the pursuit of international criminal justice on an ad hoc basis is less than satisfying. For example, while tribunals were established in the wake of World War II, armed conflict in the former-Yugoslavia, and the Rwandan genocide, similar international action has not been taken in the aftermath of the countless other tragedies, which may not have produced similar levels of victimisation or been prominently featured in the Western media's nightly news broadcasts. To avoid the pitfalls of ad hoc justice, international criminal justice requires clearly established norms that are consistently applied by a permanent international criminal court.

The purpose of a permanent international criminal court is to combine humanitarian values and policy consideration which are essential for justice, redress, and prevention, with the need for the restoration and preservation or peace. An international criminal court is the most appropriate international mechanism through which the proscriptive norms against genocide, crimes against humanity, and war crimes can become more effective instrumental norms, as opposed to being essentially the embodiment of intrinsic values reflecting international social expectations. The consistent interpretation and successive application of such norms intensifies social expectations and thereby reinforces compliance.

DRAFTING AND ADOPTING THE STATUTE OF THE INTERNATIONAL CRIMINAL COURT[10]

Preparing the Draft Statute

From 1995 to 1998, the United Nations General Assembly convened two committees to produce what was called a 'consolidated text' of the Draft Statute for

Prosecute the Major War Criminals of the European Axis; (2) The 1946 International Military Tribunal to Prosecute the Major War Criminals of the Far East; (3) The 1993 International Criminal Tribunal for the Former Yugoslavia; and (4) The 1994 International Criminal Tribunal for Rwanda. See generally Bassiouni, 'From Versailles to Rwanda', above n 8.

10 The Rome Statue of the International Criminal Court is reprinted as an appendix to this book and should be consulted in conjunction with this chapter. The ICC's Rules of Procedure and Evidence can be consulted at UN Doc PCNICC/2000/INF/3/Add 2 ['RPE'] and the Elements of Crime at UN Doc PCNICC/2000/INF/3/Add 1 ['Elements of Crime']. The following section is based largely on the author's observations made in his various leadership roles in the drafting process, *ie*, Vice-Chairman of the ad hoc Committee on the Establishment of the International Criminal Court; Vice-Chairman of the Preparatory Committee on the Establishment of the International Criminal Court; Chairman of the Drafting Committee of the Rome Diplomatic Conference. For additional background on the movement to establish an international criminal court and the drafting and negotiating process, see generally M Cherif Bassiouni, 'Historical Survey: 1919–1998' in M Cherif Bassiouni (ed), *The Statute of the International Criminal Court: A Documentary History* (1998); William Bourdon, *La Cour Pénale Internationale 13–24* (2000); M Cherif Bassiouni, 'The

the Establishment of an International Criminal Court (ICC).[11] The Ad Hoc Committee on the Establishment of an International Criminal Court (Ad Hoc Committee) met throughout 1995 to discuss major substantive and administrative issues, but did not engage in negotiations or drafting. In 1996, the Ad Hoc Committee was replaced by the Preparatory Committee on the Establishment of an International Criminal Court (PrepCom), which met through 1998. During its first year, the PrepCom also did not draft provisions of the Draft Statute because several States were not ready to proceed to the drafting stage. Indeed, a number of major states, including the United States, the United Kingdom, and China, initially felt that the PrepCom, like the Ad Hoc Committee, should only discuss issues until the political climate matured enough to allow the process to move into the drafting stage.

Had the PrepCom continued to merely discuss issues throughout 1997, it would not have been able to complete the Draft Statute by the 3 April 1998 deadline, and the Rome Diplomatic Conference (the Conference) due to start 15 June 1998, would have had to have been postponed. While some governments would have welcomed a postponement, most governments did not want the Diplomatic Conference to be delayed. Ambassador Adriaan Bos, an experienced Dutch diplomat who was the Chairman of the Ad Hoc Committee and the PrepCom, was sensitive to these concerns and cautiously moved forward. By 1997, the PrepCom had produced only an unstructured and substantially unusable compilation of all governmental proposals. To remedy the situation, an inter-sessional meeting of the Bureau and the coordinators of the different parts of the statute was held at Zutphen, The Netherlands, 19–30 January , 1998. That meeting provided some structure and streamlining for the compilation of the proposed texts. Even so, what emerged remained essentially a cumbersome accumulation of alternative governmental proposals requiring additional technical work and more extensive negotiations, particularly with regard to fundamental issues such as the definition of crimes, the nature of the ICC's jurisdictional mechanisms, and complementarity, which remained in the early stages of negotiation.

International Criminal Court in Historical Context', *St. Louis-Warsaw Trans'l*, 1999 (1999), 55; Philippe Kirsch and John Holmes, 'The Rome Conference on an International Criminal Court: The Negotiating Process', *Am J Int'l L*. 93 (1999) 2; Leila Nadya Sadat, 'The Establishment of the International Criminal Court: From the Hague to Rome and Back Again', (1999), 8 *MSU-DCL J In'tl L* 97; Fanny Benedetti and John Washburn, 'Drafting the International Criminal Court Treaty: Two Years to Rome and an Afterward on the Rome Diplomatic Conference', *Global Governance*, 5 (Jan–Mar 1999), 1; Mahnoush H Arsanjani, 'The Rome Statute of the International Criminal Court', (1999) 93 *Am J Int'l L* 22, 22-24; Christopher Hall, 'The First Proposal for a Permanent International Criminal Court', *International Review of the Red Cross*, 322 (1998), 57.

[11] See *United Nations General Assembly Resolution on the Establishment of an International Criminal Court*, G.A. Res. 51/207, UN doc A/51/627 (1996), reprinted in 'The International Criminal Court: Observations and Issues Before the 1997-1998 Preparatory Committee; and Administrative and Financial Implications', (1997), 13 *Nouvelles Études Pénales* 1. The resolution recalls the General Assembly's decision to establish a preparatory committee 'to discuss further the major substantive and administrative issues arising out of the draft statute prepared by the International Law Commission, and taking in account the different views expressed during the meetings, to draft texts, with a view to preparing a widely acceptable consolidated text.'

The Rome Diplomatic Conference

The United Nations Conference of Plenipotentiaries on the Establishment of an International Criminal Court began 15 June 1998 in Rome. After the first week of the Conference, the number of delegates (many of whom had come only for the initial ceremonies) shrank from about 5000 to approximately 2000.

The length of the Draft Statute complicated the delegates' task: it was 173 pages and consisted of 116 articles with some 1300 brackets for optional provisions and word choices.[12] Working with such a text was difficult even for those who participated in the Ad Hoc Committee and the PrepCom, let alone for those delegates who were unfamiliar with it.

To speed the pace of the discussions, Ambassador Philippe Kirsch of Canada, Chairman of the Committee of the Whole, instituted several informal working groups, which ultimately broke down into smaller informal-informal working groups. As a result of these multiple meetings, most delegates worked 10 to 12 hours a day, and those who assumed leading roles worked even longer hours. Given the hectic pace and gruelling nature of the work, the delegates' mood became increasingly pessimistic during the ensuing weeks of the Conference. Worst of all, there were few effective negotiations on the Statute's difficult provisions (which are customarily left to the end of most negotiating processes). The formation of smaller working groups and the extensive work schedule weighed most heavily on the smaller delegations.

While the breakdown into informal working groups quickened the drafting process, it also resulted in a piecemeal treatment of the Statute's articles. Each day, the Drafting Committee received only a few complete articles and an average of 10 to 15 paragraphs of disparate articles from the Committee of the Whole. Furthermore, the Drafting Committee often received different parts of a given article over a two to three week period. Formulating the Draft Statute thus resembled the assembly of a large jigsaw puzzle: the Committee had to determine how all the pieces—the separate articles or paragraphs received in this manner—fitted together. The disparity in languages, legal approaches, and drafting techniques among the various working groups further complicated the drafting process. The piecemeal transmission process also caused the Drafting Committee significant difficulties in maintaining a consistent form and style, in ensuring the uniform usage of terms, and in providing cross-references to other related articles. As a result of these difficulties, most articles required several revisions before they were finalized. Perhaps the Drafting Committee's most difficult and time-consuming task was to work in six languages simultaneously and to do its own corrections on most of the translated articles. Consequently, the 25 delegations serving on the Drafting Committee were heavily burdened.

The delegates at the Conference did not begin negotiating with a blank slate; instead, they built upon the efforts of the Ad Hoc Committee and the PrepCom.

[12] *Report of the Preparatory Committee on the Establishment of an International Criminal Court, Draft Statute and Draft Final Act*, UN Doc A/Conf.183/2/Add 1 (1998).

During the meetings of these Committees, as well as at three inter-sessional meetings, the delegates of certain active governments and some NGO representatives forged strong professional bonds, in contrast to other multilateral negotiation processes.

During the Diplomatic Conference negotiations, a coalition known as the 'like-minded states' became a significant driving force behind the Statute.[13] This diverse group emerged from the meetings of the Ad Hoc Committee and the PrepCom and ultimately grew to over 60 states.

The delegates who remained after the opening ceremonies to hammer out the Draft Statue had varying degrees of instructions from their respective governments. While delegations from developed countries typically had detailed, specific instructions, other delegations had received instructions which varied widely in their detail and specificity and particularly in the level of discretion granted to the delegation heads. Most developing countries, based on my observation, had received fairly vague instructions.

These factors, combined with the fact that many delegations did not have sufficient time to study the Draft Statute or were otherwise unready for wide-ranging negotiations, slowed the negotiating process. By 5 July, the delegates' concern over the pace of the negotiating had increased to the point that the successful outcome of the Conference was genuinely threatened. To forestall a breakdown in negotiations, Kirsch, assisted by the Bureau of the Committee of the Whole, members of the Canadian delegation, and some members of the 'like-minded states' delegations, produced a Chairman's Paper dealing with what he then saw as the major unresolved issues. Kirsch hoped that the Paper would re-focus the delegates' attention by providing them with a draft compromise. Delegations engaged in a multi-lateral process usually try to resolve their differences by extensive negotiations. At the Conference, however, some delegations adopted inflexible positions either because they did not have enough instructions or for other specific reasons. In particular, the United States exhibited greater rigidity than many had expected. Most delegations, especially those from the 'like-minded states', had bent over backwards to accommodate the United States. For example, the articles dealing with procedure and with the definition of crimes were substantially as the United States wanted. When the delegations began to grapple with such issues as the ICC's jurisdiction and the independent role of the Prosecutor, the US delegation, which had previously secured broad concessions on many points, adopted an unyielding position. Many delegations were dismayed by this display of diplomatic inflexibility, which was widely interpreted as another sign of US intransigence and as a weakness in the US negotiating approach. The US response failed to alleviate these concerns, thus confirming the delegates' negative judgements. However, it must be noted that the United States had some valid concerns that were not

[13] The 'like minded states' at the Conference included: Australia, Austria, Argentina, Belgium, Canada, Chile, Croatia, Denmark, Egypt, Finland, Germany, Greece, Guatemala, Hungary, Ireland, Italy, Lesotho, Netherlands, New Zealand, Norway, Portugal, Samoa, Slovakia, South Africa, Sweden, Switzerland, Trinidad and Tobago (representing 12 Caricom states), Uruguay, and Venezuela.

sufficiently and clearly articulated, and that these were not addressed in an imaginative fashion.

By 12 July, the gaps between the more active delegations narrowed, due to the efforts of Kirsch and those working with him. Although the United States had rejected the proposed compromise package, the other delegations were growing weary of what they perceived as the US delegation's lack of negotiating flexibility and subtlety. Increasingly, the other delegations felt that it would be better to stop giving in to the United States; they believed the United States would never be satisfied with the concessions it got and ultimately would never sign the Treaty for completely unrelated domestic political reasons. The other delegations therefore decided to go ahead with Kirsch's proposed compromise package rather than to have it unravel due to last minute US demands.

The final stages of the drafting and negotiating process involved Part 2 of the Draft Statute which addressed, inter alia, the definition of crimes, the Court's jurisdiction and triggering mechanisms, complementarity, the roles of the Prosecutor and the Security Council, and the prospective application of the Statute's substantive provisions. On the last day of the Conference, the Bureau presented the Committee of the Whole with a proposed text for Part 2 on a take it or leave it basis. The Bureau adopted that approach to forestall further discussions by the Committee of the Whole; at that late stage, additional debate would have meant the collapse of the Conference. The take it or leave it approach was a calculated risk, as some delegations could have raised procedural hurdles in the few remaining hours of the Conference.

The Conference was officially supposed to end at 1800 hours on Friday 17 July, or by midnight at the latest. To allow the delegations to study the text of Part 2, the Committee of the Whole convened after 1800 hours on that last Friday to adopt the Bureau's proposal. Due to the extraordinary efficiency of the Secretariat and the Conference staff, the text had already been integrated with the main body of the Statute, which had been previously adopted by the Committee of the Whole on 15 July. With the hours slipping away, the US and Indian delegations each sought to introduce last minute amendments to the Part 2 proposal. India, for example, wanted to limit the role of the Security Council (a change most delegations opposed), and include nuclear weapons among prohibited weapons (a change most developing countries supported). The United States primarily wanted jurisdiction to be subject to the consent of the state of nationality of the prospective defendant, but that was opposed by most states. India and the United States also wanted to limit the scope of Article 12 affecting non-State-Parties. With respect to each of the two proposed amendments, however, Norway introduced a no action motion, which is the same as a motion to table. In response to these motions, the Chairman of the Committee of the Whole acted boldly and decisively, in accord with the rules, by giving precedence to the no action motions so that the Conference could proceed.

The vote of the no action motion for India's proposal was 114 in favour, 16 against and 20 abstentions. The vote on the no action motion for the US proposal was 113 in favour, 17 against and 25 abstentions. After this second vote, the delegates burst into a spontaneous standing ovation, which turned into rhythmic applause that lasted close to 10 minutes. Some delegates embraced one another, and others had tears in their eyes. It was one of the most extraordinary emotional scenes ever to take place at a diplomatic conference. The prevailing feeling was that the long journey that had started after World War I had finally reached its destination. This historic moment was of great significance for everyone who had struggled to establish the ICC.

The Committee of the Whole adjourned at about 2100 hours; shortly thereafter the Plenary convened for its final session. This was to be a quick formal session, but to everyone's surprise, the United States asked for another vote. This time 120 delegations voted for the adoption of the Statute and the Final Act of the Diplomatic Conference, and for the opening of the Convention for signature on the next day; only seven voted against and 21 abstained.

The ICC Statute entered into force on 1 July 2002. In September of that year, the first session of the Assembly of State Parties adopted a budget,[13a] as well as the 'Elements of Crimes" and the ICC Rules of Procedure and Evidence. The preparatory work culminated in the election of the first 18 judges of the Court.[13b] At the time of this writing, the ICC Statute has been ratified by 89 and signed by 139 countries. [13c]

THE CHARACTERISTICS OF THE INTERNATIONAL CRIMINAL COURT

The Nature of the ICC[14]

The ICC is a permanent international institution established by treaty for the purpose of investigating and prosecuting individuals who commit 'the most serious crimes of international concern' (Article 1), namely: genocide (Article 6), crimes against humanity (Article 7), and war crimes (Article 8). These crimes are well defined in international criminal law and presently carry international legal obligations to investigate, prosecute, or extradite those individuals who

[13a] 30 million Euros, see ICC-ASP/1/Res. 12.

[13b] See below p 207.

[13c] See www.ICCNOW.org

[14] See generally Roy S Lee (ed), *The International Criminal Court: The Making of the Rome Statute, Issues, Negotiations, Results* (1999) (hereafter '*Making of the Rome Statute*'). For additional information on the establishment of the Court, as well as detailed commentary on its articles, *see* Otto Triffterer (ed), *Commentary on the Rome Statute of the International Criminal Court: Observer's Notes, Article by Article,* (1999) (hereafter '*Commentary on Rome Statute*'). *ICC: Elements of Crimes and Rules of Procedure and Evidence* (R Lee (ed), 2001); Leila N Sadat, *The ICC and the Transformation of International Law* (2002); *The Rome Statute of the ICC* (M Politi and G Nesi (eds) 2001); William A Schabas, *An Introduction to the ICC* (2001); *The ICC: Comment on the Draft Statute* (Lattauri (ed) 1992).See also Leila Nadya Sadat and Richard Carden, 'The New International Criminal Court: An Uneasy Revolution', (2000), 88 *Geo L J* 381; Lt Com Gregory P Noone and William Douglas, 'An Introduction to the International Criminal Court', (1999), 46 *Naval L Rev* 112.

are accused of having committed such crimes and to punish those individuals who violate these well established norms.

The ICC is a treaty-based institution which is binding only on its states parties. It is not a supra-national body, but an international body similar to other existing ones. The ICC is not a substitute for national criminal jurisdiction and does not supplant national criminal justice systems, but rather is 'complementary' to them (Articles 1, 17). The ICC does no more than what each and every state in the international community can do under existing international law. It is the expression of collective action by states parties to a treaty that established an institution to carry out collective justice for certain international crimes. The ICC is therefore an extension of national criminal jurisdiction, as established by a treaty whose ratification under national parliamentary authority makes it part of national law. Consequently, the ICC neither infringes upon national sovereignty nor overrides national legal systems capable of and willing to carry out their international legal obligations.

Complementarity of the ICC and national legal systems[15]

The ICC's jurisdiction extends to its states parties. The exercise of its jurisdiction is 'complementary' to that of the national legal systems of its states parties (Articles 1, 17). National criminal jurisdiction always has priority over the ICC, and only in two situations can the ICC exercise its jurisdiction, namely: (a) when a national legal system has collapsed; or (b) when a national legal system refuses or fails to carry out its legal obligations to investigate and prosecute persons alleged to have committed the three crimes presently within its jurisdiction or punish those who have been convicted.[16]

The principles of the primacy of national legal systems and the ICC's 'complementarity' are evident in other provisions of the Statute. Perhaps most indicative of these principles are the provisions of the Statute in Part 9 that require all requests for co-operation, including the arrest and surrender of an accused and the securing of evidence, to be directed to and executed by national legal systems. In furtherance of these principles, judicial safeguards are established in connection with the ICC Prosecutor's investigations and indictments. Article 15(4) requires the authorisation of the Pre-Trial Chamber before the Prosecutor commences an investigation *proprio motu* as opposed to when it is referred by a state party or the Security Council (Article 15).

[15] The term 'complementarity' does not exist in the English language. Rather, the 1995 Ad hoc Committee and 1996 PrepCom selected the term, which is a transposition from the French term 'complementarité', to describe the relationship between the ICC and national systems. See M Cherif Bassiouni, 'Observations Concerning the 1997–1998 Preparatory Committee's Work', *13 Nouvelles Études Pénales 5, 21* (1997). For a discussion of the principle of complementarity, see JT Holmes, 'The Principle of Complementarity', in *Making of the Rome Statute*, at 41–78; see also Timothy McCormack and Sue Robertson, 'Jurisdictional Aspects of the Rome Statute for the New International Criminal Court', (1999), *23 Melbourne U L Rev 635* 644–46.

[16] See ICC Statute, Art 17(2)–(3). The admissibility and inadmissibility of a case is discussed further below.

Applicable Law[17]

Article 10 contains the overarching principle with respect to the applicable law. Article 10 requires the application of international law whose four sources (treaties, customary law, general principles, and writings of distinguished jurists) are listed in Article 38 of the Statute of the International Court of Justice.[18] Consequently, this also means that the Treaty must be interpreted in accordance with the 1969 Vienna Convention on the Law of Treaties.[19]

Any provision in the Statute which conflicts or is inconsistent with general international law shall be subordinate to it. Furthermore, a conflict or inconsistency between any obligations arising under the Statute and other treaty obligations by states parties shall first be subject to applicable sources of international law referred to above and then to Article 21.

Article 21[20] adds specificity to the general provisions of Article 10 and there appears to be a possibility of a conflict between the ranking of sources of applicable law in Article 10 and the more specific aspects of Article 21. In accordance with the rules of treaty interpretation of the 1969 Vienna Convention on the Law of Treaties, it is the intent of the parties which is controlling, and in this case the parties did not intend to limit the well-established sources of international law referred to in Article 10 and contained in Article 38 of the Statute of the International Court of Justice. Consequently, the specificity contained in Article 21 is subordinate to the generality of Article 10 because of the intent of the drafters (if that were not the case, then the specificity of Article 21 would control over the generality of Article 10.)[21]

Another apparent inconsistency arises between Article 21 and Article 9 on Elements of Crimes in that Article 21 lists Elements of Crimes as a source of applicable law, whereas Article 9 specifically states that these 'Elements of Crimes shall assist the Court in interpretation and application of Articles 6, 7, and 8'. It should be noted that Elements of Crimes which are to 'assist the Court' (Article 9)

[17] For additional commentary on applicable law see Leila Nadya Sadat, 'Custom, Codification and Some Thoughts about the Relationship Between the Two: Article 10 of the ICC Statute', (2000), 49 *DePaul L Rev* 49 (2000), 909; Bourdon, above n 10, at 74, 110. See generally Bassiouni, *Sources*, above n 4, at 3–126. For discussion on general principles of International Law, see M Cherif Bassiouni, 'A Functional Approach to "General Principles of International Law"', (1990), 11 *Mich J Int'l L* 768.

[18] Art 38 states in pertinent part:

a. International conventions, whether general or particular, establishing rules expressly recognised by the contesting states;

b. International custom, as evidenced by a general practice accepted as law;

c. The general principles of law recognised by civilised nations;

d. (...) judicial decisions and the teachings of the most highly qualified publicists of the various nations, as subsidiary means for the determination of rules of law.

See Statute of International Court of Justice, 1983 UNYB 1334.

[19] See Vienna Convention on Law of Treaties, 1155 UNTS 331.

[20] Art 21 should have been merged with Article 10 but was not because Part 2, which contains Art 10 was not submitted to the Drafting Committee. Rather, it was sent directly to the Committee of the Whole. See M Cherif Bassiouni, *Negotiating the Treaty of Rome on the Establishment of an International Criminal Court* (1999), 443, 457–60.

[21] Because of the manner in which the Statute was drafted, it cannot be said that one provision was drafted or adopted before another one.

are to be considered a source of law which can be applied in a manner that modifies the provisions of the Statute (Articles 6–8). The Elements of Crimes were adopted by the Assembly of States Parties (Article 112) at its first session after the Treaty had entered into effect.[21a] The Assembly of States Parties, however, cannot modify the Statute by means of adopting the Elements of Crimes since amendment of the non-institutional provisions of the Statute requires the approval of a two-thirds majority of the states parties and ratification (Article 121).[22]

One of the problems likely to arise in connection with the sources of applicable law and the hierarchy of these sources is in connection with Article 31(1)(c), which concerns self-defence. This provision seems to be contrary to international law, in that it may be interpreted as providing an exonerating circumstance for what may otherwise be a war crime. If the priority in the hierarchy is given to international humanitarian law, as part of conventional or customary international law, then this provision of the statute could not be interpreted in a way that is consistent with extant international humanitarian law. However, if Article 21(1)(a)(quoted above) is applied in a literal manner, then it is the ICC Statute that is the primary source. Nevertheless, it could be argued that Article 10 is the overarching principle, and therefore Article 21 must be read in a way that is not inconsistent with Article 10.

THE JURISDICTION OF THE ICC

Preconditions to the Exercise of Jurisdiction[23]

Before the Court can exercise jurisdiction over a crime, the alleged crime must have been committed on the territory of a state party or by one of its nationals (Article 12(2)). In addition, the ICC may exercise its jurisdiction when a state which is not a state party consents to the Court's jurisdiction, and the crime has been committed on that state's territory or the accused is one of its nationals (Article 12(3)).[24]

[21a] This occurred in September 2000 at the first session of the Assembly of State Parties. See ICC Rules of Procedure and Evidence (RPE) PCNICC/2000/INF/3/Add.2); Elements of Crimes PCNICC/2000/INF/3/ Add. 1.

[22] See the remarks on amending the Statute under 'The organisation and operation of the Court', below.

[23] For additional commentary on Preconditions to Jurisdiction, see Young Sok Kim, 'The Preconditions to the Exercise of the Jurisdiction of the International Criminal Court: With Focus on Article 12 of the Rome Statute', (1999); 47 *MSU-DCL J Int'l L*; Johan D van der Vyver, 'Personal and Territorial Jurisdiction of the International Criminal Court', (2000), 14 *Emory Int'l L Rev* 1; Arsanjani, above n 10, at 26; Bourdon, above n 10, at 76–81.

[24] Art 12(3) in connection with a referral to the ICC by a non state party uses the terms 'the crime in question' instead of 'a situation in which one or more crimes within the jurisdiction of the court appear to have been committed'. In all other referrals to the ICC, by a state party or the Security Council, the Statute uses the term 'situation,' which is intended to exclude a possible selectivity of instances or individuals to be referred to the ICC on an exclusive basis. The drafting of Article 12(3) (which was part of the Part 2 package that was sent directly to the Committee of the Whole and not to the Drafting Committee) did not intend to deviate from other methods of referrals. Thus, Art

Jurisdiction of the ICC is based on the principle of territorial criminal jurisdiction, and not on a theory of universality of criminal jurisdiction.[25] While the reach of the Court's jurisdiction is universal, it does not represent the theory of universality, except for 'referrals' from the Security Council, which are not linked to the territoriality of any state, whether they are Parties or non-States-Parties. It is clearly established in international law that whenever a crime is committed on the territory of a given state, it can prosecute the perpetrator even when that person is a non-national.[26] Because of that principle, a state may extradite a non-national to another state for prosecution. Accordingly, every state has the right, in accordance with its constitutional norms, to transfer jurisdiction to another state which has jurisdiction over an individual accused of committing a crime,[27] or to an international adjudicating body. Such jurisdictional transfer is an entirely valid exercise of national sovereignty. Such a transfer, however, must be done in accordance with international human rights norms.[28] Thus, the ICC, with respect to the prosecution of a national of a non-state party who commits a crime on the territory of a state party, does not provide for anything more than already exists in the customary practice of states.[29]

Since the ICC is complementary to national criminal jurisdiction, a state party's surrender of an individual to the ICC's jurisdiction pursuant to the Treaty: (a) does not detract from its national sovereignty; (b) does not infringe upon the national sovereignty of another state (such as the state of nationality of the perpetrator or the victim); and (c) does not violate the rights of the individual whose prosecution is transferred to a competent criminal jurisdiction (which will exercise its jurisdiction in accordance with international human rights law norms).

Ratione Temporis: When the ICC May Exercise Its Jurisdiction

The ICC's jurisdiction is only prospective and therefore it does not apply to crimes that occurred before the Treaty's entry into force.[30] The relevant

12(3) must be read *in pari materia* with Article 13 ('a situation in which one or more crimes within the jurisdiction of the court appear to have been committed'). See also RPG 44, above n 14.

[25] See generally M Cherif Bassiouni, *International Extradition: United States Law and Practice*, 3rd edn. (1996), 356–67.

[26] *Ibid.* at 357.

[27] See for example the European Convention on the Transfer of Proceedings in Criminal Matters, ETS No 73, 30 (March 1978); European Inter-State Co-operation in Criminal Matters 831 (EM Rappard and M Cherif Bassiouni (eds), 1991). Surrender of individuals by one state to another is commonly done by means of extradition. See Bassiouni, *International Extradition*, 385.

[28] International human rights law norms provide for certain substantive and procedural guarantees. These norms also arise under regional conventions such as the European Convention on Human Rights and Fundamental Freedoms. See M Cherif Bassiouni, 'Human Rights in the Context of Criminal Justice: Identifying International Procedural Protections and Equivalent in National Constitutions', (1993), 3 *Duke Journal of Comparative & International Law* 235–297. See also MC Bassiouni, *Introduction to International Criminal Law*, (2003)

[29] See Bassiouni, *International Extradition*, above note 25 at 357.

[30] The ICC Statute entered into force on 1 July 2002, that is, when the treaty that embodied it had been ratified by 60 states; specifically, the first day of the month after the 60th day following the

provisions of the Statute are Articles 11 and 24, on jurisdiction *ratione temporis* and on non-retroactivity *ratione personae*.

Articles 11 and 24 overlap. This is due to the fact that most of part 2 of the Statute was drafted and accepted as a 'package' that did not go through the drafting committee.[31] In that working group there was insistence by some delegations on including Article 11 notwithstanding the fact that they knew the contents of Article 24.

The two articles must be read *in pari materia*, but even so, there will be at least one interpretive issue that will require reliance on a source of law other than the Statute, and that is how to interpret these two provisions with respect to continuing crimes, which were committed in part before the ICC's entry into force and continued thereafter. This same issue will arise with respect to war crimes arising out of Article 8 for which a state party has 'opted out for a period of seven years'.[32]

Specifically, there is a noticeable textual difference between the two articles. Article 11 speaks of the Court having jurisdiction over 'crimes committed' after entry into force. In contrast, Article 24 speaks of a person not being criminally responsible for 'conduct prior' to entry into force, without the verb 'committed'. The working group that drafted Article 24 had intentionally not used a verb to describe the conduct prior to the entry into force.[33] This was because of the sensitive political nature of this issue and the varied nuances that suggested modifying verbs had.[34] The decision to eliminate a modifying term would allow the Court to decide the question of continuing violations, which is made more difficult by the contradictory provisions.[35]

Ratione Personae: the Subjects of Criminal Responsibility[36]

The ICC's jurisdiction applies only to individuals (Articles 1, 25(1)), regardless of their official capacity,[37] who committed a crime within the jurisdiction of the Court after the age of 18 (Article 26). The ICC has no jurisdiction over states or legal entities for the commission of such a crime. A specific decision was made to

deposit of the sixtieth instrument of ratification (Article 126(1)). For states that accede to the treaty after its entry into force, the effective date of entry into force for such states is the first day of the month which follows 60 days from the deposit of that state's ratification (Art 126(2)).

[31] See Bassiouni, *Negotiating the Treaty of Rome*, above n 20.

[32] The Statute provides that a state may, at the time it becomes a state party, opt-out to delay the applicability of the ICCs jurisdiction with respect to war crimes (Article 8) for a period of seven years (Art 124).

[33] See Per Saland, 'International Criminal Law Principles' in *Making of the Rome Statute*, 196–197.

[34] Such suggested verbs included: 'committed', 'occurred', 'commenced', or 'completed.' *Ibid.*

[35] *Ibid.*

[36] See Bussioni. above n 28, at chapter 2.

[37] Art 27 ensures the irrelevance of official capacity. However, this should also be contrasted with Art 98, which might subordinate a state's duty to surrender an accused individual to the ICC based on a pre-existing international legal obligation not to surrender an individual with a third state. This distinction is discussed below.

exclude the criminal responsibility of states and organisations.[38] A state or a group as a legal or abstract entity can neither be placed on trial nor be the subject of any sanctions, including the confiscation or seizure of assets. This decision perhaps represents a regression from the precedent established at Nuremberg.[39]

Indeed, Article 9 of the Charter of the International Military Tribunal (IMT) stated that 'the tribunal may declare (in connection with any act of which the individual may be convicted) that the group or organization of which the individual was a member was a criminal organisation'.[40] The IMT held the leadership corps of the Nazi party, Gestapo, and the 'SS' as criminal groups.[41] Notwithstanding, mere membership at Nuremberg was not sufficient to impose criminal liability. Criminal responsibility would only attach to the individual who joined or remained a member of a given criminal group if the individual had the knowledge that the group was a criminal organisation.[42]

Despite its exclusion of group criminal responsibility, it is still possible for the ICC to develop a concept of individual criminal responsibility from the participation in a group. For example, Article 25 provides for criminal responsibility based on a person's contribution 'to the commission of a crime by a group of persons acting with a common purpose' (Article 25). It should be noted that such contributions must be 'intentional' and made with either 'the aim of furthering the criminal activity or criminal purpose' or made with the 'knowledge' that the group had the 'intention' to commit the crime (Article 25(d)). However, unlike at Nuremberg, under the ICC formula, mere membership even with knowledge of criminal activities is not sufficient to create liability. Rather, the individual must make some 'contribution' to the commission of the crime (Article 25(d)). What type of activity will rise to the level of a 'contribution' is a question that will be left to the jurisprudence of the Court.

Ratione Materiae: the Crimes Within the Jurisdiction of the ICC

The ICC's *ratione materiae* jurisdiction under Article 5 extends, at this time, to three well-established international crimes: genocide,[43] crimes against humanity,[44]

[38] For a discussion of the criminal responsibility of states and organisations under international criminal law, see Bassiouni, 'Sources of International Criminal Law', above n 4, at 24–31.

[39] *Ibid*.

[40] Agreement for the Protection and Punishment of the Major War Criminals of the European Axis, Charter of the International Military Tribunal, 59 Stat 1544, 82 UNTS 279 (New York: United Nations, 8 Aug 1945) ['IMT Charter'].

[41] See I Trial of the Major War Criminals before the International Military Tribunal, 256–273 (1947).

[42] For example, the IMT implemented this concept of group criminality in its judgement by declaring guilty members of the SS 'who became or remained members of the organization with knowledge that it was being used for the commission [of crimes] . . . or who were personally implicated as members of the organization in the commission of such crimes.' *Ibid* at 273.

[43] For a discussion of the crime of genocide, see Matthew Lippman, 'Genocide', *ICL*, 1, above n 4, at 589–613.

[44] For a discussion of crimes against humanity see M Cherif Bassiouni, *Crimes Against Humanity in International Criminal Law*, 2nd rev edn, (1999); Margaret McAuliffe deGuzman, 'The Road from Rome: The Developing Law of Crimes Against Humanity', (2000), 22 *Hum Rts Q*, 335.

and war crimes.[45] These three crimes presently within the ICC's jurisdiction are defined respectively in Articles 6, 7, and 8. They conform to existing international criminal law and fall within the meaning of *jus cogens*, norms which are binding upon all states and that carry obligations from which a state may not derogate.[46] The Statute also lists the crime of aggression, which has yet to be defined and is therefore not subject to the ICC's jurisdiction (Article 5(2)). Furthermore, the Court also has jurisdiction over crimes against the administration of justice and may impose sanctions (Article 70, 71).

Article 6 defines genocide in accordance with the 1948 Convention on the Prevention and Punishment of the Crime of Genocide,[47] which has been ratified by 130 states.[48]

Article 7 defines crimes against humanity[49] in keeping with Article 6(c) of the Nuremberg Charter,[50] Article 5 of the International Criminal Tribunal for the former Yugoslavia[51] and Article 3 of the International Criminal Tribunal for Rwanda.[52] However, the detail included in the ICC's article provides more specificity, and reflects the progressive evolution of customary international law.[53] Among the charges are the elimination of the armed conflict nexus, the inclusion of apartheid and enforced disappearances, a broadened definition of torture, and an expanded list of sexual offences.[54]

It should be noted that in order for crimes against humanity to occur the following elements are necessary: (a) there has to be a state policy, or a policy by

[45] For a historical overview of the evolution of formal and informal limitations on the conduct of war among Western states, see M.Howard, G Andreopoulos and M Shulman, *The Law of War: Constraints on Warfare in the Western World* (1994). See also generally *The Law of War Crimes: National and International Approaches*, Timothy McCormack and Gerry Simpson, (eds), (1997); Michael Schmitt and Leslie Green (eds), *The Law of Armed Conflict into the Next Millennium* (1998); Leslie Green (ed), *Essays on the Modern Law of War,* 2nd edn. (1999); Leslie C Green, 'International Regulation of Armed Conflicts', *ICL*, 1, above n 4, at 355–380; Yves Sandoz, 'Penal Aspects of International Humanitarian Law', *ICL*, 1, above n 4, at 393–416; Michael Veuthey, 'Non-International Armed Conflict and Guerrilla Warfare', *ICL*, 1, above n 4, at 417–438.

[46] See Vienna Convention on the Law of Treaties, at Arts 53, 64; M Cherif Bassiouni, 'International Crimes: Jus Cogens and Obligatio Erga Omnes', (1996), *59 L & Contemp. Probs* 63.

[47] Convention on the Prevention and Punishment of the Crime of Genocide, 78 UNTS 277 (New York, United Nations: 9 December 1948) reprinted in M Cherif Bassiouni, *International Criminal Law Conventions and Their Penal Provisions* (1997), 247–50 (hereafter 'Bassiouni, *Conventions*'). See also Lippman, *Genocide*, above n 43.

[48] As of June 2000.

[49] ICC Statute, Art 7. See Bassiouni, *Crimes Against Humanity,* above n 44, at 243–75; see also Darryl Robinson, 'Defining 'Crimes against Humanity' at the Rome Conference', (1999), 93 *Am J Int'l L* 43.

[50] See IMT Charter, above n 40.

[51] Statue of the International Criminal Tribunal for the Former-Yugoslavia, SC Res 827, UN SCOR, 48 Sess, 3217 mtg. (1993).

[52] Statute of the International Criminal Tribunal for Rwanda, SC Res 955, UN SCOR, 49 Sess, UN Doc S/RES/955, (1994).

[53] Art 7(1) of the ICC Statute requires that an 'attack upon a civilian population' be 'systematic' or 'widespread' as does Art 3 of the Statute of the ICTR, but Art 7(2) of the ICC requires that such an 'attack' be the product of a state's 'policy'. Thus, the element of 'policy' is a prerequisite. See Bassiouni, *Crimes Against Humanity*, above n 44, at 243–75.

[54] See generally McCormack & Robertson, above n 15, at 651–61.

non-state actors (Article 7(2)); (b) to commit the specific crimes enumerated in Article 7(1); and (c) the commission of these crimes take place on a 'widespread' or 'systematic' basis (Article 7(1)). The policy element is the jurisdictional element that transfers crimes which would otherwise be national crimes into international crimes. It is therefore a threshold element. The chapeau of the 'Elements of Crimes' adopted by the Preparatory Commission states:

> 3. "Attack directed against a civilian population" is understood to mean a course of conduct involving the multiple commission of acts referred to in article 7, paragraph 1, of the Statute against any civilian population, pursuant to or in furtherance of a State or organizational policy to commit such attack. The act need not constitute a military attack. It is understood that "policy to commit such attack" requires that the State or organization actively promote or encourage such an attack against a civilian population (footn 1).[55]

This provision also has a footnote at its end which states:

> (Footnote 6) A policy which has a civilian population as the object of the attack would be implemented by State or organizational action. Such a policy may, in exceptional circumstances, be implemented by a deliberate failure to take action, which is consciously aimed at encouraging such attack. The existence of such a policy cannot be inferred solely from the absence of governmental or organisational action.[56]

Consequently, the policy of a state, consistent with Article 7 ('widespread' or 'systematic'), must be evidenced by 'actively encouraging or supporting'. It should be noted that a failure to prevent the crimes does not create an automatic inference of encouragement or support, but rather only 'in exceptional circumstances' does a failure to prevent amount to 'actively encouraging or supporting.'[57]

The war crimes provision of Article 8 includes: (1) the 'grave breaches'[58] and Common Article 3 of the 1949 Geneva Conventions, which have been ratified by 186 states; and (2) the 'grave breaches' Protocol I of 1977[59]and Protocol II,[60]

[55] See Report of the Preparatory Commission of the International Criminal Court, Finalised Draft of the Elements of Crimes, U.N. Doc. PCNICC/2000/INF/3/Add 2 (30 June 2000).

[56] *Ibid*.

[57] *Ibid* at intro. to Art 7 para 3.

[58] Geneva Convention for the Amelioration of the Condition of the Wounded and Sick in Armed Forces in the Field, 6 UST 3114, 75 UNTS 31, Art 50 (12 Aug 1949); Geneva Convention for the Amelioration of the condition of Wounded, Sick and Shipwrecked Members of Armed forces at Sea, 6 UDT 3217, 75 UNTS 85, Art 51 (12 Aug 1949); Geneva Convention Relative to the Treatment of Prisoners of War, 6 UST 3316, 75 UNTS 135, Art 130 (12 Aug 1949); and Geneva Convention Relative to the Protection of Civilian Person in Times of War, 6 UST 3516, 75 UNTS 287. Art 147 (12 Aug 1949). See also Convention Respecting the Laws of Customs of War on Land (Second Hague IV), 36 Stat 2277 (The Hague: 18 Oct 1907); authorities mentioned above n 45.

[59] Protocol Additional to the Geneva Conventions of 12 Aug 1949, and Relating to the Protection of Victims of International Armed Conflicts of 8 June 1977 (1977 Protocol I), Annex I UN Doc A/32/144 (1977), reprinted in 16 ILM 139. See Yves Sandoz, *Commentary on the 1977 Additional Protocols* (1986).

[60] Protocol Additional to the Geneva Conventions of 12 Aug 1949, and relating to the Protection of Victims of Non-International Armed Conflicts (1977 Protocol II) Annex II, UN Doc A/32/144 (1977), reprinted in 16 ILM 1391. See Sandoz, *Commentary*, above n 59.

which are deemed part of the customary law of armed conflict. However, it has been observed that one of the most contentious issues in Rome involved the extension of the definition of war crimes to non-international armed conflict.[61] In addition, Article 8 includes, in part, that which is considered the customary law of armed conflict, including prohibitions of certain weapons.

As all three crimes within the ICC's jurisdiction are already well established in international criminal law, the ICC does not establish new crimes, but rather embodies pre-existing international criminal law. Furthermore, since the ICC is the product of a treaty and provides for only prospective application,[62] any claim that the ICC invokes a body of international criminal law not previously legislated is incorrect.

The Preparatory Commission established by Resolution F of the Diplomatic Conference provided for the Elements of Crimes pursuant to Article 9 of the Statute.[63] These 'elements' do not amend the Statute nor do they supplement the definition of the crimes presently contained in Articles 6, 7, and 8. They are merely designed to 'assist' the Court to prove these crimes.

The Elements of Crimes agreed upon in the fifth session of the Preparatory Commission (and which have to be adopted by the states parties) have clarified in varying degrees what needs to be proven. In genocide, the Elements of Crimes do not add anything of a significant nature to the general understanding of the well-established definition of genocide.[63a]

In war crimes, the Elements of Crimes introduce concepts such as military necessity, reasonableness, and unlawful conduct without setting forth an evidentiary standard by which to assess such additions.[64] Thus, these will be left to the jurisprudence of the Court on the basis of the relevant applicable sources of law contained in Articles 10 and 21.

Crimes against humanity introduces a chapeau with an explanatory footnote (quoted above). With respect to crimes against humanity, the Elements of Crimes emphasise the need to prove the policy of a state or non-state actor, by means of showing active promotion or encouragement, including omission or failure to act.[64a] It should be noted that general principles of criminal law contained in most legal systems recognise that an intentional, deliberate, or purposeful failure to act when there is a pre-existing legal duty or obligation to act

[61] See McCormack and Robertson, above n 15, at 663. Delegations arguing for the inclusion of violations in a non-international armed conflict drew support from both the Statute of the ICTR and the *Tadic* case in the ICTY. See also, below n 63 at 52–53 (containing the 'chapeau' of elements of Article 8).

[62] Art 11 and 24 expressly state that ICC jurisdiction is prospective.

[63] See generally 'International Criminal Court: Ratification and National Implementing Legislation', (2000), 71 *International Review of Penal Law* 39–221. This volume contains the ICC Statute with the Elements of Crimes and Rules of Procedure integrated into the text after the applicable provision to which they pertain.

[63a] See *ibid*, at 41-43.

[64] See Elements of Crimes, above n 10. See also, International Criminal Court, above n 63 at 52–81.

[64a] See *ibid*, at 43-52.

is part of the material element of major crimes. Consequently, it is possible to establish policy by a state or non-state actor through intentional, deliberate, or purposeful failure to act. 'Actively promoting and encouraging' obviously includes engaging in conduct by a state or non-state actor which results in the commission of crimes against humanity. In both cases, namely commission and omission (or failure to act or passive conduct), they must be accompanied by an element of at least knowledge.

With respect to all three crimes, the mental element articulated in Article 30 applies except where another mental element is specified. Article 30 requires that the material element of each crime be committed with both 'intent' and 'knowledge'.

The Elements of Crimes, probably, reveal some confusion between general intent and specific intent. For example, Article 6 (genocide) requires a specific intent; that is a general intent 'to kill', for example, with the specific intent that it is done to 'destroy, in whole or in part' a protected group enumerated in the Statute. This confusion could have been resolved by requiring a lower standard for policy makers, a general intent up to and including knowledge, because of the ability of such persons to know or foresee the consequences of their acts due to their greater access to information and to their ability to control the apparatus of the state. For lower executors, specific intent or knowledge of the overall policy which they are acting in furtherance of should be required. This knowledge would not be required however for the commission of war crimes (Article 8) because those crimes do not require a specific intent.

The three crimes overlap as to their legal elements, but the Statute does not contain a provision on how to deal with either legal overlaps or factual overlaps.[65] Similarly, the Statute does not address the problems of overlaps in respect to penalties (Articles 70–80) whenever a person is convicted of several crimes (which have similar legal elements) arising out of the same conduct. The problems of overlapping legal provisions (Articles 6, 7 and 8) will also arise in respect to the Court's determination of *ne bis in idem* (Article 20). These problems will also arise in the courts of the states parties. How the ICC judges and national judges will deal with these problems is uncertain.

Aggression and Other New or Amended Crimes[66]

A fourth crime, aggression, is provided for in Article 5(1)(d) of the Statute. The crime of aggression is not defined in the Statute, as the other three crimes within its jurisdiction, namely genocide (Article 6), crimes against humanity (Article 7), and war crimes (Article 8). But Article 5(2) provides for the eventual definition of aggression.

[65] See M Cherif Bassiouni, 'The Normative Framework of International Humanitarian Law: Overlaps, Gaps, and Ambiguities', (1998), 8 *Transnational L. & Contemp. Probs.* 199. The civilist legal systems address this problem as a *Concours ideal d'infractions*.

[66] As of 30 April 2003 aggression has not been defined. See Continuity of Work in Respect of the Crime of Aggression, UN Doc ICC–ASP/1/Res 1 (2002), Pt IV at 238.

The definition of aggression is presently under discussion in the Preparatory Commission which will likely continue until it is formally adopted as an amendment by the Assembly of States Parties at the review conference seven years from the date that the ICC enters into force.[67] This will be the first opportunity when the Assembly of States Parties can begin the process of changing the crimes within the jurisdiction of the court (Articles 121(1), 123(1)). Other crimes may be subsequently included within the jurisdiction of the Court as well, and crimes such as drug trafficking and terrorism have been discussed.[68]

The definition of aggression or any other amendment to the list of crimes must first be approved by at least two thirds of the Assembly of States Parties if consensus cannot be reached (Article 121(3)). After approval the new or amended crime will be applicable prospectively to only those states parties that have ratified the amendment one year after the deposit of their instrument of ratification (Article 121(5)).

The addition of new crimes or the amendment of existing crimes has the potential to create a disparity in the application of the Court's *ratione materiae* jurisdiction. For example, the ICC will not exercise jurisdiction over a newly defined crime or an amended version of an existing crime when committed: (1) by nationals of a state party that has not accepted the amendment; or (2) by an individual who commits acts constituting the new or amended crime on the territory of a state party that has not accepted the amendments. As such, for the non-accepting state, the Court will exercise its jurisdiction as if the amendment had never been made. Therefore, if the crime of genocide were to be amended, the Court would exercise jurisdiction over an individual as if the crime had not been amended if that individual is either a national of or allegedly commits the crime on the territory of a state that has not accepted the amended definition.

In effect, after an amendment, unless or until it is accepted by all states parties, there is the potential for varying criminal responsibility depending on which states parties' territory a crime is committed or by which states parties' national. Unlike an amendment to other non-institutional provisions of the Statute, there is no specified number of ratifications at which time the amendment enters into force for all states parties.[69]

[67] See generally the following documents prepared by the PrepCom and the Secretariat summarising various proposals: Compilations of Proposals on the crime of aggression submitted at the Preparatory Committee on the Establishment of an International Criminal Court (1996–1998), the United Nations Diplomatic Conference of Plenipotentiaries on the Establishment of an International Criminal Court (1998) and the preparatory Commission for the International Criminal Court, UN Doc PCNICC/1999/INF/2; Discussion paper proposed by the Coordinator: Consolidated text of proposals on the crime of aggression, UN Doc PCNICC/1999/WGCA/RT.1; Discussion paper proposed by the Coordinator: Preliminary list of possible issues relating to the crime of aggression, UN Doc PCNICC/2000/WGCA/RT.1; Reference document on the crime of aggression, prepared by the Secretariat, UN Doc PCNICC/2000/WGCA/INF/1.

[68] See Molly McConville, 'A Global War on Drugs: Why the United States Should support the Prosecution of Drug Traffickers in the International Criminal Court', (1999), 37 *Am Crim L Rev* 75.

[69] See below under 'The organisation and operation of the Court'.

Elements of Criminal Responsibility: The General Part

The Rome Conference failed to include a specific provision concerning the required 'material element' or *actus reus*. This resulted from a failure of delegates to agree on the inclusion of an 'omission' as a basis for imposing criminal liability.[70] Rather than using the language 'act or omission', the Statute uses the term 'conduct'. It will ultimately be left to the jurisprudence of the Court to determine at what point an 'omission' gives rise to criminal responsibility.

Pursuant to Article 25 of the Statute, an individual is criminally responsible for 'conduct' that constitutes a crime within the jurisdiction of the Court if that person (a) orders, solicits, or induces the commission of the crime that either occurs or is attempted; or (b) facilitates the commission of such a crime, aids, abets, or otherwise assists in its commission or its attempted commission.

An individual may also be guilty if that person contributes to the commission or attempted commission of a crime by a group with a common purpose (Article 25(d)). The conduct of the individual must be intentional and made either with the aim of furthering the criminal activity of the group where such activity or purpose involves the commission of a crime within the jurisdiction of the Court; or made with the knowledge of the intention of the group to commit the crime (Article 25(d)(i)–(ii)).

Moreover, criminal responsibility cannot be avoided based on: (a) the official capacity of the offender (Article 27); (b) any period of limitations (Article 29); or (c) mistake of law, unless the mistake negates the mental element (Article 32(2)).[71]

A military commander or any person effectively acting as a military commander cannot avoid responsibility for crimes committed under his or her command when that commander knew, should have known, or failed to reasonably prevent such crimes (Article 28(a)). This responsibility includes actions of subordinates if the superior: (i) knew or consciously disregarded such actions; (ii) effectively controlled such actions; or (iii) failed to take necessary preventive or repressive measures (Article 28 (b)).[72]

A person will not be criminally responsible in certain circumstances, if the person: (a) suffers from a mental disease or other capacity that diminishes the persons ability to control his or her conduct; (b) acts in self-defence; or (c) was subject to duress (Article 31).

[70] Saland, above n 17, at 212–13; Bassiouni, *Negotiating the Treaty of Rome,* above n 20, at 464.

[71] See Christine Van den Wyngaert, 'War Crimes, Genocide and Crimes Against Humanity—Are States Taking National Prosecutions Seriously?', in 3 *ICL*, above n 4, at 227–38.

[72] See Jordan J Paust, 'Superior Orders and Command Responsibility', in 1 *ICL*, above n 4, at 223–38.

INVOKING THE JURISDICTION OF THE ICC

Referring a 'Situation' to the Court: Initiation of the Investigation and Prosecution[73]

The ICC may exercise jurisdiction over a crime after a factual situation, which involves the possible commission of one or more of the crimes defined by the Statute, is referred to the Prosecutor by: (a) a state party (Articles 13(b), 14); (b) the Security Council (Article 13(b)); or (c) a non-state party (Article 12(3)). A referral by a state party must specify the relevant circumstances and be accompanied by supporting documentation (Article 14(2)).[73a]

In order to refer a 'situation' to the Prosecutor, the Security Council must be acting pursuant to Chapter VII of the United Nations Charter. Thus, the 'situation' must involve a threat to peace and security. In the event that the Security Council refers a 'situation' to the Court pursuant to Chapter VII, the Court need not concern itself with the pre-conditions set forth in Article 12(2), namely that the crimes be committed by either a citizen of a state party or on the territory of a state party. The only requirement is that the situation be one that involves a 'threat to peace and security'. It should be noted too that Security Council has the power to delay the investigation and prosecution of a 'situation' that has been referred to the Court (by either a state party (Article 13(1)) or the Prosecutor's *proprio motu* action (Article 15) for up to 12 months (Article 16). This delay will only occur pursuant to a resolution by the Security Council acting pursuant to chapter VII of the United Nations Charter in response to 'a threat to peace and security'. In addition, the Prosecutor may also initiate an investigation concerning the commission of crimes defined by the Statute after obtaining approval of the Pre-Trial Chamber (Articles 13(c), 15).

A 'situation' is the overall factual context in which it is believed that 'a crime within the jurisdiction of the court' (Article 5) has been committed. Thus, the ICC's jurisdiction cannot be triggered against a specific person, and, consequently, it cannot be used as a political instrument against anyone.

The term 'situation' cannot be interpreted in a narrow or restrictive manner that singles out a given party to a given conflict, or a given group, or military unit, nor can it be interpreted to refer to a specific occurrence without regard to its overall context. This intended meaning of the term 'situation' will of course vary from one instance to the next, but it must be determined contextually by the ICC Prosecutor, and will ultimately be subject to the judicial review of a three judge panel (Article 61), and eventual review by the Appellate Chamber

[73] See also Morten Bergsmo, 'Occasional Remarks on Certain State Concerns about the Jurisdictional Reach of the International Criminal Court, and Their Possible Implications for the Relationship Between the Court and the Security Council', (2000), 69 *Nordic Journal of International Law* 87 (discussing state concerns about the ICC's jurisdictional reach implicating the Security Council's use of the Court).

[73a] Rule 45 further notes that a referral shall be in writing; See also Lee above n 14.

(Article 82). Such judicial review at two levels, by a total of eight judges, guarantees the integrity of the process.

While there is no doubt that only a 'situation' can be referred to the ICC Prosecutor by the Security Council or a state party, there is a material error in Article 12(3), which deals with acceptance of the ICC jurisdiction by a non-state party of 'the crime in question.' The term 'crime' seems to have been inadvertently used by the unofficial drafters of this provision rather than the term 'situation' which was used with respect to referrals by the Security Council or a state party.[74] The intention was to have a non-state party refer a 'situation' that gives rise to 'a crime within the jurisdiction of the court'. It is not believed that this material error in Article 12(3) will give rise to concerns that the ICC will interpret that provision in a manner inconsistent with what is stated above.

When a situation is referred to the ICC Prosecutor, whether by the Security Council, state party, or non-state party, the Prosecutor may initiate an investigation if he or she believes that there is a 'reasonable basis' to proceed under the Statute (Article 53(1)).

A 'referral' by the Security Council, a state party, or a non-state party are all at the same level. Thus, the Security Council's 'referral' is not in any way to be understood as an obligation on the ICC Prosecutor to proceed with a prosecution. All three sources of referrals merely bring to the ICC Prosecutor's attention facts which might prompt an investigation. Whether that investigation produces sufficient evidence to constitute a 'reasonable basis' (Article 53) to prosecute will depend upon the outcome of the investigation.

The Prosecutor's *Proprio Motu* Initiation of an Investigation

Pursuant to Article 15, the Prosecutor may also initiate *proprio motu* an investigation, absent a 'referral' by a state (Articles 13(a), 14), the Security Council (Article 13(b)), or a non-state party (Article 13(b)). However, prior to undertaking an investigation, the Prosecutor must submit a request along with supporting material to the Pre-Trial Chamber (Article 15(2)) and obtain its approval (Article 15(4)) by a majority vote (at least two out of three).

In gathering supporting material or simply in evaluating whether to make such a request, the Prosecutor may seek information from reliable sources, such as states, organs of the United Nations, intergovernmental or non-governmental

[74] The small group of delegates worked with the Chairman of the Committee of the Whole to develop the text. It is clear that they did not intend to alter the essence of a 'referral', namely a 'situation.' See Bassiouni, *Negotiating the Treaty of Rome,* above n 20, at 443, 453, 457–58. It is difficult to ascertain in view of the negotiating conditions, and the drafting of this provision by a few delegates and not by the Drafting Committee (which was not referred the provisions in Part 2), what the appropriate formulation was to be. Most likely it was intended to be 'a situation giving rise to a crime within the jurisdiction of the court'. Even though most of these words are absent from the text, it is surely construed that way. Any other construction would absurdly result in non-parties having the ability to select which 'crimes' are to be investigated and which ones should not, and by implication also predetermine which party is to be investigated. Such a situation would fly in the face of all the basic principles on which the ICC's jurisdiction is founded.

organisations, and receive written or oral testimony at the seat of the Court or elsewhere (Article 15(2)). Moreover, victims are also permitted to make representations before the Pre-Trial Chamber.

The Prosecutor may commence an investigation only after the Pre-Trial Chamber determines that there is a reasonable basis to proceed with an investigation and that the case falls within the jurisdiction of the Court (Article 15(4)).[74a] If the Pre-Trial Chamber does not authorise an investigation, the Prosecutor may file subsequent requests based on new facts or evidence. (Article 15(5)).

Admissibility and Inadmissibility

Before an arrest warrant is issued, the Prosecution must seek approval of the Pre-Trial Chamber (Article 58). The Pre-Trial Chamber is to determine whether there are reasonable grounds to believe that the individual who is being sought has committed a crime within the jurisdiction of the Court. In addition, upon the individual's surrender to the ICC, the charges again must be confirmed by the Pre-Trial Chamber (Articles 60(2), 61). Thus, any investigation, initiated by any of the sources of 'referrals' (state-party (Article 13(a)), non-state party (Article 12(3)), or Security Council (Article 13(b)) or by the Prosecutor *proprio motu* (Article 15)), cannot result in a prosecution unless the criminal violation charged by the Prosecutor in the indictment is 'confirmed' by the Pre-Trial Chamber (Article 61).[74b]

The Court will determine that a case is inadmissible based on any of the following:

(1) the case is being investigated or prosecuted by a state which has jurisdiction over it, unless the state is unwilling or unable to genuinely carry out these obligations (Article 17(1)(a));
(2) the case has been investigated by a state with jurisdiction and the state has decided not to prosecute, unless the decision resulted from the unwillingness or inability of the state to genuinely prosecute (Article 17(1)(b));
(3) the person has already been tried for conduct which is the subject of the complaint (Article 17(1)(c));
(4) the case is not of sufficient gravity to justify further action by the Court (Article 17(1)(d)).

If indeed a Prosecutor defers investigation or prosecution to the state, he or she may request the state to provide information concerning the domestic proceedings (Article 19(11)).

The issue of whether a state is 'unwilling' to 'genuinely' investigate or prosecute an individual was a sensitive issue during the drafting process.[75] Indeed,

[74a] See also RPE 46-50, 102-3, see Lee above n 14.
[74b] See also Rules 121, 122, 123, 124, 125, 126 131; see Lee above n 14.
[75] See Holmes, above n 15, at 48–54.

this is necessarily a subjective inquiry. The following are the criteria that the Court will use to determine the issue of 'unwillingness': (a) the state undertakes the proceedings for the purpose of shielding the person from the ICC's jurisdiction (Article 17(2)(a)); (b) there is an unjustified delay in the proceedings that is inconsistent with an intent to bring the person to justice (Article 17(2)(b)); and (c) the proceedings are not conducted independently or impartially (Article 17(2)(c)). While these criteria outline the situations where a state is likely failing to genuinely execute its duties under international law, it fails to provide concrete examples of the factual situations that will give rise to the Court's assertion of jurisdiction over the matter. In establishing that a given state's proceeding are in good faith, the state may provide to the court evidence that 'its courts meet internationally recognised norms and standards for the independent and impartial prosecution of similar conduct'.[76]

The issue of 'inability' to prosecute was a less contentious issue during the drafting phase.[77] A state's inability to prosecute in a particular case is reflected in a total or substantial collapse or unavailability of its national judicial system that prevents it from obtaining an accused or acquiring necessary evidence (Article 17(3)). The determination of an 'inability' to prosecute is perhaps more objective than the determination of an 'unwillingness', which necessarily requires an examination into a state's motives. Situations where there is a 'total' or a 'substantial' collapse of the judiciary are generally glaringly apparent.

The Court must always satisfy itself that it has jurisdiction in any case brought before it, and indeed, on its own motion, may determine the admissibility of a case before it (Article 19). In addition, challenges to the admissibility of a case may be brought by: (a) an accused; (b) a state with jurisdiction over a case (on the grounds that it is fulfilling or has fulfilled its duties to investigate and prosecute the case); (c) the state in which the conduct occurred; or (d) the accused's state of nationality (Article 19(2)).[77a]

The Court's jurisdiction may be challenged only once by any person or state listed above, and this challenge generally must be made prior to or at the commencement of trial (Article 19(4)–(5)). Prior to the confirmation of charges, challenges will be directed to the Pre-Trial Chamber and, afterwards, to the Trial Chamber (Article 19(6)). The rulings of either chamber are appealable (Articles 19(6), 82).

If a challenge is made by a state, then the Prosecutor must suspend the investigation until the Court makes its determination (Article 19(7)). However, pending the ruling, the Prosecutor may seek authority to continue the investigation from the Court: (a) if it is necessary to preserve important evidence and the risk of destruction is high; (b) to complete a previously begun witness statement; (c) to prevent the absconding of persons in respect of whom the Prosecutor has already requested a warrant of arrest (Article 19(8)). If a case is

[76] See RPE 51, above n 10.
[77] See Holmes, above n 15, at 49.
[77a] See also RPE 58/133, 59, 60, 61, 62; and Lee above n 14.

deemed inadmissible, the Prosecutor may seek review by the Court should new facts or evidence arise (Article 19(10)).

Ne Bis In Idem[78]

The principle of *ne bis in idem* is a corollary to the principle of complementarity reflected in Article 17, which likewise prevents the Court from asserting jurisdiction when a competent national legal system has already accepted jurisdiction.

The principle *ne bis in idem* prevents persons from being tried before the Court twice for conduct that formed the basis of crimes for which the person had either been convicted or acquitted by the Court (Article 20(1)). Moreover, it prevents a national legal system of a state party from prosecuting an individual for the same conduct that formed the basis of a crime for which the person had previously been convicted or acquitted by the Court (Article 20(2)). In addition, an individual, who has been either previously acquitted or convicted by a national court for conduct that formed the basis of crimes under the Statute, may not be prosecuted by the Court (Article 20(3)). However, a conviction or acquittal by a national jurisdiction will not bar subsequent prosecution by the ICC if: (a) the purposes of the state proceedings were to 'shield the person concerned form criminal responsibility' (Article 20(3)(a)); or (b) the domestic proceedings were not conducted independently or impartially (Article 20(3)(b)).

Thus, *ne bis in idem* only prevents a second prosecution of an accused in two circumstances: (1) when the first attempt was either made by the ICC, and the second effort is by either a state party or the ICC; or (2) when the first attempt was by a national legal system (assuming that the first prosecution was independent, impartial, and not for the purposes of shielding the accused from criminal responsibility (Article 20(3)(a)-(b))) and the second prosecution is by the Court.

The principle is plainly only applicable between the ICC and a given state party. It is however not binding between states. Thus, a prosecution in one state has no effect in barring a prosecution in another, even if both are states parties to the ICC. This results from the fact that there is no internationally recognised norm or standard for the principle of *ne bis in idem*.

It should be noted that the Statute only bars re-prosecution at the point where an accused has either been convicted or acquitted. Thus, if a given national system attaches the principle at an earlier stage in a proceeding than conviction or acquittal, such a bar will conceivably have no effect on the Court's re-prosecution of the individual. A question arises as to whether a state will still be obligated to surrender to the ICC for prosecution an individual who is barred from domestic re-prosecution by virtue of the state's own domestic principles

[78] For a general discussion, see Christine van den Wyngaert and Guy Stessens, 'The International Non Bis in Idem Principle: Resolving Some of the Unanswered Questions', (1999), 48 *Int'l & Comp L Q* 779 .

concerning *ne bis in idem*. The state's *ne bis in idem* principle may vary from the Court's, and, for example, the state may attach the principle at the empanelling of a jury rather the final determination of guilt. Thus, before surrender, when the individual is granted the right to challenge the request before the national court on the basis of *ne bis in idem* (Article 89(2)), the national court will need to determine whether to apply the national standard or the Statute. While there is an obligation to comply with Court orders, there is no corresponding duty to apply the jurisprudence of the Court. Subsequently, the national court may opt to apply the domestic standard. There is of course no question of the state's obligation to surrender if the first attempt at prosecution was not independent, impartial, or was for the purposes of shielding the accused from criminal responsibility (Articles 20(3)(a)-(b)). However, questions will certainly be raised where the first attempt was made in good faith, and the state wants to ensure that its greater protection of the rights of the accused are applied.

THE COURT'S EXERCISE OF JURISDICTION

The Investigation Process

The Prosecutor, after evaluating the information that has been made available, shall initiate an investigation unless the Prosecutor determines that there is no reasonable basis to proceed (Article 53(1)). In determining whether to proceed, the Prosecutor will consider whether: (a) the information made available provides a reasonable basis to believe that a crime within the ICC's jurisdiction has been committed; (b) the case would be admissible under Article 17 (for example, whether another state with jurisdiction is currently investigating or prosecuting the case); and (c) there are substantial reasons to believe that the investigation will not serve the interests of justice taking into account the gravity of the crime and the interests of victims. However, if the Prosecutor decides not to proceed, the Pre-Trial Chamber must be informed, and either the Pre-Trial Chamber, the referring state, or the Security Council may request the Prosecutor to reconsider the decision not to proceed.[78a]

The Prosecutor's investigation must extend to cover all facts and evidence relevant to a determination of whether there is criminal responsibility, and thus both incriminating and exonerating evidence must be investigated equally (Article 54(1)). In addition, the investigation must respect both the interests and personal circumstances of the victims and witnesses and the rights of the accused (Article 54(1)).

Pursuant to Article 54(2), the investigation may be conducted on the territory of a state party in accordance with Part 9 concerning international co-operation and judicial assistance or as authorised by the Pre-Trial Chamber when the state is 'clearly unable to execute a request for cooperation due to the unavailability

[78a] See also RPE 104-10; and Lee above n 14.

of any authority or component of its judicial system capable to execute the request for cooperation' (Article 57(3)(d)). With respect to investigations on the territory of a non-state party, the ICC Prosecutor is empowered to enter into ad hoc agreements and arrangements to facilitate cooperation with the state (Article 54(3)(d)).

In conducting an investigation, the Prosecutor may: (a) collect and examine evidence; (b) request the presence and question persons under investigation, witnesses, and victims; (c) enter into agreements to facilitate the co-operation of a state, organisation, or person; (d) agree not to disclose information that the Prosecutor receives as confidential; and (e) take necessary measures to ensure confidentiality of information, the protection of persons, and preservation of evidence (Article 54(3)).

When a 'unique investigative opportunity' arises, if necessary, at the request of the Prosecutor, the Pre-Trial Chamber can authorise the Office of the Prosecutor to take measures to collect evidence that may not be available subsequently for the purposes of a trial (Article 56). A 'unique investigative opportunity' refers to the civil law concept of 'definitive and unrepeatable acts' or the 'anticipated taking of evidence'.[79] It is also related to the common law tradition of taking evidence depositions (which ensure full cross-examination) of witnesses who will not be available at trial.[80] It also refers to evidence which by its very nature cannot be reproduced at trial (e.g. mass grave exhumations) and requires a record of the manner in which it was obtained or other extraordinary measures to preserve it.[81]

Upon the Prosecutor's motion, the Pre-Trial Chamber may issue an arrest warrant if it is satisfied that reasonable grounds exist that an individual committed a crime within the ICC's jurisdiction (Article 58). The state party in which the accused is located is expected to 'immediately take steps to arrest the person in question in accordance with its laws' as well as with Part 9 of the Statute concerning international cooperation and judicial assistance (Article 59).

The Pre-Trial Chamber must hold hearings to confirm charges in the presence of the person charged (Article 61(1)). If the circumstances warrant, the charges can be confirmed in the absence of the accused (Article 61(2)).

Rights of Individuals Under Investigation[82]

Persons under investigation are granted several rights pursuant to Article 55. They shall not be compelled to incriminate themselves or be subjected to any

[79] See Fabricio Guariglia, 'Role of the Pre-Trial Chamber in Relation to a Unique Investigative Opportunity', in *Commentary on Rome Statute*, above n 14, at 737–38.

[80] *Ibid.*

[81] *Ibid.*

[82] See 'Substantive and Procedural Aspects of International Criminal Law' (GK McDonald and O Swaak-Goldman (eds) 2000) at vol I; Christoph Safferling, 'Towards an International Criminal Procedure' (2001).

form of duress, coercion, threats, or torture. They shall be questioned in a language they understand or with the assistance of a competent interpreter if necessary. Furthermore, if there are grounds to believe that a person has committed a crime within the jurisdiction of the court, prior to questioning by either the Prosecutor or national authorities pursuant to Part 9, the accused shall be informed that there are grounds to believe the accused has committed a crime, advised of the right to remain silent, provided with legal assistance,[83] and questioned in the presence of counsel.[84]

The Trial

The Rights of the Accused At Trial

A trial before the ICC must be in the presence of the accused (Article 63) with full recognition of his or her rights, including the presumption of innocence (Article 66). These rights include: (a) a public and fair hearing conducted impartially and without delay; (b) being promptly informed of the charges in a language he or she fully understands and speaks; (c) having adequate time and facilities to prepare a defence and to examine witnesses against him or her before and during the trial; (d) having the free assistance of a competent interpreter and necessary translations; and (e) not being compelled to testify or confess guilt (Article 67).

In addition to the rights contained in the text of the Statute, the Rules of Evidence and Procedure also require the Prosecutor to make pre-trial disclosures of witnesses intended to be called and copies of their statements.[85] In addition, the Prosecutor shall permit the defence to inspect evidence in the possession of the prosecution which are material for the preparation of a defence or to be used by the Prosecutor.[86]

Protection of Victims and Witness At Trial

In addition to protecting the rights of the accused, the Court must protect the victims and witnesses who participate in the proceedings (Article 68). This includes an exception to the principle of a public hearing to allow for an *in camera* presentation of evidence or by electronic or other means, particularly to protect children and victims of sexual violence. Moreover, the views and concerns of victims may be presented at appropriate stages of the proceedings as determined by the Court (Article 68(3)).[86a]

[83] See also RPE 21, above n 10 (concerning the assignment and qualification of legal counsel).

[84] See RPE 111–112, above n 10 (concerning the record of questioning and the manner in which it should be taken)

[85] See RPE 76, above n 10.

[86] See RPE 77, above n 10.

[86a] See also RPE 85–93; see above n 14

Relevant Evidence and the Protection of National Security

The Court will also rule on the relevance or admissibility of any evidence by taking into account its probative value weighed against the prejudice it might cause to a fair trial (Article 69). This should be done in accordance with the Rules of Procedure and Evidence.[86b]

The Statute contains numerous safeguards to allow states parties to protect sensitive national security information that might potentially be used as evidence at trial. States may protect national security information that is either requested of them (Article 72) or in the possession of a third state (Article 73). Furthermore, any state may intervene in a case to protect its national security information from being disclosed (Article 72(4)).

The determination of whether the disclosure of information would prejudice a state's national security is ultimately left to the state itself (Article 72). However, the state must attempt to resolve the matter with the Court and take reasonable steps to resolve a dispute about protected material either through the use of: (a) *in camera* or *ex parte* proceedings; (b) summaries or redactions of the information; or (c) other protective measures (Article 72).

Offences Against the Administration of Justice

The Court also has jurisdiction over offences against the administration of justice, including: (a) giving false testimony; (b) presenting false evidence; (c) interfering with witnesses; (d) intimidating and influencing Court personnel; (e) retaliation against Court personnel based on the performance of official duties; and (f) soliciting or accepting a bribe as an official of the Court (Article 70).[86c] These offences must be committed intentionally.

The Appeal

Decisions of the trial chamber may be appealed by either the Prosecutor or the accused (Article 81).[86d] An appeal may be raised based on: (a) a procedural error; (b) error of fact; (c) error of law; or (d) any other ground that affects the fairness of the proceedings (Article 81(1)). In addition, a sentence may be appealed (Article 81(2)). Other decisions may be appealed, including: (a) jurisdiction and admissibility; (b) a decision granting or denying the release of the person investigated or accused; (c) a decision of the Pre-Trial Chamber to take measures to preserve evidence on its own motion; or (d) a decision that involves an issue that would significantly affect the fair and expeditious conduct of the proceedings or outcome of trial (Article 82).[86e]

[86b] See RPE 63–75. See Lee above n 14.
[86c] See RPE 162–69. See Lee above n 14.
[86d] See RPE 150–52. See Lee above n 14.
[86e] See RPE 154–55. See Lee above n 14.

The Penalties and Sentencing

Pursuant to Article 77, the ICC may impose penalties for the commission of crimes within its jurisdiction. In general, a sentence should not exceed a maximum of 30 years (Article 70(1)(a)). However, a life sentence may be imposed when justified by the extreme gravity of the crime and the individual circumstances of the convicted person (Article 70(1)(b)). In addition, the Court may impose fines or the forfeiture of assets or property derived from the commission of the crime (Article 70(2)).[86f]

The sentence is to be determined by the Court, in accordance with the Rules of Procedure and Evidence, which must take into account the gravity of the crime and the individual circumstances of the convicted person (Article 78).

The death penalty has been excluded from the Statute as a penalty for the proscribed crimes. However, the Statute assures states that the penalties provided for under the statute will not affect such penalties under their national laws. Thus, states may apply their own penalties when sentencing individuals convicted under an exercise of national jurisdiction, which may or may not include the death penalty (Article 80).

The sentence of imprisonment is to be served in a state designated by the Court from a list of states parties that have expressed their willingness to accept sentenced persons (Article 103(1)). In selecting a state where the convicted person will serve the sentence, the Court will take into account factors including: (a) the principle of equitable distribution of responsibility amongst the states parties; (b) the application of widely accepted treaty standards concerning the treatment of prisoners; (c) the views of sentenced persons; (d) the nationality of the sentenced person; and (e) such other factors regarding the circumstances of the crime, the person sentenced and the effective enforcement of the sentence (Article 103(3)). In the event that no state is designated by the Court, the sentence will be served in a facility provided by the host state (Article 103(4)). The law of the state of enforcement will govern the imprisonment; however, the Court will supervise the conditions to ensure that they are consistent with international standards (Article 106).[86g]

In addition, only the Court may authorise a reduction in sentence. Such a reduction is only possible after the individual has served two thirds of a sentence or 25 years in the case of a life sentence (Article 110).[86h]

Victim Reparation[87]

The Rules of Procedure and Evidence define victims as: (a) 'natural persons who have suffered harm as a result of the commission of any crime within the

[86f] See RPE 146. See Lee above n 14.

[86g] See RPE 211–12. See Lee above n 14.

[86h] See RPE 223–24. See Lee above n 14.

[87] For the relevant norms in international law, see generally 'Basic Principles and Guidelines on the Right to a Remedy and Reparation for Victims of Violations of International Human Rights and

jurisdiction of the court'; and (b) 'organizations or institutions that have sustained direct harm to any of their property, which is dedicated to religion, education, art or science or charitable purposes, and to their historic monuments, hospitals and other places and objects for humanitarian purposes'.[88]

The Court also has the power to order the payment of appropriate reparation to the victims by the convicted person (Article 75). The Court, either by request or in 'exceptional circumstances' on its own motion, may 'determine the scope and extent of any damage, loss and injury to, or in respect of, victims' (Article 75(1)). The Court may then make an order for reparation[89] (compensation, restitution, and rehabilitation) directly against the convicted person (Article 75(2)). Before making an order, the Court may invite and take account of representations from or on behalf of the offender, victims, and other interested persons or states (Article 75(3)). By inviting comment from other interested persons the Court may take into account the needs of the victim and others who might be affected by the award, such as the offender's family or a *bona fide* purchaser of property that is to be restored. In order to facilitate enforcement of awards, the ICC Statute mandates states parties to the convention to give effect to all decisions entered (Article 75(5)). [89a]

The ICC Statute also envisions a Trust Fund for the benefit of victims and their families (Article 79).Assets of the Trust Fund may come from money or property collected through fines or forfeiture (Article 79(2)). The Court may order reparations to victims out of this fund (Article 75(2)).[89b]

The Court is powerless to order reparations from anyone other than the individual violator. Thus, even though the individual offender's acts can be attributed to the state, an order for reparations cannot be imposed on the state. However, nothing in Article 75 is to be interpreted as prejudicing the rights of victims under national or international law; and thus, these claims can be pursued in other forums (Article 75(6)).

In addition to the potential for reparation, the Statute contains other victim-centred aspccts. Specifically, the Statute envisions the creation of a Victims and Witnesses Unit (Article 43(6)). Moreover, victims are allowed to participate in several stages of the proceedings at the discretion of the court, including: (a) the Pre-Trial Chamber's decision to authorise an investigation (Article 57); and (b) the awarding of reparation (Article 75).

Humanitarian Law', UN Doc. E/CN.4/2000/62 (18 Jan 2000)(annex) ('Basic Principles to Reparation'). See also Chante Lasco, 'Repairing the Irreparable: Current and Future Approaches to Reparations', 10 *Human Rights Brief* 8-21 (2003); Raquel Adana-Pindell, 'In Vindication of Justiciable Victims' Rights to Truth and Justice for State Sponsored Crimes', 35 *Vand J Transn'l L* 1399 (2002).

[88] RPE 85, above n 10.

[89] For a description of the various modalities of reparation, *see* 'Basic Principles to Reparation', above n 87. See 'Declaration of Basic Principles of Justice for Victims of Crime and Abuse of Power', GA Res. 40/34, UN GAOR, 7th Sess (1985). See ICTY Statute, above n 51.

[89a] See RPE 94-97. See Lee above n 14.

[89b] See RPE 98; See Lee above n 14.

Enforcement Modalities and Judicial Assistance[90]

Enforcement Modalities

Enforcement modalities must go through national legal systems which enforce ICC orders and judgements (Parts 9–10). This approach further evidences that the ICC is not supranational but rather 'complementary' to national criminal jurisdiction. However, because the ICC is not a foreign legal system (such as that of a sovereign state), after ratification of the treaty, it becomes an extension of a state's national criminal jurisdiction. This is not to be confused with the idea that the ICC is an extension of national criminal justice systems. The ICC is neither part of national criminal justice systems nor an extension thereof. It is an extension of national criminal jurisdiction established by treaty and implemented by national legislation. The closest analogy is that of transfer of criminal proceedings.[91] Thus, an individual is 'surrendered' to the ICC and not extradited. A consequence of that concept is that states parties could not invoke, in opposition to surrender, their domestic laws that prohibit extradition of nationals, or other defenses.[92]

Enforcement modalities and cooperation between states will be channelled through the national legal systems of states parties, as well as co-operating non-states parties. Thus, they do not infringe upon national sovereignty nor have a supranational character.

The ICC may, however, benefit from accelerated procedures and processes not necessarily available to other states within the context of bilateral relations (Articles 86–99). However, even if the ICC has some priority in national processes, this priority does not alter the nature of the process.

Surrender of Individuals and Judicial Assistance

In general, states parties have a general obligation to cooperate with the ICC's investigation and prosecution (Article 86) and ensure that there are procedures available under national law for all forms of co-operation which are specified under Part 9 (Article 88). However, states parties may deny the request for judicial assistance with regard to the disclosure of documents, which in the opinion of the state, would compromise national security interests (Article 72, 93(4)). In such an instance the Prosecutor will take necessary measures to cooperate with the states' interests and the state shall then provide the Prosecutor with specific reasons for its denial of assistance (Article 72 (5), (6)).

Upon ratification, acceptance, approval, or accession, states designate the channel and the language by which the ICC will make requests for assistance (Article 87(1)). Non-states parties have no obligation to cooperate with a request of the court. However, the ICC may enter into ad hoc arrangements with these states (Article 87(5)). A failure to comply with a request of the Court

[90] See Lee, above n 14; Triffterer, above n 14.
[91] See generally *ICL*, 2, above n 4 (volume regarding procedural and enforcement mechanisms).
[92] See Bassiouni, *International Extradition*, above n 25, at 588–95.

by either a state party or a non-state party that has entered into an ad hoc agreement with the Court may be referred to the Assembly of States Parties or to the Security Council, if the matter had been referred by it (Article 87(7)).[92a]

A request for the arrest and surrender of an individual must be accompanied by an arrest warrant and supporting material (Article 89(1)).[92b] The supporting material should include the arrest warrant and describe the person sought and his or her probable location (Article 91(2)(a)-(b)). In addition, it should include any documents, statements, or information that is required by the laws of the requested state (Article 91(2)(c)). However, these additional requirements should not be more burdensome than those required of requests pursuant to treaty or arrangement with other states. Indeed, if possible, they should be less burdensome (Article 91(2)(c)).[92c]

Individuals may challenge the request before their national courts on the basis of *ne bis in idem* (Article 89(2)).[92d] In addition, a state need not surrender the individual if they are currently serving a sentence for a different crime. (Article 89(4)).[92e] Moreover, a state need not surrender an individual to the Court when there is a competing extradition request for the individual (Article 90). The Court's request shall take priority if the Court has already made a determination of admissibility pursuant to Article 18 and 19 (Article 90(2)). However, if the Court has not made a ruling on admissibility, the requested state may in its discretion, pending the determination of admissibility, deal with the competing request (Article 90(3))

If the competing request comes from a non-state party and the requested state is under an existing international obligation to extradite the person to the competing state, then the requested state should make its decision to extradite after considering all the relevant factors, such as: (a) the dates of the competing requests; (b) interests of the requesting state, including where the crime was committed and the nationality of the person sought and the victims; and (c) the possible subsequent surrender (Article 90(6)). Where the competing request from the non-state party is for conduct that is different than that for which the Court seeks surrender, then the requested state shall also consider the relative nature and gravity of the conduct of the individual (Article 90(7)(b))[92f].

The Court may request other forms of co-operation pursuant to Article 93(1), including the following assistance:[93] (a) identification and whereabouts of

[92a] See also RPE 176–80.

[92b] See also RPE 181–84. See Lee above n 14.

[92c] See also RPE 187.

[92d] See RPE 181.

[92e] See also RPE 183–84. See above Lee n 14

[92f] See also RPE 186. See above Lee n 14.

[93] See generally 2 *ICL*, above n 4, including: Dionysios D Spinellis, 'Securing Evidence Abroad: A European Perspective'; Bruce Zagaris, 'Gathering Evidence from and for the United States'; Edward M Wise, 'Aut Dedere Aut Judicare'; Ekkehart Muller-Rappard, 'Inter-State Cooperation in Penal Matters within the Council of Europe Framework'; Alan Ellis, Robert L Pisani and David S Gualtieri, 'The United States Treaties on Mutual Assistance in Criminal Matters'; Mohamed Abdul-Aziz, 'International Perspective'; M Cherif Bassiouni and Grace MW Gallagher, 'Policies

persons or the locations of items; (b) the taking of testimony, production of evidence such as reports and expert opinions; (c) question of persons being investigated or prosecuted; (d) service of documents; (e) facilitation of the voluntary appearance of persons before the court; (f) temporary transfer of persons; (g) examination of sites, including the exhumation of graves; (h) execution of searches and seizures; (i) the provision of records and documents; (j) the protection of victims and witness; (k) the identification, tracing, and freezing or seizure of proceeds, property and assets and instrumentalities of crime; (l) and any other type of assistance not prohibited by the law of the requested state.

Requests for assistance may be denied based on the existence of a fundamental legal principle of general application in the requested state (Article 93(3)). Moreover, requests may be denied to protect national security pursuant to Article 72 (Articles 93(4), 93(5)). Also, a state may deny assistance that requires it to violate obligations under international law concerning the diplomatic immunity of a person or property of a third state, unless the Court first ascertains the waiver of that immunity from the third state (Article 98(1)).

Requests may also be postponed when they would interfere with an ongoing investigation or prosecution of a different case (Article 94(1)). The Prosecutor may still seek measures to preserve evidence in the event of a postponement (Article 94(2)). States may postpone execution of requests when the Court is considering the admissibility of a case, unless the Prosecutor has received a special order pursuant to Articles 18 and 19 to preserve certain evidence (Article 95).

Co-operation with Respect to Waiver of Immunity

Article 98(2) sets forth an exception to the general duty of co-operation with the ICC in which a requested state would not be compelled to act inconsistently with its obligations under an international agreement necessitating its consent for the surrender of a national, unless the Court can obtain such consent. Certain agreements may also be allowed to take priority over requests from the ICC such that an individual is returned to the sending state instead of the ICC.[94]

Article 98 also raises problems as to the applicable sources of law and their hierarchy. The difficulties with Article 98 rest in the potential conflict between the obligation of a state party to cooperate with the ICC in accordance with the Statute, but yet limiting the Court when its request for cooperation is inconsistent with the 'obligations under international law with respect to the State or diplomatic immunity of a person or property of a third State. . .' Furthermore,

and Practices of the United States'; Helmut Epp, 'The European Convention'; M Cherif Bassiouni and David S Gualtieri, 'International and National Responses to the Globalization of Money Laundering'; M Cherif Bassiouni, 'Policy Considerations on Inter-State Cooperation in Criminal Matters'.

[94] See also RPE 195, above n 10 (noting that a requested state must inform the Court regarding an Art 98 obligation).

under Article 98(2) the Court is also limited in the same manner with respect to a state party's obligations under international agreements.

In essence, Article 98 subordinates cooperation to status of forces agreements, the conventional and customary international law of diplomatic immunity,[95] and the immunity of heads of states. This subordination however is inconsistent with Article 27 concerning the irrelevance of official capacity, and is a question that the Court will likely need to resolve on the basis of a higher source of law than the Statute.[96]

A compromise was reached in order to obtain a consensus, resulting in an Understanding to Rule 195. Rule 195 now reads that the Court may not proceed under Article 98(2) for a request of surrender if such request is inconsistent with international obligations set forth in an agreement mandating the consent of the Sending state. The related Understanding specifies that Rule 195 does not require the negotiation of provisions of such international agreements.

THE ORGANISATION AND OPERATION OF THE COURT

The Principal Organs of the ICC

The ICC is composed of four principal organs[97] (Article 34): (a) the Presidency; (b) an Appeals, Trial, and Pre-Trial Division; (c) the Office of the Prosecutor; and (d) the Registry. Important oversight and policy functions are carried out by the Assembly of States Parties. In addition, while the Court is not an organ of the United Nations, it will maintain a special relationship with that body.

As noted earlier, the first 18 judges of the ICC were elected during the first resumed session of the Assembly of State Parties, which took place in New York between 3–7 February 2003.[97a] The 18 judges represent the world's major legal systems and represent an equitable geographic and gender distribution (Article 36).[97b] The President and the First and Second Vice-Presidents were elected by an absolute majority of the judges and will serve for a three year term (Article

[95] See, eg, Vienna Convention On Diplomatic Relations, 1961, 500 UNTS 95.

[96] The Court could for example distinguish between the relevance of official position on the non-applicability of heads of state immunity from a substantive aspect, and yet preserve these immunities from a procedural aspect. Thus, for example, the Court may deem these immunities applicable procedurally during the period when a head of state is in an office or during a diplomat's accredited tenure in a host nation, but no longer applicable when these relevant periods are over. In any event, such a procedural immunity cannot be deemed a defense or a substantive immunity when a person is indicted or tried for the crimes listed in Art 6–8. Such a position reflects the existing status of international criminal law. See the chapter in this volume by Brigitte Stern.

[97] For additional commentary on the Organs of the Court, see Karim AA Khan, 'Art 34: Organs of the Court', in *Commentary on Rome Statute*, above n 14; see also Sadat & Carden, above n 14, at 397–403; Bourdon, above n 10, at 132–65; Noone and Moore, above n 14, at 123–27.

[97a] The judges were sworn in on 11 March 2003 in the inaugural public session held at the Hall of Knights in The Hague. A list of the first ICC judges is available at www.iccnow.org

[97b] Elected candidates by UN regional group: 3 (African States); 3 (Asian); 1 (Eastern Europe); 4 (Latin America); 7 (Western Europe and other states). By gender 7 women and 11 men.

38(1)).[97c] One division consisting of not less than six judges will deal exclusively with indictments and pre-trial matters; another division consisting of not less than six judges will compose the trial chambers; and another division consisting of four judges and the President will deal with appeals (Article 39). To maintain a distinction between trial and appellate chambers, neither the five appellate judges nor their colleagues in the trial chambers can rotate between two chambers (Article 39).

The Office of the Prosecutor will act as an independent and separate organ of the ICC (Article 42(1)). The Prosecutor will be assisted by Deputy Prosecutors; all of whom will be of different nationalities (Article 42(2)). The first ICC Prosecutor was elected by secret ballot by an absolute majority of the Assembly of States Parties (Article 42(4)) on April 21, 2003[97d]. The Deputy Prosecutors are elected in the same manner by a list of candidates proposed by the Prosecutor (Article 42(4)). The Prosecutor and Deputy Prosecutor will serve nine year terms and are not eligible for re-election (Article 42(4)). The Statute also provides protections to ensure impartiality and allows for the disqualification of a Prosecutor or Deputy Prosecutor at their request or at the request of an accused in situations where their 'impartiality might reasonably be doubted on any ground' (Article 42(8)).The Registry will be responsible for the non-judicial aspects of the administration and servicing of the Court, including setting up a Victims and Witnesses Unit (Article 43(1), (6)). The Registrar is elected by absolute majority of the judges of the ICC, and excerises his functions under the authority of the President of the Court. [97e]

The Assembly of States Parties

An Assembly of States Parties shall be constituted with certain specific prerogatives including the electing of judges, the Prosecutor, and the Registrar (Article 112). Moreover, it reviews and approves the budget, and provides support for the institution, including the ability to deal with states parties who fail to carry out their treaty obligations. The Assembly also has the power to enunciate rules for the internal functioning of the Court, and to adopt rules of procedure and evidence in conformity with the Statute.[97f] Every state party has one vote and consensus will be attempted to be reached except pertaining to matters of substance or procedure where a two-thirds majority and simple majority are necessary, respectively (Article 112 (7)(a), (7)(b)).

Many treaty-based bodies provide for such a system of governance (for example, the World Trade Organization). This system ensures that the

[97c] Judge Philippe Kirsch was elected president, while judges Aku Rueuyehia and Elizabeth Odio Benito were elected first and second vice president, respectively.

[97d] Luis Horeno Ocampo from Argentina was elected Prosecutor of the ICC in an election (by secret ballot) that took place on 21 April 2003. The election took place during the second resumed first session of the ASP held 21-23 April 2003 in New York.

[97e] As of 24 April 2003, there were two nominations for the position of Registrar.

[97f] The RPE and EC were adopted on 30 September 2003, during the first session of the ASP.

bureaucracy of the body acts in conformity with the expectations of the states parties in the fulfilment of the treaty.

Relationship of the ICC to the Security Council[98] and the United Nations

The relationship between the ICC and the Security Council is a consequence of the Security Council's power as established in the United Nations Charter, particularly chapter VII, which gives the Council exclusive political authority over matters involving the preservation, restoration, and maintenance of peace. Chapter VII, Article 39 also gives the Council the power to devise sanctions to preserve and maintain peace achieved by these results. Consequently, the Security Council has the right to refer a situation to the ICC for investigation and eventual prosecution.

In recognition of the Council's powers under Chapter VII of the United Nations Charter, the ICC recognises in Article 16 that the Security Council may ask for a suspension of proceedings before the ICC for 12 months if the Security Council deems that the situation under which the prosecution arises constitutes a threat to 'peace and security' as provided for in the United Nations Charter. Under its Charter powers, the Security Council can, by resolution, take measures that are binding upon all United Nations member states. Thus, the Security Council's suspension prerogatives in the Statute are within its Charter powers. The Statute therefore does no more than recognise the Security Council's powers; in fact, it even limits these powers.

The ICC will be brought into a relationship with the United Nations through an agreement to be approved by the Assembly of States Parties (Article 2).[99] Similarly, funding will be provided to the ICC from the United Nations. The seat of the ICC is at The Hague in the Netherlands (Article 3).

Amending the Statute

Under Article 121, an amendment cannot be proposed until seven years after the entry into force of the Statute. After an amendment has been proposed and 'no sooner than three months from the date of notification' of the amendment to the states, the Assembly of States Parties must decide by a majority present and voting whether to take up the proposal (Article 121(2)).

The Statute distinguishes between amendments of an institutional matter[100] and other types of amendments. Article 122 presents an opportunity for States Parties to amend provisions of the Statute, such as the service of judges, the President, the Prosecutor, the Staff, and the instance of their dismissal, at any

[98] See Bergsmo, above n 73, at 92–113 (discussing the Security Council's use of the ICC and possible state concerns).

[99] See Draft Relationship Agreement between the United Nations and the International Criminal Court—Prepared by the Secretariat, UN Doc PCNICC/2000/WGICC-UN/L.1

[100] These are contained in arts 35–39, 42–44, 46, 47, 49.

time (Article 122(1)). Such amendments will be adopted by consensus or, with a lack thereof, by the Assembly of States Parties with a two-thirds majority vote (Article 122(2)). These amendments will take effect six months after adoption and do not require ratification.

The adoption of other amendments requires at least a two-thirds majority vote of all states parties if consensus cannot be reached (Article 121(3)). The entry into force of the particular amendment differs however depending on the particular section to be amended.

For amendments to Articles 5–8, which would involve the addition of new crimes or modification of existing ones, the amendment will enter into force for a given state party one year after that state party deposits its instrument of ratification (Article 121(5)). The amendment will not apply to those states that have not yet deposited their instrument of ratification (Article 121(5)). However, for amendments to other non-institutional provisions, the amendment will enter into force for all states parties one year after seven-eighths of them deposit an instrument of ratification. States may withdraw immediately from the Statute, if they fail to ratify an amendment when it has been accepted by seven-eighths of the states parties (Article 121(6)). If a state seeks to withdraw on this basis it has one year from the entry into force of the amendment (121(6)).

The Statute does not permit the states parties to ratify the Treaty with any reservations or declarations and understandings (Article 120).

CONCLUSION

Without a doubt, international accountability for genocide, war crimes, and crimes against humanity is necessary to achieve justice as well as peace and reconciliation between peoples in conflict-torn areas. Thus, if it were not sufficient to rely on the intrinsic need for justice and its expectations of deterring future criminals, then it should be sufficient to recognise that international prosecution, as one of the various methods of accountability can contribute to restoring and maintaining peace. In other words, if not justice for justice's sake, or justice for the victims' sake, then justice for the sake of peace. Above all, when overlooking the victimisation of the past, international civil society breaks faith with the bonds of humanity and is condemned to repeat the worst of history's mistakes.

Whether national or international, justice never comes easily or painlessly. A justice system with the characteristics of political independence, impartiality toward all persons, fairness to the accused and the victim, effectiveness in its functioning, and transparency in its processes will have some deterring effect on potential future violators. Such a system must, however, also provide victims with redress. That is what the ICC is intended to accomplish, and if it does so, the ICC will contribute to peace. Indeed, the ICC, like its counterpart, the domestic justice systems, will only partially achieve its goals; however, it is an important step.

As the above overview reflects, the ICC is a product of compromise, and like other international and national legal institutions it must sacrifice efficiency in order to safeguards other competing interests, such as state sovereignty and the rights of those who will be impacted by its process. However, the ICC is a necessary institution for the attainment of the goals of international criminal justice. While it will not bring an end to all injustice, conflict, or international crime, its establishment is a step in the direction of providing international criminal justice.

At the Rome Ceremony on 18 July 1998, I attempted to express some of the moral, ethical and policy significance of the creation of the ICC:

> The ICC reminds governments that *realpolitik,* which sacrifices justice at the altar of political settlements, is no longer accepted. It asserts that impunity for the perpetrators of genocide, crimes against humanity and war crimes is no longer tolerated. In that respect it fulfils what Prophet Mohammad said, that 'wrongs must be righted'. It affirms that justice is an integral part of peace and thus reflects what Pope Paul VI once said, 'If you want peace, work for justice'. These values are clearly reflected in the ICC's Preamble.
>
> The ICC will not be a panacea for all the ills of humankind. It will not eliminate conflicts, nor return victims to life, or restore survivors to their prior conditions of well being and it will not bring all perpetrators of major crimes to justice. But it can help avoid some conflicts, prevent some victimisation, and bring to justice some of the perpetrators of these crimes. In so doing, the ICC will strengthen world order and contribute to world peace and security. As such, the ICC, like other international and national legal institutions, will add its contribution to the humanisation of our civilisation.
>
> The ICC also symbolises human solidarity, for as John Donne so eloquently stated, 'No man is an island, entire of itself; each man is a piece of the continent, a part of the main . . . Any man's death diminishes me because I am involved in mankind.'
>
> Lastly, the ICC will remind us not to forget these terrible crimes so that we can heed the admonishment so aptly recorded by George Santayana, that those who forget the lessons of the past are condemned to repeat their mistakes. Ultimately, if the ICC saves but one life, as it is said in the *Talmud*, it will be as if it saved the whole of humanity.

8

*Striking a Balance: Mixed Law Tribunals and Conflicts of Jurisdiction**

DIANE F ORENTLICHER

The law derived from Nuremberg has entered a new era of enforcement. Its most visible emblems are two international criminal tribunals established in the 1990s to judge atrocities committed in the former Yugoslavia and Rwanda, the birth of a permanent International Criminal Court (ICC) in July 2002, and states' unprecedented use of universal jurisdiction to prosecute crimes against the basic code of humanity. But the emerging system of transnational enforcement is much wider and deeper.

Recent years have seen extraordinary experimentalism in the design of courts that enforce the law of humanity. In Kosovo, East Timor, and Sierra Leone, tribunals have been fashioned from a blend of national and international elements. For over five years, the United Nations and Cambodia have pursued negotiations—so far inconclusive—aimed at creating a domestic court with international participation to judge Khmer Rouge-era atrocities.

Although supported by other forms of jurisdiction, this innovation has significant implications for the principle of universality.[1] By expanding state practice in prosecuting atrocious crimes, the new tribunals reinforce the conceptual underpinnings of universal jurisdiction.[2] At the same time, the hybrid courts present an alternative to universal jurisdiction. Their operation will thus help define circumstances in which the exercise of universal jurisdiction is seen as the preferred path.

* This chapter has been adapted from portions of 'The Future of Universal Jurisdiction: in the New Architecture of Transitional Justice,' *Universal Jurisdiction: National Courts and the Prosecution of Serious Crimes Under International Law*, Stephen J Macedo, (ed) (University of Pennsylvania Press, Philadelphia: forthcoming), and is published with the permission of Stephen J Macedo. I am grateful to Gregg Bloche, John Cerone and Steve Macedo for helpful comments and suggestions, and to Helen Harnett, Kathlyn Mackovjak, William Martin and JR Hamilton for research assistance.

[1] The mixed tribunals examined in this chapter rely principally on territorial jurisdiction—that is, they have jurisdiction over crimes committed in the territories where they operate.

[2] It is generally recognised that universal jurisdiction exists over conduct defined as a crime under customary international law. Since customary law is established in part by relevant state practice, the trend toward increased prosecution of certain crimes bolsters the claim that those crimes are or may eventually become subject to universal jurisdiction.

Meanwhile, the advent of international criminal tribunals and the robust use of universal jurisdiction have revitalised efforts by domestic prosecutors and judges to secure justice in the countries where atrocious crimes occurred. Faced with the prospect of their nationals being prosecuted in another state or by an international tribunal, states have new incentive to seek justice at home.

In these and other ways, international and national courts are working in tandem, sharing responsibility for enforcing the law of humanity. In the process, they are constructing a transnational jurisprudence. National courts, international tribunals, and regional and international human rights bodies are communicating across jurisdictional lines, developing a common code of humanity.

THE HYBRID COURTS

International tribunals have understandably become the pre-eminent symbol of global justice. But an important alternative is now emerging: hybrid courts composed of international and national elements.

Independent Special Court for Sierra Leone

By letter dated 12 June 2000, Ahmad Tejan Kabbah, the President of Sierra Leone, asked the United Nations to assist his country in bringing to justice those responsible for 'crimes against the people of Sierra Leone and for the taking of United Nations Peacekeepers as hostages.'[3] Ravaged by a decade of savage civil war, Sierra Leone did not have the resources to mount prosecutions itself. And yet, Sierra Leone's Justice Minister later explained, 'we came to realise ... that without ending impunity by bringing to justice those who bear the greatest responsibility for the atrocities committed in this country, we were dooming ourselves to repeat them.'[4]

On 14 August 2000, the United Nations Security Council adopted a resolution expressing its deep concern 'at the very serious crimes committed within the territory of Sierra Leone' and requesting the Secretary-General 'to negotiate an agreement with the Government of Sierra Leone to create an independent special court' with jurisdiction over serious violations of international humanitarian law as well as crimes under Sierra Leonean law.[5] On 16 January 2002, the agreement envisaged in this resolution was concluded in Freetown, Sierra Leone.[6]

[3] Letter from Ahmad Tejan Kabbah, President of Sierra Leone, to Secretary-General Kofi Annan, UN Doc S/2000/786, Annex.

[4] The Hon Solomon E Berewa, Attorney-General and Minister of Justice for the Republic of Sierra Leone, 'Remarks for Signing Ceremony for Special Court', 16 Jan 2002.

[5] SC Res 1315 (2000), preamble; paras 1 and 2.

[6] Agreement Between the United Nations and the Government of Sierra Leone on the Establishment of a Special Court for Sierra Leone, 16 January 2002 (hereinafter 'UN-Sierra Leone Agreement'). The Statute of the Special Court is annexed to the Agreement and forms an integral part thereof.

Soon after, the Parliament of Sierra Leone ratified the agreement and enacted implementing legislation.[7]

In the words of the United Nations Secretary-General, the Special Court for Sierra Leone is 'a treaty-based sui generis court of mixed jurisdiction and composition.'[8] The subject matter jurisdiction of the Special Court is defined principally in terms of international criminal law, but also includes two offences proscribed by Sierra Leonean law. [9] Although the Special Court is based in Sierra Leone,[10] a majority of its judges, its Prosecutor, and its Registrar are appointed by the UN Secretary-General.[11] The Government of Sierra Leone appoints the remaining judges, who need not be nationals of Sierra Leone.[12] The only senior official required to possess Sierra Leonean nationality is the Deputy Prosecutor.[13] Thus the Special Court is not so much a court of 'mixed jurisdiction and composition'[14] as an international court onto which national elements are grafted.

The Special Court operates alongside national courts of Sierra Leone. The two court systems have concurrent jurisdiction,[15] with the Special Court enjoying primacy when it formally requests a national court of Sierra Leone 'to defer to its competence'.[16]

[7] The Special Court Agreement, 2002, Ratification Act, 2002, Supplement to the Sierra Leone Gazette vol CXXX, No II dated 7 March 2002.

[8] Report of the Secretary-General on the establishment of a Special Court for Sierra Leone, UN Doc S/2000/915, para 9 (2000).

[9] Art 2 to 4 of the court's statute establish jurisdiction over crimes against humanity, several specified violations of international humanitarian law, and crimes that involve attacking the personnel or property of peacekeeping and humanitarian assistance operations. Art 5 establishes jurisdiction over certain offences under Sierra Leonean law. The Special Court has jurisdiction only with respect to offences committed in Sierra Leone since 30 Nov 1996. See Statute of the Special Court for Sierra Leone, Art 1(1).

[10] The bilateral agreement establishing the Special Court provides that it 'shall have its seat in Sierra Leone' but 'may meet away from its seat if it considers it necessary for the efficient exercise of its functions.' The agreement also contemplates the possibility that the court 'may be relocated outside Sierra Leone, if circumstances so require.' UN-Sierra Leone Agreement, Art 10.

[11] Statute of the Special Court for Sierra Leone, Arts. 12(1), 15(3) & 16(3). In April 2002 the Secretary-General appointed David Crane, a US national, as Prosecutor, and Robin Vincent, a UK national, as Registrar. See Reuters, 'Pentagon Lawyer Named Prosecutor in Sierra Leone', 19 April 2002. In announcing these appointments, a UN spokesman indicated that a majority of the court's judges would come from Africa. UN News Centre Report, 'Sierra Leone: Annan names prosecutor, registrar of special war crimes court', 19 April 2002.

[12] Statute of the Special Court for Sierra Leone, Art 12(1).

[13] *Ibid*, Art 15(4). A Sri Lankan national has nonetheless been appointed to serve as Deputy Prosecutor. The official may be granted honorary Sierra Leonian citizenship in order to satisfy the aforementioned requirement.

[14] Report of the Secretary-General on the establishment of a Special Court for Sierra Leone, UN Doc S/2000/915, para 9 (2000).

[15] Statute of the Special Court for Sierra Leone, Art 8(1).

[16] *Ibid*, Art 8(2). The Special Court's primacy does not extend to courts of states other than those of Sierra Leone. See Report of the Secretary-General on the establishment of a Special Court for Sierra Leone, UN Doc S/2000/915, para 10 (2000).

Extraordinary Chambers in the Courts of Cambodia

On 13 May 2003, the UN General Assembly approved an agreement with Cambodia to create a court, established under Cambodian law but operating with substantial international participation, to prosecute those most responsible for crimes committed by the Khmer Rouge when they ruled Cambodia in the mid- to late- 1970s. The agreement was the product of vexed negotiations lasting over five years. The process reached a low point on 8 February 2002, when the UN announced that it was withdrawing from the negotiations because it had concluded that, 'as currently envisaged, the Cambodian court would not guarantee independence, impartiality and objectivity, which is required by the United Nations for it to cooperate with such a court.'[17]

Negotiations were revived at the urging of the UN General Assembly, which adopted a resolution in December 2002 requesting the Secretary-General 'to resume negotiations, without delay, to conclude an agreement with the Government of Cambodia' aimed at establishing the mixed court. [18]

The negotiating process was initiated by a letter to the UN Secretary-General from Cambodia's two co-Prime Ministers, dated 21 June 1997, seeking 'the assistance of the United Nations and the international community in bringing to justice those responsible for the genocide and crimes against humanity during the rule of the Khmer Rouge from 1975 to 1979'.[19] Earlier that month, the notorious leader of the Khmer Rouge, Pol Pot, had unexpectedly become available for trial. Since their ouster from power in 1979, the Khmer Rouge had continued to operate as a guerrilla force under Pol Pot's leadership. After an internal rebellion, Pol Pot's Khmer Rouge captors expressed their readiness to surrender him for prosecution. But no international court was available to try Pol Pot and no country was willing to seek his extradition.[20] The moment of opportunity soon passed, largely because of political upheavals in Phnom Penh.[21] Pol Pot's death one year later forever deprived Cambodians of the justice

[17] Seth Mydans, 'U.N. Ends Cambodia Talks on Trials for Khmer Rouge', *New York Times*, 9 Feb 2002.

[18] GA Res 57/228, para 1 (18 Dec 2002); UN Doc A/RES/57/228 (2002).

[19] This action was preceded by the adoption of a resolution by the UN Commission on Human Rights in April 1997 calling on the Secretary-General to 'examine any request by Cambodia for assistance in responding to past serious violations of Cambodian and international law as a means of addressing the issue of individual accountability'. That resolution was apparently adopted in response to the initiative of Ambassador Thomas Hammarberg, then serving as the Special Representative of the Secretary-General on Human Rights in Cambodia. See Stephen Heder, with Brian Tittemore, *Seven Candidates for Prosecution: Accountability for the Crimes of the Khmer Rouge* (War Crimes Research Office of American University and the Coalition for International Justice, 2001).

[20] Aware that Canadian legislation provided for universal jurisdiction over crimes against humanity, the US government pressed Canadian authorities to seek Pol Pot's extradition. Canada declined, explaining that its legislation applied only when a suspect was already in Canada. Canadian officials may also have been offended by what they viewed as heavy-handed US pressure.

[21] Not long after the letter from Cambodia's two co-Prime Ministers was sent to the UN Secretary-General, then Second co-Prime Minister Hun Sen ousted the First co-Prime Minister in a coup. The coup fundamentally altered the political environment surrounding the issue of accountability.

of seeing him brought to trial but provided fresh impetus for prosecuting surviving Khmer Rouge leaders.

In their letter seeking UN assistance in bringing Khmer Rouge leaders to justice, Cambodia's co-Prime Ministers explained that their country did 'not have the resources or expertise to conduct this very important procedure' and asked the United Nations to provide the same assistance it had provided in response to atrocities in Rwanda and the former Yugoslavia—presumably meaning the creation of an international tribunal for Cambodia. But the government's consent to such a tribunal was later withdrawn. When a UN-appointed Group of Experts recommended that the United Nations establish a tribunal with jurisdiction over those most responsible for Khmer Rouge-era crimes, the Cambodian government rejected their proposal.[22] Prime Minister Hun Sen[23] said he would permit foreign participation in domestic trials, but rejected a proposal put forth by the UN's Office of Legal Affairs to establish a 'mixed tribunal' under predominantly non-Cambodian control. In the Spring of 2000, the United Nations and the Cambodian government reached an agreement in principle to establish a novel court that would be dominated by Cambodian officials but would include non-Cambodians wielding an effective veto power by virtue of a 'super-majority' voting requirement.[24]

After protracted delays, on 10 August 2002 Cambodian authorities enacted enabling legislation for the court.[25] Pursuant to the 'Law on the Establishment of the Extraordinary Chambers in the Courts of Cambodia for the Prosecution of Crimes Committed During the Period of Democratic Kampuchea', the office of the prosecutor would comprise two co-Prosecutors, one of whom must be Cambodian and the other 'foreign'.[26] Similarly, investigations would be 'the joint responsibility of two investigating judges, one Cambodian and another foreign.'[27] Judicial panels, too, would comprise a mix of Cambodian and foreign judges. At each level of the system envisaged for the Extraordinary Chambers, Cambodian judges would constitute a majority. For example, three

[22] The Group of Experts presented its report to Secretary-General Kofi Annan on 22 Feb 1999. See 'Report of the Group of Experts for Cambodia established pursuant to General Assembly Resolution 52/135 (1999)', UN Doc A/53/850, S/1999/231, Annex (16 Mar 1999). The Cambodian government rejected its central recommendations by letter dated 3 Mar 1999.

[23] Hun Sen has been the sole Prime Minister of Cambodia since ousting his co-Prime Minister in 1997.

[24] The compromise formulation was approved by Hun Sen in a meeting in April 2000 with a US intermediary, Senator John F Kerry (D-Mass.). See Seth Mydans, 'Cambodia Agrees to Tribunal Setup for Khmer Rouge Trials', *New York Times*, 30 April 2000; Colum Lynch, 'U.N., Cambodia Agree on Court for Khmer Rouge Trials', *Washington Post*, 25 May 2000.

[25] Law on the Establishment of the Extraordinary Chambers in the Courts of Cambodia for the Prosecution of Crimes Committed During the Period of Democratic Kampuchea (hereinafter 'Law on Extraordinary Chambers'). Available in English at http://www.derechos.org/human-rights/seasia/doc/krlaw.html. The history of this legislation is summarised in Stephen Heder with Brian Tittemore, *Seven Candidates for Prosecution: Accountability for the Crimes of the Khmer Rouge* (War Crimes Research Office of American University and the Coalition for International Justice, 2001).

[26] Law on Extraordinary Chambers, Art 16.

[27] *Ibid*, Art 23.

of the five judges constituting a trial court must be Cambodian.[28] Further, all judicial appointments are supposed to be made by the Cambodian government, although foreign judges are generally supposed to be appointed on the basis of nominations by the United Nations Secretary-General.[29] But, reflecting the 'super-majority' formula accepted by Cambodia in 2000, the law provides that the vote of at least one UN-appointed judge is necessary to secure a judgment of guilt.[30]

The international subject matter jurisdiction of the Extraordinary Chambers comprises genocide as defined in the 1948 Convention on the Prevention and Punishment of the Crime of Genocide, crimes against humanity, and certain violations of the Geneva Conventions of 1949 and two other treaties.[31] The Chambers' jurisdiction also includes three crimes proscribed by the 1956 Penal Code of Cambodia—homicide, torture and religious persecution—when committed between 17 April 1975 and 6 January 1979.[32]

As UN Under-Secretary-General for Legal Affairs Hans Corell has observed, the court envisaged by the UN-Cambodia negotiations is without precedent.[33] Its unique features are best understood as the product of extremely difficult negotiations between the United Nations and the Cambodian government. Explaining the UN's willingness at that time to participate in the hybrid court, in February 2000 Corell said that the court represented an acceptable balance between the sovereignty of Cambodia and the credibility of the United Nations.[34] Although Corell would have preferred that the UN exercise greater control over the proceedings, he explained that the Organisation could not force Cambodia to accept foreign control[35] —not, at any rate, without a Security Council resolution adopted under Chapter VII of the UN Charter, an option ruled out by China's certain veto.

Two years later, Corell defended the UN's decision to pull out of negotiations on the ground that Cambodia was unwilling to commit itself to the supremacy of a UN-Cambodia agreement concerning the Extraordinary Chambers over domestic law. Under these circumstances, Corell said, the UN would be implicated in a 'judicial process over which it would have had little or no control.'[36]

[28] *Ibid*, Art 9.

[29] *Ibid*, Arts 10–11. But see *ibid*, Art 46 (providing for appointment of Cambodians as a last resort 'in the event any foreign judges or foreign investigating judges or foreign prosecutors fail or refuse to participate in the Extraordinary Chambers').

[30] *Ibid*, Art 14. See also *ibid*, Art 23 (imposing similar voting requirements for decisions of pre-trial chambers).

[31] *Ibid*, Arts 4–8.

[32] *Ibid*, Art 3.

[33] Press Briefing by United Nations Legal Counsel, 8 Feb 2000.

[34] *Ibid*.

[35] See *ibid;* see also Press Briefing by Under-Secretary-General for Legal Affairs and United Nations Legal Counsel, 13 July 2000.

[36] Hans Corell, 'No Justice for Victims of the Khmer Rouge', *Int'l Herald Tribune*,19 June 2002. UN officials also cited specific features in the Aug 2002 Cambodian legislation, such as the law's failure to ensure that individuals previously granted amnesty could be tried before the Extraordinary Chambers, as a factor in their decision. See Colum Lynch, 'U.N. Ends Negotiations

When negotiations resumed, UN negotiators were able to secure assurances addressing some of the key concerns that had led them to abandon talks in February 2002, but the agreed text fell short of the Organisation's aims. And so when he presented the draft agreement to the UN General Assembly, the Secretary-General reminded the body that. 'under the terms of the draft agreement, any deviation by the [Cambodian] Government from [its] obligations... could lead to the United Nations withdrawing its cooperation and assistance from the process'.[37]

* * *

As the contrasting details of the Extraordinary Chambers and the Special Court suggest, the two models resulted from negotiations that unfolded in markedly different political contexts. In Cambodia, the United Nations has had to reckon with a government determined to retain as much control over the proposed court as possible and relatively confident of its negotiating power. In contrast, the Organisation's Sierra Leonean interlocutors were keen to establish an internationally legitimate process for prosecuting atrocities committed mainly by rebel forces opposing the government.

Both sets of negotiations have presented the United Nations with novel challenges: Its officials have had to decide how far they are prepared to go in supporting criminal proceedings they cannot fully control. So far, those challenges have stalled the creation of a hybrid court for Cambodia. Several prominent NGOs have criticised the Organisation for what they consider its readiness to compromise international standards of fair process[38] and applauded its

on Khmer Rouge Trials; Cambodians Accused of Rejecting Key Points', *Washington Post*, 9 Feb 2002. The UN's decision to withdraw from negotiations drew mixed responses from governments and NGOs. Human Rights Watch and Amnesty International and some Cambodian activists supported the Organisation's decision, arguing that participating in flawed proceedings would tarnish the UN and do a disservice to Cambodians. See Amnesty International, 'Cambodia: Flawed trials in no one's best interests', AI Index: ASA 23/001/2002, 11 Feb 2002; Colum Lynch, 'U.N. Ends Negotiations on Khmer Rouge Trials; Cambodians Accused of Rejecting Key Points', *Washington Post*, 9 Feb 2002 (quoting Human Rights Watch staff member saying 'We strongly support the U.N.'s decision to drop the negotiations'). Others criticised the decision, arguing that Cambodians' best hope for justice lies in UN participation in a court constituted to try those most responsible for Khmer Rouge crimes. See, eg, Youk Chhang, 'Cambodia Won't Easily Find Justice on Its Own', *New York Times*, 14 Feb 2002. Various governments and the European Union encouraged the UN to resume negotiations. See BBC News, 'EU urges UN rethink on Cambodia', 21 Feb 2002; Colum Lynch, 'U.N. Ends Negotiations on Khmer Rouge Trials; Cambodians Accused of Rejecting Key Points', *Washington Post*, 9 Feb 2002 (reporting that US and French officials said they hoped the UNs Feb 2002 decision would not end negotiations aimed at establishing a court to try Khmer Rouge atrocities).

[37] Report of the Secretary-General on Khmer Rouge trials, UN Doc A/57/769 (31 March 2003). As noted earlier, the General Assembly approved the agreemnt on 13 May 2003. Cambodian authorities have indicated that Cambodia would be unable to ratify the revised agreement until after general elections scheduled for late July 2003. Alan Boyd, 'Cambodia's legal system on trial', *Asia Times Online: Southeast Asia*, 20 May 2003.

[38] See Human Rights Watch, 'UN: Khmer Rouge Tribunal Flawed' (Briefing Paper, 30 Apr 2003); Barbara Crossette, 'Cambodians Will Prosecute Khmer Rouge', *New York Times*, 25 May 2000;

decision in February 2002—later reversed—to withdraw from negotiations.[39] For the United Nations, then, participating in mixed tribunals presents the risk of tarnishing its own credibility. But as UN officials have reminded critics, they do not have the option of establishing a UN-controlled tribunal for Cambodia.

Although they present special challenges, mixed tribunals may offer an attractive alternative to UN tribunals or to trials conducted by bystander states. Unlike the international tribunals for the former Yugoslavia and Rwanda, the court established in Sierra Leone will operate in the country most deeply affected by its proceedings and judgements. So, too, would the Extraordinary Chambers envisaged in the UN-Cambodia negotiations. By bringing justice home, these courts might contribute more effectively to national processes of reckoning than the remote justice dispensed in The Hague and Arusha. And by including national judges, prosecutors and staff, the mixed tribunals may help strengthen the sinews of law in countries whose systems of justice have been shattered. None of these goals can be realised, however, without adequate resources, training of court personnel, and an enduring commitment by the international community to insist upon fair process.

Internationalised National Courts: Ethiopia

Although an innovation, the mixed courts contemplated for Cambodia and established in Sierra Leone are a natural evolution of developments that have been under way for some time. Several countries that have instituted prosecutions for mass atrocities have sought guidance and support from other states, international organisations, and international NGOs.

Criminal proceedings in Ethiopia exemplify this trend. In 1992, the Ethiopian government established a Special Prosecutor's Office to prosecute individuals for certain crimes committed during the reign of the Dergue, the military junta led by Colonel Mengistu Haile Mariam that ruled Ethiopia from 1976 until 1991. The Special Prosecutor has sought technical advice from the UN Centre for Human Rights and has received both technical and financial support from several Western governments. Charges in these trials have included national and international crimes, the latter as incorporated in Ethiopian law.[40]

The role of international actors in these prosecutions has been complex. Although supportive in principle of Ethiopia's attempt to establish legal accountability for atrocious crimes, NGOs and others have criticised due

Seth Mydans, 'Cambodian Deputies Back War Crimes Tribunal to Try Khmer Rouge', *New York Times*, 3 Jan 2001.

[39] See above n 36.

[40] Art 281 of the Ethiopian Penal Code criminalises genocide and crimes against humanity. Although derived from international law, the offences are defined in the Ethiopian Penal Code somewhat differently than under international law. Art 28 of the Ethiopian Constitution provides that the criminal liability 'of persons who commit crimes against humanity, so defined by international agreements ratified by Ethiopia and by other laws of Ethiopia, ... shall not be barred by statute of limitation.' Constitution of the Federal Democratic Republic of Ethiopia, Art 28(1).

process violations attending these prosecutions, particularly the lengthy time spent in pre-trial detention without charge.[41]

UN-Administered Courts: Kosovo and East Timor

A third model of internationalised prosecutions has emerged as a byproduct of recent UN operations in post-conflict regions. In two territories administered by the United Nations, human rights crimes have been prosecuted before courts established under UN auspices, with the involvement of local personnel.

Following the 1999 war between Yugoslavia and the North Atlantic Treaty Organisation, the UN Security Council adopted a resolution pursuant to which Kosovo would be governed by the United Nations Mission in Kosovo (UNMIK) until the region's final status is determined.[42] As an interim governing authority, UNMIK has established local courts that prosecute crimes ranging from reckless driving to genocide.[43]

Like the Special Court for Sierra Leone and the Extraordinary Chambers contemplated in Cambodia, the UN-administered courts are a hybrid of local and international elements. The first International Prosecutor was a US national employed by the United Nations, and other 'internationals' serve alongside local judges.[44]

A UN-administered court system was also established in East Timor by the United Nations Transitional Administration in East Timor (UNTAET), which administered East Timor during the period beginning shortly after East Timorese voted for independence from Indonesia in August 1999[45] and ending

[41] See, eg, Human Rights Watch, 'Mengistu Haile Mariam: A Human Rights Watch background paper' (Press Release 24 Nov 1999).

[42] SC Res 1244 (1999).

[43] See Carlotta Gall, 'U.N. Mission in Kosovo Proposes to Set Up a War Crimes Court', *New York Times*, 23 June 2000; Agence France Presse, 'Serb motorist whose arrest sparked riot released on bail', 19 Dec 2000; Carlotta Gall, 'UN Court Tries Serb in Mass Killing', *New York Times*, 7 Dec 2000.

[44] For example, the presiding judge in a trial involving genocide charges was Swedish, while other members of the judicial panel were Kosovo Albanians; Carlotta Gall, 'UN Court Tries Serb in Mass Killing', *New York Times*, 7 Dec 2000. According to the *New York Times*, the Kosovo court system is 'headed by international judges and prosecutors and supplemented' by local judges; Carlotta Gall, 'U.N. Mission in Kosovo Proposes to Set Up a War Crimes Court', *New York Times*, 23 June 2000. UN officials have had trouble recruiting local Serbs to serve on these courts. An International Prosecutor has explained that foreign nationals dominate the judicial panels because '[l]ocal judges in war crimes cases, which are highly publicized and politicised, can be and are pressured by their community, both implicitly and explicitly... In [Kosovo], the judicial culture and society are not yet ready to handle the war crimes cases without internationals as neutral participants ....' Posting by Michael Hartmann to Justwatch-L@LISTSERV.ACSU.BUFFALO.EDU, 1 Mar 2002.

[45] On 15 Sept 1999, the UN Security Council authorized a peace enforcement operation to restore order in East Timor; SC Res. 1264 (1999). The Australian-led mission, known as INTERFET, entered East Timor on 20 Sept 1999 and operated there until responsibility for its administration was transferred to UNTAET. The latter was established pursuant to SC Res. 1272 (1999), which was adopted on 25 October 1999. INTERFET handed over the command of military operations in East Timor to UNTAET on 28 Feb 2000. See Susanna Linton, 'Rising from the Ashes: The Creation of a

when East Timor became independent on 20 May 2002. UNTAET Regulation No 2000/11 vested in the District Court of Dili exclusive jurisdiction over genocide, war crimes and crimes against humanity, as well as over torture, murder, and crimes of sexual violence when committed between 1 January 1999 and 25 October 1999.[46] Under another UNTAET regulation, these crimes are tried before Special Panels for Serious Crimes.[47] The Special Panels apply a combination of domestic and international law, and draw substantially upon the crimes set forth in the Rome Statute.[48] Although numerically dominated by international judges, the Special Panels include local judges.[49]

To assist the new state during its first two years of independence, the United Nations has established a Mission of Support in East Timor (UNMISET).[50] Like UNTAET before it, UNMISET now administers the Serious Crimes Unit of the judicial system. During a transitional period, this unit will continue to be headed by an international deputy prosecutor, who reports to the East Timorese general prosecutor. The UN also envisages the continuing need for participation by international judges in the Special Panels through 2003.[51]

In both Kosovo and East Timor, the UN-administered courts exercise jurisdiction that overlaps with that of purely national courts and, in the case of Kosovo, an international tribunal. How to reconcile potentially competing claims of jurisdiction among these courts presents novel questions. Consider this: In December 2000, the ICTY continued its investigation of Yugoslav atrocities committed in Kosovo in 1999—crimes for which the Hague Tribunal issued indictments against then-President Slobodan Milošević and other senior Yugoslav officials in May 1999. Meanwhile, in early December 2000 a Serbian law student went on trial before a UN-administered court in the northern

Viable Criminal Justice System in East Timor', (2001) 5 *Melbourne UL Rev* (hereinafter 'Rising from the Ashes').

46 See UNTAET Reg No 2000/11, s 10 (entered into force 6 Mar 2000).

47 UNTAET Reg No 2000/15 on the Establishment of Panels with Exclusive Jurisdiction over Serious Criminal Offenses, s 1 (entered into force 6 June 2000).

48 See Susanna Linton, 'Cambodia, East Timor, and Sierra Leone: Experiments in International Justice', (2001), 12 *Crim L Forum*, 185, 206–07 (hereinafter 'Experiments in International Justice').

49 Pursuant to UNTAET Reg 2000/15, s 22.1, each panel consists of one East Timorese judge and two international judges. The panel that presided over the first case involving charges of crimes against humanity to come to trial before the Special Panel comprised jurists from Brazil, Burundi and East Timor. See 'Dili District Court Convicts Ten Men of Crimes Against Humanity in the Los Palos Case', *Nizkor English Service*, 10 Dec 2001. Until 7 Jan 2000, when the first judges, prosecutors and public defenders were appointed to the District Court of Dili, no East Timorese had served as a judge or prosecutor. See Linton, 'Rising from the Ashes'. The new appointees 'received no training beyond a week'; *ibid*. See also Linton, 'Experiments in International Justice', at 203. The specially-constituted prosecution service for serious crimes is 'almost exclusively international in composition, with its own totally international investigation unit'; *ibid* at 204. The Court of Appeal is 'also dominated by internationals'; *ibid* at 205.

50 SC Res 1410, UN Doc S/RES/1410 (2002). This resolution establishes UNMISET for an initial period of 12 months, but contemplates a two-year period of devolution of responsibility from UNMISET to East Timorese authorities.

51 See Report of the Secretary-General on the United Nations Transitional Administration in East Timor (17 April 2002), paras 76–78, UN Doc S/2002/432 (2002).

Kosovo town of Mitrovića on charges of genocide for mass murders committed in April 1999.[52] And on 20 December 2000, a Yugoslav court in the town of Niš convicted three Yugoslav soldiers of the double murder in late March 1999 of an ethnically Albanian couple in Šušića, Kosovo.[53]

Several times zones away, in September 2000 Indonesia's Attorney General named 19 suspects in connection with violent crimes surrounding East Timor's pro-independence vote in August 1999.[54] In November 2000, the UN High Commissioner for Human Rights warned Indonesian authorities that the United Nations might create a tribunal to try those behind the violence in East Timor if domestic trials did not deliver justice.[55] On 11 December 2000, UN prosecutors in East Timor indicted ten members of a pro-Indonesia militia group and an Indonesian army officer on the charge of crimes against humanity for their alleged role in atrocities surrounding the August 1999 referendum on independence.[56] Thus, as UNTAET proceeded with trials in East Timor, a top UN official was pressing Indonesian authorities to prosecute related crimes in Indonesian courts—under threat of being superceded by an international tribunal.[57]

The Lockerbie Model

Still another innovation was born of negotiations aimed at resolving a longstanding impasse between the governments of Libya, the United States and the United Kingdom concerning the trial of two Libyan nationals believed to be responsible for the 1988 bombing of Pan Am Flight 103 as it flew over Lockerbie, Scotland en route to the United States. The explosion caused the deaths of 259 people on board the flight and 11 residents of Lockerbie who were killed when the plane crashed. Both the United States and British governments filed criminal charges against the two Libyan suspects and requested their extradition. France made a similar request in connection with a related case.

Libya refused to comply with these requests, arguing that its law prohibits it from extraditing Libyan nationals. The three requesting states next turned to

[52] Carlotta Gall, 'Serb on Trial for Genocide of Albanians in Kosovo', *New York Times*, 5 Dec 2000; Carlotta Gall, 'UN Court Tries Serb in Mass Killing', *New York Times*, 7 Dec 2000.

[53] R Jeffrey Smith, '3 Soldiers Convicted in Kosovo Atrocity; Verdict Is First by Military Court', *Washington Post*, 21 Dec 2000.

[54] Rajiv Chandrasekaran, 'Prosecutors Name 19 in East Timor Violence Probe', *Washington Post*, 2 Sept 2000. Another source reports that 18 suspects were indicted in Jan 2002: 'Indonesia: The Implications of the Timor Trials', *International Crisis Group Briefing Paper,* 8 May 2002, 5. The first three trials of these suspects began in mid-March 2002.

[55] Agence France-Presse, 'East Timor Violence Requires an Accounting, U.N. Official Says', *New York Times*, 24 Nov 2000.

[56] Rajiv Chandrasekaran, 'U.N. Names 11 in E. Timor Violence', *Washington Post*, 12 Dec 2000. Ten defendants were convicted of crimes against humanity one year later. See Judicial System Monitoring Program, 'Dili court convicts ten of crimes against humanity', 11 Dec 2001.

[57] More senior UN officials have apparently been disinclined to establish such a tribunal. In May 2002, Secretary-General Kofi Annan expressed support for efforts by the Indonesian government to prosecute officials charged with crimes of violence committed in East Timor. See AP, 'Annan downplays international tribunal for East Timor suspects', 18 May 2002.

the UN Security Council, which adopted a series of resolutions urging Libya to comply with the extradition requests[58] and imposing sanctions that were to remain in effect until Libya complied.[59]

The standoff ended in March 1999, when Libya accepted a US and British proposal to try the Libyan suspects before a Scottish court, applying Scottish law and largely following Scottish criminal procedure,[60] but located in the Netherlands.[61] Under this novel arrangement, a patch of Dutch real estate would become Scottish territory for the duration of the proceedings. The Libyan suspects were transferred to the Netherlands on 5 April 1999.[62] After repeated delays, their trial finally began at Camp Zeist in the Netherlands on 3 May 2000.[63] On 31 January 2001, the Scottish court found one of the defendants guilty of murder, but freed the second defendant because, it concluded, the prosecution had not proved his guilt beyond a reasonable doubt.[64]

The principal jurisdictional basis of the court convened at Camp Zeist is apparently the territorial principle.[65] As noted, parties to the dispute as well as the Dutch government agreed that Scotland, the site of the explosion, would extend its territorial jurisdiction to Camp Zeist for the duration of the trial. The court's authority arguably could be supported as well by a treaty-based form of universal jurisdiction.[66] But even if the arrangement were regarded solely as a unique application of the territorial principle, it would have significant implications for contemporary issues relating to international jurisdiction.

The innovation subtly bolsters the view that the ICC can exercise jurisdiction derived from the transferred jurisdiction of states—a claim that has figured

[58] SC Res 731, UN Doc S/RES/731, para 3 (1992).

[59] SC Res 748, UN Doc S/RES/748 (1992); SC Res 883, UN Doc S/RES/883 (1993).

[60] One exception is that the defendants' guilt was determined by a panel comprising three Scottish judges instead of a jury.

[61] See Paul Lewis, 'Libya Sets Date for Turning Over 2 Suspects in Lockerbie Bombing', *New York Times*, 20 Mar 1999. The proposal put forth by the US and UK was a modified version of a proposal previously made by the Libyan government for trial in a third country.

[62] See Daily Press Briefing of Office of Spokesman for Secretary-General (5 April 1999).

[63] See Martin Fletcher, 'Moment relatives faced the accused', *Times*, London, 4 May 2000.

[64] See Donald G McNeil Jr, 'Libyan Convicted by Scottish Court in '88 Pan Am Blast; 2nd Defendant Freed—Verdict Is Not Likely to End US Curbs', *New York Times*, 1 Feb 2001. The conviction of the defendant Abdel Basset Ali Megrahi was upheld on appeal on 14 Mar 2002.

[65] In respect of the Scottish victims, the court's authority is further supported by the principle of passive personality, pursuant to which states may assert jurisdiction over certain crimes when the victims are their nationals.

[66] The states involved in the Lockerbie dispute had adhered to a convention that requires states parties to prosecute or extradite individuals in their territory suspected of committing certain acts against civilian airplanes and/or their passengers. See Convention for the Suppression of Unlawful Acts Against the Safety of Civil Aviation, Arts 5 (2) and 7, 23 Sept 1971, 24 UST 564, TIAS No 7570. Whether this duty was triggered in the Lockerbie case is not altogether clear. The aforementioned treaty provisions contemplate a situation in which a state party learns that someone suspected of committing one of the proscribed acts is present in its territory. But the two Libyan defendants were transferred to Camp Zeist from Libya. Technically, however, the two 'surrendered' to Scottish authorities so that Libya could avoid having to extradite its nationals in violation of Libyan law. Once the suspects were in the custody of Scottish authorities in Camp Zeist, the UK's treaty obligation to prosecute or extradite them may have been triggered.

prominently in legal justifications for the ICC's authority over nationals of non-state parties.[67] The analogy is, to be sure, imperfect. Theoretically, Scotland did not transfer its jurisdiction to the Netherlands; it extended Scottish sovereignty to a piece of real estate in the Netherlands. Still, if this form of legal alchemy is acceptable, the claim that states cannot transfer their own jurisdictional authority to the ICC is difficult to sustain.[68]

The Lockerbie case also highlights the enduring importance of national ties in resolving jurisdictional conflicts over international crimes. It took a decade to resolve the impasse generated by Libya's insistence on its right—usually respected by international law—not to extradite its own nationals on the one hand, and the determination of British and US authorities to prosecute those believed to be responsible for a terrorist attack against *their* nationals on the other.

IMPACT OF INTERNATIONAL TRIBUNALS ON NATIONAL PROCESSES

A fundamental feature of the emerging system of transnational justice is the dynamic interplay among international tribunals, national courts exercising universal jurisdiction, and courts punishing crimes committed in their own countries. The creation of international tribunals for the former Yugoslavia and Rwanda has spurred courts in several European countries to exercise universal jurisdiction over human rights crimes committed during recent conflicts in those two regions. In turn, the existence or looming prospect of international tribunals, along with the credible threat of prosecutions based on universal jurisdiction, have revitalised national processes of reckoning in countries directly affected by mass atrocities.

Although largely unforeseen, this last development means that international criminal law is increasingly working just as it should. International human rights law does not—and should not—seek to displace national jurisdiction. The law that seeks to enforce the basic code of humanity works best when it widens the political and moral space for accountability in countries where atrocious crimes occurred. In this sense, European efforts to prosecute former Chilean President Augusto Pinochet achieved an important measure of success. Although Pinochet's legal odyssey in Europe ended when British authorities judged him unfit to face further criminal proceedings, his protracted house arrest in England had a catalytic effect in Chile. Nine months after returning home, he was formally charged by a Chilean judge in connection with disappearances occurring in the early 1970s.[69]

[67] See Diane F Orentlicher, 'The Future of Universal Jurisdiction: in the New Architecture of Transnational Justice,' *Universal Jurisdiction: National Courts and the Prosecution of Serious Crimes Under International Law*, (University of Pennsylvania Press, Philadelphia, forthcoming).

[68] The fictional nature of Camp Zeist's metamorphosis is suggested by the fact that a key condition of surrender by Libya was that the trial not take place in either Scotland or the United States.

[69] See Clifford Krauss, 'Pinochet's Arrest Ordered by Judge,' *New York Times*, 2 Dec 2000. On

To be sure, even before Pinochet was arrested in England, Chilean society had made significant progress in its national process of reckoning with the depredations of the regime he led. Even so, proceedings against Pinochet in Spain, England and other countries enlarged the political space in Chile for confronting Pinochet-era crimes.[70] Many Chileans who believed they had pressed the question of accountability as far as the political climate in Chile would bear were prompted to reconsider their calculation. Some expressed a sense of shame that Chilean victims believed they could find justice for Pinochet-era crimes, if at all, only in courts an ocean away. Stung by what they regarded as an affront to their national honour, Chilean officials who had previously accepted Pinochet's untouchability pledged that Chilean courts would dispense justice.

A similar, though less successful, dynamic lies behind efforts by Indonesian authorities to prosecute those responsible for abuses committed in the period surrounding the 1999 plebiscite in East Timor. As the United Nations considered a proposal to create an international tribunal to judge those crimes, Indonesia instituted its own criminal proceedings.[71]

These developments provide a powerful, if partial, answer to the charge, sounded by critics of Pinochet's arrest in England, that universal and international jurisdiction invade the province of domestic politics. In this view, magistrates in Spain and courts in London had no business upending the decision made by Chilean society to grant Pinochet immunity in furtherance of Chile's transition to democracy.[72] While this concern must be taken seriously, it should be tempered by a keen awareness of the constraints Chile faced when its political leaders accepted Pinochet's self-amnesty. In effect, the proceedings outside Chile helped blunt the power of General Pinochet's threat to unleash destabilising force if his amnesty were challenged.

Further, to suppose that the political leaders who accepted Pinochet's impunity represent 'Chilean society' is to silence his victims and other Chileans who opposed the General's self-amnesty. Survivors of Pinochet's torture chambers and mothers of the disappeared did not make a deal with Pinochet, nor did they accept the bargain struck by politicians. They, after all, instituted the proceedings in Spain that led to Pinochet's arrest in London.[73]

9 July 2001, a Chilean appeals court ruled that Pinochet was mentally unfit to stand trial. One year later, the ruling was reaffirmed by Chile's highest court. See 'Court Rules Pinochet Unfit to Stand Trial'. AP, 2 July 2002.

[70] See Clifford Krauss, 'High Court Voids Charges for Pinochet; Sets New Date', *New York Times*, 21 Dec 2000 ('a trial would have been unthinkable [in Chile] until General Pinochet was arrested two years ago in London on a Spanish warrant'); and the chapter in this volume by Mark Lattimer.

[71] As noted, on 1 Sept 2000, Indonesian prosecutors named 19 people, including three generals, as potential suspects. See Rajiv Chandrasekaran, 'Prosecutors Name 19 in East Timor Violence Probe', *Washington Post*, 2 Sept 2000.

[72] See David Bosco, 'Dictators in the Dock', *American Prospect* 26, 14 Aug 2000, 28–29 (quoting views of John Bolton).

[73] See Richard J Wilson, 'Prosecuting Pinochet: International Crimes in Spanish Domestic Law', (1999), 21 *Hum Rts Q* 927, 931–32.

Turning to the future, just as the prospect of proceedings against Pinochet in Spain made it more likely that he would be prosecuted in Chile, the ICC will doubtless inspire national prosecutors to pursue a greater measure of justice than they might otherwise have sought. Pursuant to the ICC Statute, the ICC will not be able to try a case that is being or has been investigated or prosecuted by a state with jurisdiction, unless that state is unwilling or unable genuinely to carry out the proceeding.[74] This requirement will help ensure that the Court's very existence will inspire more vigorous enforcement of international law by national courts.

CONSTRUCTING A COMMON LAW OF HUMANITY

Courts enforcing humanitarian law are also influencing each other through their jurisprudence. Judges are talking to each other across jurisdictional lines, shaping each other's understanding of the law and, together, constructing a common code of humanity across borders.[75]

Notably, in its most important ruling on whether General Pinochet could be extradited to Spain, British Law Lords found persuasive authority on a key issue in a decision recently rendered by a Trial Chamber of the Yugoslavia war crimes tribunal.[76] Each of the major decisions rendered by British courts in the Pinochet proceedings has also cited decisions of US and other national courts. For their part, the two UN ad hoc tribunals have repeatedly drawn upon case law of national courts, including courts exercising universal jurisdiction,[77] as well as decisions rendered by human rights treaty bodies.[78]

This phenomenon can operate as a corrective to problems that may arise when courts exercise universal jurisdiction: They may render improper interpretations of international law. At a time when the Internet makes judicial opinions readily accessible across jurisdictions, patently incorrect interpretations are likely to be 'corrected' by courts in other jurisdictions. Judicial communication across jurisdictional lines can also mitigate the risk of radically divergent interpretations of what is supposed to be a universal code.

74 ICC Statute, Art 17.

75 For discussion of the wider phenomenon of cross-fertilization among courts belonging to different legal systems, see Anne-Marie Slaughter, 'Judicial Globalization', (2000), 40 *Va J Int'l L* 1103.

76 *Pinochet No 3*, Opinions of Lords Brown-Wilkinson and Millett (both quoting *Prosecutor v Anto Furundžija*, case no IT-95-17/1-T, Trial Judgment, 10 Dec 1998).

77 See, eg, *Prosecutor v Duško Tadić*, case no IT-94-1-AR72, Decision on the Defence Motion for Interlocutory Appeal on Jurisdiction, para 57, 2 Oct 1995 (citing decision of the Supreme Court of Israel in the *Eichmann* case); See also *Prosecutor v Anto Furundžija*, above note, para 153 n 170 (citing decisions of United States federal courts).

78 See, eg, *Prosecutor v Anto Furundžija*, para 160 n 179 and n 180 (citing decisions of European Court of Human Rights and UN Human Rights Committee).

RECONCILING INTERESTS

The globalisation of justice raises a new set of challenging issues: If the same crime can be prosecuted in multiple venues, how shall we choose among them? Suppose that British authorities had determined General Pinochet medically fit to stand trial. In this (counter-factual) setting, should British authorities have extradited Pinochet to Spain, which made the first request for his surrender? To other European states that made subsequent requests for his extradition? Or to Chile, where numerous complaints had been filed against the former President? National amnesties may present another dilemma. If a society that has endured the depredations of dictatorship decides to forego or limit prosecutions, should other legal systems defer to its policy by declining jurisdiction when victims seek justice abroad?

Familiar theories of universal jurisdiction provide surprisingly scant guidance, though their very diffidence tells us something important. To understand this point and its contemporary implications, it is helpful to return to the moment when universal jurisdiction was first made widely applicable to human rights crimes—the post-war period.

When law departs abruptly from its previous path, jurists typically seek support in the closest precedent they can plausibly cite. In the post-war period, Nazi war criminals were analogised to the pirate of another age—*hostis humanis generis*, enemies of all mankind who could be punished by any state that could establish jurisdiction.[79]

The image borrowed from piracy law—an enemy of mankind—served its immediate purpose and still provides a powerful metaphor in support of universal jurisdiction for human rights crimes. Yet the analogy is not entirely apt. For one thing, frequently cited justifications for universal jurisdiction over piracy assume that no state would consider prosecution an affront to its sovereignty. But when bystander states prosecute traveling dictators, indifference may be the least likely response on the part of the defendant's home state.

Further, by its nature piracy is indiscriminate in its choice of victims; to say that the pirate is an enemy of all mankind may be an exaggeration, but it is more than a metaphor. In contrast, the claim that, 'like the pirate... before him', the torturer is now an enemy of all mankind[80] is fundamentally a moral claim. Rhetoric deployed by post-war tribunals to justify their extraordinary jurisdiction makes this plain. Consider, for example, the decision of the US Military Tribunal in the *Einsatzgruppen Case*.[81] The Tribunal emphasised that the

[79] On the conceptual link between piracy and crimes punished in the post-war period, see Kenneth C Randall, 'Universal Jurisdiction Under International Law', (1988), 66 *Tex L Rev* 785, 803–04.

[80] *Filartiga v Peña-Irala*, 630 F 2d 876, 890 (2d Cir 1980); see also *Prosecutor v Anto Furundžija*, judgment, para 147 (quoting *Filartiga*).

[81] *United States v Otto Ohlendorf et al*, IV *Trials of War Criminals Before Nuremberg Military Tribunals Under Control Council Law No 10* at 411 (1950) (hereinafter *Trials of War Criminals*).

defendants were accused '[n]ot [of] crimes against any specified country, but against humanity'.[82] It followed that 'humanity' itself could summon perpetrators to account through universal jurisdiction:

> [T]he inalienable and fundamental rights of common man need not lack for a court ... Humanity can assert itself by law. It has taken on the role of authority.
> ... Those who are indicted ... are answering to humanity itself, humanity which has no political boundaries and no geographical limitations.[83]

With the Nuremberg precedent, the Tribunal continued, 'it is inconceivable . . . that the law of humanity should ever lack for a tribunal. Where law exists, a court will rise. Thus, the court of humanity . . . will never adjourn'.[84]

When an Israeli court rendered judgment against Adolf Eichmann in 1961 it, too, invoked the metaphor of humanity to justify its extraordinary jurisdiction: 'The abhorrent crimes defined in [Israeli] Law are not crimes under Israel [sic] law alone. These crimes, which struck at the whole of mankind and shocked the conscience of nations, are grave offences against the law of nations itself ...'[85]

But if the core justification for universal jurisdiction over inhumane crimes is framed as a moral claim, an important corollary emphasises practical concerns: By their nature, crimes against humanity are unlikely to be punished in the state where they occurred. This justification had strong resonance in the aftermath of Hitler's crimes; German courts were not to be trusted to prosecute major Nazi war criminals. Thus, one US Military Tribunal operating in Germany observed that surrendering the Nazi defendants before it for prosecution by German authorities would have been the 'equivalent [of] a passport to freedom'.[86]

More recently, this rationale has been amplified by a distinct but related consideration. In many countries recently scourged by mass atrocity, the judicial system is in a state of wholesale collapse. For decades after the Khmer Rouge were routed from power, Cambodia was bereft of seasoned judges and lawyers, who were targeted for extermination in the 1970s. In these circumstances, the state where atrocities occurred may not be *able* to bring perpetrators to account.

In sum, legal justifications for universal jurisdiction over human rights crimes make two core claims: (1) certain crimes offend Humanity writ large—a claim that translates into a global entitlement to bring perpetrators to account; and (2) unless every state assumes responsibility to prosecute the perpetrators of such crimes, they will elude justice. Beneath the second rationale is an implied claim: Universal jurisdiction provides an antidote to the impunity that

[82] *Ibid* at 497.
[83] *Ibid* at 498.
[84] *Ibid* at 499.
[85] *Attorney Gen. of Israel v Eichmann*, reprinted in 36 ILR 18, 26 (Isr Dist Ct B Jerusalem 1961), aff'd, 36 ILR 277 (Isr Sup Ct 1962) (hereinafter '*Eichmann* District Court Opinion').
[86] In *re List*, 11 *Trials of War Criminals*, at 757 (US Mil Trib – Nuremberg 1948). See also *Hadamar Trial*, 1 *L Rep Trials of War Criminals*, at 53 (1949) (US Military Commission claimed jurisdiction regardless of nationality of defendants and victims and 'of the place where the offence was committed, particularly where, for some reason, the criminal would otherwise go unpunished').

accomplished despots are likely to enjoy in the countries that endured their crimes.

This rationale explains why universal jurisdiction is thought necessary, but it may not fully reflect contemporary concerns about 'transitional justice', processes of accountability undertaken to help heal the wounds of societies that have suffered savage crimes. At a time when dozens of countries are confronting the dilemmas of transitional justice and devising policies that reflect their unique experiences, the impunity rationale in support of universal jurisdiction may be too simplistic.

It does not, for example, readily accommodate the sophisticated policy devised by the post-*apartheid* South African government led by Nelson Mandela. Eschewing a blanket amnesty, South Africa established a Truth and Reconciliation Commission (TRC) with several mandates. One TRC committee was empowered to grant amnesty for political crimes on an individual basis, but could do so only if it was convinced that the applicant had fully confessed to his or her crimes. The TRC was also charged with establishing a comprehensive account of human rights violations committed during decades of *apartheid* and recommending reparations for victims.

Suppose that an individual granted amnesty by the TRC travelled to Spain, where victims of his crimes instituted criminal proceedings against him for torture. Should Spanish judicial authorities honour South Africa's policy by declining to arrest the travelling torturer? Or should the victim-petitioners, denied legal recourse in South Africa, be allowed to seek some measure of justice in Spain?

I will return to these questions shortly. First, however, I would like to explore in broader perspective how the impunity rationale for universal jurisdiction might be refined to reflect insights derived from contemporary experience.

Jurisdictional Conflicts

My principal claim is that jurisdictional clashes over human rights crimes should be resolved by considering the respective interests of relevant communities. Here, Nuremberg law provides a crucial insight. The interests of humanity—represented above all in the claims of victims and, in the rhetoric of Nuremberg, in the core values of 'civilisation'—merit special consideration. Even so, the values captured in this concept hardly obliterate the interests of other communities with substantial links to the crimes at issue, including the polity of the state where crimes occurred.

Generally, according primacy to the interests of humanity will translate into support for prosecutions before impartial tribunals that operate in accordance with international standards of fair process. Sometimes, this will point toward prosecutions outside the state where atrocities were committed. As noted, countries ravaged by mass atrocities often cannot or will not dispense justice. Even so, core values underlying postwar human rights law are best served when fair proceedings are instituted in the country that bears primary responsibility for atrocious crimes, generally the territorial state. By averting or dispelling a culture of impunity, in-country justice provides the surest guarantee that human rights will be respected in the future.

Complicating the analysis, in an age that has spawned international and mixed tribunals operating alongside national courts, principles for resolving competing claims must take account of the respective merits of various *forms* of jurisdiction. When, for example, should an international tribunal have priority over national courts? Does it depend on *which* national court has asserted a competing claim?

The basic elements of an interests-analysis approach can be found in international instruments concerned with criminal law. The ICC Statute provides especially relevant guidance in resolving conflicting claims of an international tribunal on the one hand and of national courts on the other. As for inter-state conflicts, extradition treaties provide a useful starting point for resolving competing claims among states.

As noted earlier, under the ICC Statute the ICC cannot try a suspect if a state with jurisdiction is pursuing the case, unless that state is unwilling or unable genuinely to carry out the investigation or prosecution.[87] This restriction is likely to have a salutary effect: it will provide strong incentive for states to prosecute crimes they might have been disposed to entomb in a grave of silence and denial. That national trials will avert international prosecution may also provide domestic leaders with the political cover they need to prosecute those most responsible for notorious crimes.

In this fashion, the ICC Statute strikes just about the right balance, at least insofar as it resolves competing claims between the ICC and states with significant links to the crime in question. Far from undermining state responsibility, the ICC will likely invigorate governmental efforts to provide redress to victims. At the same time, the Court remains available to dispense justice when national courts fail.

It is less clear that the ICC Statute deals adequately with situations where more than one state seeks to prosecute the same individual. Notably, the ICC could be disabled from prosecuting an individual if a bystander state instituted criminal proceedings *solely* pursuant to the principle of universal jurisdiction.[88] This result may be generally undesirable. The values that underlie universal jurisdiction are generally thought to be better served when an international tribunal acts on behalf of the international community than when a national

[87] This restriction operates even if the state has decided not to prosecute a suspect after undertaking an investigation, provided the decision was not itself a result of the state's inability or unwillingness to prosecute. ICC Statute, Art 17(1) (b).

[88] See ICC Statute, Art 17(1). Art 90 of the ICC Statute essentially seeks to preserve the ICC's right to assert jurisdiction *subject to the principle of complementarity* in situations where the Court seeks custody of a suspect from a state that has received a request to extradite that same person to another state. As noted below, this provision has somewhat more complex provisions that apply when the requested state is a party to the ICC Statute but the requesting state is not.

court purports to act on its behalf.[89] This is not to deny the value of national authorities assuming responsibility, when necessary, for enforcing the law of humanity. That countries are now exercising universal jurisdiction to punish atrocious crimes has surely deepened international society's commitment to humanitarian law. Even so, national courts are embedded in particular political communities, and to that extent may not be as well suited as international tribunals to enforce law *on behalf of the international community*.

The fact that *any* state—and many states—can defeat jurisdiction by the ICC brings new urgency to a pressing task: developing appropriate principles for resolving conflicting claims of jurisdiction among states. Normally, the question of how such conflicts should be resolved arises when a state receives multiple requests for extradition of the same person or when a country requests the extradition of an individual whom the requested state also wishes to try. Extradition treaties typically direct the requested state, in making its determination, to take into account a fairly standard set of considerations. For example, the European Convention on Extradition[90] specifies that, when a state receives multiple extradition requests, the requested state should 'make its decision having regard to all the circumstances and especially the relative seriousness and place of commission of the offences, the respective dates of the requests, the nationality of the person claimed and the possibility of subsequent extradition to another State.'[91]

The closest analogy in the ICC Statute, a provision that applies when a state party receives competing requests from the ICC and another state, directs the former to 'consider all the relevant factors,' including

(a) The respective dates of the requests;
(b) The interests of the requesting State including, where relevant, whether the crime was committed in its territory and the nationality of the victims and of the person sought; ...[92]

While these provisions provide a useful starting point, they do not provide sufficient guidance as to how relevant interests should be weighed when there are competing claims among states to prosecute the same person for crimes

[89] Notably, even the Israeli District Court that convicted Adolf Eichmann justified its exercise of universal jurisdiction as a second-best alternative to trial before an international tribunal: International law is, it asserted, 'in the absence of an International Court, in need of the judicial and legislative organs of every country to give effect to its criminal interdictions and to bring the criminals to trial'. *Eichmann* District Court Opinion, above n 85, at 26. When the US government tried to persuade Canadian authorities to seek the extradition of Pol Pot in 1997, many thought it inappropriate for Canada, which had no direct links to the crimes of the Khmer Rouge in Cambodia, to play such a leading role in punishing them. This, it seemed, was the work of an international tribunal.

[90] ETS No 24 (1957).

[91] *Ibid*, Art 17.

[92] ICC Statute, Art 90 (6). This provision addresses only situations where a state party receives with respect to the same person both a request for surrender from the ICC and an extradition request from another state (1) that is not a party to the ICC Statute; and (2) with which the requested state has a treaty obligation to extradite the person.

subject to universal jurisdiction. In these circumstances, the following considerations should supplement the guidelines provided in standard extradition treaties:

First, although a state's link of nationality to an alleged perpetrator usually counts in favour of its jurisdictional claim, this presumption is not always appropriate in respect of human rights crimes. As already noted, a chief justification for universal jurisdiction is that there is a heightened risk of impunity if, say, prosecution of a notorious dictator were left to national courts subservient to his despotic rule. A principle requiring states to institute criminal proceedings if they decline to extradite their nationals would mitigate the risk of impunity,[93] but would not prevent states from staging sham proceedings. For the same reasons, the claims of territorial states are sometimes at odds with the goal of combating impunity.

Yet human rights values themselves provide compelling reasons to give priority to prosecutions by the territorial state, provided there are sufficient guarantees of fair process. For one thing, this is the best assurance that human rights will be protected in every country through the rule of law, reliably enforced. In-country justice may also do more to advance a wounded nation's process of recovery in the aftermath of mass atrocity than the remote justice dispensed by international courts. Provided they enjoy legitimacy, trials in the territorial state are more likely than internationally-sponsored prosecutions to inspire a sense of 'ownership' by societies in which atrocious crimes occurred. Thus, the claims of territorial states should generally be given significant weight and support, including the sort of international support provided to the Special Court for Sierra Leone.

Suppose, however, a credible (and safe) judicial process is not possible in the state where atrocities occurred. And further suppose that several other states wish to prosecute the perpetrator. How should their conflicting claims be resolved? Assuming that the judicial system of each state meets international standards of fairness, it would be appropriate to prefer the claim of the state that has the most significant links to the crime in question. Since this approach would generally favour the state of nationality of the defendant and/or victim, this preference essentially amounts to a preference for 'universality plus' over jurisdiction based solely on universal jurisdiction.[94] Giving priority to the claims of states that have substantial links to the crime in question can mitigate the appearance of hubris associated with universal jurisdiction and thereby

[93] Several conventions relevant to the issues addressed in this chapter contain analogous provisions. The four Geneva Conventions of 1949 and the 1984 Convention against Torture include provisions requiring states parties to either assert jurisdiction over persons in their territory believed to have committed certain specified offences or to hand them over for trial in another state. In the view of some writers, a duty to extradite or punish also exists with respect to some human rights offences under customary international law.

[94] This is because the state of nationality of the perpetrator would generally be able to assert jurisdiction based upon the nationality principle as well as the principle of universality, while the state whose nationality the victim possesses may be able to exercise jurisdiction pursuant to the combined authority of passive personality and universal jurisdiction.

enhance the legitimacy of prosecutions in fora outside the territorial state. By honouring enduring sensibilities of state sovereignty, 'universality plus' may serve as a bridge to wider acceptance of jurisdiction based solely on the principle of universality.[95]

Amnesties

Returning to one of the most nettlesome issues raised in this chapter: how should principles aimed at resolving conflicting jurisdictional claims take account of domestic amnesty laws?

As a matter of international law, states generally are not required to give extra-territorial effect to another state's amnesty law. The state that enacts an amnesty is exercising only its own prescriptive jurisdiction; it is not enacting international law. When the amnesty covers crimes that are subject to universal jurisdiction, other states would remain free to apply their own law to the conduct at issue.[96]

More important, some amnesties are inconsistent with international law. This is clearly true with respect to blanket amnesty laws covering atrocious crimes when enacted by states parties to certain human rights treaties, and some amnesties may be incompatible with states' obligations under customary law.[97] Addressing a hypothetical situation in which a state absolved perpetrators of torture through an amnesty law, a Trial Chamber of the International Criminal Tribunal for the former Yugoslavia has observed:

> If such a situation were to arise, the national measures, violating the general principle [proscribing torture] and any relevant treaty provision, would . . . not be accorded international legal recognition. Proceedings could be initiated by potential victims if they had *locus standi* before a competent international or national judicial body with a view to asking it to hold the national measure to be internationally unlawful; or the victim could bring a civil suit for damage in a foreign court, which would therefore be asked *inter alia* to disregard the legal value of the national authorising act. What is even more important is that perpetrators of torture acting upon or benefiting from those national measures may nevertheless be held criminally responsible for torture, whether in a foreign State, or in their own State under a subsequent regime.[98]

[95] Notably, the Spanish criminal proceedings against both Argentine and Chilean military officials began with complaints filed on behalf of victims of Spanish nationality, and were thus supported by the jurisdictional theory of passive personality. The Chilean case was instituted by seven victims of Spanish descent who had been killed or disappeared in Chile, and later broadened to include petitioners who possessed only Chilean nationality. See Wilson, above n 73, at 934.

[96] Domestic courts exercising extraterritorial jurisdiction might consider whether to apply another state's amnesty law as a matter of conflicts-of-law analysis. The considerations addressed in this section would be relevant to such an analysis.

[97] See generally Diane F Orentlicher, 'Addressing Gross Human Rights Abuses: Punishment and Victim Compensation', in Louis Henkin and John Lawrence Hargrove, (eds), *Human Rights: An Agenda for the Next Century* (American Society of International Law, Washington, 1994), 425.

[98] *Prosecutor v Anto Furundžija*, Trial Judgment, see above n 76, para 155.

But let us suppose that a court were free to decide whether to give extraterritorial effect to another country's amnesty for torture. How should the court approach this issue?[99] The classic impunity rationale for universal jurisdiction would suggest that the bystander court should exercise jurisdiction despite—indeed, *in light of*—the domestic amnesty. But insights gleaned from contemporary experience suggest that this approach may be too rigid, perhaps even that bystander states should defer to some domestic policies of national reconciliation.

The complex considerations bound up in this issue are beyond the scope of this chapter. A cautionary note may, however, be in order. Pinochet's legal odyssey teaches an important lesson: It has highlighted the value of maintaining pressure for legal accountability through the credible threat of universal jurisdiction. Had Spanish and British authorities declined to pursue torture charges in deference to Chilean amnesties, civil society in Chile would have lost a powerful source of support. Instead, the proceedings outside Chile bolstered domestic efforts to secure Chile's future by confronting its past.

CONCLUSION

A new architecture of transnational justice is now taking shape. Besides the familiar models of global tribunals and universal jurisdiction, hybrid courts are being fashioned out of national and international elements. Far from displacing national prosecutions, the expanding writ of justice across borders has invigorated efforts to bring justice home. In the process, in-country justice has been transformed. No longer operating exclusively within a national frame of law, domestic courts have become embedded in a transnational process of lawmaking and enforcement.

The proliferation of forums newly able and willing to enforce humanitarian law raises novel challenges. If more than one authority—national, international, or a blend of both—seeks to prosecute the same crime, which should prevail? When, if ever, should courts feel free to disregard an amnesty conferred by another country when asked to judge atrocious crimes? The task today is to develop principled rules for resolving these dilemmas.

[99] One issue meriting further attention is whether the answer to this question should be different with respect to civil actions than in respect of criminal prosecutions based on universal jurisdiction.

PART III

Justice in National Courts

9

Pursuing Crimes Against Humanity in the United States: The Need for a Comprehensive Liability Regime

WILLIAM J ACEVES AND PAUL L HOFFMAN*

INTRODUCTION

Recent developments in international criminal law, including the establishment of the Rome Statute of the International Criminal Court and the various legal proceedings brought against Augusto Pinochet, demonstrate a revitalised commitment to investigate, prosecute, and punish serious violations of international law, including crimes against humanity.[1] These developments are part of a broader movement to end impunity by bringing perpetrators of human rights atrocities to justice.[2]

At the international level, the adoption of the ICC Statute in July 1998 and its subsequent entry into force affirm the inter-state obligation to respond to mass atrocities.[3] The ICC Statute authorises prosecution for genocide, war crimes, and crimes against humanity.[4] While genocide and war crimes are already codified in existing treaties, the ICC Statute represents the first codification of

* 9 May 2002. The authors appreciate the comments of Al Rubin and Beth Stephens. They also acknowledge the research assistance of Alina Connor, Marin Dell, Jennifer Marion, and Amy West. Of course, all errors and omissions remain the responsibility of the authors.

[1] For an overview of these two developments, see 'Developments in the Law—International Criminal Law', (2001), 114 *Harv L Rev* 1943.

[2] See generally Ellen Lutz and Kathryn Sikkink, 'The Justice Cascade: The Evolution and Impact of Foreign Human Rights Trials in Latin America', (2001), 2 *Chi J Int'l L* 1; Steven R Ratner and Jason S Abrams (eds), *Accountability for Human Rights Atrocities in International Law* (1997); Roland Bank, 'International Efforts to Combat Torture and Inhuman Treatment: Have the New Mechanisms Improved Protection?', (1997), 8 *Eur J Int'l L* 613; M Cherif Bassiouni, 'Accountability for International Crime and Serious Violations of Fundamental Human Rights', (1996), 59 *Law & Contemp Prob* 63; Diane F Orentlicher, 'Settling Accounts: The Duty to Prosecute Human Rights Violations of a Prior Regime', (1991), 100 *Yale LJ* 2537; Naomi Roht-Arriaza, 'State Responsibility to Investigate and Prosecute Grave Human Rights Violations in International Law', (1990), 78 *Cal L Rev* 449.

[3] See appendix.

[4] See generally Otto Trifferer (ed), *Commentary on the Rome Statute of the International Criminal Court* (1999); M Cherif Bassiouni, *The Statute of the International Criminal Court: A Documentary History* (1998).

crimes against humanity in a multi-lateral agreement since the adoption of the Charter of the International Military Tribunal in 1945.[5] At the domestic level, efforts to use universal jurisdiction as a basis for prosecuting serious violations of international law acknowledge a similar intra-state obligation to address mass atrocities.[6] Indeed, the *Pinochet* proceedings evince an awareness that national courts can (and should) play a role in enforcing international criminal law.[7]

While these developments reveal a broad movement to combat impunity, they also highlight the shortcomings of US policy on crimes against humanity. Simply put, the United States has not adopted a comprehensive criminal liability regime to prosecute these crimes. Instead, the United States has developed an ad hoc approach, establishing liability for several acts that could also constitute crimes against humanity. Pursuant to existing treaty obligations, for example, the United States has established jurisdiction to prosecute genocide, war crimes, torture, hostage-taking, and hijacking. In certain situations, these acts can also constitute crimes against humanity. Universal jurisdiction, however, exists for only a handful of these crimes. Thus, the United States lacks criminal jurisdiction to prosecute the majority of acts that constitute crimes against humanity when committed abroad if neither the victim nor the perpetrator are US nationals. This ad hoc approach leaves significant gaps in coverage.[8]

In stark contrast, the United States has developed a comprehensive civil liability regime that covers crimes against humanity as well as a wide range of other

[5] Agreement for the Prosecution and Punishment of the Major War Criminals of the European Axis (London Agreement), 8 Aug, 1945, 58 Stat 1544, 82 UNTS 280.

[6] See generally Princeton University, Program in Law and Public Affairs, *The Princeton Principles on Universal Jurisdiction* (2001); Symposium, 'Universal Jurisdiction: Myths, Realities, and Prospects', (2001), 35 *New Eng L Rev* 227; Hari M Osofsky, 'Domesticating International Criminal Law: Bringing Human Rights Violators to Justice', (1997), 107 *Yale LJ* 191; Benedetto Conforti & Francesco Francioni (eds), *Enforcing International Human Rights in Domestic Courts* (1997); Christopher Joyner, 'Arresting Impunity: The Case for Universal Jurisdiction in Bringing War Criminals to Accountability', (1996), 59 *Law & Contemp Probs* 153; Jeffrey Rabkin, 'Universal Justice: The Role of Federal Courts in International Civil Litigation', (1995), 95 *Colum L Rev* 2120. For concerns over the use of universal jurisdiction, see Henry Kissinger, 'The Pitfalls of Universal Jurisdiction', (Jul/Aug 2001), *Foreign Aff* 86; Clive Nicholls, 'Reflections on Pinochet', (2000), 41 *Va J Int'l L* 140.

[7] See generally Human Rights Watch, *The Pinochet Precedent: How Victims Can Pursue Human Rights Criminals Abroad* (2000); Redress, *Challenging Impunity for Torture: A Manual for Bringing Criminal and Civil Proceedings in England and Wales for Torture Committed Abroad* (2000); Amnesty International, *United Kingdom: Universal Jurisdiction and Absence of Immunity for Crimes Against Humanity* (1999); International Council on Human Rights Policy, *Hard Cases: Bringing Human Rights Violators to Justice Abroad* (1999).

[8] For similar criticisms, see Douglass Cassel, 'Empowering United States Courts to Hear Crimes Within the Jurisdiction of the International Criminal Court', (2001), 35 *New Eng L Rev* 421; Mark S. Zaid, 'Will or Should the United States Ever Prosecute War Criminals?: A Need for Greater Expansion in the Areas of Both Criminal and Civil Liability', (2001), 35 *New Eng L Rev* 447; Jordan Paust, 'Problematic US Sanctions Efforts in Response to Genocide, Crimes against Humanity, War Crimes, and Other Human Rights Violations', (2000), 96 *Waseda Proc Comp L* 3, 109; Douglass Cassel, 'The ICC's New Legal Landscape: The Need to Expand US Domestic Court Jurisdiction to Prosecute Genocide, War Crimes, and Crimes against Humanity', (1999), 23 *Fordham Int'l LJ* 378.

human rights violations. For example, the Alien Tort Claims Act allows victims of human rights violations, including crimes against humanity, to pursue civil remedies in US courts.[9] Similarly, the Torture Victim Protection Act allows victims to pursue civil remedies for acts of torture or extrajudicial killing, which may also be characterised as crimes against humanity in certain situations.[10] Since the landmark case of *Filártiga v Peña-Irala* in 1980, US courts have employed the Alien Tort Claims Act and its progeny to allow victims of human rights violations from every part of the world to pursue civil remedies against perpetrators found in the United States. In several lawsuits, US courts have recognised the status of crimes against humanity under international law and the ability of victims to seek redress for such acts.[11]

There is a significant need for a comprehensive liability regime to prosecute crimes against humanity. The ICC Statute entered into force on 1 July 2002. While the United States signed the ICC Statute on 31 December 2000, it renounced its signature on 6 May 2002 by indicating its intention not to become a party.[12] The effects of this renunciation are particularly serious with respect to crimes against humanity.[13] Both genocide and war crimes are already subject to existing multilateral agreements that establish an obligation on states to investigate and prosecute these acts. Indeed, the United States has established criminal jurisdiction, albeit limited, to prosecute acts of genocide and war crimes.[14] In contrast, there is no independent basis for prosecuting crimes against humanity in the United States. The implications of this situation are twofold. First, the United States is limited in its ability to prosecute foreign nationals for crimes against humanity. The ICC Statute establishes a court of limited jurisdiction and power. The International Criminal Court has limited temporal jurisdiction; it does not have the authority to review crimes committed before the entry into force of the ICC Statute.[15] In addition, there is no guarantee that crimes against humanity committed after entry into force will be prosecuted. The Prosecutor has discretion in deciding which cases are brought before the court and may decide to forego prosecution in some cases.[16] Political considerations may also influence member state or Security Council referrals to the court. Quite simply, not all crimes against humanity will be prosecuted by the International

[9] 28 USC. § 1350.

[10] 28 USC. § 1350 (Notes).

[11] See, eg, *Kadic v Karadzić*, 70 F 3d 232 (2d Cir 1995); *Doe v Islamic Salvation Front*, 993 F supp 3 (DDC 1998).

[12] See 'Action for Global Justice: US Signs Treaty for International War Crimes Tribunal', *Newsday*, (1 Jan 2001), at A8. But see William Orme, 'US Quits Treaty on Global Court', *Los Angeles Times*, (7 May 2002), at A3.

[13] According to the Vienna Convention on the Law of Treaties, a state that has signed a treaty is obliged to refrain from acts that would defeat the object and purpose of the treaty. Vienna Convention on the Law of Treaties, May 23, 1969, Art 18, 1155 UNTS 331. The United States, however, has not signed the Vienna Convention.

[14] 18 USC. § 1091 (genocide); 18 USC. § 2241 (war crimes).

[15] ICC Statute, Art 11.

[16] *Ibid,* at Art 53.

Criminal Court. Accordingly, there may be cases where national prosecution is the only option for punishing crimes against humanity. In the absence of criminal legislation that imposes liability for crimes against humanity, the United States will be unable to prosecute these offences even when perpetrators enter US territory. Secondly, the United States is limited in its ability to prosecute US nationals for crimes against humanity. A comprehensive set of domestic enforcement mechanisms would allow the United States to prosecute US nationals in its own courts, bypassing the need for international prosecution.[17] The ICC Statute provides such deference to national tribunals under the principle of complementarity. Given existing US concerns about the competence of international tribunals to prosecute US nationals, the implications of complementarity are particularly significant.[18] According to former US Ambassador-at-Large for War Crimes Issues David Scheffer,

> [b]oth critics and supporters of the court should find common cause in amending the federal criminal code (Title 18) and the Uniform Code of Military Justice (Title 10) to ensure that crimes under the treaty can be fully prosecuted in US courts. Current codes are simply out-dated and may deprive us of our first line of defense.[19]

US Under Secretary of State for Political Affairs Marc Grossman also acknowledged that gaps exist in United States law and that such gaps should not allow 'persons wanted or indicted for genocide, war crimes, or crimes against humanity to seek safe haven on our soil in the hopes of evading justice.'[20] Thus, domestic enforcement mechanisms will remain relevant for the United States (and other countries) even with the existence of the International Criminal Court.

This chapter examines the criminal and civil liability regimes for crimes against humanity in the United States.[21] It is divided into three sections. The first part presents a brief overview of US policy toward crimes against humanity from Nuremberg to Rome. Next, the chapter reviews the US criminal liability regime for crimes against humanity. The final part examines the civil liability regime for crimes against humanity. This overview reveals the limitations of US policy toward crimes against humanity and the need to establish a comprehensive liability regime that ensures the United States does not become a safe haven for human rights abusers.[22]

[17] Once the United States agrees to ratify the ICC Statute, it will still need to adopt implementing legislation. See generally Helen Duffy, 'National Constitutional Compatibility and the International Criminal Court', (2001), 11 *Duke J Comp & Int'l L* 5.

[18] See Katherine L Doherty and Timothy LH McCormack, 'Complementarity' as a Catalyst for Comprehensive Domestic Penal Legislation', (1999), 5 *UC Davis J Int'l L & Pol'y* 147.

[19] Ambassador David J Scheffer, 'Fourteenth Waldemar A. Solf Lecture in International Law: A Negotiator's Perspective on the International Criminal Court', (2001), 167 *Mil L Rev* 1, 15.

[20] Under Secretary of State for Political Affairs Marc Grossman, Remarks at the Centre for Strategic and International Affairs, 6 May 2002.

[21] This chapter focuses on efforts to address crimes against humanity that occurred outside the United States. It does not address crimes against humanity committed in the United States.

[22] See generally Amnesty International USA, *USA—A Safe Haven for Torturers* (AIUSA, 2002).

A BRIEF OVERVIEW OF US POLICY TOWARD CRIMES AGAINST HUMANITY

The United States has generally supported the codification and prosecution of crimes against humanity, although it initially opposed this movement.[23] Efforts to recognise the 'laws and principles of humanity' in the Treaty of Versailles were challenged by the United States, which found the concept too vague for codification.[24] During the Second World War, similar efforts met with initial opposition by the State Department and War Department. The discovery of massive atrocities perpetrated by the Nazi regime against Jews and other non-combatants led to a reversal of US policy. As a result, the Roosevelt administration adopted the memorandum 'Trial and Punishment of Nazi War Criminals' in January 1945, which acknowledged the need for the prosecution of crimes against humanity.[25] The United States subsequently supported inclusion of crimes against humanity as a separate offence in both the Charter of the International Military Tribunal and Control Council Law No 10.[26]

Almost 50 years after the Nuremberg trials, the United States renewed its support for efforts to codify crimes against humanity within the framework of international criminal law. The United States supported the establishment of the International Criminal Tribunals for the former Yugoslavia and Rwanda and the inclusion of crimes against humanity in their respective statutes.[27] The United States affirmed its commitment to the principles set forth in the respective statutes on several occasions. In an *amicus curiae* submission to the Trial Chamber of the International Criminal Tribunal for the former Yugoslavia, for example, the United States argued that

> [t]he relevant law and precedents for the offences in question here—genocide, war crimes and crimes against humanity—clearly contemplate international as well as national action against the individuals responsible. Proscription of these crimes has long since acquired the status of customary international law, binding on all states, and such crimes have already been the subject of international prosecutions by the Nuremberg and Tokyo Tribunals.[28]

[23] See generally Arieh J. Kochavi, *Prelude to Nuremberg: Allied War Crimes Policy and the Question of Punishment* (1999); Telford Taylor, *The Anatomy of the Nuremberg Trials* (1992), 15–16; Bradley F Smith, *The Road to Nuremberg* (1981); Egon Schwelb, 'Crimes against Humanity', (1946), *Brit Y B Int'l L* 23, 178.

[24] See Memorandum of Reservations Presented by the Representatives of the United States to the Report of the Commission on Responsibilities (4 Apr 1919), Annex 2, reprinted in 'Commission on the Responsibility of the Authors of the War and on Enforcement of Penalties, Report Presented to the Preliminary Peace Conference (29 March 1919)', (1920), 14 *Am J Int'l L* 95. See also M. Cherif Bassiouni, *Crimes against Humanity in International Criminal Law*, 2d edn. (1999), 63.

[25] Kochavi, above, at 160.

[26] See Telford Taylor, *Final Report to the Secretary of the Army on the Nuernberg War Crimes Trials Under Control Council Law No 10,* (1949), at 69, 108–109.

[27] See, eg, 'Letter Dated 5 April 1993 from the Permanent Representative of the United States of America to the United Nations Addressed to the Secretary-General', UN Doc S/25575 (1993).

[28] Amicus Curiae Brief of the United States, *Prosecutor v Tadić*, IT-94-I-T, Motion Hearing

The United States was also a firm supporter of efforts to draft the ICC Statute and to establish crimes against humanity as a punishable offence.[29] Throughout the deliberations of the Preparatory Committee, the United States delegation expressed its support for placing crimes against humanity within the proposed court's jurisdiction.[30] The United States also supported expanding the definition of crimes against humanity although it cautioned that these crimes should be carefully defined in the statute. For example, '[t]he US delegation, aided by the advice of experts in the NGO community, fought hard during the final sessions of the Preparatory Committee and again in Rome to include explicit reference to crimes relating to sexual assault in the text of the statute.'[31] At a broader level, the United States took the position that 'contemporary international law makes it clear that no war nexus for crimes against humanity is required.'[32] Thus, the United States argued for an interpretation of crimes against humanity that did not differentiate between internal armed conflict and crimes occurring outside armed conflict. Through its support, the United States played an integral role in ensuring the placement of crimes against humanity within the final draft of the ICC Statute. As noted by Ambassador Scheffer, '[o]ur strong support for a broad interpretation of crimes against humanity was instrumental in maintaining this principle in the draft text that would go to Rome.'[33]

Although the United States ultimately opposed the adoption of the ICC Statute in July 1998, it did so for reasons unrelated to the codification of crimes against humanity. Its principal concern lay in the possibility that US military personnel might be subjected to politically motivated prosecutions.[34] Despite these concerns, the United States signed the ICC Statute on 31 December 2000.[35] According to President Clinton, the United States signed the treaty in order to continue its tradition of moral leadership in the struggle to promote

25 July 1995), quoted in Sharon Williams, 'The Rome Statute of the International Criminal Court: From 1947–2000 and Beyond', (2000), 38 *Osgoode Hall L J* 297, 313.

[29] See generally Michael P. Scharf, 'The ICC's Jurisdiction Over the Nationals of Non-Party States: A Critique of the US Position', (2001), 64 *Law & Contemp Probs* 67, 88-90; David J Scheffer, 'The United States and the International Criminal Court', (1999), 93 *Am J Int'l L* 12.

[30] See UN Doc A/AC.244/1/Add.2, para 22 (1995).

[31] Scheffer, The United States and the International Criminal Court, above, at 16–17.

[32] Statement of the United States Delegation to the Preparatory Committee on the Establishment of an International Criminal Court (23 March 1998), reprinted in 'Is a UN International Criminal Court in the US National Interest? Hearing Before the Subcomm. on International Operations of the Senate Comm. on Foreign Relations', *105th Cong.* (1998), 129.

[33] Scheffer, The United States and the International Criminal Court, above, at 14.

[34] See, eg, Bruce Broomhall, 'Toward US Acceptance of the International Criminal Court', (2001), 64 *Law & Contemp Probs* 141; Madeline Morris, 'High Crimes and Misconceptions: The ICC and Non-Party States' (2001), 64 *Law & Contemp Probs* 13; John Seguin, 'Denouncing the International Criminal Court: An Examination of US Objections to the Rome Statute', (2000), 18 *BU Int'l L J* 85; John F Murphy, 'The Quivering Gulliver: US Views on a Permanent International Criminal Court', (2000), 34 *Int'l Law* 45.

[35] See Steven Lee Myers, 'US Signs Treaty for World Court to Try Atrocities', *New York Times*, (1 Jan 2001), at A1; Thomas E Ricks, 'US Signs Treaty on War Crimes Tribunal', *Wash Post*, (1 Jan 2001), at A1.

human rights and international accountability. Signature would also allow the United States to work with other signatories to promote US interests.

> In signing, however, we are not abandoning our concerns about significant flaws in the treaty. In particular, we are concerned that when the court comes into existence, it will not only exercise authority over personnel of states that have ratified the treaty, but also claim jurisdiction over personnel of states that have not. Given these concerns, I will not and do not recommend that my successor submit the treaty to the Senate for ratification until our fundamental concerns are satisfied.[36]

On 6 May 2002, the Bush administration announced that the United States did not intend to become a party to the treaty and, therefore, it had no legal obligations arising from its signature. It remained committed, however, to promoting accountability for genocide, war crimes, and crimes against humanity.[37]

The ICC Statute identifies eleven separate acts that constitute crimes against humanity.[38] Article 7(1) defines the following acts as crimes against humanity when committed as part of a widespread or systematic attack directed against a civilian population by someone with knowledge of the attack: (a) murder; (b) extermination; (c) enslavement; (d) deportation or forcible transfer of population; (e) imprisonment or other severe deprivation of physical liberty in violation of fundamental rules of international law; (f) torture; (g) rape, sexual slavery, enforced prostitution, forced pregnancy, enforced sterilisation, or any other form of sexual violence of comparable gravity; (h) persecution against any identifiable group or collectivity on political, racial, national, ethnic, cultural, religious, gender, or other grounds that are universally recognised as impermissible under international law; (i) enforced disappearance of persons; (j) the crime of apartheid; or (k) other inhuman acts of similar character intentionally causing great suffering, or serious injury to body or to mental or physical health.[39] Because of its recent codification in the ICC Statute, Article 7(1) represents the most authoritative interpretation of crimes against humanity in international criminal law.

[36] Statement on the Rome Treaty on the International Criminal Court, 37 *Weekly Comp Pres Doc* (31 Dec 2000), 4. See also Sean D Murphy, 'US Signing of the Statute of the International Criminal Court', (2001), 95 *Am J Int'l L* 397.

[37] See Letter from John R Bolton, Under Secretary of State for Arms Control and International Security, to Kofi Annan, UN Secretary-General (6 May 2002).

[38] See generally Simon Chesterman, 'An Altogether Different Order: Defining the Elements of Crimes against Humanity' (2000), 10 *Duke J Comp & Int'l L* 307; Daryl Robinson, 'Defining "Crimes against Humanity" at the Rome Conference', (1999), 93 *Am J Int'l L* 43; Beth Van Schaack, 'The Definition of Crimes against Humanity: Resolving the Incoherence', (1999), 37 *Colum J Transnat'l L* 787.

[39] ICC Statute, Art 7. For further elaboration, see 'Report of the Preparatory Commission for the International Criminal Court: Addendum—Part II: Finalised Draft Text of the Elements of Crimes', UN Doc PCNICC/2000/1/Add 2 (2000).

CRIMINAL LIABILITY FOR CRIMES AGAINST HUMANITY IN THE UNITED STATES

The United States does not recognise common law criminal jurisdiction.[40] That is, individuals cannot be prosecuted in the absence of criminal statutes that explicitly set forth the underlying offence. Even though crimes against humanity are recognised under international criminal law, these international rules cannot provide the sole basis for criminal prosecution in the United States. Explicit legislation is necessary to prosecute these offences.

The Constitution grants Congress the power to define offences against the law of nations. Congress has exercised this power on several occasions to establish extraterritorial jurisdiction for crimes committed abroad.[41]

The Statutory Framework

The United States has not adopted legislation to criminalise crimes against humanity as set forth in Article 7(1) of the ICC Statute. Rather, it has developed an ad hoc approach. The United States has ratified several international agreements that require member states to establish criminal liability for specified acts such as hostage-taking, genocide, torture, or war crimes, even when such acts were committed abroad. These acts can also constitute crimes against humanity when committed as part of a widespread or systematic attack directed against a civilian population by someone with knowledge of the attack.

Hostage-Taking

While hostage-taking is not specifically recognised as a crime against humanity in the ICC Statute, it can be interpreted to fall within several of the acts set forth in Article 7(1). For example, Article 7(1)(e) establishes criminal liability for 'imprisonment or other severe deprivation of physical liberty in violation of fundamental rules of international law.' Article 7(1)(k) acts as a catch-all provi-

[40] See *United States v Hudson and Goodwin*, 11 US (7 Cranch) 32 (1812); *United States v Hutchinson*, 26 F Cas 452, 453 (E D Pa 1848) (No 15,432). See generally Gary D Rowe, 'The Sound of Silence: United States v Hudson & Goodwin, The Jeffersonian Ascendancy, and the Abolition of Federal Common Law Crimes', (1992), 101 *Yale L Rev* 919.

[41] Under Art I, s 8, cl 10 of the US Constitution, Congress has the power to define and punish 'Offenses against the Law of Nations.' See *In re Yamashita*, 327 US 1 (1946); *Ex Parte Quirin*, 317 US 1 (1942). See generally Beth Stephens, 'Federalism and Foreign Affairs: Congress' Power to 'Define and Punish . . . Offenses against the Law of Nations,' (2000), 42 *Wm & Mary L Rev* 447. Congress also has the power to establish extraterritorial jurisdiction for crimes committed abroad. See generally Mark P Gibney, 'The Extraterritorial Application of US Law: The Perversion of Democratic Governance, The Reversal of Institutional Roles, and the Imperative of Establishing Normative Principles', (1996), 19 *B C Int'l & Comp L Rev* 297; Jeffrey Rabkin, 'Universal Justice: The Role of Federal Courts in International Civil Litigation', (1995), 95 *Colum Rev* 2120; Susan S Gibson, 'Lack of Extraterritorial Jurisdiction Over Civilians: A New Look at an Old Problem', (1995), 148 *Mil L Rev* 114.

sion, establishing liability for '[o]ther inhumane acts of a similar character intentionally causing great suffering, or serious injury to body or to mental or physical health.' Both provisions appear applicable to hostage-taking which, by definition, involves the use of coercive force and is a violation of international law.

The United States ratified the International Convention against the Taking of Hostages ('Hostage-Taking Convention') in 1984.[42] Article 5(2) of the Hostage-Taking Convention requires each state party to take such measures as may be necessary to establish jurisdiction over acts of hostage-taking in cases where the alleged offender is present in its territory and it does not extradite him. Congress adopted 18 USC. § 1203 to implement this obligation.[43] It provides that:

> whoever, whether inside or outside the United States, seizes or detains and threatens to kill, to injure, or to continue to detain another person in order to compel a third person or a governmental organisation to do or abstain from doing any act as an explicit or implicit condition for the release of the person detained, or attempts or conspires to do so, shall be punished by imprisonment for any term of years or for life and, if the death of any person results, shall be punished by death or life imprisonment.[44]

This section establishes jurisdiction to prosecute acts of hostage-taking that occur outside the United States in three situations: (1) the offender or the person seized or detained is a national of the United States; (2) the offender is found in the United States; or (3) the governmental organisation sought to be compelled is the Government of the United States.[45] In contrast,

> [i]t is not an offence under this section if the conduct required for the offence occurred inside the United States, each alleged offender and each person seized or detained are nationals of the United States, and each alleged offender is found in the United States, unless the governmental organization sought to be compelled is the Government of the United States.[46]

The United States has prosecuted several individuals under this statute.[47] However, none of these cases were based exclusively upon universal jurisdiction.

Genocide

While genocide is recognised as a separate offence under the ICC Statute, it can also constitute a crime against humanity. Indeed, most of the acts set forth in Article 7(1) of the ICC Statute could give rise to claims of both genocide and crimes against humanity.

[42] International Convention against the Taking of Hostages, 17 Dec 1979, 1316 UNTS 205.
[43] PL 98-473, § 2002(a), 98 Stat 2186.
[44] 18 USC. § 1203(a).
[45] 18 USC. § 1203(b)(1).
[46] 18 USC. § 1203(b)(2).
[47] See, eg, *United States v Yunis*, 924 F 2d 1086 (DC Cir 1991).

The United States ratified the Convention on the Prevention and Punishment of the Crime of Genocide ('Genocide Convention') in 1988.[48] Article VI of the Genocide Convention provides, inter alia, that persons charged with genocide or ancillary crimes shall be tried by a competent tribunal in the state where the act was committed. In order to comply with this obligation, Congress adopted the Genocide Convention Implementation Act.[49] The Act establishes criminal liability for acts of genocide.

> (a) Basic offence. Whoever, whether in time of peace or in time of war, in a circumstance described in subsection (d) and with the specific intent to destroy, in whole or in substantial part, a national, ethnic, racial, or religious group as such—
>
> (1) kills members of that group;
> (2) causes serious bodily injury to members of that group;
> (3) causes the permanent impairment of the mental faculties of members of the group through drugs, torture, or similar techniques;
> (4) subjects the group to conditions of life that are intended to cause the physical destruction of the group in whole or in part;
> (5) imposes measures intended to prevent births within the group; or
> (6) transfers by force children of the group to another group;
>
> or attempts to do so, shall be punished as provided in subsection (b).[50]

The Act provides that an offence under subsection (a)(1) may be punishable by death or imprisonment for life and a fine of not more than $1,000,000, or both.[51] In any other case, an individual may be punished by imprisonment for not more than 20 years and a fine of not more than $1,000,000, or both.[52] In addition, the Act provides a separate offence for incitement to commit genocide.

> (c) Incitement offence. Whoever in a circumstance described in subsection (d) directly and publicly incites another to violate subsection (a) shall be fined not more than $500,000 or imprisoned not more than five years, or both.[53]

The Act contains a significant jurisdictional limitation. Specifically, subsection (d) limits prosecution to the following circumstances: (1) the offence is committed within the United States; or (2) the alleged offender is a national of the United States.[54] Accordingly, the United States does not recognise universal jurisdiction for acts of genocide.

To date, there have been no prosecutions under this statute.

[48] Convention on the Prevention and Punishment of the Crime of Genocide, 9 Dec 1948, 78 UNTS 277.

[49] PL 100-606, § 2(a), 102 Stat 3045.

[50] 18 USC. § 1091(a).

[51] 18 USC. § 1091(b)(1).

[52] 18 USC. § 1091(b)(2).

[53] 18 USC. § 1091(c).

[54] 18 USC. § 1091(d).

Torture

Torture is explicitly recognised as a crime against humanity in Article 7(1)(f) of the ICC Statute.[55] It is defined as 'the intentional infliction of severe pain or suffering, whether physical or mental, upon a person in the custody or under the control of the accused; except that torture shall not include pain or suffering arising only from, inherent in or incidental to, lawful sanctions; ...'[56]

The United States ratified the Convention against Torture and Other Cruel, Inhuman or Degrading Treatment or Punishment ('Convention against Torture') in 1994.[57] Article 5(2) of the Convention against Torture requires each state party to take such measures as may be necessary to establish its jurisdiction over acts of torture in cases where the alleged offender is present in any territory under its jurisdiction and it does not extradite him. Congress adopted 18 USC § 2340A(a) to implement this obligation.[58] It provides:

> Whoever outside the United States commits or attempts to commit torture shall be fined under this title or imprisoned not more than 20 years, or both, and if death results to any person from conduct prohibited by this subsection, shall be punished by death or imprisoned for any term of years or for life.[59]

Criminal liability attaches if: (1) the alleged offender is a national of the United States; or (2) the alleged offender is present in the United States, irrespective of the nationality of the victim or alleged offender.[60] In other words, a torturer can be held criminally liable for acts of torture even when such acts occurred abroad and regardless of whether the victim or the perpetrator is a US citizen.

According to the State Department, this legislation was adopted to implement the principle of *aut dedere aut judicare* (extradite or prosecute) as set forth in Article 7 of the Convention against Torture.[61] When an alleged torturer is found within territory under US jurisdiction and the suspect is not extradited,

[55] Indeed, it was recognised as a crime against humanity as early as 1919. Christopher K Hall, 'Crimes against Humanity' in Triffterer, *Commentary on the Rome Statute*, above, at 117, 139.

[56] ICC Statute, Art 7(2)(e).

[57] See appendix. Note that the definition of torture contained in the ICC Statute is broader in scope than the definition in the Convention against Torture.

[58] PL 103-236, § 506(a), 108 Stat 463.

[59] 18 USC. §§ 2340A(a). The definition of 'torture' is codified at 18 USC. § 2340:

> 'torture' means an act committed by a person acting under the colour of law specifically intended to inflict severe physical or mental pain or suffering (other than pain or suffering incidental to lawful sanctions) upon another person within his custody or physical control; . . . .

The term 'severe mental pain or suffering' is further defined as the prolonged mental harm caused by or resulting from—

> (A) the intentional infliction or threatened infliction of severe physical pain or suffering; (B) the administration or application, or threatened administration or application, of mind altering substances or other procedures calculated to disrupt profoundly the senses or the personality; (C) the threat of imminent death; or (D) the threat that another person will imminently be subjected to death, severe physical pain or suffering or the administration or application of mind altering substances or other procedures calculated to disrupt profoundly the senses or personality; . . . .

[60] 18 USC. § 2340A(b).

[61] US Dept of State, 'Initial Report of the United States of America to the UN Committee Against Torture', UN Doc CAT/C/28/Add 5 (1999), at paras 193, 194 [hereinafter 'Initial Report'].

the United States acknowledges its obligation to submit the case to its competent authorities for the purpose of prosecution. 'Indeed, the US Department of Justice has undertaken measures to ensure that any person on US territory believed to be responsible for acts of torture is identified and handled consistent with the requirements of this provision.'[62] In hearings before the Committee against Torture, a US government delegation reaffirmed this commitment to prosecute alleged torturers found in the United States.[63]

To date, there have been no prosecutions under this statute.[64]

War Crimes

While war crimes are recognised as a separate offence under the ICC Statute, they can also be categorised as crimes against humanity.[65] When committed during time of war, most of the acts set forth in Article 7(1) of the ICC Statute could give rise to claims of both war crimes and crimes against humanity.

The United States ratified the Geneva Conventions, which codify many of the laws of war, in 1955. The Geneva Conventions require member states to search for persons alleged to have committed grave breaches of the laws of war and to bring such persons before their courts, regardless of nationality.[66] Congress did not codify this obligation until the adoption of the War Crimes Act in 1996.[67] The War Crimes Act establishes federal jurisdiction to prosecute violations of the laws of war.[68] It provides:

> Whoever, whether inside or outside the United States, commits a war crime, in any of the circumstances described in subsection (b), shall be fined under this title or imprisoned for life or any term of years, or both, and if death results to the victim, shall also be subject to the penalty of death.[69]

[62] *Ibid,* at para 194.

[63] See UN Press Release on Committee against Torture, 24th Sess (11 May 2000).

[64] But see Ellis Burger, 'INS Lacks Explanation for Suspect's Citizenship', *Sun-Sentinel* (Ft. Lauderdale, Fl.), (6 Sept 2001), at 4B; Jody Benjamin, 'Suspected Cuban Torturer Arrested', *Sun-Sentinel* (Ft. Lauderdale, Fl), (5 Sept 2001), at 4B. In Sept 2001, a suspected torturer was arrested by the Immigration and Naturalization Service and charged with immigration fraud.

[65] Bassiouni, *Crimes against Humanity in International Criminal Law*, above, at 60, 77 ('The conclusion is clear that 'crimes against humanity' are analogous to war crimes and are an extension thereof, ...').

[66] See, eg, Geneva Convention Relative to the Treatment of Prisoners of War, 12 Aug 1949, Art 129, 75 UNTS 135.

[67] See generally Zaid, above, at 462, 463.

[68] In the United States, the Articles of War regulated the laws of war until their replacement by the Uniform Code of Military Justice in 1950. See generally Jan E Aldykiewicz, 'Authority to Court-Martial Non-US Military Personnel for Serious Violations of International Humanitarian Law Committed During Internal Armed Conflicts', (2001), 167 *Mil L Rev* 74. The Uniform Code of Military Justice was in operation during the Vietnam War and regulated US prosecution of war crimes. Following the My Lai massacre, for example, Captain William Calley was prosecuted and convicted under the Uniform Code of Military Justice for premeditated murder and assault with intent to commit murder. See *United States v Calley*, 46 CMR 1131 (1973). The War Crimes Act does not replace the Uniform Code of Military Justice.

[69] 18 USC. § 2441(a). The term 'war crime' is defined at 18 USC. § 2441(c) as any conduct:

(1) defined as a grave breach in any of the international conventions signed at Geneva 12 Aug

The War Crimes Act contains a significant jurisdictional limitation. Specifically, subsection (b) limits prosecution to the following circumstances: (1) the person committing such war crime is a member of the United States Armed Forces or a US national; or (2) the victim is a member of the United States Armed Forces or a US national.[70] Accordingly, the United States does not recognise universal jurisdiction for war crimes.

To date, there have been no prosecutions under this statute.

Additional Crimes

In addition to hostage-taking and torture, the United States has established universal jurisdiction for the following acts: destruction of aircraft and aircraft facilities; violence at international airports; protection of foreign officials, official guests, and internationally protected persons; threats and extortion against foreign officials, official guests, or internationally protected persons; murder or manslaughter of foreign officials, official guests, or internationally protected persons; piracy; violence against maritime navigation; violence against maritime fixed platforms; and aircraft piracy. Table 1 lists those provisions of federal law that establish universal jurisdiction.[71]

If these acts are committed as part of a widespread or systematic attack directed against a civilian population by someone with knowledge of the attack, as set forth in the *chapeau* of Article 7(1) of the ICC Statute, they could also constitute crimes against humanity.

While the United States has established criminal liability for such acts as murder, slavery, forced labour, sex trafficking, racial persecution, the use of chemical weapons, or other weapons of mass destruction, these provisions contain significant jurisdictional limitations and do not establish universal jurisdiction.[72] Some of these provisions only apply to acts committed in territory under US jurisdiction. Other provisions only apply when the perpetrators or

1949, or any protocol to such convention to which the United States is a party;
(2) prohibited by Arts 23, 25, 27, or 28 of the Annex to the Hague Convention IV, Respecting the Laws and Customs of War on Land, signed 18 Oct 1907;
(3) which constitutes a violation of common Art 3 of the international conventions signed at Geneva, 12 Aug 1949, or any protocol to such convention to which the United States is a party and which deals with non-international armed conflict; or
(4) of a person who, in relation to an armed conflict and contrary to the provisions of the Protocol on Prohibition or Restrictions on the Use of Mines, Booby-Traps and Other Devices as amended at Geneva on 3 May 1996 (Protocol II as amended on 3 May 1996), when the United States is a party to such Protocol, wilfully kills or causes serious injury to civilians.

[70] 18 USC. § 2441(b).

[71] For similar overviews, see Cassel, 'Empowering United States Courts to Hear Crimes Within the Jurisdiction of the International Criminal Court', above, at 429–30; Christopher L Blakesley, 'Extraterritorial Jurisdiction', in M Cherif Bassiouni (ed), *International Criminal Law*, 2d edn. (1999), 33, 56–57.

[72] See 18 USC. § 241 (murder); 18 USC. § 1581 (slavery); 18 USC. § 1589 (forced labour); 18 USC. § 1591 (sex trafficking of children or by force, fraud or coercion); 18 USC. § 241 (persecution); 18 USC. § 229 (use of chemical weapons); 18 USC. § 2332a (use of certain weapons of mass destruction).

TABLE 1 Statutes Authorising Universal Jurisdiction in the United States

18 USC. § 32	Destruction of aircraft and aircraft facilities
18 USC. § 37	Violence at international airports
18 USC. § 112	Protection of foreign officials, official guests, and internationally protected persons
18 USC. § 878	Threats and extortion against foreign officials, official guests, or internationally protected persons
18 USC. § 1116	Murder or manslaughter of foreign officials, official guests, or internationally protected persons[73]
18 USC. § 1203	Hostage-taking
18 USC. § 1651	Piracy under law of nations
18 USC. § 2280	Violence against maritime navigation
18 USC. § 2281	Violence against maritime fixed platforms
18 USC. § 2340	Torture
49 USC. § 46502	Aircraft piracy

victims are US nationals. Accordingly, the United States does not have criminal jurisdiction to prosecute the majority of crimes against humanity when committed abroad and where neither the victim nor the perpetrator are US nationals.

The Case Law

There are few reported cases in the United States involving prosecution of acts that could be characterised as crimes against humanity. This can be attributed, in part, to the paucity of statutes establishing criminal liability for violations of international law committed abroad. And yet, US courts have recognised the validity of extraterritorial jurisdiction, as well as universal jurisdiction, on several occasions.[74]

[73] 18 USC. § 1117 imposes criminal liability for conspiracy to commit any of the acts set forth in 18 USC. § 1116.

[74] In addition to cases involving criminal prosecution in the United States, US courts have also discussed universal jurisdiction in the context of extradition proceedings. In *Demjanjuk v Petrovsky*, the Israeli government sought to extradite John Demjanjuk, a naturalised US citizen, for war crimes and crimes against humanity allegedly committed as a Nazi prison camp guard at Trawniki and Treblinka. Demjanjuk was alleged to have been the notorious Nazi guard 'Ivan the Terrible.' Demjanjuk challenged the extradition request on the grounds that Israel lacked jurisdiction to prosecute the murder of Jews in a Nazi extermination camp in Poland during the Second World War. The District Court noted that war crimes and crimes against humanity have long been recognised under international law. *In the Matter of the Extradition of John Demjanjuk*, 612 F supp 544 (ND Ohio 1985). Indeed, '[t]he principle that the perpetrators of crimes against humanity and war crimes are subject to universal jurisdiction found acceptance in the aftermath of World War II.' *Ibid*, at 556. The Court of Appeals for the Sixth Circuit affirmed the District Court's findings. It concluded that Israel's assertion of universal jurisdiction for war crimes and crimes against humanity was valid under international law. *Demjanjuk v Petrovsky*, 776 F 2d 571 (6th Cir 1985). 'This universality principle is based on the assumption that some crimes are so universally condemned that the

One of the earliest cases to recognise the permissibility of extraterritorial jurisdiction and the authority of Congress to establish universal jurisdiction was decided in 1820. In *United States v Smith*, the defendant, purportedly a US citizen, plundered a Spanish vessel on the high seas. He was subsequently charged with piracy under a federal statute that provided 'if any person or persons whatsoever, shall, upon the high seas, commit the crime of piracy, as defined by the law of nations, and such offender or offenders shall be brought into, or found in the United States, every such offender or offenders shall, upon conviction thereof . . . be punished with death.'[75] The defendant challenged the constitutionality of the statute. The Supreme Court determined that the constitutional power set forth in Article I, Section 8 of the Constitution to define and punish piracies, felonies committed on the high seas, and offences against the law of nations provided sufficient authorisation for the statute.[76] In addition, the Court recognised the unique quality of piracy, which justified its prosecution in national courts. 'The common law, too, recognises and punishes piracy as an offence, not against its own municipal code, but as an offence against the law of nations, (which is part of the common law,) as an offence against the universal law of society, a pirate being deemed an enemy of the human race'.[77] Indeed, the authority to punish piracy extended to all persons who commit this offence.

> And the general practice of all nations in punishing all persons, whether natives or foreigners, who have committed this offence against any persons whatsoever, with whom they are in amity, is a conclusive proof that the offence is supposed to depend, not upon the particular provisions of any municipal code, but upon the law of nations, both for its definition and punishment.[78]

In *United States v Yunis*, Fawaz Yunis was charged with participating in the hijacking and destruction of a foreign registered aircraft in Lebanon. Yunis, a resident and citizen of Jordan, was apprehended in international waters in the

perpetrators are the enemies of all people. Therefore, any nation which has custody of the perpetrators may punish them according to its law applicable to such offenses.' *Ibid*, at 582. Indeed, the Nuremberg legacy makes clear that 'there is a jurisdiction over some crimes which extends beyond the territorial limits of any nation.' *Ibid*. For these reasons, the Court of Appeals affirmed the District Court's decision. Demjanjuk was subsequently extradited to Israel.

In 1988, Demjanjuk was tried and convicted in Israel. His conviction was subsequently overturned by the Israeli Supreme Court as a result of new evidence that raised questions about his identity as Ivan the Terrible. As a result, Demjanjuk was returned to the United States. In 1993, the Sixth Circuit strongly criticised the Office of Special Investigations ('OSI') for its handling of the Demjanjuk case. See *Demjanjuk v Petrovsky*, 10 F 3d 338 (6th Cir 1993). In 2001, the OSI initiated new proceedings to denaturalise Demjanjuk, alleging that he did, in fact, participate as a Nazi concentration camp guard. See Eric Fettmann, 'The New Demjanjuk Case', *New York Post*, (6 June 2001), at 33.

75 *United States v Smith*, 18 US 153, 157 (1820).

76 *Ibid*, at 158.

77 *Ibid*, at 161.

78 *Ibid*. See also *United States v Demarchi*, 25 F Cas 814 (CCNY 1862); *United States v Klintock*, 18 US 144 (1820); *United States v Furlong*, 18 US 184 (1820). But see *United States v Kessler*, 26 F Cas 766 (CC Pa 1829); *United States v Palmer*, 16 US 610 (1818). For a discussion of several piracy cases, see Alfred P Rubin, *The Law of Piracy* (1988).

Mediterranean Sea. He was subsequently transferred to the United States, where he was charged with acts of hostage-taking and hijacking. Yunis challenged his indictment arguing, inter alia, that the United States lacked jurisdiction to prosecute him for crimes committed abroad. Both the District Court and the Court of Appeals for the District of Columbia denied the challenge, affirming US jurisdiction under the Hostage Taking Act and the Hijacking Act. Because there were three US nationals on the aircraft, the District Court did not rely exclusively on universal jurisdiction. As noted by the District Court, however, the principle of universal jurisdiction was well-established and provided sufficient basis for asserting jurisdiction over an alleged offender. 'In light of the global efforts to punish aircraft piracy and hostage taking, international legal scholars unanimously agree that these crimes fit within the category of heinous crimes for purposes of asserting universal jurisdiction.'[79] The Court of Appeals agreed that universal jurisdiction authorises criminal prosecution, even in the absence of any special connection between the state and the offence. The Court added that:

> [a]ircraft hijacking may well be one of the few crimes so clearly condemned under the law of nations that states may assert universal jurisdiction to bring offenders to justice, even when the state has no territorial connection to the hijacking and its citizens are not involved.[80]

United States v Smith and *United States v Yunis* are representative of US case law. While US courts have recognised the permissibility of universal jurisdiction, they have yet to apply it to the exclusion of other forms of jurisdiction. That is, these cases do not address instances of where the offences were committed abroad and neither the perpetrators nor the victims were US nationals.[81] Table 2 lists the status of criminal enforcement in the United States of crimes against humanity committed abroad when neither the victim nor the perpetrators are US nationals.[82] While eleven separate acts can give rise to crimes against humanity under international law, the United States has established universal jurisdiction for only three of these acts.[83]

[79] *United States v Yunis*, 681 F supp 896, 901 (DDC 1988).

[80] *United States v Yunis*, 924 F 2d 1086, 1092 (DC Cir 1991).

[81] See also *United States v Rezaq*, 134 F 3d 1121 (DC Cir 1998); *United States v Yousef*, 927 F supp 673 (SDNY 1996); *United States v Layton*, 509 F supp 212 (ND Cal 1981); *United States v Marcano Garcia*, 456 F supp 1358 (DPR 1978).

[82] Table 2 identifies statutes and cases that discuss universal jurisdiction where the act occurred outside the United States. For similar overviews, see Francisco Forrest Martin, *Challenging Human Rights Violations: Using International Law in US Courts* (2001), 253–56.

[83] Such acts as murder, extermination, imprisonment, sexual violence, or enforced disappearance could also be characterised (and prosecuted) as torture.

TABLE 2 Statutory Authority for Criminal Prosecution of Crimes Against Humanity Committed Abroad

Act	Codification	Case Law
murder	No	No
extermination	No	No
enslavement	No[84]	No
deportation or forcible transfer of population	No	No
imprisonment or other severe deprivation of physical liberty in violation of fundamental rules of international law	18 USC. § 1203	*United States v Yunis*
torture	18 USC. § 2340A	No
rape, sexual slavery, enforced prostitution, forced pregnancy, enforced sterilization, or any other form of sexual violence of comparable gravity	No	No
persecution against any identifiable group or collectivity on political, racial, national, ethnic, cultural, religious, gender, or other grounds that are universally recognised as impermissible under international law	No	No
enforced disappearance of persons	No	No
apartheid	No	No
other inhuman acts of similar character intentionally causing great suffering, or serious injury to body or to mental or physical health	18 USC. § 32 18 USC. § 37 18 USC. § 112 18 USC. § 878 18 USC. § 1116	No No No No *United States v Layton* *United States v Marcano-Garcia*
	18 USC. § 1651	*United States v Smith*
	18 USC. § 2280	*United States v Furlong*
	18 USC. § 2281 49 USC. § 46502	

[84] The United States has criminalised peonage and slavery. These provisions include: 18 USC. § 1581 (peonage); 18 USC. § 1583 (enticement into slavery); 18 USC. § 1584 (sale into involuntary servitude); 18 USC. § 1589 (forced labour); 18 USC. § 1590 (trafficking with respect to peonage, slavery, involuntary servitude, or forced labour). The language in these provisions suggests they could be used to establish universal jurisdiction although the language is not as explicit in this regard as it is for other crimes.

This overview of the criminal liability regime reveals significant limitations in the ad hoc approach developed by the United States to address crimes against humanity. Universal jurisdiction is not recognised for murder, extermination, enslavement, deportation, sexual violence, persecution, enforced disappearance, or apartheid. Accordingly, the United States does not have criminal jurisdiction to prosecute the majority of crimes against humanity when committed abroad and where neither the victim nor the perpetrator are US nationals. In addition, only a handful of cases that could be classified as involving crimes against humanity have been prosecuted in the United States although these cases did not rely exclusively on universal jurisdiction. Despite these limitations, the case law suggests that US courts will likely recognise the validity of statutes authorising universal jurisdiction for prosecuting crimes against humanity.[85]

CIVIL LIABILITY FOR CRIMES AGAINST HUMANITY IN THE UNITED STATES

The United States maintains a robust civil liability regime for punishing serious violations of international law. While federal legislation does not specifically target crimes against humanity in the civil context, several statutes establish subject matter jurisdiction or a cause of action for violations of international law. Pursuant to these statutes, US courts have addressed several civil lawsuits alleging acts that clearly constitute crimes against humanity.[86]

The Statutory Framework

In 1789, Congress adopted the Alien Tort Claims Act ('ATCA') as part of the First Judiciary Act.[87] Codified at 28 USC. § 1350, the ATCA provides 'that [t]he district courts shall have original jurisdiction of any civil action by an alien for a tort only, committed in violation of the law of nations or a treaty of the United States.'

By now, it is well-established law that the ATCA provides subject matter jurisdiction and a cause of action for damages when three conditions are met: (1) an alien sues; (2) in tort; (3) alleging a violation of international law.[88] As noted by

[85] But see *United States v Bin Laden*, 92 F supp 2d 189 (SDNY 2000).

[86] See generally Ralph G Steinhardt and Anthony D'Amato (eds), *The Alien Tort Claims Act: An Analytical Anthology* (1999); Beth Stephens and Michael Ratner, *International Human Rights Litigation in US Courts* (1996).

[87] Litigators have also relied on the grant of general federal question jurisdiction in 28 USC. § 1331 as a basis for international human rights claims with mixed results. In *Handel v Artukovic*, for example, the District Court rejected the idea that § 1331 provided subject matter jurisdiction or that customary international law provided a cause of action for claims brought by victims of wartime atrocities committed in Croatia during World War II. *Handel v Artukovic*, 601 F supp 1421, 1426–28 (CD Cal 1985). Other courts have found subject matter jurisdiction over international human rights claims under § 1331. See, eg, *Abebe-Jira v Negewo*, 72 F 3d 844 (11th Cir 1996).

[88] See, eg, *Abebe-Jira v Negewo*, 72 F 3d 844 (11th Cir 1996); *Kadic v Karadzić*, 70 F 3d 232 (2d Cir 1995); *Hilao v Marcos*, 25 F 3d 1467 (9th Cir 1995); *Trajano v Marcos*, 978 F 2d 493 (9th Cir 1992). But see *Tel-Oren v Libyan Arab Republic*, 726 F 2d 774 (DC Cir 1984), cert. denied, 470 US 1003 (1985).

the US State Department, '[h]uman rights lawyers now regularly invoke the Act in litigating international human rights principles in United States courts.'[89] Numerous violations of international law have been litigated under the ATCA, including torture, genocide, war crimes, and crimes against humanity.

In 1991, Congress enacted the Torture Victim Protection Act ('TVPA') as a complement to the ATCA and to ensure full compliance with the Convention against Torture.[90] The TVPA enables US citizens, who are not entitled to sue under the ATCA, to bring lawsuits for acts of torture or extrajudicial killing committed under the colour of foreign authority.[91] The TVPA provides, in pertinent part, that:

> [a]n individual who, under actual or apparent authority, or colour of law, of any foreign nation—
> (1) subjects an individual to torture shall, in a civil action, be liable for damages to that individual; or
> (2) subjects an individual to extrajudicial killing shall, in a civil action, be liable for damages to the individual's legal representative, or to any person who may be a claimant in an action for wrongful death.

According to the Senate Report accompanying the TVPA, torture violates standards of conduct accepted by virtually every nation and has attained the status of customary international law. 'These universal principles provide little comfort, however, to the thousands of victims of torture and summary executions around the world.... Despite universal condemnation of these abuses, many of the world's governments still engage in or tolerate torture of their citizens....'[92] The TVPA was drafted to provide a remedy for these acts.

While the ATCA and the TVPA authorise civil actions against public officials and private individuals, they do not provide a basis for actions brought against foreign sovereigns or their agents or instrumentalities. The Foreign Sovereign Immunities Act ('FSIA') is the sole basis for obtaining jurisdiction over a foreign state in US courts.[93] Under the FSIA, a foreign state is presumed to be immune from suit unless one or more of the codified exceptions to immunity apply.[94] Efforts to bring FSIA claims for human rights violations occurring

[89] Initial Report, above, at para 278.

[90] Pub L No 102–256, 106 Stat 73, reprinted in 28 USC. § 1350 notes.

[91] A similar statute, 18 USC. § 2333, authorises US citizens to bring civil actions in cases of international terrorism.

[92] S Rep No. 249, 102d Cong, 1st Sess (1991). See also HR Rep No 367, 102d Cong, 1st. Sess, pt. 1 (1991). On signing the TVPA into law, President Bush acknowledged the importance of providing a civil remedy to victims of torture. 'In this new era, in which countries throughout the world are turning to democratic institutions and the rule of law, we must maintain and strengthen our commitment to ensuring that human rights are respected everywhere.' Statement on Signing the Torture Victim Protection Act of 1991, 28 *Weekly Comp Pres Doc* (16 Mar 1992), 465–466. The Senate Report also emphasised that the enactment of the TVPA was not meant to limit the broader scope of the ATCA in any respect, especially the list of human rights violations that might be the subject of ATCA actions.

[93] *Amerada Hess Shipping Corp v Argentine Republic*, 488 US 428 (1989).

[94] 28 USC. § 1604. Pursuant to 28 USC. § 1605, these exceptions include situations of waiver, commercial activity, limited property rights, and arbitration.

outside the United States have, with rare exceptions, proven unsuccessful.[95] A recent amendment to the FSIA, however, has strengthened the ability of terrorism victims to bring actions against foreign governments. In 1996, the FSIA was amended to provide authorization for lawsuits against foreign states that allege, inter alia, acts of torture, extrajudicial killing, hostage-taking, or aircraft sabotage committed in the context of state-sponsored terrorism.[96] However, three conditions must be met in order to bring these actions: (1) the plaintiff or victim must be a United States national; (2) the foreign state must have been designated as a state sponsor of terrorism by the State Department; and (3) the foreign state must be offered an opportunity to arbitrate the claims if the actionable conduct occurred within that state's territory. Several lawsuits have been brought under the state-sponsored terrorism exception to the FSIA.[97] These cases have generated significant judgments in favour of the plaintiffs.[98]

The Case Law

To date, more than 100 lawsuits have been filed in the United States seeking civil remedies for violations of international human rights norms committed abroad.[99] These lawsuits have been filed against a variety of defendants, including foreign governments, foreign government officials, multinational corporations, and private individuals.[100] Several of these lawsuits have resulted in significant damage awards.[101]

The seminal case is *Filártiga v Peña-Irala*.[102] The case arose from the 1976

[95] The most significant exception is *Siderman v Republic of Argentina*, in which a District Court permitted an action against Argentina based on torture to proceed on the theory that Argentina had pursued the Siderman family in the United States and had thus waived its sovereign immunity under the FSIA. *Siderman v Republic of Argentina*, 965 F 2d 699 (9th Cir 1992), cert. denied, 113 S Ct 1812 (1993). The FSIA has also been the basis for several successful suits where foreign governments have committed human rights violations on US territory. See, eg, *Letelier v Republic of Chile*, 488 F supp 665 (DDC 1980).

[96] 28 USC. § 1607.

[97] These cases involved acts of terrorism, including hostage-taking and extrajudicial killing. See *Daliberti v Republic of Iraq*, 97 F supp 2d 38 (DDC 2000); *Anderson v Islamic Republic of Iran*, 90 F supp 2d 107 (DDC 2000); *Cicippio v Islamic Republic of Iran*, 18 F supp 2d 62 (DDC 1998); *Flatow v Islamic Republic of Iran*, 999 F supp 1 (DDC 1998); *Alejandre v Republic of Cuba*, 996 F supp 1239 (SD Fla. 1997); *Rein v Socialist People's Libyan Arab Jamahiriya*, 162 F 3d 748 (2d Cir 1999).

[98] To facilitate the collection of judgments in these cases, Congress recently adopted legislation that authorises payment of judgments from the US Treasury. See generally 'US Approves Payment of Frozen Cuban Assets to Relatives of Brothers to Rescue', *Int'l Enforcement L Rep* 17 (2001); Robert S Greenberger, 'Quest by Terrorism Victims to Collect Judgments From Rogue States Creates Problems for Clinton', *Wall St J* (3 May 2000), at A28.

[99] See Stephens & Ratner, above at 239.

[100] See, eg, *Doe v Unocal*, 963 F supp 880 (CD Cal 1997); *Abebe-Jira v Negewo*, 72 F 3d 844 (11th Cir 1996); *Kadić v Karadzić*, 70 F 3d 232 (2d Cir 1995).

[101] See generally Richard B Lillich, 'Damages for Gross Violations of International Human Rights Awarded by US Courts', (1993), 15 *Hum Rts Q* 207; Stephens & Ratner, above, at 343.

[102] The *Filártiga* case has been the subject of extensive commentary. See, eg, Ralph G Steinhardt, 'Fulfilling the Promise of Filartiga: Litigating Human Rights Claims against the Estate of Ferdinand Marcos', (1995), 20 *Yale J Int'l L* 65; Richard Pierre Claude, 'The Case of Joelito Filartiga and the

torture and murder of Joelito Filártiga, a 17-year old Paraguayan student, by Americo Peña-Irala, a police official in Asuncion, Paraguay. In 1979, Dolly Filártiga, Joelito's sister, discovered Peña-Irala was living in the United States. Dolly Filártiga and her father Dr. Joel Filártiga then brought an action for damages against Peña-Irala based on the ATCA. The District Court dismissed the case, holding that the term 'law of nations' does not apply to the way in which a state treats its own citizens. Because the lawsuit concerned the torture of a Paraguayan citizen by a Paraguayan official in Paraguay, the District Court concluded that the ATCA was not an appropriate basis for subject matter jurisdiction.

On appeal, the Court of Appeals for the Second Circuit reversed. After reviewing numerous multilateral, regional, and national sources of law, the Court of Appeals determined that torture was firmly prohibited by international law.

> In light of the universal condemnation of torture in numerous international agreements, and the renunciation of torture as an instrument of official policy by virtually all of the nations of the world (in principle if not in practice), we find that an act of torture committed by a state official against one held in detention violates established norms of the international law of human rights, and hence the law of nations.'[103]

This violation occurs regardless of the nationality of the parties. The Court of Appeals also upheld the constitutionality of the Alien Tort Claims Act. The Court recognised that US courts 'regularly adjudicate transitory tort claims between individuals over whom they exercise personal jurisdiction.'[104] In addition, Congress had specifically authorised federal court jurisdiction over such lawsuits alleging violations of international law by enacting ATCA. Since the law of nations formed a part of the common law of the United States, this grant of jurisdiction was authorised by Article III of the Constitution. Accordingly, the Court held that 'whenever an alleged torturer is found and served with process by an alien within our borders, §1350 provides federal jurisdiction.'[105] Upon remand, the District Court granted the plaintiffs a judgment in excess of $10 million.[106]

Since *Filártiga*, there have been dozens of ATCA and TVPA lawsuits filed in the United States. Many of these lawsuits have alleged acts that could also constitute crimes against humanity, though the litigants did not always frame their claims in this manner. In *Forti v Suarez-Mason*, for example, two Argentine citizens sued a former Argentine general, alleging numerous violations of international law, including torture, prolonged arbitrary detention, summary execution, causing disappearance, and cruel, inhuman or degrading

Clinic of Hope', (1983), 5 *Hum Rts Q* 275; Dean Rusk, 'A Comment on Filartiga v Pena-Irala', (1981), 11, *Ga J Int'l & Comp L* 311; Lisa A Rickard, 'Filartiga v Pena-Irala: A New Forum for Violations of International Human Rights', (1981), 30 *Am U L Rev* 807.

[103] *Filártiga*, 630 F 2d at 880.

[104] *Ibid*, at 885.

[105] *Ibid*, at 877.

[106] *Filártiga v Peña-Irala*, 577 F supp 860 (EDNY 1984).

treatment.[107] These acts were committed by military personnel under the command of Carlos Guillermo Suarez-Mason. Jurisdiction was premised under the Alien Tort Claims Act. The District Court held that torture, prolonged arbitrary detention, and summary execution were prohibited under international law. Accordingly, these acts were actionable under the Alien Tort Claims Act and the federal question statute.[108] In contrast, the District Court held that the prohibitions against causing disappearance and cruel, inhuman and degrading treatment had not yet attained the requisite degree of international consensus that demonstrates a customary international norm. Thus, the Court dismissed both of these claims.[109] Upon reconsideration, the District Court found the existence of an international consensus as to the prohibition against causing disappearance.[110] However, the District Court refused to recognise the existence of an international consensus as to cruel, inhuman or degrading treatment.[111]

Several lawsuits filed against Philippine President Ferdinand Marcos provide a similar example of ATCA litigation. After his overthrow in 1986, Marcos came to the United States and established residence in Hawaii. His arrival spawned a number of class action and individual lawsuits that have created a body of case law crucial to the development of ATCA litigation.[112] Ultimately, the Marcos Estate was found liable for thousands of acts of torture, summary execution, and disappearance. All of these acts could have been characterised as crimes against humanity; however, counsel for the plaintiffs elected to frame their claims in a more familiar human rights framework. In addition, the federal courts rejected the claim that Marcos was immune from civil prosecution based on sovereign immunity or former head of state immunity. Similarly, the courts rejected Marcos' attempt to argue that the cases were barred by the Act of State doctrine. Significantly, the courts found that acts of torture, summary execution, and disappearance could not be considered official acts leading to immunity from civil proceedings brought by the victims of these acts.[113]

Like the *Filártiga*, *Forti*, and *Marcos* litigation, several other courts have addressed acts that could have been framed as crimes against humanity.[114] In

107 *Forti v Suarez-Mason*, 672 F supp 1531 (ND Cal 1987).

108 *Ibid*, at 1540–1542.

109 *Ibid*, at 1542–1543.

110 *Forti v Suarez-Mason*, 694 F supp 707, 711 (ND Cal 1988).

111 *Ibid*, at 712.

112 There are numerous reported decisions arising out of this 15-year long litigation. These include: *Trajano v Marcos*, 878 F 2d 1438 (9th Cir 1989) (reversal of dismissal of all actions on act of state grounds); *Trajano v Marcos*, 978 F 2d 493 (9th Cir 1992), cert. denied, 113 S Ct 2960 (1993) (affirmance of default judgment against Imee Marcos and rejection of immunity defense); *Hilao v Marcos*, 25 F 3d 1467 (9th Cir 1994), cert. denied, 115 S Ct 934 (1995) (affirmance of preliminary injunction regarding asset transfers and rejection of argument that the ATCA does not provide a cause of action for damages); *Hilao v Marcos*, 103 F.3d 767 (9th Cir 1996) (affirmance of damage awards).

113 Thus, the approach of the *Marcos* courts was broader than the more limited refusal to accept Pinochet's immunity based on the United Kingdom's ratification and implementation of the Convention Against Torture.

114 See, eg, **Torture**: *Abebe-Jiri v Negewo*, 72 F 3d 844 (11th Cir 1995); *Xuncax v Gramajo*, 886 F supp 162 (D Mass 1995); *Hilao v Marcos*, 25 F 3d 1467 (9th Cir 1994); *Paul v Avril*, 812 F supp 207 (S D Fla 1993); *Trajano v Marcos*, 978 F 2d 493 (9th Cir 1992); *Siderman de Blake v Republic of*

contrast, only a handful of courts have actually addressed the specific offence of crimes against humanity in ATCA or TVPA litigation.[115]

In *Doe v Karadzić*, several Bosnian women filed two lawsuits in the federal district court for the Southern District of New York against Radovan Karadzić, the purported leader of the Bosnian Serbs.[116] The complaints alleged that Karadzić was complicit in numerous violations of international law committed during the Yugoslav conflict, including genocide, war crimes, and crimes against humanity. Jurisdiction was premised upon the ATCA, the TVPA, and federal question jurisdiction. The District Court dismissed the lawsuits, holding, *inter alia*, that 'acts committed by non-state actors do not violate the law of nations.'[117] The Court of Appeals for the Second Circuit reversed. Citing its earlier decision in *Filártiga*, the Court of Appeals identified three conditions that are required for jurisdiction under the ATCA: '(1) an alien sues (2) for a tort (3) committed in violation of the law of nations (ie international law).'[118] Since the first two conditions were clearly satisfied, 'the only disputed issue is whether plaintiffs have pleaded violations of international law.'[119]

While the Court of Appeals recognised the status of both genocide and war crimes under international law, its analysis of crimes against humanity is unclear. In its initial description of the case, the Court identified three claims made by the plaintiffs under international law: genocide, war crimes, and crimes against humanity.[120] In its description of the plaintiffs' asserted causes of

Argentina, 965 F 2d 699 (9th Cir 1992); *Forti v Suarez-Mason*, 672 F supp 1531 (ND Cal 1987); *Filártiga v Peña-Irala*, 630 F 2d 876 (2d Cir 1980). **Summary execution**: *Xuncax v Gramajo*, 886 F supp 162 (D Mass 1995); *Hilao v Marcos*, 25 F 3d 1467 (9th Cir 1994); *Trajano v Marcos*, 978 F 2d 493 (9th Cir 1992); *Forti v Suarez-Mason*, 672 F supp 1531 (ND Cal 1987). **Disappearance**: *Xuncax v Gramajo*, 886 F supp 162 (D Mass 1995); *Forti v Suarez-Mason*, 694 F supp 707, 711 (ND Cal 1988). **Arbitrary detention**: *Eastman Kodak Co. v Kavlin*, 978 F supp 1078 (SD Fla 1997); *Hilao v Marcos*, 103 F 3d 789 (9th Cir 1996); *Abebe-Jiri v Negewo*, 72 F 3d 844 (11th Cir 1995); *Xuncax v Gramajo*, 886 F supp 162 (D Mass 1995); *Paul v Avril*, 901 F supp 330 (SD Fla 1994); *Forti v Suarez-Mason*, 672 F supp 1531 (ND Cal 1987). **Slavery**: *Doe v Unocal*, 963 F supp 880 (CD Cal 1997). **Cruel, inhuman or degrading treatment**: *Jama v US Immigration and Naturalization Service*, 22 F supp 2d 353 (DNJ 1998).

115 See, eg, *Wiwa v Royal Dutch Petroleum Co*, 226 F 3d 88 (2d Cir 2000); *Doe v Islamic Salvation Front*, 993 F supp 3 (DDC 1998); *Doe v Unocal*, 963 F supp 880 (CD Cal 1997). In *White v Paulsen*, the District Court examined allegations of human experimentation on prison inmates in the State of Washington as a crime against humanity for purposes of a lawsuit filed pursuant to 28 USC. § 1331. *White v Paulsen*, 997 F supp 1380 (ED Wash 1998).

116 The two lawsuits were *Doe v Karadzić* and *Kadić v Karadzić*. The *Karadzić* litigation has been the subject of extensive commentary. See, eg, William J Aceves, 'Affirming the Law of Nations in US Courts: The Karadzic Litigation and the Yugoslav Conflict', (1996), 14 *Berk J Int'l L* 137; Theodore Posner, 'International Decision: Kadić v Karadzić', (1996), 90 *Am J Int'l L* 658; Michele Brandt, 'Doe v Karadzić: Redressing Non-State Acts of Gender-Specific Abuse Under the Alien Tort Statute', (1995), 79 *Minn L Rev* 1413.

117 *Doe v Karadzić*, 866 F supp 734, 739 (SDNY 1994).

118 *Kadić v Karadzić*, 70 F 3d 232, 238 (2d Cir 1995).

119 *Ibid.*

120 *Ibid*, at 236, 237. In its Statement of Interest submitted to the Second Circuit, the United States addressed genocide, war crimes, and crimes against humanity. Statement of Interest of the United States, *Doe v Karadzić*, Nos. 94-9035 and 94-9069 (2d Cir 13 Sept 1995).

actions, however, the Court did not specifically mention crimes against humanity. Rather, it identified genocide, rape, forced prostitution and impregnation, torture and other cruel, inhuman, and degrading treatment, assault and battery, gender and ethnic inequality, summary execution, and wrongful death.[121] In its analysis, the Court then grouped the plaintiffs' claims into three categories: (a) genocide; (b) war crimes; and (c) other instances of inflicting death, torture, and degrading treatment.[122] In its analysis of the third category, the Court discussed only torture and summary execution.[123] The Court did not discuss the specific concept of crimes against humanity in its analysis. Although the Court of Appeals did not specifically analyse crimes against humanity as an actionable claim under the ATCA, the Court's analysis clearly supports such a conclusion.[124] Indeed, the jury instructions prepared in the *Karadzić* litigation referenced crimes against humanity as one of the actionable claims.[125]

In *Wiwa v Royal Dutch Petroleum Company*, a lawsuit was filed in the federal district court for the Southern District of New York against two oil companies and a corporate official for violations of international law arising out of the development of an oil exploration and development project in the Ogoni region of Nigeria.[126] Widespread protests of the project were met by a brutal campaign of repression, including the execution of Ken Saro-Wiwa and eight other Ogoni activists. The complaint raised numerous violations of international law, including arbitrary arrest and detention, forced exile, torture, summary execution, and crimes against humanity. In reviewing whether crimes against humanity constituted actionable conduct under the Alien Tort Claims Act, the District Court referred to the ICC Statute and the case law of the International Criminal Tribunal for the former Yugoslavia. Based on these sources, the District Court indicated that plaintiffs seeking to establish crimes against humanity must establish three elements: (1) a violation of one of the enumerated acts set forth in Article 7(1) of the ICC Statute; (2) committed as part of a widespread attack against a civilian population; (3) by someone with knowledge of the attack.

Applying this three-part test, the District Court found that the plaintiffs' claims satisfied the definition of crimes against humanity. First, the plaintiffs'

[121] *Kadić*, above, at 237.

[122] *Ibid,* at 241.

[123] *Ibid,* at 243–44. The Court noted that both torture and summary execution are prohibited by international law when committed by state officials or under colour of law. These acts are also proscribed by international law when perpetrated in the course of genocide or war crimes. Absent such conditions, torture and summary execution are not prohibited by international law.

[124] The same can be said for other cases in which acts that would constitute crimes against humanity have been alleged. In *Doe v Unocal*, for example, the District Court rejected Unocal's motion to dismiss the plaintiffs' cause of action based on crimes against humanity, even though it did not specifically find that the plaintiffs' claims, in fact, constituted crimes against humanity. *Doe v Unocal*, 963 F supp 880 (CD Cal 1997).

[125] In the *Karadzić* litigation, default judgments were entered and the issue of damages was presented to the jury. In July 2000, a jury entered a judgment of $900 million in the *Kadic* case; in Oct 2000, a different jury entered a judgment of $5 billion in the *Doe* case. These judgments were based, in part, on the plaintiffs' crimes against humanity claims.

[126] See *Wiwa v Royal Dutch Petroleum Company*, 2002 US Dist. LEXIS 3293 (SDNY 2002).

claims of forced exile and torture involve specific acts set forth in Article 7(1) of the ICC Statute. In addition, claims of arbitrary arrest and detention could also constitute crimes against humanity. Secondly, the acts were a widespread attack committed against a specific civilian population—the Ogoni people. While the Court did not resolve whether discriminatory treatment is a necessary element to crimes against humanity, it found that the attacks arguably involved persecution against an identifiable group on political, ethnic, and cultural grounds. Third, the defendants' actions against the plaintiffs were intentional and, therefore, knowing. 'Such conduct, if proven, satisfies the definition of 'crimes against humanity' provided in Article 7 of the I.C.C., violates international law, and therefore is actionable under the ACTA [sic].'[127]

Table 3 lists the status of civil enforcement in the United States of crimes against humanity committed abroad.

TABLE 3 Statutory Authority for Civil Litigation of Crimes Against Humanity Committed Abroad

Act	Codification	Case Law
Murder	28 USC. § 1350 (ATCA)	*Doe v Islamic Salvation Front* *Doe v Karadzić* *Forti v Suarez-Mason* *Hilao v Estate of Marcos* *Kadić v Karadzić* *Mushikiwabo v Barayagwiza* *Trajano v Marcos* *Wiwa v Royal Dutch Petroleum* *Xuncax v Gramajo*
	28 USC. § 1350 (TVPA)	*Doe v Islamic Salvation Front* *Doe v Karadzić* *Kadić v Karadzić* *Mushikiwabo v Barayagwiza* *Wiwa v Royal Dutch Petroleum*
	28 USC. § 1605(a)(7)	*Alejandre v Republic of Cuba* *De Letelier v Republic of Chile* *Elahi v Islamic Republic of Iran* *Eisenfeld v Islamic Republic of Iran* *Flatow v Islamic Republic of Iran* *Rein v Socialist People's Libyan Arab Jamahiriya*
	18 USC. § 2333	No
Extermination	28 USC. § 1350 (ATCA)	*Doe v Islamic Salvation Front* *Doe v Karadzić*

[127] *Ibid*, at *30.

Act	Codification	Case Law
		Kadić v Karadzić *Mushikiwabo v Barayagwiza*
Enslavement	28 USC. § 1350 (ATCA)	*Doe v Unocal* *Nat'l Coalition Gov't v Unocal*
Deportation or forcible transfer of population	28 USC. § 1350 (ATCA)	*Doe v Unocal*
Imprisonment or other severe deprivation of physical liberty in violation of fundamental rules of international law	28 USC. § 1350 (ATCA)	*Abebe-Jira v Negewo* *Cabiri v Assasie-Gyimah* *Doe v Karadzić* *Eastman Kodak Co v Kavlin* *Forti v Suarez-Mason* *Hilao v Marcos* *Paul v Avril* *Trajano v Marcos* *Wiwa v Royal Dutch Petroleum* *Xuncax v Gramajo*
	28 USC. § 1605(a)(7)	*Anderson v Islamic Republic of Iran* *Cicippio v Islamic Republic of Iran* *Daliberti v Republic of Iraq* *Price v Socialist People's Libyan Arab Republic* *Siderman de Blake v Republic of Argentina*
	18 USC. § 2333	No
Torture	28 USC. § 1350 (ATCA)	*Abebe-Jira v Negewo* *Burma v Unocal* *Cabiri v Assasie-Gyimah* *Doe v Islamic Salvation Front* *Doe v Karadzić* *Filartiga v Pena-Irala* *Hilao v Estate of Marcos* *Kadić v Karadzić* *Mushikiwabo v Barayagwiza* *Paul v Avril* *Trajano v Marcos* *Wiwa v Royal Dutch Petroleum* *Xuncax v Gramajo*
	28 USC. § 1350 (TVPA)	*Alvarez-Machain v United States* *Cabiri v Assasie-Gyimah* *Doe v Islamic Salvation Front* *Doe v Karadzić* *Forti v Suarez-Mason* *Kadić v Karadzić*

Act	Codification	Case Law
		Mushikiwabo v Barayagwiza *Wiwa v Royal Dutch Petroleum* *Xuncax v Gramajo*
	28 USC. 1605(a)(7)	*Anderson v Islamic Republic of Iran* *Cicippio v Islamic Republic of Iran* *Daliberti v Republic of Iraq* *Price v Socialist People's Libyan Arab Republic* *Siderman de Blake v Republic of Argentina*
Rape, sexual slavery, enforced prostitution, forced pregnancy, enforced sterilization, or any other form of sexual violence of comparable gravity	28 USC. § 1350 (ATCA)	*Doe v Islamic Salvation Front* *Doe v Karadzić* *Jama v US Immigration and Naturalization Service* *Kadić v Karadzić*
	18 USC. § 2333	No
Persecution against any identifiable group or collectivity on political, racial, national, ethnic, cultural, religious, gender, or other grounds that are universally recognised as impermissible under international law	28 USC. § 1350 (ATCA)	*Doe v Islamic Salvation Front* *Kadić v Karadzić* *Mushikiwabo v Barayagwiza*
Enforced disappearance of persons	28 USC. § 1350 (ATCA)	*Doe v Karadzić* *Forti v Suarez-Mason* *Hilao v Estate of Marcos* *Xuncax v Gramajo*
Apartheid other inhuman acts of similar character intentionally causing great suffering, or serious injury to body or to mental or physical health	28 USC. § 1350 (ATCA)	No *Bodner v Banque Paribas* *Doe v Islamic Salvation Front* *Doe v Karadzić* *Jama v US Immigration and Naturalization Service*
	18 USC. § 2333	No

This overview of the civil liability regime indicates that US courts will accept an ATCA cause of action based on crimes against humanity.[128] However, there are a number of issues still to be decided in future litigation.[129] Will US courts continue to accept Article 7 of the ICC Statute as an appropriate codification of crimes against humanity?[130] Is discriminatory treatment a necessary element for crimes against humanity? Can private actors be held liable for these acts?[131] Should crimes against humanity be punished more severely than common crimes or other violations of international law? These and other questions regarding the prosecution of crimes against humanity must still be resolved.

A Critique of the Civil Liability Regime

The development of a civil liability regime in the United States has raised several concerns that implicate US foreign policy.

One concern involves the decentralised nature of the civil liability regime, which allows anyone to bring a claim against a perceived perpetrator. As a result, lawsuits have been filed by a variety of plaintiffs against a myriad of defendants, including private individuals, foreign government officials, foreign governments, and multinational corporations. Some commentators have expressed concern

[128] In the last five years, dozens of lawsuits have been filed in the United States to obtain compensation for human rights violations committed during the Second World War. See generally Michael Bazyler, 'Nuremberg in America: Litigating the Holocaust in United States Courts', (2000), 34 *U Rich L Rev* 1. Most of these lawsuits were resolved before a decision on the merits was reached. In *Iwanowa v Ford Motor Co*, for example, the District Court recognised that Ford's 'use of unpaid, forced labour during World War II violated clearly established norms of customary international law.' *Iwanowa v Ford Motor Co*, 67 F supp 2d 424, 439–41 (DNJ 1999). Notwithstanding, the Court found that the plaintiffs' claims were barred under the London Debt Agreement. These cases suggest that US courts will recognise ATCA jurisdiction over crimes against humanity committed during the Second World War, even though there are a variety of defences potentially available to the defendants in these cases.

[129] There are a number of pending ATCA cases in which some of these issues may be resolved.

[130] Recent decisions have been inconsistent on this issue. In *Cabello v Fernandez-Larios*, the federal district court for the Southern District of Florida recognised that crimes against humanity are actionable under the Alien Tort Claims Act. However, the Court chose not to use the ICC Statute to establish the status of crimes against humanity under customary international law; instead, it considered other sources including the Statutes for the International Criminal Tribunals for the former Yugoslavia and Rwanda. 'While the United States has not ratified the Rome Statute on the International Criminal Court, the US has approved the other United Nations General Assembly and UN Security Council resolutions, cited by Plaintiff Aldo Cabello as sources of law which Defendant's alleged commission of crimes against humanity violated.' *Estate of Cabello v Fernandez-Larios*, 157 F supp 2d 1345, 1360 (SD Fla 2001). In *Mehinović v Vucković*, however, the federal district court for the Northern District of Georgia relied on the ICC Statute to establish the status of crimes against humanity. *Mehinović v Vucković*, 198 F supp 2d 1322, (ND Ga 2002). 'Although the Rome Statute's definition of crimes against humanity may be narrower in scope than the customary law definition of crimes against humanity today, the evidence before this Court clearly demonstrates that the defendant has committed acts which constitute crimes against humanity under any of the applicable definitions enforceable under the ATCA.' *Ibid*, at 1353. In *Mehinović*, the district court awarded the plaintiffs $140 million in compensatory and punitive damages for numerous violations of international law, including crimes against humanity.

[131] This issue was raised but not resolved in the *Doe v Unocal* litigation.

that these lawsuits could embarrass or impede US foreign policy.[132] While these concerns are not entirely unfounded, the federal courts have developed several approaches to address cases that may implicate US foreign policy interests. For example, courts can use doctrines of judicial abstention, including the political question doctrine and the act of state doctrine, to dismiss lawsuits that are seen as an infringement on the constitutional powers of the President or Congress.[133] Even so, the courts are not likely to dismiss a lawsuit in the absence of serious concerns that rise to the level of constitutional implication. As the Supreme Court set forth in *Baker v Carr*, not all questions touching foreign relations are political questions, and 'it is error to suppose that every case or controversy which touches foreign relations lies beyond judicial cognizance.'[134]

In addition, the federal government has been quite active in addressing cases that may affect US foreign policy interests. For example, the State Department has occasionally submitted *amicus curiae* briefs to express its position on pending litigation.[135] While the United States has indicated its opposition to some litigation, it has also indicated its support in other cases. US courts have recognised that such views should be considered in their deliberations but should not be considered dispositive.

A second concern with the civil liability regime involves the notion of judicial imperialism. Some commentators argue that the federal courts are now replacing the military in leading US intervention into the affairs of foreign countries, particularly developing countries. The facts, however, belie such claims. For example, only foreign nationals can bring lawsuits under the Alien Tort Claims Act. It is difficult to characterise torture victims from Bosnia as evincing imperialist motives when they file civil lawsuits against their torturers who are also from Bosnia. Victims from Argentina, Burma, Chile, Ethiopia, Guatemala, Haiti, Nigeria, Paraguay, and Rwanda are similarly situated. This victim-centred approach of the civil liability regime undermines claims of imperialist bias.

More significantly, the civil liability regime has a strong foundation in international law. Claims of judicial imperialism are less meaningful when made by countries that have signed and ratified agreements that authorise the development of civil liability regimes. For example, the International Covenant on Civil and Political Rights and the Convention against Torture require member states to provide some form of redress to victims of human rights violations.[136] Over 120

[132] See Curtis A Bradley, 'The Costs of International Human Rights Litigation', (2001), 2 *Chi J Int'l L* 457; Anne-Marie Slaughter and David Bosco, 'Plaintiff's Diplomacy' (Sept–Oct, 2000), *Foreign Aff* 102.

[133] See *Tel-Oren v Libyan Arab Republic*, 726 F 2d 774, 823 (DC Cir 1984) (Robb, J concurring).

[134] *Baker v Carr*, 369 US 186, 211–22 (1962).

[135] Convention against Torture, Art 14; International Covenant on Civil and Political Rights, Art 3, 999 UNTS 171.

[136] See generally Sarah Joseph *et al*, *The International Covenant on Civil and Political Rights* (2000), 38; J. Herman Burgers & Hans Danelius, *The United Nations Convention against Torture* (1988), 146.

countries have ratified each of these agreements. Even customary international law recognises the validity of universal jurisdiction and the obligation of states to punish perpetrators of human rights violations.[137]

Finally, US courts can respond to the legitimate concerns of foreign governments in appropriate cases. If a foreign government has a properly functioning civil system capable of addressing these claims in a fair and efficient manner, US courts can use the doctrine of *forum non conveniens* to dismiss these lawsuits.[138] Of course, US courts should not take such drastic action in the absence of compelling evidence that foreign governments have the ability and inclination to punish serious violations of international law. US courts should be particularly wary of foreign government challenges to the civil liability regime when such challenges are made by regimes that have a history of promoting impunity.

CONCLUSION

For several reasons, the United States must develop a comprehensive liability regime to prosecute crimes against humanity.[139] International institutions remain limited in their ability to address crimes against humanity. Restrictions in temporal and territorial jurisdiction impede effective enforcement of international human rights norms by these institutions. The entry into force of the ICC Statute and US renunciation of the Statute highlight these concerns.

This brief overview of United States law and practice reveals significant limitations in how crimes against humanity are punished. While the United States has established a robust civil liability regime, it has not developed a comprehensive approach to criminal prosecution. This criminal liability regime fails to address a number of acts that constitute crimes against humanity. Moreover, it minimises the gravity of these crimes by failing to differentiate common crimes and more serious violations of international law.[140] As noted by Hannah Arendt:

> Nothing is more pernicious to an understanding of these new crimes, or stands more in the way of the emergence of an international penal code that could take care of

[137] See *Restatement (Third) of the Foreign Relations Law of the United States* § 404 (1987).

[138] See *Wiwa v Royal Dutch Petroleum Co*, 226 F 3d 88 (2d Cir 2000). See also Aric K Short, 'Is the Alien Tort Statute Sacrosanct? Retaining Forum Non Conveniens in Human Rights Litigation', (2001), 33 *NYU J Int'l L & Pol* 1001. But see Kathryn Lee Boyd, 'The Inconvenience of Victims: Abolishing Forum Non Conveniens in Human Rights Litigation', (2000), 39 *Va J Int'l L* 41.

[139] See Beth Stephens, 'Translating Filartiga: A Comparative and International Analysis of Domestic Remedies for International Human Rights Violations', (2002), 27 *Yale J Int'l L* 1; William J Aceves, 'Liberalism and International Legal Scholarship: The Pinochet Case and the Move Toward a Universal System of Transnational Law Litigation', (2000), 41 *Harv Int'l L J* 129.

[140] For efforts to identify a hierarchy of crimes under international law, see Micaela Frulli, 'Are Crimes against Humanity More Serious Than War Crimes?', (2001), 12 *Eur J Int'l L* 329; Allison Marston Danner, 'Constructing a Hierarchy of Crimes in International Criminal Law Sentencing', (2001), 87 *Va L Rev* 415; Walter Gary Sharp Sr, 'The International Criminal Tribunal for the Former Yugoslavia: Defining the Offenses', (1999), 23 *Md J Int'l L & Trade* 15.

> them, than the common illusion that the crime of murder and the crime of genocide are essentially the same, and that the latter therefore is 'no new crime properly speaking'. The point of the latter is that an altogether different order is broken and an altogether different community is violated.[141]

To effectively address crimes against humanity, the United States must adopt a comprehensive liability regime that punishes crimes against humanity *in toto*. Each act that constitutes a crime against humanity must be subject to punishment. Both criminal and civil liability must apply.[142] Jurisdiction must be universal. These crimes must not only be legislated, however; they must also be prosecuted.

[141] Hannah Arendt, *Eichmann in Jerusalem: A Report on the Banality of Evil* (1963), 272.

[142] For a recent example of such efforts, see Crimes Against Humanity and War Crimes Act, RSC, ch 24, § 6 (2000) (Can).

10

Criminal Responsibility in the UK for International Crimes Beyond Pinochet

CLARE MONTGOMERY

INTRODUCTION: THE QUESTIONS RAISED BY PINOCHET

On 24 March 1999 the Appellate Committee of the UK House of Lords delivered what has become known as the *Pinochet No 3* decision.[1] It held by a majority of six to one that Senator Pinochet as a former head of state enjoyed no immunity in respect of the offence of torture from 8 December 1988 onwards, the date by which time all three countries involved in the extradition proceedings, being Chile, Spain, and the United Kingdom, had become parties to the UN Convention against Torture. In any event, as the implementing legislation, namely section 134 of the Criminal Justice Act 1988, which made torture an offence under UK, only came into force on 29 September 1988, and since it did not permit the provisions of the Torture Convention to be applied retrospectively, torture was not a crime in the United Kingdom before that date. Hence, the double criminality rule as required by the Extradition Act 1989 was not satisfied in respect of any conduct before 29 September 1988. As a result, the decision reduced the number of charges for which Senator Pinochet could be extradited to Spain from many thousands to a single substantive charge of torture and an associated conspiracy charge.[2]

The decision has since been widely discussed and analysed. The findings reflect some of the very first judicial opinion on the enforcement by national courts of the laws prohibiting crimes against humanity, particularly as expressed in the Torture Convention. The House of Lords classified these crimes as *international* crimes in that they were prohibited under international law by treaty or customary law, and in respect of the offence of torture, the United Kingdom was obligated by the Convention to make it criminal under domestic law. The decision then addressed the extent of such criminality and

[1] *R v Bow Street Metropolitan Stipendiary Magistrate and others, ex parte Pinochet Ugarte* (*No 3*) [2000] 1 AC 147 HL(E).

[2] Further torture charges were subsequently added to the Spanish extradition request.

whether it was compatible with the national laws governing the immunity of state officials.

Despite the fact that this Convention and other treaties (such as the International Convention against the Taking of Hostages 1979, and the grave breach provisions of the Geneva Conventions on the treatment of prisoners of war and civilians 1949[3]) have been ratified by many states for long periods of time, their application before national courts has been lacking.[4] The decision thus provoked reflection on the enforcement of other international crimes within national jurisdictions.

The decision surfaced amidst a heightened focus within the international community on the appropriate means of implementing international laws that criminalise serious human rights violations and war crimes, including the establishment of the International Criminal Tribunals for the former Yugoslavia and Rwanda and the adoption of the Rome Statute of the International Criminal Court. On 5 February 2000 Tharcisse Muvunyi became the first person indicted by these tribunals to be arrested in the UK. The ICTR sought to transfer him from the UK for trial at the seat of the Tribunal in Arusha, Tanzania on charges of genocide relating to a period when he was a Lieutenant Colonel in the Rwandan army.[5]

In the wake of *Pinochet No 3* there was much speculation over whether former and current political and military leaders would be in jeopardy of being arrested and extradited if they travelled to foreign jurisdictions. The reality is that they may always have faced the risk of arrest and extradition irrespective of the decision of the House of Lords, and depending on the domestic legislation in force. What had changed was that the political will now appeared to exist to implement laws that had been available for many years. Perhaps the new commitment on the part of the international community to prosecute war crimes and crimes against humanity fuelled the efforts of the government of the United Kingdom to act when Senator Pinochet set foot in its jurisdiction.

Some criticisms were levelled at the UK government for intervening in the affairs of another state, especially since Senator Pinochet had been given an amnesty from prosecution under Chilean law. It was also suggested that it would have been more appropriate for him to be transferred to the ICC if it had been in existence.

It is evident that *Pinochet No 3* has stirred up legal questions that have lain dormant for decades. The timing of the decision could not have been more apt

[3] Art 147 of Geneva Convention IV applicable to civilians provides: 'Grave breaches... shall be those involving any of the following acts, if committed against persons or property protected by the present Convention: wilful killing, torture or inhuman treatment, including biological experiments, wilfully causing great suffering or serious injury to body or health, unlawful deportation or transfer or unlawful confinement of a protected person, compelling a protected person to serve in the forces of a hostile Power, or wilfully depriving a protected person of the rights of fair and regular trial prescribed in the present Convention, taking of hostages and extensive destruction and appropriation of property, not justified by military necessity and carried out unlawfully and wantonly.'

[4] For instance, until 1994 there were no reported cases from domestic jurisdictions for any prosecutions of grave breaches of the Geneva Conventions.

[5] See below; see also the contribution by Geoffrey Bindman in ch 13.

in light of the global emphasis on prosecuting international crimes. As the dust has settled after Senator Pinochet's return to Chile, it is imperative that the ramifications of *Pinochet No 3* are considered. This will foster a pro-active stance towards resolving the fundamental issues of accountability for serious international crimes that were revealed after Senator Pinochet's arrest. Preparations need to be undertaken in advance of the next case involving allegations of torture or other crimes against humanity, or war crimes.

THE APPLICATION OF THE DECISION TO FUTURE CASES

Pinochet No 3 represents the tip of the iceberg in proceedings concerning torture and other international crimes that are likely to arise in the future in the United Kingdom. Even though these offences may not be committed on UK territory, those who commit such crimes in other parts of the world will continue to travel to this country. The government will have to decide whether such persons will be prosecuted by UK courts, or be extradited or transferred to another jurisdiction, perhaps in circumstances contrary to the wishes of the state of which the accused is a national.

The decision of the House of Lords firmly established that conduct amounting to torture, although an international crime, was not an offence under UK law until 29 September 1988 when section 134 of the Criminal Justice Act 1988 came into force. Section 134(1) provides:

> A public official or person acting in official capacity, whatever his nationality, commits the offence of torture if in the United Kingdom or elsewhere he intentionally inflicts severe pain or suffering on another in the performance or purported performance of his official duties.

Further, it was held that under the extradition laws of the United Kingdom, Senator Pinochet could not be extradited to another country for conduct that did not constitute an offence under UK law at the time of the commission of the offence. The Law Lords interpreted the applicable section of the Extradition Act 1989, section 2, to require that Senator Pinochet's conduct be assessed in terms of the UK law applicable at the time the conduct took place.

It follows that UK courts do not have jurisdiction to *prosecute* persons for torture that is alleged to have occurred before 29 September 1988. On the basis of *Pinochet No 3*, if a former public official of the Cambodian government allegedly responsible for torturing thousands of civilians arrived at Heathrow airport tomorrow he could not be extradited or tried in the UK for any acts of torture that occurred before 29 September 1988.

Furthermore, following the rationale of *Pinochet No3*, the liability of such a public official in the UK for other international crimes, including genocide,[6]

[6] As codified in the Convention on the Prevention and Punishment of the Crime of Genocide 1951.

other crimes against humanity (including murder, rape, and inhuman treatment),[7] and war crimes (including grave breaches of the Geneva Conventions 1949)[8] would depend on whether these offences were incorporated into UK law by statute, and if so, unless the legislation provided otherwise, the official could only be prosecuted for crimes committed after the date when the legislation entered into force.

Similar points as those that arose in respect of the Torture Convention could surface in respect of the other international crimes, such as the grave breach provisions of the Geneva Conventions. The relevant provision is Article 146 of Geneva Convention IV (which is repeated as a different article in each of the four Conventions):

> The High Contracting Parties undertake to enact any legislation necessary to provide effective penal sanctions for persons committing, or ordering to be committed, any of the grave breaches of the present Convention defined in the following Article.
>
> Each High Contracting Party shall be under the obligation to search for persons alleged to have committed, or to have ordered to be committed, such grave breaches, *and shall bring such persons, regardless of their nationality, before its own courts.* It may also, if it prefers, and in accordance with the provisions of its own legislation, hand such persons over for trial to another High Contracting Party concerned, provided such High Contracting Party has made out a *prima facie* case.
>
> Each High Contracting Party shall take measures necessary for the suppression of all acts contrary to the provisions of the present Convention other than the grave breaches defined in the following Article. [Emphasis added.]

The grave breach provisions have traditionally been viewed as creating a system of universal jurisdiction for the most serious war crimes. They are enacted in UK law by virtue of the Geneva Conventions Act 1957 and the Geneva Conventions (Amendment) Act 1995. Section 1(2) of the 1957 Act provides:

> In the case of an offence under this section committed outside the United Kingdom, a person may be proceeded against, indicted, tried and punished therefore in any place in the United Kingdom as if the offence has been committed in that place, and the offence shall, for all purposes incidental to or consequential on the trial or punishment thereof, be deemed to have been committed in that place.

However, the provisions in UK law with regard to extra-territorial jurisdiction for other war crimes, for crimes against humanity, or for genocide are less far-reaching . The War Crimes Act 1991 is concerned only with crimes committed in Germany or German-occupied territory during the Second World War. The Act provides in section 1:

[7] As codified in the Nuremberg and Tokyo Charters; UN General Assembly Resolution 95(I), (1946), (Affirmation of the Principles of International Law recognised by the Charter of the Nuremberg Tribunal); and the Statutes of the ICTY (Art 5) and ICTR (Art 4).

[8] Above n 3.

(1) Subject to the provisions of this section, proceedings for murder, manslaughter or culpable homicide may be brought against a person in the United Kingdom irrespective of his nationality at the time of the alleged offence if that offence—
   (a) was committed during the period beginning with 1st September 1939 and ending with 5th June 1945 in a place which at the time was part of Germany or under German occupation; and
   (b) constituted a violation of the laws and customs of war.

(2) No proceedings shall by virtue of this section be brought against any person unless he was on 8th March 1990, or has subsequently become, a British citizen or resident in the United Kingdom, the Isle of Man or any of the Channel Islands.

New legislation was passed in the UK in 2001 which enabled the United Kingdom to respond to requests for the arrest and surrender of suspects to the ICC and which also made crimes defined in the ICC Statute offences under domestic law. Section 51 of the International Criminal Court Act 2001 provides simply:

(1) It is an offence against the law of England and Wales for a person to commit genocide, a crime against humanity or a war crime.

(2) This section applies to acts committed-
   (a) in England or Wales, or
   (b) outside the United Kingdom by a United Kingdom national, a United Kingdom resident or a person subject to UK service jurisdiction.[9]

Unlike the legislation implementing the relevant part of the Torture Convention, the extra-territorial jurisdiction created here is limited to crimes committed by UK nationals, UK residents or those subject to UK armed services jurisdiction.

It is worth noting that in the first decision of the House of Lords,[10] it was argued by Lords Nicholls and Steyn that various crimes, including genocide and torture were crimes of universal jurisdiction in customary international law and thus criminal under the municipal law of the UK. Only Lord Millett took a similar view in *Pinochet No 3* in finding that torture was crime by English law throughout the relevant period by reason of its criminality under customary international law, which was part of English law. The other Law Lords founded their views on the 'black letter' law of the treaty provisions of the Torture Convention and the corresponding national legislation.

However, even where national enacting legislation has been passed in the UK in respect of crimes under international law, prosecutions have generally not followed. For example, despite the length of time since the Geneva Conventions

[9] Art 58 makes similar provision for Northern Ireland. Parallel legislation was introduced in Scotland the same year in the form of the International Criminal Court (Scotland) Act 2001.

[10] *R v Bow Street Metropolitan Stipendiary Magistrate, ex parte Pinochet Ugarte* [2000] 1 AC 61, HL(E) (*Pinochet No 1*).

Act 1957 was passed, there have been no prosecutions in the UK under the Act. Some potential UK prosecutions for crimes under international law, and the reasons why they did not progress, are discussed by Geoffrey Bindman in his contribution to this volume.

THE IMPLICATIONS FOR THE IMMUNITY OF PUBLIC OFFICIALS

On the crucial subject of immunity,[11] *Pinochet No 3* held that immunity *ratione materiae* (in respect of official or governmental acts) was not extended to heads of state and other public officials by the Torture Convention and section 134 of the Criminal Justice Act. This immunity would usually apply to heads of state once they had left office for acts undertaken while in office under section 20 of the State Immunity Act 1978 read with section 39(2) of Schedule 1 of the Diplomatic Privileges Act 1964. But it was held that the terms of the Convention created an exception, and that the State Immunity Act had to be read in light of the UK's international obligations under the Convention and customary international law. The position was stated by Lord Saville in the clearest terms:

> So far as the states that are parties to the [Torture] Convention are concerned, I cannot see how, so far as torture is concerned, this immunity can exist consistently with the terms of that Convention. . . To my mind, these terms [of the Convention] demonstrate that the states who have become parties have clearly and unambiguously agreed that official torture should now be dealt with in a way which would otherwise amount to an interference in their sovereignty.[12]

None of their Lordships in *Pinochet No 1* or No *3* came close to suggesting that the immunity *ratione personae* (by virtue of the status as a serving head of state or public official) should be removed before national courts. A serving head of state would thus enjoy immunity before national courts for acts of torture.[13]

Heads of state still in office have, however, not enjoyed immunity for similar crimes before international courts.[14] There is also precedent for national courts not granting immunity on account of holding an official position for crimes against humanity and war crimes—the national trials that occurred in the various European countries following the Nuremberg Trial under legislation like Allied Control Council Law No 10 of 20 December 1945 and other similar domestic laws.[15] It gives rise to a situation in which the criminal responsibility

[11] See also ch 3.

[12] *Pinochet No 3*, 147.

[13] The International Court of Justice has recently held that serving foreign ministers also enjoy such immunity. See the chapter in this volume by Andrew Clapham.

[14] Including under the Nuremberg and Tokyo Charters, the Statutes of the ICTY (Art 7) and ICTR (Art 6), and Art 27 of the ICC Statute.

[15] In addition, it has been argued that the Nuremberg Tribunal's jurisdiction over crimes against humanity and war crimes was based on the sum of the jurisdiction that had always been exercised over these crimes by national courts.

of a serious offender may turn rather arbitrarily on whether an international court has been set up to deal with the matter, and if not, the accused could escape liability purely because of the shield provided by his official status. Further, as suggested below, the ICC will not serve as an automatic reference point for national courts in respect of international crimes as certain jurisdictional requisites will have to be satisfied before the matter can be tried before the ICC.

It is also not clear whether other exceptions to immunity *ratione materiae* would exist for international crimes other than torture. A short answer may be that it would depend on the municipal law, and the UKs obligations under international law, both under treaty law and customary law. Nevertheless, it may be a prudent course to ensure a measure of consistency between legislation for different offences. Disparities that may arise between liability for these offences should be avoided as they could give rise to injustices. For instance, a former head of state may enjoy immunity for official acts in respect of one international crime but not for another of a similar seriousness.

In light of the questions raised by *Pinochet No 3* consideration may have to be given to new or amended legislation to ensure that the intention of Parliament in respect of the prosecution of international crimes and extradition of suspects is given full effect. It remains a political question as to how far Parliament would be prepared to legislate to facilitate prosecution or extradition with regard to international crimes and whether with retrospective effect.

THE RELATIONSHIP WITH INTERNATIONAL COURTS

A predicament that remains to be addressed is the disparity between the jurisdiction of international courts over international crimes and that of national courts, which in accordance with the House of Lords' decision is limited by the provisions of domestic legislation. Contrary to widespread opinion, the ICC, when it comes into force, will not provide an instant solution. The ICC will not have jurisdiction over any offences that occurred before the court was established.[16] Even if the UK government had sought to transfer Senator Pinochet to the ICC (had it then been in existence), the ICC would have been bound to decline jurisdiction.

For cases that arise after the ICC is operational, there are certain other jurisdictional requirements that must be met before the ICC could be seized of the matter, the most significant being that in terms of the principle of 'complementarity' with national courts, the ICC would only have jurisdiction if the state(s) which could exercise jurisdiction is 'unwilling or unable genuinely to carry out the investigation or prosecution'.[17] In this way the ICC aims to serve as a

[16] ICC Statute, Art 11.

[17] See Art 17(1) of the ICC Statute, which is founded on the principle of 'complementarity' as laid down in the Preamble and Art 1, which states that the ICC 'shall be complementary to national

mechanism to encourage national courts to investigate and prosecute international crimes, rather an institution that erodes the authority of domestic judiciaries. Under the ICC regime, hypothetically Chile (a state which could have jurisdiction over the case) would have an opportunity to demonstrate that it was willing to conduct the prosecution (as has indeed now happened), thereby excluding the ICC's jurisdiction. The actions of the UK and Spain as states that could exercise jurisdiction would also have to be assessed under this provision.

If the case were inadmissible before the ICC, Spain's extradition request might still then have had to be adjudicated by the UK courts. In any event, the ICC Statute does not clarify whether an extradition request by a third state (like Spain) would take precedence over a referral to the ICC (for instance, by the UK).

In this sense the ICC is very different from the ICTY and ICTR, which both enjoy primacy over national courts.[18] As a result of their establishment by the Security Council under chapter VII of the United Nations' Charter, which obliges compliance from states,[19] national courts are required to defer jurisdiction to the International Tribunals. However, the Tribunals cannot try all cases, and have to be selective. Many cases concerning the conflicts that occurred in these regions have still been tried in domestic courts (for example, in Germany, Austria, and Switzerland). Similar cases could arise in the UK if a suspected war criminal was arrested, but not transferred to one of the Tribunals. Likewise, the government could be faced with a difficult choice as to whether to investigate or not if it was known that a suspect was in the UK, and not sought by an international court, or his state.

This occurred in the case of Tharcisse Muvunyi. He arrived in the UK in March 1998, and was granted leave to enter in August 1998. Despite information that was circulating in the public domain concerning his part in the genocide in Rwanda, he was not investigated or arrested by the UK authorities. It was not until 5 February 2000 that he was arrested on the request of the ICTR.

Legislation had been passed by order to ensure that those accused by the ICTY and ICTR could be transferred from the UK for trial at these Tribunals.[20]

criminal jurisdictions'. Art 17(1) and (2) set out criteria by which 'unwillingness' and 'inability' may be determined. Also see O Triffterer (ed), *Commentary on the Rome Statute of the International Criminal Court* (1999), 383–94. Arguably, the Security Council acting under ch VII of the UN Charter (as it did when the ICTY and the ICTR were established) could refer a matter to the ICC irrespective of the complementarity requirements of the ICC Statute.

[18] See Art 9 of the ICTY Statute, and Art 8 of the ICTR Statute.

[19] Art 25 in ch VII of the UN Charter provides that member states are obliged 'to accept and carry out the decisions of the Security Council'. Also see, Arts 24, 41, 48, and 49 of the UN Charter. Accordingly, Arts 29 and 28 of the ICTY and ICTR Statutes, respectively, require states to 'co-operate with the International Tribunal in the investigation and prosecution' of serious violations, and to 'comply without undue delay with any request for assistance or an order issued by a Trial Chamber'. Further, Art 103 of the UN Charter provides: 'In the event of a conflict between the obligations of the Members of the United Nations under the present Charter and their obligations under any other international agreement, their obligations under the present Charter shall prevail'.

[20] United Nations (International Tribunal) (Rwanda) Order 1996 (SI 1996/1296) and United Nations (International Tribunal) (Former Yugoslavia) Order 1996 (SI 1996/716).

The procedure provided differs from the extradition arrangements of the Extradition Act 1989, and is more akin to a 'backing of warrants' procedure. It reflects the obligatory nature of the relationship between states and the Tribunals, which is founded on the chapter VII mandate of the Tribunals. This feature will be lacking in respect of the ICC that is based on an agreement between states' parties to co-operate with each other.

Section 4(1) of each Order provides:

> Where the Secretary of State receives from the International Tribunal a warrant of arrest issued by the International Tribunal... the Secretary of State shall transmit the warrant to an appropriate judicial officer who shall... endorse the warrant for execution in any part of the United Kingdom.

The Orders further provide in Article 6(2) that where the purpose of the arrest is to enable the defendant to be brought before the Tribunals 'the appropriate order is that the person be delivered up into the custody of the International Tribunal'. Pursuant to s.6(5) the defendant may only be released if it is shown:

> (a) that the document purporting to be a warrant issued by the International Tribunal is not such a warrant...
>
> (b) that the person brought before the court is not the person named or described in the warrant,
>
> (c) where the person has not been convicted by the International Tribunal of the offence specified in the warrant or any accompanying document, that the offence is not an International Tribunal crime, or
>
> (d) notwithstanding that the offence is an International Tribunal crime, that the person would if he were charged with it in the United Kingdom be entitled to be discharged under any rule of law relating to previous acquittal or convictions.

The request from the ICTR spared the UK government the complication and possible embarrassment of having to deal any further with Mr Muvunyi. However, if the ICTR had not requested Mr Muvunyi's transfer, theoretically he could have been prosecuted in the UK for the same conduct for which he was sought by the ICTR. *Pinochet No 3* would provide a precedent for prosecution or extradition for torture that occurred after 1988. However, it is doubtful whether he would ever have been charged under UK law, perhaps for a lack of evidence, perhaps for a lack of commitment to dedicating time and resources to pursuing these offences. There is a danger that a substantial degree of inconsistency, and ultimately, unfairness could result from a failure to follow through from the *Pinochet* decision. A clear policy will have to be devised for determining whether prosecutions of international crimes are necessary or not in the circumstances of each case.

Furthermore, neither UK legislation on the Tribunals nor the statutes and rules of the Tribunals make provision for the position of an accused who, once transferred from the UK to the Tribunals, has proceedings withdrawn before the Tribunals or is acquitted. May he be returned to the UK, and could he then face prosecution? This issue was the subject of dispute in the *habeas corpus* proceedings that were brought in the *Muvunyi* case. The defendant asserted that if he was sent to Arusha there was a real risk of violation of his rights under Article 3 of the European Convention on Human Rights because he faced the threat of extra-judicial execution, particularly if he was released in Tanzania and not returned to the UK in the event that the indictment was withdrawn or he was acquitted.[21]

The leading case of the ICTR that was cited in the pleadings was *Jean-Bosco Barayagwiza v The Prosecutor*[22] in which the Appeals Chamber dismissed the indictment and ordered the appellant's release. Three of the five appellate judges ordered that he be delivered to the authorities of Cameroon, where he had been arrested, especially in light of a Rwandan extradition request for the appellant which had been denied by the courts in Cameroon. Judge Shahabuddeen dissented, stating:

> If Cameroon does not accept delivery, custody by the Tribunal is indefinitely prolonged. If Cameroon accepts delivery, at the point of time at which Cameroon does so the appellant is in the custody of Cameroon. . . it is considered that Cameroon has a duty to accept delivery of the appellant, or that, at any rate, Cameroon has some legal basis for doing so. Has it? A possible argument is that the direction to the Registrar to make the necessary arrangements for the delivery of the appellant to the authorities of Cameroon can be supported by Cameroon's obligation to co-operate with the Tribunal. But also possible is an opposing argument that a state's obligation to cooperate with the Tribunal does not extend to assisting the Tribunal to correct its own errors. Whatever may be the strength of the latter argument, Cameroon can at any rate contend that, even if its duty to cooperate can be so extended, there should be reasonable limits to that duty and that those limits would be exceeded if it were to be required to accept delivery of the appellant in this case. . . With respect, I do not appreciate how the dismissal of the extradition request justifies the conclusion 'that it is appropriate for the Appellant to be delivered to the authorities of Cameroon. . . ' . . . For these reasons, I should have thought that the proper order was to set the appellant at liberty and to direct the Registrar to provide him with reasonable facilities to leave Tanzania, if he so wishes.

It appears that this position was to some extent supported by Judge Nieto-Navia's Declaration, which stated:

> I am not convinced that it is appropriate to direct the Registrar to make the necessary arrangements to deliver the Appellant to the Cameroonian authorities ... Cameroon is under no legal obligation to accept the Appellant unless they wish to proceed with

[21] In the High Court of Justice, CO/595/2000, which application has subsequently been withdrawn on the basis that undertakings were received from the Tribunal that the defendant would be returned to the United Kingdom if proceedings were withdrawn against him or he was acquitted.

[22] Case No ICTR-97-19-AR72, 3 Nov 1999.

his prosecution. Under these circumstances, the Registrar should obtain the views of the Cameroonian authorities, and deliver the Appellant to them only if appropriate.

In an earlier decision in the *Ntuyahaga* case,[23] the Trial Chamber, having ordered that the indictment against him be withdrawn, held that it could not order the defendant who was no longer under indictment into the custody of any given state, including the host state, Tanzania. Instead, the Trial Chamber ordered, in the absence of any other charge against him, the immediate release of Bernard Ntuyahaga from the Tribunal's detention facilities.

As the decision in *Barayagwiza* was subsequently overturned on 31 March 2000 by a newly constituted Appeals Chamber on the grounds of new evidence, the finding in respect of returning him to the state where he was arrested was not implemented. The question remains open, and UK courts could yet have to consider cases that are returned from the Tribunals in the future, including the *Muvunyi* case.

THE LEGAL EFFECT OF AMNESTIES

Pinochet No 3 also demonstrates that an amnesty against prosecution for international crimes granted by one country does not necessarily bind another in the application of its law. No hard and fast rule was, however, laid down in the decision. It is unclear whether all amnesties would be overridden by the House of Lords in the same way as Senator Pinochet's was brushed aside. For example, if a former South African governmental official from the *apartheid* era arrived in the UK with an amnesty from the South African Truth and Reconciliation Commission for any crimes committed in South Africa, would the courts here respect his immunity from prosecution, and on what grounds?

The same concerns will have to be confronted by the ICC. In particular, it is uncertain whether 'truth commission' options, which result in amnesties being granted, would suffice to exclude the ICC's jurisdiction.[24] Much could depend upon the manner in which the commission was established, its guiding principles and practices, and the basis upon which amnesties were approved. Criteria will have to be developed to adjudicate these matters. Some institutions may pass the ICC's scrutiny, others may fail. For instance, a commission appointed solely by the alleged perpetrators of international crimes and designed to grant them quick amnesties from prosecution may understandably not be sufficient to bar the ICC's involvement.

23 *Prosecutor v Ntuyahaga*, ICTR-98-40-T, Decision on the Prosecutor's Motion to Withdraw the Indictment, 18 Mar 1999.

24 This is a subject that demands closer attention. For a comprehensive examination of truth commissions, see Neil J Kritz (ed) 'Transitional Justice', United States Institute of Peace, 3 (1995); and, John Dugard, 'Is the Truth and Reconciliation Process Compatible with International Law?', (1997) *South African Journal of International Law*.

CONCLUSION: CLARIFICATION AND CONSISTENCY SHOULD BE THE GOAL

Pinochet No 3 is undoubtedly a landmark decision. There are very few other national decisions that have addressed the complexities of jurisdiction over international crimes before national courts. Yet, the historic qualities of the decision are tempered by the many questions that it leaves unanswered, some of which have been highlighted in this essay.

One of the most perplexing is the extent of universal jurisdiction over international crimes in the absence of national legislation creating a jurisdictional base. Or considered from Parliament's perspective, what provision should be made in legislation for jurisdiction over international crimes? The idea of universal jurisdiction for all serious international crimes on the basis of their evolution into customary international law has not found favour. States would find it unacceptable if one state could interfere in another by arresting or seeking the extradition of an accused for crimes entirely unconnected with that state, other than a general international obligation under customary law to prosecute and punish. On the other hand, jurisdiction based upon the presence of the person on the territory of the state concerned, the location of the offences, or the nationality of the accused must be considered as options for implementation through appropriate legislation or judicial opinion. These are the indices of jurisdiction that have been relied upon in the ICC Statute to delineate the authority of the court.[25]

Whatever the acceptable limits of jurisdiction for international crimes before municipal courts, clarity, consistency and certainty must be the order of the day. The main point is that the UK government must recognise the consequences of the *Pinochet* experience and review its national policy and approach to international crimes. As a national citizen one expects no less with respect to domestic offences, like murder, assault, theft, and so forth. The enforcement of international crimes ought to be guided by the same standards. These are after all crimes which 'by their magnitude and savagery or by their large number. . . endangered the international community or shocked the conscience of mankind'.[26]

[25] See ICC Statute, Arts 12–17.

[26] *History of the United Nations War Crimes Commission and the Developments of the Laws of War* (1943), 179.

11

Civil Reparation in National Courts for Victims of Human Rights Abuse

FIONA McKAY

INTRODUCTION

As criminal prosecutions in national courts for crimes against humanity and other crimes under international law on the basis of universal jurisdiction become increasingly common, an important question for victims of these violations is whether there will be a concomitant development in the *civil* sphere that will enable them to claim compensation and other forms of reparation from perpetrators.[1] Where victims cannot obtain such a remedy in the country where the violations occurred, will other legal systems be able to provide a forum? After all, the same factors that lead to impunity for serious violations of international human rights and international humanitarian law also tend to prevent victims from obtaining an effective remedy and reparation. While civil proceedings may not by themselves be capable of delivering the same level of satisfaction to victims of serious violations as criminal proceedings, and it is often difficult to enforce any award of reparation, they do offer victims the opportunity to reveal the truth, to turn the spotlight on atrocities, to obtain an authoritative finding by a judicial body and to have their day in court. Civil actions also have certain advantages over criminal proceedings: victims have a greater degree of control than they do in criminal cases, and the level of proof required is lower.

International mechanisms do exist to provide avenues for redress for victims of human rights violations unable to obtain an effective remedy within their own domestic system, but few of these mechanisms can order and enforce awards of damages and other forms of reparation to victims. Those that are

[1] The term 'civil' here denotes a remedy in private law; a legal action that is brought by an individual rather than by the State, under the law providing rules and remedies to regulate disputes between individuals. The term 'civil' will also be used in this essay in a different sense, to describe the type of legal system derived from Roman law that applies in many countries of the world including most of Western Europe, Latin America and parts of Africa and Asia.

able to do so—such as the European and Inter-American Courts of Human Rights—can only hear cases against contracting states and relatively few cases make it through their systems. The International Criminal Court will be the first international criminal tribunal to allow victims to seek reparation from individual perpetrators.[2] In sum, it is by no means the case that international level mechanisms can fill the gap left in cases where it is impossible to obtain a remedy in the violating state. Just as in the criminal sphere, victims are turning to national courts as possible avenues for redress.

Recent years have seen a number of examples of civil litigation being entertained in the courts of one state in respect of serious violations of human rights committed in another. The possibility of bringing civil actions for violations of human rights is perceived as particularly important in legal systems based on the common law, where victims are used to claiming damages and other forms of relief in a process separate to any criminal proceedings brought by the state. But cases have arisen both in civil law countries, as part of criminal proceedings,[3] and in common law countries in separate civil proceedings where national courts have assumed jurisdiction on the basis of the defendant's presence within that jurisdiction.[4] As detailed in chapter 9, the most prolific jurisdiction has been the US, where a long line of cases has followed the 1980 decision in *Filártiga v Peña-Irala* in which the family of a man tortured to death in Paraguay sued the high ranking officer responsible after they found him living in exile in New York.[5]

The question arises whether these are isolated examples or whether they herald the arrival of 'universal civil jurisdiction'. National courts are traditionally reluctant to adjudicate regarding acts committed in another state, particularly where the acts are committed by the state itself, and they will be aware of the political sensitivity of such cases. Where the wrong committed is also a gross violation of international human rights norms, or is an international crime,[6] do

[2] See appendix. ICC Statute Art 75 obliges the Court to establish principles relating to reparation including restitution, compensation and rehabilitation, and empowers it to make an order for reparation against a convicted person.

[3] In states with a civil law system victims are able to apply to become civil parties in criminal prosecutions, which entitles them to claim reparation through those proceedings without having to institute a separate civil action. See below for examples of where this has occurred in cases involving international crimes.

[4] In the US the cases under the Alien Tort Claims Act and the Torture Victim Protection Act, in the UK the case of *Al-Adsani* and suits against corporations regarding their responsibility for violations abroad. On the US law and cases see the chapter in this volume by William Aceves and Paul Hoffman; see also Beth Stephens and Michael Ratner, *International Human Rights Litigation in US Courts* (Transnational Publishers Inc, New York, 1996). On UK law and practice see *Challenging Impunity for Torture* (Redress, London, 2000) and 'Report on Civil Actions in the English Courts for Serious Human Rights Violations Abroad', a report of the Human Rights Committee, International Law Association (British Branch), published in the (2001) 2 *European Human Rights Law Review*, 129.

[5] 639 F 2d 876 (2d Cir 1980)

[6] For a discussion of crimes under international law that give rise to universal jurisdiction, see *Final Report on the exercise of universal jurisdiction in respect of gross human rights offences*, International Law Association, 2000.

special rules apply as regards civil liability? What are the prospects of victims, by way of private legal action, obtaining reparation in the courts of another country from the state, the individual or even the corporation responsible for the violation? Is allowing such actions part of the duty of states to enforce international human rights norms? Is it likely that the line of civil cases in the US that began with *Filártiga* will be imitated elsewhere? This essay examines these questions in light of recent developments, chiefly in North America and Western Europe, and finds reason to hope for improved access to reparation for victims of serious human rights violations in the future.

RELEVANT INTERNATIONAL LAW AND PRACTICE

International law provides for both substantive and procedural aspects of the right to reparation. Under general international law of state responsibility a breach of international law involves an obligation to make reparation.[7] Provisions regarding compensation can be found in both international human rights and international humanitarian law treaties.[8] The UN adopted Basic Principles of Justice for Victims of Crime and Abuse of Power that called for steps to improve access to justice for victims, and for restitution, compensation and assistance to victims.[9] The adoption of Article 75 of the Rome Statute of the International Criminal Court constitutes recognition of the right of victims to obtain reparation from those convicted of crimes under the Statute.[10] The right to an effective remedy for violations of human rights is long established.[11] Building on this body of law, in the early 1990s the UN Commission on Human Rights initiated a process aimed at the establishment of international standards on the right to reparation for victims of violations of human rights.[12] The draft Basic Principles and Guidelines on the Right to a Remedy and Reparation for Victims of Violations of International Human Rights and Humanitarian Law that the UN is expected to adopt shortly will cover violations of both

[7] Judgment of the Permanent Court of International Justice in the Chorzow Factory (Indemnity) case, 1928 PCIJ, Ser. A, no 17, 29.

[8] For example, Art 14.1 of the UN Convention against Torture provides that 'Each State Party shall ensure in its legal system that the victim of an act of torture obtains redress and has an enforceable right to fair and adequate compensation, including the means for as full rehabilitation as possible.' The four Geneva Conventions of 1949 and their two Additional Protocols of 1977 make several references to liability for compensation. For instance, Art 91 of Additional Protocol 1 states that a party to the conflicts which violates the provisions of the Conventions or of the Protocol will be liable to pay compensation.

[9] UN Declaration of Basic Principles of Justice for Victims of Crime and Abuse of Power, adopted by the General Assembly on 29 November 1985, UN Doc A/40/881.

[10] See n 2 above.

[11] Such provision, found in Art 8 of the Universal Declaration of Human Rights, is included in many human rights treaties including Art 2.3.(a) of the International Covenant on Civil and Political Rights, Art 13 of the European Convention on Human Rights.

[12] Study concerning the right to restitution, compensation and rehabilitation for victims of gross violations of human rights and fundamental freedoms, Final report to the UN Commission on Human Rights by Theo van Boven, Special Rapporteur, UN Doc E/CN.4/Sub.2/1993/8.

international human rights and humanitarian law. Declaring that: 'The obligation to respect, ensure respect for, and enforce international human rights and humanitarian law includes, inter alia, a state's duty to ... afford appropriate remedies to victims; and provide for or facilitate reparation to victims', the Principles go on to define 'reparation' as including restitution, compensation, rehabilitation, satisfaction (including symbolic or moral measures) and guarantees of non-repetition.[13] In order to stress the importance of procedural guarantees, the Principles state that victims have a right of access to justice.[14]

In parallel with these developments in international standards, lessons have been learnt from actual experience concerning forms of reparation and how it can best be delivered. One lesson is that the form of reparation must be appropriate to the particular circumstances. In some situations payment of monetary compensation is viewed by victims as an unacceptable buy-off for loved ones killed,[15] or as a means of avoiding prosecuting those responsible,[16] or as an insufficient remedy.[17] In others, even if damages are not actually collected, the judgement of the Court is considered an important acknowledgement that violations have occurred.[18] Other lessons have been learnt about the role that can be played by truth commissions, national compensation schemes and other alternatives to judicial processes.

Adjudication of civil actions by national courts being one desirable avenue of redress for victims, what does international law have to say about states' rights and obligations in this regard? It is true that no international treaty explicitly obliges states to open their courts to civil actions by individuals in respect of serious violations in another state. But the increasing focus on the rights and interests of victims and the right to reparation, the development of international law concepts such as *erga omnes* and *jus cogens*, and of international human rights and humanitarian law standards such as the duty to bring perpetrators to justice and the right to an effective remedy, and the growing amount of state practice of the exercise of universal jurisdiction, are leading to a growing

[13] Final report of the Independent Expert on the right to reparation for victims of gross violations of human rights and humanitarian law Mr M Cherif Bassiouni, UN Doc E/CN.4/2000/62, Principles II and X.

[14] *Ibid*, Principle VIII.

[15] For instance the Mothers of the Plaza de Mayo Association in Argentina rejected any form of reparation other than bringing those responsible for disappearances to justice.

[16] The UK was criticised by the European Committee for the Prevention of Torture for its failure to take effective disciplinary and criminal action for police misconduct, fuelling a tendency for members of the public to pursue their grievances against the police through the civil courts: Report to the United Kingdom on the visit to the United Kingdom and the Isle of Man carried out by the CPT from 8 to 17 Sept 1997, Strasbourg, (13 Jan 2000), 23–31.

[17] Dinah Shelton, in *Remedies in International Human Rights Law* (Oxford University Press, Oxford, 1999), suggests that particularly in cases of gross and systematic violations, compensation can only be a partial remedy and that truth, accountability and symbolic reparation will be more important (p 357). She also criticises the European Court of Human Rights for limiting its remedial orders to declaratory judgments and compensation, and failing to direct or recommend appropriate remedies.

[18] Almost none of the successful plaintiffs in the US litigation under the Alien Tort Claims Act have actually collected the damages awarded.

acceptance that international law might permit the courts of one state to hear a civil action regarding serious human rights violations that took place in another.

Nevertheless plaintiffs in civil actions for human rights violations committed abroad will face formidable obstacles and complexities. To some extent these reflect a clash between two branches of international law. On the one hand developments in public international law since 1945 have seen increasing obligations on states to protect human rights and to combat impunity. Such developments include the concept of universal jurisdiction for certain crimes considered crimes against international law, by which states are permitted or even obliged to prosecute even though there may be no connection between their state and the crime. On the other hand, private international law has developed rules restricting the bases on which national courts may exercise extraterritorial jurisdiction in civil matters, with the objective of facilitating commerce. The result of these parallel developments has led to some uncertainty and apparent anomalies in the field of human rights. One uncertainty is whether the principle of universal jurisdiction governs the civil as well as the criminal law context. The US Restatement (Third) of Foreign Relations Law, considered an authoritative statement of US positions, maintains that international law does not preclude the application of non-criminal law on the basis of universal jurisdiction.[19] Elsewhere the implications of the overlap are either not perhaps considered relevant, such as in civil law jurisdictions where civil reparation can be claimed in the course of a criminal action, or had not until very recently been considered.[20] Additional obstacles and complexities for plaintiffs are introduced by the way in which these two branches of international law impact on, and interact with, national law, which varies enormously from one country to another.

SCOPE FOR CIVIL REDRESS FOR HUMAN RIGHTS ABUSE COMMITTED ABROAD

A victim of human rights violations wishing to pursue a remedy in a jurisdiction other than where the violation took place may try to bring an action against the responsible state, individual state officials, a head of state, or a non-state actor such as a corporation. In such an action a plaintiff is likely to encounter a number of procedural and substantive obstacles.

One important question when a court is considering a case involving harm that arose abroad will be which law the court should apply. There are three main possibilities: the law of the forum state, the law of the state where the harm arose, or international law. In cases involving serious violations of human

[19] Restatement (Third) of the Foreign Relations Law of the United States, American Law Institute, §404, comment b.

[20] The issue was first raised by human rights organisations in Nov 1998 during negotiations on a new Hague Convention on jurisdiction and enforcement of judgements, see below.

rights, which law applies on matters such as the characterisation of the act as a civil wrong, limitation periods or who is entitled to sue could be crucial. The general rule in conflict of law situations is that the governing law will be the law of the country most closely connected with the harm, normally that of the place where the harm occurred.[21] However there are exceptions, for instance in common law jurisdictions foreign law will be excluded if contrary to public policy, which would be likely to include infringement of human rights.[22] In the US *Filártiga* type cases, the courts have avoided ruling definitively on the issue but have tended to apply US federal common law as informed by international law, while paying lip service to the law of the country where the violation took place.[23]

Plaintiffs are also likely to face difficulties inherent in any cross border civil litigation such as availability of evidence, limitation periods, tracing and freezing assets, enforcement and prohibitive costs.[24] In cases raising issues of human rights, three problems likely to arise are establishing a cause of action, jurisdiction and state immunity. These will now be considered in more detail.

Is there a Cause of Action?

In many countries with a civil law system, the linking of civil with criminal proceedings provides the basis for the action in tort, at least so far as actions against individuals are concerned (where the defendant is not an individual against whom criminal proceedings may be brought, such as a corporation or a state, the victim will be forced to start a separate civil action in any event).[25] Gross violations of human rights would fall into the category of acts that give rise to both penal and civil liability: if a crime is established, an action in tort is also created. A victim may seek compensation either by starting a separate civil action, or by being joined as a 'civil party' (*partie civile*) to criminal proceedings. In France, for instance, the victim may seek damages for all types of loss in the course of the criminal proceedings.[26] While the precise way in which it works varies from one civil law system to another, the *partie civile* system has many advantages for the victim, who is given access to the dossier of evidence

[21] See for example the European Convention on the Law Applicable to Contractual Obligations 1980, Art 4. In the UK, the Private International Law (Miscellaneous Provisions) Act 1995 now governs choice of law in a tort issue.

[22] In the UK this principle was established by the House of Lords in *Oppenheimer v Cattermole*, [1976] AC 249, and subsequently enshrined in the Private International Law (Miscellaneous Provisions) Act 1995 s14(3)(a)(i). Regarding the US, see *Filártiga v Peña-Irala*, 577 F. Supp., at 863–64.

[23] Stephens and Ratner, *International Human Rights Litigation in US Courts*, 119–23.

[24] Particularly where, as in the UK, the adverse costs rule means a loser will normally have to pay the winner's legal costs and legal aid is unlikely to be available.

[25] See for example the French *Code de Procédure Pénale*, Art 2: the right to bring a civil action for reparation for harm caused by a crime, delict or contravention belongs to those who have personally suffered damage caused directly by the offence.

[26] French *Code de Procédure Pénale*, Arts 2 and 3.

and is relieved of the burden of starting a separate legal action which can be stressful, lengthy and costly.

Nevertheless there are pitfalls in the *partie civile* system. During the trial in Switzerland of *N* in April 1999, the spouse of a victim who had died in the Rwandan genocide withdrew as *partie civile* from the criminal prosecution of *N* for war crimes after being forced to choose between receiving witness protection as an ordinary witness, or remaining as *partie civile* and losing her entitlement to such protection.

Victims of human rights violations in civil law countries have tended to use the *partie civile* system primarily as a means of getting criminal proceedings off the ground. One way of starting criminal proceedings in Francophone countries, for instance, is for a victim to make a complaint to the *juge d'instruction* who, if convinced a prima facie case is made out, will commence an investigation. The recent proceedings in Senegal against former Chadian dictator Hissène Habré, the proceedings in Chad against several of Habré's colleagues, and the prosecution in France of Mauritanian Captain Ely Ould Dah, all for torture, were initiated in this way. So far few of the cases prosecuted on the basis of universal jurisdiction and initiated by victims as *parties civiles* have been concluded. In the trial *in absentia* of Argentinean Captain Astiz in France for his role in the torture and disappearance of two French nuns, victims joined as *parties civiles* were awarded one franc each by way of moral damages.[27] As more and more prosecutions on the basis of universal jurisdiction reach conclusion, it can be expected that victims will be awarded reparation.

In states with a common law tradition,[28] the separation between civil and criminal proceedings means that it is always necessary to find a separate cause of action in order to initiate a civil action. The cases founded on international human rights brought in the US that began with *Filártiga* were based on two pieces of legislation, the Alien Tort Claims Act, which confers jurisdiction on federal district courts over 'torts committed by non-citizens in violation of the law of nations or a treaty of the United States' and the Torture Victim Protection Act, which authorises civil suits for torture or extrajudicial killing.[29] As yet, there is no equivalent elsewhere of the US legislation conferring civil jurisdiction on domestic courts for human rights violations committed abroad.[30] While violations of human rights, such as those involving injuries to the person, might be characterised as existing domestic torts, this might not be sufficient to found jurisdiction.[31] The question arises whether, in the absence of legislation, states will found a tort action directly on customary international

[27] Judgment of the Cour d'Assises de Paris, 16 Mar 1990.

[28] The English common law system applies in most former British colonies around the world and has also been adopted elsewhere. It applies in the US, Australia and New Zealand, and large parts of Africa and Asia.

[29] 28 USC.§ 1350. See ch 9.

[30] The Alien Tort Claims Act and the Torture Victim Protection Act have provided the basis for tens of civil actions brought by victims of human rights violations against individuals and corporations in the US.

[31] See the discussion on jurisdiction and immunities below.

law. Although it is well established that customary international law is automatically part of the common law,[32] it is not so clear that a tort action may be founded upon a violation of international human rights law.

In the UK, the general rule is that a rule of international law needs to be specifically incorporated into UK law by legislation before it could give rise to a domestic cause of action.[33] In the case of *Al-Adsani v Government of Kuwait and Others*, the plaintiff attempted to found a tort action on customary international law. Suleiman Al-Adsani was a pilot with joint Kuwaiti and UK citizenship who had fought with the Kuwait Airforce in the Gulf War. Afterwards, in May 1991, he was allegedly abducted and brutally tortured in Kuwait by those who believed he had publicised a video that had come into his possession compromising a member of the Royal Family. Held first in a state security prison and then a palace, he claimed to have been beaten, immersed in a pool full of dead bodies and set on fire. Afterwards Al-Adsani came to the UK, where he was subjected to threats by people whom he believed to be agents of the State of Kuwait.

Al-Adsani issued civil proceedings in the UK against named individuals and the State of Kuwait seeking damages for the severe physical and mental suffering that he had endured. The matter came before the Court of Appeal twice. First, the Court was called upon to decide whether Al-Adsani should be given leave to serve the proceedings on the State of Kuwait outside the jurisdiction on an *ex parte* application, and on the second occasion to determine the matter of state immunity. Since the proceedings were halted at this stage the court did not specifically address the question of whether a tort could be founded on customary international law. Nevertheless the first bench found a good arguable case that the claim was founded on a tort (the claim was for injury to physical and mental health amounting to torture), and on both occasions the Court accepted that torture was a violation of international law, though without specifying whether this had any consequence so far as cause of action was concerned.[34]

In Australia the Federal Court addressed the question in the case of *Nulyarimma v Thompson*.[35] Here the Court had to decide claims by members of the Aboriginal community that members of the Government had engaged in genocide. The main question at issue was whether both criminal and civil proceedings could be based on the international law prohibition on genocide, in the absence of appropriate domestic legislation. Although two of the judges held that they could not, support for the claim came in the dissenting judgment of Merkel J, who asserted:

[32] *Trendtex Trading Corporation v Central Bank of Nigeria* (1977) QB 529

[33] This principle of non-justiciability was confirmed in *J.H.Rayner Ltd v Department of Trade* [1989] 3 WLR 969. Also see Murray Hunt, *Using Human Rights Law in English Courts* (Hart, Oxford, 1997), 299.

[34] Court of Appeal Judgment of 21 Jan 1994, (1994) 100 ILR 465, and 12 Mar 1996, Times Law Reports, 29 Mar 1996. The Court focused on the implications as regards state immunity. See further below.

[35] [1999] FCA 1192 (1 Sept 1999).

> In my view there is no binding authority or persuasive jurisprudential support for the Commonwealth's submission that adoption of customary international civil law or criminal law in relation to universal crimes, as such, into Australian municipal law requires legislation to that effect.[36]

In this case, since he found that the conduct complained of did not amount to genocide in any event, he found it unnecessary to consider whether genocide might give rise to civil liability.[37] In sum, the lack of legislation in most common law countries conferring a cause of action for human rights violations is likely to be a major, if not an insurmountable, obstacle to such actions.

Establishing Jurisdiction

Differences in approach between common law and civil law legal systems are also apparent when it comes to the basis on which national courts exercise jurisdiction over acts committed abroad. As already mentioned, in civil law countries separate civil actions for human rights violations are likely to be rarer given the greater extent of merger between penal and civil fault, and the fact that the victim has a right to initiate a criminal action.

Common law legal systems hold two apparently contradictory principles as regards jurisdiction. On the one hand a defendant may be sued where s/he is found, while on the other, the basis of jurisdiction is basically territorial, and there is a built-in check against the continuance of actions that have no real connection with the jurisdiction in the form of the *forum non conveniens* doctrine.

If a defendant can be served with process within the jurisdiction, a civil action in that jurisdiction can be initiated; the crucial factor is the defendant's personal presence within the jurisdiction, however briefly.[38] Such a rule, prevalent in common law systems, opens the way for opportunistic service of legal process on alleged human rights violators who travel, and some of the tort litigation in the US under the Alien Tort Claims Act and the Torture Victim Protection Act has been based on this so-called 'tag jurisdiction'.

Where a defendant is not physically within the jurisdiction, service of proceedings is only normally permitted with the consent of the court and on certain grounds. Among these grounds is that the damage was sustained within the jurisdiction. Jurisprudence from some jurisdictions suggests that it may be possible to argue successfully that although the *injury* was inflicted by human rights abuse committed in another state, the *damage* which flowed from the injury—whether physical or mental—was suffered within the jurisdiction.[39]

[36] *Ibid*, para 160

[37] *Ibid*, para 231

[38] In *Kadic v Karadzić*, 70 F 3d 232, at 247, the US District Court Second Circuit held that the fact that Radovan Karadzić was only present in the US for a short visit was irrelevant; the court had jurisdiction since the defendant was physically present and properly served. The same principle has long been upheld in other common law jurisdictions; see in the UK *Colt Industries v Sarlie* [1966] 1 WLR 440 (CA).

[39] The Canadian and Australian courts have been particularly open to this approach: see in

Where it is a corporation, rather than an individual, that is the target of the action, establishing jurisdiction has additional complexities.[40] A number of actions have been successfully initiated in the US against corporations for their role in human rights violations abroad. This is possible because corporations may be sued in the US for acts of subsidiaries in other countries, solely on the basis that they do business in the US. This 'doing business' basis of jurisdiction is unique to the US and is regarded elsewhere as exorbitant. Elsewhere there appears to be scope for actions alleging complicity of multinational corporations in human rights violations abroad, so long as the direct responsibility of the parent company or branch that is actually based in the forum state can be engaged. In three ground-breaking cases in the UK, plaintiffs have sought to establish the direct negligence of parent companies based in the UK. In the *Thor Chemicals* case, it was argued that the parent company based in England was liable in relation to its own failure to take steps to protect South African workers from exposure to mercury, and that the defendants were 'directly liable to the plaintiffs in tort for setting up and maintaining factories in South Africa which they knew or ought to have known would be unsafe for those who worked in them'.[41] Similarly in the case of *Connelly v RTZ* it was argued that key strategic technical and policy decisions were taken by the English based company in relation to a uranium mine in Namibia run by its subsidiary, where a plaintiff alleged he developed cancer of the larynx as a result of exposure to uranium dust.[42] In *Lubbe v Cape plc*, the claim was that the parent company based in England failed to take proper steps to ensure that proper working practices were followed and proper safety precautions taken in its world-wide asbestos business, while knowing that exposure to asbestos was gravely injurious to health.[43]

Initiating proceedings in common law countries is only the first step, however. Once service has been successfully effected, a defendant may ask the courts to stay the action on the basis that this is not the appropriate forum for the action (*forum non conveniens*). The criteria for this test, aimed at establishing where the case can most suitably be tried, vary somewhat between different common law jurisdictions. In the leading case of *Spiliada*, the UK House of Lords held that the court will look first to see whether there is another forum with which the action has a more real and substantial connection and, if it finds one, will normally grant a stay unless persuaded by the plaintiff that nevertheless the

Canada, *Vile v Von Wendt* (1980) 103 DLR 3d 356 and in Australia *Challenor v Douglas* (1983) 2 NSWLR 405. On service out of the jurisdiction see Redress, *Challenging Impunity for Torture*, above, 138–52

[40] See chs 11 and 12 of Menno T Kamminga and Saman Zia-Zarifi (eds), *Liability of Multinational Corporations under International Law* (Kluwer Law International, The Hague, 2000), in which Andre Nollkaemper and Gerrit Betlem examine the prospects for transnational litigation against multinational corporations before Dutch Courts.

[41] *Moses Fano Sithole and Others v Thor Chemical Holdings Ltd and Another*, judgment of the Court of Appeal, 3 February 1999, unreported.

[42] *Connelly v RTZ Corp plc*, judgment of the House of Lords, [1997] 3 WLR 373, at 376–77.

[43] *Lubbe and Others v Cape plc*, House of Lords 20 July 2000, WLR 4 Aug 2000 1545, at 1550.

interests of justice require that a stay not be granted.[44] Whilst the first part of this test will almost always favour the forum where the violation of human rights took place, the second part of the test has provided an opening for plaintiffs in a number of cases.

In *Lubbe and Others v Cape plc*, the question before the House of Lords was whether proceedings brought by more than 3,000 plaintiffs seeking damages for personal injuries and death suffered as the result of exposure to asbestos in South Africa should be tried in the UK or in South Africa.[45] Applying the first part of the Spiliada test, Lord Bingham found that the defendant was able to demonstrate that South Africa was another available forum that was clearly more appropriate than England for the action. Applying the second part of the test, however, he concluded:

> If these proceedings were stayed in favour of the more appropriate forum in South Africa the probability is that the plaintiffs would have no means of obtaining the professional representation and the expert evidence which would be essential if these claims were to be justly decided. This would amount to a denial of justice. In the special and unusual circumstances of these proceedings, lack of the means, in South Africa, to prosecute these claims to a conclusion provides a compelling ground, at the second stage of the Spiliada test, for refusing to stay the proceedings here.

In another case against a corporation, *Connelly v RTZ*, Lord Bingham said in the Court of Appeal that: '(I)t seems right to bear the international obligations of the United Kingdom in mind when the Court is invited to make an order which would have the practical effect of preventing a plaintiff pursuing his rights anywhere'.[46] Such an approach can only be strengthened by the Human Rights Act 1998, incorporating the provisions of the European Convention on Human Rights into UK law.

The UK courts have been willing to consider a range of factors in determining that a claimant will not otherwise obtain justice in the alternative forum, which bode well for a victim of human rights violations seeking to persuade a court. These include: the lack of an independent judiciary, the likelihood of inordinate delay or that the claimant would be liable to imprisonment in the other forum, and practical obstacles such as the fact that the plaintiff would have to deal with the proceedings from outside the jurisdiction.[47]

In Australia, the emphasis is rather different, with the House of Lords' 'clearly more appropriate forum test' rejected in favour of a 'clearly more inappropriate forum test'. In *Voth v Manildra Flour Mills*, the Australian High Court said the task of the Australian courts was to establish whether they were clearly an inappropriate forum, rather than passing judgement on the appropriateness of the

[44] *Spiliada Maritime Corp. v Cansulex Ltd*, [1987] AC 460.

[45] Judgment of the House of Lords, 20 July 2000, WLR 4 Aug 2000 1545.

[46] *Connelly v RTZ Corp plc*, Court of Appeal, 2 May 1996.

[47] See *The Abin Daver* [1984] AC 398 at 411, *The Vishva Ajay* [1989]2 Lloyd's Rep 558, at 560, *Purcell v Khayan, The Times*, 23 Nov 1987, *Mohammed v Bank of Kuwait*, [1996] 1 WLR 1483, at 1496.

foreign forum, which they were not equipped to do.[48] In the US the test is whether or not there is an adequate alternative forum,[49] and in the cases based on international human rights the plaintiffs have been able to demonstrate that the territorial forum is not in practice available.[50]

While its application is still relatively untested in human rights cases, the *forum non conveniens* doctrine has the potential to act as an effective test for determining whether a national court should exercise jurisdiction. Further development of this line of case law is now threatened, however, by trends towards a different approach—already entrenched in civil law systems—which takes away any discretion from the courts and instead establishes rules regarding jurisdiction which the courts must apply. In civil law systems, the basic starting point for establishing jurisdiction in civil cases is that a defendant may be sued where he is domiciled or, in the case of torts, where the tortious act was committed.[51] The Brussels Convention on Jurisdiction and the Enforcement of Judgments in Civil and Commercial Matters, to which most EU states are party, codifies these principles and excludes bases of jurisdiction considered exhorbitant.[52]

While the Brussels and Lugano Conventions apply only within Europe, negotiations began under the auspices of the Hague Conference on Private International Law to establish a new international Convention on Jurisdiction and Foreign Judgments in Civil and Commercial Matters. The proposed Convention aimed to establish a world-wide regime for the permissible bases on which courts in contracting states are entitled to assume jurisdiction.[53] It achieves this by prohibiting states from exercising jurisdiction on grounds considered exorbitant by others. Thus jurisdiction on the basis of the nationality of the plaintiff or the defendant, common in civil law countries such as France, would be prohibited together with jurisdiction on the basis of the presence of property belonging to the defendant or the service of a writ upon the defendant in that state (so-called tag jurisdiction), both possible in common law states.[54]

Such provisions would have disastrous implications for civil actions to redress human rights violations. Prohibiting tag jurisdiction and the *forum non conveniens* doctrine would threaten civil actions of the type currently possible in the US and envisaged in other common law countries, which have relied heavily on these two doctrines. Civil actions joined to criminal prosecutions for international crimes brought on the basis of universal jurisdiction or of the active or

[48] *Voth v Manildra Flour Mills Pty Ltd*, [1990] 171 CLR 538, at 557–61

[49] *Piper Aircraft Company v Reyno*, 454 US 235 (1981).

[50] Stephens and Ratner, *International Human Rights Litigation in US Courts*, 151–53.

[51] See for example the German Code of Civil Procedure, §32 (1981).

[52] Art 2 establishes the general rule that a defendant must be sued in his/her domicile, while Art 3 excludes other bases of jurisdiction and Art 5 allows actions in tort, delict or quasi-delict to be brought in the courts of the place where the harmful event occurred.

[53] The Convention also establishes a regime for the recognition and enforcement of judgements given by courts in other contracting states, which would benefit plaintiffs in human rights cases.

[54] These are among the prohibited grounds of jurisdiction listed in Art 18 of the Preliminary Draft Convention adopted by the Special Commission on 30 Oct 1999, as amended during the first part of the Diplomatic Conference, held in June 2001.

passive personality principles in civil law countries such as France, Spain and Italy could also be under threat.[55] Similarly the enforcement of civil judgments relating to human rights from, say, US courts in France, and judgments from France elsewhere, could be affected.

A coalition of human rights organisations drew these implications to the attention of delegates at the Hague Conference. They sought to preserve the current scope of civil litigation relating to human rights, and to allow the future development of such litigation.[56] The challenge was to carve out a category of more serious violations to which the list of prohibited bases of jurisdiction would not apply. The draft text, as of June 2001,[57] contained the following draft Article 18.3:

> [3. Nothing in this Article shall prevent a court in a Contracting State from exercising jurisdiction under national law in an action claiming damages in respect of conduct which constitutes—
>
> [a) genocide, a crime against humanity or a war crime]; or]
>
> b) a serious crime under international law, provided that this State has exercised its criminal jurisdiction over that crime in accordance with an international treaty to which it is a Party and that claim is for civil compensatory damages for death or serious bodily injuries arising from that crime.
>
> Sub-paragraph b) only applies if the party seeking relief is exposed to a risk of a denial of justice because proceedings in another State are not possible or cannot reasonably be required.]]

If and when the Diplomatic Conference reconvenes to finalise the Convention, there remain a number of fundamental issues on which consensus has still not been reached. Among these is the list of prohibited grounds of jurisdiction itself, and whether or not to leave a 'grey zone' of grounds that are not listed as either prohibited or required under the Convention, that would remain open for the exercise of jurisdiction under national law. If a Convention can be agreed in broadly the current format, it is likely that some form of human rights exception will be included.[58]

[55] See the Position Paper of the Fédération Internationale des Ligues des Droits de l'Homme, Paris, to the Hague Conference dated October 1999. For an explanation of these different types of jurisdiction, see ch 2 in this volume.

[56] Position Paper of the Coalition on Jurisdiction and Enforcement of Judgments to the Hague Conference in Oct 1999.

[57] Interim Text, Summary of the Outcome of the Discussion in Commission II of the First Part of the Diplomatic Conference 6–20 June 2001, available on the Hague Conference on Private International Law web site: www.hcch.net/e/conventions

[58] Although the entire sub-para 3 remains in square brackets, the majority of delegates appear to have accepted that the human rights impact of the Convention needs to be addressed. The issue remaining for discussion is how to define the exemption.

Suing States or State Officials: State Immunity

Most—though not all—cases involving serious violations of human rights will involve responsibility of state officials. Any suit against a state, state official or head of state can therefore be expected to quickly come up against a claim of immunity.[59] This is the concept that one state, or its agents, may not be sued in the courts of another (see Chapter 3). Many states have moved away from the traditional international law doctrine which held that states, heads of state and state officials are absolutely immune from all criminal or civil actions, and have adopted the doctrine of restrictive immunity. This is a qualified immunity, according to which states are immune from the jurisdiction of the courts unless specific exceptions apply. The major recognised exception is for commercial transactions, where a state acts in the private sphere (*acta jure gestionis*) rather than in its sovereign capacity (*acta jure imperii*).[60]

There are two main options open to those wishing to find a way around state immunity in civil cases alleging serious violations of human rights: one is to seek to rely on established exceptions to state immunity, the other is to find—or legislate to create—an additional 'human rights exception', bearing in mind the developing law on immunity in the sphere of international criminal law.[61]

In terms of the first possible way around state immunity, that of bringing human rights cases within existing exceptions, the scope is rather limited. In the US, a number of attempts have been made to bring suits for human rights violations under the 'commercial activities' exception to the Foreign Sovereign Immunities Act. In *Doe v Unocal Corp*, the California District Court considered whether the role of SLORC (the State Law and Order Restoration Council, the military junta that seized power in Burma (Myanmar) in 1988) and MOGE (the Myanmar Oil and Gas Enterprise, controlled by SLORC) in human rights violations during the building of a gas pipeline through Myanmar by Unocal and Total constitute commercial activity for the purposes of the FSIA.[62] The plaintiffs alleged that SLORC and MOGE used violence and intimidation to relocate villages, enslave farmers and steal their property. The Court found that despite the commercial nature of the enterprise, the acts alleged were essentially abuse of police powers and therefore 'peculiarly sovereign in nature' and did not fall within the commercial exception.[63] The action could be continued against Unocal, however.

Another exception to state immunity contained in some of the state immunity statutes which exist in common law countries, modelled on the UK's State

[59] Various forms of immunity exist in national legal systems based on international law, including state immunity, head of state immunity and diplomatic immunity. The exact extent of immunities are regulated by international treaties such as the 1961 Vienna Convention on Diplomatic Relations and the 1972 European Convention on State Immunity, and national law. See ch 3.

[60] For a comparative analysis of national law and legislation see Jurgen Brohmer, *State Immunity and the Violation of Human Rights* (Martinus Nijhoff and Kluwer, 1997).

[61] For example ICC Statute Art 27 and the House of Lords decision in *Pinochet No 3*.

[62] *Doe et al v Unocal Corp et al*, 963 F Supp 880 (CDCal 1997).

[63] *Ibid*, at 888.

Immunity Act, is an additional tort exception whereby a state is not immune from civil actions for death, injury or damage to property. However this only applies where the damage was caused by an act committed in the state where the action is brought, and is therefore not likely to assist a victim of human rights seeking to sue for acts committed in another state.[64]

In a ground breaking case in New Zealand, known as the 'wine-box' case,[65] the Court of Appeal hinted at the possible existence of a further 'public policy' exception to state immunity in the common law.[66] While such a concept could prove extremely important in human rights cases, it is unlikely to make headway in many common law jurisdictions where, unlike New Zealand, legislation exists that governs state immunity.

Unless there are further developments along the lines of the New Zealand case, the existing exceptions are likely to be of limited assistance to plaintiffs in most human rights cases. If one turns to searching for signs of emergence of a 'human rights exception', one finds the beginnings of a slow shift. So far, only in the US has legislation been introduced to lift the immunity of states for certain human rights violations. The provision, enacted in 1996 and amending the Foreign Sovereign Immunities Act (FSIA), is extremely limited in scope and politically opportunistic, applying only to 'terrorist states' and only where the claimant or victim is a US national.[67] Furthermore, execution of judgements made under the provision is extremely difficult.[68] In the UK, the human rights organisation Redress is campaigning to introduce a Redress for Torture Bill that would remove the immunity of a state in respect of an action for torture or death caused by torture.

In the UK case of *Al-Adsani v Kuwait*, it was argued that the State Immunity Act must be interpreted as subject to the overriding international law prohibition on torture which amounts to a *jus cogens* norm. The plaintiff sued both the State of Kuwait itself and named individuals for acts of torture.[69] As noted above, the case came before the Court of Appeal twice. On the first occasion, on an *ex parte* application for leave to serve the proceedings on Kuwait outside the jurisdiction, the plaintiff argued that the prohibition on torture, as a violation of a *jus cogens* norm, trumped the principle of state immunity. The Court,

[64] For example s. 1605(a)(5) Foreign Sovereign Immunities Act 1976 (US), s 5 of the State Immunity Act 1978 (UK), s 7 State Immunity Act 1979 (Singapore), s 6 Foreign States Immunities Act 1981 (South Africa).

[65] The name came from the boxes in which the voluminous documentation was contained: the case involved tax avoidance in the Cook Islands.

[66] *Controller and Auditor-General v Sir Ronald Davison* [1996]2 NZLR 278

[67] Antiterrorism and Effective Death Penalty Act of 1996, s 221, Jurisdiction for Lawsuits against Terrorist States. Immunity is lifted for torture, extra-judicial killing, aircraft sabotage and hostage taking.

[68] A further amendment to the FSIA of 1998, permitting attachment and execution of judgements against a foreign State's diplomatic or consular properties, was suspended by President Clinton in the interests of the national interests of the US, (1999), 93 *American Journal of International Law*, 181, 185.

[69] Default judgement was obtained in relation to one defendant, leaving unaddressed the issue of whether or not that individual was a state official.

albeit at this preliminary stage where Kuwait had not yet had an opportunity to put its case for immunity, agreed that the plaintiff had made out a good arguable case that Kuwait was not entitled to state immunity because 'no State or sovereign immunity should be accorded even under the State Immunity Act in respect of acts which it is alleged are properly to be described as torture in contravention of public international law' and that the reference to immunity in the SIA is to be interpreted as meaning immunity in accordance with international law under which torture is prohibited.[70] When the matter came to the Court of Appeal for a second time, after process had been served and Kuwait had come forward to claim immunity, the Court found in favour of Kuwait, holding that the State Immunity Act was comprehensive and unambiguous, and that an exception for acts in violation of international law could not be read into it.[71]

Al-Adsani then petitioned the European Court of Human Rights, arguing that by granting immunity to the State of Kuwait, the UK was denying his right of access to court and to an effective remedy contrary to Articles 6 and 13 of the Convention.[72] On 21 November 2001 the European Court rejected the claim, though by the narrowest of margins. By a majority of nine votes to eight, the Grand Chamber held that the right of access to court was not absolute and may be subject to limitations. Any limitation must pursue a legitimate aim and be proportionate to its purpose. In this instance, the Court considered that 'the grant of sovereign immunity to a state in civil proceedings pursues the legitimate aim of complying with international law to promote comity and good relations between States through the respect of another State's sovereignty', and '... measures taken by a High Contracting Party which reflect generally recognised rules of public international law on State immunity cannot in principle be regarded as imposing a disproportionate restriction on the right of access to court'.[73] While, like the dissenting judges, the majority accepted that the prohibition on torture had achieved the status of a peremptory norm, or norm of *jus cogens*, it did not 'find it established that there is yet acceptance in international law for the proposition that States are not entitled to immunity in respect of civil claims for damages for alleged torture committed outside the forum State'.[74] The minority, which apparently did not disagree with the test applied,[75] based its dissent entirely on the *jus cogens* nature of the prohibition of torture,

[70] Court of Appeal judgment of 21 Jan 1994, 12.

[71] *Al-Adsani v Government of Kuwait and Others*, Times Law Reports, 29 Mar 1996

[72] *Al-Adsani v UK*, appl no 35763/97. The applicant also alleged that the UK had failed to secure his right not to be tortured, contrary to Art 3 of the Convention read in conjunction with Arts 1 and 13, but the Court held unanimously rejected this claim, since the torture did not take place in UK jurisdiction and nor did the UK authorities have any causal connection with its occurrence, para 40, judgment of 21 Nov 2001.

[73] Paras 53–56 of the Court's judgment. The test applied is consistent with earlier cases such as *Osman v UK*, judgment of 28 Oct 98, appl no 23452/94.

[74] Para 66 of the judgment.

[75] In *Fogarty v the UK*, application no 37112/97, in which judgment was given on the same day as in *Al-Adsani*, the Court applied the same test and found, with only one dissention, that there had been no violation of Art 6.

holding that regardless of whether the proceedings were criminal or civil, a state cannot invoke hierarchically lower rules (those on state immunity) to refuse to adjudicate a torture case.

Despite the fact that Al-Adsani failed to win his case in the European Court of Human Rights, the closeness of the decision together with the sense of recognition, even by the majority, that the argument for the denial of immunity in cases involving violation of *jus cogens* norms is increasingly being heard, gives cause for optimism to the proponents of this argument. Judge Bratza, in his concurring opinion, warned that the European Court 'should be very cautious before taking upon itself the role of a forerunner', suggesting that things are indeed moving in that direction but that in his view, the Court should not be the forum for achieving this.

Another sign of movement towards a human rights exception to state immunity is the undermining of immunity afforded to *individual* state officials—as opposed to states themselves. In the US, although actions against foreign states as such have failed, the FSIA does not appear to be a bar to suits against individual state officials at least if they are acting outside the scope of their authority—and committing gross violations of human rights has been held to be outside official authority.[76] So far, this is not so in the UK where the Court of Appeal has held that the State Immunity Act must be read as 'affording to individual employees or officers of a foreign state protection under the same cloak as protects the State itself'.[77]

An additional potential obstacle for plaintiffs in litigating human rights abuses in common law countries is the Act of State doctrine, which prevents a national court adjudicating in relation to an act of a foreign government within its own territory.[78] However this seems less likely in practice to present an obstacle to such actions since it will be subject to an exception on public policy grounds.[79]

State immunity seems likely to remain a significant obstacle to extraterritorial civil actions for human rights violations in national courts. In *Pinochet* Lord Millett was untroubled by the apparent contradiction whereby a person could be acting outside their official capacity in terms of criminal liability, but not in terms of civil liability, for the same acts:

> I see nothing illogical or contrary to public policy in denying the victims of state sponsored torture the right to sue the offending state in a foreign court while at the same time permitting (and indeed requiring) other states to convict and punish the individuals responsible if the offending state declines to take action.[80]

[76] Stephens and Ratner, *International Human Rights Litigation in US Courts*, 126–31

[77] *Propend Finance Pty Ltd v Sing* (1997) Times Law Reports 238.

[78] Unlike state immunity, the principle that sovereign executive acts characterised as 'Acts of State' are not justiciable is not rooted in international law but has developed in the US and other common law jurisdictions. See ch 3.

[79] See for example in the UK *Oppenheimer v Cattermole* [1976] AC 249, at 277.

[80] *Pinochet No 3*. The House of Lords made a number of remarks about immunity under UK civil law even though the case concerned the criminal law, and such remarks were strictly *obiter dicta*.

Nevertheless, considering the decisiveness with which the House of Lords concluded that torture cannot be an official function in relation to criminal proceedings,[81] it would seem extraordinary if the distinction between civil and criminal law in this regard will stand the test of time. US courts have already overcome the hurdle as regards individual state officials in suits regarding international human rights. The *Pinochet* case and other developments in international criminal law have stressed that many forms of immunity attach not to the individual officials themselves but to the acts they perform, and that for certain types of acts immunity cannot be claimed, since these acts are simply not part of the official functions of the person concerned.

CONCLUSIONS

Signs of movement towards emergence of 'civil universal jurisdiction' are evident. The human rights litigation in the US has led to pressure in other common law countries to follow suit by introducing similar legislation to the Alien Tort Claims Act and the Torture Victim Protection Act. There is a growing sense that state immunity legislation that exists in common law countries may be out of line with international law. *Al Adsani* was decided in the English courts strictly on the basis of UK legislation, not on the basis of international law. Although the European Court of Human Rights also rejected the case, it did so by the narrowest of margins and acknowledged the existence of a general movement in international law towards a denial of immunity in cases involving violations of norms of *jus cogens* such as the prohibition on torture. The increasing exercise of universal jurisdiction for gross violations of human rights and humanitarian law has started to provide opportunities for victims in civil law systems to join the criminal proceedings as *parties civiles* and seek reparation. The human rights exception that may be established in a new Hague Convention on jurisdiction and enforcement of judgements will serve to at least preserve, and at best also encourage, the possibility of extra-territorial civil actions for human rights.

There is no suggestion that recourse to foreign courts for civil reparation should be a primary remedy. Civil remedies in countries other than where the violation took place are only required where that national system is unable or unwilling to provide a remedy. Amidst the growing pressure on states to enact legislation so as to enable their courts to provide redress to victims of gross violations of human rights where violators enter their jurisdiction, therefore, mechanisms will be needed to ensure it is in the interests of justice to go against the ordinary rules that civil tort cases should be heard in the state where the harm arose. A determination may need to be made as to whether the victim is able to obtain justice in the territorial state and whether in the particular cir-

[81] *Ibid,* Lord Browne-Wilkinson: 'How can it be for international purposes an official function to do something which international law itself prohibits and criminalises?'

cumstances it is appropriate to proceed in the forum state, for instance because evidence is available and the due process rights of defendants will be safeguarded. Since it is difficult to develop rules on such matters, it may be best to leave it to the courts to look at all the circumstances. The *forum non conveniens* doctrine and the principle of exhaustion of effective domestic remedies provide possible mechanisms.

It is likely that the law in this area will develop differently in common law and civil law countries. In states with the common law tradition, victims are more likely to resort to civil actions, either as an alternative where state authorities decline to initiate criminal action, or as a preferred option that offers them greater control. In civil law countries, developments are likely to be more closely linked to criminal prosecutions on the basis of universal jurisdiction; as the number of criminal cases based on the principle of universal jurisdiction increases, there are likely to be cases where victims successfully sue as *parties civiles* and obtain reparation.

Both developments are likely to be encouraged and informed by development of international standards relating to the right to reparation and the rights of victims generally. It can be expected that the adoption of principles by the UN will be followed by moves to define reparation, effective remedies and how they can be provided. The strong message coming from victims is that it is not enough just to make available fora for adjudicating claims. It is also crucial that developments take place at national level, in line with international instruments such as the UN Declaration of Basic Principles of Justice for Victims of Crime and Abuse of Power of 1985, and the emerging UN Basic Principles and Guidelines on the right to reparation, on issues such as the forms of reparation that are available and the process by which it is awarded.

At present there is a real possibility in some jurisdictions that a person alleged to have committed gross violations of human rights abroad could be put on trial, but that his victims would not be able to sue for civil reparation for the same acts. Formidable obstacles remain which must be tackled if potential for extraterritorial civil actions are to develop further. The largest obstacle remains state immunity. But the logic of the *Pinochet* case, despite their Lordships' comments regarding civil cases, is that a breakdown in immunity, at least for individual officials and former officials, now seems inevitable. After all, if a state official can be prosecuted and deprived of his liberty for an international crime, and if torture and such serious violations are no longer to be viewed as falling within his official functions, why cannot he also be sued for reparation by his victims?

Immunities aside, there are a number of other areas in which law reform will be needed for 'universal civil jurisdiction' to move forward. Assuming that private international law rules do not cut off the possibility, states will need to adopt legislation to establish a cause of action, provide a basis of jurisdiction and deal with state immunity and any other issues particular to that jurisdiction. If development in national practice leads to the emergence of a principle of international law recognising human rights as an exception to state immunity, limitations on jurisdiction and other norms, this category of 'international torts' will need to be defined. Existing definitions in international criminal law, the international law of human rights and international humanitarian law can be drawn upon.

Alternatively, such changes could be led by international law. In 1993 one author, Richard Lillich, proposed that other states should be encouraged to enact legislation similar to that existing in the US allowing their courts to hear civil actions brought by victims of gross violations of human rights against perpetrators found within their jurisdiction. In 1993 he wrote:

> An International Convention on the Redress of Human Rights Violations that would obligate states parties to enact legislation along these lines would be a promising first step. Such a Convention could define just what gross human rights violations were actionable, provide a common choice of law approach for courts to follow, establish general norms governing the allowance of compensatory and, especially, punitive damages, and provide for the enforcement of judgments against human rights violators wherever they may reside.[82]

Today prospects for concluding such a convention seem a good deal less remote than they did in 1993.

[82] Richard Lillich, 'Damages for Gross Violations of International Human Rights Awarded by US Courts' (1993), 15 *Human Rights Quarterly* 207, 216–17.

12

National Action Challenged: Sovereignty, Immunity and Universal Jurisdiction before the International Court of Justice

ANDREW CLAPHAM*

The International Court of Justice has jurisdiction over inter-state disputes where the states concerned consent to the Court's jurisdiction.[1] The Court can also consider requests for advisory opinions, when the request comes from an authorised UN organ or specialised agency.[2] At first sight this seems an unlikely forum for a discussion of the international law concerning individual criminal accountability and justice for crimes against humanity. But the application brought by the Democratic Republic of Congo (DRC) against Belgium on 17 Oct 2000 has prompted the Court to consider the limits of state action with regard to prosecutions in national courts for international crimes committed by foreign officials.[3]

The press release of the Court of 8 December 2000 neatly summarised the facts:

> The merits of the dispute concern an international arrest warrant issued on 11 April 2000 by a Belgian investigating judge against Mr Yerodia Abdoulaye Ndombasi—Minister for Foreign Affairs of the DRC at the time, now Minister of Education—seeking his provisional detention pending a request for extradition to Belgium for 'serious violations of international humanitarian law'. In its request for the indication of provisional measures, the DRC had *inter alia* asked the Court to make an order for the immediate discharge of the disputed arrest warrant.[4]

* I am grateful to Théo Boutruche, graduate student at the Graduate Institute of International Studies (GIIS), Geneva, for his excellent research assistance for this chapter.

[1] Art 36 of the Statute of the International Court of Justice (1945).

[2] Art 96 of the UN Charter (1945), Arts 65 to 68 of the Statute of the International Court of Justice (1945).

[3] Application instituting proceedings available on the website of the ICJ http://www.icj-cij.org/icjwww/idocket. The Provisional Measures order of 8 Dec 2000 and the final judgment of 14 Feb 2002 are also posted at this site.

[4] Release 2000/40 of 8 Dec 2000.

The Court declined to indicate provisional measures.[5] The Court focused on the fact that Mr Yerodia Ndombasi (Yerodia) was no longer Minister for Foreign Affairs after the first day of oral pleadings and had been given the post of Minister of Education. The Court stated that this involved less foreign travel and 'it has accordingly not been established that irreparable prejudice might be caused in the immediate future to the Congo's rights nor that the degree of urgency is such that those rights need be protected by the indication of provisional measures'.[6] However the Order of the Court stated that it was 'desirable that the issues before the Court should be determined as soon as possible' and that 'it is therefore appropriate to ensure that a decision on the Congo's application be reached with all expedition'.[7]

The eventual final judgment on the merits held that Belgium had violated the rights of the DRC under international law. The Court held that a foreign minister enjoys inviolability of the person and complete immunity from prosecution by the authorities of any other state. Belgium was required by the ICJ to cancel the arrest warrant 'by means of its own choosing' and 'so inform the authorities to whom that warrant was circulated'.[8]

What I propose to do in this short contribution is to use the litigation as a springboard to examine three issues of international law which arise in this context. First, is there a violation of the sovereignty of a state such as the DRC as a result of the issue of an international arrest warrant for international crimes against a foreign minister? Secondly, does international law demand immunity from criminal jurisdiction for an acting foreign minister accused of international crimes? Thirdly, what is the legitimate scope of the principle of universal jurisdiction?

The purpose of this chapter is first, to shed some light on the principles of international law involved, and, second, to suggest ways of resolving some of the apparent contradictions. International law is more than a language used by states to make their claims and counter-claims. It comprises principles and rules which permit and prohibit certain forms of action. The international legal order, if it is to command respect and co-operation, must reflect a serious attempt to combine these rules into a system which works in the common interest. One way to ensure its credibility in this context is to suggest a framework which is not only principled but coherent.

[5] On 8 Dec 2000 the Court unanimously rejected the request of Belgium that the case be removed from the Court's List, and found by 15 votes to two that the circumstances, as they presented themselves to the Court, were not such as to require the exercise of its power to indicate provisional measures, as the DRC had wished. Considerations of space preclude an examination of the questions relating to the preliminary measures requested or the complex questions of the ICJs jurisdiction related to this application. The reader is referred to the oral pleadings of 20–32 Nov 2000 and the order of the Court of 8 Dec 2000 available on the Court's website http://www.icj-cij.org/icjwww/idocket

[6] Order of the Court, 8 Dec 2000, para 72.

[7] Order of the Court, 8 Dec 2000, para 76.

[8] Judgment, 14 Feb 2002, para 78 (3) by 10 votes to six.

SOVEREIGNTY

The DRC claimed that the arrest warrant issued by the Belgian judge, Judge Vandermeersch, with regard to Mr Yerodia, for grave breaches of international humanitarian law and crimes against humanity, violated the principle that no state can exercise its power on the territory of another state. They also claimed that the arrest warrant violated the principle of the sovereign equality of states.

The claim of a violation of sovereignty suggested that the issuance of an arrest warrant infringed on the sovereignty of all states, and in particular the DRC. It somehow suggested that the request created an obligation on those states which receive the request to apply the law of the issuing state in contravention of their own law and applicable international law.

First, let us look at the effect of the warrant on the sovereignty of DRC. Sovereignty is often seen as an overarching notion from which a number of international law rules flow.[9] Sovereignty as such is a changing notion which adjusts to the developing nature of international law. The specific rule of public international law which guarantees the *sovereign equality* of states is not usually considered a *jus cogens* norm,[10] and it too adapts to the evolution of international law. [11]

[9] A Cassese, *International Law in a Divided World* (Oxford University Press, Oxford, 1986), 129.

[10] *Ibid,* 131. See also A Bleckmann, 'Article 2 (1) of the UN Charter', in B Simma (ed), *The Charter of the United Nations: A Commentary* (Oxford University Press, Oxford/New York, 1995), 89. Interestingly the International Tribunal for the former Yugoslavia has commented that the fact that a crime such as torture has achieved the status of a *jus cogens* norm means that not only are states entitled to prosecute individuals for this crime without the need to show a link to the state in question, but also that no rule of international law could undermine the rights of states to prosecute this crime. '153. While the *erga omnes* nature just mentioned appertains to the area of international enforcement (*lato sensu*), the other major feature of the principle proscribing torture relates to the hierarchy of rules in the international normative order. Because of the importance of the values it protects, this principle has evolved into a peremptory norm or *jus cogens*, that is, a norm that enjoys a higher rank in the international hierarchy than treaty law and even "ordinary" customary rules.... [footnote omitted] The most conspicuous consequence of this higher rank is that the principle at issue cannot be derogated from by States through international treaties or local or special customs or even general customary rules not endowed with the same normative force.... 156. Furthermore, at the individual level, that is, that of criminal liability, it would seem that one of the consequences of the *jus cogens* character bestowed by the international community upon the prohibition of torture is that every State is entitled to investigate, prosecute and punish or extradite individuals accused of torture, who are present in a territory under its jurisdiction. Indeed, it would be inconsistent on the one hand to prohibit torture to such an extent as to restrict the normally unfettered treaty making power of sovereign States, and on the other hand bar States from prosecuting and punishing those torturers who have engaged in this odious practice abroad. This legal basis for States' universal jurisdiction over torture bears out and strengthens the legal foundation for such jurisdiction found by other courts in the inherently universal character of the crime. ... 157. It would seem that other consequences include the fact that torture may not be covered by a statute of limitations, and must not be excluded from extradition under any political offence exemption.' Judgment 10 Dec 1998, IT9517, *Furundžija*. This issue was not addressed on appeal, see Appeal Judgment 21 July 2000, IT-95-17/1-A.

[11] See O Schachter, 'Sovereignty – Then and Now', in R St. John MacDonald, *Essays in Honour of Wang Tieya* (Martinus Nijhoff Publishers, Dordrecht/Boston/London, 1993), 671–88 at 679:

According to Antonio Cassese sovereignty grants each state a set of powers relating to its jurisdiction (we might call this the internal dimension).[12] Sovereignty also protects states from inadmissible intervention by other states in their internal affairs, it gives rise to the rule that individuals representing the state in their official capacity create obligations for the state and are not usually held individually accountable (the exception being where international crimes are at issue), and, lastly, sovereignty suggests that one state can not judge another state for acts performed in their 'sovereign capacity'. Cassese is then careful to state that there is an exception to this rule with regard to 'international crimes'.[13]

Sovereignty and Non-Intervention

With regard to the first issue of intervention, the parameters of what is considered legal action and illegal intervention, are changing. The UN General Assembly's Declaration on Friendly Relations (1970) states in two key paragraphs:

> No State or group of States has the right to intervene, directly or indirectly, for any reason whatsoever, in the internal or external affairs of another State. Consequently, armed intervention and all other forms of interference or attempted threats against the personality of the State or against its political, economic and cultural elements, are in violation of international law.
>
> No State may use or encourage the use of economic, political or any other type of measures to coerce another State in order to obtain from it the subordination of the exercise of its sovereign rights and to secure from it advantages of any kind. Also, no State shall organise, assist, foment, finance, incite or tolerate subversive, terrorist or armed activities directed towards the violent overthrow of the régime of another State, or interfere in civil strife in another State.[14]

'Like other abstract concepts of law and politics, it [sovereignty] cannot be reasonably applied without considering competing principles and the particular contextual circumstances.'

[12] Cassese, *International Law in a Divided World*, 130.

[13] *Ibid*: 'individuals can not be brought to trial and punished by foreign States for any such official act if the latter proves contrary to international law (the exceptions being international crimes)'. For the crimes to be included under international crimes in this context, see A Cassese, *International Law* (Oxford University Press, Oxford, 2001), 246. See also A Cassese and A Clapham, 'International Law', in J Krieger (ed), *The Oxford Companion to Politics of the World* 2nd edn, (Oxford University Press, Oxford, 2001), 408–11 at 409: 'at least with respect to some of those values (torture, the prohibition of crimes against humanity, in particular genocide), international rules now provide for the personal criminal responsibility of the state officials who engage in such prohibited acts, in addition of course, to the traditional state responsibility which will be triggered where the acts of the individual can be attributed to the state'. The articles on State Responsibility adopted by the International Law Commission in 2001, and annexed to General Assembly Resolution, A/Res/56/83, adopted 12 Dec 2001, specifically provide for the possibility of the same act giving rise to both individual and state responsibility under international law. See Art 58: 'These articles are without prejudice to any question of the individual responsibility under international law of any person acting on behalf of a State.'

[14] Declaration of Principles of International Law concerning Friendly Relations and

It remains clear under public international law today that 'compulsion (force arrest, seizure, search and other coercive measures within the territory of another state) is illicit, unless expressly legitimated under international law'.[15] In the present context the non-intervention principle is usually considered to cover 'intervention by physical means, in particular the use of force, which leads to concrete violations of the territorial integrity of other states'.[16] This rule would of course forbid sending law enforcement officials to another state to exercise executive jurisdiction over an individual and execute an arrest in that other state.[17] Such action is not permitted under international law, unless the state where the arrest was taking place consented to such an exercise of executive jurisdiction.[18]

But we cannot deduce from this prohibition on extraterritorial *executive* jurisdiction (jurisdiction to enforce) an absolute prohibition on extraterritorial *legislative* jurisdiction (jurisdiction to prescribe).[19] The two issues are not the same and any prohibition on legislating against extraterritorial crimes will have to come from general international law and be coherent with other obligations under international law. This distinction between legislative jurisdiction and executive jurisdiction was approved by the Select Committee of Experts on

Co-operation between States adopted by consensus on 24 Oct 1970, Resolution 2625 (XXV). See also the Declaration on the Inadmissibility of Intervention and Interference in the Internal Affairs of States, GA Resolution of 9 Dec 1981 (which did not enjoy the same degree of consensus).

[15] Extraterritorial criminal jurisdiction European Committee on Crime Problems, Council of Europe, Strasbourg 1989, ch III 'The Relationship between public international law and the law of criminal jurisdiction' at 18 in the French text version 'Competence extraterritoriale en matière pénale'.

[16] *Ibid* at 22 of the French version.

[17] 'The governing principle is that a state cannot take measures on the territory of another state by way of enforcement of national laws without the consent of the latter. Persons may not be arrested, a summons may not be served, police or tax investigations may not be mounted, orders for production of documents may not be executed, on the territory of another state, except under the terms of a treaty or other consent given.' I Brownlie, *Principles of Public International Law,* 5th edn (Oxford University Press, Oxford, 1998), 310.

[18] See above n 16 at 18 of the French version: 'On peut, dès le départ, faire l'observation suivante: le droit international interdit l'exercice de la compétence exécutive sur le territoire d'un autre Etat, si ce n'est avec le consentement de l'Etat concerné.'

[19] See G Abi-Saab, *Cours Général de Droit International Public*, vol 207 *RCADI* (Nijhoff, The Hague, 1996), 73–74: 'A cet égard on peut distinguer, avec les auteurs anglais, entre deux types de pouvoirs juridques, le pouvoir d'édicter ou de prescrire (par une législation ou par une décision spécifique) (*jurisdiction to prescribe*) et le pouvoir d'exécuter (*jurisdiction to enforce*). Le souverain territorial peut évidemment exercer les deux types de pouvoirs. Mais alors que l'exercice du pouvoir d'exécuter est strictement limité à l'assise territoriale de l'Etat, qui ne peut par conséquence souffrir aucun exercice de pouvoir par un autre Etat, l'exercice du pouvoir d'édicter peut déployer ses effets au-delà de l'assise territoriale de l'Etat, et par conséquent sur le territoire d'un autre Etat. La raison en est que l'exercice du pouvoir d'exécuter comporte la possibilité du recours à la force légale, à l'exécution forcée, qui est la forme ultime de l'exercice de la puissance publique.... En revanche, les effets de l'exercice du pouvoir d'édicter ne sont pas en eux-mêmes exécutoires, de sorte que quand ils touchents des personnes, des biens ou des relations juridiques localisées sur le territoire d'un autre Etat, leur aboutissement passe nécessairement par la reconnaissance de ces effets et ou par l'exercice par l'Etat territorial de son pouvoir d'exécuter; ce que cet Etat choisira de faire en cas d'accord, parce que le droit international général lui en impose l'obligation, ou par simple courtoisie *(comitas gentium)*.' (footnote omitted)

Extraterritorial Jurisdiction set up by the Council of Europe's European Committee on Crime Problems in 1984:

> Legislative jurisdiction seldom performs its function in isolation. Usually jurisdiction claimed by the legislature has to be implemented through the exercise of judicial and executive jurisdiction. This is not to say that the scope of established legislative jurisdiction may not be broader than the scope of executive jurisdiction. It is perfectly possible to conceive of the enforcement of legislative jurisdiction either through the exercise of executive jurisdiction by another state, or with respect to persons who have come or been brought within the reach of a state's executive jurisdiction. This should not, however, be interpreted as meaning that the scope of legislative jurisdiction is in principle without territorial limits.[20]

What these limits are remains controversial. Let us examine in more detail the contours of legislative jurisdiction under international law. What seems required by the international legal order is that where international law has created an individual crime it makes no sense to say that states can not legislate against that crime even when it is committed abroad. Where a state has legislated to ensure that it has jurisdiction to prosecute and punish at home international crimes committed abroad this can not, as such, be considered a violation of the non-intervention principle. Where the crimes at issue are international crimes such as those contained in the Geneva Conventions of 1949 these crimes are crimes under customary international law and would be international crimes wheresoever committed. If there are limits to the legislative jurisdiction of states to enact criminal legislation for acts committed abroad they would not relate to international crimes under general international law.[21] They could only relate to crimes which international law had not specified as giving rise to individual criminal liability under international law.

Issues of non-retroactivity and unpredictability would be involved here and the individual would have the right not to be tried for an 'offence on account of any act or omission which did not constitute a penal offence, under national or international law, at the time it was committed'.[22] But where general international law has prohibited certain conduct and made this a crime for which individuals are accountable under international law there would seem to be no international law prohibition on legislative jurisdiction over such extraterritorial international crimes.[23]

[20] See above n 16 at 19 of the French version.

[21] For Georges and Rosemary Abi-Saab, both grave breaches and war crimes (which have been criminalised under international law) give rise to universal jurisdiction. The difference being for them that the grave breaches regime is more stringent in that it demands that states extradite or prosecute, whilst international war crimes merely give rise to a permissive jurisdiction. They suggest that a minority opinion amongst writers would extend the obligation to extradite or punish to include war crimes. G Abi-Saab and R Abi-Saab 'Les crimes de guerre', in H Ascensio, E Decaux and A Pellet (eds), *Droit international pénal* (Pedone, Paris, 2000), ch 21, paras 54–5.

[22] Universal Declaration of Human Rights 1948, Art 11(2).

[23] The *Lotus* case, Judgment No 9, PCIJ [1927] is usually cited in this context as the Permanent Court of International Justice seems to have gone out of its way to stress that rather than extraterri-

As already stated, the strict rule of non-intervention through *executive* jurisdiction abroad is violated for example by sending officers to physically arrest someone outside the territory. But we are suggesting here that there is no rule of public international law which prevents a state from exercising its sovereignty by *legislating* for jurisdiction over international crimes committed abroad. The issue would be more complicated if a state sought to legislate for crimes committed abroad by foreigners which were not considered international crimes under general international law.[24] For present purposes we might confine our discussion to international crimes at the heart of the allegations in the *DRC v Belgium* case: grave breaches of the 1949 Geneva Conventions, war crimes under international law, and crimes against humanity.[25] For such international crimes it must be understood that all states enjoy the right to legislate against them.

We should now examine whether the actual *issuance of a warrant for arrest* might constitute an interference in the internal affairs of another state. We saw above that the essence of the non-interference rule is that it prohibits the coercion of one state by another state. Of course this could in some circumstance occur without the physical invasion of one state by officers from another.

torial jurisdiction being a violation of sovereignty it was in fact a legitimate privilege of sovereignty unless one could point to an international rule which prohibited such an exercise of criminal jurisdiction. It is worth citing the relevant paragraphs in full: 'Now the first and foremost restriction imposed by international law upon a State is that—failing the existence of a permissive rule to the contrary—it may not exercise its power in any form in the territory of another State. In this sense jurisdiction is certainly territorial; it cannot be exercised by a State outside its territory except by virtue of a permissive rule derived from international custom or from a convention' (at p. 18). Here the Court is talking about what we have described above as 'executive competence'. One cannot deduce from this that a state has no power to legislate for criminal acts committed abroad by non-nationals and with no link to the territory. This becomes clear as the judgment continues: 'It does not, however, follow that international law prohibits a State from exercising jurisdiction in its own territory, in respect of any case which relates to acts which have taken place abroad, and in which it cannot rely on some permissive rule of international law. Such a view would only be tenable if international law contained a general prohibition to States to extend the application of their laws and the jurisdiction of their courts to persons, property and acts outside the territory, and if, as an exception to the general prohibition, it allowed States to do so in certain specific cases. But this is certainly not the case under international law as it stands at present. Far from laying down a general prohibition to the effect that States may not extend the application of their laws and the jurisdiction of their courts to persons, property and acts outside their territory, it leaves them in this respect a wide measure of discretion which is only limited in certain cases by prohibitive rules; as regards other cases every State remains free to adopt the principles which it regards as best and most suitable.... In these circumstances, all that can be required of a State is that it should not overstep the limits which international law places upon its jurisdiction; within these limits, its title to exercise jurisdiction rests in its sovereignty' (pp 18–19). So in fact the assertions of legislative jurisdiction/competence are an expression of sovereignty rather than an infringement of it. The Court summarises its approach later on: 'The territoriality of criminal law, therefore, is not an absolute principle of international law and by no means coincides with territorial sovereignty' (p 20).

[24] For a discussion of the legality of prosecutions against nationals from non-parties to international criminal law treaties see MP Scharf, 'The ICC's Jurisdiction over the Nationals of Non-Party States: A Critique of the US Position', vol 64 (2001), 1 *Law and Contemporary Problems*, 98–103, and MP Scharf, 'Applicability of Treaty-Based Universal Jurisdiction to Nationals of Non-Party States', vol 35 (2001), 2 *New England Law Review* 363–82.

[25] Genocide was not an issue in this particular case. In other cases the question of a waiver of immunity through ratification of the Genocide Convention could arise.

Georges Abi-Saab suggests that an act could violate the principle of non-interference in two different categories of cases.[26] First, if 'it carries or constitutes in itself a negation of the sovereignty of the other State'. This would be so for example 'where a State exercises acts of public authority or enforcement such as the arrest of certain persons on the territory of another State without its consent, as if the latter did not exist as a sovereign State'.[27] Secondly, he suggests that it would be illegal for a state to act in a situation where that act has the effect of 'bending the will of the other State in order to force it to act in a certain manner against its will'.

It is not obvious that issuing a warrant of arrest falls within these categories. Such a warrant is in effect a request for other states to co-operate and to act according to their own national law. There is no order, no obligation, and no imposition of one national legal system on another state. Even if the crime for which the warrant had been issued could not be punished under the law of the requested state then the warrant *on its own* could not be described as amounting to an act which has the effect of *bending the will* of a state and *coercing* it to act. To constitute an unlawful interference the concern would have to be coupled with some sort of sanctions capable of forcing a state to abandon its political, economic or cultural elements.[28] It is not even the use of sanctions, such as the termination of assistance or a trade embargo, which would be itself an illegal interference, but rather their effect in extreme circumstances.[29]

[26] 'Some Thoughts on the Principle of Non-Intervention', in K Wellens (ed) *International Law: Theory and Practice* (1998), 228.

[27] *Ibid*. The other example he gives in this context may be 'the "premature recognition" of a secessionist State, which by definition, signifies the negation of the sovereignty of the State on that part of the territory that attempts to secede'. This is a reference to the recognition by the United States of the Panamanian secession from Colombia in 1903. See G Abi-Saab 'Cours Général de Droit International Public', *Recueil des cours,* 207 (1996), 382.

[28] See General Assembly Resolutions A/RES/2131 (XX) and A/RES/36/103. However these resolutions are seen as enjoying less authority than the comprehensive Friendly Relations Declaration, A/RES/2625 (XXV) of 24 Oct 1970 which details the legal principles involved. This Declaration on Principles of International Law concerning Friendly Relations and Co-operation among States in accordance with the Charter of the United Nations explains the non-intervention principle in the following way: 'No State or group of States has the right to intervene, directly or indirectly, for any reason whatever, in the internal or external affairs of any other State. Consequently, armed intervention and all other forms of interference or attempted threats against the personality of the State or against its political, economic and cultural elements, are in violation of international law. No State may use or encourage the use of economic, political or any other type of measures to coerce another State in order to obtain from it the subordination of the exercise of its sovereign rights and to secure from it advantages of any kind.... Every State has an inalienable right to choose its political, economic, social and cultural systems, without interference in any form by another State.' In the context of the 'principle of the sovereign equality of States' the Declaration specifies that sovereign equality included the following elements: '(a) States are juridically equal; (b) Each State enjoys the rights inherent in full sovereignty; (c) Each State has the duty to respect the personality of other States; (d) The territorial integrity and political independence of the State are inviolable; (e) Each State has the right to freely choose and develop its political, social, economic and cultural systems; (f) Each State has the duty to comply fully and in good faith with its international obligations and to live in peace with other states.'

[29] In the *Case Concerning Military and Paramilitary Activities in and Against Nicaragua,* ICJ Rep (1986) at 14, the International Court of Justice considered the cessation of economic aid in

Philippe Cahier draws a distinction in this context between the non-renewal of a trade agreement and the asphyxiation of a state.[30] As long as alternatives exist for the state only the latter extreme result is an illegal intervention.

The legal effects of such a request for arrest are exemplified in the European Convention on Extradition of 1957 which is of interest in the current context as it is in effect for Belgium since November 1997 with respect to the other contracting parties. Article 16(1) reads: 'In case of urgency the competent authorities of the requesting Party may request the provisional arrest of the person sought. The competent authorities of the requested party shall decide the matter in accordance with its law.' The Explanatory Memorandum on this paragraph reads: 'Paragraph 1 permits the requesting Party to request provisional arrest and it is for the requested Party alone to decide on this request'.

With regard to international arrest warrants, it is considered that any extraterritorial effects deriving from their execution is due not to any mandatory character of the warrant, but to the existence of a new source of obligation either under the municipal law of the responding state or under international law. [31] Whether or not the crime is one of universal jurisdiction is not relevant in this regard. It is also understood, that the requesting Party is the sole judge of the 'urgency' justifying the request for provisional arrest. It seems clear that a request for provisional arrest leaves the requested state to apply its own law, use its own forces for the execution of the warrant, and can in no way be seen as a form of exercise of jurisdiction to enforce by the requesting state. Nor is it a form of interference against the personality of the state or a threat to the development of a state's political, economic and cultural systems.[32]

To the extent that this issue has been addressed in the doctrine the answer seems clear. According to Rafaëlle Maison even where the suspect is not on the territory of the state concerned, judges may often have to start to look for a suspect abroad and such action could not be prohibited by a rule of international law. Most of the time it will be carried out in the context of international

April 1981 to Nicaragua from the United States, the 90% reduction in the sugar quota for United States imports from Nicaragua in 1981, and the trade embargo adopted on May 1985. The Court rejected the argument that cumulatively these actions resulted in a systematic violation of the principle of non-intervention (at paras 244 and 245). Of course the Court was not concerned with whether any of these actions might have violated treaty obligations under economic instruments. The focus was on the question of intervention and the facts of the case: 'At this point, the Court has merely to say that it is unable to regard such action on the economic plane as is here complained of as a breach of the customary-law principle of non-intervention' (para 245).

[30] P Cahier, *Changements et Continuité du Droit International*, vol 195 *RCADI* (Nijhoff, Dordrecht, 1992), 41.

[31] Under the heading 'Mandat d'arrêt dit international', Huet quotes from a French decision '"si donc un mandat d'arrêt est mis à exécution hors des frontières, ce ne peut être en vertu de sa propre force exécutoire, mais d'une autre force qui procède d'une véritable novation, et qui n'entraîne pas mis en application, dès ce moment, des dispositions du Code de procédure pénale"; cette solution découle de Crim., 29 juin 1967, JCP, 1967, II, 1532'. A Huet, *Droit pénal international* (PUF, Paris, 1994), 405.

[32] See Friendly Relations Declaration, cited above.

judicial co-operation treaties. Such action does not in any way imply a violation of the sovereignty of the state where the suspect is found. [33]

The judgement of the Court seems to interpret sovereignty as, not only encompassing the rights and duties of states under international law, but also assuming that one of the duties international law places on states is a duty to respect the dignity of other states. The judgement seems to respond to the plaintiff state's complaint that there had been an attack on the dignity of the state[34] ('a serious insult to the honour of the Democratic Republic of Congo'[35]). The judgement assumes that there is another duty on states not to hinder the ability of other states to carry out activity in the field of international relations. Claims that there were competing values to be taken into consideration, such as the struggle to prevent and punish attacks on individual human dignity, were not given any priority or recognition by the Court.

In the end the debate turns on what one chooses to understand by the term sovereignty and who should be protected. New understandings of sovereignty are emerging which may in the end reverse the priority currently accorded to the rights of the state to respect over the claims of human beings to their rights to be treated with dignity. The recent report of the International Commission on Intervention and State Sovereignty has discerned shifting meanings in this context. They propose that sovereignty be considered as responsibility:

> Thinking of sovereignty as responsibility, in a way that is being increasingly recognised in state practice, has a threefold significance. First, it implies that the state authorities are responsible for the functions of protecting the safety and lives of citizens and promotion of their welfare. Secondly, it suggests that the national political authorities are responsible to the citizens internally and to the international community through the UN. And thirdly, it means that the agents of state are responsible for their actions; that is to say, they are accountable for their acts of commission and

[33] 'En ce qui concerne l'instruction, le juge peut affirmer sa compétence pour mener des enquêtes en l'absence de l'arrestation du suspect, en l'absence même d'indices de sa présence sur le territoire national. Les "recherches" à l'étranger ne sont pas non plus exclues dans la mesure où elles sont le plus souvent effectuées dans le cadre d'une coopération répressive dont les moyens sont définis par des Conventions internationales: *elles n'impliquent en aucune manière la violation de la souveraineté de l'Etat sur le territoire duquel se trouve le suspect*. Toutefois, si on l'admet la valeur normative supérieure de certains obligations posées par le droit international humanitaire, il serait possible de déroger aux normes de coopération classiques.' R Maison, 'Les premiers cas d'application des dispositions pénales des conventions de Genève par les juridictions internes', (1995), vol 6 *European Journal of International Law*, 260–73 at 271–2.

[34] See the separate opinion of Judge Bula-Bula, the ad hoc judge appointed by DRC at paras 24, 25 and 85 where he refers to 'La dignité du peuple congolais'. Compare the approach of Judge Van den Wyngaert, ad hoc judge appointed by Belgium at p. 19 of her dissenting opinion: 'In blaming Belgium for investigating and prosecuting allegations of international crimes that it was obliged to investigate and prosecute itself, the Congo acts in bad faith. It pretends to be offended and morally injured by Belgium by suggesting that Belgium's exercise of "excessive universal jurisdiction" (Judgment, para 42) was incompatible with its dignity. However, as Sir Hersch Lauterpacht observed in 1951, "the dignity of a foreign state may suffer more from an appeal to immunity than from a denial of it".' [Footnote 88 in original reads: 'H. Lauterpacht, "The Problem of Jurisdictional Immunities of Foreign States", *BYBIL*, 1951, 232.']

[35] Oral pleadings, Prof. Rigaux, CR 2001/6, 16 Oct 2001, at 19.

> omission. The case for thinking of sovereignty in these terms is strengthened by the ever-increasing impact of international human rights norms, and the increasing impact in international discourse of the concept of human security. (ICISS 2001, p 12)

UN Secretary-General Kofi Annan has presented the issue more prescriptively: 'National sovereignty offers vital protection to small and weak States, but it should not be a shield for crimes against humanity.'[36]

By way of interim conclusion, the rule that there should be no interference in state sovereignty simply begs the question: what are the rights and duties associated with sovereignty? The majority of the judges in the *DRC v Belgium* case have assumed that the international rules which have protected the dignity of states have not been supplanted by international developments designed to protect the dignity and worth of the human person.

Turning to the second element of sovereignty mentioned above, that related to the sovereign state immunity of states for official acts committed by individuals, we can first of all distinguish this rule of functional immunity, or immunity *ratione materiae*, from personal immunity or immunity *ratione personae*. Functional immunity stems from the sovereignty principle outlined above.

Functional Immunity of State Officials

States enjoy sovereign state immunity before the courts of other states for official acts committed by individuals. This is a principle which stems from the concept of sovereignty. According to Antonio Cassese, sovereignty grants each state a set of powers relating to its jurisdiction; sovereignty also protects states from inadmissible intervention by other states in their internal affairs, and it gives rise to the rule that individuals representing the state in their official capacity create obligations for the state and are not usually held individually accountable (an assumed exception being where international crimes are at issue).[37] Sovereignty suggests that one state cannot judge another state for acts performed in its 'sovereign capacity'. As already stated, Cassese has been careful to state that there is an exception to this rule with regard to 'international crimes'. He has stated clearly that there is no immunity for state officials from the civil or criminal jurisdiction of foreign states for international crimes (including crimes against humanity and war crimes).[38] For many lawyers such

[36] Secretary-General Statement to the General Assembly on the presentation of the Millennium Report, New York, 3 Apr 2000, SG/SM/7343, GA/9705. See also Kofi Annan, 'Two concepts of sovereignty', *Economist,* 18 Sept 1999, and 'The legitimacy to intervene: International action to uphold human rights requires a new understanding of state and individual sovereignty', *Financial Times,* 10 Jan 2000. The SG is addressing the issue of 'intervention to protect civilians from wholesale slaughter' and is aware that he is suggesting a paradigm shift in thinking about sovereignty: 'Any such evolution in our understanding of state sovereignty and individual sovereignty will, in some quarters, be met with distrust, scepticism, even hostility. But it is an evolution we should welcome.' *Financial Times ibid.*

[37] Cassese, *International Law in a Divided World*, 130.

[38] Cassese, *International Law,* 90, 246.

crimes can hardly be 'official' acts under international law. The relevant working group of the International Law Commission put the point as follows:

> Although the judgement of the House of Lords in that case [Pinochet] only holds that a former head of State is not entitled to immunity in respect of acts of torture committed in his own State and expressly states that it does not affect the correctness of decisions upholding the plea of sovereign immunity in respect of civil claims, as it was concerned with a criminal prosecution, there can be no doubt that this case, and the widespread publicity it received, has generated support for the view that State officials should not be entitled to plead immunity for acts of torture committed in their own territories in both civil and criminal actions.[39]

After a careful review of provisions in recent instruments for the prosecution of international crimes, Zappalà concludes that these provisions 'are generally considered to have confirmed the existence, under customary international law, of an exception to functional immunity for those state officials who may be responsible for international crimes'.[40] The evidence which points to such a conclusion is recalled in the *DRC v Belgium* case in the separate opinion of Judges Higgins, Kooijmans and Buergenthal (at para 82). The joint separate opinion refers to the arguments developed by Bianchi that legal interpretation demands that we aim to achieve the values the legal system is supposed to be protecting.[41] There is no particular reason to suppose that the Court has refined or altered this understanding of the functional immunity rule. The actual judgment of the Court is confined to the absolute immunity of only one type of official: foreign ministers in office. The judgment does however allude to an exception to this immunity rule simply stating that a *former* foreign minister may be tried in the courts of another state for 'acts committed during that period of office in a private capacity' (at para 61). There is no explanation as to what sort of crimes are committed in a 'private capacity' but it seems unlikely that the Court wants to protect those accused of the most serious crimes under international law. It would be odd if a former minister could be tried for something clearly private, such as shop-lifting during an official visit, but not tried for war crimes involving grave breaches of the Geneva Conventions. It is worth recalling a statement of the ILC from 1996:

> It would be paradoxical to allow the individuals who are, in some respects, the most responsible for the crimes committed covered by the Code [of Crimes against the Peace

[39] Report of the work of the ILC, UN Doc A./54/10, 1999, report of the Working Group on Jurisdictional Immunities of States and their Property, appendix to the Report of the Working Group, at para 12. 'The Working Group was composed as follows: Mr G Hafner (Chairman), Mr C Yamada (Rapporteur), Mr H Al-Baharna, Mr I Brownlie, Mr E Candioti, Mr J Crawford, Mr C Dugard, Mr N Elaraby, Mr G Gaja, Mr Q He, Mr M Kamto, Mr I Lukashuk, Mr T Melescanu, Mr P Rao, Mr B Sepúlveda, Mr P Tomka and Mr R Rosenstock (ex officio)'.

[40] A Zappalà, 'Do Heads of State in Office Enjoy Immunity from Jurisdiction for International Crimes? The *Ghaddafi* Case Before the French *Cour de Cassation*', (2001), 12 *European Journal of International Law*, 595–612 at 604.

[41] A Bianchi, 'Denying State Immunity to Violators of Human Rights', (1994), 46 *Austrian Journal of Public International Law* 195–229.

> and Security of Mankind] to invoke the sovereignty of the State and to hide behind the immunity that is conferred on them by virtue of their positions particularly since these heinous crimes shock the conscience of mankind, violate some of the most fundamental rules of international law and threaten international peace and security.[42]

Furthermore, the sovereign state immunity rule has been said to apply when proceedings before a court have been instituted 'against one of the representatives of that State in respect of an act performed in his capacity as a representative'.[43] This is quite restrictive as the individual must have been acting as a representative.[44] No similar provision appears in the European Convention on State Immunity, and the final report of the International Law Association on state immunity is clear that the proposed draft Convention:

> is not intended to cover individuals, because the reasons underlying the concept of state immunity do not apply. Court action against an individual (who would then be liable with his personal estate only) does not implicate sovereignty or sovereign equality. The formal approach as applied in the distinction between diplomatic and consular immunity and state immunity is to be applied generally, ie the problem of state immunity arises only if a state is named as a party to a suit. (ILA 1994: p 466).

IMMUNITY

Sovereignty was at the heart of the arguments before the Court. But the judgment focuses in on the derivative concept of personal immunity of foreign ministers. In

[42] ILC Commentary to the Draft Code of Crimes Against the Peace and Security of Mankind, adopted by the ILC in 1996, A/48/10, commentary to Art 7 at para (1).

[43] Draft Art 7(3) in the International Law Commission's draft articles on jurisdictional immunities of States and their property, text adopted by the Commission on first reading, *Yearbook of the ILC* (1986), Volume II Part Two: 'In particular, a proceeding before a court of a State shall be considered to have been instituted against another State when the proceeding is instituted against one of the organs of that State, or against one of its political subdivisions or agencies or instrumentalities in respect of an act performed in the exercise of sovereign authority, or against one of the representatives of that State in respect of an act performed in his capacity as a representative, or when the proceeding is designed to deprive that other State of its property or of the use of property in its possession or control.' (at 9). See also the European Convention on State Immunity, Art 27: '1. For the purposes of the present Convention, the expression "Contracting State" shall not include any legal entity of a Contracting State which is distinct therefrom and is capable of suing or being sued, even if that entity has been entrusted with public functions. 2. Proceedings may be instituted against any entity referred to in paragraph 1 before the courts of another Contracting State in the same manner as against a private person; however, the courts may not entertain proceedings in respect of acts performed by the entity in the exercise of sovereign authority *(acta jure imperii)*. 3. Proceedings may in any event be instituted against any such entity before those courts if, in corresponding circumstances, the courts would have had jurisdiction if the proceedings had been instituted against a Contracting State.' The implication in the Convention is that individual immunity should be dealt with through the law of diplomatic immunity see Art 32. In the ILC commentary to draft Art 7(3), immunity *ratione personae* is discussed with regard to personal sovereigns, ambassadors and diplomatic agents (at 105).

[44] In the ILC Commentary to draft Art 3 in addition to head of state the commentary mentions: heads of government, heads of ministerial departments, ambassadors, heads of mission, diplomatic agents and consular officers, acting in their official capacities. *Ibid* at 14.

the actual judgment of 14 February 2002 the Court held, by 13 votes to three, that issuing the arrest warrant, and its international circulation, constituted violations of a legal obligation by Belgium in that these acts failed to respect the immunity and inviolability of the incumbent Minister of Foreign Affairs.

Foreign Ministerial Immunity

The Court's judgment does not focus on the general rules on functional immunity derived from state sovereignty, discussed above, but rather on what could be termed: an almost absolute personal immunity from the actions of foreign states for foreign ministers during their period in office. The Court stressed that the immunities accorded to foreign ministers were for the effective performance of their functions. It recalled the powers of a foreign minister under the law of treaties, and it stressed the fact that such a minister is recognised in customary international law as the representative of the state without the need for any recognition by other states through letters of credence. From this the Court deduces an absolute immunity for foreign ministers in office, although the judgment fails to offer any obvious evidence of the familiar requirements of state practice or *opinio juris* to confirm the existence of such a rule in contemporary international law. Three aspects of the various arguments put before the Court deserve a brief mention here.

Personal Immunity in the Face of Accusations of International Crimes

First, the judgment did not accept the argument that this presumption of immunity had to give way where the foreign minister is accused of international crimes. The Court held there was absolute immunity before foreign courts while the minister held office. The Court stated that it had:

> carefully examined State practice including national legislation and those few decisions of national Higher Courts, such as the House of Lords or the French Court of Cassation. It has been unable to deduce from this practice that there exists under customary international law any form of exception to the rule according immunity from criminal jurisdiction and inviolability to incumbent Ministers for Foreign Affairs, where they are suspected of having committed war crimes or crimes against humanity. (para 58)

The decisions which the Court alluded to were not concerned with incumbent Ministers of Foreign Affairs. In one sense then it is not surprising that they did not therefore supply the evidence for the customary rule. Nevertheless, the reasoning in those decisions can in fact be read as suggesting that the national judges in these cases did indeed think there was a rule of customary international law that would oblige them to ignore a claim of ministerial personal immunity when faced with a case concerning international crimes, such as torture, war crimes or crimes against humanity.

In the *Pinochet* case the national legislation covered sovereign or other heads of state as well as former heads of state by analogy with former ambassadors. The issue of foreign ministers was not addressed. On the other hand, considerable attention was paid to the internationalization of the crime of torture and crimes against humanity in order to determine that: certain international crimes could not be considered part of the functions of a head of state for the purposes of functional immunity of former heads of state.[45] To the extent that an incumbent head of state was considered to enjoy immunity this was primarily due to judicial recognition of the existence of clear national legislation in this regard rather than any detailed examination of the customary international law on this point.[46]

In the *Qaddafi* case, had absolute immunity been perceived to attach to a head of state, the Cour de Cassation would presumably have been free to simply dismiss the case on those grounds. However the reasoning was otherwise. The Cour de Cassation dismissed the case on the grounds that the crime of terrorism was not yet part of the customary international law exceptions to immunity ('alors qu'en l'état du droit international, le crime dénoncé, quelle qu'en soit la gravité, ne relève pas des exceptions au principe de l'immunité de juridiction des chefs d'Etat étrangers en exercise'[47]). The implication is that were Colonel Qaddafi to have been charged with a customary international law crime, then the claimed immunity may have been inapplicable, as, according to that Court, there are exceptions to the immunity of incumbent heads of state.

The Court dismisses these two cases as providing no evidence for the purposes of customary international law; but the Court itself provides us with no evidence of the customary international law rule of absolute immunity for foreign ministers. Given that both the cases referred to leave open the question whether any such rule of immunity may give way in the face of allegations of international crimes it would have been more satisfactory if the Court offered some alternative decisions which clearly recognised the absolute nature of this personal immunity rule as divined by the Court.

[45] *R v Bow Street Metropolitan Stipendiary Magistrate and Others, ex parte Pinochet Ugarte (No 3)* [1999] 2 All ER 97 (hereinafter *Pinochet No 3*).

[46] In the present context it is worth quoting part of a speech by Professor Christopher Greenwood, instructed by the Crown Prosecution Service for the Commissioner of Police and the government of Spain, in the *Pinochet No 3* hearing in the House of Lords: 'If I can distinguish between two different points there, at the previous hearings we accepted that under the State Immunity Act, as a matter of United Kingdom law a serving head of state would be able to invoke immunity, but as a matter of international law our submission has always been that there is no immunity in respect of torture and other crimes against humanity. That is why I took your Lordships yesterday to the various passages in Sir Arthur Watts' lectures in which he is referring to the lack of immunity as a serving head of state. He is talking about the position in international law.' R Brody and M Ratner (eds), *The Pinochet Papers: The Case of Augusto Pinochet in Spain and Britain* (Kluwer Law International, The Hague, 2000), 226. See also N Rodley, 'Introduction—the Beginning of the End of Immunity and Impunity of Officials Responsible for Torture' in Brody and Ratner, *The Pinochet Papers*, 3–6, where a distinction is suggested between a head of state who 'represents the dignity and authority of the state' and head of government immunity 'which probably falls under the general theory applicable to all public officials'.

[47] Arrêt, 21 Mar 2001, Cour de Cassation, Chambre Criminelle, on file with the author.

No Distinction Between Official Visits and Private Visits

Secondly, Belgium had sought to draw a distinction between official visits and private visits by a foreign minister.[48] This was a concession to the importance of ministerial effectiveness, and the arrest warrant had in fact been drafted so as to preclude arrest during an official visit to Belgium. This distinction between private and official visits was rejected by the Court.[49] The Court was primarily concerned that arrest on a criminal charge would prevent a minister from exercising the functions of that office (para 55). The Court therefore considered that the mere issuance of the arrest warrant, 'intended to enable the arrest' (para 70), breached the inviolability of the person of the foreign minister under international law. We should recall that this ruling was addressed to the particular case of a foreign minister in office. There is no reason to believe that a lower level official would enjoy such a personal immunity. Such an official would be covered by a functional immunity but the scope of this immunity will be limited to representational acts of the state.[50]

Violation of Ministerial Inviolability even in the Absence of an Arrest

Thirdly, according to the judgment, this rule protects the Minister even in the absence of any harassment, request for extradition, actual arrest or judicial proceedings. Belgium had argued that the warrant represented a request to other states and could not be considered coercive with regards to the DRC or violative of the person of the foreign minister. But the Court considered: 'even the mere risk that, by travelling to or transiting another State a Minister for Foreign Affairs might be exposing himself or herself to legal proceedings could deter the Minister from travelling internationally when required to do so for the purposes of the performance of his or her official functions' (para 55). The judgment states the circulation of the warrant violated the obligations owed to

[48] Professor Cahier had suggested a functional immunity with regard to missions abroad in the context of discussions, negotiations, and international meetings, but no such immunity for trips for pleasure: P Cahier, *Le droit diplomatique contemporain* (Publications de l'IUHEI—n° 40, Geneva/Paris, 1962) at 359–60. 'Il semble donc que, lorsqu'il se rend à l'étranger pour accomplir une mission, ce qui exclut tout traitement privilégié lorsqu'il s'y rend en voyage d'agrément, le ministre doit jouir en tout premier lieu de l'inviolabilité, ce qui le met à l'abri de toute mesure de contrainte de la part des autorités locales.' See also J Salmon, *Manuel de droit diplomatique* (Bruylant, Brussels, 1994), 539–41.

[49] The joint separate opinion by Higgins, Kooijmans and Buergenthal seems to suggest that immunities on a private visit are limited to immunity from arrest (warrant) and detention (at para 84). This would allow for a civil suit or seizure of assets but again applying the broad brush approach of the Court such action could also be interpreted as an impediment to official functions.

[50] The Draft Articles on Jurisdictional Immunities of States and their Property, as annexed to the report of the Ad Hoc Committee on Jurisdictional Immunities of States and their Property on 13 Feb 2002, UN Doc A/57/22, includes within the definition of state 'representatives of the State acting in that capacity' (Art 2(1)(b)(iv)). Note the articles are stated to be without prejudice to the immunities enjoyed by a state under international law in relation to the exercise of the functions of 'Its diplomatic missions, consular posts, special missions, missions to international organizations or delegations to organs of international organizations or to international conferences ... and persons connected with them' (Art 3 (1)).

the Congo concerning the immunity and inviolability of their foreign minister (paras 70–1). The judgment noted that the Minister had had to change travel plans for fear of possible arrest. This finding with regard to the circulation of the warrant is consistent with the Court's insistence on protecting the overall goal of foreign ministerial effectiveness by concentrating on a chilling effect which generated a legal effect. Judge Oda's dissent saw the legal effect of the warrant quite differently:

> It bears stressing that the issuance of an arrest warrant by one State and the international circulation of the warrant through Interpol have no legal impact unless the arrest request is validated by the receiving State. The Congo appears to have failed to grasp that the mere issuance and international circulation of an arrest warrant have little significance. There is even some doubt whether the Court itself properly understood this, particularly as regards a warrant's legal effect. The crucial point in this regard is *not* the issuance or international circulation of an arrest warrant but the response of the State receiving it. (para 13)

Once the Court had decided that international law protects an incumbent foreign minister from any threat of arrest, because such a rule is essential for international relations, there was no room for argument either about exceptions to this rule or the legal status of the warrant. The Court in the end found, by 13 votes to three, that the issue of the

> arrest warrant and its international circulation, constituted violations of a legal obligation of the Kingdom of Belgium towards the Democratic Republic of Congo, that they failed to respect the immunity from criminal jurisdiction and the inviolability which the incumbent Minister for Foreign Affairs of the Democratic Republic of Congo enjoyed under international law.[51]

Nevertheless, in an echo of the arguments put by the Congo, the Court stressed that it was drawing a distinction between immunity and impunity (para 60). It offered four instances where the immunity it insisted on would not be a bar to criminal prosecutions:

> First, such persons enjoy no criminal immunity under international law in their own countries, and may thus be tried by those countries' courts in accordance with the relevant rules of domestic law.
>
> Secondly, they will cease to enjoy immunity from foreign jurisdiction if the State which they represent or have represented decides to waive that immunity.
>
> Thirdly, after a person ceases to hold the office of Minister for Foreign Affairs, he or she will no longer enjoy all of the immunities accorded by international law in other States. Provided that it has jurisdiction under international law, a court of one State may try a former Minister for Foreign Affairs of another State in respect of acts committed prior or subsequent to his or her period of office, as well as in respect of acts committed during that period of office in a private capacity.

[51] At para 78(2) of the Judgment.

> Fourthly, an incumbent or former Minister for Foreign Affairs may be subject to criminal proceedings before certain international criminal courts, where they have jurisdiction.... (para 60)

The third of these examples raises a number of questions, to which we now turn.

The Immunity of Former Ambassadors and Former Foreign Ministers

The Vienna Convention on Diplomatic Relations (1961) states in its Article 31(1) that: 'A diplomatic agent shall enjoy immunity from the criminal jurisdiction of the receiving State.' This can be considered a rule of customary international law. This immunity continues only until the person leaves the country, unless the complaint relates to 'acts performed by such a person in the exercise of his functions as a member of the mission', in which case immunity continues to exist under the Convention (Article 39(2)). Until the Court's judgment assimilated foreign ministers to heads of state there was little suggestion in this treaty that foreign ministers enjoyed absolute personal immunity akin to that of diplomatic agents under the Convention, who are defined as follows: 'head of the mission or a member of the diplomatic staff of the mission'.

The Question of Immunity in Other Relevant Treaties

Following the completion of this Convention, the International Law Commission started work on a Convention on Special Missions to complement the Convention on Diplomatic Relations. There was a realisation that ad hoc special diplomatic missions fell outside the scope of the Diplomatic Relations Convention and a new Convention was eventually adopted in 1969 to ensure the proper functioning of such missions. The preamble is telling: '*Realizing* that the purpose of privileges and immunities relating to special missions is not to benefit individuals but to ensure the efficient performance of the functions of special missions as missions representing the State.' During such a special mission the members 'benefit from the ordinary principles based upon sovereign immunity'.[52]

Although neither Belgium nor the Democratic Republic of Congo are parties to the Convention on Special Missions (1969) it is worth mentioning a few of the Articles as they illustrate the extent of diplomatic immunity in this special context. The Convention draws a distinction between heads of the sending state and other participants in the special mission. The head of state is to enjoy in the receiving state or a third state all the facilities, privileges and immunities accorded by international law to heads of state on an official visit. Similarly:

> The Head of Government, the Minister of Foreign Affairs and other persons of high rank, when they take part in a special mission of the sending State, shall enjoy in the receiving State or in a third State, in addition to what is granted by the present

[52] I Brownlie, *Principles of Public International Law*, 5th edn (Oxford University Press, Oxford, 1998), 367.

> Convention, the facilities, privileges and immunities accorded by international law. (Article 21(2))

The suggestion is that international law grants immunities to foreign ministers, but a well known manual on diplomatic law in its commentary on this Article simply states:

> However, it cannot be regarded as at all certain what, if any, additional privileges and immunities are required by international law to be given to visiting heads of government or ministers. Some states may equate a head of government with a head of state, *but ministers have never been regarded under customary law as entitled to any sovereign immunities*.[53] [emphasis added]

Turning to the exact immunities contained in the Convention, the immunity from arrest and criminal jurisdiction is clear:

> The persons of the representatives of the sending State in the special mission and of the members of its diplomatic staff shall be inviolable. They shall not be liable to any form of arrest or detention. The receiving State shall treat them with due respect and shall take all appropriate steps to prevent any attack on their persons, freedom or dignity. (Article 29)

With regard to immunity from criminal jurisdiction the rule is just as unambiguous: 'The representatives of the sending State in the special mission and the members of its diplomatic staff shall enjoy immunity from the criminal jurisdiction of the receiving State' (Article 31(1)). The Article which covers former members of the mission is instructive as it is clear that the only immunity which remains is for: 'acts performed by such a member in the exercise of his functions'.[54]

The Court chose not to discuss the implications of this inapplicable Convention and dealt with the issue as they felt it was determined under customary international law.

It is interesting at this point to consider a number of texts concerning one of the latest human rights violations to be criminalised at the international level. In the draft International Convention on the Protection of All Persons from Forced Disappearance, submitted to the UN Human Rights Commission by the Sub-Commission on the Promotion and Protection of Human Rights, Article 10(2) states that 'No privileges, immunities or special exemptions shall be granted in such trials, subject to the provisions of the Vienna Convention on Diplomatic Relations.'[55] This draft Convention does not presently grant any immunity for

[53] Lord Gore-Booth (ed), *Satow's Guide to Diplomatic Practice,* 5th edn, (Longman, London, 1979) at 159.

[54] 'When the functions of a member of the special mission have come to an end, his privileges and immunities shall normally cease at the moment when he leaves the territory of the receiving State, or on the expiry of a reasonable period in which to do so, but shall subsist until that time, even in case of armed conflict. However, in respect of acts performed by such a member in the exercise of his functions, immunity shall continue to exist.' Art 43(3).

[55] UN Doc E/CN.4/Sub.2/1998/19, 19 Aug 1998, Annex.

foreign ministers or heads of government. The text is modelled on the UN Declaration on the Protection of All Persons from Enforced Disappearance, adopted by the UN General Assembly in 1992 and the Inter-American Convention on Forced Disappearance of Persons (1994), which has been in force since 1996.[56] It would seem that, on an ordinary reading of a text such as the Inter-American Convention, at least the states parties to this treaty have contracted out of any foreign ministerial immunity that might have existed between the relevant states. It can also be argued that, taken together with the UN General Assembly Resolution the texts suggest that, in the context of an international crime such as forced disappearance, states do not consider there is a customary international law obligation to grant immunity to officials other than those protected by the Vienna Convention on Diplomatic Relations.

In the pleadings before the ICJ the Congo argued that states could contract out of their duties to grant immunities to officials such as foreign ministers. They put the point clearly:

> It is quite obvious that there is no violation of immunity from suit when the State represented agrees to waive immunity. Immunity may be waived on the occasion of a specific criminal prosecution. It may also be excluded in advance, under the express terms of a treaty.[57]

The Issue of Jus Cogens

The admission by the Congo that states can contract out of any customary international law on ministerial immunity suggests a brief consideration of the relevance of *jus cogens*. The definition of a peremptory (*jus cogens*) norm is that 'it is recognised by the international community of States as a whole as a norm from which no derogation is permitted and which can be modified only by a subsequent norm of general international law having the same character.'[58] It follows that if the rule on immunities can be derogated from it is not a *jus cogens* norm.[59] No immunities are mentioned as examples of *jus cogens* norms

[56] OAS Treaty, A 60, entered into force 28 Mar 1996. Art IX of the Inter-American Convention reads: 'Privileges, immunities, or special dispensations shall not be admitted in such trials, without prejudice to the provisions set forth in the Vienna Convention on Diplomatic Relations.' Art 16 (3) of the UN Declaration reads: 'No privileges, immunities or special exemptions shall be admitted in such trials, without prejudice to the provisions contained in the Vienna Convention on Diplomatic Relations.'

[57] Mr D'Argent, CR 2001/5, 15 Oct 2001, at 22–23, uncorrected verbatim record.

[58] Art 53, Vienna Convention on the Law of Treaties (1969).

[59] The dissenting opinion of Judges Rozakis and Caflisch joined by Judges Wildhaber, Costa, Cabral Barreto and Vajić in the European Court of Human Rights in the *Al-Adsani v United Kingdom* judgment (21 Nov 2001) is unambiguous on the understanding that state immunity is not a *jus cogens* norm: 'The Court's majority do not seem, on the other hand, to deny that the rules on State immunity, customary or conventional, do not belong to the category of *jus cogens*; and rightly so, because it is clear that the rules of State immunity, deriving from both customary and conventional international law, have never been considered by the international community as rules with a hierarchically higher status. It is common knowledge that, in many instances, States have, through their own initiative, waived their rights of immunity; that in many instances they have contracted

by the International Law Commission in their recent commentary to their articles on state responsibility. In fact the reference in the draft articles to the injunction that counter-measures must respect the inviolability of diplomatic agents was moved out of the paragraph dealing with various *jus cogens* obligations (Article 50(1)) and distanced from them in a second paragraph. It was considered 'awkward to include in the list of prohibited countermeasures some obligations which were and others which were clearly not peremptory in character. Among the latter was (c) [now 50(2)(b)], since rules of diplomatic and consular inviolability can be set aside entirely in the relations between a sending and receiving State by consent.'[60]

The same articles include an article entitled 'compliance with peremptory norms'. In this context the ILC has sought to explain the consequences of pitting a peremptory norm against a non-peremptory norm. The Commentary states:

> Where there is an apparent conflict between primary obligations, one of which arises for a State directly under a peremptory norm of general international law, it is evident that such an obligation must prevail. The processes of interpretation and application should resolve such questions without any need to resort to the secondary rules of State responsibility. In theory one might envisage a conflict arising on a subsequent occasion between a treaty obligation, apparently lawful on its face and innocent in its purpose, and a peremptory norm. If such a case were to arise it would be too much to invalidate the treaty as a whole merely because its application in the given case was not foreseen. But in practice such situations seem not to have occurred. Even if they were to arise, peremptory norms of general international law generate strong interpretative principles which will resolve all or most apparent conflicts.[61]

In its commentary on the same article the ILC states: 'Those peremptory norms that are clearly accepted and recognised include the prohibitions of aggression,

out of them, or have renounced them. These instances clearly demonstrate that the rules on State immunity do not enjoy a higher status, since *jus cogens* rules, protecting as they do the "*ordre public*", ie the basic values of the international community, cannot be subject to unilateral or contractual forms of derogation from their imperative contents.' (at para 2).

[60] J Crawford, *The International Law Commission's Articles on State Responsibility: Introduction, Text and Commentaries* (Cambridge University Press, Cambridge, 2002), 50. The UKs International Criminal Court Act 2001 provides in s 23(1) 'Any state or diplomatic immunity attaching to a person by reason of a connection with a state party to the ICC Statute does not prevent proceedings under this part in relation to that person.' The logic would seem to be that states have waived all immunities regarding arrest and delivery of persons to the ICC on becoming a party to the ICC Statute. State or diplomatic immunity includes inter alia 'any rule of law derived from customary international law', s 23(6)(c). The Explanatory Notes to the Act deal with Arts 27 and 98(1) of the ICC Statute: 'These Articles mean that a State party to the ICC Statute, in accepting Article 27, has already agreed that the immunity of its representatives, officials or agents, including its Head of State, will not prevent the trial of such persons before the ICC, nor their arrest and surrender to the ICC. But non-States Parties have not accepted this provision and so the immunity of their representatives would remain intact unless an express waiver were given by the non-State Party concerned to the ICC.' (para 46). Note that the Secretary of State may after consultation with the ICC and the state concerned direct that proceedings for arrest or delivery not be taken (s 23(4)).

[61] Commentary to Art 26 at para 3 (footnote omitted). Report of the ILC, GAOR, Supp. No 10 (A/56/10) at. 207.

genocide, slavery, racial discrimination, crimes against humanity and torture, and the right to self-determination.'[62] This authoritative statement that the prohibition on crimes against humanity is a peremptory norm, and the positioning of the inviolability of diplomatic agents outside the context of peremptory norms,[63] suggests we are in the presence of a hierarchy of norms and that the resolution of any competing obligations should take into consideration such a hierarchy.[64]

The Immunities of Former Foreign Ministers

The issue which has to be addressed now is what the Court meant when it said a former foreign minister would not enjoy immunity in a foreign court (with jurisdiction) for acts committed during the period in office in their 'private capacity' (at para 60, quoted above). This type of immunity was addressed at length in the *Pinochet* litigation and speeches in the final House of Lords judgment turn on findings that, if international law has criminalised behaviour it is unlikely, to say the least, that international law meant to protect that same behaviour through an immunity describing such behaviour as an official act. The fact that in that case the crimes (torture) were described as *jus cogens* crimes was clearly influential. Some passages bear reproduction here as they reveal the influence of international legal logic.

In introducing the judgment of the House of Lords, Lord Browne-Wilkenson said:

> Although the reasoning varies in detail, the basic proposition common to all, save Lord Goff of Chively, is that torture is an international crime over which international law and the parties to the Torture Convention have given universal jurisdiction to all courts wherever the torture occurs. A former head of state cannot show that to commit an international crime is to perform a function which international law protects by giving immunity.[65]

Lord Hope discussed the point in some detail:

> The principle of immunity ratione materiae protects all acts which the head of state has performed in the exercise of the functions of government. The purpose for which they were performed protects these acts from any further analysis. There are only two

[62] *Ibid* at para 5, at. 208.

[63] See Crawford, above n 60, at 50).

[64] The dissenting opinion of Judge Rozakis *et al* in *Al-Adsani v United Kingdom* explains the effect of a *jus cogens* norm: 'For the basic characteristic of a *jus cogens* rule is that, as a source of law in the now vertical international legal system, it overrides any other rule which does not have the same status. In the event of a conflict between a *jus cogens* rule and any other rule of international law, the former prevails. The consequence of such prevalence is that the conflicting rule is null and void, or, in any event, does not produce legal effects which are in contradiction with the content of the peremptory rule.' (para 1).

[65] House of Lords, 24 Mar 1999, reproduced in Brody and Ratner, *The Pinochet Papers*, 253–4. The introductory speech is not reproduced in the *Pinochet No 3* law report.

> exceptions to this approach which customary international law has recognised. The first relates to criminal acts which the head of state did under the colour of his authority as head of state but which were in reality for his own pleasure or benefit. The examples which Lord Steyn gave [1998] 3 WLR 1456, 1506B-C of the head of state who kills his gardener in a fit of rage or who orders victims to be tortured so that he may observe them in agony seem to me plainly to fall into this category and, for this reason, to lie outside the scope of the immunity. The second relates to acts the prohibition of which has acquired the status under international law of jus cogens. This compels all states to refrain from such conduct under any circumstances and imposes an obligation erga omnes to punish such conduct.[66]

This passage is amongst the most well known concerning the judicial appreciation of the limits of immunity for those who enjoy immunity in office but only enjoy limited immunity when they leave office for acts committed in office.[67] The *Pinochet* judgment makes it clear that where there is a treaty between the forum state and the state which is claiming immunity, and that treaty foresees criminal proceedings against foreign officials, national courts will not necessarily feel obliged to grant such immunity. The inquiry becomes more difficult when we are in the presence of crimes, such as crimes against humanity, which are not covered in a treaty between the parties. Much will be written about what the ICJ could have meant by acts committed 'in a private capacity'. Because this issue was not part of the dispute it makes little legal sense to second guess here what the Court means.[68] More important is the increasing power of the argument that, if immunity is not a *jus cogens* norm, and the prohibition on committing crimes against humanity is such a *jus cogens* norm, then the presumption must be that there will be a heavy burden on any state claiming

[66] *Pinochet No 3.*

[67] The separate opinion of Higgins, Kooijmans and Buergenthal refers to evidence of state practice which underscores the view that 'serious international crimes cannot be regarded as official acts because they are neither normal State functions nor functions that a State alone can perform' (para 85). See also A Bianchi, 'Denying State Immunity to Violators of Human Rights',(1994), 46 *Austrian Journal of Public International Law* 195–229,expressly referred to in the separate opinion. See also the discussion of the *Letelier* case in CH Schreuer, *State Immunity: Some Recent Developments* (Cambridge University Press, Cambridge, 1988), 53. For a review of the practice concerning immunity and human rights violations amounting to international crimes see A Bianchi, 'Immunity Versus Human Rights: The Pinochet Case', (1999), 10 *European Journal of International Law* 237–77 at 260, presenting an argument which limits immunity in the face of international crimes based on the need for courts to interpret the law in accordance with the basic principles and goals of the relevant legal system.

[68] Cassese has examined this question and concluded that the Court should not have relied on any distinction between official and private acts, but rather, the judges should have followed the 'customary rule that removes functional immunity. National case law proves that a customary rule with such content does in fact exist. Many cases where state military officials were brought to trial before foreign courts demonstrate that state agents accused of *war crimes, crimes against humanity,* or *genocide* may not invoke before national courts, as a valid defence, their official capacity .... It would indeed be odd that a customary rule should have evolved only with regard to members of the military and not for all state agents who commit international crimes.' (footnotes and references omitted). 'When May Senior State Officials be Tried for International Crimes? Some Comments on *The Congo v Belgium* Case' (2002) 13 *European Journal of International Law* 853–75 at 870–71.

state immunity against another state seeking to prevent, investigate or punish crimes against humanity. International law recognises that the prohibition on crimes against humanity protects interests which are at the heart of modern international law. This recognition means that any other competing rules have to be given effect in a way that respects the primacy of the *jus cogens* rule.

UNIVERSAL JURISDICTION

The parties to the case asked the Court not to address the issue of universal jurisdiction. The judgment is, however, likely to be seen as having subjugated universal jurisdiction to immunity. It is also quite likely, based on what we can read in the separate and dissenting opinions, that many judges were heavily influenced in their approach to this case by their appreciation that this was an attempt to *assert universal jurisdiction over someone outside the territory*. The Court's President in his separate opinion focused on this issue. Judge Guillaume categorically asserted that the absence of an explicit clause in the 1949 Geneva Conventions obliging states to establish jurisdiction over grave breaches when the suspect is not on the territory meant that the Belgian judge had no jurisdiction to start the investigation 'in the eyes of international law'.

Again the issue here is one of perspective. From another point of view there is little state practice to suggest that starting an investigation for grave breaches of the Geneva Conventions when the suspect is not in the territory is a violation of international law. [69]This view is reflected in the separate opinion of Higgins, Kooijmans and Buergenthal when they state:

> If the underlying purpose of designating certain acts as international crimes is to authorise a wide jurisdiction to be asserted over persons committing them, there is no rule of international law (and certainly not the *aut dedere* principle) which makes illegal co-operative overt acts designed to secure their presence within a State wishing to exercise jurisdiction. (para 58)

The various separate opinions are likely to give rise to considerable confusion. It is important not to prise too many rules from these opinions. They are all predicated on what the judges saw as an important distinction between two different situations. The first is jurisdiction over persons outside the territory (a so-called 'classical assertion of universal jurisdiction'). The second is a situation concerning a 'State party in whose jurisdiction the alleged perpetrator of such offences is found', in that case the state 'shall prosecute him or extradite him'. This is

[69] For a discussion of cases in France where it was held that such prosecutions could not go ahead under French law, see Maison, (1995) 6 *EJIL* 260–73; B Stern, 'La compétence universelle en France: le cas des crimes commis en ex-Yougoslavie et au Rwanda', (1997) 40 *German Yearbook of International Law* 280–99 and B Stern, 'Universal jurisdiction over crimes against humanity under French law—grave breaches of the Geneva Conventions of 1949—genocide—torture—human rights violations in Bosnia and Rwanda [international decisions]', (1999), 93 *AJIL* 525–29.

termed 'obligatory territorial jurisdiction over persons, albeit in relation to acts committed elsewhere'. It is pointed out that 'By the loose use of language [this obligatory territorial jurisdiction] has come to be referred to as "universal jurisdiction"' (Higgins *et al* at para 41). So universal jurisdiction means different things to different people.[70] These separate opinions often seem particularly concerned with policy issues; there is concern about the risk of 'creating total judicial chaos' (Guillaume) and the 'promotion of good inter-state relations' (Higgins *et al* at para 59) when delineating the law of universal jurisdiction.

What we can know with regard to universal jurisdiction, classically asserted or loosely used, is that the issue of universal jurisdiction is not dealt with by the Court's judgement. It is the state practice adopted by states in the context of their co-operation with each other in the light of the various international criminal courts which is most likely to shape international law in this area. If we look more closely at what happened before the ICJ we can pull out some pointers as to the evolving scope of universal jurisdiction.

The complaint filed by the DRC against Belgium refers to the Statute of the International Criminal Court adopted in Rome in 1998 and suggests that this treaty can in no way legitimate the Belgian law which defines the jurisdiction of the Belgian courts over certain crimes committed abroad by non-nationals. The complaint goes on to cite Article 17 of the Statute to support the idea that not all states necessarily have jurisdiction under international law for the crimes in the Statute. Article 17(1) reads:

> Having regard to paragraph 10 of the Preamble and article 1, the Court shall determine that a case is inadmissible where:
>
> (a) The case is being investigated or prosecuted by a State which has jurisdiction over it, unless the State is unwilling or unable genuinely to carry out the investigation or prosecution; [71]

The DRC pointed to the phrase 'a State which has jurisdiction over it' to claim that this implies that there must be limits on state jurisdiction in this field. However, the drafting history reveals that this reference to jurisdiction is in the context of national authorities starting an investigation which precludes the International Criminal Court dealing with the case. There was a fear that a challenge to admissibility could come from a state which wanted to shield a defendant from international justice. Such a state could claim that it was investigating the case when in fact the courts of that state might have no jurisdiction over the case due to the inadequacy of the challenging state's internal law. According to John Holmes, the co-ordinator of the relevant texts during the drafting of the Statute:

[70] For an extensive discussion of the writing on this topic and the practice of states see Amnesty International, *Universal Jurisdiction: The duty of states to enact and implement legislation*, AI Index: IOR 53/003/2001.

[71] Para 10 of the Preamble reads: '*Emphasizing* that the International Criminal Court established under this Statute shall be complementary to national criminal jurisdictions'.

> The second new condition limited the possibility of challenge to a State "which has jurisdiction over a case". It was not enough that a State had instituted national proceedings, it must establish to the Court that it had jurisdiction in the case. This addition was intended to forestall situations where a State could challenge (and delay) the Court from proceeding with a case on the ground that it was investigating when in fact the investigation or prosecution was sure to fail because the State lacked jurisdiction even as far as its own courts were concerned. [72]

The Statute was concerned to limit the number of states that could challenge the jurisdiction of the new Court. Where a state has no legislation to try the case it would be wrong to allow that state to block an international trial of the same offence. The ICC Statute, rather than suggesting limits on state jurisdiction can be seen as actually seeking to compensate for situations where states may not have taken steps to adopt the appropriate legislation.

The real question which was, as stated above, in the minds of the judges of the ICJ, was whether universal jurisdiction actually demands the presence of the accused in the territory of the state exercising jurisdiction. Even where national legislation has limited the conduct of criminal investigations and trials to accused who are actually on the territory of the state, this may be a self-imposed limit on the way in which jurisdiction is exercised, rather than a response to any supposed rule of international law which prohibits the initiation of any criminal investigation jurisdiction over people not present in the state.

In France the *Code de procédure pénale* grants the French courts jurisdiction whenever an international convention grants jurisdiction to the French courts (Article 689).[73] According to Brigitte Stern the French courts could rely on this Article to consider the Geneva Conventions 'precisely the type of convention referred to by this article, as they provide for universal jurisdiction.'[74] So far the higher French courts have refused to allow this sort of incorporation of the Geneva Conventions due to the fact that the Conventions have been considered to be too general in their wording and because there was no specific legislation on the subject.[75] Should France adopt legislation similar to the Belgian legislation at the heart of the *DRC v Belgium* case then Article 689 of the French Code could operate to grant French courts universal jurisdiction over grave breaches of the Geneva Conventions whether or not the suspect is present on French territory.

[72] JT Holmes, 'The Principle of Complementarity', in Roy S Lee (ed), *The International Criminal Court: The Making of the Rome Statute* (Kluwer Law International, The Hague/London/Boston, 1999), 41–78 at 66.

[73] Art 689 : 'Les auteurs ou complices d'infractions commises hors du territoire de la République peuvent être poursuivis et jugés par les juridictions françaises soit lorsque, conformément aux dispositions du livre 1er du Code pénal ou d'un autre texte législatif, la loi française est applicable, soit lorsqu'une convention internationale donne compétence aux juridictions françaises pour connaître de l'infraction' (entered into force 1 March 1994).

[74] Stern, (1999), 93 *AJIL* 529, citing Art 49 of Convention I, Art 50 of Convention II, Article 129 of Convention III, and Art146 of Convention IV.

[75] Stern, (1997), 40 *German YIL* 294.

However, the suggestion that universal jurisdiction can only be exercised when the suspect is in the territory of the forum state needs to be examined more closely. States such as France may make it a condition that the suspect be on the territory for there to be prosecution and trial by the French courts with regard to certain international crimes.[76] The real question which was, as stated above, in the minds of judges, was whether the international rule on universal jurisdiction which allows for the prosecution of crimes under international law actually demands the territorial presence of the accused at the time an arrest warrant is issued—and not only at the time of the trial.

Although the higher French courts have chosen to make the legitimacy of all *actes d'instruction* dependent on presence on the territory,[77] it would be hard to extrapolate from these decisions concerning French law (and later decisions in Belgian law[78]) a general rule of international law that forbids states from starting an investigation while a suspect wanted for an international crime is not on the territory. The relevant authorities which start such an investigation in other countries may not be the judiciary; in fact the investigation and arrest may be in the hands of the prosecutor and the police. Any rule preventing the jurisdiction of the courts when the suspect is outside the territory would not translate to a situation where investigation was undertaken by non-judicial organs. There appears to be no evidence that there is a rule that the organs of the state can not start inquiries or make requests regarding a suspect who may eventually be extradited for trial to the requesting state. The detailed report by Amnesty International has highlighted the importance of such a wide jurisdiction:

> This broad type of universal jurisdiction [for international crimes] ensures that the courts of *any* state can act as effective agents for the international community. On the basis of such jurisdiction, a prosecutor or an investigating judge may commence an investigation when the exact whereabouts of a suspect are unknown, thus permitting the gathering of evidence, such as statements of victims and witnesses, while such evidence is fresh. The ability to exercise such jurisdiction will also enable prosecutors and investigating judges to file extradition requests directed to states where a suspect is located, but where the authorities are unable or unwilling to act, or to issue international arrest warrants.[79]

[76] See also International Law Association, *Final Report on the Exercise of Universal Jurisdiction in respect of Gross Human Rights Offences*, 2000, at 2: 'Under the principle of universal jurisdiction a state is entitled or even required to bring proceedings in respect of certain serious crimes, irrespective of the location of the crime, and irrespective of the nationality of the perpetrator or the victim. The only connection between the crime and the prosecuting state that may be required is the physical presence of the alleged offender within the jurisdiction of that state.' (footnotes omitted). And see the French *Code de procédure pénale* with regard to the crime of torture, 689(1) and (2).

[77] See the cases discussed by Stern, above n 69.

[78] The Yerodia prosecution, together with a number of other prosecutions for international crimes, was dismissed due to lack of powers under domestic law to proceed due to absence from the territory in the Arrêt de la Cour d'Appel de Bruxelles, Chambre des Mise en Accusation of 16 Apr 2002, *Laurent Désiré Kabila, Didier Mumemgi, Dominique Sakambi and Ndombasi Yerodia*. On appeal, however, this decision was quashed by the Cour de Cassation, 25 Nov 2002.

[79] Amnesty International, *Universal Jurisdiction*, ch 1, 14.

Of course once the suspect is arrested, the issue falls to be decided under extradition law and the suspect will be in the hands of the judiciary. At this point the question of whether the individual is to be tried for a crime or crimes which exist as crimes in both states (the double criminality rule) may apply. The requesting state may have to show that its law also includes this crime. There would not normally be an investigation into the requesting state's jurisdiction to try the crime (the non inquiry rule);[80] the key issue is whether both states allow prosecution for such an extraterritorial crime. This is clear from the European Convention on Extradition 1957 which in its Article 7(2) states:

> When the offence for which extradition is requested has been committed outside the territory of the requesting Party, extradition may only be refused if the law of the requested Party does not allow prosecution for the same category of offence when committed outside the latter Party's territory or does not allow extradition for the offence concerned.

Obviously Mr Yerodia was wanted for an offence committed outside the territory of the requesting state and was outside the territory of the requesting state. This Article suggests that whether or not universal jurisdiction is the basis for criminal jurisdiction is a question which is irrelevant for the decision whether to extradite. Where we are dealing with crimes under international law the issue is not, whether there is universal jurisdiction, but rather whether the relevant steps have been taken in national law to ensure a satisfactory trial in accordance with international guarantees. Crimes under customary international law such as genocide, crimes against humanity and war crimes presume universal jurisdiction in all states. Whether or not investigations can start before the suspect is on the territory of the investigating state is a question which has split the judges of the ICJ. The safest conclusion on this point is that it currently falls to be decided under national law.

It would be hard to find a rule which forbids international co-operation in the realm of the suppression of international crimes. In fact a recent session of the UN Sub-Commission on the Promotion and Protection of Human Rights in August 2000 adopted a resolution which actually invites states to co-operate in exactly this sphere. The Sub-Commission in paragraph 1:

> Invites all Governments to cooperate in a reciprocal manner even when there is no treaty to facilitate the task of legal authorities dealing with proceedings initiated by victims acting either within the framework of the principle of universal competence as recognised in international law or under a domestic law which establishes an extraterritorial legal competence, in particular because of the nationality of the victim or of the perpetrator.[81]

[80] See MC Bassiouni, 'Law and Practice of the United States', in MC Bassiouni (ed), *International Criminal Law: Procedural and Enforcement Mechanisms*, (Transnational, Ardsley, New York, 1999), vol II, 191–275 at 233.

[81] Resolution 2000/24 of 18 Aug 2000, adopted without a vote.

FINAL REMARKS

The International Court of Justice has applied a rule of absolute immunity for foreign ministers before the authorities of other states. It is difficult to square this result with judgements in other international courts which have proclaimed torture to be an international crime and its breach to involve a breach of a peremptory norm of international law (*jus cogens)* from which no derogation is permitted.[82]Strictly speaking the ICJs judgment is only binding on the parties to the dispute (the DRC and Belgium) in respect of this particular case.[83]It remains to be seen whether the Court's prioritisation of smooth inter-state relations over the emerging regime of international criminal law will be followed by other international courts or indeed by national courts. Some judges may feel that it is no longer appropriate to protect the dignity of a state in this way when faced with a competing good faith attempt to protect the dignity of the victims of atrocities. New precedents could quickly redefine the limits of state immunity in the face of international crimes.

The entry into force on 1 July 2002 of the International Criminal Court Statute will radically change the way immunity is perceived. Every head of state and foreign minister in the world will be potentially liable for prosecution in the new Court. It will suffice that they be nationals of a state party, or commit the acts in the territory of a state party, or that the Security Council refers a situation to the Prosecutor, or that the state of nationality or the state where the crimes occurred accepts the jurisdiction of the Court with regard to that situation. Where the accused is to be tried in this new International Criminal Court claims for immunity at the national level will be given much less weight (in particular with regard to officials from states parties to the ICC Statute).[84]Claims of immunity made by defendants who are actually before the International Criminal Court itself should be simply rejected.

* * *

Our future understanding of the notions of sovereignty, immunity and universality is uncertain. These terms will be shaped by political developments as well as legal decisions. *Justice for Crimes Against Humanity* will remain a goal for many people who are committed to ensuring better respect for the dignity of the human person. It is the efforts of these determined individuals to ensure such

[82] See International Criminal Tribunal for the Former Yugoslavia, Judgment 10 Dec 1998, IT9517, *Furundžija*; European Court of Human Rights in the *Al-Adsani v United Kingdom* judgment (21 Nov 2001), see especially the dissent of Judges Rozakis and Caflisch joined by Judges Wildhaber, Costa, Cabral Barreto and Vajić.

[83] Art 59 of the Statute of the ICJ reads: 'The decision of the Court has no binding force except between the parties and in respect of that particular case.'

[84] Consider the UKs International Criminal Court Act 2001 s 23 as well as Art 98 of the ICC Statute.

justice which will shape the new legal possibilities for accountability for international crimes. With this increased accountability it is to be hoped that there will be a greater sense of justice for the victims. But this is a struggle for all of us for such crimes against humanity, by definition, affect us all.

PART IV

Perspectives from Practitioners

13

Personal Perspectives

Political debates over the legitimacy of international justice have tended to overshadow serious discussion of the practice of international criminal law. Yet it is not an area of law in which the role of legal practitioners could be portrayed as the mechanical application of rules set by legislators. The initiative of investigating judges and human rights activists, the at times novel arguments presented in national and international courts, and the contribution of leading jurists to international legislative developments have all played a strong role in creating the current position where those who commit grave human rights abuses are move likely than ever before to be brought to justice.

This chapter presents perspectives from a range of such individuals who have been closely involved with recent developments in international justice. They draw heavily on their own experiences, whether as advocates, advisers or activists. Alternately descriptive and analytic, at times polemical, their contributions give an important insight into the operation of truth commissions, international tribunals and the practice of national prosecutions.

What emerges from many of the contributions is an appreciation of the practical impediments to bringing perpetrators to justice, which dictate circumstances in individual cases as much as the applicable law. Some suggestions are made for overcoming such obstacles. In addition to an effective International Criminal Court, the authors variously identify the need for appropriate powers and legal support for commissions of inquiry into human rights abuses, specialist resources for national prosecuting authorities in extra-territorial cases, clarification of the nature and extent of co-operation between the UN human rights mechanisms and criminal tribunals, and an international litigation strategy for pursuing leading perpetrators.

13.1 PW BOTHA BEFORE SOUTH AFRICA'S TRUTH AND RECONCILIATION PROCESS

ALEX BORAINE

One of the more difficult challenges for the international community in coming years will be the need to define the relationship between the application of criminal justice (both at the national and international levels) and the grant of national amnesties. It will be recalled that the subject of amnesty is not addressed by the Statute of the International Criminal Court or the various international human rights conventions providing for universal criminal jurisdiction at the national level. The omission suggests a limited likely effect, if any, of national amnesties against criminal prosecution outside the home state.

Below Alex Boraine, the former coordinator and deputy chairperson of South Africa's Truth and Reconciliation Commission, describes the unsuccessful efforts to bring PW Botha, former Prime Minister and President of South Africa, before the Commission, involving the issue of two subpoenas and consequential proceedings before the South African courts. The case shows how valuable evidence was gained from amnesty applications, but also illustrates the limits to the ability of a truth commission process to secure accountability, even with the unprecedented powers held by the South African TRC. However, the episode did demonstrate, at the very least, that the former head of government and state was not above the law: notwithstanding his non-participation, the Truth and Reconciliation Commission concluded that PW Botha 'by virtue of his position as a head of state and chairperson of the [State Security Council] ... contributed to and facilitated a climate in which ... gross violations of human rights could and did occur, and as such is accountable for such violations'.

South Africa's Truth and Reconciliation Commission (TRC) enjoys widespread support and many countries are looking to that model in seeking to 'come to terms with the past'. Countries as diverse as Sierra Leone, Nigeria, Ghana, Cambodia, Indonesia, East Timor, Bosnia, Serbia, Peru and Mexico have sought copies of the Act governing the Commission and the report of the Commission itself.[1] Many of us have travelled to these countries in order to discuss the relevance, if any, of the South Africa experiment.

Obviously South Africa's Truth and Reconciliation Commission cannot be imposed on any country. It was designed specifically for the conditions which prevailed at a particular time in history in that country. Other countries have different histories, different circumstances, different political pressures and social and economic environments. It would be a mistake, therefore, to imagine that the

[1] Promotion of National Unity and Reconciliation Act No 34 of 1995. The final report of the TRC is available on the official website at http://www.doj.gov.za/trc/index.html

South African model can be taken in its entirety and used elsewhere. On the other hand there is no doubt that South Africa took the truth commission model much further than any other country. In particular the South African Parliament introduced a form of amnesty for full disclosure into the working of the Truth and Reconciliation Commission. This meant that not only were victims given an opportunity to tell their stories but perpetrators, if they were to qualify for amnesty, had to tell their stories in public relating to human rights violations.[2]

Whilst many commentators acknowledge that the South African circumstances were such that the Truth and Reconciliation Commission, holding in tension as it did both victims and perpetrators, did ensure a degree of accountability without trials, nevertheless there remained concern relating to impunity. Specifically, questions have been raised as to what happens to those who were denied amnesty and indeed those who did not apply for amnesty. Mr PW Botha, who was central in the policy-making and implementation of apartheid laws, refused to appear before the Commission and has never been charged in a court of law for human rights violations. It seems that despite the widely debated circumstances surrounding Augusto Pinochet the question has hardly been raised as to how extradition impacts on someone like PW Botha, a former Minister of Defence, a former Prime Minister and former President of the Republic of South Africa. The question also relates to other cabinet members and the top echelons of the security forces.

Of course it is very difficult to assemble the necessary evidence, even in the light of widespread allegations. Furthermore, Pinochet overthrew a democratically elected government and set up a military dictatorship. Botha was much more subtle than that. He enjoyed very close co-operation with the military and the security forces so there was no real possibility of a coup. The consensus amongst whites in government, in the security forces, and in the general public was that apartheid was necessary and should be defended at all costs.

Although it was a very sensitive and difficult decision because of the possibility of stirring up the Afrikaner right wing, the Truth and Reconciliation Commission sought to call PW Botha to account. He had been not only a political organiser but also a member of Parliament of long standing, Minister of Defence, Prime Minister and State President, and was intimately linked with the policies and practices of apartheid. It was essential to have his testimony, and his refusal to co-operate with FW de Klerk when de Klerk was preparing the National Party's submission to the Commission meant that it was inevitable that we would have to approach him directly.

We were sensitive to his age. We knew that he had had a stroke, that he was not well, and also that he was potentially a rallying point for the ring wing, and we did not want to do anything to encourage further action from that source. On the other hand, we had a responsibility to the Act as well as to the country. We had listened to many first-hand experiences from victims across the

[2] See chs 3 and 8 in this volume for a discussion of whether domestic amnesties are consistent with international law.

spectrum; we had begun to hear from applicants for amnesty who described in graphic detail the actions of the security police and the military, and we felt it was extremely important that we should hear directly from the man who had been in charge of the country.

In the 1948 general election when the National Party came to power and the dreaded apartheid policy was first introduced, Botha became a Member of Parliament for the district of George. In October 1958 Botha was appointed Deputy Minister of the Interior by the late Dr HF Verwoerd and held this post until 1961. He was closely involved with so-called Coloured affairs and the implementation of the Group Areas Act. The decision to remove en masse the Coloured people living in District Six and dump them into what is called the Cape Flats was taken whilst he was Minister of Community Development and of Coloured Affairs. In 1966 he was appointed as Minister of Defence and also elected leader of the National Party in the Cape Province.

As Minister of Defence, he also became a member of the important State Security Council. This was a statutory body established to advise the government on national policy and strategy with regard to the security of South Africa. He saw himself very much as a soldier's man and regularly visited the border areas.

It was whilst he was Minister of Defence that a major South African army incursion into Angola took place in 1975. I was in Parliament by then and still remember Botha, without turning a hair, lying to Parliament and denying that South Africa was in Angola. He and the government were very strongly criticised for covering up this escapade which was widely reported in the foreign press but denied locally because of Botha's assurances. In a democratic society, he would have been forced to resign for deceiving Parliament and the South African public.

On 28 September 1978, following the resignation of Mr BJ Vorster, Botha became Prime Minister of South Africa. He retained the post of Minister of Defence, which was always his favourite calling, and also administered the portfolio of National Intelligence. From that time on, the State Security Council became the policy-making body as far as security matters were concerned. Fundamental to his term of office was his development of what came to be known as the 'total strategy' to counteract the 'total onslaught' against South Africa, linking political, economic and military forces into one concerted effort to squash the growing resistance to apartheid.

On 14 September 1984, in terms of the new constitution, Botha became State President, which combined the functions of head of state and head of government. At the opening of Parliament in January 1986, Botha announced his intention of setting up a statutory national council to review legislation affecting blacks and undertook to develop a structure to accommodate them in the central government, but of course always in a separate institution.[3]

[3] Taken in part from Shelagh Gastrow, *Who's Who in South African Politics* (Ravan Press, 1995).

In his last remaining years as State President, relationships between himself and his cabinet deteriorated seriously, but this rift was papered over. After he suffered a stroke, there was intense speculation in the media as to whether Botha would recover sufficiently to take up his responsibilities again. He finally agreed with his National Party colleagues to resign on condition that he could make the announcement on television. He did this on 14 August 1989. He continued to influence matters from his retirement home, but from that moment on he was yesterday's man.

In October 1996 I was asked a point-blank question at a press conference as to what the Commission was going to do about PW Botha's alleged role in the period of conflict in South Africa during his tenure as Defence Minister and State President. We hadn't reached any firm decision and Archbishop Desmond Tutu, the Chairperson of the TRC, was not in South Africa. Nevertheless, I put forward an approach which would involve Tutu visiting Botha at his retirement home in Wilderness. I explained that because of Botha's age and his ill health as well as his former positions, we would attempt to coax him to co-operate with the Commission. I explained that we were well aware of his previous attitude and statements which were derisory of the Commission, but nevertheless felt it would be worthwhile making a more gentle approach to see if we could persuade him to co-operate because the information he had in terms of the various offices that he had held was invaluable. I discussed this later with Tutu and he immediately agreed and we put it to the Commission and they also supported the idea that Tutu, on his own, would visit Botha. The necessary contact was made, Botha agreed to see Tutu and their meeting took place at the end of October 1996.

The visit was successful in the sense that there was no finger-waving and no shouting match took place. Mr Botha had a prepared statement and said he was willing to co-operate with the Commission in its investigations but couldn't answer question after question and it was decided that the Commission would prepare a list of questions and send them to Mr Botha for his attention. However, he also added that he had nothing to apologise for and would not seek amnesty. The Commission felt generally satisfied that the right approach had been made and immediately began to prepare a set of questions for Botha's consideration. I sent those questions on 3 February 1997. Obviously some of the worst apartheid atrocities happened in the 1980s when the Botha administration's total strategy was at its height. I stated in a press statement that 'politicians who actually formulated policy and gave instructions are surely much more responsible than those people who followed orders and therefore should be held accountable'. I also mentioned in the press statement that some of the questions related to the 1998 Khotso House bombing. According to former Police Chief, Johan van der Merwe, the instructions to carry out the bombings were issued by Botha himself. Months went by and we didn't hear a word from Botha, although his lawyers kept on assuring us that they were busy assisting him to answer the questions. In the meantime, however, we had access to the minutes of the State Security Council and we also listened to many applicants for amnesty who constantly alleged that their orders came from the very top and, on being pressed, said they had no doubt that their actions had been sanctioned by government with the approval of the State President.

The TRC took two decisions to subpoena Botha. With our own time running out and having had no reply from Botha, plus additional information we had received, it seemed to us imperative that we had to take action. The first decision to subpoena Botha was taken on 22 August 1997 and the subpoena itself was issued for Botha to appear on 14 October 1997 at the State Security Council hearing. We were informed by Botha's lawyers that he, Botha, was not well and after Botha furnished the TRC with a medical certificate the subpoena was withdrawn. A second decision to subpoena Botha was made on 22 October 1997 by the Human Rights Violations Committee.

Four broad categories of responsibility can be distilled from the sub-sections of Section 4 of the National Unity and Reconciliation Act No 34 of 1995. Firstly, those who participated directly in gross violations of human rights, secondly, those who gave orders for gross violations of human rights to be committed, thirdly, those who created a climate in which gross violations of human rights could occur and finally those who failed to act against/punish those responsible for gross violations of human rights and therefore were responsible for sanctioning/ratifying these acts or were guilty of 'official tolerance' of these acts. We had no information that Botha had participated directly in gross violations of human rights, but certainly there were strong allegations that we needed to investigate in relation to the other three sections as outlined. In order to accommodate Botha and bearing in mind his state of health, the Commission decided to hold the State Security Council hearings in George.

However, Botha, through his lawyers, told us in no uncertain terms that he would not attend and therefore would disobey the subpoena. In terms of the Act if anyone refused a subpoena issued by the Commission they were guilty of contempt and therefore our only recourse was to hand the matter over to the Attorney-General for his consideration. The Attorney-General, having considered the papers, decided to act against Botha. Botha appeared in the George Magistrate Court on 23 February 1998. The security was so extensive that the small town of George looked as though it was under siege. Security forces erected barriers at the main entrances leading into George and put a head-high razor wire barrier around the court building on the corner of York and Courtney Streets. About 100 supporters of the African National Congress (ANC) gathered on a traffic island opposite the courtroom and booed a dark-suited Mr Botha as he stepped from his BMW shortly before 9am to attend the hearing. Some of the placards carried by the demonstrating crowd read 'Botha's Miaow No Match for Madiba's Roar' and 'Afrikaner Tiger Miaow Miaow Miaow' and 'The Tiger in Africa is Behind Bars'.

In his defence Botha accused the Commission of acting in bad faith and with an ulterior motive. He claimed that an agreement had been entered into between himself and Tutu in George on 21 November 1996 and therefore the TRC was not entitled to require his presence. Tutu strenuously denied this and said on numerous occasions that he had no authority to enter into any kind of agreement with Botha and that any decisions relating to any person and the TRC had to be taken by the Commission itself.

The trial proper started in June and our major witness on behalf of the Commission was Paul van Zyl, the Commission's Executive Secretary. He was very closely cross-examined by Botha's lawyers, but they were never able to shake him from the substance of his evidence. Van Zyl set out the evidence which influenced the first decision to subpoena PW Botha. He did so under the heading 'Those who gave orders for gross violations of human rights to be committed' and quoted from allegations made in amnesty applications. The first of these was presented by Johan van der Merwe, former Commissioner of Police, and Adrian Vlok, former Minister of Law and Order. They stated that the order to blow up Khotso House, the headquarters of the South African Council of Churches, came directly from Botha. Botha's first response to these allegations was to state that the allegation was incorrect, that it was based on untested evidence and the bombing fell outside the mandate of the TRC. The Commission argued that it was precisely because Botha's version conflicted with that of Vlok that he should be called to testify before the Commission. Botha did not apply for amnesty and there was no guarantee that his version would be subjected to proper scrutiny via cross-examination. The point was also made that there was an inevitable overlap between the work of the Human Rights Violations Committee and the Amnesty Committee and the fact that Botha might have to appear before the Amnesty Committee did not preclude him from having to appear before the Human Rights Violations Committee.

The second heading under which the evidence was presented in court was 'Those who created a climate in which gross violations of human rights could occur'. A number of factors taken on their own or considered cumulatively could create a climate in which gross violation of human rights could occur. Some of these were, firstly, pressure on the security forces from political authorities. During the mid-1980s members of the security forces who were acting on the ground experienced two new influences: they were placed under tremendous pressure by their commanders to 'perform'. Further, they were urged to take the strongest possible measures to ensure that 'hot spots' were stabilised, law and order restored and violence and intimidation ended.

Secondly, the adoption of potentially ambiguous decisions by the State Security Council encouraged a climate in which state crimes could and did occur. A few examples will make the point. On 14 April 1986 the State Security Council discussed a document which listed objectives including 'to neutralise enemy leaders' and the task of the security forces 'to neutralise or eliminate enemy leaders'. A second example is the adoption by the SSC on 25 August 1986 entitled 'Strategie ter Bekamping van die ANC' ('Strategy to Oppose the ANC'). Having noted the advances made by the ANC in its onslaught against the state, the document reiterated its goal of neutralizing the ANC/SACP/SACTU[4] alliance. The following recommendations were made: (1) to neutralise the ANC leadership, (2) to prevent and control *verhoed* in relation not only to potential terrorists but also ANC sympathisers and co-workers, (3) to neutralise the power and influence of key persons and their fellow workers in the ANC.

On 10 July 1986 the SSC produced a document entitled 'Naamlys van Politiessensitiewe Persone'[5] and listed it on the agenda for the SSC as follows: 'Action to be taken against politically sensitive persons and the withdrawal of leadership figures'. (Amongst the names on that list which would enjoy the close attention of the security police were those of Archbishop Tutu and Dr Alex Boraine!) In various other documents produced by the SSC the same thread continues: the identifying and eliminating of revolutionary leaders, particularly those with charisma, and the physical destruction of revolutionary organizations inside and outside of the country.

In most SSC documents there is a failure to provide a clear and unambiguous definition for the following terms: elimination, neutralization, physical destruction, formal and informal policing, taking out, methods other than detention.

It was our view that the failure to provide a clear and unambiguous definition of these terms, particularly the term 'eliminate', was a cause of great concern in light of the evidence given by Johan van der Merwe during an amnesty application on 27 February 1997. It should be borne in mind that van der Merwe was a member of the SSC:

> *Adv du Plessis:* General, could you assist me? Commissioner de Jager asked me yesterday if in the police there was a special meaning to the word 'eliminate' or if the normal meaning of the word applied, in other words, to kill someone. Could you assist us in this regard? If someone was to talk about 'I received instruction to go and eliminate someone', is there a special meaning to that in the police or does the normal meaning apply?
>
> *Genl van der Merwe:* No, the normal meaning applied. It would be to get rid of someone, to kill someone.

It was the Commission's submission that PW Botha, in his capacity as the chairperson of the State Security Council, himself created a climate in which gross violations occurred, and should be held accountable for such violations.

The third heading under which we set out the reasons for our subpoena of Botha was 'Those who failed to act against/punish those responsible for gross violations of human rights and therefore are responsible for sanctioning/ratifying these acts or are guilty of "official tolerance" of these acts.'

The point was made that the TRC possessed information which could point to a failure on behalf of the government and the SSC to take action against

[4] African National Congress/South African Communist Party/Congress of South African Trade Unions.

[5] List of Politically Sensitive Persons.

members of the security forces responsible for gross violations of human rights. From June to August 1997, the TRC analysed a large amount of evidence presented to it concerning allegations of torture committed by the security forces. Our information indicated that the rate of torture increased more than tenfold after the declaration of the state of emergency in June 1986. The SSC, chaired by Botha, played a central role in deciding to declare the 12 June 1986 state of emergency. Further, the TRC had received statements alleging that the security forces were involved in almost 2000 acts of torture in more than 200 different venues during the time in which Botha was either Prime Minister or State President. Nowhere in the SSC minutes are there any expressions of concern about the numerous and vocal allegations of torture made throughout the 1980s and it follows that there were no measures adopted to prevent torture and punish those responsible.

The Commission told the court that after reading the minutes of the SSC and the cabinet, it had decided to hold two sets of hearings. The first would focus on the role of the various armed forces of the Government and the liberation movements respectively while the second would concentrate on the role and functions of the State Security Council. It was decided that because of Botha's active role and his chairing of the SSC, he had to be included as one of the witnesses for the second hearing, and that is precisely why he was subpoenaed.

During the Armed Forces hearing numerous high-ranking members of the South African Police, a general in the South African Defence Force and a senior cabinet minister serving on the SSC agreed that decisions taken by the State Security Council could be interpreted to authorise serious illegal acts including the murder of the political opponents of the previous government. This served to reinforce our conviction that it was vitally important to hold a hearing into the role of the State Security Council and to clarify the meaning and status of decisions it took.

A key witness in Botha's trial for contempt was ex police Colonel Eugene de Kock. The reason for his being called was that he, together with many of his colleagues and generals, maintained that the actions which they carried out, which can only be described as state violence, were not only known by senior politicians but were authorised by them. De Kock entered the small court room looking stern and pale. Botha sat in his chair, glanced at de Kock and then turned away so that he was sitting with his back to de Kock. If Botha imagined that de Kock would be in any way intimidated by being only a few feet away from him when he read his statement, he was in for a shock. I watched de Kock as he coldly described the politicians of the National Party as cowardly and as people who sold out the police and the army. Bluntly he stated, 'They wanted to eat lamb but they do not want to see the blood and guts.'[6] De Kock went on to say that he and his colleagues had been told by politicians at the highest level that they, the security forces, were fighting for the protection of their fatherland.

[6] *Cape Times*, 4 June 1998.

However, they were only fighting for the 'incestuous little world of Afrikanerdom'. De Kock went on to say, 'We did well. We did the fighting. I am proud of that. But the politicians have not had the moral guts to accept responsibility for the killing.'[7] He described himself as a lowly colonel but 'I am also an Afrikaner.'[8] However, it was as 'cowards that God would deal with the politicians'.[9] I watched Botha carefully as this vitriol was spewed out by de Kock. He was unmoving, he stared ahead and never looked at de Kock again. In the same cold and measured tones, de Kock told the court of the bombings of the ANC offices in London in 1981, Cosatu House in 1987 and the headquarters of the South African Council of Churches, Khotso House, in 1988. He told the court that he had received the Police Star for outstanding service for the London bombings and the award could only have been granted by the State President himself, who at that time was PW Botha.

He stated that he had been very surprised at the decision to bomb Khotso House, but was told by a police general that Botha was irritated and impatient about any delay in destroying the building. He described at great length how he and others carried out the attack with the clear impression that the bombing of the church headquarters was authorised by Botha himself. He told the court that the Minister of Law and Order had warmly congratulated him a few weeks after the bombing had taken place. This for him was confirmation that the orders had come from the very top. There was a hush in the small courtroom as de Kock concluded his powerful and at times emotional evidence.

You could hear a pin drop as he left the witness box and made his way out of the court. When Bishop Peter Storey gave evidence as a witness to the aftermath of the Khotso House bombing, once again Botha sat impassively. Storey told the court that he saw a group of aged pensioners covered in blood, cowering in shock from the attack. Storey, who is a powerful public speaker, was very convincing as he described the scene.

He told the court that residents were wandering around in their night clothes, in a complete daze. Some of them were bleeding, their faces and forearms were lacerated. He told the court that in his view they were extremely fortunate to be alive. These were residents who lived on old age and mentally disabled pensions in a church-owned apartment block opposite the Council of Churches headquarters where the bombing had taken place. twenty-one people were injured in the attack. It was a very moving statement and indicated just how serious the attack had been and why it was important for the Commission to clarify exactly who was responsible.

Tutu was the last witness to be called on behalf of the prosecution. He was extremely gracious, almost tentative in his opening statement. He began by expressing his greatest possible reluctance at having to appear. He told the court that he was filled with considerable distaste at having to take part in the trial

[7] *Mail & Guardian*, 5–11 June 1998.
[8] *Ibid.*
[9] *Ibid.*

and expressed his belief that this should never have come to pass. He explained to the court that he had tried to reach out to Botha out of deep compassion for him. He saw Botha as a brother long before it was politically correct to do so. He strongly denied that he had ever agreed to exempt Botha from any appearance before the Commission, stressing that he had no authority to do so. He tried to answer also the many charges that had been made, particularly by the Afrikaans media, the generals and some politicians that the Commission was out 'to get Botha'. Tutu said that he had never gloated over Botha's position as the accused in court. Nor did he ever intend to humiliate him and their interaction had been courteous and friendly. He said when one examined the events leading up to the court case, there could be no suggestion of malice by himself or by the Commission.

At the very end of the long session in the witness box Tutu was told that he could step down. He paused and, ignoring court protocol, asked if he could say a word to Botha. He looked at Botha and asked him to apologise for the distress apartheid had caused. In giving him the benefit of the doubt, he said,

> Even if you didn't intend it, I want to appeal to you, I want you to take this chance provided by this court, for you to say that while you may not have intended the suffering to happen to people, you may not have given orders to authorise anything, but if you are able to say, I am sorry that policies of my government caused you pain. Just that. It would be a tremendous benefit to all of South Africa.[10]

Later Botha reacted through his lawyers and expressed his astonishment that Tutu should have asked him to apologise, reiterating that he was not aware of anything he had done for which he should confess to the Truth Commission.

It was a tragedy that Botha never entered the witness box to respond to the allegations made against him by the Commission. It was an even greater tragedy that because of his arrogance and his insensitivity to what apartheid had done to so many hundreds and thousands of people, he defied the Commission and refused to appear before it. He maintained to the very end that he was responsible only to God and not to the Commission.

The court was adjourned and in August 1998 Botha was convicted of contravening Section 39(e)(I) read with Sections 134 and 29 of the Promotion of National Unity and Reconciliation Act No 34 of 1995 and was sentenced to a fine of R10,000 or 12 months imprisonment, plus a further 12 months imprisonment suspended for five years on condition that he did not contravene any of the provisions of the Act. His lawyers immediately lodged an appeal which was duly heard and upheld in March 1999. The appeal was upheld purely on technical grounds, namely that the notice issued by the TRC and served on Botha on 6 December 1997 was unauthorised because it was prematurely issued. It is interesting that the Appeal Court concluded its judgment with the following words:

[10] *Cape Argus*, 5 June 1998.

> This court is duty bound to uphold and protect the Constitution and to administer justice to all persons alike without fear, favour or prejudice in accordance with the Constitution and the law. Suffice it to say that the same law, the same Constitution which obliges the appellant to obey the law of the land like every other citizen, also affords him the same protections that it affords every other citizen.[11]

This is stated in conjunction with an earlier paragraph that states,

> This court is mindful of the fact that there will be many who may consider that it is unjust that the appellant should succeed in his appeal upon the basis that the appeal was upheld purely on technical grounds.[12]

It was with great distress that we learnt of the successful appeal and the question was immediately posed as to whether or not we should appeal against the decision. The fact that the Commission was itself then in suspension and that its major actors were busy elsewhere, as well as the fact that we had succeeded in making Mr Botha accept that he was answerable to the law and was not above it, and that we were able, during the course of the trial, to outline many of the very questions and allegations that we would have posed to him in a normal public hearing, meant that there was no point in taking any further action against Botha. At least it had been conclusively shown that no one is above the law.

In Botha's press statement, following his successful appeal, he expressed appreciation for South Africa's independent judiciary. He was right to do so, but when one bears in mind that the independence of the judiciary was eroded and undermined by his government when he was in power, it is an act of supreme irony. In the *Cape Argus* of Monday 7 June 1999, a leading article stated:

> The appeal judgment is a hollow victory for the aging Mr Botha. It was decided on a technical point relating to the TRCs founding legislation and its rights and duties when its life was extended to cope with the overwhelming workload. There was no finding in respect of Mr Botha's duty as a self-proclaimed law-abiding citizen to appear before theTRC and bear witness to what he knew about the multitude of gross human rights violations that occurred during his lengthy term of office... History will be the final judge of Mr Botha and there is no doubt that it will give a harsh verdict.

In the meanwhile the Commission had published its own findings in relation to P W Botha. These concluded that during the period he presided as head of state (1978-1989), gross violations of human rights and other unlawful acts were perpetrated on a wide scale by members of the former South African Police (SAP) and the former South African Defence Force (SADF), including deliberate unlawful killings, the widespread use of torture, forcible abductions, acts of arson and sabotage, and the provision of covert logistical and financial assistance to organizations opposed to the ideology of the ANC, enabling them to commit gross human rights violations on a wide scale within and beyond the borders of South

[11] Appeal Court's notes for judgment, 1 June 1999, in respect of *PW Botha v The State*.
[12] *Ibid*.

Africa. Moreover, the Commission found that under Botha's leadership, the State Security Council created a political climate that greatly facilitated the gross violation of human rights, and in which such violations occurred on a wide scale. The SSC used language that was interpreted as authorizing killings, failed to recommend action against members of the security forces involved in human rights violations, recommended to the government and helped implement states of emergency under which violations increased, and recommended support for covert projects aimed at opposing and destabilizing organisations and people opposed to the government, including the governments of neighbouring countries which were supportive of liberation movements.

The Commission specifically found that:

> Mr Botha was responsible for ordering former Minister of Law and Order Adriaan Vlok and former Police Commissioner Johan van der Merwe unlawfully to destroy Khotso House in Johannesburg (a building occupied by organizations considered by Botha to be a threat to the security of the government), thereby endangering the lives of people in and around the building. This decision greatly enhanced the prevailing culture of impunity and facilitated the further gross violation of human rights by senior members of the security forces.

The Commission concluded:

> For the reasons set out above and by virtue of his position as head of state and chairperson of the SSC, Botha contributed to and facilitated a climate in which the above gross violations of human rights could and did occur, and as such is accountable for such violations.[13]

PW Botha has faded from the South African political landscape and no legal action will be taken against him. If an International Criminal Court were in existence it would have been a different story. Whilst Botha is very old and infirm, there were many others who served with him, in particular the high-ranking officers in the security forces, who could well have been called to account. Clearly the South African experiment, with all its benefits, illustrates vividly the need for an International Criminal Court.

13.2 PROSECUTING HASTINGS BANDA IN MALAWI

SADAKAT KADRI

If an important product of South Africa's Truth and Reconciliation Commission was the collection of detailed evidence of a quality that could support future prosecutions, in Malawi the methods of a Commission of Inquiry established to look at an egregious human rights violation fatally

[13] TRC Final Report, vol 5, 223–225.

weakened the reliability of evidence available to the prosecution in a subsequent trial. One lesson to be drawn from the trial of Dr Hastings Banda, former president of Malawi, is that for public inquiries or truth commissions to assist, rather than stymie, future criminal proceedings, they need to benefit not just from good legal advice but also from appropriate powers to ensure the reliability of witnesses. Sadakat Kadri, an advisor to the Malawian DPP before the trial and counsel in the appeal, believes this should include the ability to recommend immunity from prosecution.

Banda's trial illustrates the difficulties of convicting a former head of state in national proceedings, notwithstanding the existence of compelling evidence of the criminality of the former regime. 'Was the trial worth it?', asks Kadri. He concludes that even if the trial may have had some value in contributing to 'an international scheme of deterrence', and provided a channel for passions which might otherwise have exploded into violence, the immediate effect of the not-guilty verdicts handed down by the jury was, for the local community, 'cynicism rather than catharsis'. The reader will be particularly struck by the author's observation that for many people the fairness of the proceedings stood in contrast to the inexplicability of the verdict, a salutary reminder that due process alone will not deliver justice.

The Malawi led by Dr Hastings Kamuzu Banda was not a country where human rights prospered. Although his love-hate relationship with England led him to preserve many features of British Nyasaland—most notably, its bureaucratic and policing structures, which continued to benefit from British training throughout his rule—his qualified respect for the former colonial power's institutions did not extend to the notion of judicial independence. As early as 1963, he made clear that, 'Anything I say is law. Literally law. It is a fact in this country',[14] and during his presidency, which ended only after a peaceful revolution in 1993, Malawi's legal system was characterised by an extraordinary mixture of authoritarianism and absurdity. Dr Banda's milder eccentricities were sometimes dignified by statutory authority—as when, with his Decency in Dress Act, he banned bell-bottom trousers and mini-skirts (after first defining both terms)—but the sharp end of the rule of law, Banda-style, was rather less punctilious. Following his displeasure at the acquittal of five men accused of capital murder in 1969, a verdict which he promptly overruled, he removed the country's entire criminal justice system into the hands of 'traditional' courts. These tribunals, though empowered to sentence defendants to death, dispensed verdicts which were neither appealable, reasoned or even, in most cases, recorded. The number of people who passed through the traditional courts cannot be known—and still less identifiable are the thousands who were simply incarcerated, tortured or killed without any judicial intervention at all, traditional or otherwise.

[14] See John Lloyd Lwanda, *Kamuzu Banda of Malawi: A Study in Promise, Power and Paralysis* (Dudu Nsomba Publications, 1993), 122.

Perhaps unsurprisingly, those Parliamentary sessions which occasionally occurred in his one-party state were not typified by vocal criticism. But on 17 May 1983, an unusually fractious debate took place, at which calls were made by members of his Malawi Congress Party (MCP) for the government's budgetary records to be subjected to scrutiny. Since Dr Banda was steadily creaming off a fortune which at his death would be found to amount to $319 million, he had reason to be displeased by the unexpected, if still muted, rumble of dissent within his party. Later that day, three of the country's most senior Cabinet ministers and an MP—at least two of whom were loosely associated with the calls for greater openness within the party—went missing. Two days later, they were found dead in a car near the town of Mwanza. When the corpses—shrouded in prison blankets—were returned to their families, the police officers who offloaded them from the back of their jeeps warned that they were traitors who were to be buried without ceremony. No official from the Malawi Congress Party attended their funerals. Some months later, Dr Banda made passing reference at a party rally to one of the men, warning those present that he had been a 'confusionist', but otherwise made no public comment on the deaths. Following the cue of a man who once boasted that he threw his enemies to the crocodiles, nor for a decade did anyone else.

Only in 1993, when Banda acceded to pro-democracy protests and stood down after 30 years of uninterrupted rule, did that silence come to an end. A resolution of the case was close to the top of the opposition movements' agenda, and following newspaper investigations, a Commission of Inquiry was established. After hearing from 167 witnesses, it reported its conclusions in early 1995. It found that the four men had been arrested at a roadblock outside the parliament building on the orders of the country's most senior police officer, that they had been officially signed into the country's main prison, and that they had finally been driven in marked police vehicles, hooded and bound, some 200 kilometres to a road near the Mozambican border, where they had been blasted and bludgeoned to death by a dozen uniformed police officers. In evidence before the inquiry, most members of the death squad made full or partial confessions. For his part, Dr Banda simply stated that the incident was so long ago that he could not remember whether or not he had ordered the arrests.

That was the backdrop to the case of *DPP v Banda and others*, a case in which the former president along with two of his closest political associates and two police officers were tried for having conspired to murder the four dead men. (Initial charges of capital murder were dropped, on human rights grounds.)[15] Whereas prosecutions such as those relating to torture in Pinochet's Chile and

[15] Malawi's President, Bakili Muluzi, commuted the sentences of all those on death row when he assumed office in 1994, and has done the same for all those convicted of capital murder since then. Although human rights organisations within the country have been unsuccessful in their attempts to abolish the death penalty, which commands considerable popular support at a time of rising crime, no one has been executed in the country since Banda's departure from the presidency, and President Muluzi has pledged not to sign any execution warrants while in office: see Amnesty International News Release AFR 36/03/97, 23 July 1997.

the shoot-to-kill practices of East Germany's border guards, have raised complex issues relating to sovereign immunity and retrospective penalisation, such jurisprudential niceties were almost entirely absent from the Banda case. Rather than contend, *á la* Pinochet, that hammering and shooting to death four blindfolded politicians was an unjusticiable exercise of a presidential prerogative, Banda like his co-defendants chose primarily to rely on the presumption of innocence and the right to silence, both of which had in 1995 been incorporated into the country's new constitution. (The former president was in fact tried in his absence, on the application of his counsel, after medical experts found him to be physically unfit to attend court.) Defence counsel additionally advanced a number of legal and factual theories about the deaths: on Dr Banda's behalf, it was suggested that they had been ordered by his (since deceased) Cabinet Secretary, acting on a murderous frolic of his own, while another defendant's barrister argued that his client should be acquitted because he had assassinated the four men pursuant to (unspecified) official instructions, a defence which, the common law and Nuremberg notwithstanding, was then left to the jury. The trial resulted in unanimous acquittals for all of the defendants. The prosecution appealed on several points of law, but in July 1997 the Court of Appeal refused the request for a retrial. On 25 November 1997 Dr Banda died peacefully, his name unbesmirched by any criminal conviction.

The prosecution's inability to discharge its burden throws into sharp relief some of the obstacles which a post-totalitarian state can face when it tries to use the ordinary criminal law against its former rulers and law-enforcement officials. The higher the official position once occupied by the defendant, the more difficult it will always be to establish by way of legally admissible evidence that that defendant knew of or participated in specific substantive crimes committed by persons lower down the state's pecking order. In Malawi, direct proof that the killings had been ordered by Dr Banda was impossible given that the two human links between the president and his security apparatus in 1983—namely his Inspector-General and his Cabinet Secretary—were both long dead by the time of the trial. As a result, the prosecution had to rely exclusively on circumstantial evidence against Dr Banda, and here it was regularly met with defence objections that 'it is these defendants, and not Dr Banda's system of government which should be on trial here'.

The defence stance, framed in terms of a dichotomy between collective guilt and individual justice, had an instinctive appeal; and there is little doubt that the trial judge, who was understandably anxious not to preside over a show trial, gave it considerable weight throughout. But from the viewpoint—admittedly, not entirely disinterested—of one of those who helped to prepare the unsuccessful prosecution appeal, it seems fairly clear that his solicitude to the defence concerns led him into legal error. Although few would disagree that, in general terms, the common law operates on individuals rather than groups, and according to principles of evidence more tangible than blame by association, the law of conspiracy simply does not permit of absolute distinctions between the nature of a conspiracy, the acts committed by parties to it, and the liability of each defendant for acts of co-conspirators. This was nevertheless the theoretical framework adopted by the trial judge, and the effect was to prove fatal to the prosecution case. It led him to direct the jury entirely to ignore the evidence they had heard about the murders because 'it is conceded by the defence that the four deceased did not meet their deaths in a road accident', and to take the view (which he later made explicit to the jury) that the circumstantial evidence put forward by the prosecution was in its nature inferior to other types of proof. The result of this was that he ruled inadmissible, downplayed or ignored the entire prosecution case against Dr Banda—which depended on the facts, circumstantial but indubitable, that the president's opponents had a habit of being incarcerated, exiled or suddenly killed, that his police chiefs had systematically sought his oral or written 'advice and guidance' on every arrest they ever ordered, and that for thirty years no subordinate had been known to disobey an order and live.

Regardless of the legal merits of the judge's various rulings, they illustrate some of the difficulties which may confront a prosecutor seeking to obtain convictions against a defendant whose personality once dominated a repressive state or organisation where criminality was endemic. At the risk of extrapolating from a hard case to bad law, it is at least arguable that the common law can and should develop a narrow and exceptional presumption that, where an evidential foundation is laid to show that systematic criminal brutality was practised in a state, coordinated criminal actions committed by its security force are, unless proved otherwise, evidence of conspiracy or participation against that state's ruler. The most important lesson to emerge from the Banda case however does not stem from its verdicts, or the rulings made during the trial, but from its genesis—for events which immediately preceded the trial threw their shadow over everything which was to follow.

The background to the case shows how crucial it is that any state attempting to resolve previously uninvestigated crimes clarifies, at a very early stage, whether its primary concern is to obtain criminal convictions or to establish the truth about past misdeeds. After the collapse of the Banda dictatorship, the popular demand for swift action led Malawi's new government to seek both goals. Although there is no reason why they should necessarily conflict, they may well do so—and the procedural and evidential safeguards required by any fair criminal trial mean that extremely careful thought must be given to the terms and purposes of any preliminary inquiry. In the Malawian case, the government's apparent hope that the Commission of Inquiry would gather evidence for a future prosecution was not supported by a framework which would maintain the integrity of that evidence, giving rise to problems which weakened the inquiry and all but stymied the trial.

The most important of these difficulties stemmed from the fact that, unlike South Africa's Truth and Reconciliation Commission, the public inquiry was not empowered even to consider, let alone decide, whether witnesses appearing before it should be given immunity from prosecution. The inevitable consequence was that many of those giving evidence had very good reasons to lie. Given the totalitarian nature of Dr Banda's rule, most of the politicians and civil servants who could testify as to events in May 1983 were likely to have several skeletons in their own closets—while the murderous police officers themselves stood in peril of a capital charge and had every incentive to minimise their roles in the killings. The effect was that the inquiry did very little to ensure the reliability of witnesses who might be useful to the prosecution in a subsequent trial, but simultaneously amassed reams of material which would be—and was—invaluable for the purpose of defence cross-examination. Since the prosecution would not be able to cross-examine its own witnesses, its case could not, absent fresh evidence, become any stronger than the material unearthed by the inquiry commissioners (most of whom were not legally trained)—and was very likely to become considerably weaker when tested by the defence.

After the Commission reported, the Director of Public Prosecutions was thus faced with a choice—he could either decline to prosecute a prima facie case of multiple murder, or he could select the 'most' reliable witnesses from a group of men whose testimony was inherently unreliable. The dilemma was an unenviable one and, when he chose to prosecute, the problems it would give rise to were compounded by his decision to prefer murder charges against all the relevant police officers, and then reduce them to summary offences in respect of (only) those officers he chose to rely upon. In such circumstances, defence suggestions that those still in the dock only faced trial due to an invidious abuse of prosecutorial discretion would inevitably carry weight with the jury. This in itself cannot fully rationalise the verdicts in the Banda case, but it represented the greatest single obstacle to a successful prosecution in the trial.

Since no convictions could ever have been obtained without evidence from at least some of the actual killers, this meant that the Commission of Inquiry facilitated *neither* the emergence of the truth nor the conviction of guilty men. Although the shortcomings of both inquiry and trial are in many ways specific to Malawi—for they resulted at least in part from the irony that Dr Banda's dictatorship, had left the country with the lowest proportion of lawyers to population in the world and eviscerated its country's legal culture—they also highlight how much any institutional attempt to investigate past human rights abuses will inevitably affect future attempts to try individual defendants. If such trials are to be fair in the widest sense—both safeguarding defence rights and preserving the prosecution's proper chances of conviction—a minimum requirement for any preliminary inquiry must be that it benefit from robust legal advice, and be empowered from the outset to recommend immunity from criminal proceedings once satisfied that specified criteria had been made out. Although this may mean that serious crimes go unpunished, as illustrated by the experience of South Africa's Truth and Reconciliation Commission, the Malawian experience shows that the alternatives may be no better at securing retributive justice, and are likely to be considerably less effective in terms of uncovering the full scale of criminal actions committed by a former dictatorship.

In Malawi, straitjacketed by poverty and in the throes of an AIDS epidemic of almost unimaginable scale, the history of Dr Banda's trial poses more starkly than usual the question that lawyers are wont to shy away from—was the trial worth it? Even if one assumes its value in contributing to an international scheme of deterrence and disregards the fact that Malawi is one of the 15 poorest nations in the world, the trial's benefit to the country's political, social and legal economy is by no means self-evident. One of the most common arguments used to justify the prosecution of former dictators is that a trial enables a traumatised nation to confront its past and heal its wounds—regardless of its outcome. But although an 'outcome-neutral' theory of the trial may hold in the case of the day-to-day criminal procedures of a healthy democracy, it is at least optimistic, and arguably fictional, when applied in the context of a post-totalitarian society such as Malawi.

Since the Commission of Inquiry's report left little doubt that identifiable police officers had committed multiple murders during a period when Dr Banda's iron grip over the country was notorious, the reality was that the immediate effect of the not-guilty verdicts was cynicism rather than catharsis. To many ordinary people, non-plussed that Dr Banda *et al.* had got away with it again, the jury's decision simply confirmed that when it came to a contest between the old man and the rule of law, the law stood no chance. Others suggested that the government, occupied largely by politicians who had made their careers under Dr Banda, had long viewed the trial as a means of focusing attention away from the broader range of human rights abuses committed by Dr Banda's regime, and that the verdicts resulted from the narrowness of its remit; or even that they had been rigged in order to secure Malawi's newly-democratic credentials among donor nations. These criticisms do some disservice to the country's authorities, who have established a legal right to compensation for all victims of human rights abuses under Dr Banda's government and who facilitated a trial which was remarkably fair given the highly charged emotions which surrounded the case. This very fairness does nevertheless contrast uncomfortably with the administration of ordinary criminal justice in the country. Despite strenuous efforts by many committed individuals and NGOs, cases are typified by delays measured in years, prisoners are held in appalling and sometimes deadly conditions, and the laudable provisions of the Constitution and the various international instruments to which Malawi has become a party are all too often unenforceable due to the country's chronic shortage of lawyers.[16]

[16] At the end of 1999, the country still had only five public defenders, and approximately one-third of the country's 7324 prison inmates were unconvicted remand prisoners who were awaiting trial. See US Department of State, 'Country Reports on Human Rights Practices for 1999: Malawi'. For further information on the problems facing the country's legal system, see Bar Human Rights Committee of England and Wales, 'Library Resources for Lawyers—Malawi, Botswana, Uganda—A Report to the Human Rights Policy Department, Foreign and Commonwealth Office', May 2000.

Subsequent events have certainly lent some support to the more optimistic view about the value of the trial. Few supporters of the MCP were instantly reconciled to the new order by its outcome, but the process itself provided a channel for passions which might otherwise have exploded into violence, and introduced the language of human rights into Malawi's political discourse. The MCP, both during and since the trial, has regularly accused the government of failing to live up to its legal and constitutional duties—and although its claims, like the counter-allegations made by the government, are often more rhetorical than substantial, the mere fact that the rhetoric of human rights has replaced the silent murders of the past carries with it some hope for the future. A measure of the venom that has been drawn from Malawi's body politic is perhaps indicated by the fact that since the trial, the MCP itself has begun regularly to use the judicial system to resolve its internal disagreements. And however inexplicable the verdicts may have been to many people, the palpable fairness of the proceedings—symptomised not just by the verdicts but also by the fact that the defendants faced non-capital charges and remained on bail throughout the trial—has undoubtedly contributed to a political atmosphere of relative freedom and political tolerance. The trial was at least a symbol that a clear line differentiated the politics of the new dispensation from the arbitrary despotism of Dr Banda—even if, as this article suggests, its symbolic value may at times have conflicted with, rather than complemented, a full exploration of the criminality of the former regime.

13.3 THE CONTRIBUTION OF INTERNATIONAL TRIBUNALS TO THE DEVELOPMENT OF INTERNATIONAL CRIMINAL LAW

ERIC DAVID

Eric David considers the extent to which the practice of the International Criminal Tribunals for Yugoslavia and Rwanda, and the process of negotiating the statute of the International Criminal Court, have contributed to the progressive development of international criminal law. His conclusion is unambiguous: the statutes of these bodies and their jurisprudence have helped to confirm that international criminal law exists as a discrete subject, have contributed to its codification, and enable a growing standardization of the discipline for the suppression of grave violations of international humanitarian law. Of particular note are the growing understanding on issues of procedure between common law and civil law approaches (with their different starting points) and, with regard to substantive issues, the recognition (in the Rome Statute of the ICC) of an exhaustive and generally accepted list of crimes that fall within the category of war crimes and crimes against humanity. His conclusions are not altogether positive, however, as he notes what are, in his view, adverse implications of certain judgements of the ICTR and ICTY for issues such as duress and the annulment of prosecutions.

Of all branches of the law, international criminal law has probably undergone the deepest upheavals during the last 10 years although one can question whether for the most part they really represent transformations rather than merely applications or adaptations of rules that are sometimes very old. Flowers seem new, but the seeds that gave birth to them were sown a long time ago, and one could think that it is the warming of the (international...) climate which finally allowed them to open out.

However it may be, the discipline is enjoying a boom and an impetus which would have been unimaginable, barely more than ten years ago, at the time of the Cold War.

If one tries to make an assessment and to see what will happen tomorrow, one observes that international criminal law exhibits a dual trend, anarchic on the one hand, integrated on the other hand.

The anarchic nature of international criminal law shows itself notably in the exercise by States of their repressive jurisdiction over crimes which present an extraneous element through their particular involvement with regard to mechanisms of international judicial co-operation or with regard to the legislative sources of international crimes. Now, not only does the scope of these sources and mechanisms depend on the very varied success that they meet with in the States which accept to be bound by the legal instruments establishing them, but moreover, the legal regime brought by these instruments varies from one State to another. From this point of view, international criminal law is a reflection of general international law: a disparate set of texts which contain nothing uniform and which bind an extremely variable number of States.

Nevertheless, international criminal law exists: it is applied on a daily basis and in a relatively discrete way by national judicial authorities, either through the exercise, in the domestic sphere, of extraterritorial jurisdictions, or through the implementation of provisions in international criminal law or through international judicial co-operation in criminal matters.

If the exercise of this jurisdiction is sometimes spectacular when the prosecuted persons are State authorities—for example the *Pinochet* case before the British and other European Courts, the *Habré*[17] case before the Senegalese Tribunals or the *Yerodia* case before the Belgian justice system[18]—we must make no mistake: this is only the visible part of the iceberg. International criminal law is not confined to these cases, even if their merit is to remind us that no-one is above internal or international law, and that judges have legal weapons which have been available a long time, but which were locked in old wardrobes or in the studies of university professors who were regarded as dreamers.

[17] See the contribution in this section by Reed Brody.

[18] See ch 12.

However, these cases only illustrate old rules discussed at length elsewhere in this book and on which we will therefore not dwell here.

Besides this anarchic face of international criminal law, there also exist forms of integration in international criminal law. They are found in the establishment of international criminal courts such as the International Criminal Tribunals for the former Yugoslavia and Rwanda, and the International Criminal Court. We remain however far from an absolute and general integration: the ICTs and the ICC only have jurisdiction for *some* international crimes—essentially, genocide, crimes against humanity and war crimes (Statutes of the ICTY, Art 2–5, of the ICTR, Art 2–4, and of the ICC, Art 5–8); the jurisdiction of the ICTs is furthermore confined to offences which were committed in specific States and during a specific time: the territory of the former Yugoslavia since 1 January 1991 (S/Res. 827, para 1, 25 May 1993), and Rwandan territory (including the territory of neighbouring States for crimes committed there by Rwandan citizens) between the 1 January and the 31 December 1994 (ICTR Statute, Art 1).

As regards the jurisdiction of the ICC, this is confined to offences committed on the *territory* of a State *party* or by a *national* of that State (Statute, Art 12. 2), from the entry into force of the Statute vis-à-vis the State (Art 11.2).

This *ratione gentis* jurisdiction is without prejudice to the power of the Security Council acting under chapter VII of the UN Charter to refer to the Prosecutor a situation in which crimes provided for by the Statute would have been committed (Art 13, b).

Whatever the manner, *ratione gentis* jurisdiction or jurisdiction founded on the willingness of the Security Council to act on a case by case basis, we see how the integration of international criminal law, even confined to three categories of crime, remains a mirage since it depends on the goodwill, by definition anarchic, of States.

Considered in this way, the contribution of the law of the ICTs and of the ICC to international criminal law seems to be rather slim. In reality, we observe that the law of the Statutes themselves, as well as that coming out of the jurisprudence of the ICTs, have contributed significantly to the development of international criminal and humanitarian law.

THE CONTRIBUTIONS OF THE STATUTES OF THE ICTS AND OF THE ICC TO INTERNATIONAL CRIMINAL LAW

If a good number of the legal rules in the Statutes reflect existing rules of conventional or customary law, some of them constitute real innovations. Let us consider each of the Statutes in turn.

The Statute of the ICTY

Most crimes provided for by the Statute (Art 2–5) are classic crimes in international humanitarian law: grave breaches of the 1949 Geneva Conventions, violations of the laws and customs of war, genocide, crimes against humanity. However, there is a really new crime: 'employment of poisonous weapons or other weapons calculated to cause unnecessary suffering'.

Of course, this crime corresponded with the prohibitions provided for by, inter alia, on the one hand the 1925 Geneva Protocol and the 1993 Paris Convention on chemical weapons, on the other hand provisions regarding the employment of arms which 'uselessly aggravate the sufferings' of men (1868 St. Petersburg Declaration, Preamble, 4th para; 1907 Hague Regulations, Art 23, e; 1977 1st Additional Protocol, Art 35.2; UN Convention of 10 October 1980, Preamble, 3rd para and Protocol 2 of the Convention, Art 6.2).

However, these prohibitions did not create offences: in 1991, only Article 22.2 of the Draft Code of Crimes against the Peace and Security of Mankind drawn up by the International Law Commission criminalised the use of unlawful weapons,[19] but the text was far from being brought into force, and it did not explicitly address the use of 'arms, projectiles or material calculated to cause unnecessary suffering'.

Therefore, it is important to stress the progressive nature of the ICTY Statute in criminalizing the use of this kind of weapon.

One wonders if the authors of the text realised that they had made a serious contribution to international humanitarian law. Rather, one has the impression that they were unaware that the rule they had formulated marked a departure, since the commentary on the Statute asserted that it confined the law applicable by the Tribunal to undisputed customary law, given the *nullum crimen* rule: 'De l'avis du Secrétaire général, l'application du principe *nullum crimen sine lege* exige que le Tribunal international applique des règles du droit international humanitaire qui font partie *sans aucun doute possible* du droit coutumier'.[20] [Emphasis added.]

Now, if there was a rule whose customary character was in doubt, it was the criminalisation of the use of toxic weapons or weapons causing unnecessary suffering, since we do not know of any conventional or judicial precedent for such an offence. Quite the contrary![21]

All the better for international criminal law which was enriched 'in a roundabout way' with a crime which was sorely missing and which was confirmed in the 1996 version of the Draft Code of Crimes against the Peace and Security of Mankind (Art 20 e, i)[22] and, partially, in the ICC Statute (Art 8.2, b, xvii-xx).

19 *Rapport CDI 1991*, Doc ONU A/46/10, p 293.

20 *Rapport du S.G. établi conformément au §2 de la rés. 808 (1993) du Conseil de sécurité*, Doc. ONU S/25704, 3 May 1993, p 10 para 33.

21 E David, *Principes de droit des conflits armés* (Bruylant, Bruxelles, 1999), 620, para 4.92.

22 *Ann. CDI 1996*, II, 2e partie, p 57.

The Statute of the ICTR

If the ICTR Statute is the little twin brother of the ICTY Statute, it can be distinguished by the crimes provided for: genocide (Art 2), crimes against humanity (Art 3) and violations of Article 3 common to the 1949 Geneva Conventions and its 1977 Additional Protocol II (Art 4).

We observe that the Statute refers not to 'war crimes' *stricto sensu* but to violations of Common Article 3 and of Additional Protocol II. This wording is explained by the fact that the massacres in Rwanda had been committed during civil strife and that the notion of war crimes at that time was confined to violations of the laws of war committed in an *international* armed conflict.[23]

Therefore, the Security Council criminalised acts which were forbidden but which had never been characterised *stricto sensu* as war crimes even if those acts could fall under other categories of crime (crimes against humanity, terrorism, torture). Those acts included violence to life, cruel treatment, corporal punishment, collective punishments, the taking of hostages, acts of terrorism, rape, forced prostitution, pillage, and threat of committing those acts.

Although these crimes were new offences in international criminal law, they did not violate any principle of legality or non-retroactivity of crimes and punishments inasmuch as they corresponded not only with other crimes in international law, but also with crimes provided for by Rwandan criminal law as by the domestic criminal law of the neighbouring States where the ICTR had jurisdiction (see above).

The crimes provided for in Article 4 of the ICTR Statute nevertheless remained in international criminal law a first, which has been confirmed in the *Tadić* judgment when the Appeals Chamber of the ICTY had to found its jurisdiction with regard to the crimes committed in the purely internal phases of the Yugoslav conflict.[24]

The ICC Statute

One of the outstanding contributions of the ICC Statute to international criminal law is to have specified better than had ever been done before which behaviour amounts to war crimes and to crimes against humanity.

Concerning crimes against humanity, the source of these offences mainly lay, on the one hand, in the Statutes of the IMT of Nuremberg (Art 6, c) (1945), of Tokyo (Art 5, c) (1946), of the ICTY (Art 4–5) (1993) and of the ICTR (Art 2–3) (1994), and on the other hand, in international instruments which, implicitly or explicitly, assimilated some acts to crimes against humanity: genocide (Convention of 9 December 1948), *apartheid* (Convention of 30 November 1973, Art 1), use of nuclear weapons (eg A/Res. 1653 (XVI) of the UNGA, 24 November 1961, § 1, d), forced disappearances (A/Res. 47/133, 18 December

[23] David, *Principes de droit des conflits armés*, p 583, paras 4.45/6.
[24] ICTY, *Tadić*, case IT-94-1-AR72, from para 88.

1992, preamble, 4th para). Moreover, these crimes were taken up in the ILC Draft Codes of Crimes against the Peace and Security of Mankind (1950, 1954, 1991 and 1996).

There are as many different definitions as there are sources! The definition embodied by the ICC Statute (Art 7) puts an end to those terminological variations and seems to be the one which reflects most faithfully the *opinio juris* of the international community about the crime against humanity insofar as it has been adopted by a diplomatic conference gathering some 150 States and an equivalent number of NGOs.

It is now possible to define the notion as a set of ordinary grave crimes (murders, tortures, rapes, deportations, enslavement, etc) planned and committed on a mass basis against a civilian population, during or outside an armed conflict, against citizens or foreigners, sometimes on political, racial or religious grounds. The nature of the victims (national or foreigner, civilian or military) and the goal pursued by the authors of these acts are not constituent elements of the definition, except for 'persecutions' which are qualified as crimes against humanity only if they are committed on political, racial or religious grounds.[25]

Concerning war crimes, Article 8 of the ICC Statute takes up more or less all the crimes which were in the 1949 Geneva Conventions, the 1977 Additional Protocol I, and the ICT Statutes, and it adds new crimes corresponding to violations of Geneva law or Hague law committed in an international or an internal conflict. The result is a long enumeration of extremely varied acts, but presented in a finite way contrary to the Statutes of the IMT of Nuremberg (Art 6, b) and of the ICTs (Art 3/4) which stated that the violations of the laws or the customs of war coming within the jurisdiction of these tribunals would include, '*but not be limited to*' (emphasis added), a number of acts mentioned as examples. In the ICC Statute, it is stipulated that the Court can take cognisance of violations of the laws or customs of war, '*namely*' (emphasis added), the acts enumerated in the article, therefore to the exclusion of other acts.

This limited list of offences, in accordance with the principles of restrictive interpretation of criminal law, and without prejudice to the wider crimes found in other instruments (Statute, Arts 10 and 22.3), amounts, in a way, to a penal codification of war crimes.

Another important innovation of the Statute is found in the definition of non-international armed conflicts where war crimes will come within the jurisdiction of the Court. According to Article 8.2 (f), the Court can take cognisance of crimes committed in non-international protracted armed conflicts between governmental authorities and organised armed groups or between such groups. On this point, even if the Statute does not seek to modify the existing instruments, it leads, however, to an implicit extension of the scope of the 1977 Additional Protocol II to the 1949 Geneva Conventions. The Protocol was limited to internal armed conflicts which, on the one hand, *only* pitched the

[25] See ICTY, *Tadić*, IT-94-1-A, 15 July 1999, from para 283.

government against organised armed groups, and on the other hand, were characterised by the fact that these groups effectively exercised *control* over a part of the territory (AP II, Art 1.1). The new definition in the ICC Statute, by widening the notion of armed conflict and the rules applicable in this kind of conflict, leads undisputedly to an improvement in legal protection for the victims.

On the other hand, it is regrettable that States introduced into the Statute a provision excluding criminal responsibility for those who commit crimes mentioned in the Statute on the grounds of state of necessity and/or self-defence (Art 31.1, c). The subject of deep criticism,[26] this provision led Belgium, when it ratified the Statute, to make an interpretative declaration saying that: 'En vertu de l'art. 21 § 1 (b) du Statut et eu égard aux règles du droit international humanitaire auxquelles il ne peut être dérogé [...], l'art. 31 § 1 (c) ne peut être appliqué et interprété qu'en conformité avec ces règles.'[27]

THE CONTRIBUTION OF THE JURISPRUDENCE OF THE ICTS TO INTERNATIONAL CRIMINAL LAW

It is impossible in the limited framework of the present note on the current and future status of international criminal law to make an exhaustive assessment of the contributions made by the ICTs' case-law. One can only put forward some impressions.

The leading case in the ICTs' jurisprudence is the *Tadić* decision given by the Chamber of Appeals of the ICTY on 2 October 1995. This judgment, however, concerns less international criminal law in general than international humanitarian law. Therefore, we shall not come back to this case.

Irrespective of this judgment, the ICTs' jurisprudence has helped to clarify a number of notions, even if one can also have doubts about certain decisions. These clarifications and doubts are considered in turn below.

Some Useful Clarifications

It was not States, but the jurisprudence of the ICTs which enabled the specification in international criminal law of the classical principles of individual criminal responsibility, namely, as in domestic law, the factual element (*actus reus*) and the mental element (*mens rea*).

The *actus reus* has been defined as the 'act of participation which in fact contributes [...] to the commission of the crime'.[28] It is the act itself and includes the order to commit it, the instigation, the planning, the preparation, and complicity in the offence (ICTs' Statutes, Art 7.1/6.1), provided that these acts lead

[26] See on this point A Cassese, 'The Statute of the International Criminal Court: Some Preliminary Reflections?' (1998/1), *EJIL* 154.

[27] *MB* (1 Dec 2000), 40423.

[28] ICTY, *Delalić et al.*, IT-96-21-T, 16 Nov 1998, para 326.

to the offence. According to the Trial Chamber I of the ICTR, in case of criminal participation 'the perpetrator would incur criminal responsibility only if the offence were completed'.[29]

The *mens rea* or the mental element of the offence 'is reflected in the desire of the Accused that the crime be in fact committed'[30] or 'is indicated by the requirement that the act of participation be performed with knowledge that it will assist the principal in the commission of the criminal act.'[31] The *mens rea* emerges from factual elements of the case.[32]

The behaviour of the alleged offender can reveal the criminal intention. As stated by a Trial Chamber of the ICTY, murder requires intention which

> may be inferred from the circumstances, whether one approaches the issue from the perspective of the foreseeability of death as a consequence of the acts of the accused, or the taking of an excessive risk which demonstrates recklessness[33] [. . .] in reckless disregard of human life.[34]

Another notion specified by the ICTs: a superior's criminal responsibility by omission. This principle, which appears in the statutes of the ICTs (Art 7.3/6.3) and of the ICC (Art 28), has been analysed in depth by the ICTY in the *Celebici* (*Delalić et al.*) case.[35]

After having observed that the principle was part of international customary law,[36] the Tribunal brought out three constituent elements of this head of responsibility: [37]

— the authority link between the superior and the subordinate who committed the act: the superior can be military or civilian provided that he really possesses powers of control over the actions of subordinates;[38] it does not matter whether it is *de jure* or *de facto* power, so long as the superior has the material ability to prevent and punish the offence;[39]

— the knowledge or the aptitude to take cognisance of the offence: there is no *juris tantum* presumption that the superior is aware of the offences committed by the subordinate; this knowledge must be shown on a case by case basis taking into account a number of criteria: number, type, and seriousness of

[29] *Akayesu,* ICTR-96-4-T, 2 Sept 1998, para 473.

[30] *Ibid*, para 476.

[31] ICTY, *Delalić et al.*, IT-96-21-T, 16 Nov 1998, para 326; *Tadić*, IT-94-1-T, 7 May 1997, from para 674; *Akayesu*, ICTR-96-4-T, 2 Sept 1998, para 479.

[32] *Akayesu*, ICTR-96-4-T, 2 Sept 1998, para 478.

[33] *Delalić et al,* IT-96-21-T, 16 Nov 1998, para 437.

[34] *Ibid*, para 439.

[35] IT-96-21-T, 16 Nov 1998, paras 330-401.

[36] *Ibid, paras* 333–43.

[37] Also see *Blaskić*, IT-95-14-T, 3 Mar 2000, para 294.

[38] ICTY, *Celebici*, IT-96-21-T, 16 Nov 1998, para 370; also, *Aleksovski*, IT-95-14/1-T, 25 June 1999, paras 76–78.

[39] ICTY, *Celebici*, IT-96-21-T, 16 Nov 1998, paras 354–78, more esp., 378, 735–36, 795; also *Aleksovski*, IT-95-14/1-T, 25 June 1999, paras 118–19; *Blaskić,* para 301; ICTR, *Kayishema et al.*, ICTR-95-1-T, 21 May 1999, paras 216–23, 500, 513

the offences, number of participants, place and time of the offences, etc;[40] if the acts were committed far from the superior, it will be difficult to prove that he was aware of them;[41] the jurisprudence following the Second World War insists on the obligation of the superior to inform himself;[42] the ICTY considers—in particular with regard to the *travaux préparatoires* of Article 86.2 of Additional Protocol I—that customary law imposes not an abstract obligation to inquire and to know but an obligation to react adequately when available information warns the superior that his subordinates are committing crimes;[43]

— the aptitude to prevent or suppress: no one is expected to perform impossibilities; the superior can only "be held responsible for failing to take such measures that are within his material possibility".[44]

Establishing the criteria enabling determination of the responsibility of the author of an international crime or that of his superior is one, among others, of the significant contributions of the ICTs' jurisprudence to the development of international criminal law.

On other points, some decisions of the ICTs leave the reader somewhat perplexed (below).

Some Disputable Positions

One can question the validity of some decisions of the ICTs concerning particularly the issues of duress, the annulment of prosecution and the respective gravity of war crimes and crimes against humanity.

In Romano-Germanic law States, duress is generally considered a subjective justification, also called a cause of non-imputability (or ground of exculpation),[45] ie a cause personal to the agent which suppresses the mental element (*mens rea*) required for the existence of the offence. The offence committed under duress loses its criminal character. For instance, Article 71 of the Belgian criminal code stipulates: 'Il n'y a pas d'infraction lorsque l'accusé ou le prévenu était en état de démence au moment des faits ou lorsqu'il a été contraint par une force à laquelle il n'a pu résister.'

The rule is found in the code of numerous States[46] as well as in the international jurisprudence relating to war crimes: the IMT of Nuremberg accepted the justification of superior orders only if the subordinate did not have the moral liberty to choose.[47] In this hypothesis of duress, criminal responsibility disappears.

[40] ICTY, *Celebici*, paras 384–86; *Blaskić*, para 307.
[41] ICTY, *Aleksovski*, para 80.
[42] ICTY, *Celibici*, paras 388–89; *Blaskić*, paras 322 et 329.
[43] *Ibid*, paras 387–93, 771–72.
[44] ICTY, *Celebici*, paras 394–95; *Aleksovski*, para 81.
[45] F Tulkens and M van de Kerchove, *Introduction au droit pénal*, (Story Scientia, Bruxelles, 1997) 304.
[46] See the examples mentioned by Judges McDonald and Vohrah in their individual opinion in ICTY, *Erdemović*, IT-96-22-A, 7 Oct 1997, para 49.
[47] *Procès, doc off*, 236.

Now, rather surprisingly, the Appeals Chamber of the ICTY in the *Erdemović* case, by three votes to two, concluded that duress was not a justification for a crime against humanity or a war crime;[48] the Chamber said: 'duress does not afford a complete defence to a soldier charged with a crime against humanity and/or a war crime involving the killing of innocent human beings'.[49]

In a very long individual opinion, two judges in the majority—judges McDonald and Vorah—explained on the basis of English and American law why duress could be an extenuating circumstance, but not an exculpatory justification.[50]

This motivation was strongly and convincingly criticised by the two judges in the minority, Judges Cassese and Stephen, who showed,[51] notably, that in most systems of law, duress was a ground of absolute justification for a crime, even for an international law crime, and that the Anglo-American jurisprudence invoked by the majority was not relevant.[52]

The cancellation of prosecution in the *Barayagwiza* case in 1999 is another surprising example from the jurisprudence. In this case, it will be remembered, the Appeals Chamber of the ICTR had admitted that the violations of the Statute, of the Rules and of the right of the accused to a fair process could vitiate the proceedings and lead not only to the release of the accused, but also to a cancellation of the prosecution.[53]

Such a solution was highly disputable since the Statute and the Rules provided for *nothing* in this regard; the Tribunal referred to general principles of international law, but it should have shown that these principles were *generally* recognised; now, to the precedents invoked by the Chamber, one could oppose the rule 'pas de nullité sans texte' which exists in various countries (cf. Belgian judicial code, Art. 860).

In the absence of any provision providing for the annulment of prosecution, invoking the doctrine of the abuse of process on the basis of some common law precedents was improper. The decision, which made a great fuss, was besides reviewed on 31 March 2000 on the basis of new facts brought by the Prosecutor, showing that the rights of the accused had been, in reality, only affected very marginally.[54]

Another controversial issue on which the position of some judges raises doubts: the respective gravity per se of war crimes and crimes against humanity. Can one consider, like some judges of the ICTY[55] and of the ICTR,[56] that the

[48] On this phase of the case, L Cavicchioli, 'Il costrigimento psichico come causa di esclusione della colpevolezza nei crimini contro l'umanità: il caso *Erdemovic*', (1997), *Riv. dir. int.* 373–95.

[49] ICTY, IT-96-22-A, 7 Oct 1997, para 19.

[50] *Ibid*, individ op McDonald and Vohrah, from para 43.

[51] D Turns, 'The International Criminal Tribunal for the Former Yugoslavia: the *Erdemovic* Case', (1998), *ICLQ* 472.

[52] ICTY, IT-96-22-A, 7 Oct 1997, diss. op. Cassese, from para 16.; diss. op. Stephen, from para 14.

[53] ICTR, *Barayagwiza*, ICTR-97-19-AR72, 3 Nov 1999, from para 43.

[54] ICTR, *Barayagwiza*, 31 Mar 2000, from para 54.

[55] ICTY, *Erdemović*, IT-96-22-A, 7 Oct 1997, indiv op Mc Donald and Vohrah, from para 22.

[56] ICTR, *Kambanda*, ICTR-97-23-S, 4 Sept 1998, para 14.

crime against humanity is more serious than the crime of war? Irrespective of the fact that, beyond a certain level of atrocity, it is not very meaningful to make this type of a priori, general comparison, fortunately the Appeals Chamber of the ICTY finally settled the controversy by observing that neither the Statute, nor the Rules of the Tribunal, nor the Statute of the ICC, made any distinction between the two crimes regarding punishments, and there was thus no need to consider that, whether by definition or by hypothesis, a crime against humanity was more serious than a war crime.[57]

CONCLUSIONS

As far as substantive law is concerned, the contribution of the ICTs and of the ICC to the development of international criminal law is far from being inconsiderable. The statutes of these tribunals and their jurisprudence—currently limited to that of the ICTs—contribute to codifying and standardizing the discipline in the area of the suppression of grave violations of international humanitarian law. Of course, this does not cover the whole of international criminal law, but the solutions adopted within the jurisdiction of these tribunals are often transposable to other international offences.

As far as procedural law is concerned, the ICTs and the ICC enable the Anglo-Saxon world and the Romano-civil law world to get to know each other better; if the former widely influences the procedure applied by these tribunals, the latter is not ignored; for instance, the Statute of the ICC seems to allow some participation by the victims of crime in order to obtain reparation (Arts 68 et 75).

Whether it be standardisation or a careful and limited rapprochement, it is a start towards better integration of the international community, even if it is not tomorrow that 'le monde des cités deviendra la cité du monde'(R.-J. Dupuy).

As far as politics is concerned, the ICTs and the ICC give a new dynamism to the suppression of the most serious violations of international humanitarian law. Even if the time of bloody dictatorships is far from being gone, their masters know from now on that the Tarpeian Rock is never very remote from the Capitol.

30 October 2000

[57] ICTY, *Tadić*, IT-94-1-A*bis*, 26 Jan 2000, para 69.

13.4 UK PROSECUTIONS FOR CRIMES UNDER INTERNATIONAL LAW

GEOFFREY BINDMAN

Even with the appropriate national legislation in place to prosecute extra-territorial offences, national authorities such as those in the United Kingdom have appeared reluctant to act. Geoffrey Bindman, who represented a number of victims and human rights groups in the Pinochet proceedings, addresses the possibility that Senator Pinochet could—and should—have been subject to criminal prosecution in the United Kingdom, as an alternative to the extradition proceedings to which he was subject. He describes the efforts by some of the victims and non-governmental organisations to persuade the Attorney General of England and Wales to prosecute Senator Pinochet under section 134 of the Criminal Justice Act 1988. This met initially with the response that in England there was no domestic jurisdiction over torture carried out outside the United Kingdom, at least prior to the 1988 Act, incorporating relevant provisions of the UN Torture Convention. But ultimately the Attorney General declined to initiate proceedings even in respect of allegations of torture occurring after 1988, confirming the reluctance of the United Kingdom authorities to prosecute persons in the United Kingdom who might have committed torture or other international crimes abroad. Bindman contrasts this situation with the work of units established by the police and Crown Prosecution Service to investigate UK residents suspected of offences committed during World War II, and argues that a similar coordinating unit is necessary to investigate those suspected of more recent international crimes.

Pinochet was arrested in Britain in October 1998 and compelled to remain under arrest for more than 16 months, but he was never prosecuted in Britain. His arrest took place not on the initiative of the British prosecuting authorities but as a result of an application by the Spanish government for his extradition to Spain to face prosecution in that country.

The distinction between prosecution and detention pending extradition is important. Pinochet had committed no criminal offence in British territory and British law only allows prosecution for extraterritorial offences in a small number of carefully defined situations. At common law piracy on the high seas was always an offence triable in British courts and murder by a British subject abroad is also traditionally within the domestic jurisdiction. Statutes relating to terrorism and fraud confer extraterritorial jurisdiction as does the Taking of Hostages Act 1982. UK legislation providing for an extraterritorial jurisdiction for certain war crimes and crimes against humanity is detailed in chapter 9, and includes the Geneva Conventions Acts, the War Crimes Act 1991 (which creates jurisdiction over murders committed in Europe by foreign nationals during the

Second World War), and section 134 of the Criminal Justice Act 1988, which makes enforceable in the courts of the United Kingdom provisions of the UN Convention against Torture. The Convention, which by June 2000[58] had been ratified by 119 states including Britain, Spain and Chile, requires state parties to ensure that their courts have jurisdiction over all public officials or those acting in an official capacity within their territory suspected of such crimes regardless of where the crimes took place and regardless of the citizenship of the alleged perpetrator. It is the obligation of the state to investigate the allegations and, if they are substantiated, prosecute or surrender the accused to another state which seeks extradition with a view to prosecution in its jurisdiction. Section 135 of the 1988 Act provides that a prosecution in the UK can be brought only by or with the consent of the Attorney-General.

Under this provision Pinochet could have been arrested and put on trial for torture on any of his previous visits to Britain after torture became an extraterritorial offence in 1988. On two visits before that of 1998 I was involved with Amnesty International in attempts to have him arrested, but neither attempt succeeded. On one occasion an unsuccessful application was made to the Bow Street magistrate for an arrest warrant. On the other the Attorney-General declined to order his immediate arrest but initiated a police investigation. Before it was concluded Pinochet made a hurried departure.

In October 1998, the extradition machinery worked more smoothly. It is plain in retrospect to see why. Extradition is a routine and normal process between the European states which are parties to the 1957 European Convention on Extradition (specific provisions of which, as with the Torture Convention, have been specifically enacted in United Kingdom domestic law.) The administrative authorities are accustomed to the procedures and would not be influenced by political sensitivities or by lack of familiarity with international human rights law.

Furthermore, the extradition process is designed to secure the transfer of suspected criminals between states with the minimum of formality. In practice, there is a strong presumption that an extradition request will be implemented expeditiously. It is not even necessary for the requesting state, having identified an extraditable offence in its request, to produce evidence to justify its intended prosecution.

Pinochet's lawyers had a difficult task in seeking to overcome this presumption and it required considerable ingenuity to find any plausible legal arguments. This is apparent from the fact that once the issue of immunity had been disposed of (and the issue of Lord Hoffmann's disqualification), their opposition effectively collapsed and an extradition order was made by the Bow Street magistrate. Only his medical condition saved Pinochet from the implementation of the extradition order.

It is true that there were issues relating to the identification of the relevant offences and the range of offences contained in the original request was whittled

[58] Redress Trust, *Challenging Impunity for Torture* (Redress, London, 2000), appendix 2.

down to offences of torture alleged to have been committed after the date in 1988 when the UN Torture Convention was implemented in UK domestic law and became binding on Chile and Spain as well as the UK. Even a single offence would of course be sufficient to justify extradition.

Pinochet was in Britain for some days before the Spanish extradition request was delivered. During that period he could and should have been arrested and charged under section 134 of the Criminal Justice Act 1988 with the same offences as those for which the extradition order was eventually made. Once the Spanish request had been received there was understandable reluctance on the part of the Law Officers to embark on a prosecution under United Kingdom law, though there seems no constitutional objection to that being done.[59]

Of course, the aim of bringing Pinochet to justice would have been equally satisfied by extraditing him to Spain or putting him on trial in Britain, and it is possible that the same arguments against trying him could have been advanced in either country. If, for example, he had been charged with torture in violation of British law, it would have been open to him to make the same claim to immunity as a former head of state as he in fact made in the extradition proceedings. The *habeas corpus* application made by Pinochet's lawyers to the High Court and on appeal to the House of Lords would have been essentially the same whether it challenged extradition or prosecution.

The most important difference between extradition and prosecution is that in the former the Home Secretary has a critical role. An extradition case cannot be pursued without his authority and, as emerged in Pinochet, he has the power to terminate it on forming the view that the individual whose extradition is sought is unfit to stand trial.

On the other hand the powers of the Attorney-General (or the Solicitor-General where the Attorney-General is unable to act) in relation to a prosecution under section 134 of the Criminal Justice Act 1988 may in practice be similar. His discretion in determining whether to prosecute is comparable to that of the Home Secretary in deciding whether to allow an extradition request to be pursued and it is well established that the Attorney-General may stop any prosecution whether or not he has initiated it.

However, there was much speculation at the time of Pinochet's arrest, and indeed, throughout the progress of the case, that the Spanish government would be persuaded to withdraw its extradition request. It is well known that there were strong voices in the government which were opposed to it and the highest court in Spain was asked to rule whether it could properly be withdrawn. It ruled at that stage that it could not.

[59] As noted above, s 135 requires that prosecutions are brought only by or with the approval of the Attorney-General. However, the Attorney-General at the time, Lord Williams of Mostyn QC, had been a patron of the Redress Trust, one of the organisations which, with Amnesty International and others, intervened in the extradition proceedings when they reached the House of Lords. For this reason he took no part in the case and it was left to the Solicitor-General, Ross Cranston QC, to make any necessary decisions.

The human rights organisations and victims of Pinochet's crimes were concerned that a sudden withdrawal would result in his release and rapid return home. On their behalf I therefore requested the Attorney-General to carry out the obligations imposed on the United Kingdom government by the UN Torture Convention and initiate a prosecution. While it might have been theoretically possible for him to do this simultaneously with the Spanish extradition proceedings, the point of the request was to ensure that he would be ready to act if the extradition failed.

Although the extradition process under the European Extradition Convention did not require evidence to be put before the court, evidence would be necessary in a prosecution under domestic law. That presented no problem because a substantial volume of evidence was readily available. Indeed, several victims and eyewitnesses were present in the United Kingdom. A dossier of witness statements and other documentary material was provided to the Attorney-General and to the Metropolitan Police which was responsible for the conduct of the investigation.

Nearly all the examples of torture in Chile relied on to justify the extradition request occurred between September 1973 and September 1988, when the Torture Convention was enacted in British domestic law. Evidently the jurisdiction of the Spanish court was not limited to cases arising after the Torture Convention came into effect.[60]

In British extradition law[61] the 'double criminality' rule precludes extradition for crimes which are not crimes in both the requesting and requested states but it was understood by both the Divisional Court and the House of Lords in its first decision to be sufficient to satisfy the rule that torture abroad was a crime in Britain at the time when the extradition application was made (which of course was long after section 134 came into effect). In its third *Pinochet* ruling, the House of Lords on 24 March 1999 took a different view, reversing that of the previous Lords ruling and of the Divisional Court, so that the subsequent extradition order was limited to cases occurring after 1988.

In response to my request to prosecute Pinochet directly, the Attorney-General's office argued that there was no domestic jurisdiction over extra-territorial torture before September 1988. The argument may well have been right from the outset (regardless of the position in extradition law) but it was certainly unanswerable after the Lords decision of 24 March. There was of course evidence of torture after that date so it should have made no difference to the Attorney-General's ability to prosecute in Britain. However, the evidence of Pinochet's direct responsibility in those later cases was less compelling and the prosecuting authorities were sceptical.

Over the several months from the request to the Attorney-General to prosecute in Britain and the decision by the Home Secretary to terminate the extradition proceedings, no clear-cut final response to that request was ever made.

[60] See ch 14 in this volume.

[61] See ch 10.

However, the government was mindful of its obligations under the Torture Convention. The Home Office and the Law Officers were obviously keeping in touch. The Home Secretary announced his decision to terminate the extradition proceedings on 2 March 2000 at 8 am. The Solicitor-General immediately considered whether or not Pinochet should be arrested with a view to prosecution under section 134 of the Criminal Justice Act 1988. The manner of this consideration has not been disclosed. He was of course already in possession of all the material which I had supplied and doubtless had been provided by the Home Office with the medical evidence on which the Home Secretary had based his conclusion that Pinochet was unfit to stand trial. Presumably on the basis of a similar conclusion the Solicitor-General decided not to consent to a prosecution. It did not take him long to make up his mind. Pinochet left for the airport soon after the Home Secretary's announcement and his plane left for Chile later that morning. He arrived in Chile looking fit and cheerful when photographed walking from the plane across the tarmac.

The reluctance to prosecute Pinochet in Britain after Spain had made its extradition request is hardly surprising but there is no creditable reason for the failure of the prosecuting authorities to arrest him before the extradition request and then proceed against him under section 134. When Pinochet arrived in Britain on that and previous occasions the authorities must have been aware at least in general terms of the allegations of torture made against him. Articles 6 and 7 of the UN Torture Convention require every state party in such a case to make a preliminary inquiry into the facts and, if it does not extradite the alleged offender, to submit the case to its competent authorities for the purpose of prosecution. In 1998 that did not happen, nor, after the extradition request, does there appear to have been more than the most perfunctory investigation.

Since torture outside the United Kingdom became a criminal offence in British law in September 1988[62] no prosecutions have been brought in any British court. Before the arrest of Pinochet a Sudanese physician, Dr Mahgoub, who had been found to be living and working in Scotland, was accused of participating in the torture of another Sudanese citizen while they were both in Sudan. The police and prosecuting authorities investigated the matter with a view to a prosecution under section 134. Evidence was available to support the allegation and witnesses were prepared to attend court to testify. The Lord Advocate, who in Scotland exercises the powers given to the Attorney-General by section 134, had given his consent and a trial date was fixed. However, before the trial started it appears that the Lord Advocate re-considered his decision and

[62] Alone among the judges of the House of Lords who sat in *Pinochet No 3*, Lord Millett considered that systematic torture was an extraterritorial offence in British law by 1973, when Pinochet came to power. He said: 'For my own part, therefore, I would hold that the courts of this country already possessed extraterritorial jurisdiction in respect of torture and conspiracy to torture on the scale of the charges in the present case and did not require the authority of statute to exercise it. I understand, however, that your lordships take a different view. . . I shall accordingly proceed to consider the case on the footing that Senator Pinochet cannot be extradited for any acts of torture committed prior to the coming into force of the section'.

the prosecution was withdrawn. It has been reported that the Lord Advocate on re-consideration decided that the evidence was not strong enough after all to justify pursuing the matter. The unexpected change of mind has never been satisfactorily explained.

There is good reason to believe that other perpetrators of torture and other crimes against humanity abroad have been admitted to the United Kingdom as refugees or for other reasons. Early in 2000 I was asked by the Government of Rwanda to seek the prosecution of Colonel Muvunyi, a former officer in the Rwandan army, for torture while he participated in the massacre of many thousands of fellow Rwandans. I was told that his name was listed for prosecution by the International Criminal Tribunal for Rwanda but his name was so far down the list that it might take years to reach the top. Colonel Muvunyi had been admitted to Britain some 18 months previously to join his wife who was already living in the country. I provided the Organised Crime Squad, the department at Scotland Yard responsible for investigating such cases, with a dossier of evidence and invited them to investigate. While they did not refuse to do so, the officers who came to see me to discuss the case explained that they were busy and could not give the matter priority. They promised to get in touch with me again as soon as possible. Meanwhile Colonel Muvunyi continued to live undisturbed in South London. A photograph of his home had been published in a national newspaper. Some weeks later I was telephoned by the senior police officer in charge of the case. He informed me that he had arrested Colonel Muvunyi for transfer to the ICTR in Arusha, Tanzania. He remains in Arusha awaiting trial.

I do not know why his transfer to Arusha was so dramatically accelerated but it is certainly possible that the British authorities gave some encouragement to those in Arusha in order to avoid the burden of a trial in the United Kingdom. That would have been consistent with the attitude of the British government which has already been remarked upon in the Pinochet case and which was also evident in the debates on the International Criminal Court Bill, now enacted.[63]

The International Criminal Court Act provides that those war crimes, crimes against humanity and genocide over which the International Criminal Court will have jurisdiction are also crimes under United Kingdom domestic law. Most, including torture, are already crimes under domestic law but an extraterritorial element is also desirable in order to give adequate power to the British courts to arrest, detain and surrender to the ICC anyone indicted by the ICC.

A broader reason for extending the jurisdiction of the British courts is the aim of 'complementarity' which underlies the Rome statute. The ICC cannot try every crime against humanity. The task of bringing to justice the perpetrators of such crimes belongs to the whole world community and must be shared between the ICC and the courts of the nation states which support it. The

[63] International Criminal Courts Act 2001, introduced in order to provide necessary support for the International Criminal Court.

Rome Statute itself makes this clear in its preamble which affirms:

> that the most serious crimes of concern to the international community as a whole must not go unpunished and that their effective prosecution must be ensured by taking measures at the national level and by enhancing international co-operation

and recalls:

> that it is the duty of every State to exercise its criminal jurisdiction over those responsible for international crimes.

The International Criminal Court Bill did not embody this principle of universal jurisdiction. In its first draft, jurisdiction of domestic courts was to be restricted to crimes committed within the United Kingdom or outside it by United Kingdom citizens. The minister then in charge of the Bill, Peter Hain MP, argued that prosecutions in Britain for crimes committed abroad would be difficult and inconvenient because witnesses would not be easy to interview and bring before the court. While this might be true in some cases it hardly justifies failing to put on trial those against whom the evidence is available and who would be likely to escape justice altogether if they were not tried in Britain.

Subsequently, the government agreed to extend jurisdiction to crimes committed abroad by non-UK citizens provided they were resident in the United Kingdom. Of course where there is already universal jurisdiction as in the case of torture covered by section 134 of the Criminal Justice Act 1988, that jurisdiction will remain but it leaves an anomaly. A future Pinochet could be prosecuted in Britain, as the actual Pinochet could have been, for torture, but he could not, as a non-UK resident, be prosecuted for other crimes against humanity within the jurisdiction of the ICC.

The reluctance of the British government to prosecute in Britain those present here who may have committed crimes against humanity abroad is reflected in the absence of effective administrative machinery for the investigation and assessment of such cases. An exception, however, is the War Crimes Act 1991.

Following heated Parliamentary debates and the rejection of the Bill by the House of Lords on more than one occasion, this Act gave jurisdiction to British courts over offences of murder violating the laws and customs of war committed in Germany or German-occupied territory between 1939 and 1945. Jurisdiction was restricted to UK citizens and other residents of the United Kingdom. The legislation was designed to bring to justice the perpetrators of those crimes who had come as refugees to Britain after the war and who would otherwise be able to remain in Britain with impunity. Inevitably, there were very few who had survived and those who had were unlikely to be fit to stand trial. So far there has only been one conviction under the Act and there are unlikely to be any more.

Nevertheless, the task of implementing the Act was taken seriously and special units were set up by the police and Crown Prosecution Service to investigate possible offences and offenders. These units have now been disbanded.

If it was thought appropriate to take this trouble to deal with the inevitably small number of cases which were likely to arise under the War Crimes Act, the most recent of which could not be less than 46 years old when the Act was passed, why should there not be similar units to take responsibility for crimes against humanity of more recent origin?

As my experience illustrates, there is a lack of co-ordination and of any focus of responsibility for such cases among the organs of the British government. The Attorney-General is the head of the criminal justice system and the Crown Prosecution Service has authority delegated by him for the conduct of prosecutions. The Attorney-General has a central personal role in prosecutions under section 134 of the Criminal Justice Act 1988 because his consent for any prosecution is required by the statute. Extradition is the responsibility of the Home Office but the Foreign and Commonwealth Office is responsible for matters of international law and international human rights law. The police in London are answerable to the Home Secretary but not under his direct control. The Immigration Service, which has a duty to exclude non-citizens seeking admission to Britain who are guilty of crimes against humanity, is answerable to the Home Secretary. The Lord Chancellor's Department has since May 2001 taken over responsibility from the Home Office for the Human Rights Act 1998 and human rights generally.

Doubtless there is consultation and communication between these different departments about the prosecution of extraterritorial crimes, but there is no unit or department which seems to have the main responsibility. There is a strong case for the creation of a single central body, modelled perhaps on the War Crimes Act units, to develop and implement policy in this increasingly important area.

13.5 THE UN HUMAN RIGHTS MACHINERY AND INTERNATIONAL CRIMINAL LAW

SIR NIGEL RODLEY

UN special rapporteurs and other mechanisms play an important role in monitoring and reporting patterns of human rights violation, but to be effective much of their work relies on governments granting them access. Will state authorities be less inclined to co-operate if the possibility of international criminal prosecutions grows?

Nigel Rodley, a member of the UN Human Rights Committee and until recently the Special Rapporteur on torture, describes how the experience of the UN human rights mechanisms in addressing both de facto and de jure impunity has led them to underline the importance of a strong International Criminal Court. He reflects on the interrelationship between human rights laws and institutions and the emerging institutions of international criminal justice. He appears hopeful that the criminal justice rules may themselves assist in promoting human rights protection, but he also suggests the need for caution. As the mechanisms may in their investigations of human rights violations often also be uncovering evidence of crime, they will need to conduct their inquiries with care to avoid complicating any future prosecutions. They may also need to consider their role as potential witnesses, whether a rule of confidentiality is required to secure access, and the need for a policy on the extent of co-operation with criminal tribunals.

In view of the intense interest shown by those working for the protection of human rights in the reinforcement of the norms and institutions of international criminal law, as evidenced by the key role played by human rights non-governmental organisations at the Rome conference that adopted the Statute of the International Criminal Court,[64] a note of conceptual caution needs to be struck. International legal liability is normally founded on the notion of state responsibility. It is to states that international law is primarily addressed and it is they that mainly violate its rules. Even when international law requires states to bring criminal charges against individuals, it is an obligation of state responsibility and the violation of the obligation may often be reducible to reparation in monetary form.

At least since Nuremberg, there has been a notion that international law may in some cases bypass the corporate entity of the state and address itself directly to individuals as direct bearers of responsibility under that law, involving criminal liability for failure to comply with the relevant norms. While the International Military Tribunal at Nuremberg may not have been a clear manifestation of this (it has been argued to be a pooled exercise of national jurisdictional rights),[65] certainly the principles applied by the IMT and approved by the UN General Assembly set the stage for that normative evolution. The creation of the International Criminal Tribunals for the former Yugoslavia and Rwanda and, especially, the adoption of the Rome Statute have now definitively embodied the notion normatively and institutionally at least in respect of genocide, crimes against humanity and war crimes.

Conceptually, historically and politically, the development was based on a linking idea, namely, the existence of acts whose commission envisages state prosecution on the basis of universal jurisdiction, notably 'grave breaches' of the General Conventions and acts of torture (at least on the part of state parties to the Convention against Torture in respect of nationals of such state parties (cf *Pinochet*)).

In brief, some acts may in certain contexts both engage the (vicarious) responsibility of the state on behalf of which they were committed and the

[64] See, for example, the 'On the Record' collections of the NGO Coalition for an International Criminal Court, available on the internet at www.advocacynet.org/news_vol9.html

[65] See G Schwarzenberger, 'The Problem of an International Criminal Court', (1950), 3 *Current Legal Problems* 263, 290

(direct) responsibility of the individuals involved in their commission. Usually the acts in question will also violate national laws. In sum, they are acts perceived as deserving to be treated as criminally culpable.

Most inter-governmental human rights activity is essentially aimed at addressing state responsibility. To be sure, that is the prime focus of the UN human rights machinery, be it treaty-based or Charter-based. Yet that machinery has consistently lamented the persistence of individual impunity as a cause, or at least a condition for the persistence, of the violations in question.[66]

EFFORTS OF HUMAN RIGHTS MACHINERY TO PROMOTE THE APPLICATION OF CRIMINAL RESPONSIBILITY

The interest of the UN human rights machinery (such as UN Special Rapporteurs and Working Groups) was tellingly evidenced by the fact that, in contemplation of the Rome conference, several of the mechanisms made recommendations in their reports to the 1998 session of the UN Commission on Human Rights in favour of the establishment of a strong international court.[67] I can say with authority that there was no co-ordination or orchestration of their initiatives. The relevant bodies simply were aware that such a court was of major significance, precisely in respect of their concerns about human rights violations within their mandates.

Addressing impunity is generally routine work for some mandates. For example, the Special Rapporteur on summary, arbitrary and extrajudicial executions and on torture will routinely ask governments, inter alia, what measures they have taken to establish the criminal responsibility of perpetrators of acts falling within their mandates, they will lament the absence or insufficiency of the action and make recommendations designed to prod the legal system into action against the typical *de facto* impunity. They sometimes speak out against amnesties and other measures aimed at insulating perpetrators from legal liability (*de jure* impunity). Indeed, in 1995 four of them issued an urgent appeal to the Government of Peru in respect of legislation that would provide just such an amnesty in respect of offences committed by members of the security forces in their struggle against the brutal Shining Path insurrection.[68]

A key aspect of their work is examining alleged cases of violations within their mandates, especially when on fact-finding visits to countries where

[66] Eg, 'UN World Conference on Human Rights: Vienna Declaration and Programme of Action', Part I, paras 60 and 91, (1993), 32 *Int'l Legal Materials* 1663.

[67] UN Docs E/CN.4/1998/68, para 137 (Special Rapporteur on extrajudicial, summary or arbitrary executions); E/CN.4/1998/38, paras 227–29 (Special Rapporteur on torture); E/CN.4/1998/39, ch IV (Special Rapporteur on the independence of judges and lawyers); E/CN.4/1998/54, ch IE (Special Rapporteur on violence against women).

[68] Special Rapporteurs on torture, on extrajudicial, summary or arbitrary executions, and on the independence of judges and lawyers, and Working Group on Enforced or Involuntary Disappearances: UN Doc E/CN.4/1996/35, paras 133–35.

governments have invited them. Does this mean that they may develop information that may amount to evidence of criminal activity? The answer to this question is cautiously affirmative. The aim is to identify the prevalence of the phenomenon, not make firm findings in individual cases and, even less, to identify the individual perpetrator(s). However, the reality is that certain individual alleged torturers may be identified in circumstances in which there is strong evidence relating to the offence. The recent practice, at least of the Special Rapporteur on torture and, as far as I am aware, of others, is not to focus on this aspect. Sometimes names of alleged perpetrators may be submitted to the country's authorities, though they will rarely appear in the rapporteurs' reports.

Clearly if the information referred to events taking place within the context of a genocidal campaign or of 'a widespread or systematic' attack directed against any civilian population (crimes against humanity) or of an armed conflict (war crimes), then the information could be of interest to an international criminal court. This, in turn, could lead to the possibility of requests to testify before such a court. The very possibility raises practical questions as to the storage and retrieval of information and, indeed, policy questions as to the appropriateness of testifying. The UN mechanisms will have to consider whether they are bound by or need (for example for the purpose of access) a rule of confidentiality such as the one the International Committee of the Red Cross has successfully invoked before the ICTY.[69]

POSSIBLE IMPACT OF INTERNATIONAL CRIMINAL LAW ON THE ACTIVITIES OF THE HUMAN RIGHTS MACHINERY

Evidently one hoped-for result of developments in international criminal law, especially in the expansion of international jurisdiction and increased application of universal jurisdiction, would be a decrease in the human rights violations that are also contemplated by international criminal law and are of concern to the UN human rights machinery. Whether this will be the case, either by operation of the principle of deterrence or by the awareness-raising impact of the symbolic nature of these developments, must remain speculative at this stage.

Another possible effect could be on the nature of investigations undertaken by the machinery. If the special rapporteurs or other mechanisms conclude that they may have a role as witnesses, then their processing of information will have to take account of the possibility that they may find themselves called upon to testify. In any event, they will need to be careful that their investigations (crime scenes, *corpora delicti*, interviews) are so conducted as to avoid complicating official prosecutorial inquiries.

[69] *Simić and Others*, 27 July 1999, ICTY Press Release JL/P.I.S/439-E; see Jeannet, 'Recognition of the ICRC's long standing rule of confidentiality—An important decision of the international criminal tribunal for the former Yugoslavia', *Int'l Rev of the Red Cross,* 838 (2000), 403

If, speculatively, they decide not to follow the ICRC approach (confidentiality), then that could potentially affect their access. Negotiations with governments for visits could prove more difficult, as could co-operation on the ground by officials closer to potential direct implication. In fact, there seems no sign at this stage of the feared reluctance. As far as co-operation with local officials is concerned, for example heads of police stations, there is anyway often a certain reticence to be overcome, not least because they may have a personal interest in concealing information that could point to their involvement in acts that are unlawful under national law.

It is the higher political levels that tend to be more willing to acknowledge the existence of a problem at large, even if they will support local officials' versions of the facts in an individual case. Indeed, sometimes the very invitation to a special rapporteur to visit reflects a will at some senior political level to improve the situation, the findings and recommendations of international machinery constituting support for their efforts.

Where there is often reluctance to invite the machinery is in conflict situations of the sort and level where war crimes and crimes against humanity may be resorted to in terms of counter-insurgency strategies of the security forces. It could be envisaged that in such situations the security forces would more frequently expect the political authorities to prevent intrusive scrutiny by external bodies.

In general, then, from the perspective of one who has been responsible for a UN mandate on a human rights violation that is also a crime under international law, the accent on the criminal aspect is an important contribution to addressing the problem of impunity. There is no evidence at this stage of any adverse consequence for the work of the mandate-holders. If such evidence were to appear, it would likely be because of fear of the activities resulting in the identification of individual criminal responsibility. The machinery would then be faced both with professionalising its information gathering, processing and retrieval systems, and with establishing a policy position on the nature and extent of co-operation with international (or, for that matter, national) criminal tribunals.

13.6 USING UNIVERSAL JURISDICTION TO COMBAT IMPUNITY

REED BRODY

The wide variety of national proceedings now instituted under the principle of universal jurisdiction, particularly before the Belgian courts, has led to concerns over the haphazard or partial application of international justice. Universal jurisdiction might arguably be more effective in the pursuit of perpetrators of crimes under international law if human rights activists adopted a more strategic approach. Reed Brody, the Special Counsel at Human Rights Watch, assesses the potential which now exists for the use of the concept of universal jurisdiction to combat impunity. With the Pinochet case having breathed 'new life' into universal jurisdiction, he describes some of its immediate consequences in other jurisdictions, and identifies the elements which non-governmental organisations might focus on in developing a litigation strategy aimed at 'building favourable precedents so that universal jurisdiction becomes a widely accepted and potent tool'. Amongst the elements he identifies are: the need to ensure that the perpetrator is in a state in which prosecution or extradition is legally and practically possible; strong and accessible evidence; the absence of immunities; and a broad political consensus that the use of universal jurisdiction is appropriate.

The *Pinochet* case in the UK reaffirmed the principles of international law that a country can judge the crime of torture no matter where the acts were committed, and that not even a former head of state has immunity from prosecution. But it also showed that there are countries where, if the circumstances are right, these lofty principles can actually be applied in practice.

Human rights groups described the Pinochet arrest as a 'wake-up call' to tyrants everywhere, but an equally important effect of the case has been to give hope to other victims, many of whom are now exploring how to use foreign courts to bring their tormentors to justice.[70] Britain's Law Lords, by basing their ruling on the United Kingdom's obligations under the UN Convention against Torture to 'prosecute or extradite' alleged torturers on its territory,[71] sent a powerful message to the 122 state parties to that treaty.

OBSTACLES TO THE USE OF UNIVERSAL JURISDICTION

The *Pinochet* case thus breathed new life into the principle of universal jurisdiction that every state has an interest in bringing to justice the perpetrators of particular crimes of international concern, no matter where the crime was committed, and regardless of the nationality of the perpetrators or their victims.

As previous contributors to this book have noted, such cases were until recently rare, apart from those concerning crimes committed during World War II. In the 1990s, even before *Pinochet*, a number of European countries used the universality principle to bring to justice perpetrators of brutality in Rwanda and the former Yugoslavia.[72] In July 1999, French police arrested a Mauritanian

[70] See, eg, Human Rights Watch, *The Pinochet Precedent: How Victims Can Pursue Human Rights Criminals Abroad* (HRW ,New York, updated Feb 2001).

[71] Convention against Torture, Art 7(1).

[72] Cases have been brought in Denmark, France, Germany, the Netherlands and Switzerland. See Redress, *Universal Jurisdiction in Europe. Criminal prosecutions in Europe since 1990 for war crimes, crimes against humanity, torture and genocide* (Redress, London, 1999).

colonel, Ely Ould Dah, who was studying at a French military school, on the basis of the Convention against Torture, when two Mauritanian exiles identified him as their torturer. Ould Dah, free on bail, slipped out of France in March 2000. However, in 1997, the United Kingdom arrested a Sudanese doctor residing in Scotland for alleged torture in Sudan, but later dropped the charges, apparently for lack of evidence. In August 2000, Mexico arrested Ricardo Miguel Cavallo, a former Argentine military official. Judge Balthásar Garzón of Spain has filed an extradition request for Cavallo based on the torture and 'disappearance' of over 400 people.

The use of this revived tool will not be easy, however, particularly against political leaders. The Pinochet prosecution in Spain was made possible by the compilation of information over decades first by Chilean human rights activists, then by the Chilean National Commission on Truth and Reconciliation and finally by Spanish lawyers and judges. Roberto Garretón, who served as Legal Director of Chile's pugnacious Vicariate of Solidarity during the dictatorship before becoming an Ambassador in the democratic government, proudly reflected that, 'while we did not know it at the time, the painstaking work of documentation we did then is now being used—25 years later—to bring Pinochet to justice'. Unlike many other situations of mass killings, as in Central Africa, East Timor or Central America, every Chilean victim—even the 'disappeared'—has a name and a story, and the chainofcommand leading up to General Pinochet is clear.

In addition, the fact that a country has ratified the Torture Convention, requiring it to prosecute or extradite alleged torturers, or the Geneva Conventions for alleged war criminals,[73] or that customary international law calls for the universal prosecution of the perpetrators of genocide or other crimes against humanity, is not always enough to ensure that the country's laws actually permit such a prosecution. In many legal systems, treaties must be specifically 'incorporated' into domestic law before they can be relied on, and countries often fail to do so.

Another key hurdle in future transnational prosecutions will be the political will of the countries involved. Indeed, in retrospect, what was revolutionary about the Pinochet case was not so much the rulings of the House of Lords as that London police immediately executed the arrest warrant sent by Judge Garzón, and that Britain's Home Secretary Jack Straw then twice made the diplomatically difficult decision to allow Spain's extradition bid to proceed. While the Spanish government itself was opposed to the prosecution, a strongly supportive Spanish public opinion prevented the government from opposing Garzón. Other countries might have made decisions more weighted to the political costs of a break with the international status quo.

[73] 'Each High Contracting Party shall be under the obligation to search for persons alleged to have committed, or to have ordered to be committed, such grave breaches, and shall bring such persons, regardless of their nationality, before its own courts'.

In March 2000, for instance, Ricardo Anderson Kohatsu, a Peruvian intelligence officer accused of vicious torture, was sent by the Peruvian government to testify to the Inter-American Commission on Human Rights in Washington. When NGOs denounced his presence and presented credible evidence, US law enforcement officials detained him. The State Department intervened to free Anderson Kohatsu, however, on the questionable pretext that he was entitled to immunity. In August 1999, when Izzat Ibrahim alDuri, a top aide to Iraqi President Saddam Hussein, visited Vienna to receive medical treatment, a local city councilman filed a criminal complaint against him, citing his active role in Iraq's genocide against the Kurds. Less than 48 hours later, the Austrian government let him leave the country, placing its relations with Iraq above its international treaty obligations. In November 1999, the former tyrant of Ethiopia, Mengistu Haile Mariam, wanted by the Ethiopian authorities on charges of genocide and crimes against humanity, visited South Africa to receive medical treatment. Despite calls from local and international groups for his arrest, and despite South Africa's strong human rights record, he was not apprehended and he returned to exile in Zimbabwe, where the government has sheltered him since his fall. When Abu Daoud, accused in the massacre of Israeli athletes in the 1972 Munich Olympics, was apprehended in France in 1976, Paris gave short shrift to extradition requests from West Germany and Israel and freed him four days after his capture. No European country was eager to try Kurdish rebel leader Abdullah Ocalan when he was apprehended in Italy. It's hard to imagine anyone arresting Henry Kissinger, even if a country like Laos or Cambodia were brazen enough to request his extradition.[74]

In addition, a number of former leaders accused of crimes against humanity now live peacefully in foreign countries. In addition to Mengistu now in Zimbabwe, they include Idi Amin who is being sheltered by Saudi Arabia. When asked about the possibility of Amin's extradition or prosecution, a Saudi ambassador explained to the author that Bedouin hospitality meant that once someone was welcomed as a guest in your tent, you did not turn him out. The second reign of Milton Obote as President of Uganda (1980–1985) is thought to have even exceeded the brutality of the Amin era. After he was deposed in a May 1985 military coup, Obote fled and now lives unmolested in Zambia. Generals Raoul Cedrás and Philippe Biamby, the brutal de facto leaders of Haiti were granted asylum in Panama which has refused Haiti's extradition request, even though Panama ratified the Torture Convention in 1987 and has laws allowing for the prosecution of torture committed abroad. Emmanuel 'Toto' Constant, the CIA-backed leader of Haiti's 'FRAPH' death squad who now lives in New York, is wanted by Haitian prosecutors to face charges of murder, torture and arson carried out during Cedrás' de facto rule, but US authorities have refused

[74] Kissinger has been called for questioning, however, by judges in Chile, Argentina and France probing into Pinochet-era crimes. He has not submitted himself to any of the three judges. In addition, the family of Chilean military chief Rene Schneider has sued Kissinger for damages in a United States federal court for his role in a CIA kidnapping and murder of Schneider in a 1970 attempt to foment a military uprising to block the election of Salvador Allende.

to deport or extradite him. Alfredo Stroessner of Paraguay now lives in Brazil. In July 2000, the President of the Human Rights Committee of Brazil's National Assembly called for his prosecution. JeanClaude 'Baby Doc' Duvalier, Haiti's 'president for life' is living in France. In September 1999, four Haitian torture victims filed complaints with a French prosecutor charging crimes against humanity which were rejected because France's 1994 law on crimes against humanity is not retroactive.

It may also prove difficult to convince a foreign prosecutor, or investigating judge, to initiate the investigation of a crime committed outside of his or her country which diverts human and financial resources from a local case, particularly given the expense of international cases and the possible lack of local interest. The victims and most of the evidence will be located in the territorial state (where the acts were committed). Therefore, victims, witnesses, and documents will have to be transported to the prosecuting state. This can pose enormous financial difficulties and safety issues, as well as cultural, linguistic, and legal problems. In theory, the government in the territorial state should provide assistance pursuant to the many bilateral and multilateral treaties in force, but these are procedurally cumbersome and poorly implemented. If the territorial state opposes the prosecution, as may often be the case, these hurdles will be all the greater.

A LITIGATION STRATEGY

Given these obstacles, it is likely that most successful cases applying universal jurisdiction against higher officials will have to be supported by larger non-governmental organizations (NGOs) like the Fédération internationale des ligues des droits de l'Homme (FIDH) or Human Rights Watch which are willing to put their resources behind victims' efforts and serve as a 'facilitating intermediary' between the NGOs or victims in the territorial state and the authorities in the prosecuting state.[75] This is the situation in the prosecution of Hissène Habré, as will be shown below.

I would suggest that in these efforts, the cause of justice would be best served by a litigation 'strategy' explicitly aimed at building favourable precedents so that universal jurisdiction becomes a widely accepted and potent tool. While victims will naturally seek to use all means to defeat the impunity their torturers enjoy, international NGOs should try to focus their resources on *winnable* cases, in which:

— there is active support of the NGOs (or their equivalent) in the territorial state;
— the perpetrator already is, or is likely to be, in a state in which a prosecution

[75] Another model is the London-based NGO 'Indict' which is collecting evidence for use in trials against Iraqi leaders.

would be legally and practically possible or from which he could be extradited to such a state;
- — the evidence is strong and accessible;
- — there are no immunities which would defeat prosecution,[76] and
- — there is a broad political consensus (north/south, left/right) that the use of universal jurisdiction is appropriate in the particular case.[77]

The need for such a strategy is illustrated by the imprudent use of the Belgian anti-atrocities law. A 1993 law, amended in 1999, gives Belgian courts the authority to prosecute individuals accused of genocide, crimes against humanity and war crimes regardless of the crimes' connection to Belgium or, on the face of it, the accused's presence on Belgian soil.[78] The law also explicitly bars any immunity. These aspects, combined, make the law the broadest in the world and a potentially powerful tool to combat impunity. In a landmark trial, with wide public support in Belgium, four Rwandans living in Belgium were convicted in June 2001 by a Belgian jury on charges of involvement in the 1994 genocide in their country. However, an avalanche of new cases ensued helter-skelter. [79] Some of these cases charge sitting leaders with crimes having no connection to Belgium, and most of the defendants will never come before a Belgian jurisdiction, but the filings have caused diplomatic headaches for the Belgian government and threatened to kill the goose that laid the golden egg. As a result, the law has been challenged on three fronts. First, Belgian politicians have argued that the law has turned Belgium into a magnet for all the world's human rights cases. Secondly, the Democratic Republic of the Congo (DRC) brought a successful case against Belgium before the International Court of Justice arguing that a Belgian arrest warrant for its then-Foreign Minister violated international law.[80] Finally, in the case against Israel's Ariel Sharon, an appeals court is hearing arguments that the law cannot apply to defendants who are not on Belgian soil. The likely result of these challenges will be some curtailment of the law.

[76] The question of state immunity is of course likely to arise in any prosecution of state-sponsored human rights crimes. See ch 3.

[77] The author and others discussed these criteria in a meeting which led to the publication of International Council on Human Rights Policy, *Hard cases: bringing human rights violators to justice abroad. A guide to universal jurisdiction* (1999).

[78] A requirement for the suspect to be present on the territory has however been found by a Belgian court in the Sharon case; the ruling is being appealed.

[79] Defendants include Congo Republic President Denis Sasso-Nguesso, Iraqi President Saddam Hussein, Israeli Prime Minister Ariel Sharon, Ivory Coast President Laurent Gbagbo, Rwandan President Paul Kagame, Cuban President Fidel Castro, Central African Republic President Ange-Felix Patasse, Palestinian Authority President Yassir Arafat, Chad's former president, Hissène Habré, Pinochet, former Iranian president Hashemi Rafsanjani, former Moroccan interior minister Driss Basri, and former Foreign Minister Abdoulaye Yerodia Ndombasi of the Democratic Republic of the Congo. It was the Sharon case, in particular, that began to cause a serious re-thinking of the law.

[80] See ch 12 in this volume.

THE PROSECUTION OF HISSÈNE HABRÉ—AN AFRICAN PINOCHET

The leading post-Pinochet case employing universal jurisdiction, the prosecution of Hissène Habré, largely meets the litigation criteria set forth above. In February 2000, a Senegalese court indicted Chad's exiled former dictator, Hissène Habré, on charges of torture and crimes humanity, and placed him under house arrest. It was the first time that an African had been charged with atrocities by the court of another African country. In March 2001, however, Senegal's Court of Final Appeals ruled that he could not be tried in Senegal for crimes allegedly committed in Chad. The victims are now seeking Habré's extradition to stand trial in Belgium, while the United Nations Committee against Torture has requested Senegal not to let Habré leave the country except via extradition, and Senegal has agreed to hold him. In the meantime, the case has opened new possibilities for justice in Chad itself.

Habré ruled Chad with French and US support from 1982 until he was deposed in 1990 by current president Idriss Déby and fled to Senegal. Since Habré's fall, Chadians have sought to bring him to justice. The Chadian Association of Victims of Political Repression and Crime (AVCRP) compiled information on each of 792 victims of Habré's brutality, hoping to use the cases in a prosecution of Habré. A 1992 Truth Commission report accused Habré's regime of 40,000 political murders and systematic torture. With many ranking officials of the Déby government, including Déby himself, involved in Habré's crimes, however, the new government did not pursue Habré's extradition from Senegal.

In 1999, with the Pinochet precedent in mind, the Chadian Association for the Promotion and Defense of Human Rights requested Human Rights Watch's assistance in bringing Habré to justice in Senegal. Researchers secretly visited Chad twice, where they met victims and witnesses and benefited from the documentation prepared in 1991 by the Association of Victims. Meanwhile, a coalition of Chadian, Senegalese and international NGOs,[81] as well as a team of Senegalese lawyers, was quietly organised to support the complaint. Seven individual Chadians acted as private plaintiffs, as did the AVCRP.

In a criminal complaint filed in Dakar, the plaintiffs—several of whom came to Senegal for the event - accused Habré of torture and crimes against humanity. The torture charges were based on the Senegalese statute on torture as well as the UN Convention against Torture, which Senegal ratified in 1986. The Senegalese constitution expressly states that international treaties, once ratified, have the force of domestic law. The groups also cited Senegal's obligations under customary international law to prosecute those accused of crimes against humanity.

[81] The groups supporting the case are the Dakarbased African Assembly for the Defense of Human Rights (RADDHO), all the major Chadian human rights groups, the National Organisation for Human Rights (Senegal), the Londonbased Interights, the FIDH, and the French organisation Agir Ensemble pour les Droits de l'Homme. Upon filing the complaint, representatives of these groups formed the International Committee for the Trial of Hissène Habré.

In their court papers, the groups provided details of 97 political killings, 142 cases of torture, 100 'disappearances', and 736 arbitrary arrests, most carried out by Habré's dreaded DDS (Documentation and Security Directorate), as well as a 1992 report by a French medical team on torture under Habré, and the Chadian Truth Commission report. The organisations presented the sworn testimony of two former prisoners who were ordered by the DDS to dig mass graves to bury Habré's opponents.

The case, brought as a private prosecution (*plainte avec constitution de partie civile*), moved with stunning speed. Within three days, the victims gave their closed-door testimony before investigating Judge Demba Kandji—something they had waited nine years to do! Kandji then called in Habré on 3 February 2000 and indicted him as an accomplice to torture and crimes against humanity and placed him under house arrest.

Habre's lawyers moved before the Indicting Chamber (*Chambre d'Acccusation*) of Dakar's Court of Appeals to dismiss the case, asserting that Senegalese courts had no competence over crimes committed in Chad, that crimes committed before Senegal's 1986 ratification of the Torture Convention could not be taken into account and that the prosecution was barred by the Statute of limitations. The newly elected President of Senegal, Abdoulaye Wade, whose closest advisor was also Habré's attorney, appeared to take Habré's side. The prosecutor's office, which before had been supportive, now joined Habré's motion for dismissal, and the Superior Council of the Magistracy, presided by Wade, transferred Judge Kandji off the case and promoted the president of the Indicting Chamber which was hearing Habré's dismissal motion.

The victims asserted that the Torture Convention obliged states to either prosecute or extradite alleged torturers who enter their territory and that under Article 79 of the Senegalese constitution, international treaties, once ratified, had a higher rank than ordinary law. The Indicting Chamber nevertheless ruled that Senegalese courts had no competence under Senegal's code of criminal procedure to pursue crimes that were not committed in Senegal. The court also rejected charges of crimes against humanity, asserting that Senegalese positive law contained no such crime. The victims appealed the decision to the *Cour de Cassation,* Senegal's court of final appeals.

President Wade, undeterred by international criticism, repeatedly stated that Hissène Habré would not be tried in Senegal. The *Cour de Cassation* upheld the ruling on 20 March 2001, saying that 'no procedural law gives the Senegalese courts universal jurisdiction to prosecute and to try accused [torturers] who are found on Senegalese territory when the acts were committed outside of Senegal by foreigners; the presence of Hissène Habré in Senegal cannot in and of itself be ground for the prosecution against him'.

Even before the ruling, another group of victims, supported by the same coalition, had silently filed a case against Habré in Belgium, to create the possibility of extradition to stand trial there. That case is now before an investigating magistrate who has been taking evidence and hearing dozens of witnesses brought to Belgium by the NGOs supporting the prosecution. It is expected that, barring any immediate change in Belgian law, the Belgian judge will seek Habré's extradition.[82]

The victims also announced their intention to file a petition against Senegal before the UN Committee against Torture, seeking a ruling that Senegal amend its laws to explicitly provide for the prosecution of alleged torturers, and either initiate a state investigation against Habré or compensate the victims. On 7 April, Senegal's President Abdoulaye Wade declared publicly that he had given Habré one month to leave Senegal. This abrupt decision was a tribute to the victims' efforts, but raised the possibility that Habré would go to a country out of justice's reach. The victims appealed to the Committee against Torture, which granted interim measures calling on Senegal to 'take all necessary measures to prevent Mr Hissène Habré from leaving the territory of Senegal except pursuant to an extradition demand'. Following an appeal by Kofi Annan, President Wade stated on 27 September 2001 that he had agreed to hold Habré in Senegal pending an extradition request from a country capable of organising a fair trial.

Back in Chad, Habré's arrest had an immediate impact. The Association of Victims and the NGOs gained a new stature in Chadian society, having returned from Dakar with Habré's scalp, and announced their intention to file criminal charges in Chadian courts against their direct torturers, many of whom are still in government.

On 27 September 2000, President Déby, in a reversal, met with the Victims' leadership to tell them that 'the time for justice has come' and that he would support their cases. Déby also promised to clean up his administration of former agents of Habré's political police, the DDS. On 26 October, 17 victims lodged criminal complaints for torture, murder, and 'disappearance' against former members of the DDS. The case was initially thrown out before being reinstated by Chad's Constitutional Court. In May 2001, an investigating judge began to hear witnesses. The victims' actions are a direct challenge to the continuing power of Habré's accomplices, who have begun to respond violently: in July 2001, the victims' Chadian lawyer, Jacqueline Moudeina, was seriously injured when a grenade was thrown at her by security forces commanded by one of the ex-DDS defendants.

The Habré case reveals the possibilities and the difficulties of using universal jurisdiction. There is a huge financial cost, thus far borne by the NGOs supporting the victims. Political will in the forum state is determinative. Litigation must be accompanied by campaigning and lobbying. Unless extraterritorial competence is specifically incorporated, courts may refuse to prosecute, as in Senegal. Most importantly, perhaps, prosecutions abroad can empower victims at home.

[82] Unlike many of the other cases filed in Belgium, the Habré case offers an immediate possibility of the extradition of a defendant who enjoys no immunity. As described in this article, the territorial state, the current custodial state and the United Nations are in accord with Habré's trial in Belgium.

PART V

Conclusion

14

Enforcing Human Rights through International Criminal Law

MARK LATTIMER

The significant advances in international criminal justice described in this book, made with accelerating pace over the last decade, should be seen in the context of a crisis in the international system of human rights protection. Mass abuses perpetrated by states against their own peoples within their own borders—precisely the arena in which human rights were meant to offer protection—escalated in the experience of profound and often violent political upheavals that marked the end of the Cold War.[1] *In extremis*, the carefully articulated system of international human rights norms and standards, human rights treaty-monitoring bodies, and UN and other inter-governmental human rights machinery, repeatedly failed to deliver either protection or justice.

In one sense, of course, criminal justice is always a response to a failure to protect rights. But the establishment, for example, of the International Criminal Tribunal for the former Yugoslavia by the UN Security Council in 1993 represented a concerted international response to a situation recognised as crisis.[2]

The crisis in international human rights protection is characterised both by a systemic level of material failure in the principal mechanisms for implementing human rights and, as human rights standards are augmented every year, by an ever expanding gap between normative expectation and delivery.

Shortcomings in the UN and regional mechanisms have been described at length elsewhere[3] and only a few summary remarks will be made here about

[1] See for example, PIOOM, *World Conflict and Human Rights Map*, (Leiden University, Leiden, various years); Ted Robert Gurr, *Minorities at Risk: A Global View of Ethnopolitical Conflicts* (United States Institute of Peace, Washington DC, 1993).

[2] The UN Security Council resolution establishing the Tribunal expressed 'grave alarm at continuing reports of widespread and flagrant violations of international humanitarian law occurring within the territory of the former Yugoslavia, and especially in the Republic of Bosnia and Herzegovina, including reports of mass killings, massive, organised and systematic detention and rape of women, and the continuance of the practice of "ethnic cleansing", including for the acquisition and the holding of territory,' S/Res/827 (1993).

[3] See for example Anne Bayefsky, 'Report on the UN Human Rights Treaties: Facing the Implementation Crisis' in *First Report of the Committee on International Human Rights Law and Practice* (International Law Association, Helsinki Conference, 1996) and the response by Philip Alston in Philip Alston and James Crawford, *The Future of UN Human Rights Treaty Monitoring* (Cambridge University Press, Cambridge, 2000), 501–25. For a particularly scathing critique of the

those mechanisms purporting to operate at the universal level. The six human rights treaty-monitoring bodies face a backlog of over 100 overdue state reports each, and resource constraints have led to further delays in their consideration both of state reports and of individual petitions, prompting one leading commentator to remark that 'the system, established to oversee state compliance, depends for its continued functioning on a high level of state default'.[4] The special rapporteurs, working groups and other special procedures of the UN Commission on Human Rights face all the disadvantages of reporting to a political body that only meets in ordinary session once a year. Their fact-finding work is valuable, but even where reporting is able to be made in a timely fashion, a lack of political will or co-ordination with other parts of the UN system mean that follow up action is rarely forthcoming.[5]

The UN human rights mechanisms should naturally not be criticised for failing to accomplish tasks that they are not mandated to undertake. Their achievements in furthering and legitimising international scrutiny of the human rights performance of individual states are considerable, and their weaknesses are principally due to the fact that ultimately they have to rely for implementation on the co-operation of the offending state. Neither the special procedures of the Commission on Human Rights, nor the Office of the High Commissioner for Human Rights, have any powers of enforcement beyond naming and shaming. Even the work of the treaty-monitoring bodies—often referred to hopefully as human rights implementation—is really only another institutionalised expression of *droit de regard*: authorised only to make 'comments', 'general recommendations' or to 'forward views', the committees' deliberations are of a non-judicial character and any remedies awarded in individual cases unenforceable.[6] As a rule, furthermore, international courts and treaty-monitoring bodies can only hear cases once domestic remedies have been exhausted, a process which can take years.

This highlights the greatest weakness in the international human rights system, which is that the primary responsibility under the system for policing violations falls to the same entity responsible for perpetrating them: the individual state. Human rights treaties define norms which states are legally obliged to observe, but enforcement, such as it exists, has all the features of a voluntary code of conduct, based essentially on standard-setting, the public exposure of default, and moral suasion. Even worse, states may ratify human rights treaties

African Commission on Human and Peoples' Rights, see Geoffrey Robertson, *Crimes Against Humanity* (Allen Lane / Penguin, London, 1999), 57–9.

[4] James Crawford, 'The UN Human Rights Treaty System: A System in Crisis?' in Alston and Crawford, *The Future of UN Human Rights Treaty Monitoring*, at 6. See *ibid* at 5 for detailed figures on overdue state reports.

[5] The most notorious example of this was the failure of the UN Secretariat, or indeed states, to act on information from a Commission special procedure about the situation in Rwanda, leading to what has been acknowledged by the UN as the 'preventable genocide' of 1994. See *Prevention of armed conflict: Report of the Secretary-General*, 7 June 2001, UN Doc A/55/985-S/2001/574.

[6] See for example, in the case of the UN Human Rights Committee, ICCPR Article 40(4) and Optional Protocol Art 5(3).

just so that they can claim observance, when in reality no effort is made to improve human rights performance. Remedies in public international law generally are obtained at the suit of the injured state, but in human rights law the state whose citizens suffered violations and the state accused of the conduct are one and the same.

The disparity between the growing body of international standards and their implementation prompted moves to include enforcement measures explicitly in more recent treaties. The attempt to create a worldwide criminal jurisdiction in the 1984 UN Convention against Torture thus exhibits three features which are shared by the other advances in international law described in this volume:

(1) the assumption by the international community of states of a jurisdiction to enforce rather than merely a jurisdiction to prescribe;
(2) characterisation of that enforcement jurisdiction as obligatory rather than optional;
(3) identification of the individual offender, rather than the state, as the subject of enforcement measures.

Each of these features has proved necessary to overcome what might be referred to as the obstacle of the state. The third feature, in particular, has created enough distance between the legal person of the state and the perpetrators of gross abuses of human rights as to enable state sovereignty to be reconciled, at least in part, with international enforcement measures. Conversely, the greatest problems have occurred where that distance is difficult to establish, for example where the alleged perpetrators embody the authority of the state in their role as head of state or minister for foreign affairs.

While the crisis in human rights implementation has spurred the development of international criminal law, it has also placed upon it a high burden of expectation. Human rights activists are increasingly looking to international criminal justice to perform a range of functions—from deterrence to post-conflict reconciliation—which it cannot deliver in isolation from other implementation mechanisms. We will return to these issues in revisiting some of the major themes covered by contributors to this book.

First, however, it would be useful to take a more detailed look at the problem of enforcement by considering how human rights law and international criminal law have both developed in response to a crime which, perhaps even more than torture, characterises our own era: the 'disappearance'.

ENFORCED DISAPPEARANCE: HISTORY OF A CRIME

An enforced disappearance is essentially a state kidnapping where all knowledge of the detention is denied. Victims are frequently tortured and extra-judicially executed, although sometimes they reappear (in 1991 in Morocco, for example, over 300 prisoners were released following an international campaign after being held in secret detention for up to 19 years).[7] The crime is not a new invention: for centuries, perceived opponents of governments have been made to 'disappear' in countries across the world. As a systematic tool of intimidation, expressly designed to thwart legal measures for protecting human rights, it is of more recent origin, but still used as far back as Guatemala in the late 1960s and, arguably, by French forces in Algeria a decade earlier.[8] In many Latin American states from the 1970s onwards, the use of disappearances was developed and refined to become a multi-faceted instrument of repression.

The characteristics of disappearances can be briefly summarised. From the moment of his or her abduction, the family or relatives of the victim do not know what has happened to their loved one. Enquiries or appeals to the police, local authorities, security services or the army are met with blank denials, both as regards the whereabouts of the victim, or the fact of custody. In most cases the victims are never seen again. Occasionally they may be released, often having been tortured, or bodies are found with signs of torture, making relatives in other cases fear the very worst. The fact that they never actually know means that the anguish continues day by day, year by year, with no chance to mourn, to recover or to rehabilitate.

For every individual who is disappeared, then, there are many victims in the form of family and friends who are terrorised, often cowed into silence for fear of somehow making the fate of their loved one worse, or inviting a similar fate on themselves. As abductions are often carried out by security forces in plain clothes, or by paramilitary forces or death squads with the approval or acquiescence of the state, the identity of the perpetrators is frequently unclear, bolstering impunity and heightening the paranoia of potential victims. The families of the disappeared often speak, paradoxically, of a sense of stigma or even shame as, in the absence of other explanations, the integrity of their disappeared son or daughter is itself called into question. With that, the repression is complete.

Without a place of detention, or a body, avenues of legal redress are closed off. Writs of *habeas corpus* fail when there is no *corpus*, and criminal complaints fall without an alleged perpetrator. For its effective operation, domestically or internationally, human rights law requires a victim, and in the crime of disappearance, the victim has vanished.

The UN first expressed a general concern about the practice of disappearances in a General Assembly resolution in 1978, largely prompted by events in Chile and Argentina. A UN Working Group on Enforced or Involuntary Disappearances was established in 1980. But two cases later that decade were of seminal importance in finding chinks in the state armour of secrecy and

[7] See Amnesty International, *"Disappearances" and Political Killings: Human rights crisis of the 1990s* (AI, Amsterdam, 1994), at 68.

[8] See Raphaëlle Branche, *La torture et l'armée pendant la guerre d'Algerie 1954–1962* (Gallimard, Paris, 2001); and for a recent controversial memoir by a senior army officer, see General Paul Aussaresses, *Services Spéciaux: Algérie 1955-1957* (Paris, Perrin, 2001), particularly pp 143–55 and 194–95.

impunity that surrounded the practice of disappearances: the cases of Angel Manfredo Velásquez Rodríguez and José Gregorio Saavedra González.

Manfredo Velásquez, a Honduran student, was kidnapped from a parking lot in downtown Tegucigalpa in the afternoon of 12 September 1981 by several heavily-armed men in civilian clothes driving a white Ford without license plates. The security forces denied he had been detained, but several eyewitnesses reported that he had been taken to the cells of a public security forces station in a barrio of Tegucigalpa and on that basis a petition was later filed with the Inter-American Commission of Human Rights. Following considerable difficulties in obtaining relevant evidence, not least because key witnesses in the case were assassinated, the Inter-American Court of Human Rights finally delivered its judgment in July 1988.[9] It succeeded not only in exposing the legal obfuscations with which victims are faced, but in establishing principles of state responsibility over the practice of disappearances.

The Government of Honduras raised the objection that the case was not admissible because domestic remedies had not been exhausted. The Court was informed that three writs of habeas corpus and two criminal complaints had been brought on behalf of Manfredo Velásquez between 1981 and 1984, which were either dismissed or yielded no result. The Court reasoned that if

> as the Government has stated, the writ of habeas corpus requires the identification of the place of detention and the authority ordering the detention, it would not be adequate for finding a person clandestinely held by State officials, since in such cases there is only hearsay evidence of the detention, and the whereabouts of the victim is unknown.

Noting that 'in no case between 1981 and 1984 did a writ of habeas corpus on behalf of a disappeared person prove effective', the Court rejected the Honduran Government's objection. It concluded:

> . . . during the period under consideration, although there may have been legal remedies in Honduras that theoretically allowed a person detained by the authorities to be found, those remedies were ineffective in cases of disappearances because the imprisonment was clandestine; formal requirements made them inapplicable in practice; the authorities against whom they were brought simply ignored them, or because attorneys and judges were threatened and intimidated by those authorities.

The Inter-American Court found that the state of Honduras was responsible for the involuntary disappearance of Manfredo Velásquez and required it to pay compensation, noting that 'the forced disappearance of human beings is a multiple and continuous violation of many rights under the Convention'. Referring to the general obligation of states parties under Article 1 of the American Convention on Human Rights to ensure the free and full exercise of the rights recognised by the Convention to every person subject to its jurisdiction, the Court further drew some wide-reaching conclusions regarding state responsibility:

[9] *Velásquez Rodriguez* Case, judgment of 29 July 1988, Ser C No 4 (1988).

> This obligation implies the duty of the States Parties to organise the governmental apparatus and, in general, all the structures through which public power is exercised, so that they are capable of juridically ensuring the free and full enjoyment of human rights. As a consequence of this obligation, the States must prevent, investigate and punish any violation of the rights recognised by the Convention and, moreover, if possible attempt to restore the right violated and provide compensation as warranted for damages resulting from the violation.

Furthermore, the Court made some telling remarks which go to the tendency of states to distance themselves from violations by describing them as unfortunate excesses or ascribing them to rogue elements in the security services.

> . . . any exercise of public power that violates the rights recognised by the Convention is illegal.... This conclusion is independent of whether the organ or official has contravened provisions of internal law or overstepped the limits of his authority: under international law a state is responsible for the acts of its agents undertaken in their official capacity and for their omissions, even when those agents act outside the sphere of their authority or violate internal law.

This underlines the point that the international system of human rights protection, focusing on the obligations of states, is distinct from any domestic or international criminal proceedings against individual perpetrators. Yet the human rights courts can aid criminal justice, not just in upholding victims' rights to reparation (which may include instituting criminal proceedings against alleged perpetrators), but also in exposing the mechanics of institutionalised human rights violations. In the Velásquez Rodríguez case, in contrast to a criminal action, the Honduran Government could not rely on the defence that the complainant had failed to present adequate evidence when in fact it could not be obtained without the state's co-operation.

The passing reference by the Inter-American Court to the continuous nature of the violations in the Velásquez Rodríguez case echoes another case which also played an important role in helping dismantle the wall of official impunity around enforced disappearances, this time in Chile. Like Manfredo Velásquez, José Gregorio Saavedra González was a young student, president of his high school student association. He was one of the last victims to be executed in the so-called 'Caravan of Death', an army operation in October 1973 aimed at eliminating perceived political opposition to the new Chilean military government. General Sergio Arellano Stark, officially delegated by Pinochet, led a group of army officers who toured the country by helicopter, executing at least 72 political prisoners held in prisons and detention centres. On 19 October the caravan arrived at its last stop in Calama, where José Gregorio Saavedra was held. Of the 26 prisoners there interrogated and then shot, he was one of 13 whose bodies had never been found.[10]

[10] See http://www.santiagotimes.cl/derechos/dictadura_poder_4_eng.html

The Caravan of Death took place within the time period covered by the Chilean amnesty law of 1978.[11] However, in April 1986, José's mother, Ana Luisa González filed a criminal complaint for the abduction and murder of her son. It argued that, as the victim had never been found, the abduction was an ongoing offence and was therefore not covered under the terms of the amnesty. The argument was not new, but it was persuasive: if the absence of the body in the crime of disappearance serves to impede any effective legal redress, then it should inhibit the application of a legal amnesty too.

Following a jurisdictional tussle, the case was transferred to a military court which invoked the amnesty law in order to close the case. However, the González argument set an important precedent which fed into a growing international consensus about the ongoing nature of the crime of disappearance and the fact that it amounted to long-term torture. That precedent was used a decade and a half later by another Chilean judge to crack open Pinochet's amnesty.

In 1992 the UN General Assembly adopted a Declaration on the Protection of all Persons from Enforced Disappearance[12] which stated in Article 1 that

> enforced disappearance places the persons subjected thereto outside the protection of the law and inflicts severe suffering on them and their families. It constitutes a violation of the rules of international rule guaranteeing, *inter alia*, the right to recognition as a person before the law, the rights to liberty and security of the person and the right not to be subjected to torture and other cruel, inhuman or degrading treatment or punishment.

Article 17 went on to provide: 'Acts constituting enforced disappearance shall be considered a continuing offence as long as the perpetrators continue to conceal the fate and the whereabouts of persons who have disappeared and these facts remain unclarified.' This is also now reflected in the Draft International Convention on the Protection of All Persons from Forced Disappearance,[13] where it is stated in Article 5: 'This offence is continuous and permanent as long as the fate or whereabouts of the disappeared person have not been determined with certainty.'

In the UK *Pinochet* proceedings, after the House of Lords had radically truncated the outstanding charges against Pinochet by ruling that only crimes committed after December 1988 could be considered, the magistrate at the committal hearing considered whether this could include the continuing cases of 1,198 disappeared people detailed in the Spanish extradition request. He concluded that it could, noting 'the effect on the families of those who disappeared can amount to mental torture'.[14] The very sophistication of the cruelty that disappearance inflicted had provided the key to gaining reparation for the victims.

[11] Decree law 2191, *Diario Oficial* 19 April 1978.

[12] UN Doc A/47/49 (1992).

[13] UN Doc E/CN.4/Sub.2/1998/19, annex.

[14] *Kingdom of Spain v Augusto Pinochet Ugarte*, judgement in the Bow Street Magistrates' Court, 8 Oct 1999, reproduced in Reed Brody and Michael Ratner (eds), *The Pinochet Papers* (Kluwer Law International, The Hague, 2000), 403.

Following Pinochet's return to Chile, Judge Juan Guzmán Tapia, with whom outstanding criminal complaints against Pinochet were lodged, concluded that because the bodies of 19 victims of the 'Caravan of Death' in 1973 had never been found, their kidnapping was an ongoing offence which extended beyond the term covered by the amnesty law. In a ruling in July 1999, Chile's Supreme Court upheld that decision, confirming that the amnesty law could not be applied where the victim was still missing and the death could not be certified legally.

Looking closely at the nature of enforced disappearance as a human rights violation enabled the Inter-American Court of Human Rights to establish the full burden of state responsibility for this most terrible of acts. However, it was only the recognition of disappearance as a crime of a continuing character that enabled the further practical obstacles to redress represented by the non-retroactivity of jurisdiction and amnesties from prosecution to be overcome.

JUSTICE IN SOCIETIES IN TRANSITION

The continuing nature of the crime of enforced disappearance perhaps illustrates most starkly the difficulty of the challenge faced by post-conflict societies or states in transition from dictatorship to democracy. It is a commonplace to say that cross-community reconciliation requires some form of coming to terms with the past, even if there is wide debate about what form that process should take in different situations.[15] But how is reconciliation under a new regime possible, if violations commenced under the old continue?

Civil society organisations representing the victims of enforced disappearance, including the Association of Relatives of Disappeared Persons in Chile and the Mothers of the Plaza de Mayo in Argentina, have been among the most insistent in campaigning for justice throughout long periods of political transition in their countries. The establishment of truth commissions in many Latin American countries over the past 20 years, including those in Bolivia, Argentina, Chile, El Salvador, Haiti, Guatemala, and more recently in Panama and Peru, could be seen partly as a result of that insistence. Surveying the very mixed record of these commissions, however, it is notable that hardly any led to significant criminal proceedings against the individual perpetrators of abuses and in relatively few cases was new information made available about the whereabouts of the disappeared.

Recent Chilean history is illuminating both as an illustration of how international judicial action can trigger human rights progress nationally, particularly in relation to the victims of enforced disappearance, and in what it shows about the respective roles of truth commissions and criminal proceedings (which are sometimes presented, erroneously, as alternatives).

[15] For two recent studies, see Priscilla Hayner, *Unspeakable Truths: Confronting State Terror and Atrocity* (Routledge, New York, 2001), and Martha Minow, *Between Vengeance and Forgiveness: Facing History after Genocide and Mass Violence* (Beacon Press, Boston, 1998).

On 11 September 1998 Chile celebrated its national day on the anniversary of the military coup which brought General Pinochet to power, as it had for each of the preceding 24 years. Since stepping down as President in 1990 after losing a plebiscite, Pinochet had held the status of senator-for-life. Recently retired as commander-in-chief of the armed forces, he continued to wield a profound influence over the Right in Chilean society, in particular over the military, as well as inspiring widespread fear. Criticism in the press was partly held in check by the *desacato* provisions in Chilean law, criminalizing 'contempt of authority'.

Following the 1991 report of the Chilean National Commission for Truth and Reconciliation, chaired by Senator Raul Rettig, and the successor National Corporation for Reparation and Reconciliation, which concluded in 1996 that 3,197 people had been killed or forcibly disappeared in Chile during Pinochet's rule,[16] a number of criminal cases had been brought by victims' relatives, some of which mentioned Pinochet. But Pinochet enjoyed a three-fold immunity: the first five most bloody years of his rule were covered by the amnesty law of 1978, passed by Pinochet himself; the status of senator-for-life carried with it an immunity from prosecution; and the fact that Pinochet was a former soldier enabled jurisdiction over any case against him to be claimed by a military court, where the chances of conviction were commonly agreed to be negligible. The military courts had routinely claimed jurisdiction over cases involving abuses under the former military government and closed them forthwith citing the amnesty law.

Pinochet moved freely, both in Chile and on occasional foreign trips to buy arms or meet old allies, such as Margaret Thatcher in the UK. He had once warned, reacting to calls for justice in Chile, that 'No-one is going to touch my people'. On that September day in 1998, planning his next trip to London, Pinochet himself seemed untouchable.

Two years later, following his arrest and prolonged detention in the UK, the situation in Chile was very different. Pinochet's name was now included in over 150 cases pending before the Chilean courts concerning human violations during his rule. Ten months of government-sponsored talks, known as the *Mesa de Diálogo*, had brought together military officials, the church and human rights lawyers in an attempt to pinpoint the fate of those forcibly disappeared. This implicit admission of responsibility by the military was quickly compounded by a succession of publicised admissions and denunciations by retired army officers, often seeking to limit their own responsibility by providing information on cases of torture and forced disappearance and detailing Pinochet's involvement.

The riots and right-wing backlash that had been widely predicted in some parts of the global media when Pinochet was first arrested in London never materialised. On his return, a growing majority of Chileans polled indicated

[16] *Comisión Nacional de Verdad y Reconciliación*, established under Supreme Decree No 355, signed on 25 April 1990; and *Corporación de Reparación y Reconciliación*, established under Law 19.123, Feb 1992.

that they believed Pinochet was guilty of human rights abuses and should be tried. The newly-elected President of Chile, Ricardo Lagos, emphasised: 'Let's not interfere with justice, let's let justice speak,' adding '. . . everybody in Chile, the humble and the powerful, is subject to the courts'. Even Chile's national holiday in September was shifted from the anniversary of the Pinochet coup and renamed the 'day of national unity'.

Most significantly of all, the Chilean courts had started to whittle away Pinochet's legal immunity. Defining enforced disappearance as a continuing crime had enabled the Supreme Court to rule that the 1978 amnesty did not cover Pinochet for the cases of those still missing from the 'Caravan of Death', which headed the list of those lodged with Judge Guzmán against Pinochet. On Pinochet's return to Chile, Judge Guzmán also successfully persuaded a court to lift his parliamentary immunity from prosecution as a senator-for-life. In August 2000, the Supreme Court upheld that ruling too, by a surprisingly clear margin of 14 judges to six.[17] Chile's judiciary had come a long way from the time of the military government when, in the words of the Rettig Report, 'The attitude the judiciary adopted... aggravated the ... systematic violation of human rights... by failing to grant immediate protection to persons arrested, and by according repressive agents impunity for their criminal actions...' The way was now clear for a criminal investigation and Pinochet's arrest and questioning for involvement in the enforced disappearance of 19 victims of the Caravan of Death. In the space of just two years, Chile had undergone a remarkable transformation.

The precise extent to which this transformation had been directly caused by the international proceedings against Pinochet can not of course be verifiably established and will always be subject to conjecture. Judge Guzmán himself is categoric: 'It was like a vaccination. We Chileans got accustomed to him being locked up (so to speak), to seeing his case argued before the courts.'[18] Others have called for a more 'nuanced' evaluation. José Zalaquett, another Chilean lawyer who was a member of the Rettig Commission, while acknowledging 'the enormous impact that Pinochet's detention [in London] has had in Chile', contends that 'increasing efforts to call Pinochet to account in Chile would have taken place at any rate—most likely in a different shape or on a lesser scale or at a slower pace—had the former dictator never travelled to London'.[19]

Judicial proceedings in Chile continue at the time of writing. Following medical tests and his questioning by Judge Guzmán, the Supreme Court of Justice ruled in July 2002 by a margin of four to one that Pinochet was mentally unfit to stand trial.[20] Investigations continue, however, against other former

[17] For the text in Spanish see http://www.derechos.org/nizkor/chile/juicio/desafuero2.html

[18] *Times,* London, 19 Feb 2002.

[19] José Zalaquett, 'The Pinochet Case: international and domestic repercussions' in Alice H Henkin (ed), *The Legacy of Abuse: Confronting the Past, Facing the Future* (Aspen Institute/NYU, New York, 2002), p 55.

[20] See Amnesty International, AI Doc AMR 01/006/2002, 3 July 2002.

members of the armed forces. Information on enforced disappearance cases submitted by the armed forces in January 2001 as a result of the *Mesa de Diálogo* was incomplete and included obvious errors but did provide further details on some 200 cases. As a result of the discussions, nine judges were appointed by the Supreme Court to devote their exclusive attention to enforced disappearance cases.

Meanwhile, cases against Pinochet and other senior officials of the military government continued to progress in a number of other states, maintaining the pressure for justice. In October 2000 a Buenos Aires court requested the extradition of Pinochet and six others for their alleged role in the murder of the former head of the Chilean army, Carlos Prats, and his wife in a bombing in Argentina in 1974. In November an Argentinean court sentenced Enrique Arancibia Clavel, a former Chilean secret police agent, to life imprisonment for his involvement in the bombing. In July 2001 Pinochet's arrest was also ordered by an Argentinean judge in relation to his role in Operation Condor, a co-ordinated security operation by governments in the Latin American cone which was responsible for numerous enforced disappearances, political killings and other human rights violations. In France an investigating magistrate issued international arrest warrants for Pinochet and 14 others in October 2001 in connection with the abduction and murder of five French citizens during the military government.

Considering the events following Pinochet's detention in London, it is possible to make some early reflections on the process of justice and reconciliation in Chile. Legal action in the courts of foreign states, particularly on the basis of a universal jurisdiction over the crime of torture, managed to kick-start serious judicial investigation of human rights abuses that earlier had quickly stalled. At the same time it contributed to a wide, and predominantly peaceful, transformation in public attitudes towards those responsible for grave human rights violations under the military government. The two truth commissions had published extensive accounts of violations and the effects on victims, but had never identified perpetrators or investigated criminal responsibility. They were never any substitute for a judicial process.

But the commissions were a necessary, if hardly sufficient, condition for that process to have been initiated in earnest. They performed a vital role both in documenting cases of torture and other human rights violations on which much of the *Pinochet* case would subsequently rest, and in helping Chilean society publicly to recognise what had been done in its name in the recent past.

Much existing argument presenting truth commissions as an alternative to criminal proceedings focuses on the South African experience. However the Truth and Reconciliation Commission in South Africa was exceptional, both in its wide powers to examine witness evidence and in identifying individual perpetrators. The power of the Commission to recommend amnesty for perpetrators who made full confessions and co-operated with the Commission has drawn much comment, but it should be remembered that as a general rule the

Commission process did not preclude criminal proceedings (without the threat of which there would have been few confessions), a point made forcefully by the then South African President, Nelson Mandela.[21]

The experience of transitional societies in Chile and elsewhere in Latin America indicates that truth commissions and criminal proceedings each play a distinct, but potentially complementary role in a national reconciliation process, reflecting the need to establish both state and individual responsibility for gross human rights abuses. A properly constituted truth commission can uncover the nature, scope and scale of abuses, paving the way for a statutory reparation programme for victims. With care, its investigations may also uncover evidence that can later be used in criminal proceedings,[22] including notably evidence of the widespread or systematic nature of abuse that is necessary to establish that a crime against humanity has occurred. However, new democratic governments in Latin America, trying to find some accommodation with a military apparatus of continuing power and influence, have often seen investigations stall at this point, the individual perpetrators benefiting from pardons or amnesties. With the abusers effectively hiding behind the general admission of state responsibility, the location of the disappeared remained hidden too.

The ability of international criminal justice to spur domestic proceedings depends on national pardons or amnesties not being recognised as a bar to prosecutions for crimes against international law.[23] The threshold applied by the Rome Statute of the International Criminal Court in this regard derives from the principle of 'complementarity', under which the Court can only act where a case is of sufficient gravity and a state is 'unwilling or unable genuinely' to investigate or prosecute. The criteria to determine unwillingness in a particular case are listed in Article 17(2) and include an unjustified delay in instituting proceedings, undertaking proceedings or deciding not to prosecute for the purpose of shielding the person concerned from criminal responsibility, or otherwise conducting proceedings in a manner inconsistent with an intent to bring the person to justice. As these provisions clearly relate to criminal proceedings, the award of an amnesty from prosecution would not suffice to defeat the Court's jurisdiction, although the grant of a pardon following conviction might.[24] The ICC

[21] See for example the BBC news report 'Mandela: No blanket apartheid amnesty', 25 February 1999, at http://news.bbc.co.uk/1/hi/world/africa/286468.stm See also the contribution by Alex Boraine on the *Botha* case in ch 13.

[22] But see the contribution in ch 13 by Sadakat Kadri for an example of how the activities of a commission can also inadvertently prove deleterious to the quality of available evidence.

[23] It should be noted that international humanitarian law, in the form of Art 6(5) of Protocol II Additional to the Geneva Conventions, itself calls for 'the broadest possible amnesty for persons who have participated' in an internal armed conflict, but the ICRC has stated that this does not extend to those who have committed violations of humanitarian law.

[24] See the discussion of this issue in John T Holmes, 'The Principle of Complementarity' in Roy S. Lee (ed), *The International Criminal Court: The Making of the Rome Statute* (Kluwer Law International, The Hague, 1999), 76–7. Holmes argues, referring to the *ne bis in idem* principle in Art 20, that 'The fact that a pardon or granting of parole took place shortly after a conviction may give rise to a presumption that the entire proceedings were not genuine...'

Prosecutor could, therefore, initiate a prosecution in the case of someone granted an amnesty by a national truth commission.[25]

But the ability of international justice to encourage domestic proceedings also depends on there being a functioning national justice system. In many post-conflict situations, a state's inability rather than unwillingness to act may in fact prove the harder obstacle to surmount. The ICC has the *authority* to act where there is a total or substantial collapse of the national judicial system, and the power to order reparations to victims, but this may be of little comfort where neither it nor the state concerned has the *capacity* to deal with hundreds, thousands or even tens of thousands of cases in a given post-conflict situation. The recent histories of Rwanda, Sierra Leone and Afghanistan all provide bleak examples of the problem. Such states do not have the resources available to the various authorities in Germany after World War II, when the de-nazification process instituted by the Allied Powers involved the screening of some 13 million people and the processing of over half a million through special courts,[26] and later over 91,000 Germans were tried in the Federal Republic of Germany alone for wartime participation in crimes under international law.[27] The Rwandan government has instituted new arrangements to deal with those suspected of involvement in the 1994 genocide, loosely based on a traditional village justice system. Known as *gacaca*, the system clearly does not meet international standards for fair trial, but may yet be preferable to leaving tens of thousands of alleged *genocidaires* to rot in jail for the rest of their lives.

Debate in the rapidly growing literature on transitional justice over which mechanism—if any—is more appropriate for achieving the elusive aim of reconciliation could be informed by further research into the potential complementary working of so-called 'alternatives', including truth commissions, statutory reparation programmes for victims, domestic criminal proceedings, trials before international or mixed law courts, and proceedings before other national courts under the principle of universal jurisdiction. The exact mix will depend on the situation. In some cases, as in Chile or the former Yugoslavia, the operation of international justice will have the effect of encouraging domestic criminal trials. Conversely, in some immediate post-conflict situations, as Ian Martin has pointed out, 'The best realistic objective may be not to assert immediately the claims of justice, but at least to prevent an endorsement—certainly an international endorsement—of impunity.'[28]

But that criminal justice is a necessary element in the mix is now established. Martin, former head of the UN Mission in East Timor and a former Secretary-

[25] Although the Prosecutor could presumably also use the Art 53 discretion not to proceed where an investigation or prosecution would not serve the interests of justice. This discretion is reviewable by the Pre-Trial Chamber.

[26] Neil J Kritz, 'An Overview of Developments in the Search for Justice and Reconciliation' in *The Legacy of Abuse*, 23.

[27] See ch 4.

[28] Ian Martin, 'Justice and Reconciliation: Responsibilities and Dilemmas of Peace-makers and Peace-builders', in *The Legacy of Abuse*, 83.

General of Amnesty International, draws attention to a shift in the policy of intergovernmental organizations between the 1993-1994 negotiations in Haiti over the transition from military rule, when in attempting to secure an agreement representatives of the UN and the Organization of American States actively promoted a comprehensive amnesty for military leaders even at the time gross human rights violations were still being committed, to the 1999 peace agreement for Sierra Leone, when the UN Secretary-General instructed his Special Envoy to append a disclaimer stating that the UN did not recognise the amnesty provision in the agreement as applying to war crimes, crimes against humanity and other crimes under international law. That year the Secretary-General issued guidelines to his envoys and representatives to 'assist in brokering agreements in conformity with the law', described by the Secretary-General as 'a significant step in the direction of mainstreaming human rights'.[29]

Although amnesties were discussed in the context of the 2001 UN peace talks for Afghanistan, the Bonn agreement of the 5 December contains no provision for amnesties. It requires the Afghan interim authorities to 'act in accordance with basic principles and provisions contained in international instruments on human rights and international humanitarian law to which Afghanistan is a party' (including the Geneva Conventions) and to establish, with UN assistance, a judicial commission to rebuild the domestic justice system and a human rights commission whose responsibilities include investigation of violations. The agreement also accorded the UN 'the right to investigate human rights violations and, where necessary, recommend corrective action'.[30]

INTERNATIONAL NORMS COLLIDE

The development of UN policy between the Haiti negotiations and those for Sierra Leone and Afghanistan is significant because it represents a shift in the interpretation of provisions in the UN Charter by the organization which acts as the Charter's guardian. The tension between, on the one hand, the purpose of achieving 'international co-operation ... in promoting and encouraging respect for human rights and fundamental freedoms for all' and, on the other, the principles of sovereign equality of all states and non-intervention 'in matters which are essentially within the domestic jurisdiction of any state',[31] always present in the age of human rights standard-setting, has become insistent in the emerging age of human rights enforcement. The policy of not recognising a national decision to award amnesty from prosecution in the case of crimes under international law

[29] *Ibid* at 81–2. The contents of the Secretary-General's guidelines are confidential but, according to his announcement of the 10 Dec 1999, they 'address the tensions between the urgency of stopping fighting, on the one hand, and the need to address punishable human rights violations on the other'.

[30] 'Agreement on provisional arrangements in Afghanistan pending the re-establishment of permanent government institutions', 5 December 2001.

[31] UN Charter, Arts 1(3); and 2(1) and 2(7).

may not imply a hierarchy between these provisions, in the sense of always having one trump the other, but it does establish a principle of articulation, in this case a human rights baseline below which the principle of non-intervention will not be recognised.[32]

The tension between the international protection of human rights and the exercise of national sovereignty was also of course at the centre of the *Pinochet* case. What was essentially at issue throughout was whether the allegations of torture and other international crimes were of sufficient gravity to override the immunity or immunities to which Pinochet was entitled, both by treaty and under customary international law, as a former head of state. The limits to head of state immunity are discussed at length by Brigitte Stern in Chapter 3, but to clarify my argument it would be helpful to revisit some points here.

Both the Divisional Court of the High Court of Justice[33] and two appellate committees of the House of Lords[34] which heard the case were presented with arguments on sovereign immunity, as classically set out in a series of nineteenth century court judgments in the UK and the USA. Thus in the *Duke of Brunswick v The King of Hanover*, the UK Lord Chancellor said in 1848:

> A foreign Sovereign, coming into this country cannot be made responsible here for an act done in his Sovereign character in his own country; whether it be an act right or wrong, whether according to the constitution of that country or not, the Courts of this country cannot sit in judgment upon an act of a Sovereign, effected by virtue of his Sovereign authority abroad...[35]

And in *Hatch v Baez* the US court said in 1876:

> But the immunity of individuals from suits brought in foreign tribunals for acts done within their own States, in the exercise of the sovereignty thereof, is essential to preserve the peace and harmony of nations...[36]

In *Pinochet*, then, two compelling norms of international law came into direct confrontation: the abomination of torture on the one hand and, on the

[32] Another principle of articulation between the non-intervention principle and human rights protection is arguably established by the fact that Art 2(7) of the UN Charter stipulates that the non-intervention principle 'shall not prejudice the application of enforcement measures under chapter VII', which deals with threats to international peace and security. Human rights violations perpetrated on such a scale as to constitute a threat to international peace and security (for example through creating mass refugee movements) could therefore trigger UN Security Council enforcement measures against the state concerned. That a further right to armed intervention exists under customary international law in cases of overwhelming humanitarian necessity has been argued to justify the NATO bombing of the Federal Republic of Yugoslavia over the Kosovo crisis; see for example Geoffrey Robertson, *Crimes against Humanity*, 381–2. This topic, however, is outside the scope of the present chapter.

[33] *In re Augusto Pinochet Ugarte*, UK High Court of Justice, Queen's Bench Division (Divisional Court), 28 Oct 1998, 38 ILM 68 (1999).

[34] *Pinochet No 1* and *No 3*. The judgements are all reproduced in Brody and Ratner, *The Pinochet Papers*.

[35] *Duke of Brunswick v The King of Hanover* (1848) 2 HL Cas 1.

[36] *Hatch v Baez*, 7 Hun 596 (NY 1876).

other, the principle of international comity preventing one state sitting in judgement on the sovereign behaviour of another state.

The Divisional Court heard that under the UK State Immunity Act 1978, a serving head of state, like the head of a diplomatic mission, enjoys an absolute immunity from criminal proceedings (immunity *ratione personae*), and after ceasing to be head of state retains an immunity (*ratione materiae*) 'with respect to acts performed by him in the exercise of his functions as head of state'.[37] This raised the question of whether torture and other crimes under international law could be interpreted as acts performed in the exercise of the functions of a head of state (or in the language of *Hatch v Baez*, 'in the exercise of sovereignty').

The Lord Chief Justice, Lord Bingham, concluded that they could:

> . . . a former head of state is clearly entitled to immunity in relation to criminal acts performed in the course of exercising public functions. One cannot therefore hold that any deviation from good democratic practice is outside the pale of immunity. If the former sovereign is immune from process in respect of some crimes, where does one draw the line?'

In a concurring judgment, Mr Justice Collins helped to answer Lord Bingham's rhetorical question: 'Unfortunately, history shows that it has indeed on occasions been state policy to exterminate or oppress particular groups.'

But when the House of Lords first considered the matter on appeal, it came to the opposite conclusion. Referring specifically to the language of the High Court judgment, Lord Steyn pointed out critically:

> It is inherent in this stark conclusion that there is no or virtually no line to be drawn. It follows that when Hitler ordered the "final solution" his act must be regarded as an official act deriving from the exercise of his functions as Head of State. That is where the reasoning of the Divisional Court inexorably leads.

Lord Nicholls summed up the majority view forcefully in his leading opinion:

> . . . it hardly needs saying that torture of his own subjects, or of aliens, would not be regarded by international law as a function of a head of state. All states disavow the use of torture as abhorrent, although from time to time some still resort to it. Similarly, the taking of hostages, as much as torture, has been outlawed by the international community as an offence. International law recognises, of course, that the functions of a head of state may include activities which are wrongful, even illegal, by the law of his own state or by the laws of other states. But international law has made plain that certain types of conduct, including torture and hostage-taking, are not acceptable conduct on the part of anyone. This applies as much to heads of state, or even more so, as it does to everyone else; the contrary conclusion would make a mockery of international law.

[37] S 20, State Immunity Act 1978, read with s 39, Diplomatic Privileges Act 1964.

However, the House of Lords retreated from this unequivocal position when it considered the matter again, after the earlier judgment had been set aside on the grounds that one of the judges had links with Amnesty International, an intervener in the case. This time, in a judgment notable for its divergent opinions, the majority of the seven judges hearing the case did not accept that the fact that torture or crimes against humanity were contrary to international norms was in itself sufficient to override the immunity enjoyed by a former head of state.[38] For that they required the specific authority of an international treaty between the states concerned, the 1984 UN Convention against Torture. The Convention defined torture as the intentional infliction of severe pain or suffering, whether physical or mental, 'at the instigation of or with the consent or acquiescence of a public official or other person acting in an official capacity' (Article 1), and required state parties either to prosecute suspects or to extradite them to another state willing to do so (Article 7).

The Republic of Chile, which this second time around had entered the proceedings as an intervener, accepted that torture was prohibited by international law from before the time of the Convention against Torture and that this prohibition had the character of *jus cogens* and obligation *erga omnes* (that is, that it was a peremptory norm of general international law and an obligation owed to all other states). But counsel for Chile claimed that this implied only that the norm was mandatory and could not be derogated from, and denied any implications for either immunity or the jurisdiction of a foreign national court. However, in the leading opinion, the senior law lord, Lord Browne-Wilkinson, went much further:

> The *jus cogens* nature of the international crime of torture justifies states in taking universal jurisdiction over torture wherever committed. International law provides that offences *jus cogens* may be punished by any state because the offenders are 'common enemies of all mankind and all nations have an equal interest in their apprehension and prosecution': *Demjanjuk v Petrovsky* (1985) 603 F Supp 1468; 776 F 2d. 571.

But Lord Browne-Wilkinson, with the majority of the judicial committee, had doubts as to whether the existence of the international crime of torture as *jus cogens* was sufficient in itself to ensure that the organisation of state torture could not rank for immunity purposes as performance of an official function. Once the Torture Convention came into force, however, the conflict became acute: '[The Convention] required all member states to ban and outlaw torture: Article 2. How can it be for international law purposes an official function to do something which international law itself prohibits and criminalises?'

The decisive point in the hearing was reached when their Lordships realised that, examining the Torture Convention beside the immunities applicable under treaty and customary law, they were looking at an immunity that was co-terminous with the offence. Lord Browne-Wilkinson returned to this point again and

[38] Although Lord Phillips and Lord Millett did hold such a view.

again in exchanges with counsel, who revealed that extensive searches through the *travaux preparatoires* for the Torture Convention had thrown up no reference whatever to the potential effect of the Convention on state immunity. Counsel for Pinochet claimed that this demonstrated the absence of the deliberate state consent required for the loss of immunity; counsel for the Crown Prosecution Service pointed out that if the Convention was but a 'meek little mouse' which provided only that the home state could exercise jurisdiction, one would have expected some acknowledgement to that effect in the *travaux* too.

Lord Browne-Wilkinson summed up in his judgment:

> . . . if the implementation of a torture regime is a public function giving rise to immunity *ratione materiae*, this produces bizarre results. Immunity *ratione materiae* applies not only to ex-heads of state and ex-ambassadors but to all state officials who have been involved in carrying out the functions of the state. . . . Under the Convention the international crime of torture can only be committed by an official or someone in an official capacity. They would all be entitled to immunity. It would follow that there can be no case outside Chile in which a successful prosecution for torture can be brought unless the State of Chile is prepared to waive its right to its officials' immunity. Therefore the whole elaborate structure of universal jurisdiction over torture committed by officials is rendered abortive and one of the main objectives of the Torture Convention—to provide a system under which there is no safe haven for torturers—will have been frustrated.

Seen through the black-letter prism of the English court, the manifest incompatibility between the two international norms could no longer be denied. Given that torture is, by definition, practiced by state agents, the *Pinochet* case had brought the two principles of state immunity and abomination of torture into such direct, logical conflict that it would have been a legal nonsense for the two doctrines to have survived post-*Pinochet* without some hierarchy established between them.

To paint the *Pinochet* case as a triumph of human rights over state sovereignty would be a dangerous over-simplification. For one thing, the House of Lords never questioned the fact that serving heads of state (and serving ambassadors) would retain their immunity *ratione personae* even in the face of charges of torture or another international crime, a position also held in respect of foreign ministers by the International Court of Justice in the case of *Democratic Republic of the Congo v Belgium*.[39] And Clare Montgomery, in her essay in this volume, highlights some of the many jurisdictional questions remaining over the enforcement in domestic courts of norms prohibiting international crimes. But in the House of Lords in March 1999 an inflexion point was reached: the curve turned away from absolute deference before sovereign authority towards the international enforcement of justice for torture and crimes against humanity.

[39] *Case Concerning the Arrest Warrant of 11 April 2000 (Democratic Republic of the Congo v Belgium)*, ICJ General List No 121, judgment of 14 Feb 2002; see below. For a detailed discussion of the case, see the chapter in this volume by Andrew Clapham.

This trend can be seen more clearly if we look at the behaviour of other European states involved in the *Pinochet* case. Compared to the English court, Spain's *Audiencia Nacional* had relatively little difficulty in affirming its jurisdiction when repeatedly challenged by the public prosecutor. In a key judgment on 5 November 1998, the criminal chamber of the *Audiencia Nacional*, sitting *en banc*, ruled:

> Article 2(1) of the United Nations Charter ("The Organization is based on the principle of the sovereign equality of all its Members") is not a legal norm capable of trumping the proclamation of jurisdiction of Article 23(4) [of the Organic Law of the Judicial Branch]. When the Spanish judicial organs apply that provision, they neither invade nor interfere in the sovereignty of the State in which the offence was committed; rather, they exercise Spain's own sovereignty in relation to international crimes. Spain has jurisdiction to hear the facts, derived from the principle of universal prosecution of certain offences—categorised in international law—which has been incorporated into our domestic law.[40]

Furthermore, unlike the House of Lords, the *Audiencia Nacional* held that its jurisdiction extended over relevant crimes committed *before* the incorporation of universal jurisdiction provisions into Spain's domestic law. This was on the basis that the principle of non-retroactivity of criminal law required only that torture and other abuses were recognised as substantive offences at the time they were alleged to have been committed, even if the procedural provisions facilitating jurisdiction came later.[41]

In addition to Spain, three other states—France, Switzerland and Belgium—issued requests for the extradition of Senator Pinochet. Belgium, like Spain, demonstrated that it was prepared to pursue that claim actively in the English courts. In retrospect, then, although the court judgments handed down in the UK and Spain were the most important, perhaps the greatest impact of the case came from the fact that no less than five European states, covering a range of legal traditions, made clear assertions of extraterritorial jurisdiction over Pinochet, all refusing to recognise his claim to immunity as a former head of state.

A WATERSHED IN INTERNATIONAL LAW

In his illuminating study of the history of international criminal tribunals, covering the tribunals at Leipzig after the First World War and Constantinople after the fall of the Ottoman empire, as well as those at Nuremberg, Tokyo, The

[40] Order of the Criminal Chamber of the *Audiencia Nacional*, 5 Nov 1998. See www.derechos.org/nizkor/chile/juicio/audi.html ; an unofficial English translation is included in Brody and Ratner, *The Pinochet Papers*.

[41] See Richard J Wilson, 'The Spanish Proceedings', in Brody and Ratner, *The Pinochet Papers*, 26.

Hague and Arusha, Gary Jonathan Bass notes that each case involved defeat in war. In distinction to the truth commissions and amnesties that have characterised many recent transitions from authoritarian regimes to democracy, military defeat provided an opportunity for 'the sheer imposition of justice'.[42]

This provides a further benchmark for the innovation represented by the *Pinochet* case. In enforcing an international criminal jurisdiction over a former head of state against the wishes of that state, Spain and the UK were doing something which previously had only been accomplished through war.

It had long been accepted in customary international law, stipulated in numerous treaties and reflected in the findings of the UN treaty-monitoring bodies, that there exist important limits to the exercise of sovereignty over the treatment of a state's own nationals. The status of torture as a *jus cogens* offence furthermore placed the highest obligation on all states to ensure its suppression. Yet, before *Pinochet,* an observer of international relations might well have thought that these rules were in practice incapable of international enforcement (short of armed intervention, at least), raising in turn a question mark over their very status as law. The *Pinochet* case, finally, was a high-profile example of compulsory enforcement, not under a special jurisdiction created by specific resolution of the UN Security Council, but by the judicial organs of individual states claiming an existing jurisdiction. That this—unprecedented—instance of enforcement should have created such shock waves around the world is revealing not just of the attitude of states but of the nature of international law itself, and in particular the relationship between law and practice.

A rare humorous moment in the *Pinochet* proceedings occurred in the House of Lords when counsel for Spain argued that old certainties in international law about the position of the sovereign had long since given way to newer conceptions. Lord Browne-Wilkinson interrupted to ask:

> ... at some stage ... you are going to have to tell me when things do become part of international law and when they do not. It is a point I have never understood since I was at Oxford...

Where the Oxford tutor would probably have started his explanation was with the sources of international law listed in Article 38(1) of the Statute of the International Court of Justice: (a) international conventions; (b) international custom, as evidence of a general practice accepted as law; (c) the general principles of law recognised by civilised nations; and (d), as subsidiary sources, judicial decisions and the teachings of the most highly qualified publicists or learned writers. (Note that this is not a comprehensive list and omits, for example, UN Security Council resolutions.) Lord Browne-Wilkinson's particular difficulty was with category (b), and the problem in specifying the moment

[42] Gary Jonathan Bass, *Stay the Hand of Vengeance: the politics of war crimes tribunals* (Princeton University Press, Princetown, 2000), 34. The point is arguable in respect of the International Criminal Tribunal for the former Yugoslavia at The Hague, although note that Bass was writing before the transfer of Milošević to the Tribunal.

when custom crystallises into law, depending as it does on both the 'general practice' of states and on that practice being 'accepted as law'. This last psychological element in the formation of customary law, often referred to by the expression *opinio juris sive necessitatis,* can best be glossed as a belief in legal permission or obligation.

In both the High Court and in the House of Lords there was a clear reluctance to recognise a point of crystallisation in customary law unless it was beyond dispute. Part of this appeared underpinned by a wariness towards any implied obligations other than those specifically entered into by states—and for all the human rights advocates' talk of the *jus cogens* nature of the offence of torture giving rise to a customary universal jurisdiction, a law based on state practice can hardly be said to exist until it is practised. But there was also reluctance to infer anything for the customary law of immunity from repeated obligations made in multi-lateral treaties, for example from the fact that the Nuremberg Charter, the Genocide Convention, the statutes of the International Criminal Tribunals for the former Yugoslavia and Rwanda, and the Rome Statute of the International Criminal Court all expressly provided that the official positions of heads of state did not free them from criminal responsibility. It was finally only the unequivocal inclusion of the necessary extraterritorial jurisdiction in a recent convention that, as described above, finally persuaded their Lordships not to let Pinochet go, radically limiting the temporal scope of the applicable jurisdiction in the process.

In interpreting state practice, it is necessary to draw a distinction between the law and its enforcement. As in domestic law, some international laws indisputably do exist even if their record of enforcement is poor. The prohibition on the use of force against other states is a case in point. In the *Nicaragua* case, the International Court of Justice commented:

> It is not to be expected that in the practice of States the application of the rules in question should have been perfect, in the sense that States should have refrained, with complete consistency, from the use of force or from intervention in each other's internal affairs. The Court does not consider that, for a rule to be established as customary, the corresponding practice must be in absolutely rigorous conformity with the rule. In order to deduce the existence of customary rules, the Court deems it sufficient that the conduct of States should, in general, be consistent with such rules, and that instances of State conduct inconsistent with a given rule should generally have been treated as breaches of that rule, not as indications of the recognition of a new rule.[43]

It is significant in this regard that accusations of torture made against states are habitually met with denial or excuse rather than attempts at justification. If some states torture their citizens in violation of international human rights law, they do so in the context of a near-universal prohibition on torture and neither the states in question, nor others, generally defend those acts as legal. Similarly,

[43] *Nicaragua v USA (Merits)*, ICJ Reports 1986, 14.

acts of torture committed by officials in contravention of their orders will under human rights law still fall under the responsibility of the state, but they can hardly be interpreted as evidence of state practice for the purposes of constituting customary international law.

State practice includes omissions as well as acts, but there is a danger in making positive inferences from infrequent or non-existent practice, such as the historic rarity of international prosecutions for torture or crimes against humanity (other than those connected with the Second World War). In the *Lotus* case, the Permanent Court of International Justice considered the legality of a criminal prosecution instituted by Turkey against an officer of a French steamship which collided with a Turkish vessel on the high seas leading to the deaths of eight Turkish sailors and passengers. The Court found:

> Even if the rarity of the judicial decisions to be found among the reported cases were sufficient to prove in point of fact the circumstance alleged... it would merely show that States had often, in practice, abstained from instituting criminal proceedings, and not that they recognised themselves as being obliged to do so; for only if such abstention were based on their being conscious of having a duty to abstain would it be possible to speak of an international custom. The alleged fact does not allow one to infer that States have been conscious of having such a duty; on the other hand... there are other circumstances calculated to show that the contrary is true.[44]

The two cases cited above both demonstrate how interpretations of customary law can turn on *opinio juris*, even where the reading of *opinio juris* in some ways goes against the grain of state practice. In the *Nicaragua* case the ICJ furthermore drew for its interpretation not just on the deeds of states, but also on their words, in the sense of statements made by state representatives and state participation in (non-binding) resolutions. However, while *opinio juris* qualifies state practice, it cannot exist in a vacuum, as a review of the wording of Article 38(1)(b) of the Statute of the ICJ shows. The Court felt the need to spell this out in its judgment in the *Nicaragua* case:

> Where two States agree to incorporate a particular rule in a treaty, their agreement suffices to make that rule a legal one, binding upon them; but in the field of customary international law, the shared view of the Parties as to the content of what they regard as the rule is not enough. The Court must satisfy itself that the existence of the rule in the *opinio juris* of States is confirmed by practice.

The significance of practice is of course not just confined to customary law; under the Vienna Convention on the Law of Treaties, conventional or treaty law too needs to be interpreted with regard to subsequent practice. And although the conclusion of multi-lateral treaties, under the auspices of the UN or of regional organisations, has replaced state practice as the principal engine of development of international law, practice remains its persistent mode of expression. As De Visscher has argued:

[44] *Lotus* case, PCIJ, Series A, No 10, 1927, 8.

> What gives international custom its special value and its superiority over conventional institutions, in spite of the inherent imprecision of its expression, is the fact that, developing by spontaneous practice, it reflects a deeply felt community of law. Hence the density and stability of its rules.[45]

The significance of state practice is here being somewhat laboured because in the areas covered by international human rights and humanitarian law the distinction between words and deeds has become acute. A glance at the annual reports of international human rights bodies such as Amnesty International and Human Rights Watch reveals that over half the states in the world torture their citizens, and in a considerable number of states torture and other violations are so endemic or systematic that human rights law appears to be honoured more in the breach than the observance. The prohibition of torture under customary law may be so absolute as to give it the status of *jus cogens* (a fact notably accepted by all parties to the Pinochet proceedings), but it is also a norm which is routinely ignored in practice, not just in that states have failed to use universal jurisdiction to enforce it, but in that they continue deliberately and systematically to torture their citizens.

As noted above, the recognition of law and the enforcement of law should be distinguished, but they are also closely related. Oppenheim defines law as 'a body of rules for human conduct within a community which, by common consent of this community, shall be enforced by external power'.[46] Traditionally, Oppenheim's 'external power' is the injured state acting on the self-help principle. Much has been written about how this principle has been limited by the development of prohibitions on the use of armed force, and in particular the outlawing of war in the United Nations Charter. But while self-help remains the predominant means of enforcing law that regulates relations between states, its role in enforcing that more recent part of international law which regulates the conduct of states towards their own people has been much less clear. Both the treaty form of human rights law, and the limited remedies it prescribes, make it clear that human rights *is* a matter of inter-state relations, but one which individual states have rarely seen it as their concern to enforce. Under Article 48 of the European Convention on Human Rights, states as well as individuals can bring cases to the European Court, but they have proved themselves very reluctant to do so. The UN human rights treaty-monitoring bodies have never received an inter-state complaint.

To insist that law should be perfectly binding is to ignore its fundamentally normative status. International conventions do not just codify pre-existing law: they are often a deliberate attempt to mark a departure from state practice that is perceived to be unacceptable or inadequate. But that attempt raises the stakes: it places the integrity of international law in question if practice remains

[45] Quoted in DJ Harris, *Cases and Materials on International Law* (Sweet & Maxwell, London, 1998) 45.

[46] L Oppenheim, *International Law*, 8th edn (Longmans Green & Co, London, 1955) 10.

unchanged. And the international sphere *is* different from the domestic one, in that state practice is constitutive of law as well as being, in a sense, its outcome. Thus, if practice diverges extensively and persistently from law it marks something more than an enforcement crisis: it represents a challenge to the international legal order itself.

Reflecting on the difficulty of regulating inter-state relations at the very stage when those relations had deteriorated into war, Sir Hersch Lauterpacht famously remarked that 'if international law is, in some ways, at the vanishing point of law, the law of war is, perhaps even more conspicuously, at the vanishing point of international law'.[47] Much has changed in the half century since he wrote this, not least the creation of the huge corpus of human rights law and the further growth of humanitarian law, particularly that applicable in internal armed conflicts. A general failure to observe the 100-plus multi-lateral treaties with substantive human rights or humanitarian content would put in question the basic rules that underpin the international legal order, including *pacta sunt servanda*, the constitutive principle of international law which holds that treaties are binding on the parties to them and must be performed in good faith. Rather than being placed at the end of Lauterpacht's infinite regression, human rights and humanitarian law have moved centre stage in that they have become a key test of whether international law *is* law.

We are now in a better position to appreciate fully the potential impact of recent signal cases in international criminal law. In the *Pinochet* case, five states asserted an extra-territorial jurisdiction, and both the *Audiencia Nacional* in Spain and the UK House of Lords confirmed jurisdiction on the universality principle and rejected a claim of immunity arising from Pinochet's status as a former head of state. In the *Milošević* case, an indictment was issued against a serving head of state and his transfer to an international criminal tribunal later effected by the state authorities acting under international diplomatic pressure. These were moments when legal principle became embedded in practice, and the international community acted to enforce norms which govern the conduct of states towards their own people.

Torture survivors, the families of those forcibly disappeared and the victims of other gross abuses, in Latin America, the former Yugoslavia and around the world, had long used the language of human rights to advance their claims to justice while privately despairing of ever seeing justice in practice. The joy with which these cases were welcomed by human rights activists thus partly betrayed a collective sense of relief that 'international human rights protection' added up to more than a critical resolution at a UN meeting. It was, finally, showing its teeth.

It remains of course a matter of some doubt whether the principles established in *Pinochet* will be accepted by all states. Notwithstanding the considerable symbolic value of seeing Pinochet in a magistrates' court in south

[47] H Lauterpacht, 'The Problem of the Revision of the Law of War', BYIL 29, (1952), 382.

London and Milošević in the dock in The Hague, these cases do not by themselves remove the serious concerns that persist over the enforceability of international human rights law. But together with the growing jurisprudence of the International Criminal Tribunals for the former Yugoslavia and Rwanda, the creation of new mixed law tribunals and, probably most significantly of all, the swift coming into operation of the International Criminal Court, they demonstrate a growing judicial and diplomatic consensus about the legality and practicability of enforcing human rights through international criminal justice.

THE FUTURE OF INTERNATIONAL CRIMINAL JUSTICE

In addition to the Milošević trial, the International Criminal Tribunals for the former Yugoslavia and Rwanda have seen the convictions of a former Rwandan prime minister, a former president of the Republika Srpska, and former commanding officers of the Rwandan and Yugoslav armies are in detention awaiting trial.[48] High profile witnesses at The Hague have included a serving head of state and a former US secretary of state.[49] Early predictions that the tribunals' workload would consist only of low-ranking suspects have therefore been confounded. However, proceedings before the tribunals have been lengthy and painstaking. In the eight years since they were first established, the tribunals together secured fewer than 40 convictions.

The record of the international tribunals provides a strong indication of the likely capacity of the International Criminal Court. Furthermore unlike the tribunals, the ICC—which by the end of 2002 had already secured 87 ratifications and 139 signatures—may be involved in proceedings against suspects from a wide range of states, encompassing many different situations, institutional relationships, national legal systems and enforcement modalities. Even with adequate funding, the strictly limited number of cases the ICC will therefore be able to handle has a number of implications for the future administration of justice for crimes under international law. Firstly, the optimum role for the ICC Prosecutor will involve a strategic exercise of discretion in order to concentrate on cases where the ICC can be most effective: for example, those involving senior officials where the chances of conviction are high. Secondly, the creation of further ad hoc international tribunals or mixed law tribunals to deal with specific country situations should not be discounted, particularly where there is international political will to secure justice for crimes committed before 1 July 2002 when the ICC Statute came into force. Finally, the significance of national courts remains undiminished.

[48] The individuals are former Rwandan prime minister Jean Kambanda; Biljana Plavšić, former president of the Republika Srpska; General Augustin Bizimungu; and General Dragoljub Ojdanić.

[49] Croatian President Stipe Mesić testified at the Milošević trial on 1 Oct 2002; former Secretary of State Madeleine Albright testified at the Plavšić trial in Dec 2002.

Following the *Pinochet* case, there has been a string of cases[50] around the world based on extraterritorial jurisdiction, whether on the universality principle or on the principle of passive personality, under which some states claim jurisdiction over crimes committed against their nationals abroad. This has led some human rights organisations to refer to a 'Pinochet effect' or 'Pinochet precedent'.[51] Certainly some of these cases can be seen to stem from a legal or judicial activism inspired by the *Pinochet* case. Sometimes this is rudely disappointed by the executive branch of government, as in the case of the Argentinean naval officer Alfredo Astiz whose preventive detention had been ordered by a judge in Argentina following extradition requests from both Italy and France, or the case of the Peruvian army intelligence officer Tomas Ricardo Anderson Kohatsu who had been detained by FBI agents at Houston airport in the USA. Other cases demonstrate a new readiness on the part of states to implement their international obligations to suppress crimes under international law, including a number of recent convictions of Bosnian Serbs in Germany and of Rwandans in Switzerland and Belgium. Further cases have been halted due to deficiencies in domestic legislation required to implement the UN Convention against Torture, including the case of the former Suriname military leader Desi Bouterse before the Dutch courts, and the case in Senegal against former Chadian ruler Hissène Habré.

Both in initiation and outcome, these cases indicate a very mixed record across states, one dependent on the complex interaction of legal initiative, judicial independence, national legislative environment, geo-political alliances, and chance. Most, although not all, involve assertions of extraterritorial jurisdiction by judges in European states. The perceived need to bring order to this somewhat confusing picture has led a group of leading international jurists and legal scholars, under the auspices of Princeton University, to draw up a set of principles to guide the practice and progressive development of the law on universal jurisdiction.[52] Looking at the existing case law, however, what is perhaps most immediately apparent is the difference in practice between common law and civil law systems. In common law countries, the more limited role for victims in criminal justice procedure (particularly at the early stages) and tighter rules on admissibility of evidence (particularly affecting the investigation of crimes that took place outside the state's territory) mean that universal jurisdiction cases have tended to fall at the first hurdle.

[50] See Menno T Kamminga, 'Lessons Learned from the Exercise of Universal Jurisdiction in Respect of Gross Human Rights Offenses', (2001), 23 *Human Rights Quarterly* 965–74; Redress, *Universal Jurisdiction in Europe* (Redress, London 1999); Human Rights Watch, *World Report 2002*, 600–1. See also ch 2 and the contribution by Reed Brody in ch 13. For cases of extra-territorial prosecutions of alleged war criminals from World War II and action taken by states against suspects wanted by the International Criminal Tribunals for the Former Yugoslavia and Rwanda, see chs 4 and 13.

[51] See Human Rights Watch, *The Pinochet Precedent: How Victims Can Pursue Human Rights Criminals Abroad* (HRW, New York, 2000).

[52] 'Princeton Principles on Universal Jurisdiction', www.princeton.edu/~lapa/principles.html

The *Pinochet* and *Milošević* cases both sparked predictions—sometimes expressing hope, sometimes fear—that they would lead to a succession of current and former leaders being arrested and tried abroad for crimes under international law. This is unlikely to materialise, at least in the short term. In the *DR Congo v Belgium* case, the International Court of Justice, having refused to recognise under customary international law 'any form of exception to the rule according immunity from criminal jurisdiction and inviolability to incumbent Ministers for Foreign Affairs' went on to identify four circumstances where such international law immunity did not represent a bar to criminal prosecution: in a domestic court in the minister's own country; in a foreign court when the state he or she represents has waived immunity; in a foreign court 'in respect of acts committed prior or subsequent to his or her period of office, as well as in respect of acts committed during that period of office in a private capacity'; and finally, before an international criminal court which has jurisdiction. Given that trials in the first two sets of circumstances are unlikely, it is unfortunate that the Court failed to explain what it meant in the third category by 'in a private capacity'.

In recent universal jurisdiction cases it is in fact the combination of practical impediments presented by domestic criminal justice systems, and a pronounced wariness on the part of the executive branch of governments, that has in most cases sufficed to defeat prosecutorial zeal. It is notable that those cases that have progressed to trial nearly all concern crimes for which there already exists a country-specific international criminal jurisdiction. The complementary working of international and national jurisdictions is also of course the approach followed by the ICC Statute.[53]

The doctrine of 'complementarity', which was central to the successful negotiation of the ICC Statute, in fact looks likely to be the fulcrum on which the further development of justice for war crimes and crimes against humanity will rest, enabling as it does an accommodation between national sovereignty and the enforcement of fundamental human rights. The details of this accommodation will continue to be worked out for years to come, but it will see the ICC operating both as a spur to national justice systems and as a forum of last resort. It is clear that from proceedings before the ICC itself no-one will be immune, not even serving heads of state, but a host of outstanding questions is raised by the complementarity regime and the essential point that enforcement action requested by the ICC will need to be channelled through national legal systems, whether of states parties or of co-operating non-states parties. Can states parties enter into treaty obligations with a third state not to enforce action requested by the ICC against a national of that state? In national prosecutions under the complementarity principle, could serving senior officials from a foreign state continue to claim state or diplomatic immunity? Could such

[53] See in particular the Preamble, Art 17 and Part 9. Note that unlike the International Criminal Tribunals for Rwanda and the former Yugoslavia, which enjoy primacy over national justice systems, the ICC can only act where a state is unwilling or unable genuinely to investigate or prosecute; ICTY Statute, Art 9 and ICC Statute, Art 17.

officials similarly claim international law immunities to defeat ICC-requested enforcement action by states parties?[54] How broad is the ICC Prosecutor's discretion to decide that it is not 'in the interests of justice' to proceed with an investigation or prosecution (for example, in a case where the suspect benefits from a national amnesty)? In any particular case, much may depend on the form and status of national legislation implementing the ICC Statute, but the resolution of such questions is likely to see extensive litigation (some of it possibly driven by US attempts to ensure that its nationals never appear before the ICC).

Outside the rubric of complementarity, the realistic objective of other universal jurisdiction proceedings before national courts might be to apply appropriate pressure to individual perpetrators and national justice systems in states not party to the ICC Statute, or concerning crimes which occurred before the ICC Statute came into force. On policy or tactical grounds, if not for legal ones, such cases may prove more influential if they display a territorial connection, for example with the victims of crime.[55] In many states, these proceedings are likely to require at a minimum the presence of the suspect on the territory.[56] However, in contrast to proceedings before the ICC, following the decisions of the House of Lords in *Pinochet* and the ICJ in *DR Congo v Belgium*, serving heads of state and foreign ministers will retain, while they remain in office, an absolute immunity from such criminal proceedings in foreign national courts.

In their Joint Separate Opinion in the *DR Congo v Belgium* case, Judges Higgins, Kooijmans and Buergenthal noted that:

> One of the challenges of present-day international law is to provide for stability of international relations and effective international intercourse while at the same time guaranteeing respect for human rights. The difficult task that international law today faces is to provide that stability in international relations by a means other than the

[54] For example, under s 23 of the UK's International Criminal Court Act 2001, state or diplomatic immunity conferred by connection with a state party does not prevent enforcement action, but where such immunity is conferred by connection with a non-state party, a waiver of immunity is required; the Secretary of State also has a general discretion to stop proceedings where state or diplomatic immunity is applicable. See ICC Statute Art 98.

[55] See *DR Congo v Belgium*, Joint Separate Opinion of Judges Higgins, Kooijmans and Buergenthal, at para. 59: '...the desired equilibrium between the battle against impunity and the promotion of good inter-State relations will only be maintained if there are some special circumstances that do require the exercise of an international criminal jurisdiction and if this has been brought to the attention of the prosecutor or *juge d'instruction*. For example, persons related to the victims of the case will have requested the commencement of legal proceedings.'

[56] Although not in Belgium, which has seen the widest variety of universal jurisdiction cases. On 12 February 2003 the Belgian Court of Cassation reversed an earlier Court of Appeal decision that a criminal complaint against Ariel Sharon, Prime Minister of Israel, and Amos Yaron, former chief of the Israeli Defence Forces, was inadmissible on the grounds that they were not present in Belgium, although the Court of Cassation also held that Sharon enjoyed procedural immunity from prosecution as long as he held the position of prime minister. Under legislative amendments passed in April 2003, however, new cases that have no territorial connection with Belgium can only be initiated by the state prosecutor, and there is an executive discretion in all universal jurisdiction cases not involving Belgian victims to defer the case to the accused's home state if its judicial system ensures effective access to justice for all parties. See www.sabra-shatila.be for documentation in Dutch and French.

impunity of those responsible for major human rights violations. ... Reflecting these concerns, what is regarded as a permissible jurisdiction and what is regarded as the law on immunity are in constant evolution.

If the rapid development of international justice is reconfiguring the connection between national sovereignty and the enforcement of human rights, it is in the process also subtly modifying the relationship between individual rulers and their peoples. International acceptance of the need for individual accountability for gross human rights abuses chimes with a growing national scepticism in many countries towards the immunities claimed by political or military leaders from the ordinary criminal process.[57] The potency of the principle of state sovereignty may remain, but it is not unlimited, and the potential for it to be misused by individuals is certainly becoming more tightly circumscribed. Whether it be through the waging of wars, the effects of economic sanctions, or the abuse of human rights, peoples have always been made to suffer for the decisions of their rulers. The progressive development of international justice promises that those who rule will increasingly be held to account for what they do to their people.

[57] See for example *Le Monde*, Éditorial, 'Affaires impunies?' (Paris, 7 July 2002): 'Comment accepter que ceux quit exercent des responsabilités importantes dans la vie publique puissent se soustraire aux conséquences de leurs actes? Est-il concevable que les nouveaux dirigeants portés au pouvoir en demandant à cor et à cri le rétablissement de l'autorité de l'Etat refusent de s'appliquer a eux-mêmes un tel principe?' In a separate development, Leopoldo Galtieri, the former military ruler of Argentina, was the latest Argentinian general to face domestic criminal proceedings when he was arrested on 11 July 2002 to face questioning in relation to charges of abduction, torture and homicide allegedly committed during the period of military rule (1976–1983).

APPENDICES

UN CONVENTION AGAINST TORTURE AND OTHER CRUEL, INHUMAN OR DEGRADING TREATMENT OR PUNISHMENT, 1984

The States Parties to this Convention,

Considering that, in accordance with the principles proclaimed in the Charter of the United Nations, recognition of the equal and inalienable rights of all members of the human family is the foundation of freedom, justice and peace in the world,

Recognizing that those rights derive from the inherent dignity of the human person,

Considering the obligation of States under the Charter, in particular Article 55, to promote universal respect for, and observance of, human rights and fundamental freedoms,

Having regard to Article 5 of the Universal Declaration of Human Rights and article 7 of the International Covenant on Civil and Political Rights, both of which provide that no one may be subjected to torture or to cruel, inhuman or degrading treatment or punishment,

Having regard also to the Declaration on the Protection of All Persons from Being Subjected to Torture and Other Cruel, Inhuman or Degrading Treatment or Punishment, adopted by the General Assembly on 9 December 1975 (resolution 3452 (XXX)),

Desiring to make more effective the struggle against torture and other cruel, inhuman or degrading treatment or punishment throughout the world,

Have agreed as follows:

PART I

Article 1

1. For the purposes of this Convention, torture means any act by which severe pain or suffering, whether physical or mental, is intentionally inflicted on a person for such purposes as obtaining from him or a third person information or a confession, punishing him for an act he or a third person has committed or is suspected of having committed, or intimidating or coercing him or a third person, or for any reason based on discrimination of any kind, when such pain or suffering is inflicted by or at the instigation of or with the consent or acquiescence of a public official or other person acting in an official capacity. It does not include pain or suffering arising only from, inherent in or incidental to lawful sanctions.
2. This article is without prejudice to any international instrument or national legislation which does or may contain provisions of wider application.

Article 2

1. Each State Party shall take effective legislative, administrative, judicial or other measures to prevent acts of torture in any territory under its jurisdiction.

2. No exceptional circumstances whatsoever, whether a state of war or a threat or war, internal political instability or any other public emergency, may be invoked as a justification of torture.

3. An order from a superior officer or a public authority may not be invoked as a justification of torture.

Article 3

1. No State Party shall expel, return ("refouler") or extradite a person to another State where there are substantial grounds for believing that he would be in danger of being subjected to torture.
2. For the purpose of determining whether there are such grounds, the competent authorities shall take into account all relevant considerations including, where applicable, the existence in the State concerned of a consistent pattern of gross, flagrant or mass violations of human rights.

Article 4

1. Each State Party shall ensure that all acts of torture are offences under its criminal law. The same shall apply to an attempt to commit torture and to an act by any person which constitutes complicity or participation in torture.
2. Each State Party shall make these offences punishable by appropriate penalties which take into account their grave nature.

Article 5

1. Each State Party shall take such measures as may be necessary to establish its jurisdiction over the offences referred to in Article 4 in the following cases:
   a When the offences are committed in any territory under its jurisdiction or on board a ship or aircraft registered in that State;
   b When the alleged offender is a national of that State;
   c When the victim was a national of that State if that State considers it appropriate.
2. Each State Party shall likewise take such measures as may be necessary to establish its jurisdiction over such offences in cases where the alleged offender is present in any territory under its jurisdiction and it does not extradite him pursuant to article 8 to any of the States mentioned in Paragraph 1 of this article.
3. This Convention does not exclude any criminal jurisdiction exercised in accordance with internal law.

Article 6

1. Upon being satisfied, after an examination of information available to it, that the circumstances so warrant, any State Party in whose territory a person alleged to have committed any offence referred to in Article 4 is present, shall take him into custody or take other legal measures to ensure his presence. The custody and other legal measures shall be as provided in the law of that State but may be continued only for such time as is necessary to enable any criminal or extradition proceedings to be instituted.
2. Such State shall immediately make a preliminary inquiry into the facts.
3. Any person in custody pursuant to paragraph 1 of this article shall be assisted in communicating immediately with the nearest appropriate representative of the State of which he is a national, or, if he is a stateless person, to the representative of the State where he usually resides.

4. When a State, pursuant to this article, has taken a person into custody, it shall immediately notify the States referred to in article 5, paragraph 1, of the fact that such person is in custody and of the circumstances which warrant his detention. The State which makes the preliminary inquiry contemplated in paragraph 2 of this article shall promptly report its findings to the said State and shall indicate whether it intends to exercise jurisdiction.

Article 7

1. The State Party in territory under whose jurisdiction a person alleged to have committed any offence referred to in article 4 is found, shall in the cases contemplated in article 5, if it does not extradite him, submit the case to its competent authorities for the purpose of prosecution.
2. These authorities shall take their decision in the same manner as in the case of any ordinary offence of a serious nature under the law of that State. In the cases referred to in article 5, paragraph 2, the standards of evidence required for prosecution and conviction shall in no way be less stringent than those which apply in the cases referred to in article 5, paragraph 1.
3. Any person regarding whom proceedings are brought in connection with any of the offences referred to in article 4 shall be guaranteed fair treatment at all stages of the proceedings.

Article 8

1. The offences referred to in article 4 shall be deemed to be included as extraditable offences in any extradition treaty existing between States Parties. States Parties undertake to include such offences as extraditable offences in every extradition treaty to be concluded between them.
2. If a State Party which makes extradition conditional on the existence of a treaty receives a request for extradition from another State Party with which it has no extradition treaty, it may consider this Convention as the legal basis for extradition in respect of such offenses. Extradition shall be subject to the other conditions provided by the law of the requested State.
3. States Parties which do not make extradition conditional on the existence of a treaty shall recognize such offences as extraditable offences between themselves subject to the conditions provided by the law of the requested state.
4. Such offences shall be treated, for the purpose of extradition between States Parties, as if they had been committed not only in the place in which they occurred but also in the territories of the States required to establish their jurisdiction in accordance with article 5, paragraph 1.

Article 9

1. States Parties shall afford one another the greatest measure of assistance in connection with civil proceedings brought in respect of any of the offences referred to in article 4, including the supply of all evidence at their disposal necessary for the proceedings.
2. States Parties shall carry out their obligations under paragraph 1 of this article in conformity with any treaties on mutual judicial assistance that may exist between them.

Article 10

1. Each State Party shall ensure that education and information regarding the prohibition against torture are fully included in the training of law enforcement personnel, civil or military, medical personnel, public officials and other persons who may be involved in the custody, interrogation or treatment of any individual subjected to any form of arrest, detention or imprisonment.
2. Each State Party shall include this prohibition in the rules or instructions issued in regard to the duties and functions of any such persons.

Article 11

Each State Party shall keep under systematic review interrogation rules, instructions, methods and practices as well as arrangements for the custody and treatment of persons subjected to any form of arrest, detention or imprisonment in any territory under its jurisdiction, with a view to preventing any cases of torture.

Article 12

Each State Party shall ensure that its competent authorities proceed to a prompt and impartial investigation, wherever there is reasonable ground to believe that an act of torture has been committee in any territory under its jurisdiction.

Article 13

Each State Party shall ensure that any individual who alleges he has been subjected to torture in any territory under its jurisdiction has the right to complain to and to have his case promptly and impartially examined its competent authorities. Steps shall be taken to ensure that the complainant and witnesses are protected against all ill-treatment or intimidation as a consequence of his complaint or any evidence given.

Article 14

1. Each State Party shall ensure in its legal system that the victim of an act of torture obtains redress and has an enforceable right to fair and adequate compensation including the means for as full rehabilitation as possible. In the event of the death of the victim as a result of an act of torture, his dependents shall be entitled to compensation.
2. Nothing in this article shall affect any right of the victim or other person to compensation which may exist under national law.

Article 15

Each State Party shall ensure that any statement which is established to have been made as a result of torture shall not be invoked as evidence in any proceedings, except against a person accused of torture as evidence that the statement was made.

Article 16

1. Each State Party shall undertake to prevent in any territory under its jurisdiction other acts of cruel, inhuman or degrading treatment or punishment which do not

amount to torture as defined in article 1, when such acts are committed by or at the instigation of or with the consent or acquiescence of a public official or other person acting in an official capacity. In particular, the obligations contained in articles 10, 11, 12 and 13 shall apply with the substitution for references to torture or references to other forms of cruel, inhuman or degrading treatment or punishment.

2. The provisions of this Convention are without prejudice to the provisions of any other international instrument or national law which prohibit cruel, inhuman or degrading treatment or punishment or which relate to extradition or expulsion.

PART II

Article 17

1. There shall be established a Committee against Torture (hereinafter referred to as the Committee) which shall carry out the functions hereinafter provided. The Committee shall consist of 10 experts of high moral standing and recognized competence in the field of human rights, who shall serve in their personal capacity. The experts shall be elected by the States Parties, consideration being given to equitable geographical distribution and to the usefulness of the participation of some persons having legal experience.
2. The members of the Committee shall be elected by secret ballot from a list of persons nominated by States Parties. Each State Party may nominate one person from among its own nationals. States Parties shall bear in mind the usefulness of nominating persons who are also members of the Human Rights Committee established under the International Covenant on Civil and Political Rights and are willing to serve on the Committee against Torture.
3. Elections of the members of the Committee shall be held at biennial meetings of States Parties convened by the Secretary-General of the United Nations. At those meetings, for which two thirds of the States Parties shall constitute a quorum, the persons elected to the Committee shall be those who obtain the largest number of votes and an absolute majority of the votes of the representatives of States Parties present and voting.
4. The initial election shall be held no later than six months after the date of the entry into force of this Convention. At least four months before the date of each election, the Secretary-General of the United Nations shall address a letter to the States Parties inviting them to submit their nominations within three months. The Secretary-General shall prepare a list in alphabetical order of all persons thus nominated, indicating the States Parties which have nominated them, and shall submit it to the States Parties.
5. The members of the Committee shall be elected for a term of four years. They shall be eligible for re-election if renominated. However, the term of five of the members elected at the first election shall expire at the end of two years; immediately after the first election the names of these five members shall be chosen by lot by the chairman of the meeting referred to in paragraph 3.
6. If a member of the Committee dies or resigns or for any other cause can no longer perform his Committee duties, the State Party which nominated him shall appoint another expert from among its nationals to serve for the remainder of his term,

subject to the approval of the majority of the States Parties. The approval shall be considered given unless half or more of the States Parties respond negatively within six weeks after having been informed by the Secretary-General of the United Nations of the proposed appointment.

7. States Parties shall be responsible for the expenses of the members of the Committee while they are in performance of Committee duties.

Article 18

1. The Committee shall elect its officers for a term of two years. They may be re-elected.
2. The Committee shall establish its own rules of procedure, but these rules shall provide, *inter alia*, that

   a Six members shall constitute a quorum;

   b Decisions of the Committee shall be made by a majority vote of the members present.

3. The Secretary-General of the United Nations shall provide the necessary staff and facilities for the effective performance of the functions of the Committee under this Convention.
4. The Secretary-General of the United Nations shall convene the initial meeting of the Committee. After its initial meeting, the Committee shall meet at such times as shall be provided in its rules of procedure.
5. The State Parties shall be responsible for expenses incurred in connection with the holding of meetings of the States Parties and of the Committee, including reimbursement of the United Nations for any expenses, such as the cost of staff and facilities, incurred by the United Nations pursuant to paragraph 3 above.

Article 19

1. The States Parties shall submit to the Committee, through the Secretary-General of the United Nations, reports on the measures they have taken to give effect to their undertakings under this Convention, within one year after the entry into force of this Convention for the State Party concerned. Thereafter the States Parties shall submit supplementary reports every four years on any new measures taken, and such other reports as the Committee may request.
2. The Secretary-General shall transmit the reports to all States Parties.
3. [Each report shall be considered by the Committee which may make such comments or suggestions on the report as it considers appropriate, and shall forward these to the State Party concerned. That State Party may respond with any observations it chooses to the Committee.
4. The Committee may, at its discretion, decide to include any comments or suggestions made by it in accordance with paragraph 3, together with the observations thereon received from the State Party concerned, in its annual report made in accordance with article 24. If so requested by the State Party concerned, the Committee may also include a copy of the report submitted under paragraph 1.]

Article 20

1. If the Committee receives reliable information which appears to it to contain well-

founded indications that torture is being systematically practised in the territory of a State Party, the Committee shall invite that State Party to co-operate in the examination of the information and to this end to submit observations with regard to the information concerned.

2. Taking into account any observations which may have been submitted by the State Party concerned as well as any other relevant information available to it, the Committee may, if it decides that this is warranted, designate one or more of its members to make a confidential inquiry and to report to the Committee urgently.
3. If an inquiry is made in accordance with paragraph 2, the Committee shall seek the co-operation of the State Party concerned. In agreement with that State Party, such an inquiry may include a visit to its territory.
4. After examining the findings of its member or members submitted in accordance with paragraph 2, the Committee shall transmit these findings to the State Party concerned together with any comments or suggestions which seem appropriate in view of the situation.
5. All the proceedings of the Committee referred to in paragraphs 1 to 4 of this article shall be confidential, and at all stages of the proceedings the co-operation of the State Party shall be sought. After such proceedings have been completed with regard to an inquiry made in accordance with paragraph 2, the Committee may, after consultations with the State Party concerned, decide to include a summary account of the results of the proceedings in its annual report made in accordance with article 24.

Article 21

1. A State Party to this Convention may at any time declare under this article 3 that it recognizes the competence of the Committee to receive and consider communications to the effect that a State Party claims that another State Party is not fulfilling its obligations under this Convention. Such communications may be received and considered according to the procedures laid down in this article only if submitted by a State Party which has made a declaration recognizing in regard to itself the competence of the Committee. No communication shall be dealt with by the Committee under this article if it concerns a State Party which has not made such a declaration. Communications received under this article shall be dealt with in accordance with the following procedure:

   (a) If a State Party considers that another State Party is not giving effect to the provisions of this Convention, it may, by written communication, bring the matter to the attention of that State Party. Within three months after the receipt of the communication the receiving State shall afford the State which sent the communication an explanation or any other statement in writing clarifying the matter which should include, to the extent possible and pertinent, references to domestic procedures and remedies taken, pending, or available in the matter.
   (b) If the matter is not adjusted to the satisfaction of both States Parties concerned within six months after the receipt by the receiving State of the initial communication, either State shall have the right to refer the matter to the Committee by notice given to the Committee and to the other State.
   (c) The Committee shall deal with a matter referred to it under this article only after it has ascertained that all domestic remedies have been invoked and exhausted in the matter, in conformity with the generally recognized principles of international

law. This shall not be the rule where the application of the remedies is unreasonably prolonged or is unlikely to bring effective relief to the person who is the victim of the violation of this Convention.

(d) The Committee shall hold closed meetings when examining communications under this article.

(e) Subject to the provisions of subparagraph (*c*), the Committee shall make available its good offices to the States Parties concerned with a view to a friendly solution of the matter on the basis of respect for the obligations provided for in the present Convention. For this purpose, the Committee may, when appropriate, set up an ad hoc conciliation commission.

(f) In any matter referred to it under this article, the Committee may call upon the States Parties concerned, referred to in subparagraph (b), to supply any relevant information.

(g) The States Parties concerned, referred to in subparagraph (*b*), shall have the right to be represented when the matter is being considered by the Committee and to make submissions orally and/or in writing.

(h) The Committee shall, within 12 months after the date of receipt of notice under subparagraph (*b*), submit a report.

  (i) If a solution within the terms of subparagraph (*e*) is reached, the Committee shall confine its report to a brief statement of the facts and of the solution reached.

  (ii) If a solution within the terms of subparagraph (*e*) is not reached, the Committee shall confine its report to a brief statement of the facts; the written submissions and record of the oral submissions made by the States Parties concerned shall be attached to the report.

In every matter, the report shall be communicated to the States Parties concerned.

1. The provisions of this article shall come into force when five States Parties to this Convention have made declarations under paragraph 1 of this article. Such declarations shall be deposited by the States Parties with the Secretary-General of the United Nations, who shall transmit copies thereof to the other States Parties. A declaration may be withdrawn at any time by notification to the Secretary-General. Such a withdrawal shall not prejudice the consideration of any matter which is the subject of a communication already transmitted under this article; no further communication by any State Party shall be received under this article after the notification of withdrawal of the declaration has been received by the Secretary-General, unless the State Party concerned has made a new declaration.

Article 22

1. A State Party to this Convention may at any time declare under this article that it recognizes the competence of the Committee to receive and consider communications from or on behalf of individuals subject to its jurisdiction who claim to be victims of a violation by a State Party of the provisions of the Convention. No communication shall be received by the Committee if it concerns a State Party to the Convention which has not made such a declaration.
2. The Committee shall consider inadmissible any communication under this article which is anonymous, or which it considers to be an abuse of the right of submission of

such communications or to be incompatible with the provisions of this Convention.

3. Subject to the provisions of paragraph 2, the Committee shall bring any communication submitted to it under this article to the attention of the State Party to this Convention which has made a declaration under paragraph 1 and is alleged to be violating any provisions of the Convention. Within six months, the receiving State shall submit to the Committee written explanations or statements clarifying the matter and the remedy, if any, that may have been taken by that State.
4. The Committee shall consider communications received under this article in the light of all information made available to it by or on behalf of the individual and by the State Party concerned.
5. The Committee shall not consider any communication from an individual under this article unless it has ascertained that:
   (a) The same matter has not been, and is not being examined under another procedure of international investigation or settlement;
   (b) The individual has exhausted all available domestic remedies; this shall not be the rule where the application of the remedies is unreasonably prolonged or is unlikely to bring effective relief to the person who is the victim of the violation of this Convention.
6. The Committee shall hold closed meetings when examining communications under this article.
7. The Committee shall forward its views to the State Party concerned and to the individual.
8. The provisions of this article shall come into force when five States Parties to this Convention have made declarations under paragraph 1 of this article. Such declarations shall be deposited by the States Parties with the Secretary-General of the United Nations, who shall transmit parties thereof to the other States Parties. A declaration may be withdrawn at any time by notification to the Secretary-General. Such a withdrawal shall not prejudice the consideration of any matter which is the subject of a communication already transmitted under this article; no further communication by or on behalf of an individual shall be received under this article after the notification of withdrawal of the declaration has been received by the Secretary-General, unless the State Party concerned has made a new declaration.

Article 23

The members of the Committee, and of the ad hoc conciliation commissions which may be appointed under article 21, paragraph 1 (e), shall be entitled to the facilities, privileges and immunities of experts on missions for the United Nations as laid down in the relevant sections of the Convention on the Privileges and Immunities of the United Nations.

Article 24

The Committee shall submit an annual report on its activities under this Convention to the States Parties and to the General Assembly of the United Nations.

PART III

Article 25

1. This Convention is open for signature by all States.
2. This Convention is subject to ratification. Instruments of ratification shall be deposited with the Secretary-General of the United Nations.

Article 26

This Convention is open to accession by all States. Accession shall be effected by the deposit of an instrument of accession with the Secretary-General of the United Nations.

Article 27

1. This Convention shall enter into force on the thirtieth day after the date of the deposit with the Secretary-General of the United Nations of the twentieth instrument of ratification or accession.
2. For each State ratifying this Convention or acceding to it after the deposit of the twentieth instrument of ratification or accession, the Convention shall enter into force on the thirtieth day after the date of the deposit of its own instrument of ratification or accession.

Article 28

1. Each State may, at the time of signature or ratification of this Convention or accession thereto, declare that it does not recognize the competence of the Committee provided for in article 20.
2. Any State Party having made a reservation in accordance with paragraph 1 of this article may, at any time, withdraw this reservation by notification to the Secretary-General of the United Nations.

Article 29

1. Any State Party to this Convention may propose an amendment and file it with the Secretary-General of the United Nations. The Secretary-General shall thereupon communicate the proposed amendment to the States Parties to this Convention with a request that they notify him whether they favour a conference of States Parties for the purpose of considering and voting upon the proposal. In the event that within four months from the date of such communication at least one third of the State Parties favours such a conference, the Secretary-General shall convene the conference under the auspices of the United Nations. Any amendment adopted by a majority of the States Parties present and voting at the conference shall be submitted by the Secretary-General to all the States Parties for acceptance.
2. An amendment adopted in accordance with paragraph 1 shall enter into force when two thirds of the States Parties to this Convention have notified the Secretary-General of the United Nations that they have accepted it in accordance with their respective constitutional processes.
3. When amendments enter into force, they shall be binding on those States Parties which have accepted them, other States Parties still being bound by the provisions of this Convention and any earlier amendments which they have accepted.

Article 30

1. Any dispute between two or more States Parties concerning the interpretation or application of this Convention which cannot be settled through negotiation, shall, at the request of one of them, be submitted to arbitration. If within six months from the date of the request for arbitration the Parties are unable to agree on the organization of the arbitration, any one of those Parties may refer the dispute to the International Court of Justice by request in conformity with the Statute of the Court.
2. Each State may at the time of signature or ratification of this Convention or accession thereto, declare that it does not consider itself bound by the preceding paragraph. The other States Parties shall not be bound by the preceding paragraph with respect to any State Party having made such a reservation.
3. Any State Party having made a reservation in accordance with the preceding paragraph may at any time withdraw this reservation by notification to the Secretary-General of the United Nations.

Article 31

1. A State Party may denounce this Convention by written notification to the Secretary-General of the United Nations. Denunciation becomes effective one year after the date of receipt of the notification by the Secretary-General.
2. Such a denunciation shall not have the effect of releasing the State Party from its obligations under this Convention in regard to any act or omission which occurs prior to the date at which the denunciation becomes effective. Nor shall denunciation prejudice in any way the continued consideration of any matter which is already under consideration by the Committee prior to the date at which the denunciation becomes effective.
3. Following the date at which the denunciation of a State Party becomes effective, the Committee shall not commence consideration of any new matter regarding that State.

Article 32

The Secretary-General of the United Nations shall inform all members of the United Nations and all States which have signed this Convention or acceded to it, or the following particulars:

1. Signatures, ratifications and accessions under articles 25 and 26;
2. The date of entry into force of this Convention under article 27, and the date of the entry into force of any amendments under article 29;
3. Denunciations under article 31.

Article 33

1. This Convention, of which the Arabic, Chinese, English, French, Russian and Spanish texts are equally authentic, shall be deposited in the archives of the United Nations.
2. The Secretary-General of the United Nations shall transmit certified copies of this Convention to all States.

ROME STATUTE OF THE INTERNATIONAL CRIMINAL COURT*

[* as corrected by the procés-verbaux of 10 November 1998 and 12 July 1999]

PREAMBLE

The States Parties to this Statute,

Conscious that all peoples are united by common bonds, their cultures pieced together in a shared heritage, and concerned that this delicate mosaic may be shattered at any time, *Mindful* that during this century millions of children, women and men have been victims of unimaginable atrocities that deeply shock the conscience of humanity,

Recognizing that such grave crimes threaten the peace, security and well-being of the world,

Affirming that the most serious crimes of concern to the international community as a whole must not go unpunished and that their effective prosecution must be ensured by taking measures at the national level and by enhancing international co-operation,

Determined to put an end to impunity for the perpetrators of these crimes and thus to contribute to the prevention of such crimes,

Recalling that it is the duty of every State to exercise its criminal jurisdiction over those responsible for international crimes,

Reaffirming the Purposes and Principles of the Charter of the United Nations, and in particular that all States shall refrain from the threat or use of force against the territorial integrity or political independence of any State, or in any other manner inconsistent with the Purposes of the United Nations,

Emphasizing in this connection that nothing in this Statute shall be taken as authorizing any State Party to intervene in an armed conflict or in the internal affairs of any State, *Determined* to these ends and for the sake of present and future generations, to establish an independent permanent International Criminal Court in relationship with the United Nations system, with jurisdiction over the most serious crimes of concern to the international community as a whole,

Emphasizing that the International Criminal Court established under this Statute shall be complementary to national criminal jurisdictions,

Resolved to guarantee lasting respect for and the enforcement of international justice,

Have agreed as follows

PART I. ESTABLISHMENT OF THE COURT

Article 1

The Court

An International Criminal Court ("the Court") is hereby established. It shall be a permanent institution and shall have the power to exercise its jurisdiction over persons for the most serious crimes of international concern, as referred to in this Statute, and shall be complementary to national criminal jurisdictions. The jurisdiction and functioning of the Court shall be governed by the provisions of this Statute.

Article 2

Relationship of the Court with the United Nations

The Court shall be brought into relationship with the United Nations through an agreement to be approved by the Assembly of States Parties to this Statute and thereafter concluded by the President of the Court on its behalf.

Article 3

Seat of the Court

1. The seat of the Court shall be established at The Hague in the Netherlands ("the host State").
2. The Court shall enter into a headquarters agreement with the host State, to be approved by the Assembly of States Parties and thereafter concluded by the President of the Court on its behalf.
3. The Court may sit elsewhere, whenever it considers it desirable, as provided in this Statute.

Article 4

Legal status and powers of the Court

4. The Court shall have international legal personality. It shall also have such legal capacity as may be necessary for the exercise of its functions and the fulfilment of its purposes.
5. The Court may exercise its functions and powers, as provided in this Statute, on the territory of any State Party and, by special agreement, on the territory of any other State.

PART II. JURISDICTION, ADMISSIBILITY AND APPLICABLE LAW

Article 5

Crimes within the jurisdiction of the Court

1. The jurisdiction of the Court shall be limited to the most serious crimes of concern to the international community as a whole. The Court has jurisdiction in accordance with this Statute with respect to the following crimes:
   (a) The crime of genocide;
   (b) Crimes against humanity;
   (c) War crimes;
   (d) The crime of aggression.
2. The Court shall exercise jurisdiction over the crime of aggression once a provision is adopted in accordance with Articles 121 and 123 defining the crime and setting out the conditions under which the Court shall exercise jurisdiction with respect to this crime. Such a provision shall be consistent with the relevant provisions of the Charter of the United Nations.

Article 6

Genocide
For the purpose of this Statute, "genocide" means any of the following acts committed with intent to destroy, in whole or in part, a national, ethnical, racial or religious group, as such:

(a) Killing members of the group;
(b) Causing serious bodily or mental harm to member of the group;
(c) Deliberately inflicting on the group conditions of life calculated to bring about its physical destruction in whole or in part;
(d) Imposing measures intended to prevent births within the group;
(e) Forcibly transferring children of the group to another group.

Article 7

Crimes against humanity
1. For the purpose of this Statute, "crime against humanity" means any of the following acts when committed as part of a widespread or systematic attack directed against any civilian population, with knowledge of the attack:

   (a) Murder;
   (b) Extermination;
   (c) Enslavement;
   (d) Deportation or forcible transfer of population;
   (e) Imprisonment or other severe deprivation of physical liberty in violation of fundamental rules of international law;
   (f) Torture;
   (g) Rape, sexual slavery, enforced prostitution, forced pregnancy, enforced sterilization, or any other form of sexual violence of comparable gravity;
   (h) Persecution against any identifiable group or collectivity on political, racial, national, ethnic, cultural, religious, gender as defined in paragraph 3, or other grounds that are universally recognized as impermissible under international law, in connection with any act referred to in this paragraph or any crime within the jurisdiction of the Court;
   (i) Enforced disappearance of persons;
   (j) The crime of apartheid;
   (k) Other inhumane acts of a similar character intentionally causing great suffering, or serious injury to body or to mental or physical health.

2. For the purpose of paragraph 1:
   (a) "Attack directed against any civilian population" means a course of conduct involving the multiple commission of acts referred to in paragraph 1 against any civilian population, pursuant to or in furtherance of a State or organizational policy to commit such attack;
   (b) "Extermination" includes the intentional infliction of conditions of life, *inter alia* the deprivation of access to food and medicine, calculated to bring about the destruction of part of a population;
   (c) "Enslavement" means the exercise of any or all of the powers attaching to the right of ownership over a person and includes the exercise of such power in the course of trafficking in persons, in particular women and children;

(d) *"Deportation or forcible transfer of population" means forced displacement of the persons concerned by expulsion or other coercive acts from the area in which they are lawfully present, without grounds permitted under international law;*
(e) "Torture" means the intentional infliction of severe pain or suffering, whether physical or mental, upon a person in the custody or under the control of the accused; except that torture shall not include pain or suffering arising only from, inherent in or incidental to, lawful sanctions;
(f) "Forced pregnancy" means the unlawful confinement of a woman forcibly made pregnant, with the intent of affecting the ethnic composition of any population or carrying out other grave violations of international law. This definition shall not in any way be interpreted as affecting national laws relating to pregnancy;
(g) "Persecution" means the intentional and severe deprivation of fundamental rights contrary to international law by reason of the identity of the group or collectivity;
(h) "The crime of apartheid" means inhumane acts of a character similar to those referred to in paragraph 1, committed in the context of an institutionalized regime of systematic oppression and domination by one racial group over any other racial group or groups and committed with the intention of maintaining that regime;
(i) "Enforced disappearance of persons" means the arrest, detention or abduction of persons by, or with the authorization, support or acquiescence of, a State or a political organization, followed by a refusal to acknowledge that deprivation of freedom or to give information on the fate or whereabouts of those persons, with the intention of removing them from the protection of the law for a prolonged period of time.

3. For the purpose of this Statute, it is understood that the term "gender" refers to the two sexes, male and female, within the context of society. The term "gender" does not indicate any meaning different from the above.

Article 8

War crimes

1. The Court shall have jurisdiction in respect of war crimes in particular when committed as part of a plan or policy or as part of a large-scale commission of such crimes.
2. *For the purpose of this Statute, "war crimes" means:*
   (a) Grave breaches of the Geneva Conventions of 12 August 1949, namely, any of the following acts against persons or property protected under the provisions of the relevant Geneva Convention:
      (i) Wilful killing;
      (ii) Torture or inhuman treatment, including biological experiments;
      (iii) Wilfully causing great suffering, or serious injury to body or health;
      (iv) Extensive destruction and appropriation of property, not justified by military necessity and carried out unlawfully and wantonly;
      (v) Compelling a prisoner of war or other protected person to serve in the forces of a hostile Power;
      (vi) Wilfully depriving a prisoner of war or other protected person of the rights of fair and regular trial;
      (vii) Unlawful deportation or transfer or unlawful confinement;
      (viii) Taking of hostages.

(b) Other serious violations of the laws and customs applicable in international armed conflict, within the established framework of international law, namely, any of the following acts:

(i) Intentionally directing attacks against the civilian population as such or against individual civilians not taking direct part in hostilities;

(ii) Intentionally directing attacks against civilian objects, that is, objects which are not military objectives;

(iii) Intentionally directing attacks against personnel, installations, material, units or vehicles involved in a humanitarian assistance or peacekeeping mission in accordance with the Charter of the United Nations, as long as they are entitled to the protection given to civilians or civilian objects under the international law of armed conflict;

(iv) Intentionally launching an attack in the knowledge that such attack will cause incidental loss of life or injury to civilians or damage to civilian objects or widespread, long-term and severe damage to the natural environment which would be clearly excessive in relation to the concrete and direct overall military advantage anticipated;

(v) Attacking or bombarding, by whatever means, towns, villages, dwellings or buildings which are undefended and which are not military objectives;

(vi) Killing or wounding a combatant who, having laid down his arms or having no longer means of defence, has surrendered at discretion;

(vii) Making improper use of a flag of truce, of the flag or of the military insignia and uniform of the enemy or of the United Nations, as well as of the distinctive emblems of the Geneva Conventions, resulting in death or serious personal injury;

(viii) The transfer, directly or indirectly, by the Occupying Power of parts of its own civilian population into the territory it occupies, or the deportation or transfer of all or parts of the population of the occupied territory within or outside this territory;

(ix) Intentionally directing attacks against buildings dedicated to religion, education, art, science or charitable purposes, historic monuments, hospitals and places where the sick and wounded are collected, provided they are not military objectives;

(x) Subjecting persons who are in the power of an adverse party to physical mutilation or to medical or scientific experiments of any kind which are neither justified by the medical, dental or hospital treatment of the person concerned nor carried out in his or her interest, and which cause death to or seriously endanger the health of such person or persons;

(xi) Killing or wounding treacherously individuals belonging to the hostile nation or army;

(xii) Declaring that no quarter will be given;

(xiii) Destroying or seizing the enemy's property unless such destruction or seizure be imperatively demanded by the necessities of war;

(xiv) Declaring abolished, suspended or inadmissible in a court of law the rights and actions of the nationals of the hostile party;

(xv) Compelling the nationals of the hostile party to take part in the operations of war directed against their own country, even if they were in the belligerent's service before the commencement of the war;

(xvi) Pillaging a town or place, even when taken by assault;

(xvii) Employing poison or poisoned weapons;

(xviii) Employing asphyxiating, poisonous or other gases, and all analogous liquids, materials or devices;

(xix) Employing bullets which expand or flatten easily in the human body, such as bullets with a hard envelope which does not entirely cover the core or is pierced with incisions;

(xx) Employing weapons, projectiles and material and methods of warfare which are of a nature to cause superfluous injury or unnecessary suffering or which are inherently indiscriminate in violation of the international law of armed conflict, provided that such weapons, projectiles and material and methods of warfare are the subject of a comprehensive prohibition and are included in an annex to this Statute, by an amendment in accordance with the relevant provisions set forth in Articles 121 and 123;

(xxi) Committing outrages upon personal dignity, in particular humiliating and degrading treatment;

(xxii) Committing rape, sexual slavery, enforced prostitution, forced pregnancy, as defined in Article 7, paragraph 2 (f), enforced sterilization, or any other form of sexual violence also constituting a grave breach of the Geneva Conventions;

(xxiii) Utilizing the presence of a civilian or other protected person to render certain points, areas or military forces immune from military operations;

(xxiv) Intentionally directing attacks against buildings, material, medical units and transport, and personnel using the distinctive emblems of the Geneva Conventions in conformity with international law;

(xxv) Intentionally using starvation of civilians as a method of warfare by depriving them of objects indispensable to their survival, including wilfully impeding relief supplies as provided for under the Geneva Conventions;

(xxvi) Conscripting or enlisting children under the age of fifteen years into the national armed forces or using them to participate actively in hostilities.

(c) In the case of an armed conflict not of an international character, serious violations of Article 3 common to the four Geneva Conventions of 12 August 1949, namely, any of the following acts committed against persons taking no active part in the hostilities, including members of armed forces who have laid down their arms and those placed *hors de combat* by sickness, wounds, detention or any other cause:

(i) Violence to life and person, in particular murder of all kinds, mutilation, cruel treatment and torture;

(ii) Committing outrages upon personal dignity, in particular humiliating and degrading treatment;

(iii) Taking of hostages;

(iv) The passing of sentences and the carrying out of executions without previous judgement pronounced by a regularly constituted court, affording all judicial guarantees which are generally recognized as indispensable.

(d) Paragraph 2 (c) applies to armed conflicts not of an international character and thus does not apply to situations of internal disturbances and tensions, such as riots, isolated and sporadic acts of violence or other acts of a similar nature.

(e) Other serious violations of the laws and customs applicable in armed conflicts not of an international character, within the established framework of international law, namely, any of the following acts:

(i) Intentionally directing attacks against the civilian population as such or against individual civilians not taking direct part in hostilities;
(ii) Intentionally directing attacks against buildings, material, medical units and transport, and personnel using the distinctive emblems of the Geneva Conventions in conformity with international law;
(iii) Intentionally directing attacks against personnel, installations, material, units or vehicles involved in a humanitarian assistance or peacekeeping mission in accordance with the Charter of the United Nations, as long as they are entitled to the protection given to civilians or civilian objects under the international law of armed conflict;
(iv) Intentionally directing attacks against buildings dedicated to religion, education, art, science or charitable purposes, historic monuments, hospitals and places where the sick and wounded are collected, provided they are not military objectives;
(v) Pillaging a town or place, even when taken by assault;
(vi) Committing rape, sexual slavery, enforced prostitution, forced pregnancy, as defined in Article 7, paragraph 2 (f), enforced sterilization, and any other form of sexual violence also constituting a serious violation of Article 3 common to the four Geneva Conventions;
(vii) Conscripting or enlisting children under the age of fifteen years into armed forces or groups or using them to participate actively in hostilities;
(viii) Ordering the displacement of the civilian population for reasons related to the conflict, unless the security of the civilians involved or imperative military reasons so demand;
(ix) Killing or wounding treacherously a combatant adversary;
(x) Declaring that no quarter will be given;
(xi) Subjecting persons who are in the power of another party to the conflict to physical mutilation or to medical or scientific experiments of any kind which are neither justified by the medical, dental or hospital treatment of the person concerned nor carried out in his or her interest, and which cause death to or seriously endanger the health of such person or persons;
(xii) Destroying or seizing the property of an adversary unless such destruction or seizure be imperatively demanded by the necessities of the conflict:

(f) Paragraph 2 (e) applies to armed conflicts not of an international character and thus does not apply to situations of internal disturbances and tensions, such as riots, isolated and sporadic acts of violence or other acts of a similar nature. It applies to armed conflicts that take place in the territory of a State when there is protracted armed conflict between governmental authorities and organized armed groups or between such groups.

3. Nothing in paragraph 2 (c) and (e) shall affect the responsibility of a Government to maintain or re-establish law and order in the State or to defend the unity and territorial integrity of the State, by all legitimate means.

Article 9

Elements of Crimes

1. Elements of Crimes shall assist the Court in the interpretation and application of Articles 6, 7 and 8. They shall be adopted by a two-thirds majority of the members of the Assembly of States Parties.
2. Amendments to the Elements of Crimes may be proposed by:
   (a) Any State Party;
   (b) The judges acting by an absolute majority;
   (c) The Prosecutor.

Such amendments shall be adopted by a two-thirds majority of the members of the Assembly of States Parties.

3. The Elements of Crimes and amendments thereto shall be consistent with this Statute.

Article 10

Nothing in this Part shall be interpreted as limiting or prejudicing in any way existing or developing rules of international law for purposes other than this Statute.

Article 11

Jurisdiction ratione temporis

1. The Court has jurisdiction only with respect to crimes committed after the entry into force of this Statute.
2. If a State becomes a Party to this Statute after its entry into force, the Court may exercise its jurisdiction only with respect to crimes committed after the entry into force of this Statute for that State, unless that State has made a declaration under Article 12, paragraph 3.

Article 12

Preconditions to the exercise of jurisdiction

1. A State which becomes a Party to this Statute thereby accepts the jurisdiction of the Court with respect to the crimes referred to in Article 5.
2. In the case of Article 13, paragraph (a) or (c), the Court may exercise its jurisdiction if one or more of the following States are Parties to this Statute or have accepted the jurisdiction of the Court in accordance with paragraph 3:
   (a) The State on the territory of which the conduct in question occurred or, if the crime was committed on board a vessel or aircraft, the State of registration of that vessel or aircraft;
   (b) The State of which the person accused of the crime is a national.
3. If the acceptance of a State which is not a Party to this Statute is required under paragraph 2, that State may, by declaration lodged with the Registrar, accept the exercise of jurisdiction by the Court with respect to the crime in question. The accepting State shall co-operate with the Court without any delay or exception in accordance with Part 9.

Article 13

Exercise of jurisdiction
The Court may exercise its jurisdiction with respect to a crime referred to in Article 5 in accordance with the provisions of this Statute if:

(a) A situation in which one or more of such crimes appears to have been committed is referred to the Prosecutor by a State Party in accordance with Article 14;
(b) A situation in which one or more of such crimes appears to have been committed is referred to the Prosecutor by the Security Council acting under Chapter VII of the Charter of the United Nations; or
(c) The Prosecutor has initiated an investigation in respect of such a crime in accordance with Article 15.

Article 14

Referral of a situation by a State Party

1. A State Party may refer to the Prosecutor a situation in which one or more crimes within the jurisdiction of the Court appear to have been committed requesting the Prosecutor to investigate the situation for the purpose of determining whether one or more specific persons should be charged with the commission of such crimes.
2. As far as possible, a referral shall specify the relevant circumstances and be accompanied by such supporting documentation as is available to the State referring the situation.

Article 15

Prosecutor

1. The Prosecutor may initiate investigations *proprio motu* on the basis of information on crimes within the jurisdiction of the Court.
2. The Prosecutor shall analyse the seriousness of the information received. For this purpose, he or she may seek additional information from States, organs of the United Nations, intergovernmental or non-governmental organizations, or other reliable sources that he or she deems appropriate, and may receive written or oral testimony at the seat of the Court.
3. If the Prosecutor concludes that there is a reasonable basis to proceed with an investigation, he or she shall submit to the Pre-Trial Chamber a request for authorization of an investigation, together with any supporting material collected. Victims may make representations to the Pre-Trial Chamber, in accordance with the Rules of Procedure and Evidence.
4. If the Pre-Trial Chamber, upon examination of the request and the supporting material, considers that there is a reasonable basis to proceed with an investigation, and that the case appears to fall within the jurisdiction of the Court, it shall authorize the commencement of the investigation, without prejudice to subsequent determinations by the Court with regard to the jurisdiction and admissibility of a case.
5. The refusal of the Pre-Trial Chamber to authorize the investigation shall not preclude the presentation of a subsequent request by the Prosecutor based on new facts or evidence regarding the same situation.
6. If, after the preliminary examination referred to in paragraphs 1 and 2, the Prosecutor concludes that the information provided does not constitute a reasonable basis for an investigation, he or she shall inform those who provided the information. This shall

not preclude the Prosecutor from considering further information submitted to him or her regarding the same situation in the light of new facts or evidence.

Article 16

Deferral of investigation or prosecution
No investigation or prosecution may be commenced or proceeded with under this Statute for a period of 12 months after the Security Council, in a resolution adopted under Chapter VII of the Charter of the United Nations, has requested the Court to that effect; that request may be renewed by the Council under the same conditions.

Article 17

Issues of admissibility
1. Having regard to paragraph 10 of the Preamble and Article 1, the Court shall determine that a case is inadmissible where:
   (a) The case is being investigated or prosecuted by a State which has jurisdiction over it, unless the State is unwilling or unable genuinely to carry out the investigation or prosecution;
   (b) The case has been investigated by a State which has jurisdiction over it and the State has decided not to prosecute the person concerned, unless the decision resulted from the unwillingness or inability of the State genuinely to prosecute;
   (c) The person concerned has already been tried for conduct which is the subject of the complaint, and a trial by the Court is not permitted under Article 20, paragraph 3;
   (d) The case is not of sufficient gravity to justify further action by the Court.
2. In order to determine unwillingness in a particular case, the Court shall consider, having regard to the principles of due process recognized by international law, whether one or more of the following exist, as applicable:
   (a) The proceedings were or are being undertaken or the national decision was made for the purpose of shielding the person concerned from criminal responsibility for crimes within the jurisdiction of the Court referred to in Article 5;
   (b) There has been an unjustified delay in the proceedings which in the circumstances is inconsistent with an intent to bring the person concerned to justice;
   (c) The proceedings were not or are not being conducted independently or impartially, and they were or are being conducted in a manner which, in the circumstances, is inconsistent with an intent to bring the person concerned to justice.
3. In order to determine inability in a particular case, the Court shall consider whether, due to a total or substantial collapse or unavailability of its national judicial system, the State is unable to obtain the accused or the necessary evidence and testimony or otherwise unable to carry out its proceedings.

Article 18

Preliminary rulings regarding admissibility
1. When a situation has been referred to the Court pursuant to Article 13 (a) and the Prosecutor has determined that there would be a reasonable basis to commence an investigation, or the Prosecutor initiates an investigation pursuant to Articles 13 (c)

and 15, the Prosecutor shall notify all States Parties and those States which, taking into account the information available, would normally exercise jurisdiction over the crimes concerned. The Prosecutor may notify such States on a confidential basis and, where the Prosecutor believes it necessary to protect persons, prevent destruction of evidence or prevent the absconding of persons, may limit the scope of the information provided to States.

2. Within one month of receipt of that notification, a State may inform the Court that it is investigating or has investigated its nationals or others within its jurisdiction with respect to criminal acts which may constitute crimes referred to in Article 5 and which relate to the information provided in the notification to States. At the request of that State, the Prosecutor shall defer to the State's investigation of those persons unless the Pre-Trial Chamber, on the application of the Prosecutor, decides to authorize the investigation.
3. The Prosecutor's deferral to a State's investigation shall be open to review by the Prosecutor six months after the date of deferral or at any time when there has been a significant change of circumstances based on the State's unwillingness or inability genuinely to carry out the investigation.
4. The State concerned or the Prosecutor may appeal to the Appeals Chamber against a ruling of the Pre-Trial Chamber, in accordance with Article 82. The appeal may be heard on an expedited basis.
5. When the Prosecutor has deferred an investigation in accordance with paragraph 2, the Prosecutor may request that the State concerned periodically inform the Prosecutor of the progress of its investigations and any subsequent prosecutions. States Parties shall respond to such requests without undue delay.
6. Pending a ruling by the Pre-Trial Chamber, or at any time when the Prosecutor has deferred an investigation under this Article, the Prosecutor may, on an exceptional basis, seek authority from the Pre-Trial Chamber to pursue necessary investigative steps for the purpose of preserving evidence where there is a unique opportunity to obtain important evidence or there is a significant risk that such evidence may not be subsequently available.
7. A State which has challenged a ruling of the Pre-Trial Chamber under this Article may challenge the admissibility of a case under Article 19 on the grounds of additional significant

Facts or significant change of circumstances.

Article 19

Challenges to the jurisdiction of the Court or the admissibility of a case

1. The Court shall satisfy itself that it has jurisdiction in any case brought before it. The Court may, on its own motion, determine the admissibility of a case in accordance with Article 17.
2. Challenges to the admissibility of a case on the grounds referred to in Article 17 or challenges to the jurisdiction of the Court may be made by:

    (a) An accused or a person for whom a warrant of arrest or a summons to appear has been issued under Article 58;
    (b) A State which has jurisdiction over a case, on the ground that it is investigating or prosecuting the case or has investigated or prosecuted; or

(c) A State from which acceptance of jurisdiction is required under Article 12.

3. The Prosecutor may seek a ruling from the Court regarding a question of jurisdiction or admissibility. In proceedings with respect to jurisdiction or admissibility, those who have referred the situation under Article 13, as well as victims, may also submit observations to the Court.
4. The admissibility of a case or the jurisdiction of the Court may be challenged only once by any person or State referred to in paragraph 2. The challenge shall take place prior to or at the commencement of the trial. In exceptional circumstances, the Court may grant leave for a challenge to be brought more than once or at a time later than the commencement of the trial. Challenges to the admissibility of a case, at the commencement of a trial, or subsequently with the leave of the Court, may be based only on Article 17, paragraph 1 (c).
5. A State referred to in paragraph 2 (b) and (c) shall make a challenge at the earliest opportunity.
6. Prior to the confirmation of the charges, challenges to the admissibility of a case or challenges to the jurisdiction of the Court shall be referred to the Pre-Trial Chamber. After confirmation of the charges, they shall be referred to the Trial Chamber. Decisions with respect to jurisdiction or admissibility may be appealed to the Appeals Chamber in accordance with Article 82.
7. If a challenge is made by a State referred to in paragraph 2 (b) or (c), the Prosecutor shall suspend the investigation until such time as the Court makes a determination in accordance with Article 17.
8. Pending a ruling by the Court, the Prosecutor may seek authority from the Court:
   (a) To pursue necessary investigative steps of the kind referred to in Article 18, paragraph 6;
   (b) To take a statement or testimony from a witness or complete the collection and examination of evidence which had begun prior to the making of the challenge; and
   (c) In co-operation with the relevant States, to prevent the absconding of persons in respect of whom the Prosecutor has already requested a warrant of arrest under Article 58.
9. The making of a challenge shall not affect the validity of any act performed by the Prosecutor or any order or warrant issued by the Court prior to the making of the challenge.
10. If the Court has decided that a case is inadmissible under Article 17, the Prosecutor may submit a request for a review of the decision when he or she is fully satisfied that new facts have arisen which negate the basis on which the case had previously been found inadmissible under Article 17.
11. If the Prosecutor, having regard to the matters referred to in Article 17, defers an investigation, the Prosecutor may request that the relevant State make available to the Prosecutor information on the proceedings. That information shall, at the request of the State concerned, be confidential. If the Prosecutor thereafter decides to proceed with an investigation, he or she shall notify the State to which deferral of the proceedings has taken place.

Article 20

Ne bis in idem

1. Except as provided in this Statute, no person shall be tried before the Court with respect to conduct which formed the basis of crimes for which the person has been convicted or acquitted by the Court.
2. No person shall be tried by another court for a crime referred to in Article 5 for which that person has already been convicted or acquitted by the Court.
3. No person who has been tried by another court for conduct also proscribed under Article 6, 7 or 8 shall be tried by the Court with respect to the same conduct unless the proceedings in the other court:
   (a) Were for the purpose of shielding the person concerned from criminal responsibility for crimes within the jurisdiction of the Court; or
   (b) Otherwise were not conducted independently or impartially in accordance with the norms of due process recognized by international law and were conducted in a manner which, in the circumstances, was inconsistent with an intent to bring the person concerned to justice.

Article 21

Applicable law

1. The Court shall apply:
   (a) In the first place, this Statute, Elements of Crimes and its Rules of Procedure and Evidence;
   (b) In the second place, where appropriate, applicable treaties and the principles and rules of international law, including the established principles of the international law of armed conflict;
   (c) Failing that, general principles of law derived by the Court from national laws of legal systems of the world including, as appropriate, the national laws of States that would normally exercise jurisdiction over the crime, provided that those principles are not inconsistent with this Statute and with international law and internationally recognized norms and standards.
2. The Court may apply principles and rules of law as interpreted in its previous decisions.
3. The application and interpretation of law pursuant to this Article must be consistent with internationally recognized human rights, and be without any adverse distinction founded on grounds such as gender as defined in Article 7, paragraph 3, age, race, colour, language, religion or belief, political or other opinion, national, ethnic or social origin, wealth, birth or other status.

PART 3. GENERAL PRINCIPLES OF CRIMINAL LAW

Article 22

Nullum crimen sine lege

1. A person shall not be criminally responsible under this Statute unless the conduct in question constitutes, at the time it takes place, a crime within the jurisdiction of the Court.

4. The definition of a crime shall be strictly construed and shall not be extended by analogy. In case of ambiguity, the definition shall be interpreted in favour of the person being investigated, prosecuted or convicted.
5. This Article shall not affect the characterization of any conduct as criminal under international law independently of this Statute.

Article 23

Nulla poena sine lege
A person convicted by the Court may be punished only in accordance with this Statute.

Article 24

Non-retroactivity ratione personae
1. No person shall be criminally responsible under this Statute for conduct prior to the entry into force of the Statute.
2. In the event of a change in the law applicable to a given case prior to a final judgement, the law more favourable to the person being investigated, prosecuted or convicted shall apply.

Article 25

Individual criminal responsibility
1. The Court shall have jurisdiction over natural persons pursuant to this Statute.
2. A person who commits a crime within the jurisdiction of the Court shall be individually responsible and liable for punishment in accordance with this Statute.
3. In accordance with this Statute, a person shall be criminally responsible and liable for punishment for a crime within the jurisdiction of the Court if that person:
   (a) Commits such a crime, whether as an aindividual, jointly with another or through another person, regardless of whether that other person is criminally responsible;
   (b) Orders, solicits or induces the commission of such a crime which in fact occurs or is attempted;
   (c) For the purpose of facilitating the commission of such a crime, aids, abets or otherwise assists in its commission or its attempted commission, including providing the means for its commission;
   (d) In any other way contributes to the commission or attempted commission of such a crime by a group of persons acting with a common purpose. Such contribution shall be intentional and shall either:
      (i) Be made with the aim of furthering the criminal activity or criminal purpose of the group, where such activity or purpose involves the commission of a crime within the jurisdiction of the Court; or
      (ii) Be made in the knowledge of the intention of the group to commit the crime;
   (e) In respect of the crime of genocide, directly and publicly incites others to commit genocide;
   (f) Attempts to commit such a crime by taking action that commences its execution by means of a substantial step, but the crime does not occur because of circumstances independent of the person's intentions. However, a person who abandons

the effort to commit the crime or otherwise prevents the completion of the crime shall not be liable for punishment under this Statute for the attempt to commit that crime if that person completely and voluntarily gave up the criminal purpose.

3. No provision in this Statute relating to individual criminal responsibility shall affect the responsibility of States under international law.

Article 26

Exclusion of jurisdiction over persons under eighteen

The Court shall have no jurisdiction over any person who was under the age of 18 at the time of the alleged commission of a crime

Article 27

Irrelevance of official capacity

1. This Statute shall apply equally to all persons without any distinction based on official capacity. In particular, official capacity as a Head of State or Government, a member of a Government or parliament, an elected representative or a government official shall in no case exempt a person from criminal responsibility under this Statute, nor shall it, in and of itself, constitute a ground for reduction of sentence.
2. Immunities or special procedural rules which may attach to the official capacity of a person, whether under national or international law, shall not bar the Court from exercising its jurisdiction over such a person.

Article 28

Responsibility of commanders and other superiors

In addition to other grounds of criminal responsibility under this Statute for crimes within the jurisdiction of the Court:

(a) A military commander or person effectively acting as a military commander shall be criminally responsible for crimes within the jurisdiction of the Court committed by forces under his or her effective command and control, or effective authority and control as the case may be, as a result of his or her failure to exercise control properly over such forces, where:

(i) That military commander or person either knew or, owing to the circumstances at the time, should have known that the forces were committing or about to commit such crimes; and

(ii) That military commander or person failed to take all necessary and reasonable measures within his or her power to prevent or repress their commission or to submit the matter to the competent authorities for investigation and prosecution.

(b) With respect to superior and subordinate relationships not described in paragraph (a), a superior shall be criminally responsible for crimes within the jurisdiction of the Court committed by subordinates under his or her effective authority and control, as a result of his or her failure to exercise control properly over such subordinates, where:

(i) The superior either knew, or consciously disregarded information which clearly indicated, that the subordinates were committing or about to commit such crimes;

(ii) The crimes concerned activities that were within the effective responsibility and control of the superior; and

(iii) The superior failed to take all necessary and reasonable measures within his or her power to prevent or repress their commission or to submit the matter to the competent authorities for investigation and prosecution.

Article 29

Non-applicability of statute of limitations
The crimes within the jurisdiction of the Court shall not be subject to any statute of limitations.

Article 30

Mental element
1. Unless otherwise provided, a person shall be criminally responsible and liable for punishment for a crime within the jurisdiction of the Court only if the material elements are committed with intent and knowledge.
2. For the purposes of this Article, a person has intent where:
   (a) In addition to conduce, that person means to engage in the conduct;
   (b) In relation to a consequence, that person means to cause that consequence or is aware that it will occur in the ordinary course of events.
3. For the purposes of this Article, "knowledge" means awareness that a circumstance exists or a consequence will occur in the ordinary course of events. "Know" and "knowingly" shall be construed accordingly.

Article 31

Grounds for excluding criminal responsibility
1. In addition to other grounds for excluding criminal responsibility provided for in this Statute, a person shall not be criminally responsible if, at the time of that person's conduct:
   (a) The person suffers from a mental disease or defect that destroys that person's capacity to appreciate the unlawfulness or nature of his or her conduct, or capacity to control his or her conduct to conform to the requirements of law;
   (b) The person is in a state of intoxication that destroys that person's capacity to appreciate the unlawfulness or nature of his or her conduct, or capacity to control his or her conduct to conform to the requirements of law, unless the person has become voluntarily intoxicated under such circumstances that the person knew, or disregarded the risk, that, as a result of the intoxication, he or she was likely to engage in conduct constituting a crime within the jurisdiction of the Court;
   (c) The person acts reasonably to defend himself or herself or another person or, in the case of war crimes, property which is essential for the survival of the person or another person or property which is essential for accomplishing a military mission, against an imminent and unlawful use of force in a manner proportionate to the degree of danger to the person or the other person or property protected. The fact that the person was involved in a defensive operation conducted by forces shall not in itself constitute a ground for excluding criminal responsibility under this subparagraph;

(d) The conduct which is alleged to constitute a crime within the jurisdiction of the Court has been caused by duress resulting from a threat of imminent death or of continuing or imminent serious bodily harm against that person or another person, and the person acts necessarily and reasonably to avoid this threat, provided that the person does not intend to cause a greater harm than the one sought to be avoided. Such a threat may either be:

(i) Made by other persons; or
(ii) Constituted by other circumstances beyond that person's control.

3. The Court shall determine the applicability of the grounds for excluding criminal responsibility provided for in this Statute to the case before it.
4. At trial, the Court may consider a ground for excluding criminal responsibility other than those referred to in paragraph 1 where such a ground is derived from applicable law as set forth in Article 21. The procedures relating to the consideration of such a ground shall be provided for in the Rules of Procedure and Evidence.

Article 32

Mistake of fact or mistake of law

1. A mistake of fact shall be a ground for excluding criminal responsibility only if it negates the mental element required by the crime.
2. A mistake of law as to whether a particular type of conduct is a crime within the jurisdiction of the Court shall not be a ground for excluding criminal responsibility. A mistake of law may, however, be a ground for excluding criminal responsibility if it negates the mental element required by such a crime, or as provided for in Article 33

Article 33

Superior orders and prescription of law

1. The fact that a crime within the jurisdiction of the Court has been committed by a person pursuant to an order of a Government or of a superior, whether military or civilian, shall not relieve that person of criminal responsibility unless:

(a) The person was under a legal obligation to obey orders of the Government or the superior in question;
(b) The person did not know that the order was unlawful; and
(c) The order was not manifestly unlawful.

2. For the purposes of this Article, orders to commit genocide or crimes against humanity are manifestly unlawful.

PART 4. COMPOSITION AND ADMINISTRATION OF THE COURT

Article 34

Organs of the Court

The Court shall be composed of the following organs:

(a) The Presidency;
(b) An Appeals Division, a Trial Division and a Pre-Trial Division;

(c) The Office of the Prosecutor;
(d) The Registry.

Article 35

Service of judges

1. All judges shall be elected as full-time members of the Court and shall be available to serve on that basis from the commencement of their terms of office.
2. The judges composing the Presidency shall serve on a full-time basis as soon as they are elected.
3. The Presidency may, on the basis of the workload of the Court and in consultation with its members, decide from time to time to what extent the remaining judges shall be required to serve on a full-time basis. Any such arrangement shall be without prejudice to the provisions of Article 40.
4. The financial arrangements for judges not required to serve on a full-time basis shall be made in accordance with Article 49.

Article 36

Qualifications, nomination and election of judges

1. Subject to the provisions of paragraph 2, there shall be 18 judges of the Court.
2. (a) The Presidency, acting on behalf of the Court, may propose an increase in the number of judges specified in paragraph 1, indicating the reasons why this is considered necessary and appropriate. The Registrar shall promptly circulate any such proposal to all States Parties.
   (b) Any such proposal shall then be considered at a meeting of the Assembly of States Parties to be convened in accordance with Article 112. The proposal shall be considered adopted if approved at the meeting by a vote of two thirds of the members of the Assembly of States Parties and shall enter into force at such time as decided by the Assembly of States Parties.
   (c) (i) Once a proposal for an increase in the number of judges has been adopted under subparagraph (b), the election of the additional judges shall take place at the next session of the Assembly of States Parties in accordance with paragraphs 3 to 8, and Article 37, paragraph 2;
   (ii) Once a proposal for an increase in the number of judges has been adopted and brought into effect under subparagraphs (b) and (c) (i), it shall be open to the Presidency at any time thereafter, if the workload of the Court justifies it, to propose a reduction in the number of judges, provided that the number of judges shall not be reduced below that specified in paragraph 1. The proposal shall be dealt with in accordance with the procedure laid down in subparagraphs (a) and (b). In the event that the proposal is adopted, the number of judges shall be progressively decreased as the terms of office of serving judges expire, until the necessary number has been reached.
3. (a) The judges shall be chosen from among persons of high moral character, impartiality and integrity who possess the qualifications required in their respective States for appointment to the highest judicial offices.
   (b) Every candidate for election to the Court shall:
   (i) Have established competence in criminal law and procedure, and the necessary relevant experience, whether as judge, prosecutor, advocate or in other similar capacity, in criminal proceedings; or

(ii) Have established competence in relevant areas of international law such as international humanitarian law and the law of human rights, and extensive experience in a professional legal capacity which is of relevance to the judicial work of the Court;

(c) Every candidate for election to the Court shall have an excellent knowledge of and be fluent in at least one of the working languages of the Court.

4. (a) Nominations of candidates for election to the Court may be made by any State Party to this Statute, and shall be made either:

(i) By the procedure for the nomination of candidates for appointment to the highest judicial offices in the State in question; or

(ii) By the procedure provided for the nomination of candidates for the International Court of Justice in the Statute of that Court.

Nominations shall be accompanied by a statement in the necessary detail specifying how the candidate fulfils the requirements of paragraph 3

(b) Each State Party may put forward one candidate for any given election who need not necessarily be a national of that State Party but shall in any case be a national of a State Party.

(c) The Assembly of States Parties may decide to establish, if appropriate, an Advisory Committee on nominations. In that event, the Committee's composition and mandate shall be established by the Assembly of States Parties.

5. For the purposes of the election, there shall be two lists of candidates:

List A containing the names of candidates with the qualifications specified in paragraph 3 (b) (i); and
List B containing the names of candidates with the qualifications specified in paragraph 3 (b) (ii).

A candidate with sufficient qualifications for both lists may choose on which list to appear. At the first election to the Court, at least nine judges shall be elected from list A and at least five judges from list B. Subsequent elections shall be so organized as to maintain the equivalent proportion on the Court of judges qualified on the two lists.

6. (a) The judges shall be elected by secret ballot at a meeting of the Assembly of States Parties convened for that purpose under Article 112. Subject to paragraph 7, the persons elected to the Court shall be the 18 candidates who obtain the highest number of votes and a two-thirds majority of the States Parties present and voting.

(b) In the event that a sufficient number of judges is not elected on the first ballot, successive ballots shall be held in accordance with the procedures laid down in subparagraph (a) until the remaining places have been filled.

7. No two judges may be nationals of the same State. A person who, for the purposes of membership of the Court, could be regarded as a national of more than one State shall be deemed to be a national of the State in which that person ordinarily exercises civil and political rights.

8. (a) The States Parties shall, in the selection of judges, take into account the need, within the membership of the Court, for:

(i) The representation of the principal legal systems of the world;
(ii) Equitable geographical representation; and
(iii) A fair representation of female and male judges.

(b) States Parties shall also take into account the need to include judges with legal expertise on specific issues, including, but not limited to, violence against women or children.

9. (a) Subject to subparagraph (b), judges shall hold office for a term of nine years and, subject to subparagraph (c) and to Article 37, paragraph 2, shall not be eligible for re-election.

(b) At the first election, one third of the judges elected shall be selected by lot to serve for a term of three years; one third of the judges elected shall be selected by lot to serve for a term of six years; and the remainder shall serve for a term of nine years.

(c) A judge who is selected to serve for a term of three years under subparagraph (b) shall be eligible for re-election for a full term.

10. Notwithstanding paragraph 9, a judge assigned to a Trial or Appeals Chamber in accordance with Article 39 shall continue in office to complete any trial or appeal the hearing of which has already commenced before that Chamber.

Article 37

Judicial vacancies

1. In the event of a vacancy, an election shall be held in accordance with Article 36 to fill the vacancy.
2. A judge elected to fill a vacancy shall serve for the remainder of the predecessor's term and, if that period is three years or less, shall be eligible for re-election for a full term under Article 36.

Article 38

The Presidency

1. The President and the First and Second Vice-Presidents shall be elected by an absolute majority of the judges. They shall each serve for a term of three years or until the end of their respective terms of office as judges, whichever expires earlier. They shall be eligible for re-election once.
2. The First Vice-President shall act in place of the President in the event that the President is unavailable or disqualified. The Second Vice-President shall act in place of the President in the event that both the President and the First Vice-President are unavailable or disqualified.
3. The President, together with the First and Second Vice-Presidents, shall constitute the Presidency, which shall be responsible for:

   (a) The proper administration of the Court, with the exception of the Office of the Prosecutor; and

   (b) The other functions conferred upon it in accordance with this Statute.
4. In discharging its responsibility under paragraph 3 (a), the Presidency shall coordinate with and seek the concurrence of the Prosecutor on all matters of mutual concern.

Article 39

Chambers

1. As soon as possible after the election of the judges, the Court shall organize itself into the divisions specified in Article 34, paragraph (b). The Appeals Division shall be

composed of the President and four other judges, the Trial Division of not less than six judges and the Pre-Trial Division of not less than six judges. The assignment of judges to divisions shall be based on the nature of the functions to be performed by each division and the qualifications and experience of the judges elected to the Court, in such a way that each division shall contain an appropriate combination of expertise in criminal law and procedure and in international law. The Trial and Pre-Trial Divisions shall be composed predominantly of judges with criminal trial experience.

2. (a) The judicial functions of the Court shall be carried out in each division by Chambers.
   (b) (i) The Appeals Chamber shall be composed of all the judges of the Appeals Division;
   (iii) The functions of the Trial Chamber shall be carried out by three judges of the Trial Division;
   (iv) The functions of the Pre-Trial Chamber shall be carried out either by three judges of the Pre-Trial Division or by a single judge of that division in accordance with this Statute and the rules of Procedure and Evidence.

   (c) Nothing in this paragraph shall preclude the simultaneous constitution of more than one Trial Chamber or Pre-Trial Chamber when the efficient management of the Court's workload so requires.
3. (a) Judges assigned to the Trial and Pre-Trial Divisions shall serve in those divisions for a period of three years, and thereafter until the completion of any case the hearing of which has already commenced in the division concerned.
   (b) Judges assigned to the Appeals Division shall serve in that division for their entire term of office.
4. Judges assigned to the Appeals Division shall serve only in that division. Nothing in this Article shall, however, preclude the temporary attachment of judges from the Trial Division to the Pre-Trial Division or vice versa, if the Presidency considers that the efficient management of the Court's workload so requires, provided that under no circumstances shall a judge who has participated in the pre-trial phase of a case be eligible to sit on the Trial Chamber hearing that case.

Article 40

Independence of the judges
1. The judges shall be independent in the performance of their functions.
2. Judges shall not engage in any activity which is likely to interfere with their judicial functions or to affect confidence in their independence.
3. Judges required to serve on a full-time basis at the seat of the Court shall not engage in any other occupation of a professional nature.
4. Any question regarding the application of paragraphs 2 and 3 shall be decided by an absolute majority of the judges. Where any such question concerns an individual judge, that judge shall not take part in the decision.

Article 41

Excusing and disqualification of judges
1. The Presidency may, at the request of a judge, excuse that judge from the exercise of a function under this Statute, in accordance with the Rules of Procedure and Evidence.

2. (a) A judge shall not participate in any case in which his or her impartiality might reasonably be doubted on any ground. A judge shall be disqualified from a case in accordance with this paragraph if, *inter alia*, that judge has previously been involved in any capacity in that case before the Court or in a related criminal case at the national level involving the person being investigated or prosecuted. A judge shall also be disqualified on such other grounds as may be provided for in the Rules of Procedure and Evidence
   (b) The Prosecutor or the person being investigated or prosecuted may request the disqualification of a judge under this paragraph.
   (c) Any question as to the disqualification of a judge shall be decided by an absolute majority of the judges. The challenged judge shall be entitled to present his or her comments on the matter, but shall not take part in the decision.

Article 42

The Office of the Prosecutor

1. The Office of the Prosecutor shall act independently as a separate organ of the Court. It shall be responsible for receiving referrals and any substantiated information on crimes within the jurisdiction of the Court, for examining them and for conducting investigations and prosecutions before the Court. A member of the Office shall not seek or act on instructions from any external source.
2. The Office shall be headed by the Prosecutor. The Prosecutor shall have full authority over the management and administration of the Office, including the staff, facilities and other resources thereof. The Prosecutor shall be assisted by one or more Deputy Prosecutors, who shall be entitled to carry out any of the acts required of the Prosecutor under this Statute. The Prosecutor and the Deputy Prosecutors shall be of different nationalities. They shall serve on a full-time basis.
3. The Prosecutor and the Deputy Prosecutors shall be persons of high moral character, be highly competent in and have extensive practical experience in the prosecution or trial of criminal cases. They shall have an excellent knowledge of and be fluent in at least one of the working languages of the Court.
4. The Prosecutor shall be elected by secret ballot by an absolute majority of the members of the Assembly of States Parties. The Deputy Prosecutors shall be elected in the same way from a list of candidates provided by the Prosecutor. The Prosecutor shall nominate three candidates for each position of Deputy Prosecutor to be filled. Unless a shorter term is decided upon at the time of their election, the Prosecutor and the Deputy Prosecutors shall hold office for a term of nine years and shall not be eligible for re-election.
5. Neither the Prosecutor nor a Deputy Prosecutor shall engage in any activity which is likely to interfere with his or her prosecutorial functions or to affect confidence in his or her independence. They shall not engage in any other occupation of a professional nature.
6. The Presidency may excuse the Prosecutor or a Deputy Prosecutor, at his or her request, from acting in a particular case.
7. Neither the Prosecutor nor a Deputy Prosecutor shall participate in any matter in which their impartiality might reasonably be doubted on any ground. They shall be disqualified from a case in accordance with this paragraph if, *inter alia*, they have previously been involved in any capacity in that case before the Court or in a related

criminal case at the national level involving the person being investigated or prosecuted.

8. Any question as to the disqualification of the Prosecutor or a Deputy Prosecutor shall be decided by the Appeals Chamber.
   (a) The person being investigated or prosecuted may at any time request the disqualification of the Prosecutor or a Deputy Prosecutor on the grounds set out in this Article;
   (b) The Prosecutor or the Deputy Prosecutor, as appropriate, shall be entitled to present his or her comments on the matter;
9. The Prosecutor shall appoint advisers with legal expertise on specific issues, including, but not limited to, sexual and gender violence and violence against children.

Article 43

The Registry

1. The Registry shall be responsible for the non-judicial aspects of the administration and servicing of the Court, without prejudice to the functions and powers of the Prosecutor in accordance with Article 42.
2. The Registry shall be headed by the Registrar, who shall be the principal administrative officer of the Court. The Registrar shall exercise his or her functions under the authority of the President of the Court.
3. The Registrar and the Deputy Registrar shall be persons of high moral character, be highly competent and have an excellent knowledge of and be fluent in at least one of the working languages of the Court.
4. The judges shall elect the Registrar by an absolute majority by secret ballot, taking into account any recommendation by the Assembly of States Parties. If the need arises and upon the recommendation of the Registrar, the judges shall elect, in the same manner, a Deputy Registrar.
5. The Registrar shall hold office for a term of five years, shall be eligible for re-election once and shall serve on a full-time basis. The Deputy Registrar shall hold office for a term of five years or such shorter term as may be decided upon by an absolute majority of the judges, and may be elected on the basis that the Deputy Registrar shall be called upon to serve as required.
6. The Registrar shall set up a Victims and Witnesses Unit within the Registry. This Unit shall provide, in consultation with the Office of the Prosecutor, protective measures and security arrangements, counselling and other appropriate assistance for witnesses, victims who appear before the Court, and others who are at risk on account of testimony given by such witnesses. The Unit shall include staff with expertise in trauma, including trauma related to crimes of sexual violence.

Article 44

Staff

1. The Prosecutor and the Registrar shall appoint such qualified staff as may be required to their respective offices. In the case of the Prosecutor, this shall include the appointment of investigators.
2. In the employment of staff, the Prosecutor and the Registrar shall ensure the highest standards of efficiency, competency and integrity, and shall have regard, *mutatis mutandis*, to the criteria set forth in Article 36, paragraph 8.

3. The Registrar, with the agreement of the Presidency and the Prosecutor, shall propose Staff Regulations which include the terms and conditions upon which the staff of the Court shall be appointed, remunerated and dismissed. The Staff Regulations shall be approved by the Assembly of States Parties.
4. The Court may, in exceptional circumstances, employ the expertise of gratis personnel offered by States Parties, intergovernmental organizations or non-governmental organizations to assist with the work of any of the organs of the Court. The Prosecutor may accept any such offer on behalf of the Office of the Prosecutor. Such gratis personnel shall be employed in accordance with guidelines to be established by the Assembly of States Parties.

Article 45

Solemn undertaking
Before taking up their respective duties under this Statute, the judges, the Prosecutor, the Deputy Prosecutors, the Registrar and the Deputy Registrar shall each make a solemn undertaking in open court to exercise his or her respective functions impartially and conscientiously.

Article 46

Removal from office
1. A judge, the Prosecutor, a Deputy Prosecutor, the Registrar or the Deputy Registrar shall be removed from office if a decision to this effect is made in accordance with paragraph 2, in cases where that person:
   (a) Is found to have committed serious misconduct or a serious breach of his or her duties under this Statute, as provided for in the Rules of Procedure and Evidence; or
   (b) Is unable to exercise the functions required by this Statute.
2. A decision as to the removal from office of a judge, the Prosecutor or a Deputy Prosecutor under paragraph 1 shall be made by the Assembly of States Parties, by secret ballot:
   (a) In the case of a judge, by a two-thirds majority of the States Parties upon a recommendation adopted by a two-thirds majority of the other judges;
   (b) In the case of the Prosecutor, by an absolute majority of the States Parties;
   (c) In the case of a Deputy Prosecutor, by an absolute majority of the States Parties upon the recommendation of the Prosecutor.
3. A decision as to the removal from office of the Registrar or Deputy Registrar shall be made by an absolute majority of the judges.
4. A judge, Prosecutor, Deputy Prosecutor, Registrar or Deputy Registrar whose conduct or ability to exercise the functions of the office as required by this Statute is challenged under this Article shall have full opportunity to present and receive evidence and to make submissions in accordance with the Rules of Procedure and Evidence. The person in question shall not otherwise participate in the consideration of the matter.

Article 47

Disciplinary measures
A judge, Prosecutor, Deputy Prosecutor, Registrar or Deputy Registrar who has committed misconduct of a less serious nature than that set out in Article 46, paragraph 1, shall

be subject to disciplinary measures, in accordance with the Rules of Procedure and Evidence.

Article 48

Privileges and immunities

1. The Court shall enjoy in the territory of each State Party such privileges and immunities as are necessary for the fulfillment of its purposes.
2. The judges, the Prosecutor, the Deputy Prosecutors and the Registrar shall, when engaged on or with respect to the business of the Court, enjoy the same privileges and immunities as are accorded to heads of diplomatic missions and shall, after the expiry of their terms of office, continue to be accorded immunity from legal process of every kind in respect of words spoken or written and acts performed by them in their official capacity.
3. The Deputy Registrar, the staff of the Office of the Prosecutor and the staff of the Registry shall enjoy the privileges and immunities and facilities necessary for the performance of their functions, in accordance with the agreement on the privileges and immunities of the Court.
4. Counsel, experts, witnesses or any other person required to be present at the seat of the Court shall be accorded such treatment as is necessary for the proper functioning of the Court, in accordance with the agreement on the privileges and immunities of the Court.
5. The privileges and immunities of:
   (a) A judge or the Prosecutor may be waived by an absolute majority of the judges;
   (b) The Registrar may be waived by the Presidency;
   (c) The Deputy Prosecutors and staff of the Office of the Prosecutor may be waived by the Prosecutor;
   (d) The Deputy Registrar and staff of the Registry may be waived by the Registrar.

Article 49

Salaries, allowances and expenses

The judges, the Prosecutor, the Deputy Prosecutors, the Registrar and the Deputy Registrar shall receive such salaries, allowances and expenses as may be decided upon by the Assembly of States Parties. These salaries and allowances shall not be reduced during their terms of office.

Article 50

Official and working languages

1. The official languages of the Court shall be Arabic, Chinese, English, French, Russian and Spanish. The judgements of the Court, as well as other decisions resolving fundamental issues before the Court, shall be published in the official languages. The Presidency shall, in accordance with the criteria established by the Rules of Procedure and Evidence, determine which decisions may be considered as resolving fundamental issues for the purposes of this paragraph.
2. The working languages of the Court shall be English and French. The Rules of Procedure and Evidence shall determine the cases in which other official languages may be used as working languages.

3. At the request of any party to a proceeding or a State allowed to intervene in a proceeding, the Court shall authorize a language other than English or French to be used by such a party or State, provided that the Court considers such authorization to be adequately justified.

Article 51

Rules of Procedure and Evidence

1 The Rules of Procedure and Evidence shall enter into force upon adoption by a two-thirds majority of the members of the Assembly of States Parties.
2. Amendments to the Rules of Procedure and Evidence may be proposed by:
   (a) Any State Party;
   (b) The judges acting by an absolute majority; or
   (c) The Prosecutor.

Such amendments shall enter into force upon adoption by a two-thirds majority of the members of the Assembly of States Parties.

3. After the adoption of the Rules of Procedure and Evidence, in urgent cases where the Rules do not provide for a specific situation before the Court, the judges may, by a two-thirds majority, draw up provisional Rules to be applied until adopted, amended or rejected at the next ordinary or special session of the Assembly of States Parties.
4. The Rules of Procedure and Evidence, amendments thereto and any provisional Rule shall be consistent with this Statute. Amendments to the Rules of Procedure and Evidence as well as provisional Rules shall not be applied retroactively to the detriment of the person who is being investigated or prosecuted or who has been convicted.
5. In the event of conflict between the Statute and the Rules of Procedure and Evidence, the Statute shall prevail.

Article 52

Regulations of the Court

1. The judges shall, in accordance with this Statute and the Rules of Procedure and Evidence, adopt, by an absolute majority, the Regulations of the Court necessary for its routine functioning.
2. The Prosecutor and the Registrar shall be consulted in the elaboration of the Regulations and any amendments thereto.
3. The Regulations and any amendments thereto shall take effect upon adoption unless otherwise decided by the judges. Immediately upon adoption, they shall be circulated to States Parties for comments. If within six months there are no objections from a majority of States Parties, they shall remain in force.

PART 5. INVESTIGATION AND PROSECUTION

Article 53

Initiation of an investigation

1. The Prosecutor shall, having evaluated the information made available to him or her, initiate an investigation unless he or she determines that there is no reasonable basis

to proceed under this Statute. In deciding whether to initiate an investigation, the Prosecutor shall consider whether:

(a) The information available to the Prosecutor provides a reasonable basis to believe that a crime within the jurisdiction of the Court has been or is being committed;

(b) The case is or would be admissible under Article 17; and

(c) Taking into account the gravity of the crime and the interests of victims, there are nonetheless substantial reasons to believe that an investigation would not serve the interests of justice.

If the Prosecutor determines that there is no reasonable basis to proceed and his or her determination is based solely on subparagraph (c) above, he or she shall inform the Pre-Trial Chamber.

2. If, upon investigation, the Prosecutor concludes that there is not a sufficient basis for a prosecution because:

(a) There is not a sufficient legal or factual basis to seek a warrant or summons under Article 58;

(b) The case is inadmissible under Article 17; or

(c) A prosecution is not in the interests of justice, taking into account all the circumstances, including the gravity of the crime, the interests of victims and the age or infirmity of the alleged perpetrator, and his or her role in the alleged crime;

the Prosecutor shall inform the Pre-Trial Chamber and the State making a referral under Article 14 or the Security Council in a case under Article 13, paragraph (b), of his or her conclusion and the reasons for the conclusion.

3. (a) At the request of the State making a referral under Article 14 or the Security Council under Article 13, paragraph (b), the Pre-Trial Chamber may review a decision of the Prosecutor under paragraph 1 or 2 not to proceed and may request the Prosecutor to reconsider that decision

(b) In addition, the Pre-Trial Chamber may, on its own initiative, review a decision of the Prosecutor not to proceed if it is based solely on paragraph 1 (c) or 2 (c). In such a case, the decision of the Prosecutor shall be effective only if confirmed by the Pre-Trial Chamber

4. The Prosecutor may, at any time, reconsider a decision whether to initiate an investigation or prosecution based on new facts or information.

Article 54

Duties and powers of the Prosecutor with respect to investigations

1. The Prosecutor shall:

(a) In order to establish the truth, extend the investigation to cover all facts and evidence relevant to an assessment of whether there is criminal responsibility under this Statute, and, in doing so, investigate incriminating and exonerating circumstances equally;

(b) Take appropriate measures to ensure the effective investigation and prosecution of crimes within the jurisdiction of the Court, and in doing so, respect the interests and personal circumstances of victims and witnesses, including age, gender as defined in Article 7, paragraph 3, and health, and take into account the nature of the crime, in particular where it involves sexual violence, gender violence or violence against children; and

(c) Fully respect the rights of persons arising under this Statute.

2 The Prosecutor may conduct investigations on the territory of a State:
(a) In accordance with the provisions of Part 9; or
(b) As authorized by the Pre-Trial Chamber under Article 57, paragraph 3 (d).
3. The Prosecutor may:
   (a) Collect and examine evidence;
   (b) Request the presence of and question persons being investigated, victims and witnesses;
   (c) «Seek the co-operation of any State or intergovernmental organization or arrangement in accordance with its respective competence and/or mandate;
   (d) Enter into such arrangements or agreements, not inconsistent with this Statute, as may be necessary to facilitate the co-operation of a State, intergovernmental organization or person;
   (e) Agree not to disclose, at any stage of the proceedings, documents or information that the Prosecutor obtains on the condition of confidentiality and solely for the purpose of generating new evidence, unless the provider of the information consents; and
   (f) Take necessary measures, or request that necessary measures be taken, to ensure the confidentiality of information, the protection of any person or the preservation of evidence.

Article 55

Rights of persons during an investigation
1. In respect of an investigation under this Statute, a person:
   (a) Shall not be compelled to incriminate himself or herself or to confess guilt;
   (b) Shall not be subjected to any form of coercion, duress or threat, to torture or to any other form of cruel, inhuman or degrading treatment or punishment;
   (c) Shall, if questioned in a language other than a language the person fully understands and speaks, have, free of any cost, the assistance of a competent interpreter and such translations as are necessary to meet the requirements of fairness; and
   (d) Shall not be subjected to arbitrary arrest or detention, and shall not be deprived of his or her liberty except on such grounds and in accordance with such procedures as are established in this Statute.
2. Where there are grounds to believe that a person has committed a crime within the jurisdiction of the Court and that person is about to be questioned either by the Prosecutor, or by national authorities pursuant to a request made under Part 9, that person shall also have the following rights of which he or she shall be informed prior to being questioned:
   (a) To be informed, prior to being questioned, that there are grounds to believe that he or she has committed a crime within the jurisdiction of the Court;
   (b) To remain silent, without such silence being a consideration in the determination of guilt or innocence;
   (c) To have legal assistance of the person's choosing, or, if the person does not have legal assistance, to have legal assistance assigned to him or her, in any case where the interests of justice so require, and without payment by the person in any such case if the person does not have sufficient means to pay for it; and
   (d) To be questioned in the presence of counsel unless the person has voluntarily waived his or her right to counsel.

Article 56

Role of the Pre-Trial Chamber in relation to a unique investigative opportunity

1. (a) Where the Prosecutor considers an investigation to present a unique opportunity to take testimony or a statement from a witness or to examine, collect or test evidence, which may not be available subsequently for the purposes of a trial, the Prosecutor shall so inform the Pre-Trial Chamber.
   (b) In that case, the Pre-Trial Chamber may, upon request of the Prosecutor, take such measures as may be necessary to ensure the efficiency and integrity of the proceedings and, in particular, to protect the rights of the defence.
   (c) Unless the Pre-Trial Chamber orders otherwise, the Prosecutor shall provide the relevant information to the person who has been arrested or appeared in response to a summons in connection with the investigation referred to in subparagraph (a), in order that he or she may be heard on the matter.
2. The measures referred to in paragraph 1 (b) may include:
   (a) Making recommendations or orders regarding procedures to be followed;
   (b) Directing that a record be made of the proceedings;
   (c) Appointing an expert to assist;
   (d) Authorizing counsel for a person who has been arrested, or appeared before the Court in response to a summons, to participate, or where there has not yet been such an arrest or appearance or counsel has not been designated, appointing another counsel to attend and represent the interests of the defence;
   (e) Naming one of its members or, if necessary, another available judge of the Pre-Trial or Trial Division to observe and make recommendations or orders regarding the collection and preservation of evidence and the questioning of persons;
   (f) Taking such other action as may be necessary to collect or preserve evidence.
3. (a) Where the Prosecutor has not sought measures pursuant to this Article but the Pre-Trial Chamber considers that such measures are required to preserve evidence that it deems would be essential for the defence at trial, it shall consult with the Prosecutor as to whether there is good reason for the Prosecutor's failure to request the measures. If upon consultation, the Pre-Trial Chamber concludes that the Prosecutor's failure to request such measures is unjustified, the Pre-Trial Chamber may take such measures on its own initiative.
   (b) A decision of the Pre-Trial Chamber to act on its own initiative under this paragraph may be appealed by the Prosecutor. The appeal shall be heard on an expedited basis.
4. The admissibility of evidence preserved or collected for trial pursuant to this Article, or the record thereof, shall be governed at trial by Article 69, and given such weight as determined by the Trial Chamber.

Article 57

Functions and powers of the Pre-Trial Chamber

1. Unless otherwise provided in this Statute, the Pre-Trial Chamber shall exercise its functions in accordance with the provisions of this Article.
2. (a) Orders or rulings of the Pre-Trial Chamber issued under Articles 15, 18, 19, 54, paragraph 2, 61, paragraph 7, and 72 must be concurred in by a majority of its judges.
   (b) In all other cases, a single judge of the Pre-Trial Chamber may exercise the functions provided for in this Statute, unless otherwise provided for in the Rules of

Procedure and Evidence or by a majority of the Pre-Trial Chamber.
3. In addition to its other functions under this Statute, the Pre-Trial Chamber may:
   (a) At the request of the Prosecutor, issue such orders and warrants as may be required for the purposes of an investigation;
   (b) Upon the request of a person who has been arrested or has appeared pursuant to a summons under Article 58, issue such orders, including measures such as those described in Article 56, or seek such co-operation pursuant to Part 9 as may be necessary to assist the person in the preparation of his or her defence;
   (c) Where necessary, provide for the protection and privacy of victims and witnesses, the preservation of evidence, the protection of persons who have been arrested or appeared in response to a summons, and the protection of national security information;
   (d) Authorize the Prosecutor to take specific investigative steps within the territory of a State Party without having secured the co-operation of that State under Part 9 if, whenever possible having regard to the views of the State concerned, the Pre-Trial Chamber has determined in that case that the State is clearly unable to execute a request for co-operation due to the unavailability of any authority or any component of its judicial system competent to execute the request for co-operation under Part 9.
   (e Where a warrant of arrest or a summons has been issued under Article 58, and having due regard to the strength of the evidence and the rights of the parties concerned, as provided for in this Statute and the Rules of Procedure and Evidence, seek the co-operation of States pursuant to Article 93, paragraph 1 (k), to take protective measures for the purpose of forfeiture, in particular for the ultimate benefit of victims.

Article 58

Issuance by the Pre-Trial Chamber of a warrant of arrest or a summons to appear
1. At any time after the initiation of an investigation, the Pre-Trial Chamber shall, on the application of the Prosecutor, issue a warrant of arrest of a person if, having examined the application and the evidence or other information submitted by the Prosecutor, it is satisfied that:
   (a) There are reasonable grounds to believe that the person has committed a crime within the jurisdiction of the Court; and
   (b) The arrest of the person appears necessary:
      (i) To ensure the person's appearance at trial,
      (ii) To ensure that the person does not obstruct or endanger the investigation or the court proceedings, or
      (iii) Where applicable, to prevent the person from continuing with the commission of that crime or a related crime which is within the jurisdiction of the Court and which arises out of the same circumstances.
2. The application of the Prosecutor shall contain:
   (a) The name of the person and any other relevant identifying information;
   (b) A specific reference to the crimes within the jurisdiction of the Court which the person is alleged to have committed;
   (c A concise statement of the facts which are alleged to constitute those crimes;
   (d) A summary of the evidence and any other information which establish reasonable

grounds to believe that the person committed those crimes; and

(e) The reason why the Prosecutor believes that the arrest of the person is necessary.

3. The warrant of arrest shall contain:
   (a) The name of the person and any other relevant identifying information;
   (b) A specific reference to the crimes within the jurisdiction of the Court for which the person's arrest is sought; and
   (c) A concise statement of the facts which are alleged to constitute those crimes.
4. The warrant of arrest shall remain in effect until otherwise ordered by the Court.
5. On the basis of the warrant of arrest, the Court may request the provisional arrest or the arrest and surrender of the person under Part 9.
6. The Prosecutor may request the Pre-Trial Chamber to amend the warrant of arrest by modifying or adding to the crimes specified therein. The Pre-Trial Chamber shall so amend the warrant if it is satisfied that there are reasonable grounds to believe that the person committed the modified or additional crimes.
7. As an alternative to seeking a warrant of arrest, the Prosecutor may submit an application requesting that the Pre-Trial Chamber issue a summons for the person to appear. If the Pre-Trial Chamber is satisfied that there are reasonable grounds to believe that the person committed the crime alleged and that a summons is sufficient to ensure the person's appearance, it shall issue the summons, with or without conditions restricting liberty (other than detention) if provided for by national law, for the person to appear. The summons shall contain:
   (a) The name of the person and any other relevant identifying information;
   (b) The specified date on which the person is to appear;
   (c) A specific reference to the crimes within the jurisdiction of the Court which the person is alleged to have committed; and
   (d) A concise statement of the facts which are alleged to constitute the crime.

The summons shall be served on the person.

Article 59

Arrest proceedings in the custodial State

1. A State Party which has received a request for provisional arrest or for arrest and surrender shall immediately take steps to arrest the person in question in accordance with its laws and the provisions of Part 9.
2. A person arrested shall be brought promptly before the competent judicial authority in the custodial State which shall determine, in accordance with the law of that State, that:
   (a) The warrant applies to that person;
   (b) The person has been arrested in accordance with the proper process; and
   (c) The person's rights have been respected.
3. The person arrested shall have the right to apply to the competent authority in the custodial State for interim release pending surrender.
4. In reaching a decision on any such application, the competent authority in the custodial State shall consider whether, given the gravity of the alleged crimes, there are urgent and exceptional circumstances to justify interim release and whether necessary safeguards exist to ensure that the custodial State can fulfil its duty to surrender the person to the Court. It shall not be open to the competent authority of the custodial

State to consider whether the warrant of arrest was properly issued in accordance with Article 58, paragraph 1 (a) and (b).

5. The Pre-Trial Chamber shall be notified of any request for interim release and shall make recommendations to the competent authority in the custodial State. The competent authority in the custodial State shall give full consideration to such recommendations, including any recommendations on measures to prevent the escape of the person, before rendering its decision.
6. If the person is granted interim release, the Pre-Trial Chamber may request periodic reports on the status of the interim release.
7. Once ordered to be surrendered by the custodial State, the person shall be delivered to the Court as soon as possible.

Article 60

Initial proceedings before the Court

1. Upon the surrender of the person to the Court, or the person's appearance before the Court voluntarily or pursuant to a summons, the Pre-Trial Chamber shall satisfy itself that the person has been informed of the crimes which he or she is alleged to have committed, and of his or her rights under this Statute, including the right to apply for interim release pending trial.
2. A person subject to a warrant of arrest may apply for interim release pending trial. If the Pre-Trial Chamber is satisfied that the conditions set forth in Article 58, paragraph 1, are met, the person shall continue to be detained. If it is not so satisfied, the Pre-Trial Chamber shall release the person, with or without conditions.
3. The Pre-Trial Chamber shall periodically review its ruling on the release or detention of the person, and may do so at any time on the request of the Prosecutor or the person. Upon such review, it may modify its ruling as to detention, release or conditions of release, if it is satisfied that changed circumstances so require.
4. The Pre-Trial Chamber shall ensure that a person is not detained for an unreasonable period prior to trial due to inexcusable delay by the Prosecutor. If such delay occurs, the Court shall consider releasing the person, with or without conditions.
5. f necessary, the Pre-Trial Chamber may issue a warrant of arrest to secure the presence of a person who has been released.

Article 61

Confirmation of the charges before trial

1. Subject to the provisions of paragraph 2, within a reasonable time after the person's surrender or voluntary appearance before the Court, the Pre-Trial Chamber shall hold a hearing to confirm the charges on which the Prosecutor intends to seek trial. The hearing shall be held in the presence of the Prosecutor and the person charged, as well as his or her counsel.
2. The Pre-Trial Chamber may, upon request of the Prosecutor or on its own motion, hold a hearing in the absence of the person charged to confirm the charges on which the Prosecutor intends to seek trial when the person has:
   (a) Waived his or her right to be present; or
   (b) Fled or cannot be found and all reasonable steps have been taken to secure his or her appearance before the Court and to inform the person of the charges and that a hearing to confirm those charges will be held.

In that case, the person shall be represented by counsel where the Pre-Trial Chamber determines that it is in the interests of justice.

3. Within a reasonable time before the hearing, the person shall:
   (a) Be provided with a copy of the document containing the charges on which the Prosecutor intends to bring the person to trial; and
   (b) Be informed of the evidence on which the Prosecutor intends to rely at the hearing.

The Pre-Trial Chamber may issue orders regarding the disclosure of information for the purposes of the hearing.

4. Before the hearing, the Prosecutor may continue the investigation and may amend or withdraw any charges. The person shall be given reasonable notice before the hearing of any amendment to or withdrawal of charges. In case of a withdrawal of charges, the Prosecutor shall notify the Pre-Trial Chamber of the reasons for the withdrawal.
5. At the hearing, the Prosecutor shall support each charge with sufficient evidence to establish substantial grounds to believe that the person committed the crime charged. The Prosecutor may rely on documentary or summary evidence and need not call the witnesses expected to testify at the trial.
6. At the hearing, the person may:
   (a) Object to the charges;
   (b) Challenge the evidence presented by the Prosecutor; and
   (c) Present evidence.

7. The Pre-Trial Chamber shall, on the basis of the hearing, determine whether there is sufficient evidence to establish substantial grounds to believe that the person committed each of the crimes charged. Based on its determination, the Pre-Trial Chamber shall:
   (a) Confirm those charges in relation to which it has determined that there is sufficient evidence, and commit the person to a Trial Chamber for trial on the charges as confirmed;
   (b) Decline to confirm those charges in relation to which it has determined that there is insufficient evidence;
   (c) Adjourn the hearing and request the Prosecutor to consider:
      (i) Providing further evidence or conducting further investigation with respect to a particular charge; or
      (ii) Amending a charge because the evidence submitted appears to establish a different crime within the jurisdiction of the Court.
8. Where the Pre-Trial Chamber declines to confirm a charge, the Prosecutor shall not be precluded from subsequently requesting its confirmation if the request is supported by additional evidence.
9. After the charges are confirmed and before the trial has begun, the Prosecutor may, with the permission of the Pre-Trial Chamber and after notice to the accused, amend the charges. If the Prosecutor seeks to add additional charges or to substitute more serious charges, a hearing under this Article to confirm those charges must be held. After commencement of the trial, the Prosecutor may, with the permission of the Trial Chamber, withdraw the charges.
10. Any warrant previously issued shall cease to have effect with respect to any charges which have not been confirmed by the Pre-Trial Chamber or which have been withdrawn by the Prosecutor.
11. Once the charges have been confirmed in accordance with this Article, the Presidency

shall constitute a Trial Chamber which, subject to paragraph 9 and to Article 64, paragraph 4, shall be responsible for the conduct of subsequent proceedings and may exercise any function of the Pre-Trial Chamber that is relevant and capable of application in those proceedings.

PART 6. THE TRIAL

Article 62

Place of trial
Unless otherwise decided, the place of the trial shall be the seat of the Court.

Article 63

Trial in the presence of the accused
1. The accused shall be present during the trial.
2. If the accused, being present before the Court, continues to disrupt the trial, the Trial Chamber may remove the accused and shall make provision for him or her to observe the trial and instruct counsel from outside the courtroom, through the use of communications technology, if required. Such measures shall be taken only in exceptional circumstances after other reasonable alternatives have proved inadequate, and only for such duration as is strictly required.

Article 64

Functions and powers of the Trial Chamber
1. The functions and powers of the Trial Chamber set out in this Article shall be exercised in accordance with this Statute and the Rules of Procedure and Evidence.
2. The Trial Chamber shall ensure that a trial is fair and expeditious and is conducted with full respect for the rights of the accused and due regard for the protection of victims and witnesses.
3. Upon assignment of a case for trial in accordance with this Statute, the Trial Chamber assigned to deal with the case shall:
   (a Confer with the parties and adopt such procedures as are necessary to facilitate the fair and expeditious conduct of the proceedings;
   (b) Determine the language or languages to be used at trial; and
   (c) Subject to any other relevant provisions of this Statute, provide for disclosure of documents or information not previously disclosed, sufficiently in advance of the commencement of the trial to enable adequate preparation for trial.
4. The Trial Chamber may, if necessary for its effective and fair functioning, refer preliminary issues to the Pre-Trial Chamber or, if necessary, to another available judge of the Pre-Trial Division.
5. Upon notice to the parties, the Trial Chamber may, as appropriate, direct that there be joinder or severance in respect of charges against more than one accused.
6. In performing its functions prior to trial or during the course of a trial, the Trial Chamber may, as necessary:
   (a) Exercise any functions of the Pre-Trial Chamber referred to in Article 61, paragraph 11;

(b) Require the attendance and testimony of witnesses and production of documents and other evidence by obtaining, if necessary, the assistance of States as provided in this Statute;
(c) Provide for the protection of confidential information;
(d) Order the production of evidence in addition to that already collected prior to the trial or presented during the trial by the parties;
(e) Provide for the protection of the accused, witnesses and victims; and
(f) Rule on any other relevant matters.

7. The trial shall be held in public. The Trial Chamber may, however, determine that special circumstances require that certain proceedings be in closed session for the purposes set forth in Article 68, or to protect confidential or sensitive information to be given in evidence.
8. (a) At the commencement of the trial, the Trial Chamber shall have read to the accused the charges previously confirmed by the Pre-Trial Chamber. The Trial Chamber shall satisfy itself that the accused understands the nature of the charges. It shall afford him or her the opportunity to make an admission of guilt in accordance with Article 65 or to plead not guilty.
(b) At the trial, the presiding judge may give directions for the conduct of proceedings, including to ensure that they are conducted in a fair and impartial manner. Subject to any directions of the presiding judge, the parties may submit evidence in accordance with the provisions of this Statute.
9. The Trial Chamber shall have, *inter alia*, the power on application of a party or on its own motion to:
(a) Rule on the admissibility or relevance of evidence; and
(b) Take all necessary steps to maintain order in the course of a hearing.
10. The Trial Chamber shall ensure that a complete record of the trial, which accurately reflects the proceedings, is made and that it is maintained and preserved by the Registrar.

Article 65

Proceedings on an admission of guilt

1. Where the accused makes an admission of guilt pursuant to Article 64, paragraph 8 (a), the Trial Chamber shall determine whether:
(a) The accused understands the nature and consequences of the admission of guilt;
(b) The admission is voluntarily made by the accused after sufficient consultation with defence counsel; and
(c) The admission of guilt is supported by the facts of the case that are contained in:
(i) The charges brought by the Prosecutor and admitted by the accused;
(ii) Any materials presented by the Prosecutor which supplement the charges and which the accused accepts; and
(iii) Any other evidence, such as the testimony of witnesses, presented by the Prosecutor or the accused.
2. Where the Trial Chamber is satisfied that the matters referred to in paragraph 1 are established, it shall consider the admission of guilt, together with any additional evidence presented, as establishing all the essential facts that are required to prove the crime to which the admission of guilt relates, and may convict the accused of that crime.

3. Where the Trial Chamber is not satisfied that the matters referred to in paragraph 1 are established, it shall consider the admission of guilt as not having been made, in which case it shall order that the trial be continued under the ordinary trial procedures provided by this Statute and may remit the case to another Trial Chamber.
4. Where the Trial Chamber is of the opinion that a more complete presentation of the facts of the case is required in the interests of justice, in particular the interests of the victims, the Trial Chamber may:
   (a) Request the Prosecutor to present additional evidence, including the testimony of witnesses; or
   (b) Order that the trial be continued under the ordinary trial procedures provided by this Statute, in which case it shall consider the admission of guilt as not having been made and may remit the case to another Trial Chamber.
5 Any discussions between the Prosecutor and the defence regarding modification of the charges, the admission of guilt or the penalty to be imposed shall not be binding on the Court.

Article 66

Presumption of innocence
1. Everyone shall be presumed innocent until proved guilty before the Court in accordance with the applicable law.
2. The onus is on the Prosecutor to prove the guilt of the accused.
3. In order to convict the accused, the Court must be convinced of the guilt of the accused beyond reasonable doubt.

Article 67

Rights of the accused
1. In the determination of any charge, the accused shall be entitled to a public hearing, having regard to the provisions of this Statute, to a fair hearing conducted impartially, and to the following minimum guarantees, in full equality:
   (a) To be informed promptly and in detail of the nature, cause and content of the charge, in a language which the accused fully understands and speaks;
   (b) To have adequate time and facilities for the preparation of the defence and to communicate freely with counsel of the accused's choosing in confidence;
   (c) To be tried without undue delay;
   (d) Subject to Article 63, paragraph 2, to be present at the trial, to conduct the defence in person or through legal assistance of the accused's choosing, to be informed, if the accused does not have legal assistance, of this right and to have legal assistance assigned by the Court in any case where the interests of justice so require, and without payment if the accused lacks sufficient means to pay for it;
   (e) To examine, or have examined, the witnesses against him or her and to obtain the attendance and examination of witnesses on his or her behalf under the same conditions as witnesses against him or her. The accused shall also be entitled to raise defences and to present other evidence admissible under this Statute;
   (f) To have, free of any cost, the assistance of a competent interpreter and such translations as are necessary to meet the requirements of fairness, if any of the proceedings of or documents presented to the Court are not in a language which the accused fully understands and speaks;

(g) Not to be compelled to testify or to confess guilt and to remain silent, without such silence being a consideration in the determination of guilt or innocence;
(h) To make an unsworn oral or written statement in his or her defence; and
(i) Not to have imposed on him or her any reversal of the burden of proof or any onus of rebuttal.

2. In addition to any other disclosure provided for in this Statute, the Prosecutor shall, as soon as practicable, disclose to the defence evidence in the Prosecutor's possession or control which he or she believes shows or tends to show the innocence of the accused, or to mitigate the guilt of the accused, or which may affect the credibility of prosecution evidence. In case of doubt as to the application of this paragraph, the Court shall decide.

Article 68

Protection of the victims and witnesses and their participation in the proceedings

1. The Court shall take appropriate measures to protect the safety, physical and psychological well-being, dignity and privacy of victims and witnesses. In so doing, the Court shall have regard to all relevant factors, including age, gender as defined in Article 7, paragraph 3, and health, and the nature of the crime, in particular, but not limited to, where the crime involves sexual or gender violence or violence against children. The Prosecutor shall take such measures particularly during the investigation and prosecution of such crimes. These measures shall not be prejudicial to or inconsistent with the rights of the accused and a fair and impartial trial.
2. As an exception to the principle of public hearings provided for in Article 67, the Chambers of the Court may, to protect victims and witnesses or an accused, conduct any part of the proceedings in camera or allow the presentation of evidence by electronic or other special means. In particular, such measures shall be implemented in the case of a victim of sexual violence or a child who is a victim or a witness, unless otherwise ordered by the Court, having regard to all the circumstances, particularly the views of the victim or witness.
3. Where the personal interests of the victims are affected, the Court shall permit their views and concerns to be presented and considered at stages of the proceedings determined to be appropriate by the Court and in a manner which is not prejudicial to or inconsistent with the rights of the accused and a fair and impartial trial. Such views and concerns may be presented by the legal representatives of the victims where the Court considers it appropriate, in accordance with the Rules of Procedure and Evidence.
4. The Victims and Witnesses Unit may advise the Prosecutor and the Court on appropriate protective measures, security arrangements, counselling and assistance as referred to in Article 43, paragraph 6.
5. Where the disclosure of evidence or information pursuant to this Statute may lead to the grave endangerment of the security of a witness or his or her family, the Prosecutor may, for the purposes of any proceedings conducted prior to the commencement of the trial, withhold such evidence or information and instead submit a summary thereof. Such measures shall be exercised in a manner which is not prejudicial to or inconsistent with the rights of the accused and a fair and impartial trial.
6. A State may make an application for necessary measures to be taken in respect of the protection of its servants or agents and the protection of confidential or sensitive information.

Article 69

Evidence

1. Before testifying, each witness shall, in accordance with the Rules of Procedure and Evidence, give an undertaking as to the truthfulness of the evidence to be given by that witness.
2. The testimony of a witness at trial shall be given in person, except to the extent provided by the measures set forth in Article 68 or in the Rules of Procedure and Evidence. The Court may also permit the giving of *viva voce* (oral) or recorded testimony of a witness by means of video or audio technology, as well as the introduction of documents or written transcripts, subject to this Statute and in accordance with the Rules of Procedure and Evidence. These measures shall not be prejudicial to or inconsistent with the rights of the accused.
3. The parties may submit evidence relevant to the case, in accordance with Article 64. The Court shall have the authority to request the submission of all evidence that it considers necessary for the determination of the truth.
4. The Court may rule on the relevance or admissibility of any evidence, taking into account, *inter alia*, the probative value of the evidence and any prejudice that such evidence may cause to a fair trial or to a fair evaluation of the testimony of a witness, in accordance with the Rules of Procedure and Evidence.
5. The Court shall respect and observe privileges on confidentiality as provided for in the Rules of Procedure and Evidence.
6. The Court shall not require proof of facts of common knowledge but may take judicial notice of them.
7. Evidence obtained by means of a violation of this Statute or internationally recognized human rights shall not be admissible if:
   (a) The violation casts substantial doubt on the reliability of the evidence; or
   (b) The admission of the evidence would be antithetical to and would seriously damage the integrity of the proceedings.
8. When deciding on the relevance or admissibility of evidence collected by a State, the Court shall not rule on the application of the State's national law.

Article 70

Offences against the administration of justice

1. The Court shall have jurisdiction over the following offences against its administration of justice when committed intentionally:
   (a) Giving false testimony when under an obligation pursuant to Article 69, paragraph 1, to tell the truth;
   (b) Presenting evidence that the party knows is false or forged;
   (c) Corruptly influencing a witness, obstructing or interfering with the attendance or testimony of a witness, retaliating against a witness for giving testimony or destroying, tampering with or interfering with the collection of evidence;
   (d) Impeding, intimidating or corruptly influencing an official of the Court for the purpose of forcing or persuading the official not to perform, or to perform improperly, his or her duties;
   (e) Retaliating against an official of the Court on account of duties performed by that or another official;

(f) Soliciting or accepting a bribe as an official of the Court in connection with his or her official duties.

2. The principles and procedures governing the Court's exercise of jurisdiction over offences under this Article shall be those provided for in the Rules of Procedure and Evidence. The conditions for providing international co-operation to the Court with respect to its proceedings under this Article shall be governed by the domestic laws of the requested State.
3. In the event of conviction, the Court may impose a term of imprisonment not exceeding five years, or a fine in accordance with the Rules of Procedure and Evidence, or both.
4. (a) Each State Party shall extend its criminal laws penalizing offences against the integrity of its own investigative or judicial process to offences against the administration of justice referred to in this Article, committed on its territory, or by one of its nationals;

   (b) Upon request by the Court, whenever it deems it proper, the State Party shall submit the case to its competent authorities for the purpose of prosecution. Those authorities shall treat such cases with diligence and devote sufficient resources to enable them to be conducted effectively.

Article 71

Sanctions for misconduct before the Court

1. The Court may sanction persons present before it who commit misconduct, including disruption of its proceedings or deliberate refusal to comply with its directions, by administrative measures other than imprisonment, such as temporary or permanent removal from the courtroom, a fine or other similar measures provided for in the Rules of Procedure and Evidence.
2. The procedures governing the imposition of the measures set forth in paragraph 1 shall be those provided for in the Rules of Procedure and Evidence.

Article 72

Protection of national security information

1. This Article applies in any case where the disclosure of the information or documents of a State would, in the opinion of that State, prejudice its national security interests. Such cases include those falling within the scope of Article 56, paragraphs 2 and 3, Article 61, paragraph 3, Article 64, paragraph 3, Article 67, paragraph 2, Article 68, paragraph 6, Article 87, paragraph 6 and Article 93, as well as cases arising at any other stage of the proceedings where such disclosure may be at issue.
2. This Article shall also apply when a person who has been requested to give information or evidence has refused to do so or has referred the matter to the State on the ground that disclosure would prejudice the national security interests of a State and the State concerned confirms that it is of the opinion that disclosure would prejudice its national security interests.
3. Nothing in this Article shall prejudice the requirements of confidentiality applicable under Article 54, paragraph 3 (e) and (f), or the application of Article 73.
4. If a State learns that information or documents of the State are being, or are likely to be, disclosed at any stage of the proceedings, and it is of the opinion that disclosure

would prejudice its national security interests, that State shall have the right to intervene in order to obtain resolution of the issue in accordance with this Article.

5. If, in the opinion of a State, disclosure of information would prejudice its national security interests, all reasonable steps will be taken by the State, acting in conjunction with the Prosecutor, the defence or the Pre-Trial Chamber or Trial Chamber, as the case may be, to seek to resolve the matter by co-operative means. Such steps may include:
   (a) Modification or clarification of the request;
   (b) A determination by the Court regarding the relevance of the information or evidence sought, or a determination as to whether the evidence, though relevant, could be or has been obtained from a source other than the requested State;
   (c) Obtaining the information or evidence from a different source or in a different form; or
   (d) Agreement on conditions under which the assistance could be provided including, among other things, providing summaries or redactions, limitations on disclosure, use of *in camera* or *ex parte* proceedings, or other protective measures permissible under the Statute and the Rules of Procedure and Evidence.
6. Once all reasonable steps have been taken to resolve the matter through co-operative means, and if the State considers that there are no means or conditions under which the information or documents could be provided or disclosed without prejudice to its national security interests, it shall so notify the Prosecutor or the Court of the specific reasons for its decision, unless a specific description of the reasons would itself necessarily result in such prejudice to the State's national security interests.
7. Thereafter, if the Court determines that the evidence is relevant and necessary for the establishment of the guilt or innocence of the accused, the Court may undertake the following actions:
   (a) Where disclosure of the information or document is sought pursuant to a request for co-operation under Part 9 or the circumstances described in paragraph 2, and the State has invoked the ground for refusal referred to in Article 93, paragraph 4:
      (i) The Court may, before making any conclusion referred to in subparagraph 7 (a) (ii), request further consultations for the purpose of considering the State's representations, which may include, as appropriate, hearings in camera and ex parte;
      (ii) If the Court concludes that, by invoking the ground for refusal under Article 93, paragraph 4, in the circumstances of the case, the requested State is not acting in accordance with its obligations under this Statute, the Court may refer the matter in accordance with Article 87, paragraph 7, specifying the reasons for its conclusion; and
      (iii) The Court may make such inference in the trial of the accused as to the existence or non-existence of a fact, as may be appropriate in the circumstances; or
   (b) In all other circumstances:
      (i) Order disclosure; or
      (ii To the extent it does not order disclosure, make such inference in the trial of the accused as to the existence or non-existence of a fact, as may be appropriate in the circumstances.

Article 73

Third-party information or documents

If a State Party is requested by the Court to provide a document or information in its custody, possession or control, which was disclosed to it in confidence by a State, intergovernmental organization or international organization, it shall seek the consent of the originator to disclose that document or information. If the originator is a State Party, it shall either consent to disclosure of the information or document or undertake to resolve the issue of disclosure with the Court, subject to the provisions of Article 72. If the originator is not a State Party and refuses to consent to disclosure, the requested State shall inform the Court that it is unable to provide the document or information because of a pre-existing obligation of confidentiality to the originator.

Article 74

Requirements for the decision

1. All the judges of the Trial Chamber shall be present at each stage of the trial and throughout their deliberations. The Presidency may, on a case-by-case basis, designate, as available, one or more alternate judges to be present at each stage of the trial and to replace a member of the Trial Chamber if that member is unable to continue attending.
2. The Trial Chamber's decision shall be based on its evaluation of the evidence and the entire proceedings. The decision shall not exceed the facts and circumstances described in the charges and any amendments to the charges. The Court may base its decision only on evidence submitted and discussed before it at the trial.
3. The judges shall attempt to achieve unanimity in their decision, failing which the decision shall be taken by a majority of the judges.
4. The deliberations of the Trial Chamber shall remain secret.
5. The decision shall be in writing and shall contain a full and reasoned statement of the Trial Chamber's findings on the evidence and conclusions. The Trial Chamber shall issue one decision. When there is no unanimity, the Trial Chamber's decision shall contain the views of the majority and the minority. The decision or a summary thereof shall be delivered in open court.

Article 75

Reparations to victims

1. The Court shall establish principles relating to reparations to, or in respect of, victims, including restitution, compensation and rehabilitation. On this basis, in its decision the Court may, either upon request or on its own motion in exceptional circumstances, determine the scope and extent of any damage, loss and injury to, or in respect of, victims and will state the principles on which it is acting.
2. The Court may make an order directly against a convicted person specifying appropriate reparations to, or in respect of, victims, including restitution, compensation and rehabilitation. Where appropriate, the Court may order that the award for reparations be made through the Trust Fund provided for in Article 79.
3. Before making an order under this Article, the Court may invite and shall take account of representations from or on behalf of the convicted person, victims, other interested persons or interested States.

4. In exercising its power under this Article, the Court may, after a person is convicted of a crime within the jurisdiction of the Court, determine whether, in order to give effect to an order which it may make under this Article, it is necessary to seek measures under Article 93, paragraph 1.
5. A State Party shall give effect to a decision under this Article as if the provisions of Article 109 were applicable to this Article.
6. Nothing in this Article shall be interpreted as prejudicing the rights of victims under national or international law.

Article 76

Sentencing

1. In the event of a conviction, the Trial Chamber shall consider the appropriate sentence to be imposed and shall take into account the evidence presented and submissions made during the trial that are relevant to the sentence.

2. Except where Article 65 applies and before the completion of the trial, the Trial Chamber may on its own motion and shall, at the request of the Prosecutor or the accused, hold a further hearing to hear any additional evidence or submissions relevant to the sentence, in accordance with the Rules of Procedure and Evidence.

3. Where paragraph 2 applies, any representations under Article 75 shall be heard during the further hearing referred to in paragraph 2 and, if necessary, during any additional hearing.

4. The sentence shall be pronounced in public and, wherever possible, in the presence of the accused.

PART 7. PENALTIES

Article 77

Applicable penalties

1. Subject to Article 110, the Court may impose one of the following penalties on a person convicted of a crime referred to in Article 5 of this Statute:
   (a) Imprisonment for a specified number of years, which may not exceed a maximum of 30 years; or
   (b) A term of life imprisonment when justified by the extreme gravity of the crime and the individual circumstances of the convicted person.
2. In addition to imprisonment, the Court may order:
   (a) A fine under the criteria provided for in the Rules of Procedure and Evidence;
   (b) A forfeiture of proceeds, property and assets derived directly or indirectly from that crime, without prejudice to the rights of bona fide third parties.

Article 78

Determination of the sentence

1. In determining the sentence, the Court shall, in accordance with the Rules of Procedure and Evidence, take into account such factors as the gravity of the crime and the individual circumstances of the convicted person.

2. In imposing a sentence of imprisonment, the Court shall deduct the time, if any, previously spent in detention in accordance with an order of the Court. The Court may deduct any time otherwise spent in detention in connection with conduct underlying the crime.
3 When a person has been convicted of more than one crime, the Court shall pronounce a sentence for each crime and a joint sentence specifying the total period of imprisonment. This period shall be no less than the highest individual sentence pronounced and shall not exceed 30 years imprisonment or a sentence of life imprisonment in conformity with Article 77, paragraph 1 (b).

Article 79

Trust Fund
1. A Trust Fund shall be established by decision of the Assembly of States Parties for the benefit of victims of crimes within the jurisdiction of the Court, and of the families of such victims.
2. The Court may order money and other property collected through fines or forfeiture to be transferred, by order of the Court, to the Trust Fund.
3 The Trust Fund shall be managed according to criteria to be determined by the Assembly of States Parties.

Article 80

Non-prejudice to national application of penalties and national laws
Nothing in this Part affects the application by States of penalties prescribed by their national law, nor the law of States which do not provide for penalties prescribed in this Part.

PART 8. APPEAL AND REVISION

Article 81

Appeal against decision of acquittal or conviction or against sentence
1. A decision under Article 74 may be appealed in accordance with the Rules of Procedure and Evidence as follows:
   (a) The Prosecutor may make an appeal on any of the following grounds:
      (i) Procedural error,
      (ii) Error of fact, or
      (iii) Error of law;
   (b) The convicted person, or the Prosecutor on that person's behalf, may make an appeal on any of the following grounds:
      (i) Procedural error,
      (ii) Error of fact,
      (iii) Error of law, or
      (iv) Any other ground that affects the fairness or reliability of the proceedings or decision.
2. (a) A sentence may be appealed, in accordance with the Rules of Procedure and Evidence, by the Prosecutor or the convicted person on the ground of disproportion between the crime and the sentence;

(b) If on an appeal against sentence the Court considers that there are grounds on which the conviction might be set aside, wholly or in part, it may invite the Prosecutor and the convicted person to submit grounds under Article 81, paragraph 1 (a) or (b), and may render a decision on conviction in accordance with Article 83;
(c) The same procedure applies when the Court, on an appeal against conviction only, considers that there are grounds to reduce the sentence under paragraph 2 (a).

3. (a) Unless the Trial Chamber orders otherwise, a convicted person shall remain in custody pending an appeal;
   (b) When a convicted person's time in custody exceeds the sentence of imprisonment imposed, that person shall be released, except that if the Prosecutor is also appealing, the release may be subject to the conditions under subparagraph (c) below;
   (c) In case of an acquittal, the accused shall be released immediately, subject to the following:
      (i) Under exceptional circumstances, and having regard, *inter alia*, to the concrete risk of flight, the seriousness of the offence charged and the probability of success on appeal, the Trial Chamber, at the request of the Prosecutor, may maintain the detention of the person pending appeal;
      (ii) A decision by the Trial Chamber under subparagraph (c) (i) may be appealed in accordance with the Rules of Procedure and Evidence.
4. Subject to the provisions of paragraph 3 (a) and (b), execution of the decision or sentence shall be suspended during the period allowed for appeal and for the duration of the appeal proceedings.

Article 82

Appeal against other decisions

1. Either party may appeal any of the following decisions in accordance with the Rules of Procedure and Evidence:
   (a) A decision with respect to jurisdiction or admissibility;
   (b) A decision granting or denying release of the person being investigated or prosecuted;
   (c) A decision of the Pre-Trial Chamber to act on its own initiative under Article 56, paragraph 3;
   (d) A decision that involves an issue that would significantly affect the fair and expeditious conduct of the proceedings or the outcome of the trial, and for which, in the opinion of the Pre-Trial or Trial Chamber, an immediate resolution by the Appeals Chamber may materially advance the proceedings.
2. A decision of the Pre-Trial Chamber under Article 57, paragraph 3 (d), may be appealed against by the State concerned or by the Prosecutor, with the leave of the Pre-Trial Chamber. The appeal shall be heard on an expedited basis.
3. An appeal shall not of itself have suspensive effect unless the Appeals Chamber so orders, upon request, in accordance with the Rules of Procedure and Evidence.
4. A legal representative of the victims, the convicted person or a bona fide owner of property adversely affected by an order under Article 75 may appeal against the order for reparations, as provided in the Rules of Procedure and Evidence.

Article 83

Proceedings on appeal

1. For the purposes of proceedings under Article 81 and this Article, the Appeals Chamber shall have all the powers of the Trial Chamber.
2. f the Appeals Chamber finds that the proceedings appealed from were unfair in a way that affected the reliability of the decision or sentence, or that the decision or sentence appealed from was materially affected by error of fact or law or procedural error, it may:
   (a) Reverse or amend the decision or sentence; or
   (b) Order a new trial before a different Trial Chamber.

For these purposes, the Appeals Chamber may remand a factual issue to the original Trial Chamber for it to determine the issue and to report back accordingly, or may itself call evidence to determine the issue. When the decision or sentence has been appealed only by the person convicted, or the Prosecutor on that person's behalf, it cannot be amended to his or her detriment.

3. If in an appeal against sentence the Appeals Chamber finds that the sentence is disproportionate to the crime, it may vary the sentence in accordance with Part
4. The judgement of the Appeals Chamber shall be taken by a majority of the judges and shall be delivered in open court. The judgement shall state the reasons on which it is based. When there is no unanimity, the judgement of the Appeals Chamber shall contain the views of the majority and the minority, but a judge may deliver a separate or dissenting opinion on a question of law.
5. The Appeals Chamber may deliver its judgement in the absence of the person acquitted or convicted.

Article 84

Revision of conviction or sentence

1. The convicted person or, after death, spouses, children, parents or one person alive at the time of the accused's death who has been given express written instructions from the accused to bring such a claim, or the Prosecutor on the person's behalf, may apply to the Appeals Chamber to revise the final judgement of conviction or sentence on the grounds that:
   (a) New evidence has been discovered that:
      (i) Was not available at the time of trial, and such unavailability was not wholly or partially attributable to the party making application; and
      (ii) Is sufficiently important that had it been proved at trial it would have been likely to have resulted in a different verdict;
   (b) It has been newly discovered that decisive evidence, taken into account at trial and upon which the conviction depends, was false, forged or falsified;
   (c) One or more of the judges who participated in conviction or confirmation of the charges has committed, in that case, an act of serious misconduct or serious breach of duty of sufficient gravity to justify the removal of that judge or those judges from office under Article 46.
2. The Appeals Chamber shall reject the application if it considers it to be unfounded. If it determines that the application is meritorious, it may, as appropriate:
   (a) Reconvene the original Trial Chamber;

(b) Constitute a new Trial Chamber; or

(c) Retain jurisdiction over the matter,

with a view to, after hearing the parties in the manner set forth in the Rules of Procedure and Evidence, arriving at a determination on whether the judgement should be revised.

Article 85

Compensation to an arrested or convicted person

1. Anyone who has been the victim of unlawful arrest or detention shall have an enforceable right to compensation.
2. When a person has by a final decision been convicted of a criminal offence, and when subsequently his or her conviction has been reversed on the ground that a new or newly discovered fact shows conclusively that there has been a miscarriage of justice, the person who has suffered punishment as a result of such conviction shall be compensated according to law, unless it is proved that the non-disclosure of the unknown fact in time is wholly or partly attributable to him or her.
3. In exceptional circumstances, where the Court finds conclusive facts showing that there has been a grave and manifest miscarriage of justice, it may in its discretion award compensation, according to the criteria provided in the Rules of Procedure and Evidence, to a person who has been released from detention following a final decision of acquittal or a termination of the proceedings for that reason.

PART 9. INTERNATIONAL CO-OPERATION AND JUDICIAL ASSISTANCE

Article 86

General obligation to co-operate

States Parties shall, in accordance with the provisions of this Statute, co-operate fully with the Court in its investigation and prosecution of crimes within the jurisdiction of the Court.

Article 87

Requests for co-operation: general provisions

1. (a) The Court shall have the authority to make requests to States Parties for co-operation. The requests shall be transmitted through the diplomatic channel or any other appropriate channel as may be designated by each State Party upon ratification, acceptance, approval or accession.

   Subsequent changes to the designation shall be made by each State Party in accordance with the Rules of Procedure and Evidence.

   (b) When appropriate, without prejudice to the provisions of subparagraph (a), requests may also be transmitted through the International Criminal Police Organization or any appropriate regional organization.
2. Requests for co-operation and any documents supporting the request shall either be in or be accompanied by a translation into an official language of the requested State or one of the working languages of the Court, in accordance with the choice made by that State upon ratification, acceptance, approval or accession.

Subsequent changes to this choice shall be made in accordance with the Rules of Procedure and Evidence.

3. The requested State shall keep confidential a request for co-operation and any documents supporting the request, except to the extent that the disclosure is necessary for execution of the request.
4. In relation to any request for assistance presented under this Part, the Court may take such measures, including measures related to the protection of information, as may be necessary to ensure the safety or physical or psychological well-being of any victims, potential witnesses and their families. The Court may request that any information that is made available under this Part shall be provided and handled in a manner that protects the safety and physical or psychological well-being of any victims, potential witnesses and their families.
5. (a) The Court may invite any State not party to this Statute to provide assistance under this Part on the basis of an ad hoc arrangement, an agreement with such State or any other appropriate basis.
   (b) Where a State not party to this Statute, which has entered into an ad hoc arrangement or an agreement with the Court, fails to co-operate with requests pursuant to any such arrangement or agreement, the Court may so inform the Assembly of States Parties or, where the Security Council referred the matter to the Court, the Security Council.
6. The Court may ask any intergovernmental organization to provide information or documents. The Court may also ask for other forms of co-operation and assistance which may be agreed upon with such an organization and which are in accordance with its competence or mandate.
7. Where a State Party fails to comply with a request to co-operate by the Court contrary to the provisions of this Statute, thereby preventing the Court from exercising its functions and powers under this Statute, the Court may make a finding to that effect and refer the matter to the Assembly of States Parties or, where the Security Council referred the matter to the Court, to the Security Council.

Article 88

Availability of procedures under national law
States Parties shall ensure that there are procedures available under their national law for all of the forms of co-operation which are specified under this Part.

Article 89

Surrender of persons to the Court

1. The Court may transmit a request for the arrest and surrender of a person, together with the material supporting the request outlined in Article 91, to any State on the territory of which that person may be found and shall request the co-operation of that State in the arrest and surrender of such a person. States Parties shall, in accordance with the provisions of this Part and the procedure under their national law, comply with requests for arrest and surrender.
2. Where the person sought for surrender brings a challenge before a national court on the basis of the principle of *ne bis in idem* as provided in Article 20, the requested State shall immediately consult with the Court to determine if there has been a relevant ruling on admissibility. If the case is admissible, the requested State shall proceed

with the execution of the request. If an admissibility ruling is pending, the requested State may postpone the execution of the request for surrender of the person until the Court makes a determination on admissibility.

3. (a) A State Party shall authorize, in accordance with its national procedural law, transportation through its territory of a person being surrendered to the Court by another State, except where transit through that State would impede or delay the surrender.

   (b) A request by the Court for transit shall be transmitted in accordance with Article 87. The request for transit shall contain:

   (i) A description of the person being transported;

   (ii) A brief statement of the facts of the case and their legal characterization; and

   (iii) The warrant for arrest and surrender;

   (c) A person being transported shall be detained in custody during the period of transit;

   (d) No authorization is required if the person is transported by air and no landing is scheduled on the territory of the transit State;

   (e) If an unscheduled landing occurs on the territory of the transit State, that State may require a request for transit from the Court as provided for in subparagraph (b). The transit State shall detain the person being transported until the request for transit is received and the transit is effected, provided that detention for purposes of this subparagraph may not be extended beyond 96 hours from the unscheduled landing unless the request is received within that time.

4. If the person sought is being proceeded against or is serving a sentence in the requested State for a crime different from that for which surrender to the Court is sought, the requested State, after making its decision to grant the request, shall consult with the Court.

Article 90

Competing requests

1. A State Party which receives a request from the Court for the surrender of a person under Article 89 shall, if it also receives a request from any other State for the extradition of the same person for the same conduct which forms the basis of the crime for which the Court seeks the person's surrender, notify the Court and the requesting State of that fact.

2. Where the requesting State is a State Party, the requested State shall give priority to the request from the Court if:

   (a) The Court has, pursuant to Article 18 or 19, made a determination that the case in respect of which surrender is sought is admissible and that determination takes into account the investigation or prosecution conducted by the requesting State in respect of its request for extradition; or

   (b) The Court makes the determination described in subparagraph (a) pursuant to the requested State's notification under paragraph 1.

3. Where a determination under paragraph 2 (a) has not been made, the requested State may, at its discretion, pending the determination of the Court under paragraph 2 (b), proceed to deal with the request for extradition from the requesting State but shall not extradite the person until the Court has determined that the case is inadmissible. The Court's determination shall be made on an expedited basis.

4. If the requesting State is a State not Party to this Statute the requested State, if it is not under an international obligation to extradite the person to the requesting State, shall give priority to the request for surrender from the Court, if the Court has determined that the case is admissible.
5. Where a case under paragraph 4 has not been determined to be admissible by the Court, the requested State may, at its discretion, proceed to deal with the request for extradition from the requesting State.
6. In cases where paragraph 4 applies except that the requested State is under an existing international obligation to extradite the person to the requesting State not Party to this Statute, the requested State shall determine whether to surrender the person to the Court or extradite the person to the requesting State. In making its decision, the requested State shall consider all the relevant factors, including but not limited to:
   (a) The respective dates of the requests;
   (b) The interests of the requesting State including, where relevant, whether the crime was committed in its territory and the nationality of the victims and of the person sought; and
   (c) The possibility of subsequent surrender between the Court and the requesting State.
7. Where a State Party which receives a request from the Court for the surrender of a person also receives a request from any State for the extradition of the same person for conduct other than that which constitutes the crime for which the Court seeks the person's surrender:
   (a) The requested State shall, if it is not under an existing international obligation to extradite the person to the requesting State, give priority to the request from the Court;
   (b) The requested State shall, if it is under an existing international obligation to extradite the person to the requesting State, determine whether to surrender the person to the Court or to extradite the person to the requesting State. In making its decision, the requested State shall consider all the relevant factors, including but not limited to those set out in paragraph 6, but shall give special consideration to the relative nature and gravity of the conduct in question.
8. Where pursuant to a notification under this Article, the Court has determined a case to be inadmissible, and subsequently extradition to the requesting State is refused, the requested State shall notify the Court of this decision.

Article 91

Contents of request for arrest and surrender

1. A request for arrest and surrender shall be made in writing. In urgent cases, a request may be made by any medium capable of delivering a written record, provided that the request shall be confirmed through the channel provided for in Article 87, paragraph 1 (a).
2. In the case of a request for the arrest and surrender of a person for whom a warrant of arrest has been issued by the Pre-Trial Chamber under Article 58, the request shall contain or be supported by:
   (a) Information describing the person sought, sufficient to identify the person, and information as to that person's probable location;
   (b) A copy of the warrant of arrest; and

(c) Such documents, statements or information as may be necessary to meet the requirements for the surrender process in the requested State, except that those requirements should not be more burdensome than those applicable to requests for extradition pursuant to treaties or arrangements between the requested State and other States and should, if possible, be less burdensome, taking into account the distinct nature of the Court.

3. In the case of a request for the arrest and surrender of a person already convicted, the request shall contain or be supported by:
   (a) A copy of any warrant of arrest for that person;
   (b) A copy of the judgement of conviction;
   (c) Information to demonstrate that the person sought is the one referred to in the judgement of conviction; and
   (d) If the person sought has been sentenced, a copy of the sentence imposed and, in the case of a sentence for imprisonment, a statement of any time already served and the time remaining to be served.
4. Upon the request of the Court, a State Party shall consult with the Court, either generally or with respect to a specific matter, regarding any requirements under its national law that may apply under paragraph 2 (c). During the consultations, the State Party shall advise the Court of the specific requirements of its national law.

Article 92

Provisional arrest

1. In urgent cases, the Court may request the provisional arrest of the person sought, pending presentation of the request for surrender and the documents supporting the request as specified in Article 91.
2. The request for provisional arrest shall be made by any medium capable of delivering a written record and shall contain:
   (a) Information describing the person sought, sufficient to identify the person, and information as to that person's probable location;
   (b) A concise statement of the crimes for which the person's arrest is sought and of the facts which are alleged to constitute those crimes, including, where possible, the date and location of the crime;
   (c) A statement of the existence of a warrant of arrest or a judgement of conviction against the person sought; and
   (d) A statement that a request for surrender of the person sought will follow.
3. A person who is provisionally arrested may be released from custody if the requested State has not received the request for surrender and the documents supporting the request as specified in Article 91 within the time limits specified in the Rules of Procedure and Evidence. However, the person may consent to surrender before the expiration of this period if permitted by the law of the requested State. In such a case, the requested State shall proceed to surrender the person to the Court as soon as possible.
4. The fact that the person sought has been released from custody pursuant to paragraph 3 shall not prejudice the subsequent arrest and surrender of that person if the request for surrender and the documents supporting the request are delivered at a later date.

Article 93

Other forms of co-operation

1. States Parties shall, in accordance with the provisions of this Part and under procedures of national law, comply with requests by the Court to provide the following assistance in relation to investigations or prosecutions:

   (a) The identification and whereabouts of persons or the location of items;
   (b) The taking of evidence, including testimony under oath, and the production of evidence, including expert opinions and reports necessary to the Court;
   (c) The questioning of any person being investigated or prosecuted;
   (d) The service of documents, including judicial documents;
   (e) Facilitating the voluntary appearance of persons as witnesses or experts before the Court;
   (f) The temporary transfer of persons as provided in paragraph 7;
   (g) The examination of places or sites, including the exhumation and examination of grave sites;
   (h) The execution of searches and seizures;
   (i) The provision of records and documents, including official records and documents;
   (j) The protection of victims and witnesses and the preservation of evidence;
   (k) The identification, tracing and freezing or seizure of proceeds, property and assets and instrumentalities of crimes for the purpose of eventual forfeiture, without prejudice to the rights of bona fide third parties; and
   (l) Any other type of assistance which is not prohibited by the law of the requested State, with a view to facilitating the investigation and prosecution of crimes within the jurisdiction of the Court.

2. The Court shall have the authority to provide an assurance to a witness or an expert appearing before the Court that he or she will not be prosecuted, detained or subjected to any restriction of personal freedom by the Court in respect of any act or omission that preceded the departure of that person from the requested State.
3. Where execution of a particular measure of assistance detailed in a request presented under paragraph 1, is prohibited in the requested State on the basis of an existing fundamental legal principle of general application, the requested State shall promptly consult with the Court to try to resolve the matter. In the consultations, consideration should be given to whether the assistance can be rendered in another manner or subject to conditions. If after consultations the matter cannot be resolved, the Court shall modify the request as necessary.
4. In accordance with Article 72, a State Party may deny a request for assistance, in whole or in part, only if the request concerns the production of any documents or disclosure of evidence which relates to its national security.
5. Before denying a request for assistance under paragraph 1 (l), the requested State shall consider whether the assistance can be provided subject to specified conditions, or whether the assistance can be provided at a later date or in an alternative manner, provided that if the Court or the Prosecutor accepts the assistance subject to conditions, the Court or the Prosecutor shall abide by them.
6. If a request for assistance is denied, the requested State Party shall promptly inform the Court or the Prosecutor of the reasons for such denial.
7. (a) The Court may request the temporary transfer of a person in custody for pur-

poses of identification or for obtaining testimony or other assistance. The person may be transferred if the following conditions are fulfilled:

(i) The person freely gives his or her informed consent to the transfer, and

(ii) The requested State agrees to the transfer, subject to such conditions as that State and the Court may agree.

(b) The person being transferred shall remain in custody. When the purposes of the transfer have been fulfilled, the Court shall return the person without delay to the requested State.

8. (a) The Court shall ensure the confidentiality of documents and information, except as required for the investigation and proceedings described in the request.

(b) The requested State may, when necessary, transmit documents or information to the Prosecutor on a confidential basis. The Prosecutor may then use them solely for the purpose of generating new evidence.

(c) The requested State may, on its own motion or at the request of the Prosecutor, subsequently consent to the disclosure of such documents or information. They may then be used as evidence pursuant to the provisions of Parts 5 and 6 and in accordance with the Rules of Procedure and Evidence.

9. (a) (i) In the event that a State Party receives competing requests, other than for surrender or extradition, from the Court and from another State pursuant to an international obligation, the State Party shall endeavour, in consultation with the Court and the other State, to meet both requests, if necessary by postponing or attaching conditions to one or the other request.

(ii) Failing that, competing requests shall be resolved in accordance with the principles established in Article 90.

(b) Where, however, the request from the Court concerns information, property or persons which are subject to the control of a third State or an international organization by virtue of an international agreement, the requested States shall so inform the Court and the Court shall direct its request to the third State or international organization.

10. (a) The Court may, upon request, co-operate with and provide assistance to a State Party conducting an investigation into or trial in respect of conduct which constitutes a crime within the jurisdiction of the Court or which constitutes a serious crime under the national law of the requesting State.

(b) (i) The assistance provided under subparagraph (a) shall include, *inter alia*:

a. The transmission of statements, documents or other types of evidence obtained in the course of an investigation or a trial conducted by the Court; and

b. The questioning of any person detained by order of the Court;

(ii) In the case of assistance under subparagraph (b) (i) a:

a. If the documents or other types of evidence have been obtained with the assistance of a State, such transmission shall require the consent of that State;

b. If the statements, documents or other types of evidence have been provided by a witness or expert, such transmission shall be subject to the provisions of Article 68.

(c) The Court may, under the conditions set out in this paragraph, grant a request for assistance under this paragraph from a State which is not a Party to this Statute.

Article 94

Postponement of execution of a request in respect of ongoing investigation or prosecution

1. If the immediate execution of a request would interfere with an ongoing investigation or prosecution of a case different from that to which the request relates, the requested State may postpone the execution of the request for a period of time agreed upon with the Court. However, the postponement shall be no longer than is necessary to complete the relevant investigation or prosecution in the requested State. Before making a decision to postpone, the requested State should consider whether the assistance may be immediately provided subject to certain conditions.
2. If a decision to postpone is taken pursuant to paragraph 1, the Prosecutor may, however, seek measures to preserve evidence, pursuant to Article 93, paragraph 1 (j).

Article 95

Postponement of execution of a request in respect of an admissibility challenge

Where there is an admissibility challenge under consideration by the Court pursuant to Article 18 or 19, the requested State may postpone the execution of a request under this Part pending a determination by the Court, unless the Court has specifically ordered that the Prosecutor may pursue the collection of such evidence pursuant to Article 18 or 19.

Article 96

Contents of request for other forms of assistance under Article 93

1. A request for other forms of assistance referred to in Article 93 shall be made in writing. In urgent cases, a request may be made by any medium capable of delivering a written record, provided that the request shall be confirmed through the channel provided for in Article 87, paragraph 1 (a).
2. The request shall, as applicable, contain or be supported by the following:
   - (a) A concise statement of the purpose of the request and the assistance sought, including the legal basis and the grounds for the request;
   - (b) As much detailed information as possible about the location or identification of any person or place that must be found or identified in order for the assistance sought to be provided;
   - (c) A concise statement of the essential facts underlying the request;
   - (d) The reasons for and details of any procedure or requirement to be followed;
   - (e) Such information as may be required under the law of the requested State in order to execute the request; and
   - (f) Any other information relevant in order for the assistance sought to be provided.
3. Upon the request of the Court, a State Party shall consult with the Court, either generally or with respect to a specific matter, regarding any requirements under its national law that may apply under paragraph 2 (e). During the consultations, the State Party shall advise the Court of the specific requirements of its national law.
4. The provisions of this Article shall, where applicable, also apply in respect of a request for assistance made to the Court.

Article 97

Consultations

Where a State Party receives a request under this Part in relation to which it identifies problems which may impede or prevent the execution of the request, that State shall consult with the Court without delay in order to resolve the matter. Such problems may include, *inter alia:*

(a) Insufficient information to execute the request;

(b) In the case of a request for surrender, the fact that despite best efforts, the person sought cannot be located or that the investigation conducted has determined that the person in the requested State is clearly not the person named in the warrant; or

(c) The fact that execution of the request in its current form would require the requested State to breach a pre-existing treaty obligation undertaken with respect to another State.

Article 98

Co-operation with respect to waiver of immunity and consent to surrender

1. The Court may not proceed with a request for surrender or assistance which would require the requested State to act inconsistently with its obligations under international law with respect to the State or diplomatic immunity of a person or property of a third State, unless the Court can first obtain the co-operation of that third State for the waiver of the immunity.
2. The Court may not proceed with a request for surrender which would require the requested State to act inconsistently with its obligations under international agreements pursuant to which the consent of a sending State is required to surrender a person of that State to the Court, unless the Court can first obtain the co-operation of the sending State for the giving of consent for the surrender.

Article 99

Execution of requests under Articles 93 and 96

1. Requests for assistance shall be executed in accordance with the relevant procedure under the law of the requested State and, unless prohibited by such law, in the manner specified in the request, including following any procedure outlined therein or permitting persons specified in the request to be present at and assist in the execution process.
2. In the case of an urgent request, the documents or evidence produced in response shall, at the request of the Court, be sent urgently.
3. Replies from the requested State shall be transmitted in their original language and form.
4. Without prejudice to other Articles in this Part, where it is necessary for the successful execution of a request which can be executed without any compulsory measures, including specifically the interview of or taking evidence from a person on a voluntary basis, including doing so without the presence of the authorities of the requested State Party if it is essential for the request to be executed, and the examination without modification of a public site or other public place, the Prosecutor may execute such request directly on the territory of a State as follows:

   (a) When the State Party requested is a State on the territory of which the crime is alleged to have been committed, and there has been a determination of admissibility pursuant to Article 18 or 19, the Prosecutor may directly execute such request following all possible consultations with the requested State Party;

(b) In other cases, the Prosecutor may execute such request following consultations with the requested State Party and subject to any reasonable conditions or concerns raised by that State Party. Where the requested State Party identifies problems with the execution of a request pursuant to this subparagraph it shall, without delay, consult with the Court to resolve the matter.

5. Provisions allowing a person heard or examined by the Court under Article 72 to invoke restrictions designed to prevent disclosure of confidential information connected with national security shall also apply to the execution of requests for assistance under this Article.

Article 100

Costs

1. The ordinary costs for execution of requests in the territory of the requested State shall be borne by that State, except for the following, which shall be borne by the Court:
   (a) Costs associated with the travel and security of witnesses and experts or the transfer under Article 93 of persons in custody;
   (b) Costs of translation, interpretation and transcription;
   (c) Travel and subsistence costs of the judges, the Prosecutor, the Deputy Prosecutors, the Registrar, the Deputy Registrar and staff of any organ of the Court;
   (d) Costs of any expert opinion or report requested by the Court;
   (e) Costs associated with the transport of a person being surrendered to the Court by a custodial State; and
   (f) Following consultations, any extraordinary costs that may result from the execution of a request.
2. The provisions of paragraph 1 shall, as appropriate, apply to requests from States Parties to the Court. In that case, the Court shall bear the ordinary costs of execution.

Article 101

Rule of speciality

1. A person surrendered to the Court under this Statute shall not be proceeded against, punished or detained for any conduct committed prior to surrender, other than the conduct or course of conduct which forms the basis of the crimes for which that person has been surrendered.
2. The Court may request a waiver of the requirements of paragraph 1 from the State which surrendered the person to the Court and, if necessary, the Court shall provide additional information in accordance with Article 91. States Parties shall have the authority to provide a waiver to the Court and should endeavour to do so.

Article 102

Use of terms

For the purposes of this Statute:

(a) "surrender" means the delivering up of a person by a State to the Court, pursuant to this Statute.

(b) "extradition" means the delivering up of a person by one State to another as provided by treaty, convention or national legislation.

PART 10. ENFORCEMENT

Article 103

Role of States in enforcement of sentences of imprisonment

1. (a) A sentence of imprisonment shall be served in a State designated by the Court from a list of States which have indicated to the Court their willingness to accept sentenced persons.

   (b) At the time of declaring its willingness to accept sentenced persons, a State may attach conditions to its acceptance as agreed by the Court and in accordance with this Part.

   (c) A State designated in a particular case shall promptly inform the Court whether it accepts the Court's designation.

2. (a) The State of enforcement shall notify the Court of any circumstances, including the exercise of any conditions agreed under paragraph 1, which could materially affect the terms or extent of the imprisonment. The Court shall be given at least 45 days' notice of any such known or foreseeable circumstances. During this period, the State of enforcement shall take no action that might prejudice its obligations under Article 110.

   (b) Where the Court cannot agree to the circumstances referred to in subparagraph (a), it shall notify the State of enforcement and proceed in accordance with Article 104, paragraph 1.

3. In exercising its discretion to make a designation under paragraph 1, the Court shall take into account the following:

   (a) The principle that States Parties should share the responsibility for enforcing sentences of imprisonment, in accordance with principles of equitable distribution, as provided in the Rules of Procedure and Evidence;

   (b) The application of widely accepted international treaty standards governing the treatment of prisoners;

   (c The views of the sentenced person;

   (d The nationality of the sentenced person;

   (e) Such other factors regarding the circumstances of the crime or the person sentenced, or the effective enforcement of the sentence, as may be appropriate in designating the State of enforcement.

4. If no State is designated under paragraph 1, the sentence of imprisonment shall be served in a prison facility made available by the host State, in accordance with the conditions set out in the headquarters agreement referred to in Article 3, paragraph 2. In such a case, the costs arising out of the enforcement of a sentence of imprisonment shall be borne by the Court.

Article 104

Change in designation of State of enforcement

1. The Court may, at any time, decide to transfer a sentenced person to a prison of another State.
2. A sentenced person may, at any time, apply to the Court to be transferred from the State of enforcement.

Article 105

Enforcement of the sentence

1. Subject to conditions which a State may have specified in accordance with Article 103, paragraph 1 (b), the sentence of imprisonment shall be binding on the States Parties, which shall in no case modify it.
2. The Court alone shall have the right to decide any application for appeal and revision. The State of enforcement shall not impede the making of any such application by a sentenced person.

Article 106

Supervision of enforcement of sentences and conditions of imprisonment

1. The enforcement of a sentence of imprisonment shall be subject to the supervision of the Court and shall be consistent with widely accepted international treaty standards governing treatment of prisoners.
2. The conditions of imprisonment shall be governed by the law of the State of enforcement and shall be consistent with widely accepted international treaty standards governing treatment of prisoners; in no case shall such conditions be more or less favourable than those available to prisoners convicted of similar offences in the State of enforcement.
3. Communications between a sentenced person and the Court shall be unimpeded and confidential.

Article 107

Transfer of the person upon completion of sentence

1. Following completion of the sentence, a person who is not a national of the State of enforcement may, in accordance with the law of the State of enforcement, be transferred to a State which is obliged to receive him or her, or to another State which agrees to receive him or her, taking into account any wishes of the person to be transferred to that State, unless the State of enforcement authorizes the person to remain in its territory.
2. If no State bears the costs arising out of transferring the person to another State pursuant to paragraph 1, such costs shall be borne by the Court.
3. Subject to the provisions of Article 108, the State of enforcement may also, in accordance with its national law, extradite or otherwise surrender the person to a State which has requested the extradition or surrender of the person for purposes of trial or enforcement of a sentence.

Article 108

Limitation on the prosecution or punishment of other offences

1. A sentenced person in the custody of the State of enforcement shall not be subject to prosecution or punishment or to extradition to a third State for any conduct engaged in prior to that person's delivery to the State of enforcement, unless such prosecution, punishment or extradition has been approved by the Court at the request of the State of enforcement.
2. The Court shall decide the matter after having heard the views of the sentenced person.
3. Paragraph 1 shall cease to apply if the sentenced person remains voluntarily for more than 30 days in the territory of the State of enforcement after having served the full sentence imposed by the Court, or returns to the territory of that State after having left it.

Article 109

Enforcement of fines and forfeiture measures

1. States Parties shall give effect to fines or forfeitures ordered by the Court under Part 7, without prejudice to the rights of bona fide third parties, and in accordance with the procedure of their national law.
2. If a State Party is unable to give effect to an order for forfeiture, it shall take measures to recover the value of the proceeds, property or assets ordered by the Court to be forfeited, without prejudice to the rights of bona fide third parties.
3. Property, or the proceeds of the sale of real property or, where appropriate, the sale of other property, which is obtained by a State Party as a result of its enforcement of a judgement of the Court shall be transferred to the Court.

Article 110

Review by the Court concerning reduction of sentence

1. The State of enforcement shall not release the person before expiry of the sentence pronounced by the Court.
2. The Court alone shall have the right to decide any reduction of sentence, and shall rule on the matter after having heard the person.
3. When the person has served two thirds of the sentence, or 25 years in the case of life imprisonment, the Court shall review the sentence to determine whether it should be reduced. Such a review shall not be conducted before that time.
4. In its review under paragraph 3, the Court may reduce the sentence if it finds that one or more of the following factors are present:
   (a) The early and continuing willingness of the person to co-operate with the Court in its investigations and prosecutions;
   (b) The voluntary assistance of the person in enabling the enforcement of the judgements and orders of the Court in other cases, and in particular providing assistance in locating assets subject to orders of fine, forfeiture or reparation which may be used for the benefit of victims; or
   (c) Other factors establishing a clear and significant change of circumstances sufficient to justify the reduction of sentence, as provided in the Rules of Procedure and Evidence.

5. If the Court determines in its initial review under paragraph 3 that it is not appropriate to reduce the sentence, it shall thereafter review the question of reduction of sentence at such intervals and applying such criteria as provided for in the Rules of Procedure and Evidence.

Article 111

Escape
If a convicted person escapes from custody and flees the State of enforcement, that State may, after consultation with the Court, request the person's surrender from the State in which the person is located pursuant to existing bilateral or multilateral arrangements, or may request that the Court seek the person's surrender, in accordance with Part 9. It may direct that the person be delivered to the State in which he or she was serving the sentence or to another State designated by the Court.

PART 11. ASSEMBLY OF STATES PARTIES

Article 112

Assembly of States Parties
1. An Assembly of States Parties to this Statute is hereby established. Each State Party shall have one representative in the Assembly who may be accompanied by alternates and advisers. Other States which have signed this Statute or the Final Act may be observers in the Assembly.
2. The Assembly shall:
   (a) Consider and adopt, as appropriate, recommendations of the Preparatory Commission;
   (b) Provide management oversight to the Presidency, the Prosecutor and the Registrar regarding the administration of the Court;
   (c) Consider the reports and activities of the Bureau established under paragraph 3 and take appropriate action in regard thereto;
   (d) Consider and decide the budget for the Court;
   (e) Decide whether to alter, in accordance with Article 36, the number of judges;
   (f) Consider pursuant to Article 87, paragraphs 5 and 7, any question relating to non-co-operation;
   (g) Perform any other function consistent with this Statute or the Rules of Procedure and Evidence.
3. (a) The Assembly shall have a Bureau consisting of a President, two Vice-Presidents and 18 members elected by the Assembly for three-year terms.
   (b) The Bureau shall have a representative character, taking into account, in particular, equitable geographical distribution and the adequate representation of the principal legal systems of the world.
   (c) The Bureau shall meet as often as necessary, but at least once a year. It shall assist the Assembly in the discharge of its responsibilities.
4. The Assembly may establish such subsidiary bodies as may be necessary, including an independent oversight mechanism for inspection, evaluation and investigation of the Court, in order to enhance its efficiency and economy.

5. The President of the Court, the Prosecutor and the Registrar or their representatives may participate, as appropriate, in meetings of the Assembly and of the Bureau.
6. The Assembly shall meet at the seat of the Court or at the Headquarters of the United Nations once a year and, when circumstances so require, hold special sessions. Except as otherwise specified in this Statute, special sessions shall be convened by the Bureau on its own initiative or at the request of one third of the States Parties.
7. Each State Party shall have one vote. Every effort shall be made to reach decisions by consensus in the Assembly and in the Bureau. If consensus cannot be reached, except as otherwise provided in the Statute:
   (a) Decisions on matters of substance must be approved by a two-thirds majority of those present and voting provided that an absolute majority of States Parties constitutes the quorum for voting;
   (b) Decisions on matters of procedure shall be taken by a simple majority of States Parties present and voting.
8. A State Party which is in arrears in the payment of its financial contributions towards the costs of the Court shall have no vote in the Assembly and in the Bureau if the amount of its arrears equals or exceeds the amount of the contributions due from it for the preceding two full years. The Assembly may, nevertheless, permit such a State Party to vote in the Assembly and in the Bureau if it is satisfied that the failure to pay is due to conditions beyond the control of the State Party.
9. The Assembly shall adopt its own rules of procedure.
10. The official and working languages of the Assembly shall be those of the General Assembly of the United Nations.

PART 12. FINANCING

Article 113

Financial Regulations
Except as otherwise specifically provided, all financial matters related to the Court and the meetings of the Assembly of States Parties, including its Bureau and subsidiary bodies, shall be governed by this Statute and the Financial Regulations and Rules adopted by the Assembly of States Parties.

Article 114

Payment of expenses
Expenses of the Court and the Assembly of States Parties, including its Bureau and subsidiary bodies, shall be paid from the funds of the Court.

Article 115

Funds of the Court and of the Assembly of States Parties
The expenses of the Court and the Assembly of States Parties, including its Bureau and subsidiary bodies, as provided for in the budget decided by the Assembly of States Parties, shall be provided by the following sources:
   (a) Assessed contributions made by States Parties;
   (b) Funds provided by the United Nations, subject to the approval of the General

Assembly, in particular in relation to the expenses incurred due to referrals by the Security Council.

Article 116

Voluntary contributions
Without prejudice to Article 115, the Court may receive and utilize, as additional funds, voluntary contributions from Governments, international organizations, individuals, corporations and other entities, in accordance with relevant criteria adopted by the Assembly of States Parties.

Article 117

Assessment of contributions
The contributions of States Parties shall be assessed in accordance with an agreed scale of assessment, based on the scale adopted by the United Nations for its regular budget and adjusted in accordance with the principles on which that scale is based.

Article 118

Annual audit
The records, books and accounts of the Court, including its annual financial statements, shall be audited annually by an independent auditor.

PART 13. FINAL CLAUSES

Article 119

Settlement of disputes
1. Any dispute concerning the judicial functions of the Court shall be settled by the decision of the Court.
2. Any other dispute between two or more States Parties relating to the interpretation or application of this Statute which is not settled through negotiations within three months of their commencement shall be referred to the Assembly of States Parties. The Assembly may itself seek to settle the dispute or may make recommendations on further means of settlement of the dispute, including referral to the International Court of Justice in conformity with the Statute of that Court.

Article 120

Reservations
No reservations may be made to this Statute.

Article 121

Amendments
1. After the expiry of seven years from the entry into force of this Statute, any State Party may propose amendments thereto. The text of any proposed amendment shall be submitted to the Secretary-General of the United Nations, who shall promptly circulate it to all States Parties.

2. No sooner than three months from the date of notification, the Assembly of States Parties, at its next meeting, shall, by a majority of those present and voting, decide whether to take up the proposal. The Assembly may deal with the proposal directly or convene a Review Conference if the issue involved so warrants.
3. The adoption of an amendment at a meeting of the Assembly of States Parties or at a Review Conference on which consensus cannot be reached shall require a two-thirds majority of States Parties.
4. Except as provided in paragraph 5, an amendment shall enter into force for all States Parties one year after instruments of ratification or acceptance have been deposited with the Secretary-General of the United Nations by seven-eighths of them.
5. Any amendment to Articles 5, 6, 7 and 8 of this Statute shall enter into force for those States Parties which have accepted the amendment one year after the deposit of their instruments of ratification or acceptance. In respect of a State Party which has not accepted the amendment, the Court shall not exercise its jurisdiction regarding a crime covered by the amendment when committed by that State Party's nationals or on its territory.
6. If an amendment has been accepted by seven-eighths of States Parties in accordance with paragraph 4, any State Party which has not accepted the amendment may withdraw from this Statute with immediate effect, notwithstanding Article 127, paragraph 1, but subject to Article 127, paragraph 2, by giving notice no later than one year after the entry into force of such amendment.
7. The Secretary-General of the United Nations shall circulate to all States Parties any amendment adopted at a meeting of the Assembly of States Parties or at a Review Conference.

Article 122

Amendments to provisions of an institutional nature

1. Amendments to provisions of this Statute which are of an exclusively institutional nature, namely, Article 35, Article 36, paragraphs 8 and 9, Article 37, Article 38, Article 39, paragraphs 1 (first two sentences), 2 and 4, Article 42, paragraphs 4 to 9, Article 43, paragraphs 2 and 3, and Articles 44, 46, 47 and 49, may be proposed at any time, notwithstanding Article 121, paragraph 1, by any State Party. The text of any proposed amendment shall be submitted to the Secretary-General of the United Nations or such other person designated by the Assembly of States Parties who shall promptly circulate it to all States Parties and to others participating in the Assembly.
2. Amendments under this Article on which consensus cannot be reached shall be adopted by the Assembly of States Parties or by a Review Conference, by a two-thirds majority of States Parties. Such amendments shall enter into force for all States Parties six months after their adoption by the Assembly or, as the case may be, by the Conference.

Article 123

Review of the Statute

1. Seven years after the entry into force of this Statute the Secretary-General of the United Nations shall convene a Review Conference to consider any amendments to this Statute. Such review may include, but is not limited to, the list of crimes contained in Article 5. The Conference shall be open to those participating in the Assembly of States Parties and on the same conditions.

2. At any time thereafter, at the request of a State Party and for the purposes set out in paragraph 1, the Secretary-General of the United Nations shall, upon approval by a majority of States Parties, convene a Review Conference.
3. The provisions of Article 121, paragraphs 3 to 7, shall apply to the adoption and entry into force of any amendment to the Statute considered at a Review Conference.

Article 124

Transitional Provision
Notwithstanding Article 12, paragraphs 1 and 2, a State, on becoming a party to this Statute, may declare that, for a period of seven years after the entry into force of this Statute for the State concerned, it does not accept the jurisdiction of the Court with respect to the category of crimes referred to in Article 8 when a crime is alleged to have been committed by its nationals or on its territory. A declaration under this Article may be withdrawn at any time. The provisions of this Article shall be reviewed at the Review Conference convened in accordance with Article 123, paragraph 1.

Article 125

Signature, ratification, acceptance, approval or accession
1. This Statute shall be open for signature by all States in Rome, at the headquarters of the Food and Agriculture Organization of the United Nations, on 17 July 1998. Thereafter, it shall remain open for signature in Rome at the Ministry of Foreign Affairs of Italy until 17 October 1998. After that date, the Statute shall remain open for signature in New York, at United Nations Headquarters, until 31 December 2000.
2. This Statute is subject to ratification, acceptance or approval by signatory States. Instruments of ratification, acceptance or approval shall be deposited with the Secretary-General of the United Nations.
3. This Statute shall be open to accession by all States. Instruments of accession shall be deposited with the Secretary-General of the United Nations.

Article 126

Entry into force
1. This Statute shall enter into force on the first day of the month after the 60th day following the date of the deposit of the 60th instrument of ratification, acceptance, approval or accession with the Secretary-General of the United Nations.
2. or each State ratifying, accepting, approving or acceding to this Statute after the deposit of the 60th instrument of ratification, acceptance, approval or accession, the Statute shall enter into force on the first day of the month after the 60th day following the deposit by such State of its instrument of ratification, acceptance, approval or accession.

Article 127

Withdrawal
1. A State Party may, by written notification addressed to the Secretary-General of the United Nations, withdraw from this Statute. The withdrawal shall take effect one year after the date of receipt of the notification, unless the notification specifies a later date.

2. A State shall not be discharged, by reason of its withdrawal, from the obligations arising from this Statute while it was a Party to the Statute, including any financial obligations which may have accrued. Its withdrawal shall not affect any co-operation with the Court in connection with criminal investigations and proceedings in relation to which the withdrawing State had a duty to co-operate and which were commenced prior to the date on which the withdrawal became effective, nor shall it prejudice in any way the continued consideration of any matter which was already under consideration by the Court prior to the date on which the withdrawal became effective.

Article 128

Authentic texts
The original of this Statute, of which the Arabic, Chinese, English, French, Russian and Spanish texts are equally authentic, shall be deposited with the Secretary-General of the United Nations, who shall send certified copies thereof to all States.

In witness whereof, the undersigned, being duly authorized thereto by their respective Governments, have signed this Statute.

Done at Rome, this 17th day of July 1998.

Select Bibliography

ABI-SAAB, G AND ABI-SAAB, R, 'Les crimes de guerre' in H Ascensio, E Decaux and A Pellet (eds), *Droit international pénal* (Pedone, Paris, 2000)

ACEVES, WJ, 'Affirming the Law of Nations in US Courts: The Karadzić Litigation and the Yugoslav Conflict', (1996), 14 *Berkeley Journal of International Law* 137

—— 'Liberalism and International Legal Scholarship: The Pinochet Case and the Move Toward a Universal System of Transnational Law Litigation', (2000), 41 *Harvard International Law Journal* 129

AHKAVAN, P, 'The International Criminal Tribunal for Rwanda: The Politics and Pragmatics of Punishment', (1996), 90 *American Journal of International Law* 501

ALSTON, P, AND CRAWFORD, J, *The Future of UN Human Rights Treaty Monitoring* (Cambridge University Press, Cambridge, 2000)

AMNESTY INTERNATIONAL, *'Disappearances' and Political Killings: Human rights crisis of the 1990s* (AI, Amsterdam, 1994)

—— *Universal Jurisdiction and the Absence of Immunity for Crimes Against Humanity,* AI Index: IOR 53/003/2001 (AI, London, 2001)

ANDRIES, A, DAVID, E, VAN DEN WIJNGAERT, C, AND VERHAGEN, J, 'Commentaire de la loi du 16 juin 1993 relative à la répression des infractions graves au droit international humanitaire', (1994) 74 *Revue de droit pénal et de criminologie* 1114

ARENDT, H, *Eichmann in Jerusalem: A Report on the Banality of Evil* (Viking Press, New York, 1963)

ASCENSIO, H, 'L'immunité des chefs d'Etat et des gouvernants', in CEDIN, *L'immunité pénale des gouvernants* (Pedone, Paris, forthcoming);

BASS, GJ, *Stay the Hand of Vengeance: The Politics of War Crimes Tribunals* (Princeton University Press, Princeton, 2000)

BASSIOUNI, MC (ed), *The Statute of the International Criminal Court: A Documentary History* (Transnational Publishers Inc, Ardsley, New York, 1998)

——, *Crimes against Humanity in International Law* (Kluwer Law International, The Hague/London/Boston, 2nd rev edn 1999)

—— (ed), *International Criminal Law* (Transnational Publishers Inc, Ardsley, New York, 2nd edn 1999) (3 vols)

—— and WISE, EM, *Aut Dedere Aut Judicare—The Duty to Extradite or Prosecute in International Law* (Martinus Nijhoff, 1995)

BERGSMO, M, 'Occasional remarks on certain State concerns about the jurisdictional reach of the International Criminal Court, and their possible implications for the relationship between the Court and the Security Council', (2000) *Nordic Journal of International Law* 69

BIANCHI, A, 'Immunity Versus Human Rights: The Pinochet Case', (1999) *European Journal of International Law* 10

BOISSON DE CHAZOURNES, L AND SANDS, P (eds), *International Law, the International Court of Justice and Nuclear Weapons* (Cambridge University Press, Cambridge, 1999)

Brody, Reed and Ratner, Michael (eds), *The Pinochet Papers* (Kluwer Law International, The Hague, 2000)

Broomhall, B, 'Towards the Development of an Effective System of Universal Jurisdiction for Crimes under International Law', (2001), 35 *New England Law Review* 399

——, 'Toward US Acceptance of the International Criminal Court', (2001) 64 *Law & Contemporary Problems* 141

Burgers, JH, and Danelius, H, *The United Nations Convention against Torture* (Martinus Nijhoff, Dordrecht, 1988)

Butler, AH, 'The Doctrine of Universal Jurisdiction: A Review of the Literature', (2001) 11 *Criminal Law Forum* 353

Cassel, D, 'Empowering United States Courts to Hear Crimes Within the Jurisdiction of the International Criminal Court', (2001), 35 *New England Law Review* 421

Cassese, A, *Violence et droit dans un monde divisé* (Presses Universitaires de France Paris, 1990)

Commission on the Responsibility of the Authors of the War and on Enforcement of Penalties, 'Report Presented to the Preliminary Peace Conference' (29 March 1919), (1920) 14 *American Journal of International Law* 95

Cosnard, M, 'Les immunités du chef d'Etat' in SFDI, *Le chef d'Etat et le droit international*, (Paris, Pedone, 2002)

——, *La soumission des Etats aux tribunaux internes* (Pedone, Paris, 1996)

Crawford, J, *The International Law Commission's Articles on State Responsibility: Introduction, Text and Commentaries* (Cambridge University Press, Cambridge, 2002)

Dadrian, VN, 'Genocide as a Problem of National and International Law: The World War I Armenian Case and Its Contemporary Legal Ramifications', (1989), 14 *Yale Journal of International Law,* 221

David, E, 'La loi Belge sur les crimes de guerre', (1995), 27 *Revue Belge de droit international* 668

——, *Principes de droit des conflits armés* (Brussels, Bruylant 1999)

Dimitrijević, V, 'Justice must be done and be seen to be done: the Milošević trial', (2002) 11/1-2 *East European Constitutional Review*, 59

Donnedieu de Vabres, H, *Les Principes Modernes du Droit Pénal International* (Libraire du Recueil Sirey, Paris, 1928)

Durham, H and McCormack, TLH, *The Changing Face of Conflict and the Efficacy of International Humanitarian Law* (Martinus Nijhoff Publishers, The Hague/London/Boston, 1999)

Ferencz, B, *Defining International Aggression* (Oceana, Dobbs Ferry NY, 1975) (2 vols)

——, *New Legal Foundations for Global Survival* (Oceana, Dobbs Ferry NY, 1994)

——, *Less Than Slaves* (Indiana University Press, 2002)

Garro, AM, 'Nine Years of Transition to Democracy in Argentina: Partial Failure or Qualified Success?', (1993), 31 *Columbia Journal of Transnational Law*13

Golsan, RJ (ed), *The Papon Affair: Memory and Justice on Trial* (Routledge, 2000)

Gourevitch, P, *We Wish to Inform You That Tomorrow We Will Be Killed with Our Families* (Picador, 1999)

Graditzky, T, 'Individual criminal responsibility for violations of international humanitarian law committed in non-international armed conflicts', *Int'l Rev Red Cross* 322 (1998), 29

HAYNER, P, *Unspeakable Truths: Confronting State Terror and Atrocity* (Routledge, New York, 2001)

HENKIN, AH (ed), *The Legacy of Abuse: Confronting the Past, Facing the Future* Aspen Institute/NYU, (New York, 2002)

HENZELIN, M, *Le principe de l'universalité en droit pénal international: droit et obligation pour le Etats de poursuivre et juger selon le principe de l'universalité* (Bruylant, Brussels, 2000)

HERSH, SM, *My Lai 4: A Report on the Massacre and its Aftermath* (Random House, New York, 1970)

HERZ, JH (ed), *From Dictatorship to Democracy: Coping With the Legacies of Authoritarianism and Totalitarianism* (Greenwood Press, Westport CT, 1982)

HUET, A, *Droit pénal international* (PUF, Paris, 1994)

HUMAN RIGHTS WATCH, *The Pinochet precedent: how victims can pursue human rights criminals abroad* (HRW, 2000, New York, updated February 2001)

INTERNATIONAL COUNCIL ON HUMAN RIGHTS POLICY, *Hard Cases: Bringing Human rights Violators to Justice Abroad* (ICHRP, Versoix, Switzerland, 1999)

INTERNATIONAL LAW ASSOCIATION, 'Final Report on Developments in the Field of State Immunity and Proposal for a revised Draft Convention on State Immunity' (Buenos Aires Conference, ILA, 1994)

KAMMINGA, MT, 'Final Report on the Exercise of Universal Jurisdiction in Respect of Gross Human Rights Offences' (London Conference, Committee on International Human Rights Law and Practice, International Law Association, 2000)

——, 'Lessons Learned from the Exercise of Universal Jurisdiction in Respect of Gross Human Rights Offenses', *Human Rights Quarterly* 23 (2001), 965

KELLER, AN, 'To Name or Not to Name?: The Commission for Historical Clarification in Guatemala, Its Mandate, and the Decision not to Identify Individual Perpetrators', (2001), 13 *Florida Journal of International Law* 289

KIRSCH, P AND HOLMES, JT, 'The Rome Conference on an International Criminal Court: The Negotiating Process', (1999), 93 *American Journal of International Law* 2

KISSINGER, H, 'The Pitfalls of Universal Jurisdiction', (July/August 2001) *Foreign Affairs* 86

LEE, RS (ed), *The International Criminal Court: The Making of the Rome Statute, Issues, Negotiations, Results* (Kluwer Law International, The Hague, 1999)

LINTON, S, 'Cambodia, East Timor and Sierra Leone: Experiments in International Justice', (2001) 12 *Criminal Law Forum* 185, 206

——, 'Rising from the Ashes: The Creation of a Viable Criminal Justice System in East Timor', (2001) *Melbourne University Law Review* 5

LUPI, N, 'Report by the Enquiry Commission on the behaviour of Italian Peace-Keeping Troops in Somalia', (1998) *Yearbook of International Humanitarian Law* 1

MAISON, R, 'Les premiers cas d'application des dispositions pénales des conventions de Genève par les juridictions internes', (1995) 6 *European Journal of International Law* 260

MAYFIELD, JV, 'The Prosecution of War Crimes and Respect for Human Rights: Ethiopia's Balancing Act', (1995), *Emory International Law Review* 553

MCCORMACK, TLH AND SIMPSON, GJ (eds), *The Law of War Crimes: National and International Approaches* (Kluwer Law International, The Hague, 1997)

MCDONALD, G K AND SWAAK-GOLDMAN, O (eds), *Substantive and Procedural Aspects of International Criminal Law: The Experience of International and National Courts* (

Kluwer Law International, The Hague/London/Boston, 2000)

MERON, T, 'International Criminalization of Internal Atrocities', (1995) 89 *American Journal of International Law* 554

MINOW, M, *Between Vengeance and Forgiveness: Facing History after Genocide and Mass Violence* (Beacon Press, Boston, 1998)

MORRIS, M, 'High Crimes and Misconceptions: The ICC and Non-Party States, (2001) 64 *Law & Contemporary Problems* 13

ORENTLICHER, D F 'Settling Accounts: The Duty to Prosecute Human Rights Violations of a Prior Regime', (1991), 100 *Yale Law Journal* 2537

PICTET, JS, *Commentary on the Geneva Conventions* (Geneva, International Committee of the Red Cross 1952–1960) (4 vols)

PRINCETON UNIVERSITY PROGRAM IN LAW AND PUBLIC AFFAIRS, *The Princeton Principles on Universal Jurisdiction* (Princeton University, 2001)

PRUNIER, G, *The Rwanda Crisis: History of a Genocide* (Columbia University Press, New York, 1997)

RATNER, SR AND ABRAMS, J S, *Accountability for Human Rights Atrocities in International Law: Beyond the Nuremberg Legacy*, 2nd edn (Oxford University Press, Oxford, 2001)

REDRESS, *Challenging Impunity For Torture: A Manual For Bringing Criminal And Civil Proceedings In England And Wales For Torture Committed Abroad* (Redress London, 2000)

——, *Universal Jurisdiction in Europe: Criminal prosecutions in Europe since 1990 for war crimes, crimes against humanity, torture and genocide* (Redress, London, 1999)

ROBERTSON, G, *Crimes Against Humanity* (Allen Lane / Penguin, London, 1999)

SADAT WEXLER, L, 'The Interpretation of the Nuremberg Principles by the French Court of Cassation: From Touvier to Barbie and Back Again', (1994), 32 *Columbia Journal of Transnational Law* 316

SANDOZ, Y, SWINARSKI, C AND ZIMMERMANN, B (eds), *Commentary on the Additional Protocols of 1977 to the Geneva Conventions of 1949* (International Committee of the Red Cross/Martinus Nijhoff Geneva, 1987)

SASSOLI, M, AND BOUVIER, A A, *How Does Law Protect in War?* (International Committee of the Red Cross, Geneva, 1999)

SCHABAS, W, 'Justice, Democracy and Impunity in Post-Genocide Rwanda: Searching for Solutions to Impossible Problems', (1996), 7 *Criminal Law Forum* 535

——, *Genocide in International Law* (Cambridge University Press, Cambridge, 2000)

SCHARF, MICHAEL P, 'Swapping Amnesty for Peace: Was There a Duty to Prosecute International Crimes in Haiti?', (1996), 31 *Texas International Law Journal* 1

——, 'Applicability of Treaty-Based Universal Jurisdiction to Nationals of Non-Party States', (2001) 35/2 *New England Law Review* 363

——, 'The ICC's Jurisdiction over the Nationals of Non-Party States: A Critique of the US Position', (2001), 64/1 *Law and Contemporary Problems* 67

SCHEFFER, DJ, 'The United States and the International Criminal Court', (1999), 93 *American Journal of International Law* 12

——, 'Fourteenth Waldemar A Solf Lecture in International Law: A Negotiator's Perspective on the International Criminal Court', (2001), 167 *Military Law Review* 1

SCOTT, C (ed), *Torture as Tort: Comparative Perspectives on the Development of Transnational Human Rights Litigation* (Hart Publishing, Oxford, 2001)

SEWALL, SB, AND KAYSEN, C (eds), *The United States and the International Criminal*

Court (American Academy of Arts and Sciences and Rowman & Littlefield Publishers Inc, London/Boulder/New York/Oxford, 2000)

SHELTON, D, *Remedies in International Human Rights Law* (Oxford University Press, Oxford, 1999)

SLAUGHTER, A-M AND BOSCO, D, 'Plaintiff's Diplomacy', (Sept–Oct 2000), 79 *Foreign Affairs* 102

SLUITER, G, 'Obtaining Evidence for the International Criminal Tribunal for the Former Yugoslavia: An Overview and Assessment of Domestic Legislation', (1998) *Netherlands International Law Review* XLV 87

STEPHENS, B, 'Translating Filartiga: A Comparative and International Analysis of Domestic Remedies for International Human Rights Violations', (2002), 27 *Yale Journal of International Law* 1

—— AND RATNER, M, *International Human Rights Litigation in US Courts* (Transnational Publishers Inc, New York, 1996)

STERN, B, 'La compétence universelle en France: le cas des crimes commis en ex-Yougoslavie et au Rwanda', *German Yearbook of International Law* 40 (1998), 280

——, 'Les dits et les non dits de la Cour internationale de Justice dans l'affaire RDC contre Belgique' *International Law FORUM du droit international* (forthcoming)

TAYLOR, T, *The Anatomy of the Nuremberg Trials* (Knopf, New York, 1992)

TRIFFTERER, O (ed), *Commentary on the Rome Statute of the International Criminal Court: Observer's Notes, Article by Article* (Nomos, Baden-Baden, 1999)

VERHOVEN, J, 'Les immunités de juridiction et d'exécution du chef d'Etat et de l'ancien chef d'Etat en droit international', Rapport provisoire, Institut de droit international, 2001

WATTS, SIR A, 'The Legal Position in International Law of Heads of States, Heads of Governments and Foreign Ministers', *RCADI*, tome 247, vol III (1994)

WILSON, RJ, 'Prosecuting Pinochet: International Crimes in Spanish Domestic Law', (1999), 21 *Human Rights Quarterly,* 927

WOODHOUSE, D (ed), *The Pinochet Case: A Legal and Constitutional Analysis* (Hart Publishing, Oxford, 2000)

YOUNG, RM AND MOLINA, M, 'IHL and Peace Operations: Sharing Canada's Lessons Learned From Somalia', *Yearbook of International Humanitarian Law* 1 (1998)

ZAPPALÀ, A, 'Do Heads of State in Office Enjoy Immunity from Jurisdiction for International Crimes? The *Ghaddafi* Case Before the French *Cour de Cassation*', (2001), 12 *European Journal of International Law* 595

Index